TROTSKY

Dmitri Volkogonov joined the Soviet Army in 1945, entered the Lenin Military Academy in Moscow in 1961, and transferred in 1971 to the army's propaganda department, rising to the rank of Colonel-General. A philosopher and historian by training, he began research on his biography of Stalin in 1978; seven years later, his views were regarded as unacceptable by the army's Political Administration and he was compelled to leave the political branch. He became Director of the Institute of Military History, a post he held until June 1991, when his editorship of a new history of the Second World War was attacked as 'un-Soviet'. Following the failed coup of August 1991, he became Defence Adviser to President Yeltsin. His biography of Lenin was published in the UK in 1994. He died in 1995.

Harold Shukman is University Lecturer in Modern Russian History at Oxford and a Fellow of St Antony's College, where he was also Director of the Russian Centre from 1981 to 1991. He has edited and translated the memoirs of Andrei Gromyko, Dmitri Volkogonov's biographies of Stalin, Lenin and now Trotsky, the novels of Anatoly Rybakov (*Heavy Sand* and *Children of the Arbat*), and the plays of Isaac Babel and Yevgeni Shvarts. He is general editor of Longman's multi-volume *History of Russia*, a member of the editorial board of the journal *Istoricheskii arkhiv*, published by the Russian State Archive Commission, and author of *Lenin and the Russian Revolution* and *The Blackwell Encyclopedia of the Russian Revolution*.

Further reviews for *Trotsky*:

'Volkogonov's forte as a writer is always his depiction of personality . . . Volkogonov has a sensitive understanding of the bright, forceful person that Trotsky was.'

ROBERT SERVICE, *Guardian*

reviews overleaf

'A remarkable new biography . . . an intelligent, incisive and fascinating work . . . Harold Shukman's translation is luminous.' MONICA FOOT, *Birmingham Post*

'Volkogonov's death in December 1995 deprived Russia, and the world, of a man who indefatigably investigated the disgraceful secrets of the Soviet regime . . . his great contribution is to have given us a fair display of material not previously accessible, and thus a broader and fuller account of this strange being, and therefore of the whole Soviet phenomenon.' ROBERT CONQUEST, *New Republic*

'The interest of Dmitri Volkogonov's book is threefold: it is the first full-scale biography of Trotsky from Russia; it is based on hitherto closed Soviet archives; and the author, who died a few months ago, was a prominent historian connected to Boris Yeltsin.' RADHAKRISHNAN NAYAR, *THES*

'An excellent translation by Harold Shukman.' ABRAHAM BRUMBERG, *TLS*

'The core of the book lies in the second half, which is both original and fascinating to read. Trotsky's version of his struggle with Stalin has long been known. Volkogonov is the first historian to shed light on the Soviet side of the conflict. Citing Stalin's orders to the secret police and their reports to him, he provides a comprehensive picture of the contest that ended in Trotsky's murder.' RICHARD PIPES, *New York Times Book Review*

'Volkogonov had unprecedented access to Soviet military and secret police archives . . . In this, his final book, he makes use of these sources to add telling details to the well-known outlines – revolutionary youth, exile, triumphant return, and exile again – of Trotsky's life.' ANNE APPLEBAUM, *Spectator*

DMITRI VOLKOGONOV

Trotsky
The Eternal Revolutionary

Translated and edited by Harold Shukman

HarperCollins*Publishers*

HarperCollins*Publishers*
77–85 Fulham Palace Road,
Hammersmith, London W6 8JB

This paperback edition 1997
1 3 5 7 9 8 6 4 2

First published in Great Britain by
HarperCollins*Publishers* 1996

ISBN 0 00 638070 0

Set in Linotron Janson

Printed and bound in Great Britain by
Caledonian International Book Manufacturing Ltd, Glasgow

Contents

Illustrations

(Unless otherwise indicated, all photographs are from the David King Collection, 90 St Paul's Road, London NI 2QP)

Lev Davidovich Bronshtein – Trotsky – at the age of nine, in 1888.

Trotsky in 1897.

Trotsky's father, David Leontievich Bronshtein.

Anna Bronshtein, Trotsky's mother.

Trotsky at the time of his first arrest and imprisonment in Nikolaev, 1898.

Trotsky's first exile, Verkholensk, eastern Siberia, 1900.

Trotsky with his first wife, Alexandra Sokolovskaya.

Trotsky with his daughter Zinaida in 1906.

The 1905 revolution. Demonstration of Social Democrats in St Petersburg.

Trial of the St Petersburg Soviet.

Trotsky with Alexander Helphand and Lev Deutsch at the time of their arrest in St Petersburg in December 1905.

Trotsky reading his newly-founded *Pravda* in Vienna in 1910.

Trotsky arrives in St Petersburg, 17 May 1917.

The St Petersburg Soviet meeting in the Tauride Palace, February 1917.

Trotsky's second wife, Natalya Ivanovna Sedova.

Trotsky with Soviet delegates Admiral Altfater and Lev Kamenev at the Brest-Litovsk peace talks in January 1918.

State Prosecutor Andrei Vyshinsky at the Moscow trials.

Workers demonstrating their support for the Moscow trials.

Trotsky's elder son, Lev Sedov.

Trotsky's younger son, Sergei Sedov.

Olga Kameneva, Trotsky's sister and Kamenev's wife.

Trotsky in Mexico, 1938, with Diego Rivera, Frida Kahlo, Natalya, Reba Hansen, André Breton and Jean van Heijenoort.

Trotsky dictating to one of his secretaries in the 1930s.

At the Dewey Commission's hearings in Mexico City, April 1937: Jean van Heijenoort, Albert Goldman, Trotsky, Natalya, Jan Frankel.

Trotsky with two of his security guards in Mexico.

Trotsky with Natalya on a cactus-collecting expedition, Mexico 1940.

Trotsky feeding his rabbits, 1940.

Trotsky's study after Ramon Mercader's attack, 20 August 1940.

Mercader after his arrest.

Mercader re-enacting his attack during the investigation.

Trotsky on his death-bed.

Trotsky's funeral procession, Mexico City, 22 August 1940.

Trotsky's grandson, Esteban Volkov, at his grandfather's grave in Mexico City in 1989. (*Author's collection*)

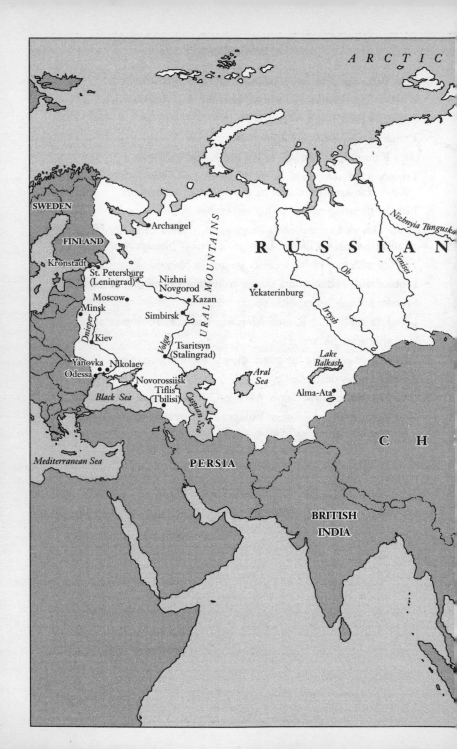

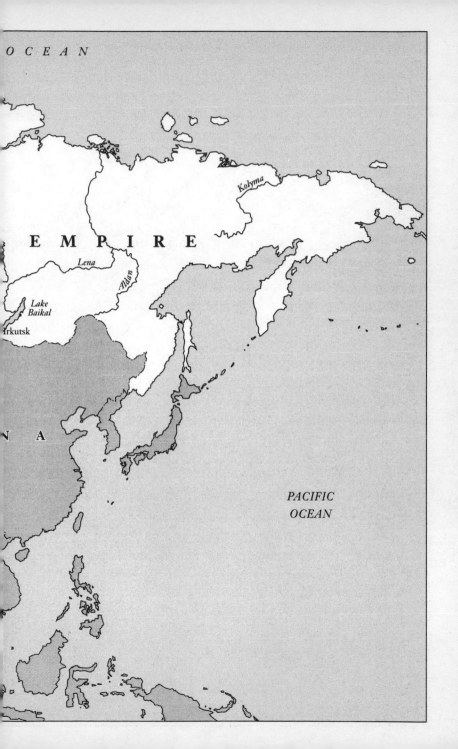

Chronological Table

(Dates according to New Style or Western Calendar)

1879	7 November	Lev Davidovich Bronshtein (Trotsky) born at Yanovka, near Yelizavetgrad (Kirovograd) in Ukraine.
	21 December	Josef Stalin born at Gori, Georgia.
1886		Trotsky begins primary school.
1888		Enters St Paul's High School, Odessa.
1896		Completes secondary education in Nikolaev.
1896–97		Joins Social Democratic revolutionary group in Nikolaev.
1898	March	Russian Social Democratic Labour Party (RSDLP) formed in Minsk. Trotsky arrested and exiled to Siberia for two years.
1899		Trotsky marries Alexandra Sokolovskaya in prison.
1900		Birth of Trotsky's first daughter, Zinaida. Lenin and Martov start their newspaper *Iskra* (The Spark).
1902		Birth of Trotsky's second daughter, Nina. Trotsky escapes from exile, adopts the name of Trotsky and leaves the country illegally. Meets Lenin for the first time in London.
1903		RSDLP splits at its Second Congress in London into Bolsheviks, led by Lenin,

		and Mensheviks, led by a group including Martov and Trotsky. Trotsky marries Natalya Sedova.
1904–06		Russo–Japanese War.
1905		Trotsky returns to Russia and takes active part in first Russian revolution.
	October	Tsar concedes political reform, including a legislative assembly, the State Duma.
	December	Trotsky elected President of St Petersburg Soviet.
1906		Trial of Trotsky and other members of St Petersburg Soviet. Birth of Trotsky's first son, Lev.
1907		Trotsky exiled to Western Siberia. Escapes abroad. First meeting with Stalin at Fifth Party Congress in London.
1908		Birth of Trotsky's second son, Sergei.
1910		Death of Trotsky's mother, Anna Bronshtein. Trotsky establishes his independent newspaper *Pravda*, which fails for lack of funds.
1912–14		Trotsky works as war correspondent in the Balkans and reporter in Paris for the newspaper *Kievskaya mysl'*.
1914		Trotsky leaves Vienna for Zurich and later Paris.
	August	Russia enters First World War.
1915–16		Trotsky collaborates with Menshevik Internationalists in Paris on newspaper *Nashe slovo*.
1916		Trotsky expelled from France to Spain, where he is arrested.
1917		Arrives in New York.
	March	Tsar abdicates. Provisional Government formed in Petrograd.
	March–May	Trotsky leaves for Russia. Arrested in Halifax, Canada. Arrives in Petrograd.
	August	Trotsky enters Bolshevik Party at Sixth Party

		Congress and becomes member of Central Committee.
	August–September	Trotsky and other Bolsheviks arrested on charges of working for Germany. Soon released.
	September	Trotsky becomes chairman of Petrograd Soviet.
	October	Military Revolutionary Committee created with Trotsky as chairman. Trotsky appointed People's Commissar for Foreign Affairs in first Soviet government.
	December	The Cheka, the Soviet political police, formed. Bolshevik–German armistice.
1918	January	Soviet–German peace talks at Brest-Litovsk. Trotsky heads Soviet delegation. Constituent Assembly dispersed by Bolsheviks after one session.
	February	Chicherin replaces Trotsky as People's Commissar for Foreign Affairs and head of Brest-Litovsk delegation.
	March	Brest-Litovsk peace treaty signed with Germany. Trotsky appointed People's Commissar for Military and Naval Affairs. Red Army founded.
	April	Civil war begins in Russia.
	July	Tsar and family executed in Yekaterinburg.
	September	Trotsky appointed chairman of the Military Revolutionary Council of the Republic.
	November	Allied–German armistice.
1919	March	Third Communist International (Comintern) founded in Moscow. Trotsky elected member of Comintern Executive Committee (ECCI).
1920	April	Poles invade Soviet Ukraine. October Armistice with Poland.
	November	Civil war ends with defeat and evacuation of White armies in Crimea.
1921	March	Anti-Bolshevik uprising of Kronstadt

		garrison. Tenth Party Congress adopts Lenin's New Economic Policy and bans the formation of factions in the Party.
1922	February	Cheka renamed GPU. Trotsky's father, David Bronshtein, dies of typhus.
	April	Stalin elected General Secretary of the Party.
	May	Lenin's first stroke.
	December	Lenin's second stroke. Formation of Union of Soviet Socialist Republics.
1923	March	Lenin's third stroke.
	April	Twelfth Party Congress.
	October	Trotsky writes to Central Committee and Central Control Commission. Statement of forty-six of Trotsky's supporters to the Politburo.
1924	January	Lenin dies. Trotsky, convalescing in the Caucasus, is absent from his funeral.
	May	Thirteenth Party Congress. Recognition of USSR from Austria, Britain, China, Denmark, France, Greece, Italy, Norway and Sweden. Death of Trotsky's eldest sister Elizabeth.
1925	January	Trotsky removed as chairman of Revolutionary Military Council and as People's Commissar for Military Affairs.
	May	Trotsky appointed chairman of the Chief Concessions Committee.
	December	Fourteenth Party Congress.
1926	March	Trotsky travels to Berlin for medical treatment.
	July	'Statement of the 13' and 'Platform of the 83'. Zinoviev expelled from Poliburo and leadership of Comintern.
	October	Oppositional statement by sixteen of Trotsky's supporters. Trotsky and Kamenev removed from Politburo.
1927	September	Trotsky expelled from Executive Committee of Comintern.

	October	Trotsky removed from Central Committee.
	November	Trotsky and Zinoviev expelled from Party.
	December	Fifteenth Party Congress.
1928	January	Trotsky banished to Alma Ata, Kazakhstan.
	June	Death of Trotsky's younger daughter, Nina Nevelson, from tuberculosis.
1929	February	Trotsky deported from USSR to Turkey.
	April	First Five-Year Plan adopted by Sixteenth Party Congress.
	July	Trotsky's *Bulletin of the Opposition* launched.
	November	Bukharin expelled from Politburo.
	December	Stalin proclaims end of NEP and start of collectivization.
1930		Trotsky's autobiography, *My Life*, published in Berlin.
1931		Trotsky's *History of the Russian Revolution* published in Berlin. Soviet rewriting of history begins under Stalin's guidance.
1932		Trotsky's book *The Stalinist School of Falsification* published in Berlin.
	February	Trotsky, with his wife Natalya and son Lev, deprived of Soviet citizenship.
	November	Trotsky briefly visits Copenhagen to give lectures.
	December	Identity cards issued to urban population in USSR. Collective farmers denied right to leave their villages.
1933	January	Hitler becomes Chancellor of Germany. Trotsky's elder daughter Zinaida Volkova commits suicide in Berlin after deep depression.
	July	Trotsky and Natalya leave Turkey for France.
	November	Diplomatic and trade relations established between USSR and USA.
1934	January	Seventeenth Party Congress, the 'Congress of Victors'. Trotsky prepares the founding of a new Fourth ('Marxist') International.

		Begins work on his biography of Lenin, which is to remain unfinished.
	September	USSR joins League of Nations.
	December	Sergei Kirov assassinated in Leningrad.
1935	June	Trotsky moves to Norway. His first wife, Alexandra Sokolovskaya, is exiled to Siberia where she dies after a few years. Part of Trotsky's correspondence is sold by his son Lev to the Institute of Social History in Amsterdam.
1936		Trotsky's nephews, Alexander and Yuri Kamenev, arrested and shot. Trotsky completes his book *The Revolution Betrayed*. Trial and execution of Zinoviev, Kamenev and fourteen others. Trial of seventeen, including Radek and Pyatakov; thirteen executed. Execution of Red Army leadership.
	November	Part of Trotsky's archive is stolen by the NKVD from the Institute of Historical Research in Paris.
	December	Trotsky and Natalya deported from Norway to Mexico.
1937	January	Trotsky arrives in Mexico and is given political asylum. Takes part in international commission intended to establish faked character of political trials in Moscow. Begins book on Stalin which is to remain unfinished. Younger son, Sergei, arrested in USSR and executed. Nephew, Boris Bronshtein, executed.
1938	February	Trotsky's eldest son Lev dies in Paris in mysterious circumstances.
	March	Trial and execution of Bukharin, Rykov and sixteen others.
	April	Trotsky's elder brother, Alexander Bronshtein, executed in Moscow.
1939	August	Soviet–German Non-Aggression Pact

		signed in the Kremlin.
	September	Germany invades Poland. USSR invades Poland. Start of Second World War. Founding congress of Fourth International in Paris.
1940	February–March	Trotsky writes his last will and testament.
	27 May	Unsuccessful attempt on Trotsky's life organized by NKVD.
	20 August	Another attempt on Trotsky's life results in his fatal wounding.
	21 August	Trotsky dies.
	December	Natalya Sedova sells remainder of Trotsky's archives to Harvard University.
1941	August	Last issue of the *Bulletin of the Opposition* published.
	October	Trotsky's younger sister, Olga Kameneva, executed.

Without doubt, Trotsky stands head and shoulders above all the other Bolsheviks, except Lenin. Lenin is of course more important and more powerful. He is the head of the revolution, but Trotsky is more talented and more brilliant.

NIKOLAI BERDYAEV

Editor's Preface

By the spring of 1987, it had become clear that the conventional Soviet treatment of modern Russian – more particularly, Soviet – history was about to undergo a fundamental shift. At first, the most dramatic revisions were conducted by a playwright and a novelist – Mikhail Shatrov in his unstaged plays, and Anatoli Rybakov in his semi-autobiographical, semi-factual novel *Children of the Arbat* – and historians were relatively slow off the mark. Then, over a brief period beginning in January 1988, the Soviet State Prosecutor announced the 'rehabilitation' of the 'Old Guard' of Bolsheviks who had been liquidated in the infamous show trials of the mid-1930s. The reason given for this belated admission of injustice was that the charges on which they had been executed were groundless, although the evidence for this discovery was not and has never been revealed.

Articles began appearing on previously taboo subjects, such as the murder of the Polish officer corps at Katyn, and new editions of encyclopedias and biographical dictionaries began to reflect a saner approach to previous 'non-persons'. Mensheviks, Socialist Revolutionaries and exterminated Bolsheviks were reinstated into Russian history, along with liberals, conservatives, White émigrés, tsarist generals and monarchist politicians.

However, Trotsky's name did not figure among the rehabilitated cohort of 1917; nor could it, since he had not been officially charged and tried, nor had he been sentenced or executed 'judicially'. He had undoubtedly figured as the chief inspirer, the *éminence grise*, the manipulator of the grand conspiracy against the Soviet state and its leaders, and his name had been a constant refrain in all the trials, including those of the Red Army élite, and was used to condemn anyone or any group suspected of real or potential hostility.

Of the rehabilitated Bolsheviks, it was above all Bukharin who first attracted a measure of interest, since it was thought that his ardent advocacy of Lenin's New Economic Policy might yield insights at a time when intellectuals and the Gorbachev government were seeking policies that could accommodate both a market and a planned economy. Other leading figures still await reassessment. As for Trotsky, a small number of short studies on his ideas has been produced in post-Soviet Russia, but their aims have been to set the record straight in terms of the facts of his life and his role in the revolution and civil war, and they have therefore concentrated on achieving as neutral, or as 'normal', a balance as possible – a laudable achievement, given the paucity of sources and the accumulated mendacity to which Soviet scholars had become accustomed over decades.

Dmitri Volkogonov was a professional soldier for most of his life, rising to the rank of Colonel-General under Brezhnev as chief of the army's Political Education Section. In the mid-1980s he became Director of the Institute of Military History in Moscow, and from that time began asking difficult questions about Soviet history. He assembled two (unpublished) volumes of data on the arrests and liquidations of the Red Army officer corps, and wrote a monumental study of Stalin which could not be published for several years. As the era of *glasnost*, or freer thinking, progressed, he became more outspoken publicly, especially about the Communist Party and its failure to move politically and ideologically with the times. Savagely attacked by the military establishment, and the Minister of Defence in person, for a generally awkward attitude and in particular for his 'anti-Soviet' interpretation of the Second World War as expressed in the draft of a new multi-volume history prepared (but never published) by his Institute, in the spring of 1991 he had little choice but to leave his post and devote himself to independent research.

His political life of Stalin (*Stalin: Triumph and Tragedy*) had been published in Russia in 1990, and had aroused strong mixed feelings, especially among hard-line Communists who saw in his denigration of the former 'father of the peoples' a dangerous trend that could lead to yet further weakening of the state's authoritarian traditions. They were to be proved right. The rising tide of criticism – of the state

and its history, and above all of the Party's claim to rule alone –
eventually inundated the leadership in an unstoppable flood. After the
failed coup of August 1991, Volkogonov became a special defence
adviser to President Yeltsin and head of the Russian Archive Declas-
sifying Commission, among other posts.

Published in Russia in 1992, Volkogonov's book on Trotsky sold
about a million copies, but received less critical attention than his
Stalin. Trotsky's legacy, unlike those of Stalin and Lenin, had long
been submerged and obliterated as a topic of debate, and his place in
Soviet history books had correspondingly been diminished to one of
no importance. For Western readers, however, Trotsky has always
been one of the most enigmatic and powerful personalities of the
Russian revolution, a Mephistophelian figure whose life ended in an
appropriately dramatic way. The absence of a balanced view of him
from the Soviet side meant that he was seen in too sharply contrasted
a light, and it is the merit of Dmitri Volkogonov's book that he has
attempted to rectify this imbalance, while also providing a unique
insight into the Soviet dimension.

This, the first full-scale political biography of Trotsky to emerge
from Russia, was made possible by the fact that Volkogonov has had
access to the relevant Russian archives that were hitherto absent from
Western studies. Isaac Deutscher was granted access to the Trotsky
papers at Harvard University by Trotsky's widow, and his three-
volume work, published between 1954 and 1963, remains a valuable
source. But Volkogonov has produced materials held by the NKVD
that reveal Soviet motives and actions as never before. His access to
the archives was complemented by his discovery of surviving members
of Trotsky's family and, most notably, of the functionaries and special
agents who were closely involved in Stalin's personal vendetta against
Trotsky and the plan to assassinate him.

After completing his *Trotsky*, Volkogonov then went on to produce
a political analysis and life of 'the last bastion to fall' in his own mind,
namely that of Lenin. If Trotsky had become at best little more than
a name, and if Stalin had been a real-life memory for millions of
Soviet citizens, Lenin had virtually been an icon for generations, an
integral part of Soviet education, a totem, a source of ritual and dogma
for national and local leaders in need of an ideological prop for a
new policy or an apt phrase to support a decision. The response to

Volkogonov's *Lenin: Life and Legacy*, when it was published in Russia in 1994, was predictably divided and extreme. Those who regarded the dissolution of the Communist Party and the dismemberment of the Soviet Union as crimes against the people were aghast at Volkogonov's temerity and disloyalty, and his book was condemned as tantamount to sacrilege. It was admired, on the other hand, by those for whom the history of the revolution and the origins of the Stalinist state had long become mere questions of history, those who had come to see Marxism-Leninism, and still more the adoration of a long-dead politician, as utterly irrelevant to the needs of the end of the twentieth century. Both sides thus recognized the book as a demolition of the intellectual foundations of the old system.

As a politician himself, Volkogonov believes that knowledge of the recent past, and especially of the origins of the Soviet state, is relevant to the needs of present-day Russia. He has seen both the rising tide of nationalism and the authoritarian response of the government he supports in the face of the problems that have surfaced with a vengeance in the former Soviet Union. His studies of the three leading figures of the revolutionary period – invaluable historical works in themselves – are meant to show the danger of combining radical politics with authoritarian tendencies. Lenin moulded his ideology from such ingredients and based the 'first workers' state' on its foundations, embedding state violence and terror in the very fabric of the new order. Stalin, once his hold on power was unchallenged, applied his hybrid policies of radicalism and reaction – rapid industrialization and terror, collectivization of agriculture and violence.

Trotsky occupied a unique position. As a militant radical during the revolution and civil war, he saw no need to adopt moderate policies once the internal threat had receded. For him, it was the threat from the capitalist world that was most pressing, and the Russian revolution was only the first stage of the world revolution that was envisaged as inevitable in Marx's understanding of history and social change. As Trotsky himself confessed in his last will and testament in 1940, he was just as committed to the revolutionary idea in his last days as he had been when he first entered the Russian revolutionary movement in the 1890s, if not more so.

Commitment to world revolution entailed for Trotsky commitment to radical domestic and foreign policies when he was still a figure with authority in the Soviet Union, and, as Volkogonov shows, it was this above all that alienated him from the rank and file of a Party that was more inclined to begin the economic reconstruction of the country than to embark on further revolutionary adventures. Certainly it would be some time before the Soviets formally abandoned the slogan of world revolution, or even their covert financial support of foreign Communist parties and front organizations in the West, but in the 1920s, when Stalin was working to consolidate his position as Party leader, Trotsky's arguments as an irreconcilable radical gave his rival the ammunition he needed to hound him out of office and ultimately out of the country.

Trotsky's expulsion from the Soviet Union coincided with the Party's adoption of the very measures he had advocated: forced collectivization of the peasants and rapid industrialization, using draconian measures wherever necessary. Volkogonov has traced the continuity between the violence and coercion of Lenin's ideas and the terror of Stalinism, and he has shown that throughout his adult life Trotsky's thinking and his actions provide a homogenous link in the chain. There is no suggestion that, had he held power, Trotsky would necessarily have unleashed the wave of terror, the purges and the show trials perpetrated by Stalin: everything Trotsky wrote on this matter argues against such a view, and in any case the question is hypothetical. The claim is, however, made by Volkogonov that Trotsky cannot be exonerated of the crime, as the author now sees it, of creating a system that behaved, while Trotsky was still a part of it and after, in a way the world has become accustomed to call 'Stalinist'.

Not all Russian revolutionaries, once they had escaped or were expelled from Soviet Russia, remained committed to the cause of universal Marxist revolution. Some became doctors and engineers, salesmen, archivists and antiquarian book-dealers, retaining only romantic memories of an adventurous youth. Trotsky shared with them a deep hatred of Stalin and his works, but, having left the Soviet Union, he remained fully active in promoting world revolution, publishing a journal, *Bulletin of the Opposition*, and establishing a Fourth (Marxist) International, as a rival to the Comintern which had become a tool of Soviet foreign policy. The fact that his venture ended in oblivion does not diminish Trotsky's image as one of the most committed revolutionaries of the twentieth century – the eternal radical, indeed – but rather shows that the ideas to which he devoted his life were both outmoded and Utopian.

The Fate of a Revolutionary

The armoured train was on its way to Kiev, rattling over the rails towards the Ukrainian capital. The passengers in one of the middle wagons were not sleeping. In the large saloon, furnished with leather armchairs and a sofa, a long table and telephone equipment, a man in an unbuttoned tunic and boots was standing at one of the spyholes. He was of medium height, with a neat beard, and above a high forehead he had a full head of hair streaked with grey. His noble Roman nose was surmounted by an elegant pince-nez. He had lively, bright blue eyes. As he stared into the darkness, searching for signs of life, he saw nothing but a vast, war-torn country languishing in ruins and deep gloom. It was August 1919.

At the table sat a young man in a flannel army shirt, pen in hand. Before him lay telegrams from the 3rd and 4th Armies of the Eastern Front, then advancing on Tobol. The southern grouping was making good progress towards Turkestan. Their reports confirmed that the leader of the White armies on that front, Kolchak's, days were numbered. The path to the east would be open. But the man in the tunic was thinking of other things. His secretary scribbled down his dictation: 'The defeat of the Hungarian [Soviet] Republic, our failures in Ukraine and the possible loss of the Black Sea coast, along with our successes on the eastern front, significantly alter our international orientation ... The situation looks different when we face the east.' In confident tone, he continued: 'There can be no doubt that our Red Army is an incomparably more powerful force on the Asian fields of world politics than it is on the European. We now face the distinct possibility of a long wait while events unfold in Europe, but a period of activity in Asia. The road to India may at this moment be more open to us, and shorter, than the road to Soviet Hungary. Our army, which by European standards is still of little importance, is capable of destroying the unstable balance of colonial relations, giving a push to and ensuring the victory of an uprising of the oppressed masses in Asia.' He sat down and continued dictating: 'Naturally, our operations in the east presuppose the building and reinforcement of a mighty base in the Urals. We must concentrate there all the labour force we had intended settling in the Don oblast. We must send to the Urals all our best scientific and technical forces, our best organizers and administrators. We must send the best Ukrainian Party people who for other reasons are now without jobs. If they have lost Ukraine, let them conquer Siberia for the Soviet revolution.'

As he went on, he outlined not merely the general strategic line of the revolution, but even provided the concrete detail: 'A cavalry corps of 30–40,000 horsemen must be formed to invade India. The path to Paris and London lies through the cities of Afghanistan, the Punjab and Bengal. Our victories in the Urals and Siberia must greatly raise the prestige of the Soviet Republic throughout oppressed Asia. We must seize the moment and somewhere in the Urals or Turkestan we must concentrate a revolutionary academy, the political and military headquarters of the Asiatic revolution, which could soon become much more effective than the Executive Committee of the Third International. Our task is to shift the centre of gravity of our international policy in good time.'[1]

The speaker was Lev Trotsky, Chairman of the Revolutionary Military Committee of the Republic, Commissar for the Army and Navy, and a member of the Politburo. His secretary was Nikolai Sermuks. In the course of his life Trotsky wrote or dictated about 30,000 documents, the great majority of which are scattered in numerous archives. Virtually everything he wrote was connected in some way with the Russian and world revolution. For him, and those like him, it was considered normal, natural and indeed obligatory to spur on the revolution. In the above notes to the Central Committee he was proposing a new strategy, calling on the Party to turn towards the east, to despatch large cavalry forces to India at a time when, as he knew perfectly well, the whole of the west and south of Russia was in flames, and the greater part of the country's industry and agriculture, as well as a third of her people, were under German control. Only the next day he was informing Lenin of the critical position in the south, and demanding a meeting of the Politburo at which measures could be taken to overcome the 'threatening danger'.[2] But he also knew that India was the Achilles' heel of the British Empire.

Even when, twenty years later, he found himself cornered in his concrete Mexican fortress, he would still dream of the world revolution. Of the millions who passed along the revolutionary path, the great majority left no trace. Trotsky, however, remains even today a topic of debate. He is remembered with hatred and respect, anger and admiration. His portrait cannot be properly painted only in black and white, but calls for a wide range of colours. Opinion on this most famous of revolutionaries has swung from glorification to anathema, until at last it is possible to accept him coolly and objectively as a vivid, complex, multi-faceted personality in the gallery of world figures.

The first study of Trotsky was probably that of G.A. Ziv, his old schoolfriend, who published a short book in New York in 1921.[3] There were also official biographies. One, compiled by order of the Central Committee in May 1924, was entitled 'Bronshtein (Trotsky) Lev Davidovich, also known as "Lvov", "N. Trotsky", "Yanovsky", and by the literary pseudonyms of "Antid Oto", "Takhotsky", "Neophyte", and others'. This five-page document was accompanied by a note which stated that 'Comrade Trotsky's biography, with the list of his publications, has been compiled by Comrade [Evgeniya] Bosh by order of Istpart [the Central Committee section dealing with the history of the Party and the October Revolution], and is to be kept in the Secret Section of Istpart for use by research workers'.[4]

These early biographies are uncontroversial and superficial, containing only the bare facts of Trotsky's life. Fifteen years later his image would be presented in the Soviet Union as malevolent, bloodthirsty, repellent. Addressing the February/March 1937 Central Committee Plenum, Stalin would describe the Trotskyists and their leader as 'a barefaced gang of wreckers, spies and murderers'.[5] The Soviet press depicted Trotsky as the source of all evils, and for the next fifty years continued to heap odium on him as on no one else. Gradually the old abuse gave way to new myths, claiming that Trotsky was a bloodstained maniac hungry for personal power, that he was in every way the forerunner of Stalin. Over the last few years, Trotsky has

become a subject of more balanced judgement, a personality symboliz-
ing not merely the radicalism of the Communist idea, as it was
expressed in the uncompromising and Utopian nature of Bolshevik
plans, but also in its tragic realization. Trotsky was at the birth of the
Soviet state, he was one of the architects of the Soviet totalitarian
bureaucratic system whose baleful effects have yet to be eradicated
from Russian life.

It was Trotsky's fate that he was able to synthesize an unbending
faith in Communist ideals with the criminal mercilessness of the dictatorship of the proletariat, that he could be both one of the inspirers
of the Red Terror and its victim. He was, in my view, unique in that
he combined what was most attractive about the Russian revolutionaries with the most repugnant aspects of Bolshevism. Early in the
century, Trotsky had read the prophetic words of the anarchist Prince
Kropotkin:

> All revolutionaries dream of the revolution as an opportunity to liqui-
> date their enemies legally ... of conquering power, of creating an
> all-powerful, all-knowing state which will deal with the people as sub-
> jects and subordinates, ruling them with the help of thousands and
> millions of bureaucrats of all kinds ... They dream of a 'committee
> of public salvation', whose purpose is to get rid of anyone who dares
> to think differently ... Finally, they dream of restricting the initiative
> of the individual and of the nation itself ... to make sure the nation
> chooses leaders who will think for it and make laws in its name.[6]

Trotsky marked this passage with a query, but both he and the
Bolshevik leadership acted according to Kropotkin's formulation with
no such questioning.

I have come to see, in writing my studies of Lenin, Trotsky and
Stalin, that each one complements the other historically. Lenin
emerges in revolutionary history as the inspirer, Trotsky as the agitator and Stalin as the executor, the one who carried out the idea.
The swerves, the collisions and the tragedies of Soviet history can be
observed in sharp relief when seen through the prism of these three
personalities. In this respect, the biographical method is quite effective, for it allows one to analyze an entire historical layer of time
through the personal fabric of a human existence. In the draft of one
his articles, Trotsky underlined the phrase: 'If personalities do not

make history, then history makes itself by means of personalities.'[7]

Trotsky enjoyed many triumphs, the most significant being that of October 1917. Having tasted this victory, it might have seemed to him that things would go on in this way for a long time, if not forever. And yet, soon after the end of the Civil War, he felt himself to be virtually superfluous in the ordinary world of everyday concerns. Everything pointed to his being made for big events, for worldwide glory, but the world revolution had stumbled, and even the 'Asiatic' one had not occurred. One tragedy after another now began to dog Trotsky's life. He lost all his jobs, was exiled, deported, wandered the globe in search of a safe hiding place from Stalin's assassins, and while virtually every member of his family, as well as countless numbers of his comrades, were meeting violent deaths. Labelled 'Trotskyist', it was not only genuine supporters who were being liquidated, but also millions of compatriots who were merely suspected of any lack of loyalty to the dictatorial regime. It is amazing that Trotsky managed to survive ten years in emigration, considering the scale of Stalin's manhunt for him. Two months before he was assassinated, he wrote: 'I can say that I live in this world not in the dimension of rules, but in that of exceptions.'[8] The life of this revolutionary was almost magical, a meteoric flight into world fame, and a long, long drama of struggle, hopes and disappointment, ending with the last act in Mexico.

Trotsky himself, his gaze fixed on the mirror of history, did not regard his life as tragic. At least, in 1930, in exile on the Turkish island of Prinkipo, he could write: ' "And what of our personal fate?" I hear you ask. I do not measure the historical process by the yardstick of personal fate ... I don't recognize personal tragedy. I recognize the replacement of one leader of the revolution by another.'[9] In practice, of course, he was able to lose the fight, but not to abandon hope. He knew very early on that, as far as history was concerned, his defeat might come to be seen as more worthy than victory in a different battle.

Trotsky's biographers enjoy a rich store of materials left by their subject, in the form of books, articles, pen-portraits, memoirs, essays. His wife, Natalia Sedova, recalled that he had intended writing a series of major books, but 'everyday events ... pushed them to one side'. His book on Stalin was forced on him by a combination of financial need and his publishers. Several times he said he wanted to write a 'pedestrian' book that would earn him enough money to be able to 'entertain himself writing about things that interested him. But he never managed,' Sedova wrote. 'He was not capable of writing pedestrian books.'[10]

Trotsky was one of the first of the Soviet leaders to exploit the intellectual potential of his secretaries to the maximum. His every speech and note, prepared or spontaneous, was carefully recorded, transcribed and printed. Most of the twenty-one volumes of his collected works that he managed, with a few gaps, to publish before his exile in 1927 consist of his reports, speeches and newspaper articles.[11] Another important source are the archives, including the Houghton Library at Harvard, which contains some 20,000 documents, including 3000 letters; the International Institute of Social History in Amsterdam, which houses more than 1000 letters, including Trotsky's correspondence with Lenin; and part of the Nicolaevsky Collection at the Hoover Institution. Archives inside Russia, which have been completely closed until very recently, include the former Central Party Archives, the Central State Archives of the October Revolution, those of the Soviet Army, the Ministry of Defence, the Committee for State Security, and a number of others. The majority of the documents in this book are published for the first time.

Another important source was the testimony of relatives of Trotsky who had by some miracle survived, and a number of people who had met or known him personally. Among these, I would like to express my gratitude to Trotsky's niece A.A. Kasatikova, his great-nephew V.B. Bronshtein, and the wife of his younger son Sergei, O.E. Grebner; to one of his stenographers, N.A. Marennikova, and one of Stalin's secretaries, A.P. Balashov; to N.A. Ioffe, D.T. Shepilov, A.K. Mironov, V.M. Polyakov, N.G. Dubrovinsky, D.S. Zlatopolsky and F.M. Nazarov, all of whom had relations with the family or with Trotsky himself; and among the remaining 'Trotskyists', to I.I. Vrachev, Stuart Kirby, and the late Tamara Deutscher, widow of Trotsky's best biographer, Isaac Deutscher.

I have also been fortunate enough to have talked to senior Soviet security officers whose knowledge of Trotsky's fate went beyond hearsay. These include P.A. Sudoplatov, Ye.P. Pivonravov and A.N. Shelepin. From the end of the 1920s until 20 August 1940, when he was liquidated on Stalin's orders, Trotsky was kept under constant surveillance by the special services, the GPU, OGPU and NKVD, the latter body knowing more about him than he could ever have suspected. Stalin was kept regularly informed about his every move, and on occasion Trotsky's writings found their way to Stalin's desk even before they were published. I have used the correspondence of the NKVD field unit that penetrated Trotsky's entourage, and have had numerous conversations with the people responsible for carrying out the Central Committee's order to assassinate him.

Among Western authors whose works I have consulted, Isaac Deutscher's three-part biography stands out, as do the efforts of Yuri Feltshinsky; Baruch Knei-Paz's monograph is a fundamental work, while others who have contributed to 'Trotskology' include Dale Reid, Michael Jacobson, Joel Carmichael, Isaac Don Levine, Harold Nelson and Robert Tucker. Only recently have Russian scholars approached the subject, and among them I should like to mention Yu.I. Koroblev, V.I. Startsev, N.A. Vasetsky, Y.A. Polyakov and P.B. Volobuev.

I began working on my three 'portraits' many years ago, gradually gathering little-known material, facts, publications and personal testimony. Had I observed proper methodology, Lenin should have come first, followed by Trotsky and then Stalin. The reason they have appeared [in Russia] in reverse order is not accidental. The book on Stalin, who now personifies Russia's historic failure, was written by 1985, at a time when an honest critical analysis of Lenin was simply impossible. Soviet prejudice against Trotsky continues even now to be very strong, and in 1987 the Party could still speak of the great service done by higher Party circles, led by Stalin, in 'the victory over Trotskyism'. Thanks to decades of brainwashing, most people in the Soviet Union are not even aware that Marxism in Russia developed in three stages: Leninism, Trotskyism and Stalinism, all of them deriving from the same root. Despite some major differences, what all three men shared was reliance on social violence, a belief in the absolute certainty of only one ideology, and the conviction that they had the right to dispose of the destinies of nations.

I have tried to describe the evolution from freedom to the unfreedom that characterized the dominant social thinking of the time. Before October 1917, all Russian revolutionaries clamoured for freedom of speech, yet when Maxim Gorky declared that Bolshevik violence was 'the path to anarchy, the end of the proletariat and of the revolution', the Bolsheviks took harsh measures not only against Gorky's paper *Novaya Zhizn*, but against all the free press. At a meeting of the Council of People's Commissars (Sovnarkom) chaired by Lenin in December 1917, Trotsky proposed even 'harsher measures against the bourgeois press and foul slanders on the Soviet regime'.[12] Almost without realizing it, he and the others were confining freedom to a reservation where in due course the time would come to liquidate it altogether. Here lay the paradox of Bolshevism: having proclaimed freedom as the aim of their revolution, they did not see that they were taking it away not only from the 'ex-people', but also from those they had promised to make 'everything', the people who had trusted them. It was the party-cum-state they invested with freedom, then the bureaucratic machine, and finally the dictator.

To the end of his life, Trotsky did not see that many of the fundamental tenets of Marxism, which he never doubted, were profoundly wrong. But it was precisely the false ideas of the dictatorship of the proletariat and of class war that lay at the root of the future tragedy, and it was the process of making these postulates into immutable principles, to which Trotsky remained faithful all his life, that led the country to its historic failure. A political portrait of Trotsky, therefore, is also an account of the fate of freedom in Russia, without doubt a tragic story.

When in March 1922 Lenin wrote, in his secret letter to the Politburo, 'If it is necessary to achieve a particular political goal by means of a number of cruel measures, then they should be carried out in the most energetic way and in the shortest possible time,'[13] Trotsky was in complete agreement with him. This was the deeply ingrained flaw in Russian Jacobinism, of which Trotsky was one of the most eloquent exponents. However pitiful the results of his efforts, to the end of his life Trotsky never ceased to peer into the future, believing fanatically, as he did, in the coming of the world revolution.

1

At the Turn of the Century

The leaders of the October revolution were born during the reign of Alexander II (1855–81), a time when, arguably, the tsarist regime experienced the first tremors of its own demise, when the 'tsar-liberator' was blown up by a bomb thrown by members of the terrorist group 'People's Will'. The Russian Empire was lagging behind the West, and the small but significant intelligentsia was the first section of society to feel and express its disillusionment, although the peasants and the workers had not yet lost their age-old delusion of 'the good tsar'.

By the turn of the century that atmosphere had changed. It was a difficult and confused time. The gentry had long lost their power and were growing still weaker, the burgeoning working class was generating revolutionary discontent, while the taciturn peasantry, oppressed by hopelessness, harboured the potential for violent rebellion. Revolutionary ideas were being spread with increasing vigour by intellectuals claiming to speak in the name of the hapless. Some were calling for enlightened reform, others preaching extreme radicalism, including individual terror. The Church meanwhile, as well as the police and the censor, did its utmost to strengthen the throne. Those with perspicacity, however, were able to sense in the barely detectable subterranean tremors the approach of a time of great change and convulsions. Just as one can almost smell the approaching spring in February, so the turn of the century in Russia was felt to be the time before the storm.

The Bronshteins

The life of Jews in Russia was governed to a great extent by the constraints of the Pale – that is, the broad corridor from the Baltic to the Black Sea, roughly following the old Polish frontier, and within which the great majority of the Jewish population were compelled to reside. Russia proper, or the provinces outside the Pale, was mostly off-limits to Jews. The rules which governed the Pale were themselves arbitrary, being both extended and narrowed by Alexander I and Nicholas I. When they were narrowed, some Jewish families, unwilling to suffer the restraints of life in some pathetic *shtetl*, or townlet, moved to the south of Russia, to what in Soviet times would be called 'virgin lands'. The government encouraged settlement on the fertile northern shores of the Black Sea where, as well as Russians, Ukrainians, Greeks and Bulgarians, a small number of Jewish colonists also settled – though they were rather exceptional, since agriculture and cattle-raising were not occupations associated at that time with the Jews. The Bronshteins, who came from a *shtetl* near Poltava, close to the centre of present-day Ukraine, were one such exception.

Trotsky's father, David Bronshtein was a tough and enterprising farmer. He bought about 250 acres from a retired Colonel Yanovsky near the small town of Bobrinets, in the more southerly province of Kherson, and by dint of hard labour and close-fisted resourcefulness, and by the constant acquisition of more and more land, became a substantial landowner. During the revolution he was to find himself caught between two fires: the Whites saw him as the father of a Red leader, while to the Reds he was a rich private farmer and exploiter. A number of telegrams of the time show that Trotsky's relatives were spared by neither the Whites nor the Reds. Having lost his estate, David Bronshtein, with the help of some local Reds, cabled his son: 'On Denikin's orders, Uncle Grigory, his wife and cousin, Lev Abramovich Bronshtein, have been arrested and taken to Novorossiisk as hostages. Their situation is very serious. I ask you to do everything to obtain their release and to inform us of the result in Odessa.'[1]

Trotsky helped his dispossessed father by setting him up as the manager of a requisitioned flour mill near Moscow. David Bronshtein retained a life-long admiration for his son, although he could not understand how his family could have produced a revolutionary. Totally illiterate, only towards the end of his life did David manage to make out some words, and then only in order to decipher the titles of the books and articles his youngest son was publishing. He died of typhus in 1922.

Trotsky's mother, Anna, was a typical Jewish town dweller from Odessa, where she had received a modest education. She married David for love, thus condemning herself to the life of a peasant, no easy option for a city girl. She managed, however, to adapt, and also to introduce some elements of culture into the family's life as countryfolk. Whenever opportunity allowed Anna spent her time reading, occasionally ordering books by post, and did all she could to ensure an education for her eight children, of whom only Lev, two sisters and a brother survived beyond childhood.

Leib (Lev) Bronshtein was born on 25 October 1879 (7 November according to the Western calendar, which the Soviet regime adopted on 1 February 1918). In the brief autobiography he submitted in 1919 for the Party's official record, he wrote that he was 'born in the village of Yanovka, Kherson Province, district of Yelizavetgrad, on the small estate of my landowner-father'.[2] In fact, the family already owned more than 250 acres, was renting another 500, had a steam-operated mill, plenty of various livestock, and was employing peasant labourers by the dozen. Lev's childhood, of which he wrote little, was not, he recalled, one of hunger and cold, as the family was already comfortably off. 'But it was a bleak sufficiency', for the family 'strained every muscle and directed every thought towards work and savings', and children were accorded little space in such an environment. 'We were not deprived, except of life's generosity and tenderness.' Childhood for Lev had been neither the 'sunny meadow' enjoyed by a small minority, nor the 'dark cave of hunger, violence and misery' suffered by the majority. 'It was the grey childhood of a petty bourgeois family, in the countryside, in the sticks, with wide-open spaces and narrow, mean interests and values.'[3] Perhaps the young Lyova learned some of the realities of life as he kept notes for his father, of how much they were getting for their wheat, how many pounds of grain a peasant had brought for milling, how much the poor peasants were earning.

Another facet of his childhood was closely associated with his mother, and with the mostly successful efforts she made to imbue her children with a love of knowledge. Trotsky recalled the long winter nights, the house buried in snow higher than the windows, when his mother loved reading to them, stumbling over a word or a complicated phrase, and showing her delight when one of the children offered an explanation. 'But,' he wrote, 'she read with persistence, tirelessly, and during the slack hours on winter days, we could hear the steady hum of her voice as we entered the porch.'[4] Perhaps it was on such nights that his mother sowed the seeds of a culture that would soon produce rich fruit.

Perhaps also the sight of the life led by the impoverished peasants, who came in their hundreds to reap the Bronshteins' harvest, shocked the future Marxist. Barefoot and dressed in rags, they worked for pennies, and were fed a basic vegetable soup, porridge and bread. They slept in the open and under the ricks when it rained.

Undoubtedly, one influence on the mind of the young Trotsky was that of school. His first school was a *heder*, or Jewish primary school. His progress there was mediocre, for he lacked Yiddish, the medium of instruction, and neither the Hebrew alphabet nor the prayer book could have had any meaning for him. Indeed, religious observance was of little more than symbolic importance to the family in general. But he did learn to read and write Russian, and had barely mastered the grammar when he began writing verses which, unlike the poetic efforts of the young Stalin, appear not to have survived.

In 1888 M.F. Shpentser, a relative of his mother who would later become a publisher in the south of Russia, got the boy into a good state school in Odessa – no simple matter, as a quota operated, according to which Jewish children must not exceed 10 per cent (in some cases 5 or 2 per cent) of the pupils in a school. In his own official file, Trotsky recorded that he had attended St Paul's High School and was always top of his class.[5] Despite the fact that ordinary high schools differed from gymnasia, which also taught Classics, in that they devoted more time to the natural sciences and mathematics, Trotsky managed to read many of the major works of Russian and Western literature. He fell foul, however, of the French teacher, a Swiss called Bernand, and was expelled for a year, an event he apparently regarded as sufficiently important in his revolutionary development to mention in his official record. Rejecting sports and other recreational activities, he excelled in all subjects and remained top of the class, and the ease with which he accomplished this feat was to leave a perceptible mark on his character for the rest of his life. He was extremely self-assured, self-assertive and somewhat condescending towards his schoolmates. His biographer G.A. Ziv, who knew him in those years, later wrote that 'the key feature of Bronshtein's personality was that everywhere and always he had to be first, the other facets of his psyche serving only as secondary elements'.[6]

Nature had endowed Trotsky with bright blue eyes, thick black hair, regular features, the gift of elegance and a talent for dressing well. He had many admirers and as many detractors, for talent is rarely forgiven, and in time, moreover, the sense that he was exceptional generated in him marked egoistic and egocentric traits. This was underlined by the fact that, even when he was popular, he had no close friends, for friendship demands equality. From childhood on, Trotsky was unwilling to recognize his intellectual equal in anyone, except possibly in Lenin, and even then only after October 1917. Trotsky recalled nothing good of his schooldays, which he characterized as 'if not black, then grey. I can hardly think of a single teacher whom I might remember with affection.'[7] He would often say that there were too many mediocrities in the world, and he did not suffer fools gladly.

Beyond the confines of the school, however, he met and was influenced by many varied personalities. His cousin Shpentser, in particular, imbued him with a love of books – both their content and the physical process of making them. As a youth Trotsky became familiar with all the stages of book production, and the feel of a book fresh off the press remained a source of intense pleasure throughout his life. As for writing, the pen became and was to remain his chief weapon. Studying literature and the production of newspapers stimulated his interest not only in the Russian classics, but also in Western culture and civilization. In this respect he was not unusual. The Russian Empire was backward in many respects, and this backwardness was felt most acutely by the progressive intelligentsia, which longed for bourgeois democratic freedoms, a liberal order and cultural advance. For the Jewish intelligentsia the Russian Empire was a world of pogroms, discrimination, the Pale of Settlement. Before he ever visited the West, Trotsky had imbibed European culture and values, and his Westernized views would influence his thinking when he later formulated his Theory of Permanent Revolution, or declared that the outcome of the Russian revolution depended on the timing of the world conflagration, or advocated that some aspects of European culture be introduced into Russia.

High school, first in Odessa and then in the neighbouring city of Nikolaev, gradually distanced Lev Bronshtein from his family. When he visited the farm in Kherson, where his father was now doing so well, he felt stifled by the narrowness of this little world, dominated as it was by the constant struggle for success, profit, advantage. He was developing a powerful, flexible, sharp mind, ever seeking to understand the new and the unfamiliar, and he brought it to bear on the contrast between what he saw in the city and what greeted him on his returns to the countryside. Trotsky spent his childhood and adolescence in a petty bourgeois milieu, and although later he would throw off the mentality of acquisition and consumption, some of the traits which he had inherited would resurface in later years.

Like many middle-class revolutionaries at the early stages of their political lives, Trotsky was capable of rapid, sometimes very dramatic, shifts of direction. Thus, he came to Marxism soon after vehemently rejecting it as a teenaged Populist.* Having collaborated with the Mensheviks at one time, after the revolution he called for the harshest measures against them. He was, perhaps, one of the first proponents of the Red Terror which he would later condemn. Though a lifelong Marxist, he retained some elements of middle-class revolutionary-mindedness, spontaneity and fanaticism. He was, however, utterly consistent in his total rejection of Stalinism, a fact chiefly motivated by personal considerations.

Trotsky's family could not of course have created the revolutionary in him, but it gave him an insight into petty bourgeois life, permitted him to obtain an education, and supported him financially right up to the revolution. In this respect, his position was greatly preferable to that of the majority of revolutionaries. Thanks to his versatility, moreover, he also had access to a variety of other sources of financial support; from lecturing, grants from charities and earnings from journalism.

As Trotsky's involvement in the revolutionary movement deepened

---

* Populism, made up of vaguely socialist, peasant-oriented ideas, dominated a large section of educated Russian youth in the 1870s–1890s.

in the late 1890s, his ties with his family weakened. David Bronshtein, according to his son, became harsher as he became richer, the burdens on him growing heavier as his business expanded, and his children became more of a disappointment to him.[8] The main disappointment was that none of his four children wanted to carry on the business. The elder son, Alexander, acquired an education and worked as an engineer in the sugar industry, continuing to do so after the revolution. After Trotsky was deported in 1929 Alexander publicly disowned him, but he was nevertheless exiled internally, then arrested, and finally, on 25 April 1938, shot. Trotsky's elder sister Liza died of natural causes in 1924. His younger sister Olga married the leading Bolshevik Lev Kamenev. Trotsky maintained the closest relations with her as long as he was in the Soviet Union. Branded the sister of the chief 'enemy of the people', however, she had little chance of survival. Arrested in 1935 and shot in 1941, she outlived her two young sons, who were shot in 1936.

Trotsky's mother died in 1910, after writing to him that she did not expect to see him again. He was outside Russia at the time and could not attend her funeral. The fate of most of his family, like his own, was a tragic one. For Olga Grebner, the wife of his younger son Sergei, Trotsky had been like a leper: 'He brought misery to everyone he came in contact with,' she told me. In his 'supplementary statement' of 24 August 1934 on the death of his elder son Lev Sedov, Trotsky wrote: 'Yagoda [head of the security organs] caused the premature death of one of my daughters, and drove the other to suicide. He arrested my two sons-in-law who simply disappeared without trace. The GPU arrested my younger son, Sergei ... and he then disappeared.'[9] Sergei perished in 1937, his elder son was murdered in Paris in 1938, and most of his relatives, even distant ones, would be liquidated in due course.

The Path of Revolution

Trotsky loved mathematics, whose abstract world fascinated him with its mystery, its logic and its inexhaustible possibilities. He dreamed of studying it at Novorossiisk University, and might have become a scientist, but the only 'universities' he was to attend were those of the Russian prison system. His revolutionary career began when he left high school, aged seventeen.

He was staying with relatives whose two grown-up sons had taken up socialist ideas. Although he was ever-open to new ideas, Lev expressed indifference for 'theoretical utopias' and was amused by the brothers' assertion of 'the historic value of socialism', preferring instead to study his textbooks. Once he had been drawn into argument by his cousins, however, the socialist way of thinking would stay with him for the rest of his life, and ideological, political struggle would become his *raison d'être*.

His political development was accelerated when his cousins introduced him to Franz Shvigovsky, a Czech who cultivated an orchard for a living and who had formed something of a commune with Populist friends. Trotsky later recalled how, as a seventeen-year-old, he used to visit this 'undefined radical' and read Mikhailovsky, Kareyev, John Stuart Mill, and 'an atrociously printed copy of the Communist Manifesto'. He remembered that only Alexandra Lvovna Sokolovskaya, a midwifery student from Odessa six years his senior, was reading Marx's *Capital*: 'In 1896–97 I was an opponent of Marx (whose works I didn't read).'[10] It was from Alexandra that Trotsky first heard an argued case for Marxism. He hated losing a debate, but he had nothing substantial to oppose to Alexandra's cool, balanced arguments. Relying on logic and intuition alone, he managed to maintain his dignity. She would smile as he tried vehemently to expose the 'inconsistency of Marxism', sensing perhaps that Populism was closer to his outlook, as he had not absorbed the iron 'determinism' to be found in Marxism. Given his self-assurance, he was more at home with a theory that advocated 'critically thinking personalities', brilliant heroes who could rise above the mob, idols capable of raising the masses to great causes. His attacks on Marxism were youthful outbursts against a dry theory of which he knew nothing.

There was in the young Trotsky a streak of revolutionary romanticism. He was an advocate of the personal principle, a pioneer for moral reasons. Sokolovskaya's arguments, nevertheless, gradually eroded his self-confidence and caused him intellectual confusion. Soon political debate became suffused by a sudden rush of feeling between the antagonists, despite their deep differences of 'doctrine'. Out of vanity and in a spirit of contrariness, Trotsky decided to 'destroy Marxism' publicly. He filled his first article with epigrams, quotations and venomous shafts, and later wrote that 'luckily it was not published, and no one, including me, was any the worse for it'. It was to have been the basis of a play he planned to write with Alexandra's brothers, the central theme of which would be the conflict between the Marxists and the Populists, but this, too, came to nothing.

When he went home on vacation in 1897, Trotsky shocked his parents by making seditious remarks about the Tsar: 'You see, father, at the first audience he gave to the nobility he declared, "I shall uphold the principles of autocracy as firmly and unflinchingly as my unforgettable late father …"'

'Quite right,' responded David Bronshtein.

'But then the Tsar went on to declaim, in his excited state, that the men of the zemtsvo [locally elected self-governed assembly] "must give up their senseless dreams"! "Senseless"! and the word in the text of his speech was "groundless".'

'So what?'

'The Tsar shouted the words "senseless dreams" so loudly that the Empress, who doesn't know much Russian, asked one of the grand duchesses what he'd said, and was calmly told, "He says they're all idiots." And Utkin, the governor of Tver province, was so badly shaken by the Tsar's shouting, he dropped the gold tray he was carrying. "A bad sign for the coronation," whispered the old retainers, as they watched Vorontsov-Dashkov, on his knees, picking up the gifts.'[11] He added: 'The world you and the rest of society are living in has gone sour. It's all got to be changed. We've got to get rid of the Tsar and achieve freedom! Yes!'

'What are you talking about?' his father exploded. 'You'd better think again! It's not going to happen for 300 years! Where did you get these ideas? Don't you ever go near that layabout Shvigovsky again!'

The argument led to a temporary rift, and Lev, feeling himself liberated, refused his father's financial support. After a few months in Shvigovsky's commune, the 'rebel' made peace, but in practice his law-abiding parents' authority over him was now a thing of the past, and most of his actions were carried out against their wishes. His radicalism, and that of his friends, meanwhile deepened. They were

much affected by the news in 1897 that a student called Vetrova had
burned herself to death in the Peter-Paul Fortress in St Petersburg.
Although the reasons for this act never became clear, to the members
of the 'orchard commune' it was plainly a protest against the autocracy. Ziv recalled that Lev suggested he join a workers' union which
he and his friends had organized, and which had decisively rejected
Populist ideas. 'It's purely social democratic.' 'Who belongs?' Ziv
asked. 'The avant-garde of youth: revolutionary-minded students and
workers!'[12] The South Russian Workers' Union was named in honour
of a body that had been dispersed by the police a quarter of a century
earlier.

Lev Bronshtein, now known by the alias of Lvov, and his friends
organized several small circles among the dockworkers of Nikolaev,
at which they read newspapers, pamphlets and consciousness-raising
proclamations. The work of the 'Union' was to copy and duplicate
social democratic texts for distribution among the workers on the
wharves and in other workplaces. Its leaders had little experience,
and their attempts at secrecy were primitive. The group was easily
penetrated by police agents, and on 28 January 1898 Bronshtein,
Shvigovsky and others were arrested. Writing to the Party historian,
Nevsky, on 5 August 1921, Trotsky recalled that 'it was the workers
in the prison who made me a Marxist, above all Ivan Andreyevich
Mukhin'.[13] From Nikolaev prison Trotsky was moved first to Kherson
and then to Odessa. He describes his 'grand tour' of Russia's gaols in
his autobiography. He was in Odessa prison for about two years while
his case was being investigated. There was no trial. He and three
others were sentenced to four years in exile, while the rest, including
Sokolovskaya, were given shorter terms. Trotsky then spent about
five months in Moscow transfer prison and three at Irkutsk in Siberia.
He did not waste a single day of his imprisonment, constantly seeking
to improve his mind. Much later, when asked what was his favourite
pastime, he replied, 'Intellectual activity: reading, thinking and,
perhaps, writing.'[14]

While they were in the Butyrki prison in Moscow, Trotsky and
Sokolovskaya requested permission to get married from the prison
authorities, who had no objection, and the couple informed their
parents. Alexandra's were not opposed, but the Bronshteins would
have none of it. Trotsky wrote to Alexandra at this time and the letter

has been preserved in the archives. For the rest of his life Trotsky remained sensitive on this matter, which was understandable enough, considering the feelings of his second wife. In 1922, when he learned that the Party's historical journal *Proletarskaya revolyutsiya* intended to publish his personal correspondence with Alexandra, he wrote to the editor: 'I'm not dead yet; people I corresponded with are still alive, so don't exert yourself to turn us into historical material for Istpart [the special commission on the history of the party and the revolution]. If Istpart has a different view, I'm prepared to take the matter to the Politburo. Until the Politburo discusses the matter, please don't publish.'[15] His wishes were complied with.

It now seems reasonable, seventy years later, to lift that ban. On the eve of their marriage, he wrote to Alexandra:

Shurochka,[16] I have a whole lot of news for you (however uninteresting). I met my mother the day before yesterday. The meeting ended in a complete rift – which is really for the best, don't you think? This time I counter-attacked and things became rather nasty. I turned down their help. I just got a letter from your father: what a nice man! He's not angry that I've broken with my parents, he seems pleased ... He says it removes the issue of material inequality ... I'm sitting so close to you now that I can almost feel your presence. Next time you go downstairs for exercise, say something, as I'm bound to hear you. Try, Sashenka! I'm finding it hard ... I want to hear your voice and I want to see you ... What if they won't let us get married? It's impossible! There have been times (hours, days, months) when suicide seemed the most decent way out. But I hadn't got the nerve ... The Siberian taiga will be the test of our civic sensibilities. Anyway we'll be happy there! Like the gods on Olympus! I've repeated this to myself so many times, and I still want to keep on repeating it ...[17]

In less than three years Trotsky would abandon Alexandra in the depths of Siberia with their two tiny daughters, never to return to his first family again, and blaming 'fate' for the separation.

Trotsky's personal correspondence makes it plain enough that he married Alexandra for love, and yet in his autobiography he devotes no more than half a paragraph to the event, and even tries to give the impression that it had been dictated by revolutionary expediency:

As well as I can remember, it took about three weeks before we came to the village of Ust-Kut. There I was put ashore with one of the

women prisoners, a close associate of mine from Nikolaev. Alexandra
Lvovna had one of the most important positions in the South Russian
Workers' Union. Her utter loyalty to socialism and her complete lack
of any personal ambition gave her an unquestioned moral authority.
The work that we were doing bound us closely together, and so, to
avoid being separated, we had been married in the transfer prison in
Moscow.[18]

Why did the eighteen-year-old Trotsky need a marriage which he
would later try to depict as virtually fictitious? Perhaps because, in all
his writings, he felt the need to invoke noble, moral motives and
decency, whereas his first love and first marriage had been short-lived.
He could hardly fail to mention the relationship in his autobiography,
but to invoke their 'work' as the reason for staying with a woman who
'lacked personal ambition' was acceptable to him.

The story of Trotsky's first marriage suggests unadorned pragmatism, an urge to free himself from a burden in order to move on to
higher things. In fairness to Trotsky, for a long time he attempted
(not very energetically) to retain the link with his wife and children.
Following his deportation to Turkey in 1929, his elder daughter, Zina,
visited him (his younger daughter, Nina, had died the previous year).
Alexandra had hoped that being with her father would help Zina to
cope with her emotional problems, but she felt like a stranger in his
house. It was decided that she needed treatment in Berlin, and Trotsky
did his utmost to obtain it for her. After a course of therapy, however,
he wrote to Alexandra in Moscow that she 'should be thinking about
a room' for Zina to come back to. A few weeks later, however, he was
faced with the sad task of informing his first wife of their daughter's
death.

It is true that when Alexandra was in trouble in 1935, and was
exiled merely for being Trotsky's first wife, he frequently talked about
her, his daughters and his grandsons to his second family, and was
worried about what would happen to them. He recorded in his diary
on 2 April 1935, having just heard that Alexandra had been deported
to Siberia:

I don't think [she] has been politically at all active during the last few
years, both because of her age and the three children on her hands.
Several weeks ago in *Pravda*, in an article devoted to the fight against
'remnants' and 'dregs', the name of [Alexandra] was also mentioned –

in the usual hoodlum manner – but only in passing; she was accused of having exerted a harmful influence – in 1931! – on a group of students – I think of the Institute of Forestry. *Pravda* could not discover any later crimes. But the very mention of her name was by itself an unmistakable sign that we must expect a blow in this direction too.

Three days later, after much agonized talk about the fate of his younger son Seryozha, Trotsky wrote: 'N[atalie, his second wife] has thought more about A[lexandra].L. than about Seryozha: it may be, after all, that Seryozha is not in any trouble, but A.L. at sixty years of age has been sent somewhere to the far north.'[19]

Deep in Siberian exile at the turn of the century, as he describes in colourful detail in his autobiography, Trotsky set about establishing a programme of work. He carried on with his education, and also took his first successful steps in journalism. He dropped his first revolutionary alias, 'Lvov', in favour of 'Antid Oto', and articles over this signature began appearing in the local newspaper *Vostochnoe obozrenie* (Eastern Review). He was willing to write on any topic – the Siberian village, the position of women in Siberia, the local authorities and the role of local government. He wrote essays on Nietzsche, Gogol, Uspensky and Herzen. He was invariably categorical in his judgements – in a piece on a popular writer, entitled 'The History of Literature, Mr Boborykin and Russian Criticism', he wrote: 'Mr Boborykin has written a book on the European novel . . . but, strange to relate, no one, apart from the author, can understand it.'[20] This was a style Trotsky would carry with him throughout his life: peremptoriness and an unwillingness to compromise on his values, a lack of fear of saying exactly what he thought to anyone, a readiness to go against established norms. It was this approach that made him many supporters. But it created still more enemies.

He managed to send a number of articles abroad, where Russian émigré circles noticed the literary talents of the unknown correspondent. Also unknown to them was the fact that these works were not the result of long and painful labour, but the fruit of rapid composition, sudden inspiration when thoughts seemed to fly onto the page. Trotsky did not suffer from the common complaint of writers, for whom, as Simon Nadson put it, 'there is no greater torture than the torture of finding a word'. He wrote quickly, sharply, emphatically. Some of the pieces he wrote as a young man show an obvious desire to dazzle with erudition, to cite the latest literary and scientific authorities or the classics, often for no obvious reason. And exile in Siberia gave him plenty of time and opportunity to engage in literary study.

His Siberian exile became for Trotsky, in his countless reminiscences, one of the peaks of his personal service to the revolutionary cause. In February 1923, at the behest of his friend Max Eastman, Trotsky wrote an account of his exile:

> We shared an apartment with a Polish shoemaker called Mikshei. He was a wonderful comrade, attentive, caring, a great cook, except that he drank, and the more he drank, the more he wanted to. We divided our time between domestic chores and reading. We cut firewood, swept, washed the dishes, helped Mikshei in the kitchen. We read all manner of things: Marx, socialist writings, world literature. There was journalism: I began writing for *Vostochnoe obozrenie*. I kept my literary writing for the night. Often until 5 or 6 a.m. I retained this habit into later life, my Vienna period . . . On one occasion they wouldn't hand over my mail at the post office. I protested furiously. They fined me three roubles. I heard about this at Verkholensk, whence I was soon to escape. So my fine was never paid, along with my many other debts to tsarism.[21]

Not for nothing did Krzhizhanovsky, Lenin's agent in Samara, nickname Trotsky 'The Pen'. He would record practically every meeting he ever had, all his conversations, speeches and appearances. It would be hard to find another Russian revolutionary who wrote so much, in such detail and so eloquently about himself. It is hard to accept his assertion in the preface to his memoirs that he had become accustomed 'to viewing the historical perspective not from the standpoint of my personal fate'.[22] On the contrary, a feature of his rich literary output is his tendency, however unwitting, to discern manifold historical events precisely through the prism of his own personality. He added that no one had succeeded in writing an autobiography without writing about themselves, and that is so. But he also wrote a great deal about himself, even when he was not writing his autobiography.

Ust-Kut boasted a small library which had been built up by exiles. Of all the books he found there, Trotsky was most impressed by a two-volume collection of Gleb Uspensky, whose tales and essays he at first approached with distrust, only to find he could not put them down. When the paraffin ran out and the lamp finally failed, he felt as if he had been living in one of Uspensky's Russian villages, with its pain, its burdens and its ignorance. Later, when Trotsky's 'Westernism' also embraced literature, he still retained a special place for Uspensky. He marked in the writer's diary a passage which read:

> ... the whole village laboured for one manor house. Without excuse or protest, the village had to work day in, day out, year in, year out. The squire, who owned the village, could change from good to bad, but this meant nothing to the village, the same work was expected whether the squire was a conservative, a liberal or even a radical, in a word, whoever took up residence in the manor house. Whoever lived there, they demanded the same thing: work, work which filled most of the day, most of the year, all one's life – work not for oneself ... All this resulted in a perfectly defined ideal for the being called a peasant.[23]

Uspensky became Trotsky's model for the pieces he himself wrote on village life in Siberia, a way of life that soon palled for a personality eager to find room for self-expression and to become known. Ust-Kut and Verkholensk became detestable, and Trotsky felt cramped by the miserable hovels along the single muddy street. When his writing began to attract attention he felt the need for a bigger stage. Trotsky heard in 1902 that two or three of his pieces had somehow reached *Iskra*, the social democratic paper edited by Lenin, and that they had made a good impression. He decided he could remain no longer in Siberia, but must get to Petersburg, to Moscow, to the capitals of Western Europe, where he felt he was needed. After much agonizing, he finally told Alexandra that he planned to escape. She did not object, although one can imagine what it must have cost her: she would have to remain behind in the depths of the Siberian taiga with two infants, her second baby having just arrived, and with little hope of reunion with her husband. But in her eyes Lev was a genius, and was destined to become famous. She thought she was being true to the revolutionary cause by sacrificing him in the name of her ideals. She would sacrifice everything in due course: her husband, her daughters, her sons-in-law, grandchildren, and finally herself.

Trotsky obtained permission from the local authorities on 20 February 1902 'to travel on for one day to Irkutsk, and not to stop anywhere en route without compelling reasons'.[24] At Irkutsk he told friends of his plan to escape, and that summer he duly carried out his plan. Alexandra's words of farewell as he left her were: 'Go, a great future awaits you.' Escape turned out not to be at all difficult. He was concealed in a cart under a load of hay and set off back to Irkutsk, where he was given clothes and a passport, in which for the first time he used the name, chosen it seems haphazardly, by which the world would come to know him. 'Trotsky' was the name of one of the warders in Odessa prison, an impressive and handsome figure of a man.

Alexandra was unable to keep her husband's escape secret for long. Within two days a cable was on its way from Verkholensk to the governor of the province, with a copy to the police chief: 'Yesterday, Leiba Bronshtein went absent without leave. Twenty-three years old, five foot ten, dark brown hair, goatee beard, wears spectacles. According to his wife, Bronshtein left for Irkutsk. Signed Police Superintendent Ludvig.'[25] A fuller description would soon appear in the records of the Okhrana:

> Bronshtein, (Lev) Davidov, also Nikolai Trotsky and Yanovsky, deprived of all rights, son of a colonist, Russian [i.e. a Russian subject], writer. Arrested in 1898 in connection with the 'South Russian Workers' Union' case in Odessa. Exiled for four years under open surveillance. Went into hiding from Verkholensk on 21 August and was placed on wanted list No. 5530 on 1 September 1902.[26]

Trotsky stopped for a week at Samara, where Iskra's Russian base was located, and a week later continued towards London. Travelling on his false passport, he crossed into Austria illegally, managing to reach Vienna before running out of funds. There he located Victor Adler, the founder of the Austrian Social Democratic Party. He later described Adler as a man with a face so expressive that he was not merely good, but was too good not to find mitigating circumstances for one's sins. When Adler opened the door of his apartment, Trotsky greeted him with, 'I am Russian . . .' to which Adler replied, 'You don't have to tell me, I already had time enough to guess.'[27]

Early one morning in October 1902, Trotsky made his way to the one-room flat occupied by Lenin and his wife Nadezhda Krupskaya at the London address given to him in Zurich by Pavel Axelrod, one of the editors of *Iskra* and a venerated figure in the social democratic movement. He knocked, as instructed, three times. Krupskaya came to the door and called out, 'It's The Pen!' While she was paying off the cabbie, Trotsky was already showering Lenin with news from Russia. Lenin, ten years Trotsky's senior, saw in the young firebrand someone who might open a new chapter in the Russian revolutionary movement. Now, virtually trapped in his bed as Trotsky pulled his chair closer, Lenin listened as the young man talked and talked, gesticulating and barely taking breath, singing like a bird that has just been released from its cage.

European Bivouac

Trotsky spent about a third of his life in exile, and each spell would have its own political and moral tone. If the second 'bivouac' in Turkey (February 1929 to July 1933) was to be 'the long wait', and the third in Mexico (January 1937 to his death in 1940) an 'exile of embitterment', then his first was one of 'enthusiastic discovery'. These three phases of his life lie at the base of his ideas on 'permanent revolution' and the role of the Fourth International.

Emigration had long figured in the political and intellectual life of Russia. When Nicholas Berdyaev became an émigré in 1922 he asked himself: 'What Russian ideas have I brought with me to the West?' and replied: 'I have brought awareness of the conflict between personality and world harmony, between the individual and the social, a conflict which cannot be resolved within the confines of history.'[28]

The young Bronshtein brought with him a thirst for knowledge and the riches of European culture. This was where he must preserve his identity and adapt to the new social and intellectual milieu. The Russian intelligentsia in those days existed as it were in two dimensions: one located in Russia, nearby, familiar, but in which it was difficult to realize one's ideas of free thinking; the other in Western Europe, with its tradition of greater political and intellectual tolerance. Western Europe was more than a source of high culture for the Russian intelligentsia. It became a place where ideas and initiatives were generated and sent back to Russia in the hope of accomplishing revolutionary changes there. Russian intellectuals had always possessed an unusually high order of spirituality and faith in eternal ideals. Many of them had gone to Europe intending no less to serve their motherland than to save themselves.

A particularly powerful group of revolutionary Marxist intellectuals in emigration around the turn of the century included Lenin, Plekhanov, Martov, Potresov, Dan, Axelrod and Vera Zasulich, all of them in one way or another making a mark on the theoretical preparation of the revolutions of 1917. It was to this revolutionary Mecca that Trotsky, barely twenty-three years old, came in the autumn of 1902. He had been drawn by the possibility of contributing to *Iskra*, the social democratic newspaper edited by two generations of revolutionaries: the 'oldies' (*stariki*), consisting of Plekhanov, Zasulich and Axelrod, and the 'young ones', Lenin, Martov and Potresov. Lenin at once saw in Trotsky 'a man of exceptional abilities, staunch, energetic, who will go further'.[29] Trotsky began writing at once. In November 1902 *Iskra* published his first article. He wrote for the newspaper about strikes and revolutionary traditions, exile and the Second International. He also contributed to other newspapers. His range was exceptionally wide, hinting perhaps at dilettantism. The archives contain a large number of his manuscripts, published and unpublished – there is even one entitled 'On Somnambulism'.

At Lenin's suggestion, in March 1903 Trotsky was co-opted onto *Iskra*'s editorial board with a consultative vote. His relationship with the highly educated Iskra group left its mark on him. He was especially attracted to Zasulich, Martov and Pavel Axelrod, to whom he dedicated his first major work, a 1904 article entitled 'Our Political Tasks'. By this time relations between Trotsky and Lenin had become strained, as he revealed in the article, in which he was as negative about Lenin as he was positive about Axelrod, of whom he wrote: 'he is the true and watchful guardian of the interests of the proletarian movement ... a genuine proletarian ideologist ... Axelrod doesn't write in the form of "articles", but mathematically concise formulae, from which others, including Lenin, compose their own numerous articles.'[30]

Trotsky moved into the house in Holford Square, King's Cross, where Lenin, Martov and Zasulich were living. They met several times a day to discuss the news as well as the articles they were writing. Trotsky could not conceal his admiration for Vera Zasulich, who had become famous throughout Russia in 1878 when a jury had acquitted her of the attempted assassination of General Trepov, the governor-general of St Petersburg. A brilliant, rebellious nihilist, her reminiscences fired the imagination of the young revolutionary. She belonged to the generation of Russian revolutionaries for whom radicalism was part of their nature. Trotsky declared that she was for him 'a legend of the revolution'. These were not empty words. Trotsky thought in radical categories. He never favoured half-measures.

At first, Trotsky's relations with Martov were excellent. Martov was a brilliant journalist with a talent for graphic, deep analysis of the most complex issues, and Trotsky genuinely admired him. But soon after the October revolution he would write of his former idol: 'Martov is undoubtedly one of the most tragic figures of the revolutionary movement. A gifted writer, an original politician, a shrewd Marxist intellectual . . . he will go down in the history of the workers' revolution as a big minus . . . Martov became the most refined, subtle, elusive, perceptive politician of the dull-witted, vulgar and cowardly petty-bourgeois intelligentsia.'[31] For Trotsky, evaluation of another's position was more important than their personal relations, and the independence of his own ideas on any subject was pre-eminent. This was something the editors of *Iskra* would soon discover, notably at the Second Congress of the Russian Social Democratic Workers' Party.

Without standing on ceremony, Trotsky scrutinized the members of the *Iskra* board, people who had become legends for many revolutionaries. The leading figure among them was Georgi Valentinovich Plekhanov, a frequent visitor to London from Switzerland, where he normally resided. In the West since January 1880 and noticeably cut off from Russia, Plekhanov was nevertheless regarded as 'the father of Russian Marxism'. Theoretical soundness, rigorous logic, encyclopaedic knowledge and an eloquent pen had made him a genuine master of the doctrine. He greeted Trotsky with caution, if not outright hostility, and his initial guardedness soon grew into a firm dislike which he retained to the end of his days. He was totally against Trotsky being co-opted onto the editorial board, and was studiedly cold when they met. Isaac Deutscher suggested that this antipathy derived from the fact that they were both excellent writers and sharp-witted debaters with a tendency to histrionics, and each had a high opinion of himself.[32] But while Trotsky's star was plainly rising, Plekhanov's was waning. Trotsky was the youthful enthusiast, Plekhanov the ageing sceptic. When Plekhanov came to London, Zasulich told him that Trotsky was a genius, to which Plekhanov sourly replied, 'I shall never forgive him for it.'

As for Trotsky's contributions to the paper, Plekhanov often complained that they were lightweight, high-flown and florid, and that they lowered the theoretical and political tone. This criticism was justified, as Trotsky often resorted to aphorism, quotation and eloquence as a substitute for depth. Although he was less outspoken on the subject than Plekhanov, Lenin took a similar view. Trotsky never learned to accept criticism coolly, but it is possible that he learned from these early lessons to moderate his style. Yet he was unable to establish good relations with Plekhanov. In 1917 Plekhanov referred, in private, to Trotsky as 'the revolution's lover', a sarcastic quip to which Trotsky would reply in good measure. When Plekhanov died in June 1918, Trotsky said in a speech: 'There can be no greater tragedy for a political leader who has spent decades saying that the Russian revolution can develop and come to victory only as a revolution of the working class, than to refuse to take part in the working-class movement at the very moment of its victory.'[33]

Having brought Trotsky into the paper, Lenin soon advised him not to limit himself to journalism, but also to use his talents as an orator. Apart from the many Russian émigrés, there were Englishmen, Frenchmen, Germans and Swiss who were interested in Marxism, the situation in Russia and the prospects for socialism, and Trotsky duly began giving speeches and lectures in London, Brussels, Paris and Zurich. The constant contact with well-known revolutionary figures quickly broadened the young man's horizons, but it also strengthened his belief that his abilities were a special gift, that he was exceptional. Trotsky wanted this be recognized by others, and would indulge in theatrical gestures and extravagant turns of phrase in order to achieve an effect.

Trotsky always knew he was going to leave his mark on history, and early on he began meticulously saving his papers. The archives contain rough drafts of speeches and articles, marginal notes on newspapers and calendars, and a large collection of newspaper cuttings in which his name was mentioned. He was right to think he would become famous: that, after all, was his aim. This does not diminish him as a revolutionary, but it does suggest that for him the revolution was a vehicle of self-expression. Ego meant more to him than to many other leaders, apart from Stalin, who wore the cloak of modesty while he was eaten up with the hunger for power and glory. Trotsky was essentially different from Stalin in that from an early age he strove for intellectual greatness. Power and glory were not his passion, as they were Stalin's, but the inevitable attributes of intellectual superiority. Intellectual recognition was for Trotsky immeasurably more important than official posts or political status.

The London period of Trotsky's emigration lasted only a few months, and ended in the summer of 1903. It was marked by visits to other countries and cities. The great public interest in enigmatic Russia, the attention Trotsky attracted to himself, the opportunity to mix with the legends of the European labour movement, and the realization that Russian social democrats could hold their own, intellectually, culturally and in the boldness of their plans, were exciting discoveries. Living in Paris from 1903, he immersed himself in French life, and felt the pulse of a different parliamentary culture from that of England. At the same time, he never failed to stress the backwardness of Russia. The admiration Trotsky expressed for Western culture and the achievements of bourgeois democracy led him in due course to argue that the victory of socialism in Russia was critically dependent on the forces of revolution in the West.

Trotsky's correspondence with Alexandra, still languishing in Siberia with their two infant daughters, very quickly diminished. His first wife had lost her attraction, and he had not given himself time to experience the joy and pain and cares of fatherhood. His little family had, in his word, receded into the 'irretrievable'. When his parents came to Paris in 1903, hoping to make peace with their son, and his mother tried to remind him of his duty to his wife and children, he gently asked her not to discuss the matter again. His father was secretly delighted, for he had always been convinced that Alexandra had led his son astray. As for his mother, she was happy to see all the newspaper cuttings about the son she so admired. She read the headlines about him aloud, while old David listened approvingly. When they left for home, they gave him money and also promised to take care of Alexandra and the two girls. It offended their Jewish sensibilities to leave the family of their own son penniless.

Trotsky's enemies, beginning with the proto-fascist groups known generally as the Black Hundreds and continuing with the anti-Semites in Russia today, have always stressed his Jewish origins, sometimes even connecting his actions with the 'Zionist conspiracy', 'Jewish intrigues', Freemasons and so on. In fact he was never a Zionist. He was a leader who happened to be a Jew, and for some that has always aroused suspicion. There were occasions when he suffered from his Jewish background. He declined Lenin's offer of the job of Interior Commissar in the first Bolshevik government, declaring that 'people wouldn't understand the appointment of a Jew to that position'. He no doubt had in mind the prejudices surviving in the public mind that associated this post with the tsar's penal system. Genrikh Yagoda would have no such qualms when Stalin offered him the job. Trotsky never forgot he was a Jew, chiefly because his enemies constantly reminded him. He was, however, never a nationalist, a Zionist, or a racist. His was unequivocally an internationalist outlook.*

In February 1932 he wrote to one of his followers, Kling:

You ask me what my attitude is to the Jewish language? My reply is, the same as to any language. If in my autobiography I really used the word 'jargon', it is only because in my childhood the Jewish language was not called 'Yiddish', as it is now, but 'jargon', at least, that's what the Jews in Odessa called it, and nothing derogatory was intended. You say [that in my book I write] 'I'm called an assimilationist'? I really don't know what to make of this word. Of course, I am opposed to Zionism and any other form of self-isolation by the Jewish workers . . .[34]

In May 1932, Jewish-American workers wrote to Trotsky on the Turkish island of Prinkipo, informing him that they had just founded a Jewish newspaper. He replied: 'The existence of an independent Jewish publication must serve not to isolate the Jewish workers, but on the contrary must make them accessible to ideas which will unite all workers into one revolutionary family.'[35]

In 1919, when he was Chairman of the Revolutionary Military Committee and War Commissar, he received a letter from Murom in Vladimir Province, from a Korean Communist called Nigay, who

* See B. Knei-Paz, *The Social and Political Thought of Leon Trotsky*, Oxford, 1978, pp. 533–55, for a masterly analysis of Trotsky's views on Jewishness and Zionism.

wrote that dark rumours were circulating in Russia to the effect that 'the motherland has been conquered by Yid commissars. All the country's disasters are being blamed on the Jews. They're saying the Communist regime is being supported by Jewish brains, Latvian rifles and Russian idiots.' To save the country from destruction and betrayal, Nigay advised Trotsky 'to create a mighty Jewish army and to arm it to the teeth ... The Jews are no worse than Tatars or Latvians, and they've got their own regiments.'[36] In reply, Trotsky asked his assistant Butov to send Nigay some of his articles on the internationalist character of the Russian revolution.

Trotsky was aware of anti-Semitic prejudice when he was at the peak of his power, but when his position became shaky he felt it all the more, as a letter he wrote to Bukharin on 3 March 1926 shows:

> I am writing this letter by hand (although I have lost the habit), because I'm ashamed to dictate what I have to say to my stenographer ... The secretary of the cell (of whom I told you) writes [that they're saying], 'The Yids in the Politburo are kicking up a fuss.' And yet again no one has reported it to anyone, and for the same standard reason: he would be kicked out of the factory. The author of the letter is a Jewish worker. He also decided not to report those who are saying 'The Yids are agitating against Leninism.' His reasoning: 'If others, non-Jews, are keeping quiet, it's awkward for me ...' In other words, members of the Communist Party are afraid to report to the Party organs about Black Hundreds-style agitation, because they're afraid they, not the Black Hundreds, will be sacked ... You'll say I'm exaggerating! How I wish I were. Anyway, let's go to the cell ourselves and check it out ...[37]

Bukharin was at the time an ally of Stalin's, however, and would go nowhere with Trotsky.

In a letter written when he was in exile on Prinkipo, Trotsky replied to a question about the creation of the Jewish autonomous region in Birobidzhan: 'The Jewish question has become a component part of the world proletarian revolution. As for Birobidzhan, its future is tied to that of the Soviet Union. The Jewish question, as a result of the whole of Jewish history, is international ... The fate of the Jewish people can be determined only by the complete and final victory of the proletariat.'[38] However erroneous and naive his reliance on class struggle and revolution to solve the 'Jewish question', this is convincing evidence of Trotsky's deep and lasting hostility to Zionism.

In all his wanderings, he remained above anti-Semitic attacks on himself.

Among the émigrés in Paris in the early years of the century was a young, clever, attractive (and married) woman called Natalya Sedova. The daughter of rich parents, she had been expelled from her ladies' college in Kharkov for free thinking and reading seditious literature, and was now studying the history of art at the Sorbonne. As she recalled, the autumn of 1902 was a time when the Russian colony in Paris was inundated with lectures. The Iskra group, of which she was a member, brought in Martov, then Lenin, then Trotsky, billed as a young comrade who had escaped from exile. Natalya recalled that his speech was very successful, and that the colony was delighted. She and Trotsky soon got to know each other better, and she showed him the Louvre and disclosed her past life to him. The relationship developed quickly, and she soon left her husband to live with the young revolutionary. They were to remain strongly attached for the rest of their lives, sharing his triumphs, as well as his ostracism and persecution. Her support was often acknowledged by Trotsky as his mainstay during his worst moments. He always felt grateful to Paris that he had met her there.

The time he spent abroad, from the autumn of 1902 to early 1905, when he returned to Russia, was perhaps the happiest of his life, despite his comment that Paris was 'like Odessa, only Odessa's better!' Sedova, who mocked this attitude, remarked that he was so 'utterly absorbed in political life' that other things 'were a bother, something unavoidable'.[39] It was also a time of self-affirmation, learning, discovery, establishing a wide circle of acquaintances and attracting admiration. The provincial revolutionary from the south of Russia was beginning to see himself almost as a hero.

The Paradox of Trotsky

The Russian radicals showed great persistence. The First Congress of the Russian Social Democratic Labour Party was held in Minsk in March 1898 but, with only nine delegates, it was more symbolic than real. The party was proclaimed to exist, but it was no more than a name, as all but one of the delegates were arrested within two weeks. The only document of importance to survive from the meeting was the RSDLP Manifesto, written by Peter Struve, who was himself in the process of self-redefinition and would shortly emerge as the organizer of Russia's first liberal movement, the Union of Liberation, forerunner of the Constitutional Democratic Party formed in 1905.

Lenin and the other editors of *Iskra* set about convening a proper constituent, second congress of the party, and this duly met in the summer of 1903. The delegates assembled first in Brussels, but then moved to London when the attention of the Russian secret police proved too intrusive. Twenty-six Marxist organizations were represented by forty-three delegates, Trotsky holding the mandate of the Siberian social democrats. He had gained a reputation as a practised underground operator who despite his youth had already experienced prison and exile. He arrived in Brussels in the company of Lenin's younger brother Dmitri, and at once threw himself into the work of the congress, making speeches, taking part in debates and discussing resolutions.

The congress opened in the warehouse of the so-called House of the People in Brussels before moving to a chapel off Tottenham Court Road in the West End of London. The agenda of some two dozen items included the composition of the congress itself, the place of the Jewish Workers' Union (known by its Yiddish name of the Bund) in the RSDLP, the party programme, the national question, demonstrations, risings, terror, the attitude to be adopted towards the Party of Socialist Revolutionaries (SRs) who had formed in the previous year, election of the Central Committee, the editorial board of *Iskra* and so on. As it transpired, only two or three issues assumed lasting significance. At first things went smoothly, but then the issue of the Bund almost split the congress in half. The Bund had already acquired considerable influence and organizational strength over a wide area of the Pale of Jewish Settlement, and had also extended its writ to the Jewish social democratic organizations in the south of Russia, where new communities of Jewish workers and artisans were settling in growing numbers. Now, at this crucially important meeting of the party, and having experienced the heavy-handedness of Iskra's agents in Russia, the Bund wanted to be recognized as the sole representative of Jewish workers in the party and to be left to run its own affairs. It was demanding not only equal, federal status with the bodies claiming central authority, like Iskra and the party central committee, but also supported resolutions which would recognize national cultural autonomy as a programme point and thus implicitly extend national status to the Jews, despite their lacking a territory.

About half the congress delegates were of Jewish origin, and in effect the result of the debate would determine whether the party was to be governed by nationalist or internationalist principles. Since the non-Bundist Jewish delegates supported the Iskra line, the congress opted for internationalism. Trotsky and Martov, both Jews, were staunch defenders of the Iskra line, even though within a few days they would be at daggers drawn with Lenin. With characteristic passion Trotsky castigated what he called the narrow nationalism of the Bund, which he claimed would impede the creation of a united and strong party in multi-national Russia. His attacks on the Bund were so fierce he earned the nickname of 'Lenin's cudgel'. He argued that if the Bund were allowed a special place in the party, other factions would demand the same, and that to accord special conditions to all the national groupings would destroy the idea of an all-Russia party. The Bund, he argued, was moving towards separatism which, once it was established within the party, would extend to the structure of the socialist state when it came into being.

Lenin won the day on this issue, and the congress adopted a resolution which roundly rejected the principle of federative relations between the party and the Bund as one of its constituent parts, and declared the Bund to be an autonomous component of the party.[40] These terms were unacceptable to the Bund.

Meanwhile, the delegates began discussing the party statutes, and a row blew up over the first point, which concerned the definition of membership. At first glance the two variants, proposed by Lenin and Martov respectively, appeared almost identical. Lenin proposed that a member should support the party not only with material help, but also by 'personal participation', whereas Martov proposed 'personal co-operation'. This terminological distinction, as the split revealed, signified two different approaches to what a member should be. Lenin's definition expressed a desire to create a strictly centralized organization in which members would carry out specific demands, chief of which should be participation in revolutionary activity.

Martov, on the other hand, wanted to open up the party into a broad association of sympathizers.

The issue became the pretext for Martov and his supporters to attack Lenin for other problems that had emerged among the supporters of Iskra in their closed sessions. Lenin had proposed reducing the size of the editorial board from six to three – himself, Martov and Plekhanov – which had been seen as offensive to the other three, Pavel Axelrod, Vera Zasulich and Alexander Potresov, all highly respected figures. Lenin might have been forgiven for wanting an efficient and productive organization, considering how few articles the latter three had contributed (eight, six and four, respectively), compared to his own, Martov's and Plekhanov's output (thirty-two, thirty-nine and twenty-four), but he succeeded only in creating a hostile atmosphere, so that when the issue of membership arose in the general assembly of the congress, the rift emerged. Trotsky declared that he could neither understand nor forgive the removal of the three editors, even though Lenin had referred to them in extremely cordial terms. Martov and Trotsky started accusing Lenin of rudeness and of usurping power.

The two allies of yesterday, Lenin and Martov, were now denouncing each other fiercely and exposing the hidden meaning behind the two rival formulations of party membership. The two simple words, 'participation' and 'co-operation', split the delegates. At first, Plekhanov was on Lenin's side, while Trotsky supported Martov. As Trotsky later described the event: 'At the congress, Lenin won Plekhanov over, although only for a time. Plekhanov evidently sensed something at the congress. At least he told Axelrod, in discussing Lenin: "Of such stuff Robespierres are made."'[41]

Lenin was disappointed by Trotsky, on whom he had counted for support, and who during the earlier sessions had been an ardent advocate of a strong, centralized party. Both during and between the sessions Lenin and his brother Dmitri tried to persuade Trotsky, in the friendliest way, that he had not thought through his position. Trotsky, however, was more influenced by his personal feelings, and he felt closer to Martov and Axelrod than to Lenin. For his part, Lenin recognized – at a time when he was still capable of self-criticism – that the split had occurred at least partly as a result of his own behaviour. Shortly after the congress, he wrote to Potresov, his friend and colleague from the earliest days of his revolutionary activity in St Petersburg: 'I ask myself why we should part and become lifelong enemies! I am going over all the events and impressions of the congress, I am aware that I often acted and behaved with appalling irritation, "crazily", and I am prepared to admit my guilt to anyone, if something generated by the atmosphere, the reactions, the retorts, the struggle and so on, can be described as guilt.'[42]

Trotsky recalled what he had thought of Lenin's behaviour in the autobiography he wrote in 1929, after his deportation from the USSR: 'His behaviour seemed unpardonable to me, both horrible and outrageous . . . My break with Lenin occurred on what might be considered "moral" or even personal grounds. But this was merely on the surface. At bottom, the separation was of a political nature and merely expressed in the realm of organization methods.' He concluded: 'Whatever I may say about it . . . the second congress was a landmark in my life, if only because it separated me from Lenin for several years.'[43] Neither Trotsky nor his many biographers seem to have noticed the profoundly paradoxical nature of the young revolutionary's own behaviour. Before addressing this issue, however, we should look at another question of great significance for understanding both the Russian and the Soviet philosophy of history, and Trotsky's political character.

For many years, scholars have interpreted the Second Party Congress, and especially the split over the membership issue, primarily as a question of organization, of what kind of party this was to be, a fortress or an association. This was not the main issue, however. The origin of the conflict lay deeper. Since the introduction of Marxism into Russia, its basic concept was interpreted and understood by the intelligentsia in different ways. Some accepted only its most radical features, those associated with the idea of smashing the old state apparatus, establishing a dictatorship of the proletariat and liquidating the exploiting classes.

Another section of the new Marxists emphasized the social democratic principles in the doctrine, principles which could be secured and consolidated not only by revolutionary, but also by reformist methods. (Indeed, the first party programme advocated democracy, secret suffrage, inviolability of the person, freedom of thought, speech, press, movement, assembly, strikes and trade unions, the right to education in one's native tongue and so on.) This division of approach gave rise, on the one hand, to those who thought terror, coercion and expropriation were permissible, and on the other to those who wanted to compel the capitalists to make concessions through compromise. It is thus correct to assert that the split at the Second Congress occurred not over the organizational question, but over a difference in the theory and practice of revolutionary methodology. The congress formalized the coexistence of two parallel tendencies: one radical, revolutionary and uncompromising, which would characterize the Bolsheviks; the other reformist, evolutionary and parliamentary, which was to become the hallmark of those henceforth known as Mensheviks. As Martov was to write in 1919, in his posthumously published work *Mirovoi bol'shevizm* (World Bolshevism): from the outset, 'Lenin was sceptical about the democratic resolution of social-political problems, trusting instead in economic vandalism and military force.'[44]

The paradox of Trotsky lay in the fact that while by his very nature he was a radical, or leftist, he supported the reformists and the moderates. The future, and lifelong, advocate of world, permanent socialist revolution was giving his support to Martov, of whom he would later write: 'Hilferding, Bauer, Renner and even Bernstein himself, all of them better educated than Martov, are by comparison clumsy apprentices when it comes to the political falsification of Marxism.'[45] Yet the paradox is illusory. Despite his intellectual brilliance and elegance, and the skill with which he was able to express complex ideas, in many respects Trotsky was at that time still relatively superficial about many things. What appeared to be encyclopaedic knowledge was often unsupported by serious analysis. It did not occur to him that by siding with Martov, he was in opposition to himself. He would understand this in due course, but the momentum of the conflict kept him in opposition to Lenin for many years.

He soon tried to correct or mitigate his situation by adopting centrist positions. Of this he himself wrote: 'I was not formally a member of either of the two factions. I continued to work with Krasin [a Bolshevik] ... At the same time, I kept in touch with the local Menshevik group, which was following a very revolutionary policy.'[46] However, he felt compelled by the logic of the ideological conflict to continue his opposition to Lenin. Shortly after the congress, in his

'Report of the Siberian Delegation', he wrote that 'the congress thought it was doing constructive work; it was only destructive ... Who could suppose that this assembly, convened by Iskra, would mercilessly trample over Iskra's editorial board? Which political crystal-gazer could forecast that Martov and Lenin would step forth ... as the hostile leaders of hostile factions? All this has come like a bolt from the blue ... this man [Lenin], with the energy and talent peculiar to him, assumed the rôle of the party's disorganizer.'⁴⁷

In his account of the congress, Trotsky accused Lenin of wanting to 'seize power' and ruling with 'an iron fist'. The democratic 'Westernizing' principle was dominant in Trotsky at that time. His criticism reached a temporary peak in his article 'Our Political Tasks', published in Geneva in 1904 and dedicated to 'My dear teacher, Pavel Borisovich Axelrod'. That dedication alone would provide ammunition for Stalin when he attacked Trotsky at the Central Committee Plenum of October 1927.⁴⁸ In his article, Trotsky accused Lenin of three sins: alienating the revolutionary forefathers from the revolutionary movement, 'impermissible devastation' of the Economists (i.e. the gradualists in the movement), and usurping power in the party. Giving the Central Committee special powers, he rightly perceived, would open the path to one-man dictatorship. Identifying him with Robespierre, he referred to 'Maximilien Lenin' as 'an adroit statistician', 'a slovenly lawyer', 'a rabble-rouser', ' a malicious man', and much more. It was a wholesale condemnation. According to Trotsky, Lenin had 'submerged the question of tactics in "philosophy"' and confused party practice with the party programme. Lenin was so obsessed with keeping the organization 'pure', so obsessed with spies, that he lost sight of 'the need to struggle against absolutism and of that far greater struggle, the emancipation of the working class.'⁴⁹

In attacking his former mentor, and in fiercer terms perhaps than any other Marxist revolutionary hitherto, Trotsky paid little attention to argument – there were few to which he might have resorted – and relied instead on youthful ardour. He plainly underestimated Lenin's political potential. Perhaps he thought that ultimately Lenin would lose his dominant position. Despite possessing immeasurably greater prophetic power than, say, Stalin or even Lenin, this was not to be either the first or last time that he would be mistaken.

Trotsky would often have to justify his 'non-Bolshevism' to those who chose to remind him of it. When during his last exile one of his supporters informed him that Tolheimer, another former supporter, was accusing him of 'anti-Leninism', he responded that he had not been a Bolshevik until 1917:

> But I believe that even when I was in disagreement with the Bolsheviks, I was closer to Lenin than Tolheimer is now. If I came to Lenin later than some other Bolsheviks, that doesn't mean I understood him less than they did. Franz Mehring came to Marxism a lot later than Kautsky and Bernstein, who had come under Marx and Engels's direct influence in their youth. That didn't prevent Franz Mehring from being a revolutionary Marxist to the end of his days, and Bernstein and Kautsky from ending their days as pathetic opportunists. It is absolutely true that Lenin was against me on a number of key issues, but why should it follow that Tolheimer is right against me? I cannot understand that.[50]

As a 'Jacobin' himself, at the beginning of the century Trotsky was accusing Lenin of radicalism; as a 'centrist', he accused Lenin of wanting to concentrate power in the party's central bodies; as an admirer of Robespierre, he repudiated Lenin as a potential dictator. This paradox was linked, on the one hand, with Trotsky's substitution of ideas by people: he saw the exit of Axelrod and Zasulich from *Iskra*'s editorial board as a tragedy and Lenin, the architect of the drama, as a usurper. On the other hand, many of the arguments he advanced at that period were intuitive and emotional, rather than rational. His sharp mind had not yet matured for deep intellectual thinking.

It irked Trotsky greatly that his sarcasm and trenchant observations went mostly unanswered by Lenin, who in one of his letters to his mistress Inessa Armand commented: 'That's Trotsky for you!!! Always the same, evasive, underhand, posing as a leftist, but helping the right while he still can.'[51] Trotsky's most savage comment on Lenin came in a private letter to the Menshevik member of the Duma Nikolai Chkheidze in March 1913, in which he called Lenin a master in the art of stoking up quarrels, 'a professional exploiter of any backwardness in the Russian labour movement ... The entire structure of Leninism is at present based on lies and falsification and carries within it the poisonous seeds of its own destruction ...'[52] This was probably the worst criticism Trotsky ever wrote about Lenin, and characterizes their extremely strained relations before 1917. In that tumultuous year, however, Trotsky witnessed what convinced him was Lenin's primacy in intellectual power, but also his harsh actions on the political and social plane. To the end of his life, he was to admire Lenin as a real leader.

From 1917 to Lenin's death, their collaboration was close and constructive. Trotsky became not only the second man of the revolution, but closer to Lenin than any other in his radicalism and determination. Together, they were the joint architects of the Soviet system. In his *Diary in Exile*, Trotsky wrote on 10 April 1935:

> Lenin and I had several sharp clashes because, when I disagreed with him on serious questions, I always fought an all-out battle. Such cases, naturally, were memorable for everyone, and later on much was said and written about them by the epigones. But the instances when Lenin and I understood each other at a glance were a hundred times more numerous, and our solidarity always guaranteed the passage of a question in the Politburo without disputes. This solidarity meant a great deal to Lenin.[53]

It should be stressed that Trotsky's early criticism of Lenin was very close to the truth, especially in his attacks on Lenin's harshness, intolerance and peremptoriness. Leaving Lenin's politics aside, his attitude to theory embodied a destructively nihilistic approach to bourgeois social thought in general. 'Not a single word of the philosophy or political economy of any of these philosophers should be believed,' he wrote in 1908 in his study 'Empiricism and Historical Materialism'.[54] This negativity was noted by Nikolai Valentinov, a former Bolshevik and former Menshevik who, as an émigré in Paris, wrote informative memoirs of his meetings with Lenin. Marxism, Valentinov remarked, was objective truth as far as Lenin was concerned, whereas everything else was either feeble-mindedness or charlatanism.[55]

Following the Second Congress, but especially between the 1905 revolution and February 1917, Trotsky expended the greater part of his prodigious energy on the factional struggle. He was very good at making enemies of his friends, and this often placed him in the crossfire between both sides. Losing allies before making new alliances was not a failing unique to Trotsky, however, but was rather a feature of Russian revolutionary life.

Ensign Arbuzov

In February 1905 Trotsky arrived in Kiev bearing a passport issued in the name of an Ensign Arbuzov. Changing his name was nothing new – Lvov, Yanovsky, Vikentiev, Petr Petrovich, Yanov, and of course Trotsky, had been used so far. Only a month before, he had been immersed in the normal business of a Russian revolutionary abroad – making speeches, writing articles, arguing and debating, and meeting interesting people. The news of 'Bloody Sunday' in St Petersburg, however, when troops had fired on a peaceful procession of workers and their families on 22 January 1905, had shaken the entire émigré colony. Even the unceasing polemics between the Bolsheviks and Mensheviks became slightly more muted. *Iskra*, now in the hands of the Mensheviks, battled with Lenin's *Vpered* (Forward), while Plekhanov was writing venomous articles against Lenin with the aim of isolating him as a 'Russian Jacobin'. Bloody Sunday and the ensuing public mood now augured the possible chance of proving one faction or another correct.

The political temperature inside Russia, especially in factories and universities, was rising rapidly, but while all the exiles' eyes were turned towards the east, not everyone was inclined to return to take part in the events. Life abroad had come to suit many of them, and observing and analyzing Russian politics from outside had become a habit they were unwilling to break. Trotsky, though, was incapable by nature of staying away from the action. He was no spectator, but a participant in and maker of history, and his illegal return to Russia was inevitable.

The events of the 1905 revolution have been sufficiently described and analyzed for there to be no need to go over them again in detail here. Instead, certain facets of Trotsky's activities deserve our attention, especially as they have either been ignored or distorted in the Soviet version. The 'retired ensign' arrived in Kiev in the guise of a respectable and successful entrepreneur. His second wife,* Natalya

---

* Trotsky and his first wife, Alexandra, had separated by 1903. It is not known when – or even if – he married Sedova. Their sons were always called Sedov, rather than Trotsky, and common-law marriages were normal among revolutionaries.

Sedova, had arrived ahead of him, found them an apartment and established contact with the local revolutionaries, notably a young engineer called Leonid Krasin, a Bolshevik who was closely associated with Lenin and who helped Trotsky acquire a rapid understanding of the situation in the country at large and among the social democrats in particular. Like many other social democrats of both camps, Krasin was committed to bringing the two warring factions together.

Soon Trotsky was turning out articles on a wide range of subjects. The liberals, especially those who had recently abandoned Marxism, came in for his special attention. In an article published in *Iskra* under the pseudonym 'Neophyte' and entitled 'A Word About Qualified Democrats', he wrote:

> The worst kind of democrats are the ex-Marxists. Their main feature is a constant hatred, gnawing and aching like a bad tooth, towards the social democrats. They are punishing our party for their own past, or maybe for their present. Marxism 'spoiled' them, some for life. If they ever had a link with the proletariat and its party, it has been severed completely now. These qualified democratic gentlemen should recognize the political moral: one can fool oneself, but not history.[56]

Trotsky particularly had in mind Peter Struve and similar former social democrats who were now seeking – and failing – to find a compromise with the tsarist regime.

With Krasin's assistance, Trotsky reached St Petersburg, where he at once plunged into the revolutionary maelstrom, sitting on strike committees, writing proclamations for posting all over the capital and distribution in the factories. When Sedova was arrested in May, however, Trotsky, who had been living illegally in the apartment of a Colonel A.A. Litkens, went into hiding in nearby Finland. Although it was an integral part of the Russian Empire, Finland, with its substantial Swedish élite minority, was ruled somewhat differently from the other borderlands and also, thanks to its burgeoning nationalist movement, was generally friendly towards the Russian left. Indeed, the Finnish Social Democratic Party, founded in 1899, was a legal body, unlike any other political party in the empire at the time. Russian revolutionaries on the run from the authorities therefore regarded Finland as the nearest safe haven.

While hiding out for three months in an isolated guest-house,

Trotsky wrote dozens of articles and pamphlets which were sent to the capital. In a May Day address to the workers, aimed at raising their flagging morale, he wrote:

> Listen, Comrades. You are afraid of the tsarist soldiers. But you are not afraid to go day in and day out to the factories and mills where the machines drain your blood and cripple your bodies. You are afraid of the tsarist soldiers. But you are not afraid to hand over your brothers to the tsarist army where they perish in the great unlamented cemetery of Manchuria.* You are afraid of the tsarist soldiers. But you are not afraid of living day in and day out under the authority of the bandit police, the barracks hangmen, for whom the life of a working proletarian is cheaper than the life of domestic cattle.[57]

With equal vigour, he addressed the soldiers and sailors:

> For a long time you have not understood the demands of the people. Your superiors and your priests lied to you and slandered the people. They kept you in ignorance. They stirred you up against the people. They forced you to stain your hands with the blood of the workers. They turned you into hangmen of the Russian people. They brought upon your heads the terrible curse of mothers and children, wives and old men ... Soldiers! Our state is like a vast battleship on which the tsarist authorities run riot, while the tormented people moan. We have only one way out: we should follow the example of the *Potemkin* and throw the whole gang which rules us overboard and take the governance of the state into our own hands.† We will determine the course of this battleship called Russia! Soldiers! When you come face to face with the people, raise your rifles! The first bullet should be for the officer who gives you the order to fire. Let the hangman fall at the hand of an honest soldier.[58]

When a large naval force under Admiral Z.P. Rozhestvensky engaged the Japanese, commanded by Admiral Togo, in the Straits of Tsushima on 14 May 1905, the tsarist fleet suffered a devastating defeat, losing eleven battleships and fifty-eight smaller vessels in a single day. Russia was in a state of shock, and Trotsky immediately rushed out a long proclamation calling for an end to the shameless

---

* Where Russia was fighting and losing a war with Japan.
† The mutiny on the battleship *Potemkin* would enter the canon of revolutionary legends, and be immortalized in Eisenstein's film of 1925.

slaughter. 'The fleet,' he wrote, 'was utterly destroyed. Nearly every ship was sunk, all the crews have either been killed, wounded or taken prisoner. The admirals are either injured or in custody . . . The Russian fleet is no more. It was not the Japanese who destroyed her, but the tsarist government . . . It is not the people that need this war! It is the governing clique, which dreams of seizing new lands and wants to extinguish the flame of the people's anger in blood.'[59]

In his Finnish hide-out, Trotsky knew the police were looking for him, but when the general strike of October broke out, he could not restrain himself from returning to St Petersburg. The Bolsheviks had been expecting the strike to occur on the first anniversary of Bloody Sunday, but instead it was triggered by the St Petersburg Council of Workers' Deputies – the Soviet – headed by a non-party lawyer, G.S. Khrustalev-Nosar, well respected as a workers' defence counsel. Trotsky was elected Khrustalev-Nosar's deputy. The Soviet's first meeting took place on 13 October and Trotsky appeared two days later, at once attracting attention with his energy, passionate speeches and radical proposals. The Soviet's authority soared. It began publishing a newspaper, *Izvestiya* (News), which called for an eight-hour day and for recognition of the newspaper as the expression of the workers' interests. Delegations came to the Soviet at the Institute of Technology and waited for instructions. Tension in the capital mounted. An Executive Committee of the Soviet was formed with three members each from the Bolsheviks, Mensheviks and Socialist Revolutionaries (SRs), as well as representatives of other organizations. Prominent among the Bolsheviks was Sverchkov, while Trotsky was the dominant Menshevik and Avksentiev the dominant SR. Khrustalev-Nosar supposedly stood above party loyalty, but it would not be long before he joined the Mensheviks.

The strike-wave rolled further and further afield. The government all but lost its head, but then took a step that visibly slowed down the revolutionary momentum: on 17 (30) October, Nicholas II issued a Manifesto promising constitutional rights. That night crowds carrying red flags emerged onto the streets of the capital and demanded the removal of hated administrators, a general amnesty and punishment of those responsible for Bloody Sunday. The Tsar's concessions had been interpreted by the crowds as a victory for the people. The rights granted included civil rights based on the inviolability of the person, freedom of conscience, speech, assembly and unions, and undertook that no law should be passed without the approval of the State Duma, a body still to be elected on a franchise yet to be defined. In Soviet historiography, the Manifesto of October 1905 has always been dismissed as a cunning move, forced on the Tsar by circumstances. But it is also possible to see it as a major step towards constitutional monarchy and hence a bourgeois democracy.

Like the Bolsheviks, Trotsky regarded the Manifesto as a half-victory. It gave pause to the liberals and the middle class, as well as to a large part of the intelligentsia which had demonstrated against the autocracy and now feared the possibility of anarchy. Sergei Witte, the prime minister who had earned the title of Count for his brilliant diplomacy at the Portsmouth (USA) peace conference with the Japanese in August 1905, wrote in a frank report to the Tsar that Russia had outlived its present political system and needed a law-governed state, based on the principles of civil liberty.[60] He advocated finding an accord between 'the intellectual tendencies and the new form' without resorting to force. The Tsar's October Manifesto made many think again. Parties were formed, patriotism found its voice, as did that of property, and the Russian wagon began to lumber to the right.

But not everyone in the government shared Witte's views, and it was those who wanted to crack down with force on the troubles who gained the upper hand, especially the Tsar's Palace Commandant and close confidant Dmitri Trepov, who advised that no bullets be spared in suppressing the disorders. Lenin, who was still in Geneva, and the Soviet in the capital sensed that the tsarist edifice, though shaken, would withstand the shock: only the cities and only the workers had risen. The government as always would be able to rely on the vast, ignorant mass of the peasantry, especially those in the army. The revolutionaries realized that neither their dream of establishing a dictatorship of the proletariat, nor their minimum programme – the overthrow of tsarism and the formation of a provisional revolutionary government – would occur.

None of the social democratic leaders doubted that the dictatorship of the proletariat would come in due course. An enormous crowd gathered at St Petersburg University on 30 October to listen to various speakers. The Bolsheviks viewed the Manifesto as a great victory. Trotsky, introduced as 'Yanovsky', soon captured the crowd's attention and declared: 'Citizens! Now that we have our foot on the neck of the ruling clique, they promise you freedom. Don't be in a hurry to celebrate the victory, it is not yet complete. Is paper money worth as much as gold? Is the promise of freedom the same as freedom itself? What has changed since yesterday? Have the gates of our prisons been flung open? Have our brothers come home from savage Siberia?' He concluded: 'Citizens! We are strong. We must defend liberty with the sword. The Tsar's Manifesto is nothing but a piece of paper. Today they gave it to you, tomorrow they will tear it into bits, as I do now!' Waving the text of the Manifesto to right and left, Trotsky demonstratively shredded it, letting the wind carry the pieces away.[61] The crowd was highly impressed by this new and unknown tribune of the revolution.

The peasants did not support the workers, nor was it possible to mobilize them. On the whole, the army remained loyal, and the workers were virtually without arms. The liberal intelligentsia were terrified by the scale of the workers' uprising. In hoping for a lasting revolutionary front, the social democrats had expected the impossible. Trotsky was peremptory and unjustifiably harsh in his condemnation of the intellectuals, especially the academics, whom he accused of doing whatever dirty work the government asked of them: 'There is no police action the professors are not willing to carry out.'[62] With the uncompromising attitude which was his hallmark, he lambasted the middle classes, the liberals, the university professors and the fellow-travellers of the revolution. The titles of some of his articles convey their flavour: 'Professors Play Political Concierge', 'Professors' Newspaper in Smear Campaign', 'Kadet Professors as Peasant Spokesmen'.[63] 'The revolution,' he wrote, 'has left the Philistines [the bourgeoisie] without a newspaper, it has extinguished the electric light in their apartments and painted on their walls a fiery message of some new vague but great ideas. The Philistines wanted to believe, but did not dare. They wanted to rise up, but could not.'[64]

Trotsky's antipathy to the liberals was a function of his radicalism, and he was frequently excessively harsh in his attacks, even on occasion suggesting that the liberals deserved as much hatred as tsarism. In the draft preface of his book on the 1905 revolution (published in German in 1907) he wrote: 'The author is in no way trying to hide from the reader his hatred of the tsarist regime, that vicious combination of the Asiatic knout and the European stock market, or his contempt for Russian liberalism, that most insignificant and spineless of political parties in the world gallery.'[65] For the Russian Jacobins, a liberal professor was no better than a policeman.

Recognizing that the revolution was beginning to flag, the Soviet passed a resolution, proposed by Trotsky, calling for an end to the October strike. Armed vigilante groups began forming in order to prevent pogroms and to defend demonstrations and labour newspapers, as well as the Soviet itself. As Trotsky began to emerge as the leading figure in the Soviet, a degree of rivalry developed between him and Khrustalev-Nosar who, having no party affiliation, lacked strong convictions on many issues. Several years later, Trotsky wrote two devastating pieces on Khrustalev, going so far as to mention reports in the bourgeois press that he had been arrested in Paris for theft:

> Khrustalev shone with a dual light, one for the party, the other for the masses. But both lights were reflected, coming from somewhere else. Khrustalev's own rise in no way corresponded to the visible rôle he was called upon to play, and even less to the legendary popularity claimed for him by the popular press. Georgi [Khrustalev-]Nosar's own fate was deeply tragic. Morally unstable, he was crushed by history which heaped burdens on him beyond endurance. His romantic image was fabricated by the fantasy of the bourgeoisie, fed by the press. He has smashed that image into smithereens, and himself with it.[66]

Trotsky's judgement of his erstwhile comrade may well have been accurate, but it was unworthy of him to kick the man when he was down. Savagery towards his rivals was one of his less attractive traits.

During the revolution Trotsky flourished. He succeeded in altering the line of the Menshevik newspaper *Nachalo* (Beginning), so that even Zinoviev, never one of his warmest admirers, was able later to write: 'When *Nachalo* was taken over by [Trotsky and Parvus] they gave it quite a Bolshevik character.'[67] Trotsky's utterances in the press had an air of assurance, firmness and determination: 'The Soviet of Deputies declares: the Petersburg proletariat will fight its ultimate battle with the tsarist government not on the day of Trepov's choice, but when it suits the organized and armed proletariat.'[68] He gave the impression that this was not his first revolution, and his manner greatly impressed the workers.

When Trotsky was in exile some three decades later, and being hunted down by Stalin's killers, an attempt was made to use his actions as a young revolutionary against him, and the name of Khrustalev-Nosar was resurrected for the purpose. A report to Stalin and Voroshilov from Beria and Yezhov, dated 28 October 1938 and possibly the last such report signed by Yezhov, declared that in the preface of a book by Khrustalev-Nosar entitled *From the Recent Past*, 'Trotsky-Bronshtein is named as having been an agent of the tsarist Okhrana since 1902.' The report further indicated that Khrustalev had been executed in 1919 in Pereyaslavl 'on Trotsky's direct orders, with the aim of removing this witness to his collaboration with the Okhrana'. The search for evidence against Trotsky had, according to this report, discovered that the Nizhni Novgorod soviet had initiated an investigation on 30 March 1917, and that Trotsky, Khrustalev and Lunacharsky – who died in 1933 – had been named there as Okhrana informers. Finally, Beria and Yezhov claimed that they had found a report from the Quartermaster-General of the Imperial Army Staff Headquarters, dated 30 March 1917, numbered 8436, and addressed to the Provisional Government, to the effect that 'a military agent in the USA had cabled that Trotsky had sailed from New York on the SS *Christiania Fjord* on 14 March, and that, according to British intelligence, Trotsky was in charge of peace propaganda in America, paid by the Germans and by persons sympathetic to them'.[69]

Stalin evidently found the whole concoction either unconvincing or of insufficient value, and it was not used against Trotsky. It has proved impossible to find Nosar's book, but it is known that his relations with Trotsky turned bad soon after their first meeting. The Soviet security organs, or NKVD, may well have suspected Nosar's involvement with the tsarist police and thought to implicate Trotsky by means of this crude fabrication.

In his fifty-two days in the Petersburg Soviet, Trotsky showed himself to be an uncompromising revolutionary leader. Soviet history depicted him as having split the labour movement and ignored the peasantry and army, but in its prejudice failed to take account of the circumstances in which Trotsky was acting. What may become clear to historians is usually unclear to the participants in historical events, when the pressure of necessity may exceed that of reflection. Trotsky made his mistakes in action. He himself rated the experience of 1905 highly. In 1919, commenting on events in Germany in an article entitled 'The Creeping Revolution', he wrote:

> The Russian working class, which has achieved its revolution, received an invaluable inheritance from the previous epoch in the form of a centralized labour party. The Populist movement [of the 1870s], the terrorist campaigns of the People's Will [of the 1880s], the underground agitation of the first Marxists [of the 1890s], the revolutionary demonstrations in the early years of the century, the October general strike and the barricades of 1905, the revolutionary 'parliamentarism' of the Stolypin era [1906–14] which was closely linked to the underground, all this prepared a large pool of revolutionary leaders.[70]

Khrustalev-Nosar was arrested at the end of November 1905 and a new presidium was elected, consisting of Trotsky, Sverchkov and Zlydnev, with Trotsky the recognized leader. By now, however, it was plain that the government had gone on to the offensive, and the revolutionary floodwaters began to recede. One of the Soviet's last decisions – inspired by Alexander Helphand-Parvus – was to call on the population not to pay any taxes until the government had fulfilled all its economic and political promises. This provided the government with the excuse to arrest the entire Soviet leadership on 3 December. The Soviet under Trotsky's chairmanship was actually discussing calling for a new general strike when the police burst in. The building had been surrounded and the officer-in-charge had begun reading his orders, when Trotsky interrupted him: 'Please don't interfere with the work of the Soviet. If you wish to speak, kindly give your name and I will ask the assembly if they wish to hear you.' The officer was lost for words. Trotsky took advantage of the hiatus by calling on the next speaker. He then asked the officer to say his piece and the order was heard in deathly silence, after which Trotsky announced in a matter-of-fact voice: 'There is a proposal to take note of the gendarme officer's statement. And now you may leave the meeting of the Soviet Workers' Deputies.' The officer departed in a state of complete confusion. Trotsky then proposed that the Soviet members prepare themselves for arrest by destroying documents that might be used to incriminate them, and also by breaking any weapons they might possess. Almost at once, the hall was invaded by a company of gendarmes and the members seized, although not before Trotsky managed to cry out: 'See how the Tsar carries out his October Manifesto! See!'

Trotsky's actions during the revolution and his behaviour at his trial convincingly demonstrated that an outstanding personality had arrived on the political scene, one for whom the revolution was the highest value. Characteristically, his actions were the more unpredictable, decisive and inspired, the more critical the situation. He never doubted the high purpose of his life and never regretted his choice of vocation. Six months before his death, he wrote in his will: 'If I had to begin all over again I would of course try to avoid this or that mistake, but the main course of my life would remain unchanged. I shall die a proletarian revolutionist, a Marxist, a dialectical materialist and, consequently, an irreconcilable atheist.'[71] He saw the failure of the 1905 revolution as no more than a historical rehearsal.

Trotsky used the twelve months of incarceration from December 1905 to January 1907, which he spent first in the Kresty prison and then the Peter-Paul Fortress in St Petersburg, to good effect, exploiting to the full the lenient conditions allowed to political prisoners. He wrote numerous articles and proclamations which he gave to his wife, who, like the rest of his family and other comrades at large, could visit him twice a week, and which she in turn handed over to the legal and illegal press for publication. His cell, according to eyewitnesses, resembled nothing so much as the study of a busy academic, with books and magazines and newspapers piled and strewn everywhere. Trotsky also tried to maintain the tenuous link with his first family by writing several times to his first wife, Alexandra Sokolovskaya. On 17 May 1906, for instance, he wrote:

Dear friend,
    Haven't you received my last letter? I sent it to your father's address. It was mostly about my views of the two factions (as you had asked me) ... My situation is unchanged. The trial has been postponed to 19 October. I sit in solitary confinement and get three to four hours' exercise a day ... My parents brought me a photograph of the girls – I wrote to you about it. They are both wonderful in their own way. Ninushka has such a face – frightened and yet slyly inquisitive at the same time. And Zinushka's is so thoughtful. Someone here managed to put a smudge on Zinushka's face. If you have a spare picture, please

send it. So, they've dissolved the Duma. I took a bet that it was going to be a hooligan government, and I was right . . .[72]

One of his articles, entitled 'Peter Struve in Politics', aroused a good deal of interest for the vehemence with which it lambasted the liberals as fellow-travellers, but not allies, of the revolution. But the chief product of this period was a long article entitled 'Results and Perspectives', in which for the first time he expounded his concept of the permanent revolution. It was an idea that would in time become the chief weapon to be used against him, namely that 'accomplishing the socialist revolution within national limits is impossible . . . The socialist revolution is becoming permanent in a new and broader sense of the word: it will not be complete until the triumph of the new society has taken place throughout the entire planet.'[73] We shall return to this theory in due course. For the moment, suffice to say that, while today it may seem hopelessly outmoded, at the time its significance lay in pushing out the national limits of the movement and offering high ideals to the proletariat.

Recognizing that the revolution had foundered on the ancient rocks of the autocracy, that it had struck at St Petersburg and Moscow and a few other cities, but not acquired nationwide dimensions, Trotsky nevertheless believed that the rehearsal had succeeded. In his elegant, easily read handwriting, he wrote: '1905 opened with events that created an irrevocable divide between the past and the present. They drew a line in blood below the era of the springtime – the childhood – of political awareness.'[74] Without childhood there can be no maturity, and Trotsky never forgot the value of the political education he and others received in the first Russian revolution, which permitted them to leave their 'childhood' behind.

Trotsky viewed the forthcoming trial as an important opportunity to address a nationwide audience, and he made careful preparation. In his speech, the notes for which are preserved in the archives, he explained the failure of the workers' rising, and noted that the army had not joined the revolt, despite the soldiers' meetings that had taken place in a wide range of Russian cities in the European part of the empire, as well as the Caucasus. 'As a rule,' he wrote, 'the leaders were "qualified" soldiers, usually local lads. The majority, i.e. the peasant recruits, sappers or artillerymen, absorbed the new mood slowly. In the end, for both us and the government, it was all a matter of time.'[75]

The prisoners resolved among themselves to adopt a defiant attitude, to expose the existing order, to speak of the Soviet's goals of social justice and concern for the workers' interests, but above all to deny that they had had any intention of using armed force to change the system. Article 126 of the Criminal Code, passed on 26 March 1903, made it plain that anyone found guilty of using explosive devices or weapons in an attempt to overthrow the existing order would be sentenced to eight years' hard labour or deportation to Siberia.[76] To avoid this outcome, when he addressed the court Trotsky tried on the one hand to expose the decay and unpopularity of the tsarist regime, and on the other to show that the Soviet had had no definite plan for an uprising: 'No matter how important weapons might be, it is not in them that great power resides, gentlemen judges. No! It is not the ability of the masses to kill people, but their own great willingness to die that in our view, gentlemen judges, determines the victory of the popular rising.'[77]

Trotsky's mother and father attended throughout the trial. 'During my speech,' he later recalled, 'which she could scarcely understand, she wept silently. She wept more when a score of attorneys for the defence came up to shake my hand ... My mother was sure that I would not only be acquitted, but even given some mark of distinction.'[78] The fourteen accused members of the Soviet were in the end not sentenced to hard labour, but to a life sentence of exile in the Siberian village of Obdorskoe, on the River Ob beyond Tyumen and above the Arctic Circle, some 600 miles from the nearest railway station and more than 500 from a telegraph point. The day before their departure, on 23 January 1907, the convicts were issued with grey prisoners' trousers, heavy coats and fur hats. They were also allowed to keep their own clothes. The travel document issued in his name indicates that, apart from his clothes, Trotsky was also given leg-irons and shackle-linings, a fur lining, a pair of trousers, gloves and a bag.[79] The shackles were issued only as a warning, and were not generally put on prisoners unless they attempted to escape. Before his departure, Trotsky managed to send a farewell note for publication in the illegal press, ending with the words: 'We depart with profound faith in the people's early victory over its age-old enemies. Long live the proletariat! Long live international socialism!'[80] The letter was signed (in Russian alphabetical order) by N. Avksentiev, S. Vainshtein-Zvezdin, I. Golynsky, P. Zlydnev, M. Kiselevich, B. Knunyants-Radin, E. Komar, N. Nemtsov, D. Sverchkov-Vvedensky, A. Simanovsky, N. Stogov, L. Trotsky, A. Feit and G. Khrustalev-Nosar.

Trotsky described the journey to Siberia in a short book, *There and Back*, and also most graphically in his autobiography.[81] Even as he was leaving to begin his life sentence he was planning to escape, for despite there being more than fifty gendarmes escorting the fourteen convicts, the regime was a lenient one compared to what would come under Stalin. At the small town of Berezov the party was given a two-day rest, and here, coached by his fellow-prisoner Feit, a trained physician, Trotsky faked an attack of sciatica. He was permitted to remain behind with two guards while the rest of the party continued on its way north, and with the help of a local peasant he made his break. It was a daring escape along the River Sosva and across the boundless expanse of the snow-covered plain. After a trek lasting a week and covering about 500 miles, and with the help of Siberian tribesmen at various tiny settlements, who sold him deer and a sleigh, Trotsky reached the Urals. Posing first as a member of a polar expedition and then as an official, he reached the railway on horseback and at the station was observed with indifference by the secret police as he unburdened himself of the fur coats he had been wearing.

The records of the police's efforts to recapture him were discovered in 1922 among the papers of the Okhrana in Nikolaev. When it was suggested to Trotsky that this material be given to the Museum of the Revolution 'as a document of enormous historical value', his secretariat replied that they wanted it 'for the biography of the leader of the proletarian revolution'.[82] He was already preening himself before the mirror of history.

Having arrived back in St Petersburg, Trotsky was reunited with Natalya Sedova, who helped him escape to Finland, where he found Lenin and Martov living in neighbouring villages. He gained the impression that the Mensheviks were 'recanting the mad acts of 1905', while 'the Bolsheviks were not recanting anything, and were getting ready for a new revolution'. Martov 'as always had many ideas, brilliant and subtle ones, but he had not the one idea that was more important than any other: he did not know what to do next'. Lenin, meanwhile, 'spoke approvingly of my work in prison, but he taunted me for not drawing the necessary conclusions, in other words, for not going over to the Bolsheviks. He was right in this.'[83]

It is noticeable in his autobiography that whenever possible Trotsky tries to minimize his differences with Lenin, repeating time and again that although he was not in the Bolshevik camp, he had nonetheless abandoned the Mensheviks. This was not in fact so. Up until 1917 Trotsky was in virtually permanent opposition to Lenin, at times conducting veritable war, and was none too fastidious in his choice of insults. Indeed, he adopted the same abusive tone towards Lenin as the latter used against his own opponents, accusing him of 'reckless demagoguery', 'lack of mental agility' and, as a philosopher, being 'beyond help'.[84] The tendency to descend to mud-slinging was a trait common to most of the Russian revolutionaries.

While essentially a leftist in outlook, Trotsky also harboured reformist ideas which to a great extent can be explained by the company he kept when in exile in the West. In due course he would come to mix his radicalism with his reformism, and this dualism would last until the tumultuous events of 1917.

After a short and extremely cool meeting with Lenin, Trotsky retired to the tucked-away village of Oglbu, and then, with the help of contacts in Helsinki given to him by Lenin, a false passport and some gold coins from his father, he made his way to Stockholm.

The Viennese Chapter

Trotsky spent the next ten years abroad, seven of them in Vienna and the rest in Switzerland, France, Spain and, finally, the United States. Throughout this period he collaborated with Austrian and other European social democrats. Vienna represented a long pause in the hectic life of the advocate of permanent revolution, but it reveals much of interest about his character. Stalin was right when he pointed out that Trotsky's strength emerged when the revolutionary tide was rising and that his weakness showed when the revolution was receding. Trotsky was a man of action. Condemned to a long period of passive waiting, he concentrated on journalism and on maintaining ties with

Russian émigrés and Western social democrats, whether organizers or Marxist theorists. Even the Fifth Party Congress, held in 1907 in London, failed to inspire him with renewed energy.

It was at this congress that the first meeting took place between Trotsky and Stalin, although Trotsky later claimed he could not recall having noticed the taciturn Georgian, then bearing the alias 'Ivanovich', who for the entire three weeks of the meeting uttered not a single word to the assembly. And this despite the fact that the congress debated and banned any further bank robberies for the benefit of the party – the notorious 'expropriations' – such as those carried out in the Caucasus by Bolshevik-sponsored gangs. As Trotsky would later repeatedly recall, Stalin had been directly implicated in these affairs, as had the Bolshevik leadership around Lenin. In a 1930 article entitled 'On Stalin's Political Biography' he wrote: 'In 1907 Stalin took part in the Tiflis bank raid ... One wonders why the official biographies are too cowardly to mention this?'[85] The General Secretary evidently had his own views of the bank robberies, but he never divulged them.

Stalin, for his part, could not have failed to notice the slim young man with blue eyes, long hair and pince-nez who addressed the congress with such self-assurance and who was invariably surrounded by other delegates during the intermissions. Trotsky used the opportunity of the assembly to air aspects of his theory of permanent revolution, emphasizing in particular that a prerequisite was an alliance of the workers and peasants. Despite the closeness of these notions to those of Lenin, Trotsky's old ties to the Mensheviks still held him back. He voted for resolutions proposed by both wings of the party, to such an extent that it seemed peace had been declared between himself and Lenin. The writer Maxim Gorky, who was present at several sessions, did his best to enhance the truce, but in vain. Trotsky was too committed to his own independence, his unorthodoxy and originality, and evidently felt that he could maintain his star image better by cutting across party lines. Lenin's remark in a letter to Gorky after the Congress that Trotsky's behaviour could often be explained by his need to show off was quite justified.[86]

After the Congress Trotsky returned to Vienna, where he and Sedova settled down. Fluent in German and French, less so in English, this most 'European' of Russian revolutionaries soon felt at home. He quickly re-established contact with Parvus, who had been exiled with him to Siberia in 1906 and who had similarly escaped. It was Parvus who originated the idea of permanent revolution, a fact Trotsky acknowledged in recognizing the debt he owed to this remarkable personality, of whom more will be said in a later chapter.

Trotsky never lost his warm feelings for Parvus, whose role in the revolutionary movement was to become so controversial. It was Parvus who in 1907 introduced him to the 'Marxist Pope' of the Second International, Karl Kautsky, a meeting Trotsky later described:

> A white-haired and very jolly little old man with clear blue eyes greeted me with the Russian 'Zdravstvuyte' ['Hello']. With what I already knew of Kautsky from his books, this served to complete a very charming personality. The thing that appealed to me most was the absence of fuss, which, as I later discovered, was the result of his undisputed authority at that time, and of the inner calm which it gave him ... One got little conversation with Kautsky. His mind was too angular and dry, too lacking in nimbleness and psychological insight. His evaluations were schematic, his jokes trite.[87]

Trotsky was nonetheless impressed by the sheer scale of Kautsky's thinking, and when the meeting was over Trotsky felt that everyone there was a head shorter than the little old man. During the First World War, however, which radically altered alignments among the social democrats, Trotsky would write in quite different terms about Kautsky, all traces of his admiration gone:

> Kautsky's entire authority was based on the reconciliation of opportunism in politics with Marxism in theory ... On its very first day, the war brought the dénouement, the exposure of the entire falseness and rottenness of Kautskianism ... 'The International is an instrument of peace, not war ...' Kautsky clung to this vulgarism like a lifebelt ... pushing Marxism towards Quakerism and crawling on all fours before [President] Wilson.[88]

Trotsky collected notes on all his meetings and, if the occasion arose, would then compose brief thumbnail sketches for publication, usually in unflattering terms, if other social democrats were concerned. It should be noted, however, that many, if not most, of the leaders of both wings of the Russian party shared his lack of delicacy when it came to personal criticism. They were all steeped in politics, and moral considerations came very low in their order of priorities.

The Vienna interlude was also one of personal development, during which Trotsky greatly broadened his knowledge. He attended meetings connected with a wide range of interests, including Freudian psychoanalysis. Of this he wrote in January 1924 in a letter to the great physiologist Ivan Pavlov:

> During the several years that I spent in Vienna I came into quite close contact with the Freudians, I read their works and even attended some of their meetings . . . In essence, psychoanalysis is based on the idea that psychological processes are the complex superstructure of physiological processes . . . Your theory of conditioned reflexes, it seems to me, embraces Freud's theory . . . The sublimation of sexual energy, a favourite sphere of Freudian teaching, is the construction of conditioned reflexes on the sexual base.[89]

Psychoanalysis was only one of many fields of intellectual exploration in which Trotsky indulged himself in those years, and intellectual curiosity remained with him all his life.

Trotsky's image and his intellect seem to embody the indisputable fact that Russia lay between Europe and Asia – that it was Eurasian. The majority of the Russian population at that time bore more Asiatic and Slavonic than Western and European characteristics. The issue was not one of different levels of civilization, so much as a capacity for absorbing and synthesizing different cultures. In Russians like Axelrod, Dan, Parvus and Plekhanov, who lived for many years in Europe, national elements of consciousness were gradually displaced by cosmopolitan elements. They felt at home everywhere. While they may readily have accepted universal human values, however, they lost something else, without which it was impossible fully to feel the pain, the suffering and the hopes of their own motherland. For Trotsky, the European experience enhanced his ability to view the revolutionary aims in his own country through the prism of the international socialist movement.

In Vienna Trotsky was active mostly among the Mensheviks, and was therefore viewed by his Western friends as a centrist. He wrote more often than any other Russian socialist for Kautsky's monthly *Neue Zeit*, in which he explained for Western social democrats the split between the Mensheviks and the Bolsheviks, which they found hard to understand and in which they were reluctant to interfere. In this respect, Trotsky seemed to them to be serving a conciliatory, rational and attractive role. For instance, he organized a conference of various Russian organizations in August 1912. Eighteen voting delegates, ten consultative delegates and five guests turned up from Menshevik groups and the Jewish Bund, but the exchange of recriminations that occupied much of the time resulted in nothing emerging from the meeting. As was always to be expected on such occasions, there was a police informer present who duly submitted his report to the Moscow Okhrana in October 1912.[90]

Among the German social democrats Trotsky was closest to Rosa Luxemburg, Karl Liebknecht and Franz Mehring, although he also socialized with their ideological opponents, a fact that put the radicals on their guard. For his part, he put personal feelings before 'unity' or 'solidarity'. When in 1916 Mehring celebrated his seventieth birthday, Trotsky associated the name of Rosa Luxemburg with his congratulations: 'Mehring, Luxemburg and I are on the same side of the trenches that run throughout the entire capitalist world. In Franz Mehring and Rosa Luxemburg we celebrate the nucleus of the revolutionary German opposition to which we are bound indissolubly as brothers in arms.'[91]

Of Karl Liebknecht Trotsky wrote in different terms:

> expansive, easily aroused, he stands out in sharp relief against the background of the orderly, faceless and indistinguishable party bureaucracy . . . Liebknecht has always felt a semi-stranger in the house of German social democracy, with its internal regularity and its constant readiness to compromise . . . His genuine and deep revolutionary instinct has always steered him, through the inevitable zigzags, onto the right path.[92]

Trotsky wrote about virtually everyone he ever met; not the dry, colourless sketches typical of other political commentators, but vivid portraits that brought his subjects to life. The time he spent in Vienna among so many interesting and original intellectuals could not but enhance the development of his own mind, help to refine his political judgement and broaden his erudition. People who witnessed him giving speeches testify that he could think on his feet, shape images instantly, define trends, identify essentials. He did not learn his speeches in advance, but would create them as he spoke, always producing something new and original. He could hold the attention of the leaders of the Second International or St Petersburg workers or soldiers of the 2nd Nikolaev Regiment with equal effect. It was a talent that derived from an amazing ability to absorb ideas and also to enter the minds of his audience. Whether friendly or hostile, no one could long remain neutral towards Trotsky. He was universally regarded as an extraordinary, larger-than-life figure.

During this second exile in the centre of Europe, when his interests revolved around the Russian factions, European parliamentarism and new trends in German social democracy, Trotsky was nonetheless for ten years in the revolutionary 'provinces'. Although a virtually professional critic of the parliamentary system, he seems not to have noticed that in Russia, thanks to the 1905 revolution, a Russian form of parliament had been born. The Bolshevik boycott of the First and Second State Dumas, as well as their active participation in the Fourth, provided ample food for thought about the use the working class might make of parliamentary methods of struggle. All this passed Trotsky by, not so much because of geographical distance as because of his sceptical attitude to the Russian parliament as such. He was not unique in this. The Bolsheviks also despised the parliamentary system. At the Second Comintern Congress in March 1920, Lenin would say that the task facing Communism was 'the destruction of parliamentarism'. In general, his second exile cut Trotsky off from revolutionary events in Russia, both legal and illegal.

Trotsky and his second family – a son, Lev, had been born in 1906 and another, Sergei, in 1908 – settled into a modest three-room apartment in Vienna, the most notable feature of which was the heaped newspapers and piled books on every available surface. He maintained his family mostly from his earnings as a journalist. He worked for a long time as a reporter for the radical Kiev newspaper *Kievskaya mysl'* (Kiev Thought), but also right up to the revolution he received money from his father. He was therefore much better off than most political émigrés, who were often reduced to beggarly conditions as they tried to find the price of their next meal. Trotsky's material security enabled him to devote himself to his writing, to be independent, to travel from capital to capital more often than others, to attend seminars and conferences, and so on. He could also develop his interest in art, visiting museums and galleries, and writing articles of professional standard on artistic topics for the Kiev newspaper. He took Natalya to the Vienna Opera, but confessed that his appreciation of music was no better than primitive. The second exile, while it was a lengthy hiatus, was also a time when Trotsky grew in stature as a theorist, journalist, writer and politician.

While analyzing Trotsky's writings and speeches during his time abroad, I was struck by the absence of (almost) any sign of nostalgia for Russia, any longing to see his father's house or to revisit the scenes of his childhood. Most people, when cut off from their homeland, yearn for their roots. Memories, scraps of news, old photos – everything carries a special meaning. But neither Lenin nor Trotsky, nor many other revolutionaries, could step onto Russian soil without the risk of being sent straight back to Siberia. The Moscow branch of the Okhrana had issued a warrant for Trotsky's immediate deportation to hard labour in Siberia should he be apprehended within the Russian borders.[93] The memoirs of many Russian revolutionaries of that time reveal frequent attacks of nostalgia for the scent of fresh snow, the crunch of sleigh-runners, the faces of their dear ones, and other memories of home. Trotsky felt no such longings. Perhaps he was one of the first 'citizens of the world' for whom home is where they happen to be. The Europeanization of his heart and mind, the gradual absorption of different cultures, and the mental identification of his motherland with the autocracy, generated in him immunity to nostalgia. He was, like his comrades, also a thoroughly political animal in whom there was little or no room for feelings of organic bonds with the land of one's forefathers, with its songs and customs and the graves of ancestors.

A very rare, if not unique, reference to nostalgic feeling for Russia is to be found in one of Trotsky's reports from the front in the Balkan wars of 1912–13, published as his 'Balkan Letters'. As he passed through the Bulgarian province of Dobrudja in 1912, he became painfully aware of its similarity to the steppes of Kherson and of Yanovka, where two years earlier his mother had died, and he had been unable to attend her funeral:

The road is just like a Russian road. Just as dusty as our Kherson road. Hens run out from under the horses' hooves, as they do in Russia, and the [Ukrainian] horses wear Russian harness, even [the driver's] back looks Russian ... Dusk falls. There is a smell of grass and the dust of the road ... It is quiet. One's feet itch and it feels as though we're off on our holidays ... to Yanovka.[94]

Such moments of reminiscence are rarely to be found in Trotsky's writings.

In September 1912 *Kievskaya mysl'* had asked Trotsky to write a series on the explosive situation in the Balkans. The pay and conditions were good, the political climate in Europe was calm and 'Antid Oto', as he called himself, therefore accepted the offer. He was required to cover two national wars, in each of which both sides were the losers. Lurking in the background were the big powers, the Russian and Austro-Hungarian empires, England and other countries. The bone of contention was Macedonia, then a Turkish province, to which Serbia, Bulgaria and Greece each laid claim. They could only free Macedonia from Turkey, however, if they combined, and the Balkan League was therefore formed. The trigger for the outbreak of war was a Turkish massacre of two Macedonian villages. On 13 October 1912 Bulgaria delivered a note to Turkey, in the name of the League, which amounted to an ultimatum. No reply was forthcoming. Hostilities began and by December Serbia, Bulgaria and Greece had taken most of Macedonia. Turkey asked for an armistice, but peace was not made until 30 May 1913, when a treaty was signed in London. The representatives of the great powers succeeded in dividing the fruits of the conflict in such a way as to satisfy nobody. All the parties began making claims against each other, with the result that in June 1913 hostilities broke out between the erstwhile allies and the Second Balkan War began. Serbia, Montenegro and Greece fought against Bulgaria, and were joined by Romania and the Ottoman Empire. Bulgaria was defeated within a month. A second peace treaty was signed in Bucharest in August 1913, according to which Macedonia was divided between Serbia and Greece, while Dobrudja went to Romania. The war left all the parties dissatisfied and had merely created new sources of tension. It was Trotsky's task to convey information and to comment on all this to his Russian readers.

The more than seventy articles he sent from the front comprise the sixth volume of his collected works. Most of them are brilliantly lucid and informative, revealing as plainly as anything else he wrote his mastery as a writer. He was not an unbiased chronicler, however. He blamed the Balkan situation on the negative role played by 'the hand of tsarism' and its Pan-Slavist ideology. It was inconceivable to him that Russia could have any legitimate interest in 'this Pandora's box', despite the competing claims of the great powers in the area. At first, his reports expressed sympathy for the South Slavs, but as he saw their hope of Russian help grow, his tone began to change, and he suddenly started defending the Turks, who were facing defeat. This at once drew a howl of protest in Sofia, Belgrade, Kiev and St Petersburg. When he wrote about the allies' 'bestial' treatment of the Turks, the Bulgarians banned him from visiting the front. Trotsky's hostility towards the slavophiles mounted as he recognized the interference from the Russian capital. In 'Open Letters' to the Bulgarian poet Petko Todorov and the leader of the Russian liberal party (the Constitutional Democrats), the historian Paul Milyukov, Trotsky defended his view of the war from an internationalist, rather than nationalist, position. It is also true that on several occasions, his understanding of the causes of the senseless slaughter was superficial.

Trotsky returned to cover the Second Balkan War and again defended the underdog, except that now it was the Bulgarians, and he had to write about the atrocities of the new victors. Reporting the war as an act of 'anti-civilization', Trotsky also attempted to give his own views as to the best arrangement for the Balkans when the conflict was over. As early as 1909 he had written: 'Only a unified state of all the Balkan nationalities on democratic-federative principles – like Switzerland or the North American republic – can bring internal peace to the Balkans and create the conditions for the mighty development of its productive forces.'[95] During the war itself, he often expressed what he plainly knew to be a virtually Utopian idea. He pointed out the irony of a world in which, although 'we have learned to wear braces, write clever leading articles and make Milka chocolate; when it comes to deciding on how to get several tribes to live together on Europe's abundant peninsula, we are powerless to find any other means than mass mutual destruction'.[96] The idea of a Balkan federation would be resurrected by Stalin after the Second World War, with the sole result of spoiling relations between Bulgaria and Yugoslavia.

A marked feature of Trotsky's reportage from the Balkans was its strong note of pacifism, a doctrine he would be strongly opposing only a few years hence. Echoing the resolution of the Zimmerwald Conference held in Switzerland in September 1915, when radical social democrats from the belligerent countries of the First World War voted to oppose the conflict, he would write: 'The workers must reject the Utopian demands of both bourgeois and socialist pacifism. The pacifists are planting new illusions in the place of the old ones and are trying to recruit the proletariat in the service of these illusions.'[97]

At the time, however, the pen of Antid Oto (and L. Yanov, another pen-name) was producing 'Utopian illusions' one after another, as what he saw conflicted with his intellectual analysis of the war, its causes and its remedies. His notes include an essay that recognized this fact:

> I went to the Balkan war believing it to be not only probable but also possible. But when ... I realized that many people I knew – politicians, editors and university teachers – were already guarding the frontier, standing at the front line rifle in hand, and that they would be the first to kill and be killed, then the war, which I had so easily speculated about in my thoughts and my articles as an abstraction, seemed to me unbelievable and impossible.[98]

He described a scene at a small railway station in Serbia:

> we met a transport of prisoners – 190 Turks and Arnauts. They got them out of the wagons and took them off to the town, to the barracks or the prison. It was not the first picture of grief and human degradation I had seen in my life, and especially here in the Balkans. But I had never seen such as this. One hundred and ninety wounded, mutilated, sick men, clad in rags and tatters with the last remnants of human clothing somehow wrapped round their miserable bodies. Many still had shreds of footwear, others had rags clinging to their feet. It was cold and raw, but about a third of them were completely barefoot. These prisoners ... were the most accurate picture of war, whether it's a defensive or offensive war, colonial or national. Any honest and intelligent artist must put this picture on his canvas. It will be far more horrible than any of Vereshchagin's symmetrical horrors or those of Leonid Andreev.[99]

In another report, dated Belgrade, 28 September 1913 and signed L. Yanov, he wrote:

The women of the East are human beasts of burden, their unwashed breasts hanging out of their blouses, carrying their babies, sacks tied to their backs and over their arms, as they struggle to get onto the train, pushing their bundles along in front of them with their knees. Behind them are peasants, blackened forever by the soil and the sun, gnarled, bow-legged, bent low ... The young women are dressed in flea-ridden sarafans. Hunched, black-clad old women with goitres are leaning on staves and sitting on a bench for three, four or five hours at a stretch, silent and still. What awful, enduring patience they have![100]

Trotsky's 'Balkan Letters' were those of a politician and journalist who had looked into the seething cauldron of the Balkans. He of course did not know that within a decade he would be engulfed in another war, not as a chronicler, but as one of the chief actors in a long and bloody drama. Antid Oto's miniatures drew the veil from the awful face of war, but while condemning it, in his theoretical reflections he continued to speak of the 'lifelessness of the humanistic, moralistic view of war'. He still believed that war could be uprooted by war. At the time, perhaps, no one could know how Utopian this idea really was. It was not pacifism that had the capacity to become a future world trend, but it was war that would displace men's reason by force and that would be forever seen as true history.

In Ahasueras's Footsteps

I met Trotsky's daughter-in-law, Olga Grebner, in 1989, in the aptly-named Leningrad old people's home 'Veterans of the Scene'. Several times she referred to Trotsky as 'Ahasueras'. According to ancient legend, the Jew Ahasueras was condemned to eternal wandering as punishment for having given Christ succour during a short pause on the way to His crucifixion. It had never been Trotsky's intention to bear a cross, even one the son of a Jewish settler in Russia might have been burdened with. Yet for most of his life he was to carry the cross of suffering and glory, disappointment and unquenchable hope, all as punishment for his love of the revolution.

In 1913, his Balkan assignment completed, Trotsky returned not to his own home but to Austria, where his family awaited him. Despite having many admirers and followers, and despite his great popularity, Trotsky had few friends. Among these was Semen Lvovich Klyachko, a Russian socialist who had lived abroad for more than forty years and who would die less than a year before the February 1917 revolution. Klyachko left little trace of his activities on the revolutionary movement because, Trotsky wrote, 'he had all the abilities necessary to attain great prominence in politics, except that he hadn't the necessary defects'.[101] Trotsky was fond of Klyachko not only for his gentle character and exceptional mind, but also for his 'cosmopolitan' qualities. Klyachko had been his own man in the social democratic organizations of New York, London, Vienna, Paris, Berlin and Rome. If it had not been for the revolution of 1917, Trotsky might also have remained a 'citizen of the world'. Klyachko's cosmopolitan attitudes impressed Trotsky, who loved to think in terms of the world revolution. After her husband had died, Anna Konstantinovna Klyachko was one of the first people Trotsky wrote to when he entered his last exile in 1929:

> We are living on the island of Prinkipo, where I was once supposed to have attended a world conference at the invitation of Lloyd George. Although nothing came of Lloyd George's initiative, geographically speaking it wasn't a bad idea; one has complete isolation from the rest of the world and beautiful scenery. The view from our windows on all sides is of improbable beauty. The only drawback is the mosquitoes which appear at night, despite the cold spring.[102]

Back in Vienna, Trotsky threw himself once again into the world of party discord, the party by now being firmly and permanently divided into two camps. Attracted as before by Bolshevik radicalism, Trotsky was drawn by his personal sympathy for the Mensheviks, and thus he stuck to his previous position. He expected a new revolutionary wave to rise and tried to keep up his contacts with his former comrades in the St Petersburg Soviet. One such was Dmitri Fedorovich Sverchkov, with whom Trotsky started a chess match by correspondence.[103] In May 1922 Sverchkov, then deputy chief of the Petrograd railway system, would ask for Trotsky's protection, and would give a lengthy account of his own past support for the now-powerful member of the Politburo and military chief of the Republic. Sverchkov wrote to Trotsky that in the summer of 1917, when Trotsky was arrested by the Provisional Government, the newspapers were baying for harsh retribution and I was afraid you might be shot. I was then a right-wing Menshevik and fiercely opposed to the Bolsheviks. Earlier, in 1909 in Paris, during a Central Committee plenum, I had learned from Martov, Dan and others about the way the Bolsheviks had commandeered the inheritance which the factory-owner Shmidt had left for the RSDLP.* In 1917 Martov, whom I believed without reservation, talked about the deceptions used by the Bolshevik Centre in order to use the inheritance without dividing it up with the other faction of the party ... A lot of very harsh words were said at that time at Menshevik gatherings about the Tiflis expropriations and the laundering by Bolsheviks abroad of the stolen 500-rouble notes. I believed it all because Martov and co. and Shmidt's relatives – his sister and her husband whom I met in Paris – talked about it with such certainty.

Sverchkov went on to say that in 1917 he had written all this down in a letter to the Ministry of Justice and in return 'asked them to release you on my own cognizance. In my letter I contrasted you with the Bolshevik Centre, and in order to protect you and also to gain the Kerensky government's confidence in myself, I spoke all the more harshly about the Bolsheviks.' He then mentioned that a major publication about the Bolshevik demonstration of July 1917 was about to come out and that it would include his letter to the Kerensky government: 'The publication of this letter will make my work extremely difficult, if not impossible, as it will be used to discredit my speeches and destroy my authority.' Trotsky was not concerned now with Bolshevik practices of the past and was content to instruct his assistants, Butov and Sermuks, to make a few phone calls in order to save Sverchkov's position.[104]

On 28 June 1914, the day Crown Prince Franz Ferdinand was assassinated in Sarajevo, Trotsky wrote a piece for *Kievskaya mysl'* giving his impressions of the scene in Vienna: 'The large area in front of the War Ministry was packed. And this was not "the public", but the real people, in their worn-out boots, with fingers gnarled. There were young people and schoolchildren, but there were also many adults and not a few women. They waved yellow and black flags in the

---

* Two young Bolsheviks were given the task of marrying Shmidt's two daughters in order to secure the money. See Volkogonov, *Lenin: Life and Legacy*, pp. 57–61, for a fuller account.

air, sang patriotic songs, someone shouted "All Serbs must die!" '[105]
Trotsky perceived that nationalistic, chauvinistic and patriotic passion
had already overturned arguments based on reason, morality and
simple self-preservation, but even he could not know that within a
month, at the beginning of August, the majority of European social
democrats would capitulate before the militarism of their own governments and vote for war credits. 'I did not expect the official leaders
of the International, in case of war, to prove themselves capable of
serious revolutionary initiative,' he would later recall. 'At the same
time, I could not even admit the idea that the Social Democrats would
simply cower on their belly before nationalist militarism.'[106] The declaration of war and mobilization had, he wrote, 'somehow wiped off
the face of the earth all the national and social contradictions in the
country. But it is nothing more than a historical postponement, a sort
of political moratorium. New redemption dates have been written on
the promissory notes, but they will still have to be paid.'[107] From that
time until the end of his life, Trotsky was hostile to the social democrats. He would later write: 'The way things have turned out, one can
say with complete objectivity that during the imperialist war German
social democracy turned out to be the most reactionary fact in world
history.'[108] The only path left to him was that which led to the radicals,
that is, the Bolsheviks.

On 2 August 1914 Austria's chief of political police, Herr Geyer,
hinted to Trotsky that next morning an order might be issued for the
detention of Russians and Serbs. 'Then your advice is to leave?' 'The
sooner the better.' 'Good. I will leave with my family for Switzerland
tomorrow.' 'Hmm . . . I should prefer that you do it today.'[109] The
Austrian authorities began interning Russians (among them Lenin,
who was near the Russian–Austrian border at the time), and Trotsky
left Vienna for the last time. The exodus from Vienna by the Russian
colony was a hasty one. At first most of them, including Trotsky
and his family, made for Switzerland, where Lenin – after a quick
release from custody – and Zinoviev, Radek and Bukharin also took
refuge.

In January 1919, when he was at the peak of his fame, Trotsky
would once again be involved in Austrian affairs: as chairman of the
Revolutionary Military Council of the Soviet Republic, he notified
the Moscow Centre for Prisoners of War and Refugees: 'I have

received the following telegram from Tsarev; Austro-Hungarian prisoners of war at Tsarev Camp, Astrakhan province, abandoned to the
whim of fate, exhausted by waiting for repatriation, request that you
exert your influence on the appropriate Russian authorities to effect
their earliest despatch.'[110] Using his tremendous authority, Trotsky
could help Austrians return home.

Within three days of the votes for war credits in the parliaments
of the belligerents, Trotsky had written an article, 'The War and the
International', in which he took the same line as Lenin, even though
they were still at daggers drawn: peace without indemnities or annexations, and peace to be had only by turning the workers' bayonets
against their own governments. It was here that Trotsky uttered an
idea which others found Utopian: in order to prevent further war, the
proletariat must form a United States of Europe, and then go on to
struggle for the creation of a United States of the World.

Trotsky liked to prophesy, although many of his prophecies failed
to materialize. He was convinced that after the October revolution,
even if world revolution was not accomplished within the next few
years, at least the revolution in Europe would erupt at once. He was
also to be proved wrong about the withering away of small nation
states. He was, however, remarkably accurate in the predictions he
made about his own country. As early as 1915 he declared that Russia
would be able to leave the war only with the aid of revolution. He
lived the revolution, waited for it and did all he could to hasten what
he called the 'festival of the oppressed'. His impatience for revolution
echoed that of the great anarchist Mikhail Bakunin, fifty years earlier.
In a conversation with the Russian thinker Alexander Herzen, Bakunin
had said, on hearing that the Poles were unlikely to rise now that the
Tsar had freed the Russian peasants, 'What about Italy?' 'It's quiet.'
'And Austria?' 'Also quiet.' 'Turkey?' 'It's quiet everywhere, and it's
hard to foresee anything.' 'What are we to do, then?' asked a perplexed
Bakunin. 'Surely we don't have to go off to somewhere like Persia or
India to get things going! It's enough to make you go crazy. I can't
just sit and do nothing.'[111]

Trotsky had spent only six weeks in Switzerland when an offer
came from *Kievskaya mysl'* to go to Paris and view the European
conflagration 'from the Eiffel Tower'. The formalities were quickly
arranged. (This was not at all the situation he would face in 1933,

when a visa took an inordinately long time. When permission finally came, he remarked to his supporter in Paris Maurice Parizhanin: 'I was surprised to receive your telegram . . . I can hardly imagine that the French government would give me a visa when it is seeking friendship with Stalin.'[112] By then, the doors of practically every state were being slammed in his face. This letter, by the way, was only one of dozens that were intercepted by the GPU-NKVD and laid on Stalin's desk.)

Trotsky stayed for two years in France. At the same time as sending his stories to *Kievskaya mysl'*, he contributed to the anti-militarist Menshevik newspaper *Nashe slovo* (Our Word). In Paris he became friendly with one of its leading lights, Antonov-Ovseenko, a friendship that·was firm and long-lasting. He also got to know the Bolshevik intellectual and aesthete Anatoly Lunacharsky better, as well as other prominent Bolsheviks who would soon be at the heart of the revolutionary events in Russia. Lenin's *Sotsial-demokrat* and the non-factional *Nashe slovo*, in which Trotsky soon became the driving force, contained articles not only about the war, but also about the unseen, subterranean tremors that were beginning to shake the flagging Russian empire.

Although it was a radical newspaper, *Kievskaya mysl'* was in favour of waging the war to a victorious conclusion, and Trotsky therefore had to resort to circumlocution in his pieces. It willingly published articles against Germany and, more reluctantly, that were critical of the Entente. It was possible to write more freely in *Nashe slovo*, however. Every day Trotsky went to the Café Rotonde, where he could sit and read the major European newspapers and talk with Martov, Ryazanov, Lunacharsky and others. News about events was harder to come by than the bad wartime coffee. The war was dividing old allies among the socialists and putting them on opposing sides of the barricades. When he heard that Zasulich, Potresov and Plekhanov supported the war, Trotsky was shocked.

During this time, Trotsky strengthened many of his old ties with French socialists, especially Alfred Rosmer who was to remain a friend for the rest of his life. In September 1919 Trotsky wrote to Rosmer and other leaders of the French Communist Party, Loriot and Donat, to encourage their activities:

Despite the blockade, with which Messieurs Clemenceau and Lloyd George and others are trying to throw Europe back to the barbarism of the Middle Ages, we are closely following your work from here, watching the growth of the ideas of revolutionary communism in France. I am personally delighted every time I hear that you, my dear friends, are standing in the front rank of the movement that must give rebirth to Europe and all mankind. The harsher the triumph of militarism, vandalism and social treachery of bourgeois France, the more severe the rising of the proletariat will be, the more decisive its tactics, the more complete its victory ... We know that the cause of communism is in firm hands. Long live revolutionary proletarian France! Long live the world socialist revolution![113]

After a long interval, Trotsky met Lenin again in September 1915 at the Swiss mountain village of Zimmerwald, where thirty-eight delegates from belligerent and neutral countries had gathered to hammer out a common position on the war. In effect, they had symbolically crossed the barbed wire in order to show the solidarity of their hatred for the war. Calling for the transformation of the imperialist war into a civil war, Lenin's position was the most revolutionary among the delegates, and also the most tragic in its consequences. Trotsky took a different line, calling for an end to the war 'without victors or vanquished'. Although Lenin did not acquire a majority, the Zimmerwald Conference witnessed the revival of the radical wing of the socialist movement as the precursor of the Third (Communist) International.

Meanwhile, Trotsky's affairs encountered difficulties. In Marseilles, where shipments of new 'cannon-fodder' from Russia arrived, a riot erupted among the Russian troops. It was savagely put down, and several of the arrested soldiers were found to be in possession of copies of *Nashe slovo* with anti-war articles by Trotsky. The reaction came swiftly: the newspaper was closed down and Trotsky was ordered out of the country. Protests by émigré and socialist friends were to no avail. Trotsky was afraid the French authorities might hand him over to the Russian government as an act of allied solidarity, and asked for permission to go to either Switzerland or Sweden. On 30 October 1916 he was ordered to leave France, and two gendarmes turned up to escort him to the Spanish border.[114] Within days of arriving in Spain, Trotsky was arrested by the Madrid police as a 'known anarchist'. After several weeks in gaol, where he kept up a barrage of protest against his treatment, he succeeded in having himself, his wife and children put on board an old passenger ship, the *Monserrat*, bound for the USA. 'Farewell, Europe!' he wrote in his diary. 'Though not quite: this Spanish ship is part of Spain, its passengers are part of Europe, most of them her outcasts.'[115]

While he was on board the *Monserrat*, Trotsky wrote to many of his friends in various countries. To Alfred Rosmer he wrote: 'For a long time I watched through the mist as that old scoundrel, Europe, slipped further away . . .' He stood with his wife and sons at the rail of the ship as it passed the towering cliffs of Gibraltar, thinking they were leaving Europe forever.

2

The Madness of Revolution

'The sea was very rough at this time of the year, and our boat did everything to remind us of the frailty of human life. The *Monserrat* was an old tub little suited for ocean voyages. But during the war the neutral Spanish flag lessened the chances of being sunk. The Spanish company charged high fares, and provided bad accommodation and even worse food.'[1] Standing on deck and staring at the grey horizon, Trotsky must have wondered what he was to do with himself in the country where, in his view, 'the heart is ruled by the moral philosophy of the dollar'.

His sons went to school in New York and quickly learnt English. They had already acquired French in Paris and German in Vienna, and were growing up in a cosmopolitan environment and shared their father's life. Trotsky spent two months giving lectures in New York, Philadelphia and elsewhere. He met Nikolai Bukharin, Alexandra Kollontai and Grigori Chudnovsky, as well as a few other revolutionaries, but he had barely found his feet among his compatriots when exciting and at first incomprehensible news began arriving from Russia. It was reported from Petrograd that on 15 March two members of the Duma, Alexander Guchkov and Vasili Shulgin, had visited the Tsar in his headquarters at Pskov and accepted his abdication in favour of his brother, Grand Duke Michael. The Duma members had done their level best to save the monarchy, as was made clear by the leader of the liberals (Kadets), Paul Milyukov, who was reported as saying: 'We cannot leave the question of the form of our state structure open. We are thinking of a parliamentary and constitutional monarchy.' When Trotsky read this he flung the newspaper down in disgust and cried: 'The Kadets have crawled into the prompter's box and are chanting their old line!' His wife was more philosophical: 'Lyova, what would you expect?' Later, when he was back in Russia, Trotsky would learn that Michael had said he would only accept the crown if it were the will of the people, as expressed in a constituent assembly, and since neither the early convocation of such a body, nor indeed Michael's own safety, could be promised by the members of the Provisional Government, Michael had followed Nicholas's example and abdicated. Three hundred years of the Romanov dynasty came to an end, and Russia was without a monarchy.

But what of the socialists? Where was Lenin? How would relations between the Bolsheviks and the Mensheviks be affected? Meanwhile, the news was dizzying. Could it really be true that the Red Flag was flying over the Winter Palace? Meetings that Trotsky attended in New York were triumphant. He was almost never at home. Having heard the news of the February revolution, he at once determined that his place was back in St Petersburg, now named Petrograd, and on 27 March, together with his family and some other Russians, he boarded the Norwegian steamer *Christiania Fjord*, bound for Europe.

When the ship was searched at the Canadian port of Halifax, the Trotsky family and a number of other Russian passengers were arrested. While in detention they learned that the British government had reported that Trotsky was travelling to Russia at the expense of the German government and with the intention of overthrowing the Provisional Government. Indeed, after his arrival in Petrograd the local newspapers continued to print this story. The issue remained controversial for decades, and conclusive proof was not available until the early 1990s, when access was finally obtained to Lenin's archives. These revealed that the Bolshevik Party had been covertly receiving large sums from the German government, with which they financed their propaganda among the troops and workers following the February revolution. But as early as 1917 well-informed observers were in no doubt that the Bolsheviks owed a great deal to financial aid from Germany, funnelled into Lenin's coffers by various channels and under different names.

After several protests against Trotsky's arrest appeared in the Bolshevik newspaper *Pravda*, the Provisional Government felt compelled to cable Halifax and request the release of the interned Russian citizens, and within three weeks, on 18 May, Trotsky was in Petrograd, as yet unsure which wing of the party he would join. All he was sure of was that he would join the revolution.

The Revolutionary Flood

After an absence of ten years, Trotsky was back on his native soil. He was greeted by friends at Petrograd's Finland Station, where a short speech was delivered by Moisei Uritsky, an old friend of Menshevik days and a collaborator on *Nashe slovo*. Trotsky's sons gazed around in amazement at this strange place, where people spoke Russian on the street and wore scarlet ribbons on the lapels of their greatcoats, indicating their support for the February revolution. Trotsky was among the last of the well-known exiles to return. He wasted no time and, once the family was established in a one-room apartment, he went to the Smolny Institute, a former college for the daughters of the nobility where the Petrograd Soviet was now in session. As the president of its predecessor of 1905, it was a natural thing to do.

When he arrived the meeting was being chaired by the Menshevik Nikolai Chkheidze, whom he knew well. The members of the Soviet gave Trotsky a cool reception. Neither the Menshevik majority nor the Bolshevik members were sure which side was going to benefit from Trotsky's arrival – nor was Trotsky himself yet sure which way he would jump. His record of 1905, however, assured him a non-voting seat on the Executive Committee, and there he sat, listening with growing surprise as his new colleagues debated which portfolios to accept in the Kerensky government that was being described in the press as 'the symbiosis of ten capitalists and six socialists'. (The first, predominantly liberal, composition of the Provisional Government had proved to be unviable, and at this moment efforts were being made to bring socialists from the Soviet into it, in the hope that further disorder and disruption could be averted.) Although Trotsky had been following events as closely as possible while abroad, he now found himself faced with new questions to which he had no immediate answers. Asked to speak by his former pupil Matvei Skobelev, he tried to say something in general terms about the revolution.

'We see,' he began, 'that Russia has opened a new era, a new era of blood and iron, a struggle no longer of nations against nations, but one of the oppressed classes against their rulers.'[2] The Menshevik leader Irakli Tsereteli and the Socialist Revolutionary leader Viktor Chernov, both advocates of continuing the war to a victorious conclusion, showed their anxiety. They saw danger for themselves in Trotsky's line.

Trotsky was aware of Lenin's 'April Theses', embodied in an article in *Pravda* of 20 April 1917, in which he had criticized Plekhanov for his chauvinistic 'defensism'. There Lenin had also formulated a position for which Russia was not yet ready: 'Not a parliamentary republic – returning to that from the Soviet of Workers' Deputies would be a step backwards – but a republic of Soviets of workers' and poor peasants' deputies from all over the country, from the bottom up.'[3] Rejection of the parliamentary principle, in a country where the first shoots of democracy had barely appeared, would in due course damage the very idea of socialism itself. Trotsky was used to Lenin's harsh tone of voice, but Plekhanov surprised him by the sharp, crude, uncompromising note he adopted. Trotsky hardly recognized the style of his old mentor in Plekhanov's article 'Lenin's Theses and why Delirium can Sometimes be Interesting', especially in such phrases as 'Lenin never was strong on logic', 'the reporter of *Edinstvo* [Unity] was quite right to describe Lenin's speech as delirious', 'Lenin's first thesis was written in a world of fantasy where there are no dates, no months, but only the devil knows what.'

Trotsky, who had written a number of articles on Plekhanov – and who would write another on him when he died in 1918, in which he would give him his due as a theorist, but also describe him as a 'conciliator' and 'nationalist', both terms of abuse in the Russian Marxist canon – was surprised by the old man's categorical tone. Plekhanov had after all embodied social democratic values in their most developed form. He had ended his article on Lenin:

> I firmly believe that . . . in Lenin's calls to fraternize with the Germans, for the overthrow of the Provisional Government, the seizure of power and so on and so forth, our workers will see them just for what they are, namely, a crazy and extremely harmful attempt to sow anarchist disorder in the Russian Land. The Russian proletariat and the Russian army will not forget that if they do not immediately and severely rebuff

this . . . attempt, then it will tear out the young and tender sapling of our political freedom by the roots.

Trotsky did not agree with Plekhanov, and could not know that time would prove 'the father of Russian Marxism' right. Trotsky sensed that the revolutionary arena was both uniting and dividing people, and that he must define his own position: the revolution would not tolerate neutrality.

Trotsky's centrist course at first took him to the Inter-district Committee of the RSDLP, known by its Russian diminutive 'Mezhrayonka'. Founded in St Petersburg in 1913 by revolutionaries seeking to bridge the gap between the two social democratic factions, during the war the remnants of its membership adopted a similar radical position to that of Trotsky, and close to that of Lenin. By the time Trotsky returned to Russia, the Mezhrayonka consisted of about 60 per cent Bolsheviks and the rest radical Mensheviks. Many of Trotsky's friends, most of them intellectuals, were to be found there. As 'Europeanized' revolutionaries, they were facing the difficult choice between Bolshevik radicalism and Menshevik parliamentarism. For Trotsky, it was like returning to his Paris days.

Petrograd was seething. The streets were thronged by continuous euphoric meetings, and from the moment he left his apartment early in the morning until he returned late at night, Trotsky moved from meeting to meeting, from assembly to committee, engaging in speeches, debates and discussions. He took a week or two to get his bearings, to see who was who, who the emerging leaders were. He observed that slowly but surely the Bolsheviks were taking the leading rôle – unsurprisingly, perhaps, since they had come out so firmly against the war. But the memory of several years of intellectual discord with Lenin still held Trotsky back. At a meeting of the Mezhrayonka of 10 (23) May, when the issue of the group's self-definition was being discussed, he said: 'I cannot call myself a Bolshevik . . . We should not be expected to recognize Bolshevism.'[4]

Lenin noticed Trotsky's arrival in the capital. At first he lumped him together with Mensheviks such as Martov, whom he dismissed as 'hesitant petit bourgeois',[5] but he read Trotsky's speeches and took note of their undertones. During this ideological intermission Trotsky frequented the newspaper offices of various tendencies, where he would meet old friends such as Lunacharsky, Maxim Gorky, Nikolai Sukhanov, Matvei Skobelev and Lev Kamenev, who was married to his sister Olga. Trotsky would sound his brother-in-law out on the Bolsheviks' position and try to divine Lenin's attitude towards him at that moment, since he knew how close Kamenev was to the Bolshevik leader. Their intimacy, indeed, was demonstrated in 1922 when, after falling ill, Lenin handed over a large part of his personal papers to Kamenev for publication. Trotsky evidently harboured some dislike for Kamenev, as appears in his book *The February Revolution*:

A Bolshevik virtually since the foundation of Bolshevism, Kamenev was always on the right wing of the party. Not devoid of theoretical grounding and political common sense, and with his great experience of the factional struggle in Russia and a fund of political observations in the West, Kamenev was better able than many other Bolsheviks to grasp Lenin's general ideas, but only in order to give them as peaceful a slant in practice as possible. He could not be relied on to give an independent decision or to initiate any action himself. An outstanding propagandist, orator and journalist, not brilliant, but thoughtful, Kamenev was especially valuable in discussions with other parties and for sounding out other social circles, though when he returned from such forays something of the other party's mood would always have rubbed off on him. Kamenev's characteristics were so plain to see that almost no one ever misjudged his political profile.[6]

From his conversations with Kamenev, Trotsky gained the impression that Lenin and the Bolshevik Central Committee were taking an extremely cautious attitude towards him, and he received direct evidence of this when he met Lenin at a joint Mezhrayonka–Bolshevik session where the entry of the Mezhrayonka into the Bolshevik party was discussed. Lenin was the undisputed leader of the Bolsheviks, who better than most realized that momentous social upheavals were on their way, and he saw a unique historical opportunity for the party which he did not want to lose. Moreover, he wanted to bring over to his side such eminent and popular figures as Martov, Plekhanov and Trotsky. The first two were lost causes, being committed social democrats and of no use to the Bolsheviks, while Trotsky was still a potential ally. For his part, Trotsky felt a new wave of revolution rising and had no intention of being left standing. As he grew closer to the Bolsheviks, his relations with Lenin gradually improved. As he would later write: 'Lenin's attitude to me went through several phases in 1917. First he was reserved and content to wait and see. The July days brought us together at once. When I launched the campaign to boycott the Pre-parliament, against the majority view among the leading Bolsheviks, Lenin wrote "Bravo, Comrade Trotsky!"'

Within a month of his arrival in Petrograd, Trotsky became one of the stars on the revolutionary meetings circuit. In the summer and autumn his presence was in huge demand and he rarely declined an invitation to appear. He often spoke at meetings in tandem with Lunacharsky, another popular speaker among the revolutionary crowds of soldiers, sailors and workers. Trotsky's favourite venue was Kronstadt, the island fortress some twenty miles from the capital in the Gulf of Finland, where the soldiers and sailors represented the most radical element of the armed forces.

The mood of the people was becoming more and more desperate, as the promises of the February revolution failed to be realized: the abolition of the autocracy was not followed by peace, nor by the redistribution of land to the peasants. The Bolsheviks seized on the mood of the workers, soldiers and peasants and did their utmost to nudge them into an increasingly radical state. On 4 (17) July, news of the Russian army's rout in Galicia reached the capital, coinciding with a huge anti-war demonstration organized and led by the Bolsheviks in what might have turned into a bid for power. The right-wing press blamed the Bolsheviks for the army's failure, and reports appeared with growing frequency alleging Lenin's links with the German General Staff and claiming that he was playing the Kaiser's game in order to knock Russia out of the war.

Trotsky wrote of this period that the Bolsheviks did not waver: despite the 'thunder and lightning of philistine bourgeois public opinion in July, they were not frightened by the slander, the lies and persecution. They set their sights on the distant target, while at the same time shortening the timetable and speeding up events.'[7] Russian public opinion provided fertile soil, however, for anything that would help explain the Russian army's defeat, and the finger of accusation was pointed firmly at the Bolsheviks. They for their part would continue to deny any collaboration with the Germans, even after the October revolution. For instance, Trotsky received a telegram from the Bolshevik Foreign Commissar Chicherin in January 1919, reporting that

In January 1918 Russian counter-revolutionaries sent Colonel Robins
[of the American Red Cross] a number of documents showing there
was a link between the German government and Lenin and Trotsky.
Robins conducted an investigation and questioned Galperin who admitted that many of the documents had been in the hands of the Kerensky
government and are obvious forgeries ... The former publisher of
Cosmopolitan Magazine, Verna Sisson, agreed with Robins, but later
changed his mind.[8]

The Bolsheviks preferred not to raise the subject after October,
and to do so meant risking one's life. Before the revolution, however,
things were different. The accusation was a serious one, and it was
difficult to refute it. Many newspapers were writing about Bolshevik
treachery and espionage. A good deal of concrete evidence of Bolshevik–German collaboration was collected, and more came to light
in the ensuing years. For example, General Erich Ludendorff, who
had been in the German High Command during the war, wrote in
his memoirs in 1919: 'In helping Lenin to get back to Russia [through
Germany] our government took a special responsibility upon itself.
From the military point of view the enterprise was justified. Russia
had to be brought down.'[9]

One of the most diligent investigators of the crimes and misde-
meanours of Russian socialists was Vladimir Burtsev, a member of the
Socialist Revolutionary Party who in 1908 had exposed one of the
most daring and effective police infiltrators in his party, Yevno Azef,
and who pursued the Bolshevik–German link with equal tenacity.
He wrote: 'All these years I have asserted the same thing: we must
pursue and beat the Bolsheviks.' In one of his many articles, entitled
'My Challenge to the Traitors and their Defenders', which was sent
from Paris to Moscow by local Soviet agents in 1922, he wrote that
since August 1914 the Germans had transmitted to the Bolsheviks
more than 70 million marks. 'As early as the summer of 1917, openly
and in the press under my own name, I accused Lenin and a dozen
of his comrades by name: Trotsky, Kamenev, Zinoviev, Ganetsky,
Kollontai, Lunacharsky, Nakhamkes, Rakovsky and others of treason
to Russia and of having had relations with the Germans during the
war and I demanded their immediate arrest and trial.'[10]

In July 1917 the Provisional Government decided to act on the
evidence it had collected, even though it was not totally conclusive,

and ordered the arrest of Lenin, Zinoviev, Kamenev and a large number of other Bolsheviks. At the height of the furore Trotsky met Lenin, evidently during a joint session of the Central and Petrograd Party Committees on 4 (17) July. When the question whether the accused should appear in court was discussed, Trotsky said they should turn the court into a revolutionary tribunal. Kamenev supported this view, but Lenin and most of the others felt, with some reason, that the government would take the opportunity to deprive the revolution of its leaders and thus be able the more easily to damp it down. The government moreover had already used troops to close down *Pravda*. It should also be noted that Lenin was by nature very cautious, and would not take risks with his own life.

Three or four days after Lenin, Zinoviev and Kamenev had gone into hiding, Trotsky published a carefully composed open letter to the government:

> Citizen Ministers! I know you have decided to arrest Comrades Lenin, Zinoviev and Kamenev. But the arrest order does not include me. Therefore I think it essential to draw your attention to the following facts: 1) In principle, I share the views of Lenin, Zinoviev and Kamenev and I defend them in my newspaper *Vpered* and in my many public speeches. 2) My position on the events of 3–4 July coincides with those of the above-mentioned comrades.[11]

Trotsky continued to make speeches declaring himself, like Lenin, a sworn enemy of the government, and labelled as a scoundrel anyone who called the leaders of the revolution German spies. Most of his listeners at that dangerous moment kept silent, even though they may have shared his position, but many others shouted abuse and threats.

Remaining at large, Trotsky continued to goad the government, accusing it of criminally continuing the war and of wanting to deprive the people of the fruits of the February revolution. After tolerating this for a week and a half, the government finally sent a detachment of officers to arrest him. In the packed Kresty Prison, familiar to him from 1905, he found his friends Lunacharsky and Antonov-Ovseenko, Raskolnikov and Kamenev, as well as many others from both wings of the RSDLP and the Socialist Revolutionaries. The following day Nikolai Sukhanov, the Menshevik chronicler of the revolution, announced to the massed crowd at the Cirque Moderne, where Trotsky had been due to speak, that he was under arrest. A howl of indignation erupted, and Sukhanov and Martov barely managed to prevent a riot by passing a resolution of protest. Sukhanov later wrote that rumours had been spread by right-wing agitators to the effect that Lenin, Trotsky and Lunacharsky had wanted to establish a three-man dictatorship and seize power, thus putting an end to the revolution.[12] This only inflamed passions further. The fact that Trotsky's arrest became an item of importance in the press and a topic of widespread debate at workers' meetings throughout the city demonstrated his rapid ascent to local fame, despite his not having yet declared himself as a Bolshevik or Menshevik – or perhaps because of it.

Repeating his actions of 1905, Trotsky took up his pen in prison and wrote a number of articles on the issues of the day, becoming more and more revolutionary as he wrote. Raskolnikov later recalled Trotsky in prison: 'When he went out for a stroll, wearing his foreign cape and soft felt hat, Comrade Trotsky would at once be surrounded by a group of comrades and a lively discussion on politics would ensue ... In his cell, however, he spent from morning till night writing intensively.'[13]

Trotsky's authority rose after his arrest, even if it had taken place virtually at his invitation. A few days after it had occurred, the Sixth Congress of the RSDLP opened in semi-legal circumstances. Many of those who would have taken part as leading members were either in hiding or in prison, among them, of course, Lenin. His intellectual and political influence, however, was much in evidence. Indeed, it was his interpretation of the political scene that echoed throughout the proceedings, namely that as long as the counter-revolution was in the ascendancy, the possibility of seizing power by peaceful means did not exist. The question of an armed uprising therefore was at the top of the party's agenda. The radicalism of the Bolsheviks emerged more sharply from this moment. As Kerensky later put it, Lenin chose the path of tragic developments: the imperialist war of nations was being turned into a civil war of the classes.[14]

The Sixth Party Congress was of enormous importance for Trotsky, who was elected an honorary chairman in his absence. After preliminary discussion and agreement, the Mezhrayonka, which could boast some 4000 members, was accepted into the party. They consisted of Menshevik-Internationalists, Bolshevik-Conciliators, and Trotsky.

Thus, his party membership was resolved while he was in prison. Along with him, Lunacharsky, Volodarsky, Ioffe, Manuilsky, Uritsky and many other intellectuals became full-fledged Bolsheviks. Trotsky's authority rose still higher when he was elected a member of the new party Central Committee by only three votes less than were cast for Lenin.

Meanwhile, the government could find no serious grounds for holding Trotsky, while he for his part declared a hunger-strike and refused to answer any questions. On 2 September he was released on bail of 3000 roubles, paid by the Petrograd Soviet. Since his arrest the political situation had changed dramatically, and Kerensky now felt he needed the support of the Soviets to resist an attempt by his commander-in-chief, General Kornilov, to crush the radical and anti-war elements in the capital and install a tough military leadership to defend Russia, which was still at war. Kerensky, meanwhile, was afraid that an anti-Soviet putsch would threaten his own precarious position, and as a result he found himself on opposing sides with his own army chief.

Trotsky, Lunacharsky, Kamenev, Kollontai and others were released, much to the disgust of the Kornilovites. General Lukomsky, chief-of-staff first to General Brusilov and then to Kornilov himself, recalled that after the events of July, 'to general consternation the Provisional Government, having crushed the Bolshevik demonstration, appeared criminally weak. Lenin, who could easily have been arrested, was given the chance to escape. Trotsky was released from prison. Traitors to the country, working with German money and openly calling for an end to the war and a peace "without annexations or reparation", were not only not punished with the full force of the law, but they were given the opportunity to start their destructive work in the capital and the army once again.'[15] The Provisional Government had become a scarecrow that had ceased to scare the crows. The many memoirs of this period, published abroad in the 1920s by men who had been associated with Kerensky's government, focus much of their indignation at the course of events precisely on the government's failure to deal forcefully with the anti-war agitation.

In the middle of September 1917 the Democratic Conference opened in Petrograd, a forum of sorts for those political parties which were committed to finding an appropriate form of government through dialogue. These included all the socialist parties and the liberal Constitutional Democrats (Kadets). It might conceivably have succeeded, had the Mensheviks and SRs not wavered and finally opted for a compromise with the Bolsheviks in preference to a coalition with the Kadets. This meeting was a significant one for Trotsky, who had for the first time been asked by the Central Committee to explain the Bolshevik position. According to eye-witnesses, his speech made a huge impression. He had prepared it with care, aware of its importance for his future. Sukhanov recorded that this was one of Trotsky's most brilliant speeches, devoid of the usual polished phrases and metallic clarity of his voice, and more in the nature of an intimate conversation with his audience. In his speech Trotsky demanded the arming of the Red Guards, the largely Bolshevik militia composed of deserters and workers who had been armed by the party: 'only by this means can we create a genuine bastion against counter-revolution'. If the Bolsheviks' proposals on the war were going to be rejected, he went on, 'then the armed workers of Petrograd and the whole of Russia will defend the fatherland of the revolution against the soldiers of imperialism with heroism unheard of in Russian history'.[16] At the end of the speech Trotsky condemned the falsification of the figures on representation at the Democratic Conference, and demonstratively walked out with the Bolshevik delegates. It was an ominous sign that the Bolsheviks had chosen the path of armed uprising.

Lenin approved of Trotsky's behaviour and, as a result, when elections for the Executive Committee of the Petrograd Soviet took place on 25 September the Bolsheviks proposed Trotsky as chairman, and he was duly elected. In his speech of thanks he promised that he would do his best to make his second stint as chairman more successful than the first, in 1905. Two sentences in this speech stand out: 'We will conduct the business of the Petrograd Soviet in the spirit of full freedom for all parties. The hand of the leadership will never be raised to oppress the minority.'[17] Despite the fact that on this occasion the principle of proportional representation was observed, Trotsky's laudably democratic sentiments would quickly be forgotten by him and the rest of the Bolshevik dictatorship. He would support measures to liquidate revolutionary pluralism, and would let his fine words about safeguarding the majority slip into history.

Trotsky's transformation into a Bolshevik was thus complete. The conflict in him between loyalty to the political culture of Western social democracy and left radicalism was resolved. He emerged as a committed left revolutionary and radical Bolshevik.

The Power of Myths

Until the end of his days, Trotsky, who was vilified by Stalin as a spy, scum of the earth, double-dealer, murderer, falsifier and imperialist agent, fought against the big lie that Soviet history had become, even though he had taken part in inventing it. In 1932 he wrote:

> The revolution explodes the social lie. The revolution is true. It begins by calling things and the relations between things by their proper names ... But the revolution itself is not an integral and harmonious process. It is full of contradictions ... The revolution itself produces a new ruling stratum which seeks to consolidate its privileged position and is prone to see itself not as a transitional historical instrument, but as the completion and crowning of history.[18]

Thus was created the lie against him, he concluded. And it was a lie against history. Trotsky, however, never admitted, even to himself, that he had been among the creators of the conditions which accommodated the lie so comfortably.

One of the most persistent myths of the revolution is that Trotsky, among other Bolshevik leaders, wanted to delay the armed uprising to coincide with the opening of the Second Congress of Soviets. This notion was persistent in Soviet sources until well into the late 1980s.[19] In reality he did not oppose the armed uprising, which for Lenin had become, in Melgunov's words, an obsession.[20] On the contrary, he fought hardest to realize the dream – so rapidly had he become an orthodox Leninist – but his preferred scenario was that the uprising should take place under the aegis and leadership of the Bolshevik Central Committee, but also as the expressed will of the Congress of Soviets. The Bolshevik slogan 'All power to the Soviets' implied that the uprising would have a much broader social base than one carried out in the name of the Bolsheviks alone. All the revolutionary forces in Russia would be involved, world opinion would see for itself that

Lev Davidovich Bronshtein – Trotsky – at the age of nine, in 1888, wearing the customary uniform of a pre-high school pupil.

Trotsky in 1897.

Trotsky's father, David Leontievich Bronshtein, became a farmer in southern Ukraine in the year Trotsky was born, 1879.

Anna Bronshtein, Trotsky's mother.

Trotsky photographed by the police at the time of his first arrest and imprisonment in Nikolaev, 1898.

Trotsky's first exile, Verkholensk, eastern Siberia, 1900 (he is second from the left in the back row).

Above: Trotsky with his first wife, Alexandra Sokolovskaya, in the summer of 1902. They were married in prison in Moscow in 1900 and exiled to Siberia with their daughter of ten months, Zinaida.

Left: Trotsky with his daughter Zinaida in 1906.

The 1905 revolution. Demonstration of Social Democrats in St Petersburg in October.

Trial of the St Petersburg Soviet. Trotsky is second from the left in the second row.

Trotsky with Alexander Helphand (Parvus, left) and Lev Deutsch at the time of their arrest in St Petersburg in December 1905. They would be sentenced to exile in Siberia for life in December 1906, and escaped in 1907.

Left: Trotsky reading his newly-founded *Pravda* in Vienna in 1910. Lenin appropriated the title in 1912.

Below: Trotsky arrives in St Petersburg from the USA on 17 May 1917.

Above: The St Petersburg Soviet meeting in the Tauride Palace, February 1917. Council, or Soviet, sessions were of this mass character. The Executive Committee of the Soviet, although numbering only two dozen or so members, was generally mobbed by hundreds of soldiers' and workers' delegates from the front and local factories.

Left: Trotsky's second wife, Natalya Ivanovna Sedova, whom he met in Paris in 1903. Photographed in the 1930s.

Trotsky with Soviet delegates Admiral Altfater and Lev Kamenev (both on right) at the Brest-Litovsk peace talks in January 1918.

the revolt was not the consequence of a narrow conspiracy by one radical party – which of course it was – but as the will of 'broad progressive circles' of Russian society.

The threat of a strong anti-Bolshevik move was a real one. From Staff HQ, General Dukhonin sent a message to the Petrograd Soviet, as well as to the press and the government, declaring: 'In the name of the army at the front we demand the immediate cessation of Bolshevik violence and complete subordination to the Provisional Government, which is empowered by the total agreement of the organs of democracy and is the only government capable of bringing the country to the Constituent Assembly – the master of the Russian Land. The active army supports this demand by force.'[21] The threat was real, but Dukhonin's confidence was exaggerated, for he did not take account of the demoralization and erosion of the army's internal bonds, which were rapidly draining its strength. The army wanted only one thing, and that was peace, and the only way to achieve it seemed to be by a revolutionary exit from the war. The socialists who supported Kerensky were not prepared to go that far, and he continued to rely on them. The revolution appeared to be the only way out of the impasse.

Trotsky made this the *leitmotiv* of all his speeches. On 21 October he transported an audience of soldiers and workers by declaring: 'The Soviet government will destroy the misery of the trenches. It will give the land and it will heal the internal disorder. The Soviet government will give away everything in the country to the poor and to the troops in the trenches. If you, bourgeois, have two fur coats, give one to a soldier ... Have you got a warm pair of boots? Stay at home. A worker needs them.' His audience was in ecstasy and, as Sukhanov recorded, it seemed they might suddenly burst into singing a revolutionary hymn without further ado. 'A resolution was proposed that they stand up for the workers' and peasants' cause to their last drop of blood ... Who's in favour? As one, the thousand-man audience shot their hands up.'[22]

It is difficult to understand why Lenin, still in hiding, should, in a letter written on the evening of 24 October to the Central Committee, 'urge the comrades with all my strength that everything is now hanging by a thread. Whatever the cost, this evening, this night, we must arrest the government, first disarming the cadets etc. (and fighting

them if they resist). We mustn't wait!! We could lose everything.' He
went on: 'The government is wavering. We must beat it, whatever
the cost.'[23] It may be, as has been suggested, that Lenin was consciously raising the tension, having taken as accurate some of the press
reports about the danger of a renewed threat from the military, à la
Kornilov. The old ideas about democracy were falling like dead leaves
from the trees. The more familiar notion of the conspirator, committed to an obsessive single goal, took stronger hold.

The very word 'beat' signalled the shift from the peaceful path to
that of violence, and this soon came to dominate the Bolshevik mentality. The weak attempts undertaken by the Mensheviks to apply
liberal methods to change this course only brought the wrath of the
radical Bolsheviks down on their heads. Soon, on 19 December 1917,
Trotsky would call on the 'iron steamroller of the proletarian
revolution to crush the spinal column of Menshevism'.[24]

Was Trotsky wrong to link the beginning of the uprising with the
opening of the Congress of Soviets, and to expect the Soviets to pass
a resolution liquidating the Provisional Government and ratifying
revolutionary power? He was not in favour of delaying the uprising,
as Soviet historians repeatedly asserted. Instead he wished to 'legitimize' the uprising by establishing it on a broader popular base. He
believed that only the Congress would bring the hesitant elements
onto the side of the revolution, that it would create a favourable
attitude abroad towards it, and help to imbue the minds of the masses
with revolutionary ideals.

The Military Revolutionary Committee of the Petrograd Soviet
was the body which headed the preparation and conduct of the
October armed uprising, and Trotsky's part in its creation and functioning is beyond dispute. Since this body was brought into being as
an adjunct of the Petrograd Soviet, Trotsky, as the chairman of the
Soviet, naturally took the leading rôle in it. In what is arguably his
best book, *The History of the Russian Revolution*, he wrote:

> The decision to create a Military Revolutionary Committee, first raised
> on the ninth [of October], was passed at a plenary session of the Soviet
> only a week later. The Soviet is not a party; its machinery is heavy . . .
> [The] Conference of Regimental Committees had demonstrated its
> viability, the arming of the workers was going forward. And thus the
> Military Revolutionary Committee, although it went to work only on

the twentieth, five days before the insurrection, found ready to its hands a sufficiently well organized dominion. Being boycotted by the Compromisers, the staff of the Committee contained only Bolshevik and Left Social[ist] Revolutionaries; that eased and simplified the task. Of the Social[ist] Revolutionaries only Lazimir did any work, and he was even placed at the head of the bureau in order to emphasize the fact that the Committee was a Soviet and not a party institution. In essence, however, the Committee, whose president was Trotsky ... relied exclusively on Bolsheviks. The Committee hardly met once in plenary session with delegates present from all the institutions listed in its regulations ... [It] was the general staff of the insurrection.[25]

After Lenin died, and the history of the revolution began to be hastily rewritten, the party's Military Revolutionary Centre emerged as having played the leading part. This was a purely symbolic body that had been created as part of the Military Revolutionary Committee. No record exists of its activity, nor would one expect to find any, since its alleged work was in fact performed by the Committee. Its membership, however, included Stalin, who embarked in the middle of the 1920s on the task of enhancing his own position in 1917 at the expense of Trotsky's. This was initially difficult to do, since Trotsky's role in 1917 was well known to have been endorsed on numerous occasions by Lenin himself.[26]

After the death of Lenin, Stalin produced his own, somewhat different view of Trotsky in 1917: 'I have to say that Trotsky played no special rôle in the October uprising, nor could he have done, since, as chairman of the Petrograd Soviet, he had to carry out the wishes of the relevant party bodies which monitored his every step ... Trotsky could play no special part either in the party or in the October uprising as a relative newcomer to our party in the October period.'[27] It was after this assertion by Stalin that Trotsky was dropped into what George Orwell called the 'memory hole', and remained there until very recently.

Russian attitudes to the revolution itself are another matter. As our minds have freed themselves of dogma and mystification, it has become clear that what happened in 1917 was the most tragic mistake. Before waiting for the aims of the February revolution to be accomplished, the Bolsheviks proclaimed the transition to its socialist phase. In these circumstances it seemed that the revolution could go further

only by bringing forward the dictatorship of the proletariat in ugly
and terrible forms.

On the eve of the tenth anniversary of the October revolution,
Istpart, the special commission on the history of the party and the
revolution, sent a questionnaire to all participants in the events of
1917. After some hesitation a questionnaire was also sent to Trotsky,
who was by then being slandered and attacked in increasingly harsh
terms. Dispirited, but neither yielding nor broken, Trotsky decided
to reply to the questions in detail. He attached a letter and sent it
back to Istpart on 21 October 1927. He knew that even if at best his
answers would be shelved indefinitely in the party archives, one thing
in history was sure: that in the end the truth would come out. Until
the end of his life, he hoped for historical rehabilitation and believed
in the invincibility of the human mind. He had never doubted the
timeliness of the socialist revolution. Nor did he doubt that in due
course the veil would be torn from Stalin – 'the second Lenin' – and
show him to be an emperor with no clothes.

Everything Trotsky wrote in his reply to Istpart was either true or,
in some cases, a subjective judgement that did not quite correspond
with what actually happened. He included his letter in his book *The
Stalinist School of Falsification*, which he published in exile in 1932, a
book which throws a good deal of light on the way Stalin created the
myth of the 'two leaders' of October, while condemning so many
other Bolsheviks to oblivion. Under the heading 'The Falsification of
the History of the October Uprising, the History of the Revolution
and the History of the Party', Trotsky wrote to Istpart:

> What is the sense in asking me to describe my part in the October
> rising, when the entire official apparatus, including yours, is working
> to hide and destroy or at least distort all traces of my participation? I
> have repeatedly been asked by dozens and hundreds of comrades why
> I remain silent and why I say nothing about the glaring falsification of
> the history of the October revolution and of our party, aimed against
> me. I have no intention here of settling the question of these falsifica-
> tions: one would need to write several volumes to do it. But allow me
> in response to your questionnaire to point to a dozen or so examples
> of the conscious and malicious distortion of recent events which is now
> being perpetrated on a mass scale, and which is sanctioned by the
> authority of all kinds of institutions and is even going into the
> textbooks.[28]

Trotsky wrote bitterly of the way some Bolsheviks had rapidly altered their view of him under the new political conditions. He cited what F. Raskolnikov had written in 1923: 'Trotsky regarded Vladimir Ilyich with enormous respect. He placed him above all other contemporaries whom he had met in Russia or abroad. One could detect the tone of the devoted pupil in the way Trotsky spoke about Lenin ... Any trace of their pre-war differences was utterly obliterated. There were no differences between their tactical positions. This rapprochement, which had been discernible already during the war, became complete from the moment of Lev Davidovich's return to Russia; after his very first speeches, all of us old Leninists felt that he was one of us.'[29] Trotsky then quoted Raskolnikov's 1927 review of the third volume of his collected works, published in 1924 and 1925: 'So, what was Trotsky's own position in 1917? He still saw himself as belonging to a general party, together with the Mensheviks ... He had not yet clarified his attitude towards Bolshevism and Menshevism. He still occupied a wavering, undefined position, neither one thing nor the other.'[30] Trotsky exposed the poverty of the Stalinist falsifications with consummate ease. He compared what Stalin was now saying about his part as chairman of the Petrograd Soviet with what he had said on the same subject on 6 November 1918: 'All the practical work of organizing the uprising was done under the direct leadership of Chairman of the Petrograd Soviet Trotsky. One can say with certainty that the party is obligated for the rapid move of the garrison onto the side of the Soviet and the capable handling of the work of the Military Revolutionary Committee first and foremost to Comrade Trotsky.'[31] Stalin had written this in an article in which, paradoxically, he had warned against exaggerating Trotsky's rôle. Trotsky commented on this that 'an honest man, even if he has a poor memory, will not contradict himself, while a disloyal, unscrupulous, mendacious man always has to remember what he has said in the past in order to avoid disgracing himself'.[32]

It should be remembered that Trotsky wrote this letter in 1927, at a time when he was cornered and the object of constant political vilification, while Stalin was rising rapidly to the peak of power. It took great courage on his part to attempt to restore the picture of events as they were in 1917, especially his view of Stalin's rôle at the time:

However unpleasant it may be to rummage in the garbage-can, allow me, as a fairly close participant and witness of the events of the time, and now as a spectator, to state the following. Lenin's rôle requires no elaboration. I was meeting Sverdlov very frequently at the time, I would ask him for advice and for support from others. Comrade Kamenev who, as is well known, occupied a special position which he himself long ago acknowledged as incorrect, nevertheless took a most active part in the uprising. Kamenev and I spent the decisive night of the twenty-fifth at the offices of the Military Revolutionary Committee, answering enquiries on the telephone and sending out instructions. But, despite my most strenuous efforts, I simply cannot answer the question of what precisely was Stalin's rôle in those decisive days. Not once did I ask him for advice or assistance. He showed no initiative whatsoever.[33]

Trotsky then sheds light on the question of the Military Revolutionary Centre, which Stalinist apologists were promoting only because Stalin had been a member of it. Here he caught them red-handed:

In an obvious oversight by the Stalinist historians, *Pravda* of 2 November 1927 published a precise extract from the minutes of the Central Committee of 16 (29) October 1917, which states that 'the Central Committee is organizing the Military Revolutionary Centre with the following membership: Sverdlov, Stalin, Bubnov, Uritsky and Dzerzhinsky. This Centre is part of the revolutionary Soviet committee.' In other words, the Centre merely supplemented the Military Revolutionary Committee, which was headed by Trotsky, who, as he himself sarcastically concluded, need hardly have belonged to the same body twice. How hard it is to correct history after the event.[34]

Two final passages from Trotsky's book will suffice to show how he exposed and ridiculed the efforts of the falsifiers. He singled out for special mention Yaroslavsky and Lunacharsky. After the revolution and civil war, Yaroslavsky had written of Trotsky:

Comrade Trotsky's brilliant literary and publicizing activity has earned him the universal title of 'king of the pamphleteers' ... We see before us the most profound giftedness ... we see a man most profoundly dedicated to the revolution, a man who has grown up to be a tribune, with a tongue as finely honed and flexible as steel, a tongue that can cut his enemies down, and a pen which scatters a wealth of ideas like handfuls of artistic pearls.[35]

As for Lunacharsky, he had written:

When Lenin was lying wounded [after being shot in August 1918], fatally, as we thought, no one could express our feelings towards him as well as Trotsky. In the appalling storms of international events, Trotsky, the other leader of the revolution, who was utterly disinclined to sentimentalize, said: 'When one thinks that Comrade Lenin might die, it seems one's whole life has been useless, and one feels one doesn't want to go on living.'[36]

Ninety per cent of Yaroslavsky's falsification, Trotsky claimed, was devoted to rewriting his part in the revolution, while Lunacharsky would write whatever he was ordered to, like an obedient secretary. They and the countless others who came after them were creating new myths by which in time the whole country would be made to bend before Stalin and his entourage. Trotsky's finest hours occurred in the revolution and civil war, and it was precisely these that were the main object of camouflage and distortion and that were ultimately erased from the popular memory.

The Oracle of the Revolution

Every revolution creates the hope that it is possible to destroy the old way of life overnight and to open the door to a new one. Excessive expectations soon give way to great disappointment. Usually, counter-revolutionary interests will exploit the disillusionment. History has no examples of the villain being magically cast into the gutter and a free rein given to the hero. It has long been observed, however, that the peak of a revolutionary crisis, when passions are at their highest and ready to explode, is generated not only by social, economic and political processes, but also by individuals who help to create that pressure.

It is not given to every intelligent or even talented person to strike a spark from a crowd, to make the crowd believe in a slogan, or to be able to divert hundreds and thousands of people by a few passionate phrases and to convince them to follow an idea. Trotsky was thus gifted, capable of using theatrical ploys, not as an end in themselves, but in order to make the fundamental truths of the revolution clear to the crowd. He was the orator-in-chief of the revolution. Watching the rare film footage of him, or hearing recordings of his voice, or reading his countless speeches, it seems he was not merely an orator with a God-given talent, but also that he was imbued with a rare inspiration and dedication to the false idea which he fed into people's minds. When he spoke, he seemed to become intoxicated by words, by the sheer pleasure of his ideas, and aware of his own intellectual power.

Trotsky himself recalled the time of the revolution with pleasure. 'Life was a whirl of mass meetings,' he wrote:

> When I arrived in Petrograd, I found all the revolutionary orators either hoarse or voiceless. The revolution of 1905 had taught me to guard my voice with care, and thanks to this, I was hardly ever out of the ranks. Meetings were held in plants, schools and colleges, in theatres, circuses, streets and squares. I usually reached home exhausted after midnight; half-asleep I would discover the best arguments against my opponents, and about seven in the morning, or sometimes even earlier, I would be pulled painfully from my bed by the hateful, intolerable knocking on the door, calling me to a meeting in Peterhof, or to go to Kronstadt on a tug sent for me by the navy boys there. Each time it would seem to me as if I could never get through this new meeting, but some hidden reserve of nervous energy would come to the surface, and I would speak for an hour, sometimes two, while delegations from other plants or districts, surrounding me in a close ring, would tell me that thousands of workers in three or perhaps five different places had been waiting for me for hours on end. How patiently that awakening mass was waiting for the new word in those days![37]

Sukhanov noted Trotsky's hectic schedule: 'Tearing himself from the work in revolutionary headquarters, he would fly from the Obukhovsky factory to the Trubochny, from the Putilov to the Baltic shipyards, from the Riding Academy to the barracks, and seemed to be speaking simultaneously in all places. Every Petrograd worker and soldier knew him and heard him personally. His influence, both on the masses and at headquarters, was overwhelming.'[38]

Paradoxically, Trotsky, whose knowledge of the life of a worker was only superficial, who had never experienced a day of army life, nor known what it was to be a university student in Russia, could nevertheless fire the imaginations and echo the feelings of worker, soldier and student alike. His opponents even accused him of toying with the masses by disguising himself as a working man. The Socialist Revolutionary M. Gendelman, for instance, predicted that 'the same working masses who lift the "worker" Trotsky high, will trample on Bronshtein the intellectual.'[39] Trotsky's favourite venue was the Cirque Moderne. He turned the hall into a 'psychological massage centre' for thousands of people, urging them on to revolution. He recalled that even his opponents recognized his supremacy in this place, and did not attempt to speak in it. He usually went there in the evenings:

> My audience was composed of workers, soldiers, hard-working mothers, street urchins – the oppressed underdogs of the capital. Every square inch was filled, every human body compressed to its limit. Young boys sat on their fathers' shoulders; infants were at their mothers' breasts. No one smoked. The balconies threatened to fall under the excessive weight of human bodies. I made my way to the platform through a narrow human trench, sometimes I was borne overhead. The air, intense with breathing and waiting, fairly exploded with shouts and with the passionate yells peculiar to the Cirque Moderne.[40]

Once, as Trotsky was walking home from a meeting late at night, he heard footsteps behind him. Pulling out his Browning revolver, he whipped round and confronted a young man who, it turned out, had been tailing him regularly. 'Why are you following me? Who are you,' Trotsky demanded to know. 'My name's Poznansky, I'm a student. Please let me accompany and protect you. As well as friends, you have a lot of enemies.' 'Thanks, but I'm not accustomed to having bodyguards. I think I'm protected by the revolution itself!' 'Then I can be its representative for your protection.' Henceforth, when the master orator delivered his speeches, to one side sat Poznansky, taking down his every word in a notebook. From that time until Trotsky was deported from the USSR, Poznansky was at his side, showing not only his capacity for selfless devotion, but also an ability to catch any word of his master's and to note it down in a form that would be usable in an article. Thanks to such people as Poznansky, as well as Sermuks, Glazman, Butov and other assistants, Trotsky was able to begin collecting his personal archive right at the beginning of the revolution, and could thus publish articles and books, partly based on his speeches. In his final exile he devoted a great deal of effort to preserving his archives, but he could not have imagined in his worst nightmare that his carefully preserved materials, as well as those under the care of his elder son, Sedov, would also be 'cared for' by agents of the NKVD. At the end of 1937, for instance, N. Yezhov reported to Stalin that 'the Trotsky documents being held by Sedov were photographed by an agent in Paris on 7–10 November 1937'.[41]

The audience at the Cirque Moderne in 1917, Trotsky noticed, was made up mostly of soldiers and sailors, and he therefore conducted his 'conversation' with them on the war. They told him: 'The war is destroying us. Every day we suffer more heavy losses. There's no bread, no firewood or coal. Things are getting worse by the day. The situation at the front is unbearable. The troops in the trenches are not properly clothed, shod or fed. They see no end to the war, no way out.' According to these 'delegates from the front', the troops were saying that if peace was not signed by 1 November, they would end the war their own way. 'We need peace. This government is incapable of giving us peace. The question of a fourth winter campaign and the blood of Russian soldiers will be decided, as it was before, by the stockmarkets of London and New York, and not by the Russian people.'

The audience waited for Trotsky to offer the solution: 'We must address the people and the armies directly and propose an immediate armistice on all fronts.' Only a genuinely revolutionary regime could make such an approach, 'a government based on the army, the navy, the proletariat and the peasantry – the All-Russian Soviet of Workers', Soldiers' and Peasants' Deputies'.[42] Trotsky urged his audience to support the Social Democratic parties if they wanted to get back to their villages and their families. They should not believe the conciliators and fake revolutionaries in the Provisional Government. Only the Bolsheviks could give them peace, land and bread. After the meeting, Poznansky typed up the speech – with some judicious editing by its author, who was all too aware that the Provisional Government still held power – and it was duly printed in the press.

These big meetings were also an opportunity for Trotsky to catch a glimpse, however fleeting, of his two daughters, Zina, now aged sixteen, and Nina, a year younger. He met their mother, Alexandra

Sokolovskaya, only two or three times in the entire time he was back in Russia until his exile in 1929, although during the worst periods of hunger and privation he was able to give his first family some assistance.

Mass meetings were not the only venue for Trotsky to employ his prodigious oratorical talent. He was also highly effective at congresses and plenary sessions of party bodies, as well as in meetings of soviets and committees. At a session of the Petrograd Soviet he raised the question of the Military Revolutionary Committee, on which the youthful SR Lazimir produced a report. Formal decisions had already been taken that this body should be created, with sections for defence, supply, communications, a workers' militia, an information bureau, despatch room and command-post.[43] The Provisional Government was now insisting on transferring the most revolutionized troops from the capital to the front, and Lazimir proposed that the Committee should decide how many to keep in Petrograd, as well as maintain contacts with the forces of several districts outside the capital, take measures to supply the revolutionary units with arms and provisions, protect the population from pogroms and safeguard the revolutionary order in the city.

The Mensheviks Broido and Astrov, as well as the SR Ogurtsovsky, expressed doubts about the Committee. Broido – who would be one of Stalin's assistants in the People's Commissariat for Nationalities for a while after the revolution – denounced the Committee as a Bolshevik device for seizing power, which would be 'the funeral of the revolution'. The Mensheviks, he declared, would therefore not join the Committee. Trotsky replied: 'Never before have we been so far from Broido and his party, and the Menshevik tactics so disastrous, as is now the case. They say we are forming a headquarters for the seizure of power. We make no secret of it, all the representatives from the front who have spoken here have all declared that if there isn't an armistice soon, the troops will abandon the front.'[44] It was on such occasions that Trotsky was seen to be not merely an effective debater, but also capable of expressing a clear and precise radical political position. For this he earned the title 'the Danton of the Russian revolution'.

In his report on the activities of the Military Revolutionary Committee, Trotsky told the Petrograd Soviet that the government's

efforts to transfer troops from the capital had been frustrated, and he
declared that the Committee was now guided by the slogan 'All Power
to the Soviets': 'This slogan is going to become reality in the next
phase, the phase of meetings of the All-Russian Congress of Soviets.
Whether it will lead to an uprising or an action will depend not only
and not so much on the Soviets, as on those who are still holding
onto state power against the will of the people.' Speaking with total
assurance, he went on:

> There is a half-regime which the people don't believe in and in which
> it doesn't believe itself, since it is internally dead. This half-regime is
> waiting for a historical broom to sweep away the genuine power of the
> revolutionary people . . . If this ephemeral regime makes a mad attempt
> to resuscitate itself, the popular masses, organized and armed, will repel
> it decisively . . . If the government tries to use the twenty-four or
> forty-eight hours left to it to stab the revolution in the back, we declare
> that the vanguard of the revolution will answer blow for blow, and steel
> for iron.[45]

Asked how he felt about having Left SRs in the Military Revolutionary Committee, Trotsky replied that only two of the five members
were from that party, and that there were no differences of principle
among them. When he was then asked the Soviet's attitude to the
municipal government, which was opposed to its purposes, he replied
almost without thinking, 'We're going to disperse the city Duma.' It
was, however, also observed that Trotsky had to bluff and improvise
in reply to the questions of whether bridges linking the centre of the
city to the working-class suburbs would be closed, how the matter of
food distribution would be handled, and whether an uprising would
be supported by troops at the front. Even so, he did it with aplomb.

The closer the date of the uprising approached, the more Trotsky
was called upon to speak; and he did so probably more often than
any other revolutionary leader at the time. To a huge and 'ecstatic'
gathering on 22 October, he promised: 'if you support our policy to
bring the revolution to victory, if you give the cause all your strength,
if you support the Petrograd Soviet in this great cause without hesitation, then let us all swear our allegiance to the revolution. If you
support this sacred oath which we are making, raise your hands.'[46] A
forest of hands was his answer.

Naturally, Trotsky's demagogic fireworks alarmed the more moderate fellow-travellers of the revolution, to say nothing of those further to the right. Gorky described them as outrageous,[47] while Milyukov in later years defined the bulk of the revolutionaries, including Trotsky, as state criminals.[48] It was only to be expected that this would be the view of a representative of the regime that was overthrown by the Bolsheviks. As for the final verdict of history, many decades would have to pass before it was pronounced.

Trotsky's emphasis on the importance of the Soviets, and his relatively lesser stress on the Bolshevik party, was of great significance. Indeed, as he was to be accused subsequently, he recognized that the Soviets had a much broader social base than any single political party could claim. In fact this was an unobtrusive way of making revolution by a party into one by the people, while working to realize the resolution of 10 October passed by the secret session of the Central Committee calling for an armed uprising. It was from that moment that one can count Trotsky as a true Leninist. A member of the Bolsheviks for barely two months, within two weeks of the uprising he had become a member of the first Politburo of the Central Committee alongside Lenin, Zinoviev, Kamenev, Stalin, Sokolnikov and Bubnov. Thus he was to witness the dissension among the party leadership when Zinoviev and Kamenev voted against the armed uprising.

This notorious meeting of the Central Committee took place on 22 October at the apartment of the Menshevik Sukhanov, a sworn opponent of an armed uprising. Sukhanov himself was absent, and it was his wife, a Bolshevik, who had arranged the session, which was to last ten hours, without his knowledge.[49] A few days later, Kamenev and Zinoviev published their opposition to the Central Committee's decision in *Novaya zhizn'*. They wrote that they were not the only Bolsheviks who felt that to launch an armed uprising 'only a few days before the Congress of Soviets would be impermissible and fatal for the proletariat and the revolution ... To stake everything on an uprising in the next few days would be an act of desperation. Our party is too strong and has before it too great a future to take such steps.'[50] Kamenev and Zinoviev would frequently repent this act in public. Their statement of October 1917 would hang over their heads like a curse.

Alongside Lenin

All of Stalin's efforts notwithstanding, there can be no argument about the fact that Trotsky was perceived – by admirers and detractors alike – as second only to Lenin in the revolution. *Rabochaya gazeta* of 6 November 1917 published an unsigned article entitled 'The Beginning of the End' which declared: 'Lenin's and Trotsky's programme means the intensification of the terror and the deepening of the civil war. A return to freedom and civil peace are the slogans of yesterday's friends and today's enemies. The "socialism" of Lenin and Trotsky is based on the "military revolutionary committee" and the bayonets of the Petrograd and Kronstadt garrisons.'[51] In his newspaper *Novaya zhizn'*, Gorky repeatedly published attacks on the two leaders. On 7 November the paper declared: 'Lenin, Trotsky and their fellow-travellers are already poisoned by the toxin of power, as demonstrated by their shameful attitude to freedom of speech, freedom of the individual and all the rights for which [the democrats] struggled. These blind fanatics and unscrupulous adventurers are racing at breakneck speed towards something they call "social evolution", but they are in fact on the path to anarchy, the ruin of the proletariat and the revolution.'[52]

Novaya zhizn' put forward the view that the Bolshevik seizure of power was little more than an unfortunate episode, and that things would soon return to their proper place. For example, the philosopher and economist Vladimir Bazarov, who had been both a founding member of the Bolshevik faction and a philosophical opponent of Lenin, wrote that the Bolsheviks' intention to divide the democratic camp would destroy the revolution:

> Naturally, however, the terrible president of the Smolny republic, N. Lenin, who is obsessed by the maniacal notion of a 'Soviet' state, will never see this elementary truth. This elementary truth will never be recognized by the excellent L. Trotsky and the phalanx of revolutionary conquistadors who are attached to him and who are playing the leading rôle in contemporary Bolshevism. Experience has shown the Leninist obsessions to be incurable. As for the conquistadors, they have not the least concern for the institutions they have created. Their psychology is simple: the day, even if only the hour, is mine, and I will look

beautiful in a classically revolutionary pose with the stamp of Robes-pierrean tragedy on my brow.[53]

The Mensheviks and liberals hoped that the Bolsheviks would not last long, and it seemed likely that their hopes might be fulfilled. Lenin and his comrades, however, saw further than their critics. For as long it was still possible – no later than December 1917, when the Bolshevik political police, the Cheka, was formed – the liberal press attacked the new regime, while the non-Bolshevik revolutionary parties condemned the dispersal of the Pre-Parliament, the arrest of the socialist ministers and the dictatorial measures adopted by the radicals, and viewed Lenin's regime as 'an enemy of the people and the revolution'.[54]

It is worth noting that while it was the losers who first employed the ominous term 'enemies of the people', resurrected from the lexicon of the French revolution, as early as 28 November 1917 Lenin chaired a meeting of the Council of People's Commissars – his new government – which passed a decree, tabled by him, 'on the arrest of leading members of the central committee of the party of enemies of the people [Constitutional Democrats] and their trial by revolutionary tribunal'. Ironically, the only member of the government to vote against this decree was Stalin,[55] perhaps as a sign from a relatively unnoticed member of the team that he too wished to be heard.

The report on the state of affairs was given at that meeting by Trotsky, who outlined the situation in Petrograd, described the counter-revolutionary movement that was beginning to take shape in the Don region and the Urals, and described the links between the Kadets and General Kaledin's forces, concluding that the Kadet central committee was the centre of counter-revolution and calling on 'all the labouring and exploited' to take up arms.[56] This was the death-knell for the Kadets' political activity in Russia. The Left SRs and Menshevik-Internationalists were, it seems, prepared to collaborate with the Bolsheviks on social issues, the Left SRs in particular making their cooperation last until the summer of 1918, although neither they nor the Bolsheviks made any special efforts to preserve it. The Bolshevik intention to hold a monopoly of power soon came to dominate their behaviour. Trotsky, who before the coup had declared that 'the minority will not be hurt', now supported Lenin's objection to allowing the 'conciliators' into the Soviet government.

After defeating Kerensky's attempt on 6–14 November to move troops under General Krasnov to Petrograd, the Bolsheviks held a memorable meeting of the Petrograd Party Committee. The 'heretics', Zinoviev and Kamenev, who had opposed the armed uprising, now proposed the creation of a so-called 'homogenous socialist government', which would include SRs and Mensheviks. Nogin and Lunacharsky suggested that what was needed was a socialist coalition. Lenin calculated that such a government would have a majority of Mensheviks and Right SRs, and was adamantly opposed. Trotsky supported him with equal vigour, a fact Lenin much appreciated. Neither side was willing to compromise, yet again ignoring the possible chance of establishing a more moderate system. The 'infallible' Lenin and his closest ally, Trotsky, committed a fatal mistake. Governing alone from the middle of 1918, the Bolsheviks condemned themselves to permanent isolation, and were able henceforth to maintain themselves in power only by the use of force and coercion.

Trotsky's book *The Stalinist School of Falsification* includes a photocopy of the minutes of this meeting of the Petrograd Party Committee. When the issue of inviting Mensheviks and SRs to enter the new government was raised, Lenin declared: 'I can't even talk about this seriously. Trotsky said such a union was impossible a long time ago. Trotsky understood this and since then there hasn't been a better Bolshevik than he.'[57] These words were not included in either the 1929 or 1958 edition of the minutes. Trotsky referred to them frequently in his writings to show that he had taken a correct position on the issue of 'homogenous government', i.e. that of Lenin. In the book, moreover, he admitted that when he had been in disagreement with Bolshevik positions in the past he had been in the wrong,[58] thus refuting the oft-repeated accusation of the Stalinists that 'Trotsky and his few close friends entered the party not in order to work for it, but to shatter and blow it up from within.'[59]

Not everyone accepted Trotsky as a major leader. Among the Bolsheviks there were those who would not forgive him his non-Bolshevik past, while for the population at large it was his Jewish origins that got in the way. The charge was made frequently enough that Lenin was 'surrounded by Jews'. Among the communications Lenin received on this subject was a telegram from an old member of the People's Will, a Bolshevik sympathizer called Makari Vasiliev: 'To save

Bolshevism, you should forgo a number of extremely respected and popular Bolsheviks: the Soviet government would be defended and supported by the immediate resignation of Zinoviev, Trotsky and Kamenev, whose presence in the highest and most influential positions does not reflect the principle of national self-determination.' Vasiliev also demanded the 'self-removal of Sverdlov, Ioffe, Steklov and their replacement by people of Russian origin'.[60] Neither Lenin nor the other leaders took any notice of such exhortations, dismissing them as an expression of low consciousness at a time when the international principle underlying the revolution was genuine and powerful. But anti-Semitism was very much in evidence. As Boris Savinkov, then in Warsaw, wrote: 'There are peasants who hate the Jewish people because some Jewish commissars requisition their livestock and grain. There are Red Army men who hate the Jewish people because some Jewish political commissars send them to the slaughter. There are [White officer] volunteers who hate the entire Jewish people because Jewish members of the Cheka are executing their families ... But anti-Semitism will only disappear when Russia is a genuinely democratic state. As a Russian, I am hurt by Jewish suffering.'[61]

Trotsky had striven for nothing in his life as zealously as he strove for the revolution, as if only the revolution could give him the opportunity he needed for full self-expression. He had succeeded also in convincing Lenin of his dedication to the Bolshevik cause. When the Bolsheviks were drawing up their list of candidates for elections to the Constituent Assembly, Lenin wrote: 'Such a large number of inexperienced people (such as Larin) who only recently joined our party is quite impermissible. There must be special scrutiny and correction of the list ... It goes without saying that ... no one would dispute, for instance, the candidacy of Trotsky, first of all because as soon as he arrived he took up an internationalist position; secondly, he strove to bring the Mezhrayonka into the party; thirdly, in the difficult days of July he was on top of the situation and a dedicated supporter of the party of the revolutionary proletariat.'[62]

The day after the coup, *Pravda* proclaimed: 'Comrades, with your blood you have guaranteed that the master of the Russian land, the All-Russian Constituent Assembly, shall convene on time.' In the elections that took place in November, however, the Bolsheviks received only a quarter of the seats, and Lenin declared: 'The republic of

Soviets is a higher form of democracy than the bourgeois republic with the Constituent Assembly.'[63] On 23 November the Bolshevik Central Committee ordered the arrest of the commission in charge of the elections and convocation of the Constituent Assembly. When the commission protested, Stalin, who had been deputed to handle the affair, stated peremptorily that 'the Bolsheviks are not interested in what these people think of the Council of People's Commissars. The Commission had committed forgeries . . .'[64]

After many delays, the Constituent Assembly finally opened on 5 (18) January 1918. It was a sad spectacle in which the assembled deputies from different parties and factions had no common political language. There was whooping and shouting. Chernov, elected Chairman, tried to shout above the din: 'The simple fact of the opening of the first session of the Constituent Assembly proclaims an end to the civil war between the peoples of Russia.'[65] It was clear to everyone that the Bolsheviks had no intention of allowing the Assembly to continue, since they could not control it. The debates were still going on, however, at five in the morning, when a sailor – one Anatoly Zheleznyakov – mounted the stage, tugged at Chernov's sleeve and loudly announced to the hushed assembly: 'Comrade Dybenko [the Navy Commissar and effectively the head of the Red Guards] wants those present to leave the hall.' Attempting to preserve his dignity, Chernov replied: 'That is for the Constituent Assembly to decide, if you don't mind.' Armed Red Army men and sailors appeared in the doorways. Zheleznyakov said: 'I suggest you leave the hall, as it's late and the guards are tired.'

The Left SRs supported the Bolsheviks, and Russian parliamentarism was laid to rest for decades to come. The newspapers at first wrote that the elections to the Assembly had been based on the old, unjust law passed by Kerensky, which gave an advantage to the greater part of the population, namely the peasantry. Of course the Bolsheviks, who now had a majority in the Soviets, had no intention of sharing power with the Assembly, where they were in a minority. It was a choice between the Soviets and the Assembly, and it was one that had been made long before. Without hesitation, Trotsky was with Lenin. The sympathy of the masses was outwardly with the Soviets, but power there was in fact in Bolshevik hands. The idea of the Assembly had already dimmed, which explains why its dispersal provoked no mass demonstrations. It was only later that the people realized that the Bolshevik ship of state was on a straight course towards totalitarian dictatorship.

With a quarter of the seats in the Assembly, and a further quarter held by the Left SRs, the Bolsheviks might have created a powerful coalition, but by early 1918 they were in no mood to share power. Lenin explained the SR election victory as a consequence of the fact that between 17 October, when the electoral registers were published, and 12 November, when the elections took place, peasants 'could not yet know the truth about the land and peace, could not distinguish between their friends and their enemies, the wolves in sheep's clothing'.[66] Some responsibility for this lost opportunity to follow a pluralist path must also be laid on the Socialist Revolutionaries, who did not want to remain in the position of the Bolsheviks' junior partners for a long time.

The October coup transformed Trotsky's relationship with Lenin from that of comrade to that of friend. Trotsky recalled the scene as they awaited the opening of the Second Congress of Soviets:

Late that evening ... Lenin and I were resting in a room adjoining the meeting-hall, a room entirely empty except for chairs. Someone had spread a blanket on the floor for us; someone else, I think it was Lenin's sister, had brought us pillows. We were lying side by side; body and soul were relaxing like overtaut strings. It was a well-earned rest. We could not sleep, so we talked in low voices. Only now did Lenin become reconciled to the postponement of the uprising. His fears had been dispelled. There was a rare sincerity in his voice. He was interested in knowing all about the mixed pickets of the Red Guards, sailors and soldiers that had been stationed everywhere. 'What a wonderful sight: a worker with a rifle, side by side with a soldier, standing before a street fire!' he repeated with deep feeling. At last the soldier and the worker had been brought together! Then he started suddenly. 'And what about the Winter Palace? It has not been taken yet. Isn't there a danger in that?' I got up to ask, on the telephone, about the progress of the operations there, but he tried to stop me. 'Lie still, I will send someone to find out.' But we could not rest for long. The session of the Congress of Soviets was opening in the next hall.[67]

For as long as it was still functioning, *Novaya zhizn'* continued to issue ominous warnings about the consequences of the Bolshevik coup.

Its main target was the new regime's resort to the use of force.
Unsigned articles bore the unmistakable mark of Martov and his fellow Mensheviks Dan and Abramovich. On 29 October an article
entitled 'The Bolsheviks in Power' argued that

> the coup of 25 October had Lenin and Trotsky as its chief actors, but
> the true initiators were Kerensky and Tsereteli . . . It is the front-men
> who are now in 'power'. But only the most superficial observer might
> think that they are going to play this comic opera through to the end.
> In fact we are witnessing the greatest of tragedies which threatens the
> country with endless miseries and the destruction of our revolutionary
> gains . . . We reject root and branch the very method of the seizure of
> power which was carried out by the isolated forces of the Bolsheviks
> with the assistance of military 'operations'. The greatest convulsions
> in accordance with the Bolshevik programme are now inevitable.[68]

With the possible sole exception of the peace negotiations at Brest-
Litovsk, on all questions of major substance faced by the Bolsheviks
in both the October coup and the civil war Lenin and Trotsky were
at one. In his magnum opus on the revolution, and in many other
works, Trotsky invariably defended Lenin, who was for him 'an outstanding leader', and with whom, whether alive or dead, he took no
issue. The question is, why? There are several explanations. First and
above all, Trotsky realized that if he were to change his political
direction yet again, it would mean his intellectual death. Political life
allows only one substantial revision, otherwise one loses credibility
with one's past comrades as well as one's new friends. Further, Trotsky
had seen during October that Lenin's views were extraordinarily close
to his own. Finally, he did not want to quarrel with the memory of
the leader of the Russian revolution because he was determined to
explode the myth that Stalin was 'the Lenin of today'. Throughout
his theoretical and political writing, he tried to show that he alone
had always understood Lenin, and that he alone had since October
1917 remained true to Lenin's ideas.
    Even when he was discussing steps and decisions Lenin had taken
that for some reason had not been supported by the Central Committee, Trotsky did not condemn him. In 1932, for example, he
wrote:

Lenin insisted on the uprising taking place during the Democratic Conference: not a single member of the Central Committee was in favour. A week later Lenin suggested that Smilga organize an uprising headquarters in Finland and from there strike a blow at the government, using the sailors . . . At the end of September Lenin regarded postponing the rising for three weeks, until the Congress of Soviets, as disastrous. In fact, the uprising, which was delayed until the eve of the Congress, was completed while it was still in session. Lenin proposed that the struggle be launched in Moscow on the assumption that it could succeed there without a battle. In fact, the uprising in Moscow, despite the previous victory in Petrograd, lasted eight days and cost many lives.

Scrupulously enumerating Lenin's failed proposals, Trotsky resisted any further temptation to blame him. On the contrary, 'Lenin was not a machine for turning out infallible decisions. He was "merely" a genius, and nothing human was alien to him, including the capacity to make mistakes.'[69]

Trotsky's attitude to Lenin was in this respect enviable, since he could recognize Lenin's genius while attacking the deification that was to bedevil Soviet intellectual life for decades to come. The iconization of Lenin led both to the impoverishment of his ideas and the growth of dogmatists who, in alliance with the bureaucrats, were responsible for much that he might not have approved of. Trotsky saw him, in other words, as a man and not as a god. Even in 1927, when he was in disgrace and at Stalin's mercy, he had the courage to defend Lenin from iconization, from the mortification of dogmatic reverence and his transformation into yet another Marxist saint. In an unpublished article entitled 'On Unctuousness' he wrote:

the dead Lenin seems to have been reborn: there you have the solution of the riddle of the risen Christ. He has been resurrected for us yet again . . . The real danger begins when the bureaucracy makes attitudes towards Lenin and his teaching a subject of automatic reverence. Speaking, as always, in simple terms, [Lenin's widow] N.K. Krupskaya has warned against this as well as another danger. She said there shouldn't be too many monuments to Lenin and that unnecessary and useless institutions shouldn't be created in his name.[70]

At an evening of reminiscences held on Lenin's birthday, three months after his death, Trotsky gave a long speech which demonstrated his ability to fathom the depths of another personality, to

perceive the philosophy of another's existence, and to detect qualities
that others might fail to notice. He remarked that already artists and
writers were talking about Lenin – for example, Maxim Gorky: 'But
he did not understand Ilyich, approaching him as he did with the petty
bourgeois sugariness of the intellectual that became so characteristic of
Gorky in his later years.' Lenin, according to Trotsky, 'had a mighty
inner seething revolutionary impatience which he tamed with will
power and mind . . . He was permeated with faith in mankind; in the
moral sense he was the highest kind of idealist, he believed in man's
ability to reach heights of which we can only dream.' Trotksy also
saw that Lenin had an ominous side, his faith in the strength of
dictatorship: 'Vladimir Ilyich said that the greatest danger was that
the Russians are good men . . . When General Krasnov was released
on his word of honour, it seems that only Ilyich was against it, and
then he gave in to the others and threw up his hands . . . When the
dictatorship of the proletariat was discussed in his presence, he would
always say – exaggerating to make the point clearer – "What sort of
dictatorship do we have! What we have is a mess, just bunglers" . . .
Generally speaking, he maintained an even temper; his emotional state
was uneven, but thanks to his unusual emotional restraint he always
appeared in control to the highest degree.' Trotsky perceptively noted
that 'the study of the psychology of our leaders will help people in
the future to understand our epoch'. From his own exalted position,
it was possible for Trotsky, given his extraordinary powers of observation, to penetrate Lenin's internal world, to see the demon in him,
rather than the god, the Robespierre of the Russian revolution.

For all his vanity, Trotsky recognized that Lenin was intellectually
more powerful and enjoyed greater authority than he. He was very
proud of the fact that it was his own name that invariably figured next
to that of Lenin in the revolutionary, counter-revolutionary and liberal
press. Sukhanov, the chronicler of the revolution, more than once
blamed Trotsky no less than Lenin for the 'collapse' of Russia, for
the 'great troubles' and for the 'destruction of democratic hopes'. In
November 1917, for example, *Novaya zhizn'* published an article by
him entitled 'The Dictatorship of Citizen Lenin', in which he wrote
with the bitterness of the defeated: 'Who cannot see that what we
have is not a "Soviet" regime, but a dictatorship of the respected
citizens Lenin and Trotsky, and that their dictatorship rests on the

bayonets of the soldiers and workers they deceived and who were given unpaid bills in place of fabulous, but non-existent riches?'[71]

Having assumed the role of 'second man', Trotsky often – especially in the later period – placed himself next to Lenin, while making it plain that this was no accident. In a piece entitled 'Petrograd' he wrote: 'In the Smolny, with Comrade Lenin and myself present (I don't remember the precise date), a meeting of the garrison was convened.'[72] Other Bolshevik leaders were also present, but Trotsky singled out only two names. Similarly: 'When Lenin and I held a meeting of officers of the Petersburg garrison, where the officers against Kerensky had gathered . . .'[73] In his memoirs, Trotsky very often mentions the personal meetings, conversations and relations of trust that he had with Lenin, presuming with good reason that by emphasizing the intimacy of his relationship with the leader of the revolution he would better secure his own image: 'On the twenty-fifth the Second Congress of Soviets opened. And then Dan and Skobelev came to the Smolny and just happened to pass right through the room where Vladimir Ilyich and I were sitting. He was wrapped up in a bandage, as if he had toothache, wearing enormous spectacles and a cheap cap and looking very odd. But Dan, who had a sharp and practised eye, nudged Skobelev, winked and went out. Vladimir Ilyich also nudged me: "They recognized me, the scoundrels."'[74]

Unquestionably, during the October revolution and the civil war a high degree of mutual trust developed between Lenin and Trotsky, of the kind that exists between like-minded men committed to the same task. It is also true that as personalities they remained very much themselves. In 1917 Lenin saw a completely new Trotsky, active and adhering to the revolutionary idea, and as a rule accepting Lenin's views without argument. Nor was this mere political conformism: it was a coincidence of aspirations. It was no doubt Trotsky's finest hour, an amazingly fortunate confluence of personal, historical and political circumstances, in which he could reveal the essence of his personality to the maximum, as well as his deepest wishes and dreams. He believed that the revolution justified any measure one might take and that it would transform the world. He had yet to discover that it would engender hopes that would be bitterly disappointed.

Possibly Lenin was the man to understand the destructive revolutionary principle embodied in Trotsky, a principle Trotsky himself acknowledged graphically at a meeting of the Politburo in July 1919, which he recalled in his memoirs. He remarks that he had become aware of the rumours circulating about the harshness of his alleged criminal order in August 1918 to execute the regimental commander and political commissar of the Eastern Front for having withdrawn their troops from battle positions:

> Only once did I remark, at the meeting of the Politburo, that if it had not been for the ruthless measures at Sviyazhsk, we would not be holding our meeting. 'Absolutely,' Lenin picked it up, and then and there he began to write very fast, as he always did, in red ink at the bottom of a blank sheet that bore the seal of the Soviet of People's Commissaries [Council of People's Commissars]. It read: 'Comrades, Knowing the strict behaviour of Comrade Trotsky's orders, I am so convinced, so absolutely convinced, of the correctness, expediency, and necessity for the success of the cause of the order given by Comrade Trotsky, that I unreservedly endorse this order.' 'I will give you,' said Lenin, 'as many forms like this as you want.' ... Lenin gave his signature in advance to any decision that I might consider necessary in the future. And these were decisions that carried life or death with them. Could there be greater confidence of one man in another? The very idea of this extraordinary document could have come to Lenin only because he knew better than I did, or else suspected the source of the intrigue [against Trotsky] and thought it necessary to strike back at it with the utmost vigour.[75]

To those in the know, it was clear that information about executions at the front carried out on Trotsky's orders was being spread by Stalin and Voroshilov. At a Central Committee Plenum in 1927, for instance, Voroshilov accused Trotsky of arresting army commanders and commissars without grounds. Trotsky interrupted him and cried out: 'You are uttering a bare-faced lie, like the dishonourable scoundrel you are, when you say I executed Communists!' 'You're a scoundrel yourself and an out-and-out enemy of our party! Anyway, the hell with him,' Voroshilov retorted angrily. 'Don't think I'm going to sit here in silence while you accuse me of shooting Communists,' Trotsky exploded. At this, Podvoisky exclaimed, 'You did shoot Communists. I'll show you the list of those who were shot.'[76]

The question of the terror and repression during the civil war, of which Trotsky was one of the initiators, will be discussed in the following chapter. For the moment, it is important to underline the fact that Lenin was always in favour of the most rigorous measures to secure the battle-worthiness of the Red Army. He believed Trotsky was sufficiently severe to bring the front to order, to end desertion, panic-mongering and partisan action, and for his part Trotsky recognized this as the highest form of trust. Trotsky expressed his own attitude to Lenin perfectly plainly: 'I realized only too well what Lenin meant to the revolution, for history and to me. He was my master. This does not mean that I repeated his words and his gestures a bit late, but that I learned from him to arrive independently at the same decision.'[77]

The years of the revolution and civil war were unquestionably the high point in Trotsky's life, at least partly because he was seen as standing alongside Lenin, with whom he was in almost complete harmony. Their intellectual and political collaboration was based on their shared fanatical attachment to the idea of revolution and the radical restructuring of Russia. Neither of them felt the tragedy of a revolution occurring in a backward peasant country with weak democratic traditions. Both had decided that it was possible to 'skip over' the bourgeois-democratic stage and proceed straight to the building of socialism, settling the needs of democracy *en route*. In practice, the revolution which brought the people peace and land took away the more important quality of their lives, liberty.

The Brest-Litovsk Formula

One of the principal reasons for the bloodlessness of the October coup was the haste with which the war-weary nation turned towards peace. The Bolshevik peace policy, expressed in the first decree of the Soviet regime, was immensely popular with millions of ordinary people. Once the Bolsheviks had gained their immediate objective, they were obliged to make good on their promise and leave the war.

On 20 November 1917, as the newly appointed Commissar for Foreign Affairs, Trotsky formally circulated the embassies of Russia's allies with the news that Russia was now ruled by a government of Soviets under the chairmanship of Vladimir Ilyich Lenin. The new

government had issued a decree on peace which was to be considered
as a proposal for an immediate armistice on all fronts and the immediate opening of peace negotiations. The peace envisaged by Lenin's
government, the note continued, would exclude reparations and
annexations, and would be based on the principle of national self-
determination.[78] This and subsequent communications from the
Soviet government and foreign commissariat were ignored.

Trotsky relates in his memoirs that he was reluctant to take office:

> From my youth on, or, to be more precise, from my childhood on, I
> had dreamed of being a writer. Later, I subordinated my literary work,
> as I did everything else, to the revolution . . . After the seizure of power,
> I tried to stay out of the government, and offered to undertake the
> direction of the press . . . Lenin would not hear of it, however. He
> insisted that I take over the commissariat of the interior, saying that
> the most important task at the moment was to fight off a counter-
> revolution. I objected, and brought up, among other arguments, the
> question of nationality. Was it worth while to put into our enemies'
> hands such an additional weapon as my Jewish origin?

The majority of the Central Committee agreed with Trotsky.
Sverdlov proposed instead that he take charge of foreign affairs, 'and
thus I came to head the Soviet diplomacy for a quarter of a year'.[79]

Within a few days of entering the government, however, Trotsky
found himself absorbed once more in the affairs of the Petrograd
Soviet and the Military Revolutionary Committee, where he was also
bombarded by questions about his activities as Foreign Commissar
and asked when he was going to publish the secret agreements made
by the Tsar with the Entente powers on the post-war division of the
territory of the defeated countries. He was able to tell the deputies
that in the three days since his appointment he had spent only one
and a half hours at the ministry, where he thought it proper to say
farewell to the outgoing staff, and had not yet had time to publish
the secret treaties.

Indeed, when he had first entered the foreign ministry, he was
greeted with the news that no one had come to work. When Trotsky
demanded that the staff all be assembled, however, it transpired that
there were in fact many of them in the building. In a few words
Trotsky explained their new duties and declared: 'Whoever is willing

to work in good faith can stay.' The new commissar was listened to with gloomy faces, but no keys or papers were handed over to him. The next day he sent a sailor, Markin, who without fuss and *pour encourager les autres* arrested Prince Tatishchev and Baron Taube, two foreign ministry officials who, like many others in that particular ministry, had survived the fall of tsarism and the Provisional Government period intact. Things then began to go more smoothly. The keys appeared and files of papers were laid out. Markin found what seem to have been two young experts, called Polivanov and Zalkind, and they began to sort out the classified documents and prepare the secret treaties for publication. But it was only when Georgy Chicherin was appointed as Trotsky's successor in February 1918 that new assistants were found and a new 'proletarian' style emerged.

The Bolshevik victory of October had barely been achieved when it became clear that the new regime's first priority must be to end the war. They had promised the people land, bread and peace. They had begun to distribute the land, and that should bring bread. But peace depended not on the Bolsheviks alone. The country watched and waited while the new government under Lenin's chairmanship deliberated at sessions lasting up to eight hours over a multitude of unfamiliar problems. The Council of People's Commissars was learning the business of administration on the job. Many of the problems being addressed were of fundamental importance for the creation of Bolshevik statehood, even if they were tackled by improvisation and guesswork. At first it was food supply, transport and fuel that occupied much of the government's attention, but soon came the turn of foreign affairs, as the people began to demand the return of the troops to their villages. The hope that the Germans would agree to a quick armistice, however, was not realized, and it was a full month before hostilities ceased on the Eastern Front.

On 27 November 1917 the Sovnarkom debated the composition of the delegation that would negotiate an armistice with the Germans. It was decided that it should consist of Ioffe, Kamenev and the female Left SR Bitsenko.[80] On 2 December the group duly signed an armistice at Brest-Litovsk, and on 9 December peace talks began. On 24 December Trotsky went to Brest-Litovsk to take over as head of the Soviet delegation.

Trotsky reported to Lenin every day, and at first it seemed things were going according to plan. German Foreign Minister Richard von Kühlmann announced that the Central Powers agreed with the Russian proposal to conclude a general peace without annexations or reparations, but only on condition the Entente agree to these terms. Trotsky again asked the Western Allies to support this formula, but again he met a wall of silence. Meanwhile, the Soviet government started demobilizing the Russian Army. On 27 December Kühlmann declared that, in the absence of an Allied response, the Central Powers could not now accept the Soviet concept. Then, on 5 January 1918, it was announced that Germany and Austria-Hungary would make peace on condition that 150,000 square kilometres of Russian territory were ceded to them. Cynically exploiting the right of national self-determination, pronounced by the Soviet government, Germany made peace conditional on Ukraine being given independence, on Poland and Lithuania being detached from Russia, as well as parts of Latvia and Belorussia and the Moonsund archipelago in the Baltic, while the border south of Brest-Litovsk was to be agreed with the government of independent Ukraine.

Trotsky was already in Brest when these conditions were put. On the way from Moscow, he had seen for himself that the Russian trenches were all but empty and that there was nothing to stop the Germans from advancing at will. The Austrian Foreign Minister, Count Czernin, later recalled that the German officer escorting Trotsky through the front line reported that the Soviet Commissar had observed the scene with a growing sense of gloom.[81] When Trotsky reported the position to him, Lenin at once replied that he should sign the 'predatory peace', although he also said that he, Lenin, must first consult the Central Committee and Sovnarkom. The issue produced a dramatic reaction in the leadership and led to the first real split since October.

Those who resolutely opposed signing the 'predatory peace treaty', and who were immediately dubbed 'Left Communists', were firmly convinced that revolutionary Russia, with the help of the international proletariat, was capable of giving a rebuff to German imperialism. Their belief in an imminent European revolution was very strong. It was at 'Left Communist' insistence that the Sovnarkom allocated two million gold roubles for revolutionary propaganda abroad. Trotsky himself, moreover, brought with him to Brest-Litovsk several bundles of pamphlets and leaflets addressed to the soldiers of the Austro–German bloc. He also took with him Karl Radek, a fiery agitator and talented pamphleteer, showing that he not only believed in the imminence of a German revolution, but was determined to do his best to make it happen. It was therefore not surprising when on 9 January General Hoffmann and von Kühlmann protested at the 'agitational appeals of the Soviet government'. Next day Trotsky decisively swept their protests aside: 'We, the representatives of the Russian Republic, maintain for ourselves and our fellow citizens full freedom to propagate republican and revolutionary socialist convictions.'[82]

As he paced the cobbled streets of the old fortress of Brest in the evenings with Kamenev, Pokrovsky and Karakhan, Trotsky agonized over how to extract Russia from the war without damaging her revolutionary reputation. He recognized that by undertaking separate peace negotiations the Russian delegation was giving the Central Powers a major advantage. Kühlmann made it abundantly clear, even if in camouflaged form, that the Russians were at Brest to sign a surrender, and that all of Trotsky's high-flown rhetoric about justice and the rights of nations to peace and self-determination were nothing but revolutionary cosmetics. He who had the power would call the tune. Kühlmann seems to have been unaware that the Central Powers were themselves standing on the brink of disaster.

Trotsky told his comrades that in Petrograd Lenin had instructed him, during a break in the talks, to prolong the verbal battle as much as possible. If the Germans issued an ultimatum, he had said, the Russians would have to sign on their terms. Kamenev had protested that it would be impossible to drag the talks out indefinitely, as 'the Germans simply won't allow it'. Trotsky replied that there was hope that the revolutionary stance of the Soviet delegation would raise revolutionary tension in the Central Powers. In this belief, he fought hard on almost every point of the treaty in the talks.

Czernin devotes several pages of his memoirs to the talks at Brest-Litovsk, and evidently found Trotsky a worthy adversary: 'Trotsky is undoubtedly an interesting, clever man and a very dangerous opponent. He has outstanding oratorical talent and an ability to make swift and effective retort such as I have rarely seen, and with the insolence characteristic of his race.' Czernin also noted that Trotsky was capable of cynicism: when Czernin asked what terms Russia would accept,

Trotsky replied that 'he was not as naive as we thought. He knew perfectly well that force was the weightiest of arguments and that the Central Powers were capable of seizing Russia's provinces.'[83] Commenting on the preamble to the peace treaty, which loftily proclaimed that the sides 'wish to live in peace and friendship', Trotsky dismissed this wording with: 'Some friendship, when one of the friends wants to rob the other ... Let it be a closer friendship. Only the word "eternal" is missing.'

Trotsky kept Moscow fully informed of progress at the talks by courier and direct telegraphic line. One particular record of such calls is worth reproducing, as it smacks of the doctoring so much material was subjected to under Stalin's auspices. It reads:

1. Lenin here. I've just received your special letter. Stalin isn't here and I haven't been able to show it to him yet. I think your plan is discussible. Shouldn't we just postpone its final stage until after a special session of the TsIK [Central Executive Committee] has passed it? As soon as Stalin gets back I'll show him your letter. Lenin.

2. I want to consult Stalin before replying to your question. A delegation from the Kharkov branch of the Ukrainian Central Executive Committee is going out to you today and they have told me the Kiev Rada [Central Government] is on its last legs. Lenin.

3. Stalin has just arrived and we are going to discuss the matter and give you our joint reply. Lenin.

Tell Trotsky we request a break in the talks and his return to [Petrograd]. Lenin.[84]

This was first published in 1929 in the journal *Proletarskaya revolyutsiya*, after Trotsky's deportation from the USSR.

The official chronicle of Lenin's life shows that Lenin discussed the issue with Stalin between 10.50 p.m. and 11.30 p.m. on 3 January 1918.[85] It seems surprising, though not inconceivable, that Lenin should find it impossible to reply to Trotsky until he had consulted Stalin. On 11 January Kühlmann asked Trotsky: 'What means of expression would a newly emerged national unit have for making known in practice its wish for independence, and in particular for secession.?'[86] Trotsky replied that the question of the future of the self-determining provinces. i.e. Ukraine, Poland, Lithuania and Kurland, would be decided in conditions of complete political freedom and the absence of any kind of outside pressure. But 'elections can

take place only after the withdrawal of foreign troops and the repatriation of refugees and exiles'.[87] It is possible that Trotsky had asked
for Lenin's view on this issue, and that Lenin in turn had wanted to
discuss it with Stalin, as Commissar for Nationalities.

The authenticity of the document, however, is flawed on the
grounds that when Trotsky was finally anathematized and 1937–38
came, the Soviet Union witnessed not only its 'night of the long
knives', but also a time when Stalin's henchmen put their hands to
falsifying the past. Among them were some well-known figures.
Whether willingly or not, on 7 May 1938 Yelena Stasova and Vladimir
Sorin, both secretaries of the Central Committee at the time of Brest-
Litovsk, drew attention to the need to 'elaborate more precisely' the
Central Committee's minutes on Brest-Litovsk and to correct 'the
incorrect light they throw on Stalin's rôle in this matter'. Stalin evi-
dently approved of this initiative and circulated the letter to Molotov,
Voroshilov, Zhdanov, Kaganovich and Andreev for their comments.

Among other things, the Stasova–Sorin letter recalled that Central
Committee sessions of 1917 and 1918 had not been recorded
verbatim:

> Rough notes were kept by three members, Stasova, Sverdlov and Ioffe,
> who themselves took part in discussion and were therefore unable to
> keep a detailed and substantive account. The words inserted by the
> secretaries in Lenin's speech of 23 February [1918], 'Stalin is wrong
> when he says we cannot sign', and the phrase attributed to Comrade
> Stalin at the same session, 'We might not sign, but begin peace negoti-
> ations', both represent a misunderstanding and are in plain contradic-
> tion to all the speeches Comrade Stalin made on the Brest-Litovsk
> peace.[88] The minutes of the meeting of 23 February are in the hand
> of Ioffe, who was at the time a rabid Trotskyist who fought tooth and
> nail against signing a peace accord and was of course not concerned to
> ensure maximum accuracy and thoroughness in writing down the
> speeches of his opponents, Lenin and Stalin.

Sorin and Stasova then offered to make the necessary corrections
in any new editions of Lenin's works on this subject.[89] It is not hard
to imagine the nature of such corrections.

In reality, during the Brest-Litovsk talks Stalin took a passive, centrist position, waiting to see how things would turn out. After he
became Lenin's successor it was important for him to reshape the past

in order to show himself as a true Leninist, while Trotsky's line must
be shown as treacherous. This despite the fact that at the Seventh
Party Congress on 8 March 1918, Lenin himself had said:

> I must touch on Comrade Trotsky's position. There are two sides to
> his activity: when he began the talks at Brest, he exploited them brilli-
> antly for agitational purposes and we were all in agreement with him.
> He has cited a conversation he and I had, but I want to add that we
> had agreed to hold out until the German ultimatum, and give in after
> the ultimatum ... Trotsky's tactics, as long as they were aimed at
> procrastination, were correct; they became incorrect when it was
> announced that the state of war was terminated and the peace treaty
> was not signed.[90]

Stalin had not even been present at that congress, and could thus
have had no influence on the outcome of the debate as to the rightness
or otherwise of the decision to sign the Treaty. In 1938, though, it
would have been a simple matter for him to produce a fake telegraph
tape in order to alter the historical record, in order to enhance his
own image and to continue the work of dismantling and destroying
Trotsky's.

Before the second round of talks began on 30 January 1918, Trotsky
was well aware that the Soviet government was ever more deeply
divided over the question of war and peace. On 8 January a meeting
of Bolshevik leaders and a number of delegates from the Third All-
Russian Congress of Soviets had been aroused to fierce debate by
Lenin's ideas on the peace talks. Voting had resulted in fifteen for
Lenin's position, a separate peace which met Germany's territorial
demands; thirty-two for 'revolutionary war'; and sixteen for Trotsky's
line of 'neither peace nor war'. The next day the Central Committee
had debated the issue and voted two for 'revolutionary war', eleven
against, and one abstention. Twelve were for prolonging the peace
talks, with one against. Nine favoured Trotsky's line, with an equal
number opposed.

Trotsky was as committed as ever to his idea of permanent revolution. On 13 January a combined session of the Bolshevik Central
Committee and the Left SRs in the government took place at which
a majority voted in favour of Trotsky's formula, which was then proposed at the Third Congress of Soviets. It was a formula derived

entirely from a 'revolutionary' assessment of the world situation, but revolution in Europe at that moment was less likely than it appeared to Trotsky. He told the delegates at the Third Congress of Soviets:

A genuinely democratic and universal peace is only possible when the victorious world revolution erupts. We believe in it ... We are going late tonight to Brest-Litovsk in far better conditions than when we left there. We have obtained the opportunity to tell Kühlmann that his militaristic quarantine, by which he was hoping to protect the land-owners of Kurland from the contagion of revolution, is ineffectual, as has been shown by [the revolutionary events in] Vienna and Budapest. Nor shall we meet there the representatives of the [Ukrainian govern-ment], as the Ukrainian Central Executive Committee of Soviets has recognized the Council of People's Deputies as the only body empowered to negotiate for peace ... They cannot threaten us with an offensive, as they cannot be sure the German soldiers will take part in one. We shall go on demobilizing our army without hesitation, for we are continuing to form the socialist Red Guards.

He ended his speech in characteristic manner:

And if German imperialism attempts to crucify us on the wheel of its military machine, then ... we shall appeal to our elder brothers in the West and say: 'Do you hear?' And the international proletariat will respond – we firmly believe this – 'We hear!'[91]

As if ideologically hypnotized, Trotsky had been pushed into an extreme leftist position by his faith. Despite having lived so long in Western Europe, and having persistently criticized the social demo-crats for their indecision and their flirtation with reformism, after the victory of October his belief in the inevitability of revolution in Europe was reignited with renewed force. And it was this revolution, he believed, that would fatally weaken the Central Powers.

In his writings, Trotsky maintained that at the joint Bolshevik–SR meeting on 25 January it was his view that had prevailed, but no documentary record of that meeting has been found.

On his return to Brest-Litovsk, Trotsky wrote to Lenin: 'We declare we end the war but do not sign a peace. They will be unable to make an offensive against us. If they attack us, our position will be no worse than now ... We must have your decision. We can still

drag on negotiations for one or two or three or four days. Afterwards
they must be broken off.'[92]

Still believing in the imminence of a European revolution, Trotsky
would not accept the counsel of his military advisers, Admiral V.
Altfater, General A. Samoilo and Captain V. Lipsky, nor the possibility
of a new German offensive. Even after Count Czernin, the head of
the Austro-Hungarian delegation, had come to him secretly at his
quarters and warned him that the Germans were preparing an offensive, urging him, 'They will advance! Don't fool yourself!', he would
not alter his position. Whether this was due to an exaggerated faith
in his own judgement, or to his doubt that the Germans were capable
of renewed fighting, or a desire to shock the world, or an attempt to
provoke a revolutionary mood in Europe, or simply a mental lapse,
it is impossible to state with assurance. One thing is certain, however,
and that is that the Brest-Litovsk epic revealed Trotsky's highly original approach to a fraught situation. It also revealed his self-confidence.
Zinoviev remarked on this when he wrote: 'Trotsky sometimes creates
the kind of political platform on which only one man can stand,
Comrade Trotsky himself, for on that platform there is literally no
room even for those who think like him.'[93] Trotsky not only loved
the revolution, he loved to be at its centre.

On 10 February 1918 General Hoffmann instructed his aides to
hang a map on the wall showing which Soviet territories the Central
Powers proposed to annex. Trotsky was faced with a dramatic choice.
The Germans had made it plain they would countenance no more
procrastination in the talks and would 'act in accordance with their
national interests'. On that memorable last day of Trotsky's presence
at the talks, he issued a concluding statement full of revolutionary
conviction and passion. Departing from his usual custom of speaking
without notes, he stuck to his prepared text:

> We are removing our armies and our people from the war. Our peasant
> soldiers must return to their land to cultivate in peace the fields which
> the revolution has taken from the landlord and given to the peasants.
> Our workmen soldiers must return to the workshops and produce, not
> for destruction but for creation. They must, together with the peasants,
> create a socialist state.
>
> We are going out of the war. We inform all peoples and their
> governments of this fact. We are giving the order for a general demobil-

ization of all our armies opposed at present to the troops of Germany, Austria-Hungary, Turkey and Bulgaria. We are waiting in the strong belief that other peoples will soon follow our example.[94]

A deafening silence fell on the delegates, broken only by General Hoffmann's exclamation, '*Unerhört!*' ('Unheard of!'). Trotsky's terms were indeed unprecedented: the war would cease and the army be demobilized, yet the peace treaty remained unsigned. In calm response, Trotsky stated: 'We have exercised our authority and are returning to Petrograd. Here is the text of the official declaration of the delegation of the RSFSR on the cessation of war.' The document he laid on the table read:

> In the name of the Council of People's Commissars, the government of the Russian Federal Republic informs the governments and peoples united in war against us, the Allied and neutral countries, that, in refusing to sign a peace of annexation, Russia declares, on its side, the state of war with Germany, Austria-Hungary, Turkey and Bulgaria as ended. The Russian troops are receiving at the same time an order for a general demobilization on all lines of the front.[95]

As the delegates started leaving the former officers' mess where the talks had taken place, the head of the German delegation, Kühlmann, stated in a loud, threatening voice that in view of what had happened, military action would be resumed. Without turning his head, Trotsky retorted, 'Empty threats!'

After he returned to Petrograd, Trotsky was deeply convinced that he had both secured Russia's exit from the war and dramatically put imperialism to shame. Despite the harsher terms now proposed, with Turkey claiming a number of Transcaucasian provinces into the bargain, he seemed unable to accept that his position was based on purely moral grounds and took no account of the cynicism of politics. Intoxicated by his 'success' at Brest-Litovsk, on 16 February he said in a speech at the Petrograd Soviet:

> Let Kühlmann go back to Germany and show his workers his treaty and explain to them why our signature is not on it. I regard an advance by German troops against us as extremely unlikely, and if you reckon it in percentages, then it would be ninety against and ten for ... To send German troops to Russia now, when Russia has publicly declared that it has left the state of war, would unquestionably mean provoking

a mighty revolutionary protest by the German workers . . . The step
we have taken in relation to the security of our country is the best one
to take at this moment.[96]

Deep disappointment was swift in coming. On 18 February, only
two days after Trotsky's euphoric speech, Austro-German troops
began an advance along their entire front without encountering any
resistance. A somewhat shaken Trotsky sent an urgent note to the
German government:

> Today, 17 February, we have heard . . . from General Samoilo . . . that
> on 18 February at twelve noon a state of war will be resumed between
> Germany and Russia. The government of the Russian Republic assumes
> that the telegram we have received did not originate from the people
> whose signature appears on it, but is a provocation . . . We request
> clarification of this misunderstanding be given on the radio.[97]

There was, however, no misunderstanding, and German boots were
soon tramping through the streets of Dvinsk, Minsk, Pskov and dozens
of other Russian towns and villages. Trotsky's self-confident, revolutionary and open diplomacy, and his boastful '90 per cent' assurance
that the Germans would not advance, had been exposed as costly
posturing.

In the evening of 18 February, after a fierce debate with the Left
Communists, the Central Committee by seven votes to five, with one
abstention, supported Lenin's decision to sign the 'indecent, predatory' treaty. Next day, 19 February, Trotsky prepared the text of a
cable to the German government which both he and Lenin signed.
It stated: 'The Council of People's Commissars finds itself compelled,
in the present circumstances, to declare its agreement to sign a treaty
on the terms proposed . . . at Brest-Litovsk. The Council of People's
Commissars declares that a reply to the precise terms of peace proposed by the German government will be given without delay.'[98] Simultaneously, Trotsky carried out Lenin's instruction to write an appeal
from the Sovnarkom, to be signed by Lenin, entitled 'The Socialist
Fatherland is in Danger', for publication in *Izvestiya* on 22 February.
  Trotsky later recalled that the draft of the appeal had been discussed
with the Left SRs, who were offended by its title. Lenin, on the other
hand, thought it excellent: 'It shows at once that our attitude to the

defence of the fatherland has shifted 180 degrees. That's just what's needed.'

One of the final points in the draft called for the execution on the spot of anyone who gave assistance to the enemy. The Left SR Shteinberg, who had inexplicably been swept into the revolution and even into the Sovnarkom as People's Commissar for Justice, objected to this as 'contrary to the spirit of the uprising'. 'On the contrary!' Lenin exclaimed, altering the stress on his words to add irony, 'this is precisely the real revolutionary spirit. You surely don't think we're going to come out of this as victors if we don't use the most severe revolutionary terror?'⁹⁹

The Bolshevik leadership was acting in two directions: first, to sign a just peace as quickly as possible, and secondly to form units of the Red Army and partisan detachments to repel the forces of intervention. On 21 February, when the German ultimatum was received, it became clear that the conditions on offer were even more onerous. Berlin postponed the deadline for forty-eight hours. The Central Committee met on 23 February. Lenin's proposal to accept the new terms immediately was supported by seven, with four against and four abstentions. The vote must have been influenced to some extent by his threat to resign as Chairman if his resolution was not passed. Still, he won his majority only because Trotsky and his supporters abstained.

The same day the full government, the All-Russian Executive Committee, met and debated until the next morning. Here Lenin succeeded in getting a majority of 126 to 85, with 26 abstentions. He and Trotsky at once cabled Berlin their acceptance of the conditions and announced that a new Soviet delegation would be on its way to Brest-Litovsk. The new team was composed of G. Sokolnikov as its chief, G. Petrovsky, G. Chicherin and L. Karakhan, with A. Ioffe, V. Altfater and V. Lipsky as consultants. It had proved difficult to find delegates, as no one wanted the 'honour' of signing the devastating, if unavoidable, treaty. The delegation left on the morning of 24 February. The railway had already been destroyed in places and part of the journey had to be covered by hand-cart or even on foot. Sokolnikov refused to enter any further discussion of the terms, and signed the treaty on 3 March, declaring that the whole world would see it as an act of imperialistic violence.

Whatever he would say later about this important episode of his life, Trotsky's position was undoubtedly more damaging than Lenin's had been, although both of them would be vindicated by the end of 1918, when the Habsburg and Hohenzollern dynasties collapsed and the Brest-Litovsk Treaty was annulled. Lenin had in effect foreseen that the Treaty would not last long, and he was right. Trotsky later acknowledged Lenin's foresight in general terms, but still maintained that his own position had not been altogether wrong.

Trotsky's position on Brest-Litovsk was best expressed in his speech to the extraordinary 'secret' congress of the Party that took place on 6–8 March 1918 with forty voting delegates, and that finally supported Lenin's line only after he had spoken no fewer than eighteen times. Trotsky spoke for an hour on 7 March, and made a statement on the following day. His speech was extremely frank and consistent in revealing his mistakes and partiality, as well as his intentions and judgements. Describing the general situation in the country, he declared: 'However clever we are, whatever tactics we invent, we can only be saved in the full sense of the word by a European revolution.' Of his reasons for abstaining at the Central Committee on 23 February, he stated that 'on the question of whether there are more chances on that side or this, I think there are not more on the side Comrade Lenin is on.' He then tried in effect to show that he had carried out the Party's orders. 'Everyone, including Comrade Lenin, told us: "Go and tell the Germans to make their formulations clear, condemn them, and at the first opportunity break off the talks and come back." We all saw this as the essence of the negotiations ... there was only one voice in the Central Committee calling for an immediate signing of the peace, and that was Zinoviev's ... he said that by procrastinating we would made the terms of peace worse, so we should sign at once.' Trotsky repeated that his formula, 'neither war nor peace', had been correct: 'If I were made to repeat the talks with the Germans on 10 February, I would repeat what I have done.'

He went on: 'We are retreating and rearming ourselves, as far as it is within our strength to do so. We are carrying out the scenario envisaged by Comrade Lenin; we shall withdraw towards Oryol, evacuate Petrograd and Moscow. I ought to tell you that Comrade Lenin has said that the Germans want to sign the peace in Petrograd. A few days ago we were thinking along those lines ... The capture

of Petrograd is a real threat, and for us it would be a terrible blow
... Everything depends on the speed at which a revolution in Europe
is provoked and developed.' He stressed that the decision on this
question in the Central Committee had depended on his vote, 'because
some comrades shared my position. I abstained and in that way showed
that I was not going to take upon myself the responsibility for a future
split in the Party. I would regard it as more sensible to withdraw than
to sign a peace that would have created a fictitious breathing-space,
but I cannot take responsibility for leadership of the Party in such
circumstances.'

What did he mean by taking 'responsibility for leadership of the
Party'? Was he implying the possibility of his personally heading the
Party? Lenin, after all, had declared that he would leave the government if he were in a minority on peace. Or did Trotsky have collective
leadership in mind? It is impossible to answer this question unequivocally, but it is clear that had Lenin resigned, Trotsky would have been
the chief candidate to succeed him. In the circumstances, Trotsky
behaved wisely in abstaining while occupying a different position from
Lenin's, as did his supporters Ioffe, Dzerzhinsky and Krestinsky, thus
allowing Lenin to obtain a majority. Trotsky also showed far-
sightedness in taking a step that would prevent a split, even if meant
letting through the policy of 'peace at any price'.

Instead, Trotsky did his best to preserve his dignity and his revolutionary honour. When the Seventh Party Congress finally approved
Lenin's proposal, Trotsky made a brief statement: 'The Party Congress, being the highest institution of the Party, has indirectly rejected
the policy I and others pursued as members of our delegation at
Brest-Litovsk ... Whether the Party Congress wanted this or not,
its last vote has accomplished just that, and I therefore resign from
whatever responsible posts our Party may have placed upon me.'[100]
He had already resigned as Foreign Commissar on 22 February.

Judging by his speeches of the period and what he wrote later, in
February–March 1918 Trotsky genuinely believed that the 'indecent
peace with Germany' was not a moral defeat for the revolution so
much as an act of capitulation. The Party, he felt, had crossed a line
beyond which the chances for the survival of the revolution had been
sharply diminished. In this, he was closer in spirit to the Left Communists, especially once the Germans had intensified their demands.

There was a moment when he felt the complete defeat of the revolution was a real possibility. As he said at the Seventh Party Congress:

> we are retreating not just topographically, but also politically . . . If we allow this retreat in the name of an open-ended breathing-space to develop, then . . . the proletariat of Russia will be in no condition to preserve class power in its own hands . . . The present breathing-space can be reckoned to last no more than two or three months at best, and most likely only weeks and days. In this time the question will be made clear of whether events are going to come to our assistance, or we will declare that we appeared too soon and are going into retirement, going back into the underground . . . But I think that, if it comes to leaving, we should do it like a revolutionary party, fighting to the last drop of blood for every position.[101]

Having miscalculated Germany's intentions and power, Trotsky was turned in one day from the hero of the talks into a historical failure. This would become a dominant theme in all subsequent Soviet writing, most notoriously in Stalin's *History of the Communist Party of the Soviet Union: Short Course*: 'Despite the fact that in the name of the Central Committee Lenin and Stalin insisted on signing the peace, Trotsky as chairman of the Soviet delegation treacherously disregarded the direct orders of the Bolshevik Party . . . It was monstrous. The German imperialists could not have asked for more from this traitor to the interests of the land of the Soviets.'[102] But history has a way of putting things in their proper place. Trotsky's miscalculation was a matter of timing. The revolutionary rise did indeed come in Europe, after all. A revolution in Germany in November 1918 disposed of the Hohenzollern dynasty and caused the annulment of the Brest-Litovsk Treaty. Trotsky's mistake had been to expect the revolution to follow a programme, rather than to erupt spontaneously. He had shown strength of will in the name of the revolution to overcome his own ego, as he said at the Seventh Congress: 'We, who abstained, demonstrated an act of great self-restraint in sacrificing our egos for the sake of Party unity . . . You have to tell the other side that the path they have taken has a real chance of success. But it is a dangerous path that could lead to the saving of lives, while depriving them of meaning.'[103]

At Brest-Litovsk Trotsky had wanted too much. He had wanted to get Russia out of the war, to raise the German working class and preserve the prestige of revolutionary Russia. It was his misfortune, rather than his fault, that these aims could not be accomplished all at once. He had shown that a revolutionary cannot be a mere executive. Above all, he had been terrified at the thought that the revolutionary flame in Russia would be stamped out by the German jackboot. For him, the Russian revolution was the great prologue to the world conflagration which he spent his life advocating. He was that rare individual who can be sustained by a single idea until his dying breath. For that particular idea to be realized, however, it needed violence, violence and still more violence.

On the Bloody Divide

All revolutions are bloody. The October revolution was bloodless, but it was only the beginning. The transfer of power in Moscow, for instance, was quite different. Political upheavals often provoke civil wars, and class hatred draws a bloody divide between compatriots. The Russian intelligentsia was especially afraid of civil war and was desperate to avoid it. Several years before 1917, in his book *Free Russia*, Merezhkovsky wrote: 'The decisive moment arrives in every revolution when someone has to shoot someone else and to do so with a light heart, the way a hunter will shoot a partridge ... The question of violence, metaphysical, moral, personal, social, arises in every revolution.' Discussing the fate of Russia's revolutions – that of 1905 which had just passed and, as he sensed, the coming one – he predicted: 'Who knows, maybe the grandeur of Russia's emancipation resides in the fact that it has never succeeded, just as the excessive rarely succeeds; but the excessive of today may be tomorrow's norm in all things.'[104] Merezhkovsky was concerned about the premature nature of the coming revolution. Was this the irrational fear of the intellectual before a social cataclysm, or a gloomy prediction? He was not alone in fearing the approaching upheavals, bringing with them, in his words, 'state-revolutionary murder'.

Even Plekhanov feared the spectre of violence that lurked behind the revolution. This was one of his reasons for rejecting outright the October coup. As a Marxist, he believed that socialist revolution would be justified in Russia only when the proletariat made up the majority of the population, thus effectively postponing it to the distant future. Not long before he died, tormented by the fact that he was being denigrated as a 'bourgeois degenerate' and 'counter-revolutionary' in many Petrograd newspapers, he resolved to remain true to his beliefs and to state plainly his views on what had transpired. In an 'Open Letter to the Petrograd Workers' he asserted: 'Having seized political power prematurely, the Russian proletariat will not accomplish the social revolution, but will only provoke a civil war which in the end will force the proletariat to retreat far back from the positions conquered in February and March of [1917].' Plekhanov had lived for many years in Western Europe as a typical social democrat, and was thus utterly incapable of accepting or reconciling himself to the course of events. 'Their consequences,' he went on, 'are already extremely unfortunate. They will be incomparably more unfortunate, if the conscious elements of the working class do not speak out loud and clear against the seizure of power by one class or, still worse, one party. Power should rest on a coalition of all the vital forces of the country, that is, on all those classes and elements that do not want to restore the old order ... The conscious elements of our proletariat must protect it from the huge misfortune that can befall it.'[105]

Among the misfortunes threatening Russia, Plekhanov, like Martov and other leading Mensheviks, regarded civil war as one of the worst. Their attitude to civil war was what divided the Bolsheviks and their allies from the Menshevik groups which above all valued democracy, even if it was of a manifestly bourgeois kind. Lenin's view, that civil wars 'represent a natural and in certain circumstances inevitable continuation, development and intensification of class struggle',[106] was fully shared by Trotsky, who did not expect the old owners and masters to give way easily. Indeed, Lenin and Trotsky were almost invariably linked as the main target of anti-Bolshevik criticism. For example, in an article entitled 'For the Workers' Attention', Maxim Gorky wrote: 'Vladimir Lenin is establishing the socialist order in Russia the Nechaev way, or "across the swamp at full steam ahead". Having compelled the proletariat to agree to the abolition of freedom of the press, Lenin and his stooges have thus made it legitimate for the enemies of democracy to shut people's mouths by threatening anyone who does not agree with the despotism of Lenin and Trotsky with starvation and violence.'[107]

In Russia the civil war started in October 1917, although it did not gather real momentum until the summer of 1918, and was virtually over by the beginning of 1921. Lenin might claim that it was provoked by international imperialism, but the generals who organized the White movement were not under the orders of foreign capitalists. They acted independently. Writing of the period from 24 October to 1 November (Old Style) 1917, Kerensky recalled: 'In fact, the days of our campaign on Petrograd were the days when the civil war flared up and overran the whole country and the front. The heroic stand of the officer cadets in Petersburg on the twenty-ninth, the street battles in Moscow, Saratov, Kharkov and elsewhere, the fighting between those true to the [February] revolution and the rebellious units at the front – all this showed that we were far from being alone.'[108]

After the Seventh Party Congress in March 1918, Trotsky was without a job until Lenin raised the question of who should run the military administration. Who was capable of creating a new military organization that would be able to resist the enemy's regular army? Who could breathe life into the old army? The German offensive of the previous month had shown that the triumvirate governing the Commissariat for Military Affairs – N. Krylenko, N. Podvoisky and P. Dybenko – were not up to handling the difficult task of creating a regular Red Army. Furthermore, they held leftist views on military organization which Lenin did not approve, although he was not prepared to put a military expert of the old school in charge either, as it would have been unacceptable to both the army and the people. After long deliberation and consultation with Sverdlov, Lenin chose Trotsky, a man who was as remote from the problems of military organization, tactics and strategy, as it was possible to be.

We shall deal in a later chapter with Lenin's reasons for choosing Trotsky. For the moment, suffice it to say that on 14 March 1918, the day he resigned as Foreign Commissar, Trotsky replaced Krylenko as Commissar for Military Affairs, the order appointing him being signed by Lenin, as Chairman of Sovnarkom, Karelin, as Commissar for State Property, and Stalin, as Commissar for Nationalities.

Trotsky's change of appointment coincided with the transfer of the Soviet government to Moscow because of the threat posed to

Petrograd by renewed German military activity in the Baltic. He arrived in the new capital a week after Lenin, and on his first evening there he held a meeting of the military collegium of the Commissariat at which he attempted to define the chief guidelines of military construction. Next day he issued his first order, requesting the army's accommodation department urgently to refurbish the former Alexander Military School for use as the Commissariat for War.[109]

The revolution, however, was more than plans, ideas and plots. It was also boundlessly chaotic, a time of arbitrary violence, licensed aggression and unwarranted demands from the masses. The Bolshevik leaders soon became aware of this, as the Central Committee began to receive a flood of complaints about 'requisitions', 'expropriations', unsanctioned 'revolutionary punishment'. Often these actions took the form of grabbing for oneself. For instance, in May 1918 Trotsky received a telegram from a commissar called Pozern to the effect that 'the second Petrograd conference of the Red Army voted for a resolution on the need to fix their wages at 300 roubles'. Realizing that to concede to such a demand would be to open the floodgates, Trotsky replied: 'I refuse to take responsibility for your breaking of Soviet government decrees.' On the reverse of the message he wrote a further explanation to be given to the troops: 'The wages of the Red Army are not fixed by the Petrograd Red Army men but by the Soviets of Workers', Peasants' and Red Army Deputies of the whole of Russia ... Wages have been fixed at 150 roubles. I regard Red Army men who make demands to raise pay at a difficult time for the republic as bad soldiers of the revolution.'[110]

Unbridled violence would soon become the order of the day in the Russian civil war. As a rule prisoners were not taken. Kolchak's troops would raise injured Red Army men on their bayonets, and the savagery practised by the Reds was no less widespread or cruel. Trotsky issued orders to shoot Red Army men found guilty of cowardice, or who ran from the field of battle or were caught looting. Top of his list for execution were commanders and commissars who abandoned their positions. The front would be ravaged by typhus. Both Reds and Whites would execute hostages. Life would become cheap. Blind class appeal would become stronger than human sympathy, pity, wisdom or good judgement. Russia would be drenched in her own blood.

Trotsky formulated his political views on the eve of the civil war most graphically in a report to the Moscow City Bolshevik Party Conference in the spring of 1918, and in two speeches at workers' meetings on 'Our Friends and Our Enemies' and 'On the Soviet Government's Domestic Tasks'. He included these pieces in a separate section of volume seventeen of his collected works under the title 'The Basic Tasks of the Soviet Regime in the Spring of 1918'. It was a period he described as 'an internal hitch', when the October revolution was being seen by some 'as either an adventure or a mistake'. He justified the 'hitch' as the heritage of tsarism, the crimes of the autocratic system, the mistakes committed by Milyukov and Kerensky. 'The tsarist bureaucrats and diplomats were even guilty of the Brest-Litovsk Treaty because it was they who had got us into the appalling war, wasting the people's property, robbing the people whom they kept in ignorance and slavery ... This treaty is a tsarist promissory note, a promissory note of Kerensky and Co. It is a cruel crime that has burdened the working class with the huge responsibility for the sins of the international imperialists and their servants.'[111]

Trotsky outlined his views on power thus: 'In the political and directly militant sense, the October revolution took place with unexpected and incomparable success.'[112] He declared that there could be no reconciliation between the classes: 'either the dictatorship of capital and the landowners, or the dictatorship of the working class and the poorest peasantry', while the Constituent Assembly would have been 'a great conciliation chamber, a great compromising institution of the Russian revolution'.[113] Further, he says of the Constituent Assembly that it was good only for 'a general roll-call', showing who was for whom. As for 'revolutionary creative work, it was of no use. We are not about to share power with anyone. If we were to stop halfway,' he went on, 'then it wouldn't be a revolution, it would be an abortion, if you'll excuse the expression. A false historical delivery.'[114] Trotsky did not want an abortion of democracy, but a successful birth of the Bolshevik dictatorship.

The Bolsheviks had no room in their concept of power for any other parties, including those, like the Mensheviks and Socialist Revolutionaries, who had swum with them in the revolutionary stream for decades. Single-mindedness, a monopoly on revolutionary truth and the conviction that no one else could be right, united the Bolsheviks, and with them, Trotsky. As early as April 1918 he voiced a thesis that is painfully similar to the ominous formula advanced by Stalin in the 1930s: 'The further and the more the revolutionary movement develops, here and abroad, the more tightly the bourgeoisie of all lands will close ranks.'[115] Stalin would reshape the thesis as the sharpening of the class war, but in one country.

In the spring of 1918 Trotsky declared: 'Yes, we are weak, and that is our greatest historical crime, because one cannot be weak in history. The weak become the prey of the strong.'[116] In the preface to his 1918 pamphlet 'The October Revolution', he stressed: 'The facts alone of the way the October revolution took place are a ruthless contradiction of seminarist metaphysics. You can repeat as often as you like that it would have been better to obtain power for the working class by means of the universal franchise ... but history is not written according to a recipe in a cookbook, even if the book is in kitchen Latin ... The proletariat gets power by the right of revolutionary force. And if some confused Marxist theorist starts getting under their feet, then the working class will step over that theorist, as over much else.'[117]

A significant aspect of Trotsky's speeches in the spring of 1918 concerned the labour organization of society, underlining the need for revolutionary order and discipline. He published his speech to a conference of the Moscow City Party Organization under the title 'Labour, Discipline and Order will Save the Soviet Republic'. The disorder of society during the revolution he explained as the result of the upsurge of freedom in the downtrodden individuals which 'like the roach, lived and died the way a swarm of locusts lives and dies'. Yesterday, such an individual was 'a man of the masses, he was nothing, a slave for the tsar, the gentry, the bureaucracy, a component in the factory-owner's machine', and then suddenly he felt himself to be a person. 'That is what caused the flood of disorganizing impulses, the individualistic, anarchistic, destructive tendencies which we have observed especially among broad sections of the declassed elements, in the old army, and also among certain sections of the working class.'[118]

Trotsky made his own recommendations as to how the regime should deal with the chaos, sabotage, anarchy, Communist arrogance and lack of competence. Above all he advised the severe limitation of 'collegial' principles. During the period of consolidation, collegia, or boards, were being formed at every level of the state and economic hierarchy. Soon, however, the consequences of unbridled democracy and the absence of personal responsibility were felt throughout society. On 29 April 1918, the VTsIK agreed to strengthen the principle of one-man management, centralization and an active policy of employing bourgeois experts. A month earlier, the Central Committee, with Trotsky present, had discussed 'the Central Committee's general policy'. It was established that 'the period of the conquest of power is over, basic construction is under way. It is essential to bring knowledgeable, experienced and businesslike people into the work. Sabotage by intellectual groups has been broken, the engineers are coming over to us, we must make use of them.'[119]

In effect, it was this policy that Trotsky propagated in his speeches. Some Left SRs, and many leading Bolsheviks also, feared that this step might lead to the downgrading of democracy and the growth of bureaucracy. Like Lenin, Trotsky argued for the introduction of iron discipline and the harshest of measures against overt and covert enemies. He stated that 'the rural bourgeoisie will be the chief enemy of the working class, it wants to starve the Soviet revolution out . . . We warn the kulaks that as far as they are concerned we shall show no mercy.'[120]

Trotsky believed that enlightenment changed people. 'There are many high and beautiful spiritual values: there is science and art, and they are not accessible to the working people, because the workers or peasants are forced to live like convicts, shackled to their wheelbarrows. People with a spiritual cast of mind must be prepared to say to themselves, "Yes, perhaps I shall perish in the struggle that is now going on. But what is the enslaved life without enlightenment and under the heel of the oppressors, when compared to the glorious death of a fighter?"'[121] Like a true radical, Trotsky advocated the path of sacrifice, a path that would lead in time to the socialism of sacrifice.

Naturally, as Commissar for War, Trotsky devoted much thought and writing to questions of military construction. 'The question of forming an army,' he wrote, 'is for us a question of life and death.' Three or four years later, when preparing his earlier articles for publication in his collected works, he seems to have recalled something V.V. Shulgin had written about military force during turning-points in history. Shulgin was an exiled politician, a former member of the State Duma and one of the two emissaries from the Provisional Government-to-be to accept Nicholas II's abdication. In a series of articles, later collected and published as *Dni* (The Days), he wrote of the revolution, which he called 'the Devil's plaything': 'A lost war always threatens [to bring] revolution . . . But revolution is immeasurably worse than a lost war. Therefore, the guards must be kept for the sole and honourable task of fighting against the revolution.'[122] Trotsky determined that first the Red Guards and then the Red Army were needed to fight counter-revolution and the intervention. The revolution would not survive without force.

Trotsky was both a pragmatist and a dreamer. He was capable of withdrawing from the prosaic tasks of everyday life and floating on high, gazing far into the 'Communist distance'. He could fire others with a belief that what he was saying was true. When on 14 April 1918 he sketched an outline of the future for which they would have to struggle and suffer and sacrifice, he held his audience in thrall. His words cast the seeds of great hopes:

> We shall build a unified fraternal state on the land which nature has given us. We shall plough that land and work it on a collective basis, we shall turn it into a flowering garden, where our children will live, and our grandchildren and great-grandchildren, as if they were in paradise. People used to believe in the legends about paradise; they were dreams of people in ignorance and misfortune, they were the longings of oppressed people for a better life. People wanted to live more justly, more purely, and people said there must be such a paradise even in the next life, in an unknown and secret place. But we say that we, the toiling people, will build paradise here in this world, for everyone, for our children and grandchildren forever.[123]

His audience gave him the expected stormy ovation.

Trotsky was speaking of heaven on an earth that had been ruined by war and two revolutions and that was now to face another three long years of bitter civil war. Dreams of paradise would be overwhelmed by the armoured trains, the music of liberty drowned by the clash of cavalry sabres and salvos, hopes for peace would be crushed by typhus and starvation. And against the background of Russia's suffering, Trotsky would rise to the peak of his power and reputation.

3

The Ninth Wave of the Vendée

While he was in his first place of post-Soviet exile, in Turkey from the end of 1929, Trotsky planned to write a book on the Russian civil war and the formation of the Red Army. But, as he wrote to Yelena Vasilievna Krylenko, sister of the People's Commissar of Justice and wife of the Trotskyist Max Eastman, a fire at his villa destroyed a large number of his books and documents on the subject.[1] Trotsky's copy of this letter was one of many stolen from him in the 1930s by the NKVD. There is no indication in the archives of the special services as to whether the fire was an accident or was caused by the NKVD, but in any event, the book was never written.

The carnage of the civil war was defined by another Bolshevik, A.S. Bubnov, as 'a model of the escalation of the bourgeois-democratic revolution into the proletarian socialist revolution'. The civil war, he wrote in 1928, 'advanced this process'.[2] It was this 'escalation' that raised Trotsky to the summit of his power. He welcomed the war, in which he saw the chance both to eliminate all the exploiting classes in Russia and to push the workers of other countries towards the world revolution. In the autumn of 1918, when it was suggested in Moscow that boats carrying grain on the Volga should fly the Red Cross flag as a safety measure, Trotsky sent a telegram to Lenin protesting: 'I consider it impermissible to let through ships flying the flag of the Red Cross. The charlatans and fools will think the delivery of grain means there is a chance of conciliation and that the civil war is not a necessity.'[3] To the Russian Jacobins, the internecine slaughter was a necessary means to achieve their great goal.

The 'Laws' of Revolution

By early March 1918, Trotsky had become Commissar for Military (and later also Naval) Affairs. At the same time he was made Chairman of the Supreme War Council of the Republic. Why did Lenin choose Trotsky for these posts? First, Lenin recognized that organization of the military, a key factor in the survival of the revolution, would require an ability to make political judgements, as well as zeal and determination, a talent for exhortation of the masses, and the ability to bring spontaneous Bolshevik actions and the herd instinct under central control. The holder of this post also needed to be popular and to have political weight and authority in the Party. Lenin believed that Trotsky was such a man.

Lenin also came to see that it was impossible to create a battle-worthy Red Army without the help of military specialists, the generals and officers of the old army, a notion many Bolsheviks, among them some leaders, found unacceptable. Trotsky was firmly behind Lenin on this issue. Indeed, it was Trotsky who, before being appointed to his new position, had suggested the setting up of a Supreme War Council to be composed of former generals who were willing to collaborate. The Council was headed by commissars, but its main functions were carried out by these military specialists under the leadership of the former chief-of-staff of the General Staff of the tsarist army, General M.D. Bonch-Bruevich, a brother of one of Lenin's most trusted colleagues, Vladimir Bonch-Bruevich.

The opposition to the use of military specialists from a number of prominent Bolsheviks forced Lenin to make some significant changes. His opponents had resisted abolishing the elective principle for the appointment of commanders and wanted to preserve the role of the soldiers' committees, and were prepared to accept former officers only under strict control as 'consultants'. The German advance, however, soon exposed the weakness of Red Guard units which applied these principles.

Trotsky later recalled that he had resisted taking the job at first, but was persuaded when he found he could not think of anyone better:

> Was I prepared to do military work? Of course not. I had not even had the benefit of service in the Tsar's army. My army-service years I

had spent in prison, in exile, and abroad. In 1906, the court deprived me of all civil and military rights ... I did not think of myself as in any sense a strategist, and had little patience with the sort of strategist-dilettantism that flooded the party as a result of the revolution. It is true that on three occasions – in the war with Denikin, in the defence of Petrograd, and in the war with Pilsudski – I took an independent strategic position and defended it first against the high command, and again against the majority of the Central Committee.[4]

Lenin made the correct choice in appointing Trotsky. What he lacked in military knowledge and technique, he made up for in his broad political approach to questions of defence and military organization, as well as in his astonishing energy and the ability to inspire people.

Trotsky applied himself to his new post with all the vigour expected of him. He made speeches, wrote papers, gave instructions and received a stream of visitors. Recalling that period of his life, he wrote:

The Cavalry building, opposite the Poteshny Palace, before the revolution was the living quarters of the officials of the Kremlin. The entire lower floor was occupied by the commanding officer. His apartment had now been made into several smaller ones. Lenin and I took quarters across the corridor, sharing the same dining-room. The food at the Kremlin was then very bad. Instead of fresh meat, they served corned beef. The flour and the barley had sand in them. Only the red Ket caviar was plentiful, because its export had ceased. This inevitable red caviar coloured the first years of the revolution, and not for me alone ... Lenin and I met a dozen times a day in the corridor, and called on each other to talk things over ... The little cloud of the Brest-Litovsk disagreements had dispersed, leaving never a trace. Lenin was very cordial and considerate both to me and to my family. He often stopped our boys in the corridor to play with them.[5]

Trotsky saw his chief task as the 'revolutionary education' of the masses in uniform. Problems of strategy, operations and tactics, of which he knew nothing anyway, tended to be put to one side. He sought an intellectual or ideological 'flux' with which to weld the peasants, workers and lower middle class into a single revolutionary family, which would be bound not only by a sense of moral responsibility, but also by judicial means, with the threat of revolutionary punishment for not obeying an order.

On 22 April 1918, the VTsIK approved Trotsky's 'socialist military oath'. In six points it covered the meaning of military service, the duty and honour of a soldier, the obligation to study military affairs, willingness to come to the defence of the Soviet Republic at the first call, sparing neither 'one's strength nor one's life', and ended: 'If with malicious intent I renounce this my ceremonial promise, then let general scorn be my lot, and let me be punished by the stern hand of revolutionary law.'[6] Generations of Soviet soldiers swore an oath close to this, never realizing that its author was the 'despised fascist hireling, Trotsky', as he is described in Stalin's history of the Party.

Among the issues Trotsky dealt with in 1918 was that of the mass mobilization of the workers and peasants, which he regarded as an absolute necessity that was being inadequately carried out. There were far too few naturally gifted people available to convert shapeless assemblies into the revolutionary units of a regular army. What was needed were commissars, political organizers and teachers, the experience and knowledge of the old officer corps.

The First All-Russian Congress of Military Commissars met in June 1918 to hear Trotsky expound in simple terms two fundamental tasks of commissars in the army: to give the soldiers a political education, and to control the actions of the command staff. Recognizing that voluntary recruitment could not produce more than a third of the army's needs, and that too many 'useless elements – hooligans, idlers and dregs – had been let in', he argued that it was 'the responsibility of commissars to work ceaselessly to raise awareness in the depths of the army and mercilessly to root out the undesirables'. He pointed out that the commissars were 'the direct representative of the Soviet regime in the army, and defenders of the interests of the working class . . . If a commissar notices that a military leader represents a danger to the revolution, then he has the right to deal ruthlessly with the counter-revolutionary, including execution.'[7]

There were some Left SRs among the military commissars, and Trotsky described the Left SR Krivoshein, for instance, as 'a wonderful provincial commissar' in Kursk. Soon, however, the Bolshevik monopoly would be extended to every facet of state activity. Like the other leaders, Trotsky was not troubled by the fact that the commissars were 'defenders of the interests of the working class' in an army that was overwhelmingly made up of peasants.

Trotsky was the chief protagonist of the idea of using military specialists. In the summer and autumn of 1918 he published a series of articles with such titles as 'The Officer Question', 'On the Officers Deceived by Krasnov', 'NCOs to Your Posts!', 'NCOs', 'On Former Officers', 'Military Specialists and the Red Army'. It was in the last of these, written on 31 December 1918, that Trotsky expounded most fully his ideas on the use of former tsarist officers. In it he dealt with the criticism he had endured from comrades on this issue: 'When the nagging became persistent, I had to resort to pragmatism rather than logic: "So, can you give me ten divisional commanders, fifty regimental commanders, two army commanders and one front commander – today? And all of them Communists?" In reply, my "critics" would smile meekly and change the subject.'[8]

Plainly, the regime would choose a Communist commander over a non-Communist one, but, as Trotsky pointed out, the regime did not have that choice. Another criticism that required rebuttal was that officers were defecting to the enemy. 'There have been quite a few such cases,' he admitted,

> mostly of officers in important posts. But rarely do people talk about the loss of entire regiments through a [Communist] commander's lack of training, because a commander did not know how to maintain communications, had not put out pickets or field patrols, had misunderstood an order or could not read a map. If I were asked what had caused us the most damage up to now, treachery by former professional officers or the lack of training among new commanders, I would personally find it hard to give a reply . . . Cases of treason and treachery by former officers are known about in general, but unfortunately neither the general public nor even inner Party circles know enough about regular officers who honestly and consciously have given their lives for the cause of workers' and peasants' Russia. Only today a commissar told me about a captain who was in command of nothing more than a unit and who declined a higher command because he had become closely attached to his soldiers. That captain died in battle a few days ago.[9]

When confronted by a concrete case of treachery, however, Trotsky was implacable and merciless, as the case of A.M. Shchastny shows. Captain First Class Shchastny, commander of the Baltic Fleet, was arrested on 27 May 1918 on Trotsky's orders and arraigned before the Supreme Tribunal of the Republic on 20–21 June, charged with organizing a counter-revolutionary coup. Trotsky – the sole witness – brought as evidence the text of a speech that Shchastny was to have made to a naval congress: 'The whole speech from beginning to end, despite its apparent cautiousness, is indisputable documentary proof of a counter-revolutionary plot . . . It was a particular political game, a big game, aimed at seizing power. But when gentlemen admirals and generals start playing their personal political games during a revolution, they must be prepared to take the responsibility for such games when they go wrong. Admiral [sic] Shchastny's game has gone wrong.'[10] The trial was brief. Shchastny was shot on suspicion of conspiracy, but no evidence was brought, other than Trotsky's, and there were no defence witnesses. This was the first political trial in Soviet Russia at which the death sentence was imposed, and it is worth noting that it was a breach of the law in itself. The extreme nature of the revolutionary laws, while combating one evil, was capable of creating a greater evil. Trotsky was an ideal executor of such laws.

The Red Army's crushing of the Kronstadt revolt, which occurred during the Tenth Party Congress of March 1921 when the once-loyal garrison rebelled against Bolshevik policies, gave a perfect illustration of Trotsky's capability in this sphere. When he was told about the uprising, he at once dictated an address:

> To the population of Kronstadt and the rebellious forts. I order all those who have raised their hand against the socialist Fatherland to lay down their arms immediately. Recalcitrants must be disarmed and handed over to the Soviet authorities. Commissars and other representatives of the regime who have been arrested [by the insurgents] must be released at once. Only those who surrender unconditionally can count on the mercy of the Soviet Republic. I am simultaneously issuing instructions to prepare to crush the insurgency and the insurgents with an iron hand.[11]

The address was signed by Trotsky, as People's Commissar, S.S. Kamenev, as commander-in-chief of the armed forces, commander of 7th Army Tukhachevsky, and chief-of-staff Lebedev.

Years later, when his rôle in Kronstadt was mentioned in the West, Trotsky tried to justify his actions in his *Bulletin of the Opposition* and in letters to his supporters. These letters, of which there were several hundred, quickly found their way into the hands of the NKVD.

Noting that the revolution had its own laws and that it recognized only the strong, Trotsky wrote on one occasion: 'During the years of the revolution, we had frequent clashes with Cossacks, peasants, even with groups of workers (groups of Urals workers formed a volunteer regiment in Kolchak's army) . . . In various parts of the country so-called "Green" peasant detachments were formed that did not recognize either "Reds" or "Whites". The "Greens" often clashed with the "Whites" and suffered heavy losses; and of course they were given no quarter by the "Reds".'[12]

The use of terror and violence by both sides in the civil war is well illustrated by memoirs in the collection *Arkhiv russkoi revolyutsii*, published in Berlin in the 1920s. Former White officer V.Yu. Arbatov recalled: 'The head of the Cheka in Yekaterinoslav, Valyavka, used to release a dozen or so prisoners into a small, high-walled yard at night. Valyavka himself with two or three comrades would go into the middle of the yard and open fire on these utterly defenceless people. Their cries could be heard throughout the town on those quiet May nights . . . The Whites were no better; they would loot any town they entered for a whole day.'[13]

If the period from October 1917 to March 1918 was what Lenin called 'the victorious triumphal march of Bolshevism',[14] then from March, when Trotsky became War Commissar, began the long counter-revolutionary rebound. And if the 'triumphal march' was accompanied, in Lenin's words, 'less by military action than agitation',[15] then the counter-revolutionary wave was a bloody one. Every day Trotsky read reports of new uprisings, White advances, landings by intervention expeditionary forces sent by former allies of pre-Soviet Russia to stifle the revolution, the defection of entire units and garrisons. In the volume of his collected works devoted to the civil war, he called the period beginning in March 1918 'the first wave of the counter-revolution'.

There was the revolt led by Kaledin in the Don region, Dutov's campaign in the Southern Urals, Dovbor-Musnitsky's uprising in Belorussia, the German and Austro-Hungarian advance into Ukraine, the incursion by Turkish forces into the Transcaucasus, rebellions by Armenian Dashnaks and Azerbaijani Mussavatists. Little blue flags showing the locations of anti-Bolshevik forces were appearing in increasing numbers on the map hanging on the wall of Trotsky's office. He was in constant consultation with representatives from the fronts, he called in former regular officers, telephoned Lenin in his efforts to do something to alter a situation that was rapidly becoming catastrophic. He formed a commission under his own chairmanship to discuss the creation of an army air force,[16] and also concerned himself with land forces. He sent a telegram to his deputy, Ye.M. Sklyansky: 'It is essential to start producing tanks in the Urals or in other plants, using tractor parts, if possible. The presence of a certain number of tanks on the southern front would have enormous psychological significance.'[17] At a critical moment in the spring of 1919 Trotsky was prepared to take an appalling step. He cabled Moscow: 'It is necessary to find a possible way of using asphyxiating gases. We must find a responsible person to head this responsible work.'[18]

Trotsky's own responsibilities were extraordinarily wide-ranging – from setting up courses for camouflage[19] to proposals for improving the purging of Soviet institutions locally and catching deserters,[20] requisitioning a repair rail-car from the tsar's former train for one of his aides,[21] issuing orders to throw cowards out of the army,[22] and sending the following telegram to Sverdlov, with a copy to Lenin: 'I categorically insist Stalin be recalled. The Tsaritsyn front is going badly, despite superior forces.'[23] The work of Trotsky's department in those difficult days of spring and early summer 1918 bears the stamp of spontaneity and improvisation, if not simply chaos. The new regime was facing its worst moments. Only when Denikin was approaching Tula in 1919 would the situation seem worse. Meanwhile, there was the intervention of the British, French, American and Japanese forces at Murmansk, Archangel, in Turkestan, the Caucasus and Vladivostok, and the revolt of the Czech Legion.* New political formations made their appearance in the reports: in Samara there was the Committee of Members of the Constitutional Assembly, an SR government in Yekaterinburg, a Directory in Ufa, Hetman Skoropadsky, and many more. Trotsky later wrote of this period: 'Could much more be needed to overthrow the revolution? Its territory was now

---

* The Czech Legion consisted of former prisoners-of-war from the Austro-Hungarian Army who were trying to make their way home by a circuitous route eastwards through Russia. They became a significant military factor in the civil war in Siberia.

reduced to the size of the ancient principality of Muscovy. It had hardly any army; it was surrounded by enemies on all sides. After Kazan would have come the turn of Nizhni-Novgorod, from which a practically unobstructed road lay open to Moscow.'[24]

On 29 July 1918 Lenin convened an extraordinary joint meeting of the VTsIK and the Moscow City Soviet, at which he made a speech on the present position, followed by Trotsky, whose speech was given the now-familiar title 'The Socialist Fatherland is in Danger'. Lenin declared that the Soviet Republic was again embroiled in a war foisted on it by internal and external counter-revolution. Since the future of the Republic depended on the outcome of this war, the slogan 'Everything for the Front', must be the top priority. Trotsky also spoke of the seriousness of the situation, but stressed the fact that it was not hopeless, and that the energy of the revolution had not yet dried up. Many of the solutions he proposed, however, were harsh, even savage.

'Our Red Army units,' he declared, 'lack the necessary mental and fighting cohesion, as they don't have the fighting experience . . . Here in this hall we are some 2000 people or more, and the overwhelming majority of us share the same revolutionary point of view. We are not a regiment, but if they made us into a regiment right now and armed us and sent us to the front, I don't think we'd be the worst regiment in the world. Why? Is it because we are trained soldiers? No, it's because we are united by a particular idea, inspired by the firm awareness that at the front history is putting the question point-blank, and we must either win or die right there.'[25] He at once transformed this idea into a concrete proposition, that every army formation should have its own rock-hard Communist nucleus, what he called 'the heart of the regiment and the company'. The most politically conscious workers, Communists and agitators should be sent to the front from Moscow, Petrograd and other cities. 'The Petrograd Soviet,' he announced, 'has already decided to send a quarter of its staff, numbering about 200 members, to the Czechoslovak front as agitators, instructors, organizers, commanders and fighters.'

As for dissident ex-tsarist officers, 'they must be curbed with an iron bit'. All former officers who refused to collaborate should be registered and 'locked up in concentration camps'. If any officer with command rights should behave suspiciously, 'then it stands to reason the accused – there can be no argument about it, the question is open

and shut – must be shot ... There is no one in the high command
who should not have a commissar to the right and left of him, and if
a specialist is not known to us as someone dedicated to the Soviet
regime, then the commissars are duty-bound to keep a constant watch
on him, not taking their eyes off him for a single hour. And if these
commissars, standing to right and left with revolvers in their hands,
see that specialist falter and betray, then he must be shot in good
time.'[26] 'The commissar's right of the revolver,' Trotsky said, was no
more than the inevitable expression of 'the severity of the proletarian
dictatorship'.[27]

After Lenin and Trotsky had made their speeches, a resolution
drafted by Trotsky was passed, reflecting his arguments and proposals.
In these harsh times, he and Lenin were in their element.

Head of the Revolutionary War Council

When the revolution, in Trotsky's words, reached 'its lowest point',
the VTsIK issued a special decree on 2 September 1918 declaring
that the socialist Fatherland was in danger and the Soviet Republic a
military camp. The same decree created the Revolutionary War Council of the Republic, the supreme military-political organ. Sverdlov
proposed Trotsky as chairman. A few weeks earlier, Trotsky and a
group of Communist agitators had travelled to the eastern front,
where the position was close to catastrophic. Simbirsk, and then
Kazan, had fallen to the Whites. Trotsky's train could get no further
than Sviyazhsk, a large station before Kazan. Throughout the journey
from Moscow he had conferred with the other leaders, giving instructions on what military and organizational measures they must take.
During one such meeting, a Communist worker asked: 'What's to be
done with Left SR commissars, and how should we regard them in
general?' Without hesitating, Trotsky repeated what he had said on
9 July 1918 at the Fifth All-Russian Congress of Soviets: 'The party,
led by a small clique, that could be so insane as to oppose the will
and the consciousness of the overwhelming majority of workers and
peasants, killed itself off forever on 6 and 7 July. That party cannot be resurrected!' 'Does that mean we get rid of all of them?' the

excitable agitator asked. 'Leave only those who publicly condemn the [Left SR] uprising and break with the adventurists!'

At the Fifth Congress of Soviets, Trotsky had been charged by Lenin with explaining the uprising of the Left SRs: 'Should the whole party be blamed for the actions of its leaders?' Such leaders, he said, were foolish and ignorant. 'Comrade Lenin has spoken here of Spiridonova as a most honest person, a sincere person. But woe to the party whose most honest people have to resort to slander and rabble-rousing in the struggle!' By demanding a renewed war with Germany, they were trying to fool the masses. But 'the regime is now facing the most critical question, the question of war and peace. If the regime cannot answer this question, and a bunch of rogues think they can, then we have no power.'

To a hushed audience in the Bolshoi Theatre, Trotsky outlined the details of the Left SR uprising. A contingent of 2000 men, some guns and around sixty machine-guns, had seized the telegraph office and the People's Commissar for Posts, Podbelsky, held Dzerzhinsky and opened random fire on the Kremlin: 'When we saw some, fortunately only a few, of their shells fall into the precinct, we thought to ourselves, the Sovnarkom is a natural trap for the Left Socialist Revolutionaries.' Bolshevik units, he went on, were posted at the Cathedral of Christ the Saviour, on Passion Square at Pushkin's monument, on Arbat Square and in the Kremlin. Seven days later, after Podvoisky, Muralov and Vatsetis had done their work, the insurgents moved away towards Kursk Station. Units which had come from Petrograd and the western border provinces to help the insurgents were disarmed without incident. The only small skirmish took place at the Corps of Pages, where a Left SR unit was disarmed: ten Bolsheviks were killed and ten injured.[28]

Thus ended the brief alliance between the Bolsheviks and the Left SRs. Trotsky proposed, and the Congress passed, a resolution declaring that henceforth there could be no place for Left SRs in Soviets of Workers' and Peasants' Deputies.[29] Many aspects of the affair were left unexplained. For instance, on whose orders did the Left SR Blyumkin assassinate the German Ambassador Count Mirbach on 6 July 1918? Was it a decision of the Left SR Central Committee? Why was there no proper investigation? One thing is plain, and that is that the assassination gave Lenin the chance to settle the score with the

Left SRs. In a telegram to Stalin in Tsaritsyn, Lenin gave the order to start mass terror against them.

All that, however, was in the past. Now, Trotsky had to try to make a breakthrough or expect the worst and to die in the last battle. In his memoirs of this time he wrote:

> The army at Sviyazhsk was made up of detachments which had retreated from Simbirsk and Kazan, and of assisting units rushed in from all directions. Each unit lived its own distinct life, sharing in common only a readiness to retreat – so superior were the enemy in both organization and experience. Some White companies, made up exclusively of officers, performed miracles. The soil itself seemed to be infected with panic. Fresh Red detachments, arriving in vigorous mood, were immediately engulfed by the inertia of retreat. A rumour began to spread among the local peasantry that the Soviets were doomed. Priests and tradesmen lifted their heads. The revolutionary elements in the village went into hiding. Everything was crumbling; there was nothing to hold to. The situation seemed hopeless.[30]

Even before his arrival at Sviyazhsk, on 8 August Trotsky had dictated his Order No. 10:

> The struggle with the Czecho-White Guards is taking too long. Slovenliness, carelessness and faint-heartedness in our ranks are our enemies' best allies. In the War Commissar's train, where this order is being written, there is a Military Revolutionary Tribunal which has unlimited powers. Comrade Kamenshchikov, whom I have made responsible for defending the Moscow–Kazan railway line, has seen to the creation of concentration camps at Murom, Arzamas and Sviyazhsk, where shady agitators, counter-revolutionary officers, saboteurs, parasites and speculators will be locked up, except for those who will be shot at the scene of the crime or sentenced by the tribunals to other punishment.[31]

In a telegram to the Revolutionary War Council of the Eastern Front, Lenin declared: 'The entire fate of the revolution now stands on one card: a quick victory over the Czechoslovaks on the Kazan–Urals–Samara front.'[32] The Supreme War Council was sending everything it could find to the eastern front. The former tsarist generals on the Supreme War Council, who readily collaborated in repelling external enemies, participated less willingly in organizing campaigns against the internal counter-revolution. Lenin rebuked the Council for their delay and demanded the despatch of trained units.

By the time Trotsky arrived 11,500 men had been shipped there, plus nineteen field guns, 136 machine-guns, sixteen aircraft, six armoured trains and three armoured cars.[33] This was as much as the beleaguered Soviet Republic could do, but Trotsky knew well that the Red Army was facing significantly superior forces: 50,000 bayonets and sabres, up to 190 field guns and twenty armed river vessels.[34] Trotsky agreed with the advice of the specialists to shift from the unit form of organization to the old, classical arrangement of three divisions, a cavalry corps and an air squadron to each regiment. By the end of August five armies had been formed on the eastern front, numbering in all about 70,000 men, more than 250 field guns and over 1000 machine-guns.[35]

While I.I. Vatsetis was engaged in reorganizing the eastern front for a counter-offensive, a White brigade under Colonel V.O. Kappel carried out a raid on the rear of 5th Army and also attacked Sviyazhsk, from where a route to the centre of the country could be opened up. Trotsky's train was at Sviyazhsk. 'This move caught us quite off our guard,' he later recalled. 'We were afraid to disrupt the already shaky front, and so we withdrew only two or three companies. The commander of my train again mobilized everyone he could lay his hands on, both in the train and at the station, including even the cook. We had a good stock of rifles, machine-guns and hand-grenades. The train crew was made up of good fighters. The men took their posts about a [kilometre] from the train. The battle went on for about eight hours, and both sides had losses. Finally, after they had spent themselves, the enemy withdrew. Meanwhile the break in the connection with Sviyazhsk had stirred up Moscow and the whole line.'[36]

On Trotsky's orders, a field court martial sentenced every tenth deserter to death, including the regimental commander and commissar. In defending his decision to have them executed, Trotsky stressed as late as 1927 that they had been shot not as Communists, but as deserters. A special commission exonerated him. Nevertheless, throughout the civil war, and after it, rumours circulated to the effect that Trotsky had personally executed commissars and commanders.

When Trotsky managed to communicate this event to Lenin, having been cut off for some time, Lenin replied in a coded cable: 'I received your letter. If there is superiority and the soldiers are fighting, then special measures should be taken against the high command.

Shouldn't we tell them that henceforth if there is delay and failure we're going to apply the model of the French revolution and put Vatsetis on trial and even execute him, as well as the army commander at Kazan and the top commanders? I advise you to bring in many known energetic and militant people from [Petrograd] and other places on the front.'[37]

Trotsky evidently felt that Lenin's radical telegram had been provoked by his news about Kappel's breakthrough. Whether or not his actions caused in him a conflict of reason and conscience, the fact is that neither Vatsetis nor the commander of 5th Army was charged. In any case, next day Trotsky was handed a telegram from Sverdlov informing him that Lenin had been wounded in an assassination attempt, how dangerously was not yet known, that the country was calm and that Trotsky should come to Moscow at once.[38] There he found the Party leaders in a sullen mood, 'but they were absolutely unshakeable. The best expression of this determination was Sverdlov. The physicians declared that Lenin's life was not in danger, and promised an early recovery. I encouraged the Party with the prospects of success in the east, and returned at once to Sviyazhsk.'[39]

In his 'encouraging' speech to the Party on 2 September 1918, Trotsky declared:

A new front has been created alongside those which we already have – in Vladimir Ilyich's chest cavity, where even now life is struggling against death and where, as we hope, the struggle will end in victory for life. On our military fronts victory takes turns with defeat; there are many dangers, but all the comrades undoubtedly recognize that this front, the Kremlin front, is now the most worrying . . . As for the front I have just come from, I regret to say I cannot report decisive victories, but I can say with complete confidence that there are victories ahead; that our position is strong and steady; that a decisive breakthrough has taken place; that we are now insured against major surprises, and each week will strengthen us at the expense of our enemies.[40]

Trotsky remained himself: as long as there was the smallest chance, he was optimistic. And he soon fulfilled his promise of victory. On 5 September he approved an order by the front commander to commit two armies to a counter-offensive.

In Moscow meanwhile a campaign of Red Terror was unleashed in response to the attempt on Lenin's life. Hundreds of people were shot, some of them publicly. As the former assistant of a revolutionary tribunal, S. Kobyakov, recalled: '[There was] a wave of executions. During the day in Petrovsky Park, with the public there, they executed former Minister of Justice Shcheglovitov, former Minister of the Interior Khvostov, former Director of the Police Department Beletsky (he tried to escape but was caught and shot), former Minister Protopopov, Archpriest Vostorgov and dozens more.'[41]

Not long before the capture of Kazan, Trotsky under the command of F.F. Raskolnikov took part in a raid on the city involving four torpedo-boats that had come via the river system from the Baltic, and a number of armed river steamers. He experienced all the emotions a soldier feels under fire. Elements of 5th Army working together with units of 2nd Army and a river-landing force under the command of N.G. Markin liberated Kazan on 10 September, the Red Army's first big victory on the eastern front. Trotsky later explained the nature of this victory: 'Inside the units, the [commissars] acquired the importance of revolutionary leaders, or direct representatives of the dictatorship. The tribunals demonstrated to everyone that revolution, when in mortal danger, demands the highest sacrifice. Propaganda, organization, revolutionary example and repression produced the necessary change in a few weeks. A vacillating, unreliable and crumbling mass was transformed into a real army.'[42]

As soon as he heard of the capture of Kazan, Trotsky dictated Order No. 33: '10 September will enter the history of the socialist revolution as a festival. Units of 5th Army tore Kazan out of the hands of the White Guards and Czechoslovaks. It is a turning-point . . . Soldiers and sailors of 5th Army, you took Kazan. It is to your credit. Those units and individual fighters who particularly distinguished themselves will be appropriately rewarded by the workers' and peasants' government . . . In the name of the Council of People's Commissars I say thank you, comrades!'[43]

After the success on the Volga, with the liberation of Kazan, Simbirsk, Khvalynsk and other cities, Trotsky was given the task of coordinating and directing the actions of countless other fronts. He paid great attention to the deployment of cadres. More than fifteen armies were staffed by the most varied commanders, and if chiefs-of-staff were in the main former tsarist officers, the commissars were mostly Trotsky's own appointees. Practically every one of them who

survived the civil war would perish in the purges of the 1930s. Any
reference in a personal file to an association with Trotsky was fatal.

Trotsky soon established businesslike contact with front commanders, commissars and army commanders, but his nature ruled out
the likelihood of any special warmth. He was universally appreciated
for his mind, his energy and his political vigour, but it was also felt
that he liked to exhibit his intellectual superiority. He therefore lacked
close personal supporters among the senior military commanders. Perhaps this was also due in part to their awareness of a lack of military
professionalism in a chief who rarely gave a strategic or operational
order.

He was ubiquitous, his train constantly travelling from one front
to another; he worked hard to secure supplies for the troops, and his
personal involvement in the use of military commissars at the front
brought positive results. The army chiefs, moreover, saw in him the
'second man' of the Soviet Republic, a major political and state official,
a man with enormous personal authority. His rôle in the sphere of
strategy was therefore political, rather than military.

From the start of the civil war Trotsky had bad relations with a
number of military and political leaders, one of whom was Stalin. In
October 1917 he did not know Stalin, and barely noticed the
Caucasian who carried out the orders of Lenin, Sverdlov, Zinoviev
and Kamenev so punctiliously. When at the end of May 1918 Stalin
and Alexander Shlyapnikov were appointed general controllers of food
supply in the south, Trotsky learnt of it only from a Sovnarkom
decree. Then Stalin, while remaining People's Commissar for Nationalities, became a member of the Military Revolutionary Committee
of the Southern Front. His behaviour soon began to irritate Trotsky,
as Stalin on several occasions went over his head straight to Lenin on
military issues, and sometimes simply ignored Trotsky's direct order.

Lenin soon saw what was going on, as a telegram from him to
Trotsky suggests: 'If you don't have this and all deciphered . . . telegrams instantly, then send Stalin the following coded telegram over
my signature: Address all military communications to Trotsky as well,
otherwise there could be a dangerous delay.'[44] To a telegram from
Lenin on the need to help the Caucasian front, Stalin replied: 'I don't
see why concern about the Caucasian front has first of all to be put
on me . . . The question of strengthening the Caucasian front falls

squarely on the Revolutionary Military Committee of the Republic, whose members, according to my information, are in perfectly good health, and not on Stalin who is anyway overloaded with work.'[45] Lenin's reply was laconic: 'The job of speeding up the supply of reinforcements from the South-western Front to the Caucasian Front is yours. Help must be given in every possible way, without squabbling over departmental responsibilities.'[46]

On more than one occasion relations between Trotsky and Stalin were so strained that they resorted to Lenin as the final arbiter. Trotsky could not forgive Stalin for his cavalier attitude to the Revolutionary Military Committee of the Republic, especially as he received complaints from the front of the crude, arbitrary and harsh nature of Stalin's orders and judgements. Trotsky tried several times to have him removed from military work. In early October 1918 he wrote to Sverdlov, with a copy to Lenin:

> I categorically insist that Stalin be recalled. The Tsaritsyn front is going badly, despite our superior forces. Voroshilov can command a regiment but not an army of 50,000 men. Still, I'm leaving him in command of 10th Tsaritsyn Army on condition he takes orders from the commander of the Southern [Front] Sytin. Up to now the Tsaritsyn people have not sent even their operational reports to [me]. I ordered them to present operational and intelligence reports to me twice a day. If this order is not carried out tomorrow, I'm going to put Voroshilov and Minin on trial and announce it in orders throughout the army ... [Army command at] Tsaritsyn must either obey orders or get out. All our armies are successful except the Southern Front, especially the Tsaritsyn front, where we have colossal superiority of force but total anarchy in the leadership. Things could be brought under control in twenty-four hours with your firm and decisive support. At any rate, this is the only way I can see for myself.[47]

Lenin felt compelled, 'for the good of the cause', to try to reconcile the two men. For example, on 23 October he sent Trotsky a telegram giving the contents of a conversation with Stalin, with an account of Stalin's assessment of the position at Tsaritsyn and his wish to improve relations with the Revolutionary Military Committee. Lenin concluded: 'In reporting all these statements of Stalin to you, Lev Davydovich, I would ask you to consider them and to reply, first, whether you are willing to have it out with Stalin face to face, and secondly,

whether you consider it possible, under certain concrete circumstances, to remove the earlier friction and work together, as Stalin so
much wants. As far as I am concerned, I think it is necessary to exert
every effort to work together with Stalin.'[48]

Lenin's efforts were unsuccessful. Both men were too ambitious,
capricious and vain, even though it was Stalin's insubordination that
had triggered their conflict. Throughout the civil war, Stalin repeatedly ignored Trotsky's authority and went over his head to Lenin,
who to some extent sympathized with Trotsky, knowing him to be
the more able and creative man, and with a far greater range of influence than Stalin.

In June 1920 Stalin sent a demand to Lenin from the front: '[Either]
we make a real armistice with [White General Baron] Wrangel and
thus gain the possibility of transferring one or two divisions from the
Crimean front, or we abandon all negotiations with Wrangel, not wait
for him to recover his strength but strike at him now and, having
smashed him, release forces for the Polish front. The present position,
which offers no clear solution to the Crimean question, is becoming
intolerable.'[49] Lenin sent this on to Trotsky with a note: 'This is
obviously utopian. Wouldn't it cost too many lives? We would be
losing a multitude of our soldiers. This has to be gone over ten times
and tested. I suggest replying to Stalin: "Your proposal about an
offensive into the Crimea is so serious that we have to inform ourselves
and think about it arch-cautiously. Wait for our reply. Lenin and
Trotsky." '[50]

Once again Stalin was breaking the rules on subordination. Trotsky's view was that Stalin's suggestions be submitted to the commander-in-chief of the south-western front, A.I. Yegorov. Lenin
agreed, and added in his note of reply, 'There's more than a hint of
whim here. But it must be discussed quickly.'[51] Stalin approached
Trotsky only in extreme circumstances, always officially and imper-
sonally. For his part, Trotsky, as his senior in rank, never let slip an
opportunity to point out to Stalin the failure of units in which he,
Stalin, was a member of the Military Revolutionary Committee. For
instance, in one of his coded telegrams he wrote:

Bring Serebryakov or Stalin to the apparatus and ask for immediate
decoding and reply. Information about Budenny's corps is giving con-

cern. According to a detailed account from Pyatakov, Budenny's army is looting the population, there is drunkenness at headquarters which threatens disintegration of Mamontov's corps. Also in the political sense serious difficulties may result if the corps breaks up. It is apparently absolutely essential that the most serious measures be taken: tighten up the commanders, drawing Voroshilov's and Shchadenko's special attention to this, check the Communist cells, bring to book some of the commanders and commissars who are guilty of looting and drunkenness, in general establish a proper regime in the corps and save it from disintegration. Perhaps the shakiest units of the Cavalry Army should be removed to the reserves soon and restored to order, otherwise they could fall apart altogether, if they have to face Makhno. Please let me know what you have done or propose to do about this.[52]

No reply from Serebryakov or Stalin has been found, but it seems plain that, in sending such telegrams, Trotsky was as concerned to make Stalin submit to his authority as he was about the state of the forces. The chief difference between them, however, was over the issue of the military specialists. Trotsky shared Lenin's position, but Stalin was generally distrustful, suspecting treason and plots at every turn. On two occasions, once from Tsaritsyn with the support of Voroshilov and Minin, and again from Petrograd with Zinoviev, Stalin demanded that the Central Committee alter its policy on military specialists, accusing Trotsky of 'indulging' treachery. He achieved the final solution of this matter in the mid-1930s when he liquidated almost every former tsarist officer who had served in the Red Army as a commander or commissar.

The Revolutionary Military Committee operated as a military-political organ, directing the strategy of the commanders-in-chief and field headquarters. Trotsky rarely interfered in operational or strategic issues, relying instead on I.I. Vatsetis, S.S. Kamenev and other specialists. But he ensured that the Party's instructions and Lenin's orders were carried out at the front. Since the autumn of 1918 he had wanted to introduce an element of planning into military actions, especially on the operational and strategic levels. On his orders, for example, Vatsetis drew up a plan of action for the winter campaign of 1918–19. Trotsky approved it and sent it to Lenin. The aim of the plan was to strengthen the Republic's defence capabilities, build up strategic reserves and systematically destroy the internal and external

enemy in Ukraine, the Donbass, the Caucasus, the Urals and Siberia.
Events would cause changes in this and similar plans, but the documents show that Trotsky and his Revolutionary War Council were
not acting impulsively. The leaders of the revolution were learning
not only the art of governing the social and political processes evoked
by the October coup, but also how to organize the defence of the
Bolshevik state.

The White Movement

The founders of Trotsky's adversaries, the Whites, were Generals
M.V. Alexeev, L.G. Kornilov and A.M. Kaledin. The White movement began in November 1917 when Alexeev sent an address to all
officers who wanted to reject the 'yoke of Bolshevism'. The address
included a call to convene in Novocherkassk in southern Russia, where
it was intended to form volunteer units. Only some 200 officers from
Petrograd, Moscow and Kiev answered the call at first, but they were
quickly followed by a group of officers from the Romanian front under
Colonel Drozdovsky, then by Kornilov's assault regiment and a host
of smaller groupings of generals and colonels. The Volunteer Army
barely numbered 4000 men at first, and Denikin was given command
of the Volunteer Division. When under Bolshevik pressure the Whites
had to withdraw to the Kuban – the first 'ice campaign' – Kaledin
shot himself in a fit of depression, and Kornilov was blown up by a
shell. From 13 April 1918 the Volunteer Army came under the command of Denikin, who soon became the dominant figure of the White
movement in the south of Russia.

The Whites' political programme was succinctly expressed by Denikin at the opening of the Kuban parliament on 1 November 1918:
'Bolshevism must be crushed. Russia must be liberated ... There
shouldn't be a Volunteer Army, a Don, Kuban or Siberian Army.
There should be a single Russian Army, with a single GHQ, single
command, endowed with full power and responsible only to the Russian people as its future legal supreme authority.'[53] Denikin's main
idea, which was shared by the White officer corps, was 'the most rapid
restoration of Great, Unified, Indivisible Russia'. While the Germans

were still occupying Ukraine and other provinces, Denikin's policy was 'neither peace nor war with the Germans'. He would consider the question of chasing out the Germans only after the White movement was established.

With the death of Alexeev in October 1918 Denikin became commander-in-chief of the Volunteer Army. He established unstable communication with Admiral A.V. Kolchak, who had some 400,000 men under his command in eastern Russia, with General N.N. Yudenich in the north-west and General Ye.K. Miller in the north. No unification of these commands, however, was ever achieved. Against his own better judgement, in May 1919 Denikin recognized Kolchak's supremacy as 'Supreme Ruler of the Russian State and Supreme Commander of the Russian Armies'. As a token of his gratitude, Kolchak appointed Denikin his deputy in the south. Although shortly before his death, in one of his last orders as 'Supreme Ruler', Kolchak reported that it had been decided that supreme all-Russian power should be handed over to Denikin,[54] the latter did not long remain commander-in-chief.

In the words of former professor of the Imperial Military Academy N.N. Golovin, those who 'saw the [Volunteer Army] as a feat overshadowed by suffering and martyrdom are right. And those who saw the dirt that stained the clean banner are also right.' An epic accompanied by filth, in Denikin's words, heroism flanked by savagery, compassion by hatred. Denikin called the civil war a 'Russian graveyard', where both Reds and Whites shed rivers of blood: 'The methods used to torment and destroy Russians were varied, but the system of terror that was applied openly and with rampant brazenness was invariable. In the Caucasus the Chekists cut people down with blunt sabres over graves dug by the victims themselves; in Tsaritsyn they suffocated people in the dark, stinking holds of barges ... We shall never know the number of those killed by Bolshevik terror' (the figure given by Golovin for 1918–19 alone is 1.7 million). Denikin also recognized that 'the mounting wave of Cossack and Volunteer forces left a filthy stain in the form of rape, pillage and pogroms against the Jews'.[55] According to various estimates, the total number of victims of the White and Red terror, famine and disease, including those who fled the country altogether, amounted to 13 million. Morality in Russia fell to a low level, as Trotsky realized, although his explanation was rather limited: 'The demoralization brought about by starvation and profiteering was greatly exacerbated by the end of the civil war. The phenomenon of the so-called "bagmen" [who collected grain in the villages for black-market deals in the cities] became so prevalent that it threatened to stifle the revolution.'[56]

Boris Savinkov, an SR who fought on the White side but eventually became reconciled to the Soviet regime, called the civil war a struggle by the Whites for the old, worn-out past, which had no chance: 'The Reds mobilize and requisition, and the Whites do, too. As hated as the names Lenin and Trotsky are those of Krivoshein and Glinka. Until the White cause becomes the peasants' cause, they will not succeed. Whoever can turn the struggle against the Bolsheviks into a struggle for a new peasant Russia will beat the Bolsheviks.'[57]

The White forces began as a motley assortment which included the Kornilov Regiment, the St George Regiment, three battalions of officers, a cadets' battalion, a regiment of students from Rostov and a couple of batteries. As they regrouped in the Cossack territories of the Don and Kuban, however, and gathered a continuous flow of people and supplies, some of it from Russia's former allies, Denikin was able to raise the stakes. Soon his army numbered tens of thousands.

With the revolution of November 1918 in Germany and the end of the war, Lenin was able to annul the 'indecent' peace of Brest-Litovsk, and the Germans left the south of Russia. It was not, however, only the Bolsheviks' hands which were now freed by the so-called breathing-space, but also those of the Entente powers which had decided to help the White movement end the 'Russian troubles'. During this time the territory of the former vast empire was like a disturbed ant-hill in which parties and governments surfaced and vanished, where the people had no idea what to expect tomorrow, where life was going on outside the law, the old laws having been abolished, the new ones as yet unknown, where millions of worried, disoriented and often outraged people were ready to support the Reds one day and the Whites the next, or were desperately seeking a way out of their homeland altogether to escape further disasters.

Denikin, meanwhile, was not wasting time. While Kolchak was suffering defeat after defeat – a series of misfortunes that ended in his execution by Bolsheviks at Irkutsk in January 1920 – Denikin was gaining great victories. At the Seventh Congress of Soviets on 7 December 1919, Trotsky declared that 'Denikin was undoubtedly far more of a danger to us than Kolchak. Kolchak depended on the slender thread of the Siberian railway, whereas Denikin could spread across the wide Russian plains with his horses.'[58] The summer and autumn of 1919 saw Denikin's greatest successes. At the end of June in Tsaritsyn, which his forces had taken, he issued the order for three major groups 'to seize the heart of Russia – Moscow'. Overcoming the unorganized resistance of the occasional Red Army unit, Denikin's troops moved towards the capital. Maintaining his outer calm, while rejoicing inwardly, he read the reports sent by cavalry corps commander Mamontov, who had broken through far to the north in an audacious attack.

In October Denikin's headquarters staff felt that their goal was at hand. Only a couple of hundred kilometres remained. Voronezh was captured, then Oryol, and Tula must be next. The question was, would Denikin replace Kolchak as 'Supreme Ruler of Russia'? He had already formed a Special Convention, later transformed into a government, but while he was anticipating the pleasure of imminent victory, he failed to observe that the Bolsheviks were regrouping and creating major cavalry formations in readiness for a mighty counter-attack.

Speaking to a meeting of Party workers in Penza on 29 July 1919, Trotsky remarked: 'Our retreat in the south took place because Denikin had greater force than us. Now we've got greater force than Denikin. He has no reserves, we have inexhaustible reserves. We have more cavalry than our adversary, and we are adding to it at a rapid rate ... Denikin has outreached himself. Having seized a vast territory, he now has to create a regime to hold onto it, but since Russia has broken into two camps, Denikin is compelled to invite into his government the old landowners, former governors and land captains ... That's the best propaganda against Denikin ... One cavalry army is not enough for Denikin to consolidate his extended front, so he has had to resort to forced mobilization of workers and peasants, and this means he is sowing the seeds of disintegration in his army. I think this autumn we shall deliver the decisive blow against Denikin.'[59] Both the analysis and the prognosis were correct.

General A.S. Lukomsky later recalled in Berlin that no one in the White camp had noticed the rise of discontent among Denikin's troops in the rear: 'Thieving and requisitioning, the excesses of the old bosses who had returned, and the deterioration of conditions for the poorest sections of the population, all this undermined Denikin's rear.' The order making units responsible for their own supplies led to a hunt for 'the spoils of war'. Intelligence reports also told Trotsky that Denikin's position had become insecure. At the end of June 1919 in Voronezh Trotsky wrote: 'The Denikin bands that are moving up from the south are not the vanguard of Anglo-French troops, no, they are the entire army that the counter-revolution is capable of deploying against us. Behind Denikin's back there is nothing but a hostile rear.'[60]

The horrified local population saw their 'saviours' as little more than marauding gangs. The Volunteer Army, stretched along a broad front, was unable to withstand the powerful blows of the Red divisions, and its retreat southwards was more rapid than its advance on Moscow had been. Denikin rushed about giving orders and threw his last reserves into the most threatened sectors, but to no avail. By the end of 1919 the Red Army was already in Rostov on Don and Novocherkassk, and was approaching Novorossiisk. Denikin, who did not expect to be forgiven by the White movement for his failure, wrote an order, in tone something like a testament to his followers. It called for Russia to be restored to its former unity and indivisibility, for order to be restored and the struggle against Bolshevism to be continued to the end; all resistance to the authorities, whether from left or right, should be punished, by extreme means if necessary; the form of government, although a matter for the future, must not be imposed by force; foreign policy must be based solely on Russian national interest; Russian territory must never be offered in exchange for help; the government must treat all classes equally; the press, if cooperative, should be helped, if dissident, tolerated, if destructive, eliminated.[61]

These views reflected the outlook not only of those actively engaged in opposing the Bolsheviks, but also of a broad section of liberal and democratic opinion. It was a theme to which Denikin was to return. In the autumn of 1921, by now an émigré in Brussels and 'despite the difficulties and inadequacy of working in refugee conditions, without archives, materials or the opportunity to exchange views face to face with participants in the events', Denikin decided to write his five volumes of memoirs. In his preface he wrote:

After the overthrow of Bolshevism, along with the enormous work of restoring the moral and material strength of the Russian people, the question of the preservation of Russia's existence as a state will arise with an urgency unknown in the history of the fatherland. For already outside Russia's borders the gravediggers are rattling their spades. They will not wait. The Russian people will arise in strength and reason from the blood, the dirt, the spiritual and physical poverty.[62]

Only eighteen months before writing these words, Denikin had watched the utter destruction of all his hopes and plans. He had seen Novorossiisk packed as contingent after contingent of his troops had retreated southwards under the blows of the Red Army. General Kutepov, who had been in charge of defending the city, had told Denikin that his demoralized forces could not hold out for more than another twenty-four hours. Denikin could not forget the sight of men being crushed in the stampede for the ladders onto the evacuation ships, or of the officers who shot themselves in desperation when they failed to get on board: 'Many animal instincts surfaced in the face of the impending danger, as naked passion overcame conscience and man became ferocious fiend to man.' Denikin was one of the last to embark on the British destroyer *Captain Sacken* with his chief-of-staff General Romanovsky, on 22 March 1920.

About 40,000 soldiers had managed to get into the Crimea. Denikin had tried to regroup and to raise their morale, but their dissatisfaction with him mounted rapidly. To have been almost within reach of Moscow and now to be stranded in the Crimea and doomed to defeat meant someone had to be blamed. Among the best elements of the Russian officer corps military honour was the highest value, and Denikin was not one to wait until the War Council expressed its lack of confidence in him. He wrote to the chairman, General A.M. Dragomirov:

Respected Abram Mikhailovich, For the three years of the Russian troubles I have led the struggle, devoting all my strength and bearing authority like a heavy cross laid on me by fate. God did not bless with success the troops I led. And although I have not lost my faith in the viability of the Army and its historic calling, the inner link between the leader and the Army has been broken. I can no longer lead it.

In his last order, Denikin appointed Lieutenant-General Baron Peter Wrangel as his successor, and ended: 'To all who have accompanied me honourably in this hard struggle, I humbly bow. God, give the Army victory and save Russia.'[63]

A sworn enemy of Bolshevism to his dying day, Denikin never grasped the fact that it was not the 'socialists' who had made the revolution as much as the tsarist regime which had dragged the country into a senseless war, exhausting the people and creating the conditions for revolution. The February revolution had not succeeded because it failed to give the people either land or peace. The Bolsheviks exploited this fact and gave the people both, while taking away the liberty acquired in February. The value of land and peace without liberty, of course, was altered. Denikin failed to understand this great paradox, and explained the Russian tragedy purely in terms of Kerensky's tolerance and Lenin's deceit.

The death throes of the White movement continued for a long time. Denikin learnt that following Soviet amnesties of 1921 and 1924 for the lower ranks, many soldiers returned to Russia. Officers who found emigration too painful and who returned to Russia met a harsher fate. For instance, at the end of 1921 former commander of Crimea corps Lieutenant-General Ya.A. Slashchev, artillery inspector Major-General Milkovsky, Colonels Gilbikh and Mizernitsky and Captain Voinakhovsky returned voluntarily to Soviet Russia. Reporting this to the press, Trotsky added: 'Whoever tries to use the magnanimity of the toilers' state against the Soviet Republic will be severely punished ... The Soviet Republic must remain vigilant.'[64]

During the purges of the 1930s, the last of the White officers who had returned home were liquidated. Large numbers of participants in the movement, however, remained beyond Soviet borders. In 1925 Wrangel's Russian Council calculated that the number of Russian refugees who were capable of being mobilized in Germany, France, Yugoslavia, Greece, Turkey, China, Latvia, Czechoslovakia and Bulgaria amounted to 1,158,000 men.[65] All of them, according to a document obtained by Red Army intelligence, considered themselves to be loyal to the 'White idea' – no doubt this was an exaggeration. Nevertheless, the 'Russian All-Army Union', which combined various elements and committees of former Volunteers, survived a long time, and the publication of newspapers and magazines gave evidence that there was life in the White émigré community.

Despite their strong anti-Communist attitudes, the Whites abroad did not identify Bolshevism with the regime. In the latter part of the 1930s, when war was looming, many émigrés saw that Germany and the Western democracies would try to settle their differences at the cost of the Soviet Union. In Paris, Milyukov organized a 'defence movement' which included a number of White leaders, among them Denikin. Its aim was 'to unite the émigrés and cooperate to the best of its ability in the defence of Russia'. In Moscow such patriotism, coming from former Russian citizens, was incomprehensible, and the chief of Red Army intelligence, Corps Commander M.S. Uritsky, reported to the leadership: 'One can see this movement as a sign of the disintegration of the émigré milieu.'[66] During the upheaval of Hitler's invasion of the USSR, only a handful of White émigrés found it possible to offer their services to Fascism.

If Denikin's explanation of the White defeat ignored the deep social causes of Russia's disintegration, at least he was able to face the fact that the monarchy could not be restored and that democracy was an inevitability. He believed that 'a host of Russia's problems cannot be solved by revolution. What is needed is evolution.' For many years the Whites lived with the memory of a Russia long gone. There were others who took a different view. Berdyaev, for example, in his book *Self-Awareness*, wrote: 'I never believed in the White movement and had no sympathy for it . . . I put my trust only in Bolshevism being overcome internally. The Russian people would liberate itself.'[67] Denikin's last words before he died in Paris in 1947 were, 'Alas, I shall never see a rescued Russia.'

Within the Noose

On 2 June 1919 Trotsky published an article entitled 'The Ninth Wave' in the newspaper *V Puti* (On the Road), which was printed on board his special train. In it he wrote: 'What we are experiencing at the moment is the ninth wave of the counter-revolution. It presses on us on the Northern and Southern Fronts. It threatens Petrograd. But at the same time we know for sure that the counter-revolution has gathered its last forces, it is committing its last reserves to battle.'[68]

Stating that 'the counter-revolution was greatly strengthened during the past year by the lethal weapons supplied by the Anglo-French bandits', he declared: 'We now know for certain that when we have dealt with Kolchak and Denikin, we shall make the Soviet Republic completely inviolable and give a mighty push to the revolution in Europe and the whole world. Behind the forces Denikin, Kolchak, the White Estonians and White Finns have fielded against us, the counter-revolution has nothing more to give. It is staking everything on the Southern Front, on the east and on Petrograd, and so is the world counter-revolution.'[69] What he omitted to say was that this was just as true for the revolution itself.

An understanding of how it was that Trotsky's mere presence at the front raised the troops' morale and led to the meteoric rise of his reputation may lie in an account of a tour he made in September 1918 which is to be found among the papers of 4th Army, eastern front senior headquarters adjutant Savin. The notes were written on 22 September 1918 in the village of Pokrovsk, Samara province, during one of Trotsky's whistle-stops. They give an exhaustive description of Trotsky's behaviour among the troops, and help to explain his popularity, his *modus operandi* and the political and military consequences of his visits.

Having been told that Trotsky's train was due to arrive next day at Saratov, 4th Army HQ sent a commander and a commissar by boat to meet him there. Savin's account continues:

9.37 a.m., to sounds of brass band playing national anthem, Trotsky's train pulls in, troops of Saratov garrison lined up. Trotsky greeted by thunderous 'Hurrah!' ... Reception committee introduced; Trotsky inspected troops and thanked everyone for coming (local Soviet chiefs absent) ... Convoy of automobiles drove to quay ... Boat arrived at Pokrovsk 12.15 ... Guard of honour. Headquarters chief Bulgakov gave report. At HQ Trotsky inspected every section. The commander reported on position (pointing out poor supply). Trotsky gave instant orders to improve supply. He spent 1 hour and 45 minutes at HQ. Left for quay. Greeted by Marseillaise. Gave speech from deck. Thunderous 'Hurrah'.
    Trotsky left for Volsk. Again met by national anthem. Gave speech. Called for earliest possible capture of Samara. Thunderous 'Hurrah'. Arrived at Balakovo. Again speech. Again troops lined route, gave

speech from automobile. Ordered each Red Army man present should receive month's pay (250 roubles) as gift. We arrived at Khvalynsk. Again parade. Trotsky gave speech. We drive to Volsky Division at front in village of Popovka. Formed international regiment. Trotsky gave speech in Russian, Lindov in German. Trotsky's remarks: 1. Divisional chief Gavrilov has gone to pieces and behaved like a disorderly soldier; 2. The regiments have no sentries; 3. The international regiment mustered slowly, practice 'alerts' are needed; 4. Communications are bad; 5. There is too much independence in the units, they don't follow HQ's orders; 6. HQs are too far from the troops; 7. They want automobiles and warm clothing. But on the whole the revolutionary spirit and discipline in Volsk division are strong, it has no place for disintegrating units.

We set off (19 September, 9 a.m.) down Volga to Pokrovsk ... [We] arrive in Saratov at 1.45 p.m. Trotsky makes speech to large meeting in People's Palace. Commissar Sharskov reported. Dealt with supply problems of provincial military committee. Left for Nikolaevsk (arrived 20 September 11.15 a.m.). Guard of honour, lined route, 'hurrah'. Decided to form new division and call it 2nd Nikolaevsky with Comrade Chapaev as chief. As commander of 1st brigade, Chapaev dug in his heels and refused command of 2nd division: 'I've got used to this, I've settled in.' People said: 'The fact is Comrade Chapaev, steppe eagle that he is, has used purely partisan tactics since the front opened.' He doesn't obey HQ orders. On occasion he has set off with his detachment and disappeared, only to turn up after a while with booty and prisoners. According to eye-witnesses, wherever Chapaev showed up, the local population were terrorized. His savagery is well known to many. A legendary personality. Trotsky persuaded Chapaev [to take the post].

Trotsky spoke at meeting in theatre in the evening. Doled out 250 roubles to each soldier in village of Raevskoe. Exclaimed: 'Forward, to Samara!' Also gave cigarette-cases to distinguished soldiers.

In Bogorodskoe troops reported there were turncoats. They'd been captured. Comrade Trotsky at once ordered a revolutionary tribunal within twenty-four hours to try the turncoats: 'All those found guilty of desertion are to be shot on the spot.' 3rd and 4th Regiments lined up outside village. All dressed anyhow, one even in a top-hat. They included some old men. 'So, you want to fight?' Trotsky asked one. 'Yes, I do!' Trotsky made a speech with the call 'On to Samara!' Talked about desertion in 1st and 2nd Regiments, said they'd be shot today.

Asked who had distinguished themselves in battle. Told there were twenty men. They stepped forward. But it turned out there were only eighteen gifts. Trotsky gave one of the last two the watch off his own wrist and the other got his Browning. All the rest were promised 250 roubles each. They shouted 'hurrah'. We had travelled 200 [kilometres] in the car that day.

[Trotsky] made following remarks: the division is strong and is burning to take Samara. But they carry out orders and commands badly. Chapaev says: I don't trust HQ and don't intend to recognize their bits of paper.

Accompanying Comrade Trotsky on his journey were a photographer and film cameraman who captured on film important episodes of the trips and individual people of interest to the Russian Soviet Republic and who can serve as a political example for other countries to show the proletariat are struggling against the capitalist yoke.[70]

Savin's notes suggest that Trotsky was not primarily concerned to enhance his own popularity, but rather to stress the significance of the new central authority, the significance of the supreme command of the Republic, as well as his own confidence in the triumph of the revolution. He used every stopover as a chance to meet ordinary soldiers. His brief, twenty–thirty-minute speeches helped to raise general awareness among the soldiers, but he took every opportunity to give them a concrete target, e.g. to capture Samara. In Trotsky, ex-peasants, now bearing arms, saw not merely their own 'boss', but also one of the highest representatives of the new authorities. Savin's notes show Trotsky as an astute demagogue who recognized the need to deliver something against the larger promises: silver cigarette-cases – looted, incidentally, from tsarist stores – his own wristwatch and personal revolver helped to build his image as a legend of the revolution. A thorough-going populist, he knew that his fame enormously enhanced whatever he said to the semi-literate troops. There was something very un-revolutionary, even commercial, in the hand-out of cash – perhaps the price of a bottle of moonshine or a packet of cheap cigarettes – but he knew his public, the poorest peasants, who valued a kopeck earned. The order to shoot deserters, issued in the same businesslike way as the distribution of the cigarette-cases or instructions to improve supplies, taught the people that violence and coercion were not the products only of war, but also hallmarks of the new regime.

No other Bolshevik leader thought of bringing along with him two secretaries, a photographer and a film cameraman, whose efforts were intended to immortalize his image for future generations. There were some attempts to depict Trotsky as a great military leader, but it was well known that he was not this, nor even a military specialist of average ability. He was a dilettante in this field. When a labour activist from Chicago called Arthur Allen referred to Trotsky as a 'one of a dozen of the greatest military leaders', a Miss J. Allen responded: 'The civil war in Russia was fought mostly by officers of the old army, on both sides. Trotsky is an agitator, not a military leader.'[71] And, indeed, his orders bear the stamp of a politician committed to carrying out the Bolshevik line. He kept this unflattering exchange among his papers.

Trotsky was especially sensitive to any conflict with an ethnic dimension. When on 3 July 1919 he received reports that Red Army units were running riot among the population of Bashkiria, he at once sent a threatening order over the direct line: 'Apparently indisputable facts testify to the criminal, bestial attitude of some units on the Eastern Front towards the Bashkir population and Bashkir troops who have come over to the Soviet side. Moreover, although until now only verbal reprimands have been issued, I regard severe and exemplary punishment of anyone found guilty of shameful acts of violence against the Bashkir people as necessary. Report actions taken and punishments carried out.'[72]

Threat of severe repression was Trotsky's style of operation. In November 1918 he sent a telegram to the war council of 9th Army, with a copy to Sverdlov: 'We must use an iron fist to force divisional and regimental commanders to go onto the offensive at any cost. If the position doesn't change by next week, I will have to use severe repression against the commanders of 9th Army . . . I require an exact list on 1 December of all units that have not fulfilled their battle instructions.'[73]

One of the most significant sources of armed support for the White cause came from the Cossack population, encouraged no doubt by the policy of terror pursued against them by the Bolshevik regime as 'the social base of the counter-revolution'. Moscow sent plain instructions 'for the complete, rapid and decisive annihilation of the Cossacks as a distinct economic group, the destruction of their economic foundations, the physical destruction of Cossack administrators and officers, in general of the entire Cossack leadership'.[74]

It was in this spirit that the 'decossackization' began. The predictable response was a rising of people who knew how to fight, for it had been their traditional rôle to defend the Russian Empire. Lenin demanded that the speediest and most merciless means be used to crush the rebellion, and Trotsky issued a special order 'to destroy the nest of dishonourable traitors. These Cains must be annihilated, no mercy must be shown to any settlement that gives resistance. Mercy only for those who hand over their weapons voluntarily and come over to our side ... You must cleanse the Don of the black stain of treason within a few days.'[75]

One of Trotsky's chief concerns, as the chief organizer of the military effort, centred on the social questions that reflected the difficulties being experienced by the new regime. In a letter to the Revolutionary Military Committees of the fronts and the armies headed 'More Equality', he developed his ideas on social justice in the army:

> We are living in a period of transition. We have to use shock methods in the distribution of both means and manpower, that is, we must first of all guarantee that the most important branches of state work are supplied with people and goods ... in giving everything to the front, we are depriving working men and women of education, food, and the supply of essentials. This is all understandable. But there are people who use these priorities for their own ends. We should not only realize that everything we get in the army is at the cost of the people, but also that there should be more equality in the army itself. Any soldier will understand that the first pair of boots and the first cape should be given to the commander. When a car is used for jolly jaunts in front of exhausted Red Army men, or when commanders dress up to the nines in front of their ragged fighters, it can only cause irritation and disgruntlement. In itself privilege, we repeat, is occasionally an inevitable and for the moment insurmountable evil. Blatant over-indulgence in privilege is not just an evil, it is a crime ... Especially demoralizing and destructive is the abuse of goods when rules and regulations are also being broken. This applies above all to parties with drink, women and so on.

Trotsky remarks that the 'obedient and uncomplaining soldier' is not the best sort; on the contrary it is the quick, observant and critical soldier, who sees that leadership based on the illegal abuse of privilege undermines the fighting capacity of the Red Army.[76] Trotsky's orders to the front commanders to ensure social justice were not only aimed at securing the army's fighting abilities, but also the viability of the young state.

As early as September 1918 Trotsky had secured the appointment as Deputy War Commissar and Deputy Chairman of the Revolutionary Military Council of Efraim Markovich Sklyansky, a former member of the first War Commissariat created in 1917. A young army doctor who had become a Bolshevik in 1913, Sklyansky, an amateur in strategic and operational matters, was favoured by Trotsky for his energy, assiduity, organizing skills and efficiency. Sklyansky was a model executive. All of Trotsky's communications from his train went through him, as he was the link between Trotsky and the political and economic organs of the republic. During halts at Kharkov and Liski in May 1919, for example, Trotsky cabled Sklyansky: 'If Okulov isn't needed in Ukraine, I suggest he be sent immediately to the Western Front as a member of the Revolutionary Military Council and that he tour the front with his commission and sort the units out'; 'Troops mobilized in Novgorod and Pskov provinces can be sent to the Western Front, but not Zinoviev'; 'I would have spoken against the appointment of Unshlikht in case he took it as a demotion. If he agrees, I don't object to his appointment'; 'My first train was in a crash on 16 May . . . There were no losses. A radical inspection of the track is needed'; 'It is necessary to find a possible way of using asphyxiating gases. We must find a responsible person to head this responsible work'; 'Isn't my carriage ready yet? It's impossible to go on living in it any longer, as apart from everything else it leaks.'[77] Dozens of such messages were sent by Trotsky to Sklyansky every day.

Among Sklyansky's equally numerous replies was the following, dated 19 May 1919:

Stalin has reported that the front is being brought to order, three punitive companies have been sent to Luga, Gatchina and Krasnoe Selo; all forward forces have been mobilized and despatched to the front line. Zinoviev is going to Luga, Stalin to Staraya Rusa, the disorderly sixth division has been taken in hand and is coming to order, the divisional commanders of the sixth showed cowardice and confusion

and have been set aside. They need cavalry. Stalin gave a positive report
of the navy. Semashko has been set aside. Shatov has been appointed
to the Revolutionary Military Council of the Western Front. Reinforcements are being hurried by every available means. Stalin thinks a new
Communist front is needed.[78]

From the mass of documentation generated by Trotsky during the
civil war it is plain that, for what he perceived as the good of the
revolution, he was prepared to apply any and all means, including
the manufacture and use of poisonous gas. Deceit and manipulation
were standard practice for the Bolsheviks, and Trotsky proved himself
to be a master exponent. In January 1920 he received a telegram from
the Ukrainian Anarchist military leader Nestor Makhno, explaining
why he, Makhno, was not willing to go to the Polish front. While
continuing 'peace talks' with Makhno, Trotsky maintained contact
with the Revolutionary Military Committee through Stalin, to whom
he cabled: 'Do you think it would be possible to encircle Makhno
right away and carry out a complete liquidation? It would probably
be possible to destroy his artillery base if we sent some entirely reliable
people there posing as anarchists. Makhno uses hardly any security
measures, so we could most probably destroy his ammunition stores.'[79]
Stalin replied: 'The encirclement of Makhno was started a few days
ago and will be accomplished by the ninth. The order [for him] to
move against the Poles was issued with the intention of collecting
extra material against Makhno.'[80] Thus, even while Makhno was still
an ally, his termination was being planned and executed.

It seems that the main explanation for Trotsky's immense popularity was the impression he gave that he was capable of sacrificing
himself in the name of the idea. The people, above all, saw his dyna-
mism, his decisiveness, his constant movement, they heard his passionate speeches and sensed his implacability, and many were taken with
his originality. For instance, when the noose was tightening around
the throat of the republic, there were growing demands from 'bourgeois specialists and instructors' who had been mobilized to be sent
back to their former places of work, to the institutes, factories and
offices that were 'in a state of collapse'. Trotsky was tired of refusing
these constant requests and at the end of June 1919 signed Order
No. 118 which said, *inter alia*: 'I forbid anyone to approach me with
such requests in future, otherwise I shall publish the names of the

petitioners for general circulation as the names of citizens who are trying to use legal means to become deserters.'[81] No further requests were made.

Trotsky was everywhere an object of discussion and argument. In its regular 'Leaders of the Revolution' column the newspaper of 7th Army, *Krasnyi Shtyk* (Red Bayonet), wrote:

> In a short space of time he has performed a near miracle: he has created a wonderful army and led it to victories. Trotsky himself is always at the front, the real front where the fighting is eye to eye, where stray bullets do not distinguish between ordinary Red Army men, commanders or commissars. The train and the boat he lives on have frequently come under artillery- and machine-gun-fire. But Trotsky somehow doesn't notice these inconveniences. Under enemy fire, as during the revolution itself, he goes on working and working and working ... No one knows where Trotsky takes a rest.'[82]

It is true that Trotsky worked prodigiously, but it is also true that he did not make an effort to curtail such panegyrics in the press which was under his own control. Dedication to the revolutionary idea did not prevent him from being vain, from posturing before the mirror of history.

It often seemed to him that one decisive blow was needed to scatter the counter-revolution. At the beginning of April 1919 he wrote another of his countless articles on his train. This one was entitled 'What Does Russia Need?' : 'The attack on Kolchak will be of decisive importance. The destruction of his army will not only secure the Urals and Siberia for Soviet Russia, but will make itself felt at once on all other fronts. The annihilation of the Kolchakites will lead immediately and inevitably to the total annihilation of Denikin's Volunteers ("volunteers" under the lash) and the ultimate disintegration of the White Guards, the Estonian, Latvian, Polish and Anglo-American forces in the west and east.'[83] The breakthrough in the east was indeed accomplished, but it did not lead to the alleviation of the other fronts.

Speaking on 26 August 1919 to a joint meeting of the Moscow Soviet and trade union delegates, Trotsky was forced to admit: 'It is true, comrades, that we are facing an unpleasantness, not a military failure, but an unpleasantness in the full sense. That is the breakthrough by Mamontov's cavalry. If this breakthrough is viewed as a cavalry raid, then it was carried out successfully.' Trotsky did not spell out the fact that in the space of one month Mamontov's 9000 men had gone through five provinces, pausing in dozens of towns in an attempt to raise an anti-Soviet rebellion, and finally in September 1919 managing to join up with Denikin's army. The Red infantry without cavalry had proved powerless to stop Mamontov's advance. During the attack Trotsky had issued Order No. 146, entitled 'Into Battle with the Bandits of Mamontov's Gang'. In it he wrote: 'I give warning: Mamontov's cavalry will pass and the Soviet Republic will remain. Fallen men and women workers and peasant men and women will be avenged. The counter-revolutionary vipers will be crushed. Their property will be confiscated and handed over to the poor ... Any help given to Mamontov's bandits, direct or indirect, is treason to the people and will be punished by shooting.'[84] Mamontov, however, was elusive.

After the Mamontov raid, Trotsky issued a new slogan: 'Proletarian, to horse!' He also issued a new order, offering a reward for every Cossack from Mamontov's forces captured dead or alive. 'Prizes will include leather tunic, boots, watches, [several dozen pounds] of food-stuffs and so on. Also, everything found with the captured Cossack, his horse and saddle, will go to the captor.'[85]

The end of Denikin, Trotsky told his audience at the Moscow Soviet, would be the beginning of the world revolution: 'We shall crush and smash Denikin, for he has no reserves. Like the Transcau-casus, Georgia and Azerbaijan, so Afghanistan, Baluchistan, India and China won't wait for us. Soviet Hungary, with a radius of seventy–eighty kilometres, has fallen temporarily. But what is an area of sev-enty–eighty kilometres around Budapest compared to the thousands of kilometres that we have taken over for Soviet Russia? ... To our Hungarian comrades we say: "Wait, brothers, wait! You have less time to wait than we expected!" And, turning to the east, we must say to the people of Asia: "Wait, oppressed brothers, you have less time to wait than we thought!" '[86]

But the much desired world revolution refused to ignite, and relief on one front did not eliminate mortal danger elsewhere. Trotsky was, however, right to say that Soviet Russia had no frontiers, only fronts. A week after his promise to the Moscow Soviet to finish off Denikin, he declared at a special meeting of the Petrograd Soviet: 'There is an outpost in the west from which we cannot withdraw as much as a kilometre, where we cannot yield to the enemy so much as one square kilometre of territory. That outpost is the Petrograd front. [Petrograd] still remains our eye on the Baltic turned on Western Europe.' He assured his audience that the world struggle would be decided 'not in the Finland sector, nor the Estland sector, but would be resolved on the entire surface of the earth'. The 'question of Finland's future and Estland's future will be settled on the way'. Pointing out that Russia was being torn apart, Trotsky declared that 'there are moments when revenge becomes a matter of revolutionary expediency ... And we shall show an example of this in Finland. Finland will be the first to fall into the hands of the Red Army which will take revenge for the policy of encirclement ... We shall attack the Finnish bourgeoisie in a crusade of devastation, we shall destroy them without mercy.'[87] He asserted that the destruction of Yudenich and his accomplices would be the final breakthrough in the struggle against counter-revolution and the intervention.

It was not so much that Trotsky was naive. He was not, but was an adventurist who depicted reality as he wished it to be, rather than as it was. This often led him to promise an early victory, future happiness, universal brotherhood and a worldwide Soviet republic. Perhaps it was this aspect of Trotsky – the prophet of a happy future – that drew the crowds. Perhaps it was that he realized that one must promise something to people who were up to their knees in blood, that one must inspire them with something and point to great goals that were close at hand and attainable. He could, as we have seen, be extremely harsh with his subordinates, but he was equally able to vent his frustration on Lenin, as a barbed telegram of 1919 shows:

I reported that the [Revolutionary Military Committee of 12th Army] is utterly powerless. Zatonsky has been despatched to the south, but he is quite unsuitable for this mission. Semenov and Aralov are depressed. They need at least one fresh man. I've been told that Lashevich is going to Kozlov where he is completely unnecessary. No one is going to [12th Army] which is virtually non-existent. After twenty-four hours and waiting in feverish expectation, I get either bureaucratic questions about which commanders to send or instructive explanations that 12th and 14th Army commanders are subordinate to the commander-in-chief, a fact of which we here were, of course, in utter ignorance. I earnestly ask Moscow to desist from the policy of fantastic apprehensions and panic decisions.[88]

When confronting concrete strategic issues, Trotsky took the advice of his assistants and military specialists, and when he departed from this rule he tended to produce plans that verged on the delirious. En route in his train from Bologoe to Petrograd, he summed up his thoughts on ways to save the northern capital in an article entitled 'Petrograd Defends itself from Within', published in *V puti* on 18 October 1919. Writing that Yudenich must be destroyed, he declared:

> The best thing for us, from the purely military point of view, would be to allow Yudenich's gang to penetrate the very walls of the city, as it would not be difficult to turn Petrograd into a huge trap for the White Guard forces ... Having broken into the gigantic city, the White Guards would find themselves in a stone labyrinth, where every house would represent a quandary as to whether it was a threat or a mortal danger to them. Where would the blow come from? From the window? From the attic? From the cellar? Round the corner? From everywhere! ... An artillery bombardment of Petrograd might of course cause damage to individual buildings, it might destroy a certain number of inhabitants, women and children. But several thousand Red fighters, deployed behind barbed-wire fortifications, barricades, in cellars or in attics, would be at negligible risk ... Two or three days of such street-fighting would be enough to turn the gangs that had broken through into a frightened, hunted herd of cowards who either in groups or individually would give themselves up to unarmed passers-by or women.

Admittedly, Trotsky concludes the article by pointing out that street-fighting would cause 'accidental victims and the destruction of cultural treasures. That is one of the reasons the commanders should not let the enemy into Petrograd.'[89]

Trotsky's military thoughts reveal quite graphically his super-revolutionary views. He belonged to that category of people who believe that the end justifies everything. How lightly he admits that his plan might mean destroying 'a certain number of inhabitants, women and children', as if this were a mere trifle. For such people human life – if it is another's – is as nothing when set against the goal, the ideal, the dream. Despite their attractive features and personal qualities, the minds of such people are often very dangerous.

Trotsky's Special Train

The myths about Trotsky's train were numerous. Red Army men came to expect that it would bring them long-awaited reinforcements, artillery and ammunition, as well as the legendary leader of the army himself, whose personal example would create a breakthrough on the front. Commanders and commissars, on the other hand, awaited Trotsky's peremptory orders with trepidation. Everyone, however, believed that Trotsky's arrival meant that 'things would get going'. More was said than written about the train, but the archives hold much information about this unique symbol of Trotsky's operational revolutionary leadership of the fronts in the civil war.

In the summer of 1922 the chief of the Central Board of Military Communications, M.M. Arzhanov, proposed that the train be shown at the jubilee exhibition of the Red Army and Navy. Trotsky deputed Ya.G. Blyumkin to draft plans. In December 1922 Blyumkin reported:

> There is to be a section at the exhibition on 'The train used by PredRVSR [Chairman of the Revolutionary Military Committee of the Soviet Republic] Trotsky'. A vast plan will show all of the train's journeys over four years and the places where it stopped, was in battle and derailed. Publications printed on the train will be displayed on special boards, notably files of the newspaper *V puti*, copies of orders, pamphlets. Lists of train personnel will be displayed, and a memorial board of train-niks [Blyumkin's term, *poezdniks*] who fell in battle. Battle honours bestowed on the train will be exhibited with a guard of honour. Before the exhibition opens there will be a 'History of the Train Week', during which memories of the crew will be gathered on special questionnaires.[90]

What was the 'special rôle' played by Trotsky's train, on which Blyumkin laid such stress in his memorandum? Years later, in exile on the island of Prinkipo, Trotsky wrote:

> My train was hurriedly organized in Moscow on the night of 7 August 1918. In the morning I left in it for Sviyazhsk, bound for the Czecho-Slovak front. The train was continually being reorganized and improved upon, and extended in its functions. As early as 1918, it had already become a flying apparatus of administration. Its sections included a secretariat, a printing-press, a telegraph station, a radio

station, an electric-power station, a library, a garage, and a bath. The train was so heavy that it needed two engines; later it was divided into two trains. When we had to stop for some time at a section of the front, one of the engines would do service as courier, and the other was always under steam. The front was shifting constantly, and one could take no chances.[91]

At first the train consisted of twelve carriages and carried about 250 people, including a bodyguard of Latvian Riflemen, a machine-gun unit, a group of agitators, a communications crew, a team of drivers, a unit of track repairmen and other specialized personnel. The first chief of the train was S.V. Ciccolini, and among the long-standing staffers were two old Bolsheviks, S.I. Gusev and P.G. Smidovich. When the train was divided into two, an aviation unit of two aero-planes was added, as well as several automobiles and even a band.[92]

Always concerned for his creature comforts, Trotsky provided the train with cooks, secretaries and bodyguards, as well as adequate supplies. He also saw that his staff was well paid by putting the train chief and his own secretary on the same scale as a divisional commander.[93] He expected to be greeted by senior officials at stopping-places, with a guard of honour and due protocol. Instructions issued by the chief of the train ordered that 'People should not crowd around People's War Commissar Comrade Trotsky's carriage,' and that 'When People's War Commissar Comrade Trotsky leaves his carriage he should not be accompanied by an indiscriminate heap of comrades who just happen to turn up, but only by people appointed for this purpose.'[94] Already the young republic was creating its own rituals for the worship of its leaders. The revolution, whose purpose had been to install people's power, quickly created a cohort who spoke and acted in the name of the people. Trotsky's train, although it performed a necessary function, acquired the attributes that would become characteristic of one-man rule.

Trotsky liked his train to go fast, and anyone found guilty of holding it up for any reason was likely to be penalized. His secretary, M. Glazman, once cabled Lenin from Astrakhan: 'Comrade Trotsky's special train arrived at Baskunchak at 9 o'clock on the seventh and hence took ten hours to cover 230 versts [about 150 miles]. In accord-ance with Trotsky's orders I request that the reasons for such a slow movement of the special train be discovered and that the guilty answer for it. Inform us urgently when the order has been carried out.'[95]

Trotsky spent more time on his special train than he did working in the Commissariat. According to some estimates, he travelled more than 200,000 kilometres during the civil war, many of his trips being to the southern front, which he regarded as the most difficult and most dangerous.

Besides the trusted bodyguards Trotsky selected for his entourage – most of them young workers, sailors and intellectuals – there were always several dozen Communists. Trotsky often appointed new commissars and commanders from among this group. The train was highly protected: the carriages were all armoured, machine-guns were placed on the footplates and the crew itself was armed to the teeth. 'They all wore leather uniforms, which always make men look heavily imposing,' Trotsky later recalled:

> On the left arm, just below the shoulder, each wore a large metal badge, carefully cast at the mint, which had acquired great popularity in the army . . . To keep the men on the alert while we were travelling, there were frequent alarms, both by day and by night. Armed detachments would be put off the trains as 'landing parties'. The appearance of a leather-coated detachment in a dangerous place invariably had an overwhelming effect. When they were aware of the train just a few kilometres behind the firing-line, even the most nervous units, their commanding officers especially, would summon up all their strength.[96]

The train had its own internal order, some aspects of which testify not only to its rapid evolution as a new organ of military administration, but also to the significance Trotsky imparted to the train as such. The activities of its numerous personnel were circumscribed by a host of instructions. In the event of an emergency, train-chief Voldemar Ukhenberg laid down that 'the alarm signal would consist of three shots or three alarm whistles from the locomotive . . . Duty telephonists must under no circumstances leave their telephones . . . Anyone who disobeys these instructions will be arrested at once and handed over to a Military-revolutionary court.'[97] Apart from the train's security guards, Trotsky had his own personal bodyguards, twelve in all at the end of 1918.[98] Among his other duties the chief of Trotsky's own guards, Nikolai Sharapov, had a special licence 'to acquire food products for [Trotsky] for cash at the stopping-places'.[99]

In Nezhin, for instance, Sharapov presented the following order to the city food committee: 'I request the urgent release of the following items for the personal consumption of Comrade Trotsky: fresh game – ten pieces, butter – five lbs, greens (asparagus, spinach, green cucumbers) . . .'[100] The date on the order was 6 May 1920, when the entire Volga region and much of Russia was suffering an appalling famine.

Every day, circumstances permitting, Ukhenberg submitted a written report on the train's affairs to Trotsky. On 7 November 1918, the first anniversary of the revolution, he wrote:

> 2. The chairman of the Saratov Provincial Executive Committee, Comrade Vasiliev, has asked me to request that you speak today at their celebrations of the October revolution . . . 3. I petition you to amnesty the offenders on your train on the occasion of the October revolution: a) Fedor Gorin, for drunkenness and attempting while under the influence to shoot the train's head of security; b) Martin Burkan, in connection with Petrovsky's escape from arrest. 4. I request your instructions as to the distribution of the 3,500,000 papirosy [cigarettes] sent from Moscow as gifts for the front. 5. Many personnel are carrying flour that they have bought with their own money . . . May train personnel engage in trade and on what scale? 6. In view of the loss of a large quantity of various uniforms from the train, I request clarification as to whether personnel are to be released on arrival in Moscow.[101]

The train had special compartments for telegraphic and radio communication, and Trotsky remained in constant contact with Moscow. On 3 April 1919, for instance, he sent a long report on the condition of four armies. In 4th Army, he wrote,

> the 22nd Sharpshooters Division is committing looting, rape and anti-Communist agitation in the Muslim language [sic, presumably Tatar]. In Orlov-Kurilov regiments the Communists have to work semi-legally; casual recruits want to be released. In 1st and 5th companies of the Penza regiment, kulak elements are carrying on agitation, the Communists play cards . . . In the Penza division of 1st Army almost all the units have disintegrated, they do not carry out battle orders, the mood is one of panic, especially in the Petrograd regiment where a battalion has dispersed. Nothing is known of 2nd Army. In 3rd Army, Orenburg regiment of 30th Division is exhausted; they are poorly clothed . . . Bogoyavlensk regiment lacks underwear. Putilov artillery regiment is

running a commune. Lesno-Vyborg regiment lacks uniforms. The morale of Petrograd regiment is good. Red Eagles regiment lacks weapons, medicines, boots, and the men are tired.[102]

Trotsky later recalled that, after ascertaining the needs of a division on the spot, he would hold a conference in the staff-car or dining-car, 'inviting as many representatives as possible, including those from the lower commanding force and from the ranks, as well as from the local party organizations, the Soviet administration, and the trade unions ... These conferences always had immediate practical results. No matter how poor the organs of the local administration might be, they always managed to squeeze a little tighter and cut down on some of their own needs to contribute something to the army ... A new group of Communists would be drawn from the institutions and put immediately into an unreliable regiment. Stuff would be found for shirts and for wrappings for the feet, leather for new soles, and an extra hundredweight of fat. But of course the local sources were not enough.'[103] Trotsky would then wire Lenin or Sklyansky with requests for the extra supplies.

On arriving at a station close to a headquarters or a front, two or three trucks and Trotsky's personal automobile would be unloaded from the train. Usually twenty or thirty soldiers armed with machine-guns would accompany him to the units. There was always the risk of an ambush, and Trotsky took great care to protect himself. He was invariably surrounded by his bodyguards, his 'lads' in their creaking, tight leather tunics. Nadezhda Alexandrovna Marennikova, who worked in Trotsky's secretariat and was extremely close to his entourage, told me: 'Almost every day he seems to have had his health checked by doctors. But the main thing was he was always being guarded. Well guarded. Always several bodyguards. Frunze,* for whom I also worked, only had one. Trotsky was an exceptional man, outstanding even, but he was something of a coward.' Certainly, the train served above all as a mobile administrative organ, but the greater part of it was devoted to accommodating Trotsky and his security personnel.

Trotsky's visits to the front were motivated partly by his need to

---

* Mikhail Frunze, a Red Army commander who succeeded Trotsky as Military Commissar in 1925 and died the same year while undergoing surgery.

know the position, but also, perhaps chiefly, to raise morale. It was his suggestion that the Order of the Red Banner be created in September 1918. When he received his first batch of the decorations in January 1919, however, he was disappointed, and cabled Sverdlov: 'The Red Banner medal is impossible, it's too crude and the fixing device is so cumbersome that it's practically impossible to wear. I'm not going to distribute any, as it would cause general disappointment. I insist no more be made or issued to the military administration. We waited several months for the medal, but what we've got is a porter's name-plate, except that it's not as convenient. The medal should be three or four times smaller and made of better material.'[104] Feeling, perhaps, that this was not enough, he also cabled Yenukidze, Sverdlov's chief secretary: 'The negligence shown in making the medals for the Red Banner is quite unacceptable ... Everyone's waiting, yet we're incapable of producing the medal. To debate how much cheaper it would be in silver is ludicrous. We're talking about pennies. The medal needs to be three times smaller. The rim should be gilded. The work should be of higher quality.'[105]

When the decoration began being issued in massive numbers to the troops as an incentive, it started to lose its value. In January 1920 Trotsky received a cable from Voroshilov, Budenny and Shchadenko: 'The Revolutionary-Military Council of the Cavalry Army requests the release of 300 Red Banner medals for decorating the troops.' Trotsky's reaction was instant: 'Too many! 50 to 75 can be sent.'[106] Sensing that this form of morale-boosting had got out of hand, he cabled Moscow: 'Decorations issued by the Revolutionary Military Council without ratification of the TsIK should be resubmitted for such ratification.'[107] Sometimes he objected to the decoration of a particular individual. He cabled Sklyansky: 'I regard the decoration of Tukhachevsky with the Red Banner on the army's anniversary as quite inappropriate. It's a purely monarchical way of giving awards ... Tukhachevsky doesn't personify the army, he should be rewarded in accordance with his war service, not because it's the army's anniversary.'[108] In the long term, Trotsky lost the argument, and it was precisely 'the monarchical way' that came to be applied in the Soviet Union.

As soon as the military councils started awarding medals, the question arose of what to do when a soldier, commander or commissar distinguished himself further. Trotsky's solution was simple: 'Many Red Army men, especially pilots, have the order of the Red Banner and difficulties arise over decorating them again when they perform further brave feats. The only way out is to decorate them a second and third time, not with a new medal, but by fixing to the original medal small numbers – two, three, four, and so on. I propose this be done as soon as possible by the presidium of TsIK.'[109]

Trotsky was not yet aware that on 22 November 1919 he would himself be decorated with the Red Banner. The order read: 'Comrade Lev Davidovich Trotsky, having accepted the VTsIK's commission to organize the Red Army, has displayed indefatigability and indestructible energy in his appointed task. His huge efforts have been crowned with brilliant results . . . In the days when Red Petrograd came under direct threat, Comrade Trotsky, in setting off for the Petrograd front, took the closest part in the organization of the brilliantly executed defence of Petrograd, inspiring with his personal bravery the Red Army units under fire at the front.'[110] In September 1920, along with Sklyansky, S.S. Kamenev and Lebedev, Trotsky was also awarded a 'sword of honour of native design'.[111]

The greater part of what Trotsky wrote on the train was collected and published between 1922 and 1924 in five volumes. He recognized that he could not have accomplished so much without help:

All my work in the train, literary and otherwise, would have been impossible without my assisting stenographers, Glazman and Sermuks, and the younger assistant, Nechaev. They worked all day and all night in the moving train, which, disregarding all rules of safety in the fever of war, would rush over shaken ties at a speed of seventy or more kilometres an hour . . . I would watch in wondering gratitude the movements of the hand that, despite the incessant jerking and shaking, could inscribe the finely shaped symbols so clearly. When I was handed the typed script half an hour later, no corrections were necessary. This was not ordinary work; it took on a character of heroic sacrifice.'[112]

Glazman and Sermuks were rather more than 'stenographers', and Trotsky did not name all of his immediate staff who, amounting to more than twenty, probably outnumbered the entourage of any other revolutionary leader.[113] He was perhaps more aware than his colleagues of the need for highly educated staff who were capable of grasping ideas rapidly and composing the appropriate document or collecting data, organizing the execution of an order, and so on.

That he would set up a printing-press and publish a newspaper on his train was perhaps inevitable, given the fact that all his life he had in effect been a journalist. The message he most frequently conveyed was that the entire course of the civil war now depended on the success of the particular front and forces located at the place where he happened to have stopped. He would alight from the train, followed not only by his team of assistants but also by bales of his newspaper *V puti* and pamphlets and addresses which would be distributed at once among the Red Army men and the local population. They would be despatched to the regiments, pinned up on garrison bulletin boards, read aloud by company literates, with the result that many fighters became convinced that the war really did depend on them: the thing would be settled here – after all, Trotsky himself had arrived.

The White leaders knew the importance Trotsky, and indeed the regime, attached to propaganda, and they made efforts to counter it with campaigns of their own, sometimes in new and unexpected ways. In May 1919, for instance, Sermuks showed Trotsky several copies of an order, supposedly signed by Trotsky, which had been removed from the walls of railway stations by Red Army men. The 'order', dated 1 May 1919 and printed in precisely the same format used by Trotsky's press, read:

> After a period of time in which I sold out Russia, which is alien and hateful to me, I achieved the highest power thanks to the hooligan-sailors of Kronstadt and with material help from the Germans. I now govern the remnants of Russia in fear of my death and to the misfortune of all who love Russia. Our cause is quite hopeless, also on the fronts of which I have lost count; all I can see is that the borders of my kingdom are shrinking; within only a year I have lost bountiful Siberia, Turkestan and in a week or so the entire Perm region will have gone, Ukraine doesn't recognize us, we have lost Riga, Pskov has left us and soon there will be no Petrograd ... We are not sorry for Russia, and therefore as before, comrades, we will go on stealing, ruining the labouring peasantry, destroying industry, causing violence and excesses, bestiality, deception.

The document was signed 'Leiba Trotsky-Bronstein' and listed all his posts.[114]

'Why did they tear them down?' Trotsky asked. 'They shouldn't have. No one would believe such a forgery. They should have pasted up my latest order alongside.'

The editor of *V puti* was the former head of the Moscow training battalion, Berezovsky, who also compiled reports on the fronts for *Izvestiya*. Trotsky had issued a general order to all HQs requesting full cooperation with him.[115] Berezovsky began by lauding the War Commissar, but Trotsky quickly put a stop to this, sending a memo to his editor: 'The leading article of No. 18 contains references to me. I regard it as highly inappropriate that such eulogies should appear in a paper printed on our train. I request you to keep personalities out of the paper as far as possible.'[116] Trotsky had no need of petty flattery, having long been used to thinking in terms of epochs and continents.

He took the issue of propaganda very seriously, and expected others to do no less. At the beginning of June 1920 he cabled Karl Radek, who was in charge of 'Polish agitation', with copies to Alexandrov, the deputy chief of the political section of the Revolutionary Military Council, the Central Committee Secretariat, Steklov, editor of *Izvestiya*, and Bukharin, editor of *Pravda*:

> Our agitation on Poland so far in no way corresponds to the importance of events and only touches the masses superficially . . . 1. We must organize flying street meetings on, for instance, the capture of Borisov. Totally precise slogans must be issued from one centre . . . 3. Slogans attacking the Polish bourgeoisie must be posted on every street, at all stations, terminals and so on . . . 4. The poets must be mobilized for this. Up to now practically no poems have been written about the war with Poland. 5. We must bring in the composers, ordering them to compose for the victory of the international over the tune of Polish chauvinism. I suggest we start with a small 'special commission' of poets, playwrights, composers, artists, film-makers, and then, after working out a definite programme, with prizes, create an intellectual-artistic meeting of Proletcult under the slogan 'The Mobilization of the Arts against the Polish Landowners'.[117]

Trotsky established a political section on the train itself, whose task was both to undertake the political education of the crew and to recruit reserve commissars at the stopping-places.[118]

On most of their return trips to Moscow, Trotsky's staff would deposit hundreds of files in the Commissariat, including Trotsky's orders, intelligence data, correspondence on the conduct of the war, details of 'unrest in various towns and localities', materials on 'arrests and investigations, supply questions, cables about leave of absence and apartments'.[119]

The train enjoyed a high degree of autonomy when it came to obtaining weapons and ammunition, equipment and food supplies, usually of the highest quality. When Trotsky discovered that the Tsar's garage with five automobiles had survived, he at once requested the People's Commissar of Transport to transfer them to his train.[120] Thanks to Trotsky's efforts, train personnel enjoyed certain benefits, including cooks and doctors, and there is a note from Trotsky requesting a warm winter coat for one of his staff, Alexander Pukhov, 'who really needs one badly. I request he be authorized to obtain one without having to wait.'[121] Even at the height of the war, Trotsky issued passes for his men to go on leave, for instance three weeks at the end of 1918 for one Comrade Spiridonov.[122]

Apart from his wife, Trotsky had no close friends. Instead, he had what Stalin would later call 'staff'. This was not the same as domestic staff, but rather a silent, terrified socialist staff who, for the privilege of the slave, for the possibility of being somewhat higher than ordinary mortals, were willing to carry out the leader's every wish. Trotsky was one of those who laid the foundations of this numerous and essential attribute of the bureaucratic Moloch.

The Whites and the intervention forces frequently subjected the train to artillery and aircraft bombardment, and several times it was mysteriously derailed. As Trotsky later recalled: 'The train earned the hatred of its enemies and was proud of it. More than once the [Socialist Revolutionaries] made plans to wreck it. At the trial of the [SRs], the story was told in detail by Semenov, who organized the assassination of Volodarsky* and the attempt on Lenin's life, and who also took part in the preparations to wreck the train.'[123]

Later in Berlin, perhaps with the connivance of the Cheka, Semenov published an account of the SRs' terrorist actions, in which

---

* Volodarsky, the Petrograd Commissar for Press Propaganda and Agitation, was assassinated in July 1918.

Trotsky (standing to the left of the left-hand rail) being filmed on the Eastern Front with his armoured train, 1918.

Trotsky visiting the Western Front during the Civil War.

Above: Trotsky talking to a young Red Army recruit.

Right: Trotsky with his deputy Sklyansky and chief of staff S.S. Kamenev (in pointed hat), August 1921.

Right: Recruiting poster for the Red Army.

Below: Red Army men in 1918. The first recruits were poorly equipped and wore rag-tag uniform.

The Red Army captures Kazan, September 1918.

Trotsky's armoured train at Tsaritsyn, 1918.

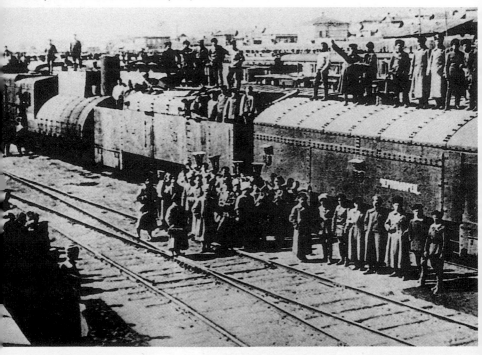

Sketch of Trotsky by
F. Malyavin, 1920.

The Red Army advancing over the frozen Baltic to suppress the sailors and soldiers of the Kronstadt garrison rebelling against Bolshevik policies, March 1921. Bolshevik delegates at the Tenth Party Congress in Moscow were among the assault force.

Interrogation of a sailor by government forces at Kronstadt, 1921.

Lenin, Trotsky and Voroshilov among Red Army men after the suppression of the Kronstadt revolt.

The Praesidium of the Second Congress of Comintern, Moscow, 1920.

Trotsky inspects the Red Army at a parade honouring the Third Congress of Comintern, 1921.

he wrote that, after the murder of Volodarsky, 'we planned the assassination of Lenin and Trotsky'.[124]

The savagery of the war left its mark on Russia. It is hard now to accept that in order to establish the Idea so much blood had to be shed. One of the high priests of that Idea hurried from place to place in his special armoured train. It never occurred to him to doubt whether the great idea could be built on the pinnacle of a heap of his countrymen's skulls. The fact is, any dictatorship needs terror. And Trotsky, like the other leaders of the revolution, knew it.

The Dictatorship and Terror

Radically-minded Russian revolutionaries had for decades believed that, in a country where the peasantry were the overwhelming majority, only a dictatorship of the proletariat would be capable of moving society in the desired direction. Thus, the unrestrained use of violence against the enemies of the dictatorship was justified in their minds. To a considerable degree the Bolsheviks were compelled by their opponents to use force and by the manifest failure of their economic policy to resort to extreme measures. Lenin had to admit that 'on the economic front and with our attempt to go over to Communism, by the spring of 1921 we had suffered a more serious defeat than anything inflicted on us by Kolchak, Denikin or Pilsudski, far more serious and far more fundamental and dangerous. Our economic policy was isolated from the grass roots.'[125]

In the unstable circumstances that reigned throughout the country, the situation in the Red Army was also unstable. Typical of the reports Trotsky was receiving from the Cheka in different localities was one dated 15 May 1919, covering Ukraine. In Kiev province anti-Semitic agitation was widespread. Jewish members of the Cheka in Uman district were being captured by the population and shot, and the local villages were anti-Soviet. In Berdichev district Red Army units were running riot, perpetrating pogroms under the slogan 'Beat the Yids, smash the Cheka – they're our enemies'. Vasilkovsk district was rife with banditry, counter-revolutionaries and 'every other kind of scum'. There were constant risings, looting, murder, attacks on the Cheka.

'In one case practically the entire staff of the local Cheka were murdered by bandits. The leather factory was razed to the ground by Red
Army men.' In Tarashchansk, when a gang of twenty bandits was
approaching, the Red Army commander assembled his men and asked
them if they wanted to fight: they voted to abandon the town. The
gang entered Tarashchansk, opened the army stores and started selling
goods to the population. Similar accounts of wholesale banditry, pogroms and Red Army failure came from all over Russia.[126]

The peasantry had been allowed by the Bolsheviks to take the land,
but now they were being subjected to seizure and requisitioning. The
Soviet regime had been forced to change its policy towards the peasantry, differentiating between the various levels of the agrarian population and using extreme measures in the process. In an article entitled
'The Governing Principles of [Our] Policy in the Don Region',
Trotsky outlined the regime's attitude to the Cossacks:

> We explain to the Cossacks by word and show them by deed that our
> policy is not one of revenge for the past. We do not forget anything,
> but we are not avenging the past . . . We watch carefully to ensure that
> the Red Army does not commit pillage and rape as it advances. Firmly
> aware that any excess by Red Army forces . . . would become a major
> political fact and create the most enormous difficulties, we nevertheless
> demand everything the Red Army needs from the population, we collect
> everything in an organized way through the food committees and we
> are careful to pay fully and promptly . . . We deal demonstratively with
> elements that penetrated the Don during its cleansing.[127]

'Organized' and 'demonstratively' were of course euphemisms
intended to conceal coercion and violence.

The mood among the peasants could not but be felt also by the
Red Army, which consisted mostly of peasants, as Trotsky was well
aware. He wrote to Lenin in December 1919: 'All the information
from the localities confirms that the emergency tax has greatly aroused
the local population and is having a bad effect on the ranks. It is the
mood of most of the provinces. In view of the poor food situation it
would seem necessary to halt the emergency tax or to moderate it
sharply, at least as far as the families of serving men are concerned.'[128]

The sufferings of the villages and other causes of discontent among
the Red Army soldiers, not least the successes of the White armies,

created a mood of unrest and a wave of desertion. Commanders, faced with chaotically retreating units shouting 'We're surrounded!' resorted to the sort of coercion that is customary in time of war, the threat of the firing-squad. But what was permissible on the battlefield soon became a key feature of the Soviet system. Trotsky found the situation perfectly normal, and never revised his views. Later, in his memoirs, he wrote: 'An army cannot be built without [repression]. Masses of men cannot be led to death unless the army command has the death penalty in its arsenal. So long as those malicious tailless apes that are so proud of their technical achievements – the animals that we call men – will build armies and wage wars, the command will always be obliged to place the soldiers between the possible death at the front and the inevitable one in the rear.'[129]

Repression was in Trotsky's view a component part of military structure, a method for educating both officers and men. A telegram he sent to the Revolutionary Military Committee of the Western Front in 1919 is characteristic: 'One of the most important principles of educating our army is never to leave a single crime or misdemeanour unpunished . . . Repression must follow immediately upon a breach of discipline, for repression is not an end in itself, but is directed towards didactic, military aims . . . Breaches of discipline and disobedience . . . must be subjected to the harshest punishment.'[130] It was Trotsky's belief that the threat of harsh punishment would compensate for the low level of awareness, conviction and training of the army rank and file. Curiously, like Lenin, Trotsky regarded consciousness as the foundation of discipline, yet he stressed that fear and arrest should be used to instil discipline.

He told his commanders to set an example in the field, but also to command with an iron fist and not to flinch from using their weapons to maintain order. When someone pointed out to him that not all commanders and commissars had revolvers, he at once cabled Lenin: 'The absence of revolvers creates an impossible situation at the front. It is impossible to maintain discipline without a revolver. I suggest Comrades Mironov and Pozern requisition revolvers from everyone who is not on active duty.'[131] The threat of punishment gradually entered the structure and functioning of the army, and also entered people's minds as a moral norm, 'revolver law', the revolutionary imperative, proletarian necessity.

On 26 November 1918 Trotsky wrote to a number of army military councils, with copies to Lenin and Sverdlov: 'I draw your attention to the fact that 9th Army is working very poorly. Its HQ's orders are not being carried out, the army is marking time . . . The divisional and regimental commanders must be made to go over to the attack at any price. If the position does not change in the course of the next week, I shall be compelled to apply severe repression against the commanding personnel of 9th Army.'[132] In due course he was able to acknowledge the achievements of 9th Army: '8th and 9th Armies have gone over to victorious offensives. The first steps have made significant advances: there are many prisoners and much booty. I demand merciless punishment for the deserters and shirkers who are paralyzing the will of 10th Army . . . No mercy for deserters and shirkers. Commanders and commissars answer for disobedience and cowardice. Advance!'[133]

All civil wars are inordinately bloody, but the sheer scale of the Russian civil war made it one of the most violent in recorded history. And its violence was expressed not only in military, but also in economic, social and spiritual terms. Addressing an audience of Chekists on 7 November 1918, Lenin declared: 'When we are reproached for our harshness, we wonder how people could have forgotten the most elementary Marxism. What is important for us is that the Cheka is directly involved in bringing about the dictatorship of the proletariat, and for that reason its rôle is invaluable. There is no other way to the liberation of the masses than by means of violence against the exploiters.'[134] It seemed completely normal that the regime should employ the most violent means to attain its ends. Lenin could send a telegram to Trotsky in Sviyazhsk, thanking him for his good wishes for Lenin's health and adding: 'I'm sure the crushing of the Kazan Czechs and White Guards, as well as the kulak-bloodsuckers who support them, will be carried out with an exemplary lack of mercy.'[135]

Trotsky, however, would apply 'an exemplary lack of mercy' to more than just 'kulak-bloodsuckers'. Thousands of peasants were driven into the Red Army, many of them only recently released from the trenches of the First World War and with no appetite for wading through any more mud, taking part in bayonet charges or being fed on by lice. Battalions and regiments were melting away as soon as they were formed, as Red Army men scattered to their homes. Desertion acquired mass proportions. S. Olikov, who had been engaged on recapturing deserters, wrote an interesting study of the subject in the 1920s, in which he noted that desertion reached particularly high numbers in the second half of 1918 and the first half of 1919: 'In the first two weeks of their punitive and agitational operations, the [desertion] commissions produced 31,683 men who were either caught or returned voluntarily. The next weeks saw 47,393 such cases. In a few months as many as 100,000 were caught. Only force, the threat of execution (and many were executed mercilessly), forced thousands of men to return to the front.'[136] Trotsky realized he would never build an effective army as long as the epidemic of 'boycotting the war' continued, and hence a large number of desertion commissions was formed, at divisional, army and front levels. On 2 June 1919 Lenin and Sklyansky co-signed a special Defence Council order according to which deserters who failed to report to their units or to the authorities 'will be regarded as enemies and traitors of the toiling people and will be sentenced to severe punishment, including execution'.[137]

On his first trip to the front Trotsky dictated a number of extremely harsh orders on deserters. On 30 August 1918, for instance, he reported that: 'Yesterday 5th Army field court martial sentenced twenty deserters to death. First of all, commanders and commissars who had abandoned the posts entrusted to them were executed. Then cowardly liars who had tried to pass as unfit. Finally, a number of Red Army deserters who refused to atone for their crime by agreeing to fight in the future.'[138]

Such measures helped, but not invariably. Fear prevented many from escaping to their homes, but not everyone. There were also many deserters who were motivated by political considerations. Thousands of the former tsarist officers who had been swept into the army were divided into three categories by Denikin in his study of the civil war:

The first, very few in number, were those who 'stood on the Bolshevik platform', that is, they were either sincere Communists or 'Octobrists' [i.e. sympathizers since the coup], in any event sufficiently compromised by their close association with the bloody work of the Bolsheviks to be denied a place outside the Soviet system ... A second group, equally small in number, were the so-called 'counter-revolutionaries' who actively worked against the Soviet regime, despite the repression,

Cheka persecution and terror. They took part in scattered outbreaks, uprisings, assassination attempts, defection to the White armies, and so on. Finally, the third group, and the most numerous, were flung into the Red Army by hunger, fear and compulsion, and they shared the fate of the Russian intellectuals who had become specialists.[139]

Denikin and other commanding White officers did their best to persuade former tsarist officers either to leave the Red Army or not to join it. One of Denikin's orders, calling on men to leave the Red Army at once, warned those who refused that they would be cursed by the people and tried by a 'stern and pitiless court martial' of the Russian Army.[140] The order was circulated clandestinely in the Soviet Republic and some officers obeyed it, with the result that even more severe repression followed. Former tsarist officers continued to go over to the Whites, nevertheless. In response, Trotsky instituted hostage-taking. On 2 December 1918 he cabled the Revolutionary Military Council at Serpukhov:

> I ordered you to establish the family status of former officers among command personnel and to inform each of them by signed receipt that treachery or treason will cause the arrest of their families and that, therefore, they are each taking upon themselves responsibility for their families. That order is still in force. Since then there have been a number of cases of treason by former officers, yet not in a single case, as far as I know, has the family of the traitor been arrested, as the registration of former officers has evidently not been carried out at all. Such a negligent approach to so important a matter is totally impermissible.[141]

Similar reports and orders were sent by Trotsky to other army chiefs. To Kazan he cabled:

> 11th Division has revealed its utter uselessness. Units are still surrendering without a fight. The root of the evil is in the command staff. Obviously, the [Regional Military Commissar] has concentrated on the combat and technical side and forgotten about the political. I suggest a strict watch be kept on recruited personnel and that command responsibilities be given only to those former officers whose families reside within Soviet borders, and that they be informed by signed receipt that they are responsible for the lives of their families.[142]

Former officers themselves were also held as hostages, and many would be shot when one of their fellow ex-officers went over to the Whites. Trotsky asked Dzerzhinsky to let him know whether there were 'still any former officers who had been taken hostage in concentration camps and prisons. If so, where are they and how many?'[143] Any method was appropriate, in Trotsky's view, if it prevented the disintegration of the Red Army. He formulated the hostage policy in an order of 2 November 1919: 'Families of traitors must be arrested at once. Traitors themselves must be registered in the army's black book, so that after the imminent and final triumph of the revolution, not a single traitor can escape punishment.'[144] In 1920 he ordered that 'families found guilty of aiding Wrangel will be deported beyond the Baikal'.[145]

When on 25 October 1918, however, Trotsky proposed at the Central Committee that all officers being held hostage be set free, it was decided that only those 'who did not belong to the counter-revolution' would be released. 'They will be recruited into the Red Army, at which time they will submit the names of their family and be told that the family will be arrested, should they go over to the White Guards.'[146] According to Denikin, however, rumours about treason and treachery were exaggerated. In two years, he received reliable information from a former general of the Soviet headquarters staff that only one case of material significance had occurred for certain.

The most difficult category to make fight was the rank and file. Trotsky relied particularly on Communists and commissars, and on the whole his expectations were fulfilled, although not invariably. There were cases when entire units abandoned their positions and fled the field of battle. With Moscow's approval, Trotsky took the major decision of placing blocking units behind unreliable detachments, with orders to shoot if they retreated without permission. Thus, when Stalin applied this policy in 1941–42, he was merely applying the experience of the civil war under new conditions.

Blocking units appeared for the first time in August 1918 on the eastern front in 1st Army under the command of Tukhachevsky, who was the first to issue orders to shoot. In December 1918 Trotsky ordered the formation of special detachments to serve as blocking units. On 18 December he cabled: 'How do things stand with the blocking units? As far as I am aware they have not been included in our establishment and it appears they have no personnel. It is absolutely essential that we have at least an embryonic network of blocking units and that we work out a procedure for bringing them up to strength and deploying them.'[147]

Trotsky was not content to issue general orders, but gave specific instructions on how the new units were to be used. He told Ivanov, chief of the blocking units:

> Evidently in many cases blocking units are doing no more than holding individual deserters. In fact the role of the blocking units during an attack must be more active. They must be deployed closely behind our lines and when necessary give a shove to stragglers and the hesitant. As far as possible, blocking units must have at their disposal either a truck with a machine-gun or a light vehicle with a machine-gun, or, finally, some cavalry with machine-guns.[148]

There were occasions when blocking units were used to restore order in the rear following a panic retreat. On 19 May 1919 Sklyansky reported to Trotsky: 'Stalin reports: the front is being brought to order, three punitive companies have been sent to Luga, Gatchina and Krasnoe Selo. Zinoviev is going to Luga, Stalin to Staraya Rusa, the scattered 6th Division has been brought together and order is being restored, the divisional commander, who showed cowardice, has been removed.'[149]

Deserters were to be treated in various ways, according to their behaviour. Trotsky ordered that: 'Every deserter who turns up at divisional or regimental HQ and declares, "I am a deserter but I swear I shall fight honourably from now on," is to be forgiven and allowed to fulfil the high duties of a warrior in the Workers' and Peasants' Army. A deserter who offers resistance to arrest shall be executed on the spot.'[150]

Trotsky used every means available to him to strengthen morale: threats, arrests, encouragement, rewards, appeals to class instinct, political education. Once, on reading a routine report on desertions, he dictated a cable to the War Commissariat: 'I suggest as a punishment for the Army and Navy that black collars be worn by deserters who have been returned to their unit, by soldiers who refuse an order or have committed pillage and so on. Anyone wearing a black collar who is caught committing a second crime shall be doubly punished. Black collars shall be removed only in the event of exemplary behaviour or military valour.'[151] This idea was not adopted by the leadership, thus sparing thousands from public shame.

Generally, however, Trotsky's harsh line on discipline was supported. Typical of the sort of communication he sent to Lenin on this subject was the following:

> The cause of the shameful failures on the Voronezh front is the total collapse of 8th Army. The chief blame falls on the commissars who have not brought themselves to use tough measures. Six weeks ago I demanded stern punishment for deserters from the Voronezh front. Nothing was done. Regiments wander from place to place, leaving their positions at will and at the first sign of danger ... The field tribunals then went to work. The first executions of deserters took place. The order was announced placing responsibility for harbouring deserters on Soviet deputies, Committees of the Poor and heads of households. The first executions had their effect. I hope a breakthrough will be achieved in a short time. More tough Communists are needed. I'm staying at the Voronezh front until things are in order.[152]

The tribunals were at work throughout the civil war. An especially large number of executions took place in 1918–19, although 1920 and 1921 were not far behind. According to a participant: 'The new courts were called tribunals (as in the time of the Great French Revolution). The sentences of these courts could not be appealed. Sentences were not ratified and had to be carried out within twenty-four hours.'[153] Of course, many of the victims were genuine enemies of the Soviet Republic, but the overwhelming majority were simple peasants who either had no idea of what was happening or no wish to die for the 'Commune'.

The total number of those sentenced to death by the military tribunals is not known, but a figure for Russian and Ukrainian executions in 1921 has been compiled from the evidence of cables formulated and signed by the Deputy Chairman of the Military Collegium of the Supreme Tribunal, V. Sorokin, and its director of statistics, M. Strogovich. The figure is 4337,[154] but 1921 was a less 'fruitful' year than its predecessors.

Although Trotsky was better informed than most about desertion and other shameful events taking place in the army, he reacted with anger when the press wrote about it. On 14 July 1919, over the direct

line to Sklyansky, he conveyed his indignation in a memorandum to
the Central Committee about articles by various 'idlers who are trying
to discredit the army'. He was especially incensed by pieces written
by Tarasov-Rodionov which had appeared in *Izvestiya*, and which were
'a shameful and false slander of the Red Army, depicting the entire
command staff as traitors, members of the Revolutionary Military
Councils as brainless and incapable of using the Communists, and so
on and so on . . . Tarasov-Rodionov is a dubious Communist.'[155]

Trotsky reminded the Central Committee that he knew of Tarasov-
Rodionov from another era: 'In June 1917 he was, it seems, a Left
SR, and when he was called in for questioning about the events of
July he behaved like a coward and renegade and traitor . . . Later he
wormed his way into the Soviet regime,'[156] and became a divisional
commander. Trotsky was close to the truth about Tarasov-Rodionov's
character: in 1935, when his Left SR past and his pre-revolutionary
criticism of Stalin caught up with him, Tarasov-Rodionov wrote to
Voroshilov, the Defence Commissar: 'The Left SR rebellion was a
veiled attempt by Trotsky and his followers to seize power from Lenin
in order to disrupt the Brest treaty. The Left SRs were used as the
skirmishers of the rebellion, but behind them were forces led by Trotsky and his accomplices.' In other letters, Tarasov-Rodionov repented
of his 'renegade letters of July 1917 concerning the true Bolshevik,
Stalin', managing meanwhile to inform on Kamenev, with whom he
was personally acquainted. Despite signing his letters as 'constantly
true to the Party and devoted to you', his fate had already been
sealed.[157]

The fact that mass executions were taking place at the front was
known to many Party members, and it was discussed at the Eighth
Party Congress in connection with concern over the arrest of Communists. Trotsky's response was a lengthy letter to the Central Committee in which he explained the reasons for his position. He argued that
nothing the Congress Commission had decreed contradicted the army
administration's policy in practical terms, 'as it has been carried out
up until now with the approval of the Central Committee . . . Precisely
because I have observed at too close quarters difficult, even tragic
episodes in the active armies, I know all too well how great the temptation is to replace formal discipline with so-called "comradely" or
domestic discipline, but I also know all too well that such a change

would signal the total disintegration of the army.'[158] He then analyzed the case of a Communist who had been executed on the basis of his representations and a decision of the court, and argued that the serious situation at the front had made it necessary: 'The army can be held together only by the greatest exertion, supporting discipline from top to bottom by means of the toughest and in many cases harshest regime. The opposition's slogan is "Loosen the screws!" My point of view is that the screws must be tightened.' He ended on a tough note: 'It is important that the centre . . . not be infected with panic and not fall in with the psychological schemes of the Voroshilovs and Osinskys. Comrade Zinoviev's report raises serious concern that he is looking for a solution precisely on the path of weakening the regime and adapting to the fatigue of certain elements of our Party. To the extent that the Central Committee bureau has approved Comrade Zinoviev's report, I would like to think it has not approved this part of the report, for otherwise I would see no chance of the Party's success in the forthcoming difficult struggle.'[159]

To achieve a set goal, Trotsky's usual course of action was to opt for the most extreme measures. In June 1919 he ordered the Revolutionary Military Council of 8th Army: 'Pride of place must now be given to the work of the tribunal, which must be strongly reinforced. Punishment must follow immediately after the crime. During the cleansing of a wide strip it seems the command staff of the army did not take proper measures to seize from the population the maximum number of carts, nor to mobilize all those capable of bearing arms and to transport them to the rear, in case they became available to the enemy. Circumstances demand that measures of severe military dictatorship be applied.'[160]

Even when a shortage of uniforms or poor food was at issue, Trotsky invariably explained it in class terms. Reporting to the Central Committee on Ukraine, he wrote: 'The well-fed kulak, his rifle well-concealed, looks with contempt at the Red Army man, barefoot and hungry, and the [soldier] feels unsure of himself and humiliated. We have to run a hot iron down the spine of the Ukrainian kulaks – that will create a good working environment.'[161]

They were harsh times. Those who wanted to stifle the revolution were harsh, as were its defenders. Berdyaev rightly observed that 'truth has ceased to interest both sides'. Harshness was, as it were, programmed by the unswerving Bolshevik aim of installing the dictatorship of the proletariat. Lenin himself admitted that 'dictatorship is a harsh word, a difficult, bloody, tormenting word, and such words are not uttered idly'.[162] Force was the natural expression of the dictatorship, according to the leader of the revolution. Execution was for him just another way of settling social and political problems. He could, for instance, write that 'false informers must be prosecuted more sternly and punished by shooting'.[163] That Lenin was the chief Jacobin of the revolution was something Maxim Gorky had observed when he wrote in November 1917 that Lenin 'is talented, he has all the qualities of a "leader", but also, what is essential for that rôle, an absence of morality and a purely lordly, merciless attitude to the lives of the masses'.[164] In the last analysis, it was neither Lenin nor Trotsky who mattered. A doctrine based on the primacy of the dictatorship of the proletariat and class war, if it is adopted as a political programme, will find appropriate leaders, even if those leaders attempt to limit the dictatorship by so-called revolutionary legitimacy.

Presenting Trotsky, therefore, as a resolute advocate of repression at the front does not mean that he was personally lawless, at least in formal terms. He acted within the framework of Bolshevik military policy, 'with the approval of the Central Committee' and with the aid of the tribunals. A letter of 6 May 1919 from him to the leadership of 2nd Army demonstrates this:

> Respected Comrades: From a conversation with the chief and commissar of 28th Division, I have established that shootings without trial have taken place in 2nd Army. I do not doubt for one minute that the people who were subjected to this punishment deserved it fully. This is guaranteed by the composition of the Revolutionary Military Council. Nevertheless, executions without trial are totally impermissible. Naturally, in a war situation, under fire, commanders and commissars and even other ranks might be compelled to kill a traitor or provocateur on the spot if they had tried to sow disorder in our ranks. But apart from this exceptional situation . . . executions without trial and without the judgement of a tribunal cannot be permitted at all . . . I suggest 2nd Army organize a sufficiently competent and energetic tribunal with circuit sections and also terminate shootings without trial in all divisions.[165]

This document appeared at a time when lynch law was common in many units, and regarded as normal. Within two months Trotsky published another order, No. 126:

> Comrades, Red Army men, commanders, commissars! Let your just anger be directed only against the enemy with a gun in his hand. Be merciful to prisoners, even if they are obvious scoundrels. Among prisoners and refugees there may be many who entered Denikin's army either from ignorance or under the lash. I order that under no circumstances should prisoners be shot, but should be sent to the rear . . . All cases of disobedience must be reported and a Revolutionary military tribunal must be sent immediately to the scene of the crime.[166]

It appears from these documents that Trotsky was trying to contain the rampant harshness and lynch mentality within a framework of martial law.

Anatomy of War

Trotsky's chief influence on the formation of military policy was felt at the Eighth Party Congress, even though he was not present. He returned to Moscow in early March 1919 partly to deal with a host of problems at the Revolutionary Military Council, but mainly because the Party Congress which was due to take place later that month would discuss, among other things, the military issue. Trotsky intended telling the Central Committee that the army command was planning a major effort to break the combined forces of the interventionist and White armies in Ukraine, as well as on the Karelia to Rovno sector, during the coming spring. These campaigns were crucial to the defence of the main economic and political centres of the country.

Trotsky intended to give the Congress a detailed picture of the military position and to formulate a series of basic tenets on the building of the Red Army, knowing that there was serious opposition to his views among Party members at the front and in Moscow. He had been made particularly aware of this on 15 February 1919 when he put into action his statute on garrison and sentry duty and the first part of his field manual on war of movement. These documents had been drawn up by former tsarist officers, who naturally took most of their ideas from the practical manuals of the old Russian army, a fact at once noticed by commissars who saw this as an attempt to resurrect 'the old order'.

That, however, was only half the trouble. Trotsky also learnt that his work as War Commissar was being openly criticized by many well-known Party leaders. On the whole he was unconcerned by such criticism, since he always consulted Lenin and kept him informed. In effect, he had been practising Central Committee policy, whether on the question of recruitment or the struggle against desertion.

At this time, news was coming in that German forces under General von der Goltz were moving towards Riga and that Polish troops were advancing on Minsk. This information did not exercise Trotsky particularly, as he knew no large numbers were yet involved. But then very disturbing news came from the east. Kolchak, having recovered from the losses of 1918, was advancing westwards. According to intelligence he had 150,000 infantry and cavalry against the Red Army's 100,000 on the eastern front, and in his rear he had the potential support of large numbers of intervention forces.

Analyzing the situation in March 1919, Vatsetis later wrote: 'It was entirely clear to me that Kolchak's advance on the Middle Volga was a grandiose demonstration aimed at using energetic pressure to draw a large number of our armed forces to the Eastern Front, and then by falling back to suck them further into Western Siberia, that is, away from our main theatre of war, especially from the Southern Front, where we were preparing to deal with Denikin.'[167] A month later, Lenin came to the same conclusion: 'Kolchak's offensive,' he told a meeting of factory committees and trade unions in Moscow, 'which is inspired by the Allies, is aimed at drawing our forces from the Southern Front in order to allow the remnants of the White Guards and the Petliurists [forces of the Ukrainian nationalist leader Simon Petliura] to reorganize themselves. We shall not move a single company from the Southern Front.'[168] Of the position in March 1919, however, the historian A. Anishev noted that 1st, 2nd, 4th and 5th Armies had begun a general withdrawal: 'The troops showed all the signs of disintegration associated with a retreating army. Desertion and defection to the Whites assumed significant proportions, there was unrest in the ranks and entire regiments were breaking up.'[169]

Telegrams from the front disrupted Trotsky's plans. He had intended to report to the Congress that after a short breathing-spell a decisive offensive could be launched in several directions. But the enemy was ahead of him. A Central Committee meeting of 14 March 1919 approved a motion by Trotsky calling for all military personnel, including himself, to leave at once for the front.[170] When the army delegates heard this there was a determined protest, their main argument being that the situation at the front was not catastrophic. Moreover, they argued on 16 March, if they were all to leave for the front 'the units at the front might see it as a sign that the centre did not want to hear the voice of the army'. Some even thought it was a trick. The session decided that Trotsky should leave at once for the front, but that Sokolnikov should announce to a meeting of front delegates that the directive on their departure had been rescinded and that only those should go who felt that their presence at the front was essential. The question of military policy was placed at the top of the Congress agenda.[171]

Before leaving for the front Trotsky met Sokolnikov on 16 March for what turned out to be a brief conversation. Trotsky presented his ideas on the need to build a regular, professional permanent army, free of domination by the Party. It seems likely that his ideas had already been seen by Lenin, for on 21 March at a plenary session of the Congress it was Lenin who spoke as the chief advocate of Trotsky's theses. Trotsky left instructions with his supporters about how they should defend his ideas. He was depending especially on Alexei Okulov, but Okulov arrived late for the meeting.[172]

Sokolnikov began his report to the Congress, outlining Trotsky's nineteen points[173] and explaining that the Central Committee's military policy was structured 'in the way it is expressed in Comrade Trotsky's theses'.[174] He then laid out the principles for forming a regular army. Included in Trotsky's points was the idea of putting former officers of the old army into command positions, as well as raising the profile of military commissars and Communist cells in units and on naval ships. A firm supporter of Trotsky, Sokolnikov continued: 'On the question of military specialists the issue is not entirely a military one, but one of general principle. When the question was raised of bringing former engineers into the factories, and using former capitalist organizers, you recall that the Left

Communists published the harshest "super-Communist" criticism, which asserted that to return an engineer to the factory would mean returning capital to the commanding heights. And now we have the perfect analogy of that criticism, but in the military field. They say that by returning former officers to the army we are resurrecting the old officer class and the old army. But these comrades are forgetting that alongside the commander stands the commissar, the representative of Soviet power.'[175] Sokolnikov reproduced exactly what Trotsky had wanted him to say, but he did it without the brilliance and conviction the author of the ideas would have brought, a fact Zinoviev alluded to when he later gave a report on the Congress to the Party activists in Petrograd.[176]

Had Trotsky addressed the Congress he would no doubt have stressed the fact that there was still a large measure of support for Party domination in the army, practised in particular by Voroshilov, who was under Stalin's protection. Two months earlier in January 1919, for instance, Trotsky had informed Lenin on the direct line: 'If you want to know what Tsaritsyn is, read Okulov's report which consists entirely of factual material and reports from commissars. I consider Stalin's protection of the Tsaritsyn tendency as a most dangerous sore, worse than any treason or treachery by military specialists ... Rukhimovich is Voroshilov's other name [i.e. both were equally hostile to military specialists]; in a month we shall have to eat the Tsaritsyn dish ... Rukhimovich is not alone, they support each other firmly, raising ignorance into a principle ... Artem should be appointed, but not Voroshilov and not Rukhimovich ... I ask you once more to read Okulov's report on the Tsaritsyn army carefully to see the way Voroshilov has demoralized it with Stalin's collaboration.'[177]

Lenin had been told the day before in a cable from Pyatakov that Trotsky was determined not to use Voroshilov at the front. Trotsky had utter contempt for Voroshilov, whom he regarded as a poor war leader and a defender of anti-professionalism in the army. In October 1918, for instance, Trotsky had cabled Lenin: 'Voroshilov can command a regiment, but not an army of fifty thousand men,' and he threatened to put Voroshilov on trial for failing to carry out his instructions.[178] Thus, Trotsky would have plenty to say had he stayed for the Congress.

After Sokolnikov it was the turn of Smirnov to speak. Smirnov, a member of the Revolutionary Military Council of 5th Army, was Trotsky's chief opponent, and his tone was accusatory. He claimed that 'the general command of all the armed forces is extremely unsatis-factory', and referred to the dangerous leaning in army construction 'towards the mechanical resurrection of structures of the old army, including those which were once conditioned not by the demands of military technique, but by the class relations of the pre-revolutionary order, and which are organic relics of the autocratic-serf order'.[179] Smirnov's speech, which expressed the views of the so-called 'military opposition', pushed the Party back towards militia-style thinking in military construction, to the abolition of single command and stern discipline. Of particular harm to Trotsky's position was Smirnov's insistence that military specialists not be put in positions of command.

The fact that sixty-four delegates spoke on the military question at the Congress indicates the interest and feeling it generated. The most vigorous of Trotsky's opponents was Voroshilov, whose hostility dated from the autumn of 1918, when, as commander of 10th Army with Stalin, he had shown insubordination and blatant persecution of specialists. Trotsky had turned to Lenin and got his support, as first Voroshilov and then Stalin were withdrawn from Tsaritsyn. Voroshilov tried to show that all the successes of the Tsaritsyn army had come only because 'the command staff was not made up of the men of [the old] general staff, not made up of specialists'. He described this army as 'close to our ideal'. Without naming Trotsky, it was clear who his target was. During the session of the military section, some-one placed officers' epaulettes on the table, enabling Voroshilov's supporters to claim that Trotsky was facilitating the defection of specialists to the Whites.

At this, Okulov, who had been savaged by Voroshilov, spoke up: 'I beg your attention for a moment. Officers' epaulettes have appeared here on the table. This is their history. When Comrade Trotsky was in Tsaritsyn, as a result of a discussion with many of the comrades who were there, it was suggested to the Council (of 10th Army) that some sort of marks of distinction should be devised . . . They were designed from sketches I had made of the Red Star, sewn in gold and silver thread . . . This scheme, which did not receive approval, was known also to Comrade Voroshilov. The scheme was sent somewhere and somehow buried. When I was leaving Tsaritsyn, with the enemy only a few kilometres away, a close colleague of Comrade Shchadenko dragged out these same epaulettes and started up a campaign to the effect that general staffer Yegorov was taking seventy traitors with him and that the epaulettes had been prepared on Trotsky's instructions with the idea of handing 10th Army over to the Whites. And that filthy provocation has now been dragged up here at the Congress.'[180]

In the absence of Trotsky and a necessary degree of resistance, the 'military opposition' gained the upper hand. A roll-call vote on Smirnov's theses received thirty-seven against twenty for Trotsky's. In effect, the vote reflected the influence of the 'Left Communists' who were especially active in the first half of 1919, and it was thus leftist revolutionary principles for building and running the army that emerged from the Congress. Trotsky had feared this outcome. He received Sklyansky's daily and gloomy reports on the proceedings, hoping in his heart that Lenin would come to the rescue and defend his position, for otherwise, he feared, the difficulties would not only come from the external enemy, but also from short-sightedness and pseudo-revolutionism on the domestic scene. And he was right. What Sokolnikov had failed to do, however, Lenin set out to achieve.

At the evening session of 21 March Lenin listened attentively to the speeches. Aralov produced a survey of the situation at the fronts, Yaroslavsky outlined the course of the debate and the differences that had surfaced in the military section, and Safarov criticized Trotsky's ideas and called for the introduction of 'Party hegemony in the army'. Then Okulov, while defending Trotsky's theses, said that it was not the operational command, 'but the Communist command', i.e. not the specialists, who were making huge mistakes, not only in the military but also in the political sphere. He cited some facts: the political commissar of 1st Steel Division reported that there was flogging in the detachments; the political commissar of Trotsky Regiment 'beats the men'; instant field courts martial were being set up and were sentencing Red Army men to corporal punishment. Okulov wanted to show the delegates that the incompetent military leadership was also politically inept.

Voroshilov claimed that 'there was little truth' in Okulov's speech, and urged that 'we should not place great hopes in our specialists, even if only because these specialists are different people'. He referred several times to 'Comrade Stalin', whose own speech, delivered in a flat, quiet voice, also sharply criticized Okulov and hence also Trotsky and the Centre. 'I say this,' Stalin stated, 'in order to lift the shame that has been heaped on the army by Comrade Okulov.' As always, Stalin was taking a middle position, criticizing Trotsky's line, and hence also the Central Committee's, while agreeing partly with it, and borrowing something from Smirnov while rejecting the rest. In one thing, however, he was consistent, and that was the use of force: 'I have to say that those non-worker elements who form the majority of our army, the peasants, will not fight for socialism, they will not! They don't want to fight voluntarily. Our task then is to force them to fight, to make them follow the proletariat not only in the rear but also at the front, force them to fight imperialism.'[181] No one objected to this line, all were agreed that the dictatorship of the proletariat must compel the peasants to hand over their grain, to pay taxes and to fight for the new regime.

Trotsky, for all his leftism, understood that in order to stand fast and create a shield for the defence of socialism it was necessary to use the experience of the 'despised imperialists', the experience of the old army and military history. He showed that, for all his intellect, he was also pragmatic. When the Congress closed, for instance, he cabled the central organizing bureau of the Party, the Orgburo: 'I enclose herewith the minutes of a meeting of military delegates . . . According to a Congress resolution, the Central Committee must as soon as possible settle the question of Party committees in the army. The minutes contain valuable material on this, as the issue of Party commissions was subjected to detailed discussion and voting.'[182]

It was inevitable that Trotsky would make many enemies. Not only because of his execrable non-Bolshevik past, nor because, like others, he made serious mistakes, and not only because he unexpectedly stood firm over the military specialists and defended intelligent practices borrowed from the old army. Many could not accept his way of working, his hardness and inflexibility, but above all his independent judgement and superior intellect. Lenin knew that had Trotsky been present, his powers of presentation and analysis would surely have won the day.

To defend both Trotsky and the Central Committee's policy, therefore, Lenin took the floor. He opened by declaring that the Central

Committee had been conscious of the loss it was inflicting on Congress by sending Trotsky back to the front, and then launched into an attack on Trotsky's critics. 'When Comrade Goloshchekin said that the military administration was not following Party policy . . . this was a crazy accusation. You bring not a shadow of argument.' He spoke sharply against partisan thinking: '[One] can hear it in all the speeches of Voroshilov and Goloshchekin . . . What Voroshilov said bears awful traces of partisan thinking. That's an indisputable fact. Comrade Voroshilov says: we had no military specialists and we had 60,000 losses. That is frightful.' Lenin defended Okulov: 'Comrade Voroshilov came out with such monstrous things as that Okulov had destroyed the army. That is monstrous. Okulov was following Central Committee policy.' (None of this would help Okulov in the 1930s.) He summed up: 'This is a historic transition from a Party-run to a regular army, the Central Committee has discussed it dozens of times, but here it has been said that all that has to be thrown out and that we must start again. Never and under no circumstances.'[183]

Sokolnikov had also described Trotsky as the executor of Party policy and had added: 'For us it was clear that the issue was not only to overturn previous Party policy; had the Congress put the question thus, it would have been necessary also to take the conduct of that policy . . . out of Comrade Trotsky's hands . . . We would ask, whom would the opposition put in Trotsky's place? I don't even ask the quest. on seriously.'[184]

The fact that he received support at the Congress did not mean that Trotsky was an infallible war leader: far from it. Some of his mistakes were significant. He had quickly grasped the central operational fact about the Red Army: its fronts were all internal, and when necessary, troops could be moved from one front to another. The Whites and intervention forces lacked this advantage. But occasionally, as a military non-professional, Trotsky's understanding of operational conditions was superficial. For instance, in the spring of 1919 forces of the eastern front under the command of S.S. Kamenev delivered a powerful counter-attack against Kolchak. The Whites fell back and headed east, pursued by the Reds. On 6 June Vatsetis, with Trotsky's approval, ordered the transfer of some units to the southern front, which was under pressure. Commander of 5th Army Tukachevsky later wrote that Trotsky's directive 'met a hostile reception on the Eastern front and at the Party Central Committee'.[185] Other commanders, namely S.I. Gusev, M.M. Lashevich and K.K. Yurenev, bluntly asserted that Trotsky's directive was 'a major fatal mistake which could cost us the revolution'.[186] The Central Committee wanted to continue the pursuit of Kolchak and effectively rescinded the order given by Trotsky and Vatsetis. Trotsky, on Vatsetis's suggestion, removed Kamenev as front commander, for insubordination, but Lenin intervened and Kamenev regained his post.[187] It was a serious blow to Trotsky's authority.

A second blow occurred in July 1919, when the Central Committee rejected Trotsky's plan for an offensive against Denikin across the Donbass. The plan was later adopted – and during the Stalin cult attributed by Voroshilov to the General Secretary – but the initial rejection depressed Trotsky and led him to tender his resignation as War Commissar. Lenin, who understood Trotsky's temperament, persuaded the leadership to bolster his morale by issuing a clear motion of support: 'The Orgburo and Politburo ... have come to the unanimous decision that ... Comrade Trotsky's resignation at this moment is absolutely impossible and would do the greatest harm to the Republic, and they therefore insist that Comrade Trotsky not raise this matter again and that he continue to carry out his functions to the full.' The resolution was signed by, among others, Lenin and Stalin.[188]

Trotsky remained at his post. There were still many enemies to be defeated. The war, however, eventually came to an end in 1920, and as it did, so Trotsky's star began to wane. Within five or six years official Soviet historiography would draw a thick line through his name on the list of civil war leaders. In accordance with a decision of the Politburo, in 1928–30 a three-volume work entitled *The Civil War of 1918–21* was published. The editor, A.S. Bubnov, managed in his forty-page preface not to mention the former War Commissar's name once. By 1930, when the third volume came out, new names appeared which had not even been mentioned in the first volume. After noting the particular role played by Lenin, the editor produced the following remarkable statement: 'An enormous part in establishing the strategic aims (that is, the overall strategic leadership) was played by several members of the Bolshevik old guard, above all by Comrade Stalin.'[189]

The long night of the Stalin cult had begun, and with it the cynical reshaping and rewriting of history. Trotsky was finally cast into the Orwellian 'memory hole'. From the hero of the civil war he was made into its anti-hero.

4

The Hypnosis of Revolution

Less than four months before his death, in an open letter to the Soviet workers entitled 'You are Being Deceived', Trotsky wrote: 'The aim of the Fourth International is to spread the October revolution throughout the world,' and ended with the call that had given meaning to his life: 'Long live the world socialist revolution!'[1] Such fanatical faith in an idea – and one which turned out to be so ephemeral – is rare indeed. He would die with his faith intact and with profound conviction in the triumph of Communist ideals.

Speaking in May 1924 at the Fifth All-Union Congress of the Construction Workers Union, he expressed his belief in the imminence of world revolution, declaring: 'We have just received news that the German Communist Party appears to have got 3,600,000 votes ... There is as yet no Communist government in Germany. But the workers' regime is coming!'[2]

In 1924 Trotsky still had no inkling that the sparks of the October revolution were incapable of igniting a worldwide conflagration. He held a starkly simple view of the coming collapse of the old order. The fossilized structures which perpetuated the coexistence of rich and poor, truth and lies, tyranny and slavery, were intolerable to him. He devoted his entire life to the task of maintaining the revolutionary temperature at which the exploitative features of the state would melt, and melt forever. The anomalous nature of such a personality today is one which nevertheless fits into twentieth-century history.

Permanent Revolution

The name of Trotsky has always been associated with the enigmatic term 'permanent revolution'. Shortly before his deportation from the Soviet Union, in an article entitled 'The Permanent Revolution and the Lenin Line', he wrote: 'As soon as I am free of more important and pressing affairs, I shall complete my work on permanent revolution and distribute it to the comrades. The French say, "as long as the bottle has been opened, the wine must be finished".'[3] The credit for having opened the bottle, however, belonged not to Trotsky, but to Alexander Helphand, also known as Parvus.

Little has appeared in Soviet historiography about this intriguing personality. A member first of the Russian and then of the German Social Democrat Party, he was born in Odessa in 1869 and emigrated to Western Europe where he became a well-known journalist and theorist. During the 1905 revolution, like Trotsky, he returned to Russia and took an active part in the events, notably starting up a newspaper, *Nachalo* (The Beginning). In a series of articles written in the last years of the previous century, Parvus had formulated his idea of permanent revolution, although the idea itself in fact originated with Marx and Engels, who had written: 'While the democratic petty bourgeoisie want to end the revolution as soon as possible ... our interests and our tasks require the revolution to continue uninterrupted until all the more or less possessing classes have been removed from predominance and the proletariat has gained power.'[4] With this proposition in mind, Parvus saw permanency of revolution as the sequential replacement of one revolutionary stage by the next. Trotsky was familiar with these ideas and discussed them in his meetings with Parvus, but he was always vague about their origins, perhaps because he did not want to put his own authorship in doubt. He first expounded the concept of permanent revolution in a 1906 article entitled 'Results and Perspectives', defining it as 'the elimination of the boundary between the minimum and maximum programmes of social democracy ... locating a direct and spontaneous base in the European West.'[5] Trotsky's reticence about Parvus may also be connected with more complicated political considerations.

After the defeat of the 1905 revolution, Parvus was exiled to Siberia, but soon escaped, resurfacing in Germany. In fact, he was not greatly interested in social democratic ideas, but was very keen to become rich. When the First World War broke out he saw his opportunity and established a trading enterprise in surgical instruments, pharmaceuticals, contraceptives and other medical products, shipping them from Scandinavia through the Baltic to Germany and other countries in the region and soon becoming a millionaire. He is known to have given substantial financial support to the Bolsheviks, and he played the role of intermediary between the German High Command and the Bolsheviks, with whose help the German government hoped to weaken the Russian war effort, thus freeing the German army to concentrate on the western front, where the imminent arrival of American troops threatened to boost the Allies.[6]

The idea of transporting Lenin through Germany to Russia in a 'sealed train' was Parvus's. The German Chief of Staff, General Erich von Ludendorff, wrote unequivocally in his memoirs: 'In sending Lenin to Russia, our government took upon itself a special responsibility. His journey through Germany was justified from the military point of view; Russia had to be made to fall.'[7] While Ludendorff did not mention Parvus in his memoirs, the fact is that Lenin's most trusted agents, Ganetsky and Kozlovsky, received large sums of money from Parvus. The Bolshevik denial of this fact was as vigorous as it was unconvincing: the fact alone that they could maintain seventeen daily newspapers with a circulation of more than 300,000, while complaining of empty Party coffers, was proof enough that funds were coming from somewhere, and that it was a source they preferred to keep secret. Former tsarist police General A.I. Spiridovich, using documents from the St Petersburg prosecutor's office, established that the Bolshevik Central Committee received money from abroad via Parvus, Ganetsky, Kozlovsky and Sumenson, a female relative of Ganetsky's. In the course of 1916, for instance, Madame Sumenson withdrew from her current account 750,000 roubles which had been deposited there by various individuals.[8]

In 1905 Lenin wrote in the newspaper *Proletarii*: 'To the extent of our strength and that of the conscious and organized proletariat, we will start at once to go over from the democratic revolution to the socialist revolution. We are for uninterrupted revolution. We will not stop halfway.'[9] Such notions would later be condemned as 'Trotskyist renegadism'.

The essence of Trotsky's idea of permanent revolution was contained in a number of articles written during the 1905 revolution, in which he reiterated the belief that

> this odd name of 'permanent revolution' expresses the notion that the Russian revolution, which is confronting bourgeois aims, cannot stop at that . . . The revolution cannot settle the immediate bourgeois tasks except by putting the proletariat in power. And the latter, having taken power, will not restrict themselves to the bourgeois framework of revolution . . . In breaking out of the limited bourgeois democratic framework of revolution, by force of historical necessity, the triumphant proletariat will be compelled also to break out of the nation-state framework, that is, they will have to strive consciously to make the Russian revolution the prologue to world revolution.[10]

The idea of permanent revolution is an entirely Marxist one, as we have seen, and its critics always omitted to note one of its most important features, namely the stress on the totality of the revolutionary process, in time, scale, aims and means. This totality, however, ignored the objective conditions: whether the shift was necessary, whether the masses were ready for more activity and so on. At its basis was the idea of revolution as the highest good. It represented the primacy of the subjective over the objective, revolution for the sake of revolution. Mankind, the individual, the nation and the masses remained somewhere on the sidelines, or were at best a means for achieving this total revolution. And it was here that the idea embodied a tendency to resort to coercion.

It is apparent today that it is indeed possible to 'give history a shove', but only at a great price to be exacted later. Trotsky himself wrote in 1905 that 'while the anti-revolutionary aspects of Menshevism are already being expressed, the anti-revolutionary aspects of Bolshevism threaten an enormous danger only in the event of a revolutionary victory.'[11] What he then meant by the anti-revolutionary aspects of Bolshevism was its tendency to commit 'excess'. Permanent revolution could thus be defined as the historical expression of excess.

In the preface to his book *The Permanent Revolution* Trotsky wrote that, while idling the time away in Alma-Ata, he had looked over his old works on the subject, 'pencil in hand',[12] and noted that the first

Russian revolution had occurred a little over half a century after a period of bourgeois revolutions in Europe and nearly thirty-five years after 'the episodic uprising of the Paris Commune'. Europe had already lost the habit of revolution, while Russia still had no experience of one. Permanent revolution, he argued – citing Marx – meant that the revolution went on to socialist undertakings and ended with the liquidation of class society. What today seems a naive notion was shared by many at the time. Indeed, in the early years after the October coup, the Bolsheviks practised the postulates of this doctrine in all but name, and not only in the early years: throughout the Soviet period the regime gave assistance to countries and peoples where revolutionary conditions were 'ripening'. It was enough to recognize the 'anti-imperialist character' of this or that regime for the Soviet government to discuss supplying major material, financial, economic and military aid. This policy made 'Trotskyists' of all the Soviet leaders.

With the end of the civil war the Bolshevik leadership came to the bitter realization that the longed-for world revolution had not occurred. They had to come to terms with their own, Russian, revolution. Was it capable of surviving? Could socialism be built in one country? What future would socialism have within national limits? Trotsky answered these questions in the firm negative: 'The completion of the socialist revolution within national limits is unthinkable ... it will not be accomplished until the final triumph of the new society throughout the planet.'[13] Here lay the main reason for the savage attacks on his theory: he could not believe in the possibility of socialism in one country. In fact he had asserted that 'the socialist revolution begins on the national level, develops on the international and is completed on the world level.'[14] Thus he did not deny the viability of socialism in the first country where it appeared, but saw its completion in purely global terms.

Soon after Lenin's death and a brief lull in the internecine war among the leaders, the struggle re-emerged with renewed vigour. Trotsky was frequently ill during this period and spent much time in the south of the country, where he was working on the first drafts of his reminiscences of Lenin. In Kislovodsk he wrote his 'Lessons of October' – the preface to the third volume of his collected works – in which he put all the leaders in 'their historic places', and also demonstrated that his ideas on the shift from the bourgeois democratic revolution to the socialist revolution were correct and irrefutably proven by Russian history itself.

This was something the triumvirate of Stalin, Zinoviev and Kamenev could not stomach. Meeting at Kamenev's apartment on 16 October 1924, they devised a detailed plan for their first mass attack on Trotsky, one of their main weapons being to expose the flaws in his theory of permanent revolution. The order was issued, and dozens of articles were published, meetings held and speeches given by the triumvirate themselves and other Party leaders, all aimed at compromising Trotsky, reducing his role in the revolution and civil war and creating a new public image of him as a hollow ideologist. Trotsky was shaken and all the more hurt because he knew the campaign was inspired by the Party leaders. Now virtually isolated among the leadership, he tried to explain his silence as a desire not to incite an internal Party conflict. The draft of a letter to *Pravda*, entitled 'A reply to numerous enquiries', has survived in the archives. In it Trotsky wrote: 'I am not replying to certain specific articles that have appeared recently in *Pravda*, guided as I am by considerations of protecting the Party's interests, as I understand them.'[15]

After publication of his 'Lessons of October', Trotsky continually faced questions about his theory of permanent revolution. In May 1924, speaking to newspaper workers, he said: 'The comrades are asking what is the relationship of the theory of permanent revolution to Leninism? Personally, it has never entered my head to treat the question as one of practical relevance. The idea was merely the theoretical anticipation of the future course of events. The events which the theory anticipated took place: the October revolution was achieved. Now the question of permanent revolution is one of theoretical-historical interest, not current interest.' In order to stress the fact that Lenin had been in agreement with him, he continued: 'Did I have any differences with Comrade Lenin over the seizure of power in October or in peasant policy, in October or after?' He gave the firm answer: 'I did not.' He went on: 'The comrades who have "recoiled" from October are now, after the event, all too clever about "errors" in the theory of permanent revolution. If there were errors in it, it did not prevent me from going right through the October revolution side by side with Lenin. The attempt after the event to create Trotskyism in opposition to Leninism is nothing less than a falsification.'[16]

The attacks continued, however. At the beginning of 1925 Trotsky received through the post a pamphlet, just published, entitled 'The Theory of Permanent Revolution of Comrade Trotsky', with a preface by I. Vardin, one of the Party's 'official' theorists.[17] The chapter titles alone told much: 'Rebellion on One's Knees', 'Comrade Trotsky's Tale of How Comrade Lenin became a . . . Trotskyist', 'The Superficiality and Flippancy of Comrade Trotsky's Statements'. Vardin's preface set the tone for the rest of the pamphlet by dismissing the theory of permanent revolution as 'having nothing in common with Bolshevism'.[18] The theory had been dragged into the open on Stalin's orders, and Trotsky's early writings dredged up, in order to puncture his image as a hero of October and the civil war, and to parade him before the Party as a sceptic with a Menshevik attitude. As we have seen, by the mid-1920s Trotsky had written hundreds of political and theoretical articles, books and pamphlets, many of them wrongheaded, written in the heat of the moment and not claiming to be holy writ, but Stalin and his accomplices had to rake over his pre-revolutionary writings in order to find evidence of his 'Menshevism' and 'anti-Marxism'.

Everything connected with the theory of permanent revolution reveals Trotsky not only as a theorist but above all as a personality. His convictions were integrated and politically consistent; he never ceased to advocate revolution. He was accused of scepticism and capitulationism because he linked the building of socialism in Russia with the victory of the international revolution. Lenin had made precisely the same point many times. And Stalin, too, once he had unseated Trotsky, declared that the final victory of socialism was possible only when socialist principles were proclaimed in most of the world, although in his case the theory, as always, was dictated by pragmatic need and above all personal interest. For Trotsky, Russia could be 'towed into socialism by the advanced countries', since in the final analysis permanent revolution for Russia outside the context of world revolution was a hopeless cause.

'The World Soviet Federation'

In the Manifesto of the Second Congress of the Communist International of 1920, composed by Trotsky and signed by all the leaders of international Communism including Lenin, Zinoviev and Bukharin for the Russians, under the heading 'Soviet Russia' appear the following words: 'The Communist International has proclaimed the cause of Soviet Russia as its own. The international proletariat will not sheathe its sword until Soviet Russia has been made a link in the federation of Soviet republics of the whole world.'[19] In both content and style, the manifesto was purely Trotsky's.

During the civil war he had kept himself informed of the world situation through the radio on his train, and he firmly believed that revolution was about to break out in many other countries. At the beginning of January 1919, on behalf of the Central Committee, he sent the following message to the Spartacists in Germany and the Communist Party of Austria: 'The demise of the bourgeoisie and the victory of the proletariat are equally inevitable. Your victory is inevitable, comrades!'[20] Since in style and conviction he was so in tune with the cause of international Communism, Trotsky was asked by the Executive Committee of Comintern (ECCI) to compose many of its documents, especially its manifestos and appeals. In April 1919, for instance, he penned the May Day greetings to the workers of the world: 'Another year has passed and still we have not cast off the yoke . . . A year has passed and the helm is still in the hands of the bourgeoisie.' As a result, 'we must not moderate our attacks, and our offensive must be on a wider front with wider columns – that's the slogan for this May Day . . . The chance may occur any day when a bold move by the Communist vanguard can bring the working masses behind it and when the conquest of power becomes the order of the day.'[21]

The entire Bolshevik leadership then believed in the world revolution and a 'World Soviet Federation'. In July 1921 Lenin asserted: 'Before the revolution and indeed after it, we thought that either immediately or at least very soon the revolution would occur in countries which were most developed in capitalist terms.'[22] None perhaps was as firmly convinced of this as Trotsky, and the question arises: what were the origins of such conviction?

Trotsky held not only the materialist views of Marxism, inextricably bound up with Hegel's dialectics; he also harboured a tendency to turn subjective elements into absolutes, such as consciousness, willpower, the determination of leaders, organizations, groups and classes. The inevitability of world revolution, he believed, derived from the peculiarity of the historical process, which he formulated in the following way: 'Under the lash of external necessity, backwardness has to make leaps. From the universal law of inequality another law emerges which for the lack of a better name we can call the law of combined development, in the sense that several stages of the process merge ... and archaic forms amalgamate with more modern ones.'[23] He disagreed with M.N. Pokrovsky, L.B. Kamenev and N.A. Rozhkov who asserted that the historical process did not allow for the skipping over of stages. 'Their point of view,' Trotsky wrote, 'was essentially that the political supremacy of the bourgeoisie must precede the political supremacy of the proletariat; the bourgeois democratic republic must be an extended political school for the proletariat; the attempt to skip this stage is, [they say], adventurist; if the working class has not gained power in the West, then how can the Russian proletariat set itself the same task?'[24]

In response to these objections, Trotsky advanced as an argument Russia's peculiar development which enabled her to skip over a number of 'non-obligatory' stages and to stand in the vanguard of the revolutionary process. The contradictions in the world had long prepared the need for a revolutionary explosion, he claimed, and what was needed was the detonator. Russia could supply this need, precisely because she was able to skip certain stages. 'Just as France skipped the Reformation,' he wrote, 'so Russia skipped the stage of formal democracy.'[25]

Later, when he was in exile on the Turkish island of Prinkipo, Trotsky roundly criticized Stalin for failing to grasp these arguments: 'The "theorizing" Stalin made a great song and dance about the "law of uneven development" and "not skipping over these stages". Stalin to this day does not understand that uneven development is precisely the skipping over of stages (or remaining for too long at the same stage) ... Such foresight requires an understanding of historical unevenness in all its dynamic reality, and not simply chewing the permanent cud of quotations from Lenin.'[26]

While maintaining some caution in his conversations with the other leaders and in the Politburo, Trotsky nonetheless made frequent proposals for initiating the world revolution. It was, for instance, on his initiative that large amounts of money were sent to Germany in 1918 for revolutionary propaganda and speeding up the 'ripening' of the masses. He it was who suggested that two or three cavalry corps be formed in the southern Urals for despatch to India and China, although this proposal was not taken up. In August 1919 Trotsky sent a telegram to Zinoviev and Rozengolts, insisting that special brigades be left on the Estonian front 'to collaborate in the imminent eruption of the Estonian revolution'.[27] There are cables in the archives from Trotsky to the Hungarian revolutionary government with offers to come and help them. The Warsaw campaign of 1920 was undertaken not only to crush Pilsudski's intervention, but also 'to give aid to the Polish workers struggling for their freedom'. In Trotsky's view, 'in order to sovietize Poland' the Polish workers and peasants should be seen 'as future Polish Red Army men', and everything should be done 'to popularize the biographies of the most prominent Polish Communists, such as Dzerzhinsky, Marchlewski, Radek and Unshlikht'.[28] These ideas reveal not only Trotsky's lack of understanding of the national mood in Poland, but also an apparent failure of imagination: Dzerzhinsky, although a Pole, was head of the Cheka and deeply hostile to Polish nationalism, while Radek and Unshlikht were of Jewish origin and therefore unlikely heroes of the Polish working class. At the same Party plenum of 3 April 1922 which appointed Stalin General Secretary, Trotsky proposed 'organizing a counter-propaganda campaign abroad'. The Central Committee recruited Suvarin and Krestinsky for the job under Trotsky's general guidance.[29]

Even when he was fully occupied by the civil war, Trotsky retained a constant interest in the international revolutionary movement, took an active part in the work of the ECCI and often went abroad with Communist and worker delegations. On 19 April 1921 Sermuks gave Radek, who was responsible for German affairs at the time, Trotsky's analysis of the situation there: the German Social Democratic and trade union organizations were opposing radical action and were thus 'a most important cause of the passivity and conservatism among the working masses . . . We must systematically shake the working masses with the aim of undermining the unstable equilibrium.' The workers must be made to understand that the general strike of March 1921 (which had developed into an armed uprising by the Mansfeld miners and which had been crushed) 'once again revealed the blatant treachery of the Social Democrats'.[30]

Trotsky was disappointed by the failures of the revolutionary movement, especially in Germany. They represented not merely the collapse of hope for the revolution, but a deep personal hurt. Above all he blamed the Communist Party of Germany. When a new revolutionary upheaval in 1923 did not culminate, as he had predicted, in the assumption of power, he expressed his bitterness:

> The main reason why the German Communist Party surrendered its exceptional historic positions without a fight is that the party has not managed to shake off the inertia of yesterday's policies, which were meant to last for years, and to put the question of seizing power into its agitation, its actions, organization, propaganda and resources. Time is an important element in politics, especially at a revolutionary moment. Lost months can take years, even decades, to make up for.[31]

For Trotsky, Comintern was an instrument by which to achieve the Communists' main idea, the victory of the world socialist revolution. Speaking at its Third Congress on 2 July 1921, he called the hiatus in the revolutionary process 'a temporary hitch, a slowing-down'. But he was convinced that capitalist development, despite its momentary rises, was on a downward curve, 'while the curve of revolution, despite all its setbacks, is rising all the time'.

During the organization of this congress, Trotsky had had to make extraordinary efforts to ensure that it did not end in disaster. Yenukidze, who had been charged with organizing the domestic arrangements, had been unable to provide the delegates with decent living conditions. Complaints poured in, as well as imprecations that the Russian Communist Party was not even capable of dealing with such a simple matter. When he heard about this, Trotsky at once sent a 'top secret' note to Lenin and other members of the organizing committee:

> I have just been informed by comrades, whose objectivity and reliability I trust unconditionally, that a state of utter desperation rules in the organization of the Congress. Arriving delegates are plunged into a desperate position. Despite the fact that we were expecting one

thousand people and only three hundred have turned up, delegates are being housed eight to ten in a room. They lack the minimum facilities. It's the same with the dining-room and so on. The worst thing is the rude lack of concern being shown to arriving delegates. They have no mattresses or pillows on their beds, no wash-basins . . .

Lenin was reluctant to become involved in such a routine matter, but quickly proposed setting up a 'commission with extraordinary powers', as 'I am out of town. I've taken a few days off because of ill health.'[32] Zinoviev, meanwhile, suggested moving the congress to Petrograd, 'where proper arrangements for every delegate are guaranteed'.[33] With some scepticism, Trotsky rejected Zinoviev's proposal but went along with Lenin's, ensuring that his own deputy, Sklyansky, was appointed the commission's chairman. Sklyansky in turn recruited Trotsky's entire staff, as well as the catering services of the Moscow garrison, and a degree of normality was quickly restored.[34]

Trotsky even insisted on seeing what food was being given to delegates, who were housed at the Hotel Lux, a house on Novinsky Boulevard, and the Continental Hotel. Breakfast consisted of bread, butter, tea and sugar, plus sausage at the Continental; lunch provided soup, meat – usually lamb – with mashed potatoes, bread, tea and sugar; and for supper soup, sausage, bread, tea and sugar.[35] Even with the intervention of the top leadership and the mobilization of all available resources, the ruined country could barely feed the three hundred revolutionaries whose task it was to ignite revolution throughout the world. No doubt it was this more than anything that motivated Trotsky's concern for the well-being of the delegates.

Trotsky's fanaticism had been well noted in the West, where the press depicted him as an anarchist insurrectionary, an extreme Communist radical, or an agent of Jewish finance capital. At the height of the civil war the White press agency in Yekaterinburg published a pamphlet entitled 'Sad Recollections (about the Bolsheviks)'. Its author, Sergei Auslender, provided sketches of the Bolshevik leaders, above all of Trotsky: 'This international speculator has subdued Russia, he is shooting old army generals, lives in the Kremlin Palace and commands the Russian army . . . He knows how to bring out the worst and most foul in his slaves.'[36] In November 1921 a pamphlet entitled 'Jewish Bolshevism' was published in Munich with an extended preface by Alfred Rosenberg, the Nazi ideologue. The burden of this work was to show that the Russian revolution in its content, ideas and leadership was thoroughly Jewish: 'From the day of its inception, Bolshevism was a Jewish enterprise.' By manipulating the number of Jewish People's Commissars, Rosenberg tried to show that 'the proletarian dictatorship over the dazed, ruined, half-starved people is a plan that was devised in the Jewish lodges of London, New York and Berlin'. Its leading executors were also Jews, chief among them being Trotsky-Bronstein, and their aim was world revolution.[37] This sort of slanderous publication was aimed not only at discrediting the revolution, but also its leaders.

In February 1925 the Foreign Department of OGPU acquired a top secret report by a British envoy entitled 'Trotsky and the Russian Revolution'. Describing Trotsky's defeat in the Party debates, the diplomat nonetheless asserted that he was still the most powerful political figure in Russian Bolshevism and that he was capable of undertaking 'international revolutionary affairs', adding that the stabilization of the regime meant it would gain time 'for its great universal historic experiment, greater than the overthrow of tsarism and the destruction of the bourgeoisie in the October revolution'. After the death of Lenin, the report continued, Trotsky was 'the most significant personality in socialist revolutionary Europe'.[38] OGPU circulated copies of this report to Stalin and chiefs of the various security agencies.

Trotsky's fanatical belief in the imminence of world revolution sometimes defied reason. Ignoring the historical facts, in his 1924 article 'Five Years of Comintern' he asserted:

From the historical point of view, European capitalism has run its course. It has not developed significantly productive forces. It has no further progressive role to play. It cannot open any new horizons. If this were not so, then any thought of the proletarian revolution in our age would be tilting at windmills ... [The] bourgeois order will not fall of its own accord. It has to be overthrown and only the working class can overthrow it by revolutionary means ... History is challenging the workers, as it were saying to them: you must know that if you do not overthrow the bourgeoisie, you will perish beneath the ruins of civilization.

Trotsky often lamented the fact that the world revolution had not begun in the advanced countries like the USA, England or Germany; had it done so, it would have stood a better chance. In 'Five Years of Comintern' he declares bitterly: 'History evidently spins its thread from the other end.' He nevertheless remained an optimist, although not perhaps such a zealous one. Speaking at the Fourth Comintern Congress of 5 November–5 December 1922, he declared that the decline of revolutionary activity was 'a temporary process'. Future success required 'winning the confidence of the majority of the working class', for then, 'convinced by experience of the rightness, firmness and reliability of the Communist leadership, the working class will shake off its disappointment, its passivity and temporizing, and then the new era of the last assault will open. How near is the hour? We cannot predict.'[39]

Willing to wait for years for the new upsurge, Trotsky never doubted that it would come. Such tenacity is capable of blinding even the most talented intellectual, but even he had to admit, when analysing the world situation, that the hour of world revolution had receded. Gazing above the heads of the delegates, as it were into the future, he declared:

It would be wrong to treat the entire world revolutionary movement alike ... The revolutionary movement in America ... is receding decades into the distance. Does this mean that revolution in Europe must be compared to America? Of course not. If backward Russia did not (and could not) wait for revolution in Europe, still less will or can Europe wait for revolution in America ... [We] can state with confidence that victory of the revolution in Europe in the course of a few years will rock the mighty American bourgeoisie.[40]

Trotsky had no doubt as to what sort of Europe would emerge from the proletarian revolution. Marxist projections, mostly empty of real content, emerged as semi-utopias. Even half-ruined, bloodstained, debilitated Soviet Russia served for Trotsky as a model of future post-revolutionary state structure. In an article on the idea of the 'United States of Europe', intended for *Pravda*, he wrote: 'We shall not try here to predict the pace at which the unification of the European republics will take place, nor what economic and constitutional forms will emerge, nor the degree of centralization reached by the European economy in the first stage of the workers' and peasants' regime. We can safely leave all that to the future, bearing in mind the experience already gained by the Soviet Union.'[41]

Any future federation of states, in Trotsky's view, could only be on the basis of the socialist revolution: 'We are of course talking about a European socialist federation as a component part of a future world federation, and such a regime can only be brought in by the dictatorship of the proletariat ... [It] will not stop at the European phase. Through our Soviet Union it will open up for itself a way into Asia and thus open for Asia a way into Europe. We are talking, in other words, of a stage.'[42]

Convinced as he was that the Red Army would bring to other peoples freedom and the opportunity to unite with Russia in the 'World Soviet Federation', Trotsky's orders included the demand that national self-awareness be respected. On 30 November 1919, for instance, he circulated an address to be read to all units of Red forces entering Ukrainian territory: 'You are crossing Ukraine's borders. As you destroy Denikin's bands, you are cleansing a fraternal country of violators ... Woe betide anyone who uses armed force against the toilers of a Ukrainian town or village. Let the workers and peasants of Ukraine feel secure under the protection of your bayonets. Don't forget: your job is not to conquer Ukraine, but to liberate it.'[43] He expressed the same idea to the troops as they entered Poland: '[The] land you are entering belongs to the Polish people. We have thrown back the Polish [middle class] and we will break its back ... You are approaching Warsaw. Enter it not as a conquered city, but as the capital of independent Poland.'[44]

The tone, however, became harsh whenever there were signs of disagreement with the Soviet regime. For instance, on 27 January 1921, when the Menshevik government of independent Georgia ignored demands from the Bolsheviks in Moscow, Trotsky sent a telegram to the Revolutionary Military Council of the Caucasian front: 'If the Soviet Republic were forced against its will to give an armed rebuff to the provocative policy of Georgia, do you think you have sufficient forces and supplies for the purpose, bearing in mind the occupation of the territory and so on ... What demands would you have to make for food supplies to maintain an army and Soviet institutions in Azerbaidzhan, Armenia and Georgia in the event of having to occupy them?'[45] Once 11th Army had entered several regions of Georgia, however, Lenin warned the Red Army 'to treat the sovereign organs of Georgia with special respect and pay particular attention and care towards the Georgian population ... Report any breach or any friction or misunderstanding with the local population, however trivial.'[46] The goal had been achieved and therefore the aim now was to mollify the national mood: the ultimate objective was to bring the 'World Soviet Federation' closer.

Thus, Trotsky's views on world revolution were not restricted to theory. He initiated many practical proposals. On 29 July 1924, at a meeting of the board of the Military Science Society, he stressed the need to compose a 'Manual of Civil War' which leaders of socialist revolutions could use as a handbook, pointing out that if the leaders were not prepared, any uprising was doomed to failure. At the critical moment of a revolutionary event, he said, 'the circumstances are characterized by an extremely unstable equilibrium: the ball is at the point of the pyramid. Depending on the hit, it can go in either direction. Thanks to the firmness and determination of our leadership, our ball went in the direction of victory. In Germany, policy sent the ball towards defeat.'[47] A 'Manual on Civil War', he was convinced, 'would become a necessary element in higher-level military-revolutionary training.'[48] The euphoria of the post-October days had passed, and now was the time to prepare for the world revolution.

In September 1921 the leader of the German Communist Party, Heinrich Brandler, had come to Moscow and asked for Trotsky to be sent to Germany to organize an uprising. In the face of Trotsky's apparent reluctance to go, the Politburo decided to send Pyatakov and Radek instead, while making it plain that the strategy of the German uprising would be planned in the Kremlin. Zinoviev, as Chairman of Comintern, was very keen to encourage an uprising. It is difficult to establish exactly what role Trotsky played, although he met Brandler on several occasions. He was in favour of an uprising, but thought it should be postponed in view of the lack of preparation. Brandler, however, was not in a position to hold back, especially as a weak flame of rebellion was already alight in Hamburg. The workers' enthusiasm and resistance lasted only a few days, however. The soil lacked the proper revolutionary fertilizer.

Trotsky greeted the news that the German uprising had failed with disappointment. Whether he had declined to take part because he sensed failure is impossible to say. Perhaps his work as chairman of the Revolutionary Military Council was too pressing? Whatever the case, the fact is that when a concrete opportunity to practise 'permanent revolution' presented itself, he had been absent.

The Politburo started looking for culprits. The names of Brandler, Zinoviev, Radek, Pyatakov and Trotsky came up in the heated debate. Many thought that Trotsky had simply wanted to stay out of the fight. At Zinoviev's insistence, the ECCI found its chief scapegoat in Brandler, who was defended rather weakly only by Trotsky, Radek and Pyatakov.

The failure in Germany served Trotsky as a reminder: the world revolution required prolonged and thorough preparation, but it was not a manual on civil war that was needed, and it was Stalin, not Trotsky, who would implement the idea of world revolution, albeit in a different form, after the Second World War, and without Comintern's slogans. The anti-imperialist struggle aimed not only at the national and social emancipation of peoples, but also at the spread of socialism. Neither Lenin nor Trotsky nor Stalin saw that the idea of dividing the world along class lines by means of the dictatorship of the proletariat was doomed. After the October revolution it seemed natural that unlimited force could be used against some in order to achieve happiness for others, and the idea that world revolution was inevitable was equally accepted by the Bolsheviks as natural. If this was so, why were such non-proletarians as Lenin, Stalin and Trotsky necessary? Lenin did not live to see what would come of his 'plans'. Until August 1940 Trotsky believed that the experiment had been started and aborted. Stalin succeeded in making the Gulag the symbol of the country where the first socialist revolution had occurred. Had the 'World Soviet Federation' ever been created, it would have conformed to the Stalinist model.

Terrorism and Communism

Terrorism and Communism was the title of a book Trotsky published in 1920 in Petrograd in response to one Kautsky had brought out in Berlin in 1919 under the same name. Together, the two books provide an eloquent comparison of attitudes from opposite ends of the spectrum of European social democracy. Throughout the two hundred pages of his polemical argument, Trotsky employed language that had become characteristic of Russian political argument: Kautsky was a 'hypocritical conciliator', 'unworthy falsifier', 'besmircher' and 'total zero', among many other things. Trotsky's counter-arguments, meanwhile, exposed just how wrongheaded were many of the notions he shared with the rest of the Bolshevik leadership and which they had enshrined in law.

Trotsky attacked Kautsky for complaining about Soviet practice, while failing to offer an alternative:

> The Bolsheviks were not alone in the arena of the Russian revolution; we have seen and still see – whether in power or in opposition – SRs (no less than five groupings and tendencies), Mensheviks (no less than three tendencies), Plekhanovites, Maximalists, Anarchists . . . Absolutely all 'shades of socialism' – to use Kautsky's language – have tested their strength and shown what they want and what they are capable of . . . The political keyboard ought to be wide enough for Kautsky to find an appropriate Marxist tone for the Russian revolution. But he is silent. He cannot stand the Bolshevik melody which offends his ears, but he doesn't look for another. The conclusion is obvious: the old ballroom pianist doesn't want to play the instrument of revolution at all.[49]

In a sense, Trotsky was right: to a social democrat who believed in the constructive nature of social and economic reform, the revolution was an irrelevance.

When composing his reply to Kautsky, Trotsky asked Tomsky to provide him with some statistics to help him 'smash Kautsky for good'.[50] Kautsky, who had espoused the doctrine of the dictatorship of the proletariat before the turn of the century, recoiled from its Russian manifestation as 'coercion of the majority by the minority'. In support of Kautsky, Potresov wrote: 'Only Kautsky has raised the issue of the incompatibility of the proletarian socialist revolution and violence . . . The dictatorship of the proletariat is totally obsolete, it is a tribute to the past.'[51] Kautsky had written that only by achieving a majority in parliament could social democracy open a path to socialist change. To this Trotsky replied:

In order to write a pamphlet on the dictatorship [of the proletariat], one needs an inkwell and a batch of paper, and maybe a few ideas in one's head. But in order to establish and consolidate a dictatorship [of the proletariat], one has to prevent the bourgeoisie from undermining the state power of the proletariat. Kautsky obviously thinks it can be done with some whining pamphlets . . . [Whoever] rejects terrorism in principle, i.e. pressurizing and intimidating methods against fierce and armed counter-revolution, must also reject the political supremacy of the working class and its revolutionary dictatorship. Whoever rejects the dictatorship of 'the proletariat, rejects the social revolution and abandons hope of socialism.[52]

In practice, this meant Trotsky's issuing orders, such as one he sent to the military commander at Vologda on 4 August 1918: 'Root out the counter-revolutionaries without mercy, lock up suspicious characters in concentration camps – this is a necessary condition of success . . . Shirkers will be shot, regardless of past service . . .'[53] The message was clear, whether it was for Kautsky or a Red Army commander at the front: there would be no socialism without violence and coercion.

Trotsky and the other leaders genuinely believed that they possessed the 'revolutionary right' to determine the lives of millions of people, though many doubted the existence of such a right. Even Boris Savinkov, himself a past advocate of coercion, could write: 'The Russian people does not want Lenin, Trotsky and Dzerzhinsky, not just because the Communists are mobilizing and shooting people, seizing their grain and ruining Russia. They don't want them for the simple reason that . . . no one elected them.'[54] Trotsky shared Lenin's view that only the Communists could express the workers' interests, and it was from this belief that all of Bolshevik privilege and self-importance sprang. Speaking at a conference of Communist military school cells on 10 December 1922, Trotsky declared: 'We say, following Napoleon, that every Red Army man and every recruit has a marshal's baton [in his knapsack], but we also say that the baton is given only to Communists.'[55]

Thus, a group of people who had not been elected or appointed by the people quickly learned how to manipulate the people's interests and needs to their own advantage. They also soon learned how to exploit the privileges and benefits for which they had recently so harshly attacked the tsarist ruling élite. It was considered natural for every leading figure to have his own country house – in Trotsky's case the palace and great estate at Arkhangelskoe, a thirty-minute ride from Moscow, that had belonged to the Yusupovs – a personal physician, a large staff, good food, luxury automobiles, and so on. When Trotsky went to the Crimea in October 1922 on routine business, he was accompanied by a large security force and two automobiles for which two extra railcars had to be attached to the train.[56]

Kautsky, in his book, had identified democracy as the sole means to achieve the ideals of socialism. Trotsky's response was mocking:

> History has not turned the nation into a debating society where the transfer to socialist revolution is passed by a polite vote of the majority. On the contrary, violent revolution was necessary precisely because the urgent demands of history were powerless to cut a path for themselves through the apparatus of parliamentary democracy . . . When the Russian Soviet regime dispersed the Constituent Assembly, it seemed to the leaders of Western social democracy if not exactly the end of the world, then at least a crude and arbitrary break with the entire socialist past.[57]

In defence of Kautsky, Potresov had written: 'By their demonstrative dispersal of the Constituent Assembly, by their universal destruction of liberty, by establishing an officially permitted way of thinking, the Bolsheviks since the very first days of their statehood injected into the public mind a spirit that is hostile to democratic civil society.'[58] Trotsky could declare unequivocally that 'it is triply hopeless to try to come to power by way of parliamentary democracy.'

To Kautsky's call for new elections to the Constituent Assembly, Trotsky replied that this would not happen 'because we see no need for the Assembly. If the first Constituent Assembly could still play a momentary progressive role by sanctioning the Soviet regime convincingly for the petty bourgeois elements . . . the fact is the Soviet regime does not need the blessing of the Constituent Assembly's tarnished authority.'[59]

Trotsky was even harsher in his response to Kautsky's views on the use of terror, or the use of coercion. Lamenting the widespread idea that 'terrorism is the essence of revolution', Kautsky had written: 'The revolution brings us terrorism practised by socialist governments. The Bolsheviks in Russia embarked first on this course and have therefore been roundly condemned by all socialists who do not take the Bolshevik point of view.' He then attacked the system of hostage-taking. Trotsky replied: 'The form of repression or its degree is of course not a question of principle. It is a pragmatic question . . . The widespread use of shootings in the civil war is explained by this simple, but decisive fact . . . Only someone who rejects in principle (in words) all and any violence, and therefore any war or any uprising, can condemn state terror by the revolutionary class on "moral" grounds. And to do so one simply has to be a hypocritical Quaker.'[60] Red terror, he argued, was often provoked by White terror, but he failed to recognize that, by rejecting the social democratic path of reform, the Bolsheviks had, willingly or otherwise, limited their own choice of methods. For Trotsky, revolution was synonymous with violence, which, like Kautsky, he called terror.

Kautsky had also raised the question of the role of the Party and its attitude to the peasant issue, arguing that by substituting the dictatorship of the Party for the dictatorship of the Soviets and in 'destroying or driving other parties underground', the Bolsheviks had eliminated the possibility of political competition. Trotsky replied: 'The Bolshevik–Left SR bloc, which lasted a few months, ended in a bloody rift. True, as far as the bloc was concerned, the rift cost our unreliable fellow-travellers more than it cost us.' A regime of alliances, agreements, deals and concessions did not appeal to Bolsheviks in principle, Trotsky admitted.[61] In relation to the peasants, he claimed, the monopoly of power had made possible a number of harsh lessons for the kulaks and middle peasants, as a result of which 'the fundamental political goal has been achieved. The mighty kulak class, if it has not been completely destroyed, has been deeply shaken, its self-confidence undermined. The middle peasants, who lack political form, are starting to see the leading workers as their representatives.'[62]

Trotsky expressed himself most fully at the Third All-Russian Trade Union Congress of April 1920 when he addressed the question of the methods to be used in building the new society. A Menshevik delegation of thirty-three, headed by Dan, Abramovich and Martov, attended and vigorously opposed Trotsky's report. Abramovich was especially irreconcilable, and roundly condemned Trotsky's basic idea of forced labour. If socialism required the militarization of labour, he exclaimed, 'how does it differ from Egyptian slavery? The pharaohs

built the pyramids by forcing the masses to work.' Universal compulsion, the social democrats perceived, represented a major threat to
socialism in general. After emigrating to the West (first to Berlin in
1920, then to France and finally to the USA in 1940), Abramovich
kept up the struggle against Bolshevism, but he also attempted to
enter into a dialogue with them. At the beginning of 1926 the foreign
department of OGPU reported that he had attempted to meet Soviet
representatives to discuss the return of Mensheviks to the USSR to
participate in the work of building socialism. According to the agency
report, Abramovich himself did not expect that such negotiations
would succeed.[63] Other contacts were made. On the eve of the publication of Stalin's 1936 Constitution, Dan and Abramovich wrote an
open letter to the All-Union Congress of Soviets, stating that the
Mensheviks and Bolsheviks had 'common goals' and differed only over
methods. The path proposed by the Mensheviks, they claimed, had
been more viable because 'it would have protected the toiling masses
from suffering and sacrifice, and maintained the chance to build democratic socialism'.[64] The dwindling Menshevik party abroad was still
trying to bring the Soviet Communists 'back to democracy'. Despite
their title – 'The Foreign Delegation of the RSDLP' – these were
the last Mohicans of Russian social democracy. Trotsky never revised
his negative view of them.

    The speeches Trotsky made at the Trade Union Congress of 1920,
and which had been approved by the Politburo, were interesting –
however deeply flawed their reasoning – because their author was
like no other leader, his arguments, style and content being original,
inimitable and striking. Dressed in tight leather, his hair still abundant,
calculating the effect of his gestures, his pauses and intonation, he
was every inch the military commissar from the front. (As early as
1918, he had cabled Sklyansky to send him a new leather uniform and
boots.[65]) He opened his speech in an original way by declaring that
'as a rule, man tries to avoid work ... You might say that he is a
rather lazy animal,' and from this he deduced that 'the only way to
attract the labour force needed for economic tasks is by introducing
labour conscription'.[66] The argument would have been unanswerable
had it applied to a crisis, but in fact it was applied as a fundamental
principle and for a long time to come: '[We] must make it clear to
ourselves once and for all that the very principle of labour conscription

has replaced the principle of free labour as radically and irreversibly as socialization of the means of production has replaced capitalist ownership.'[67] Trotsky's advocacy of forced labour evokes Abramovich's question as to how such a form of socialism differed from Egyptian slavery.

Translating his thoughts on labour conscription into practical measures, Trotsky said: 'The movement of mobilized labour must be effected over the shortest distance. The number of mobilized workers must correspond to the scale of the economic job in hand. Tools and food supplies must be secured for mobilized [workers] in good time ... Mobilized [workers] must feel sure when they are at work that their labour is being used prudently ... Wherever possible direct mobilization should be substituted by a labour task, that is, by imposing on a district the obligation to deliver, say, so many cubic [metres] of firewood by such and such a date, or to transport so many [kilograms] of pig-iron to such and such a station by cart and so on.'[68] The armed forces, which were gradually being run down as the civil war approached its end, were used as the starting point for this process, and Trotsky oversaw the conversion of at least seven full armies into labour forces. Translated into Stalinist terms, such notions acquire a horrific meaning and remind us that Trotsky was one of those who initiated totalitarian coercion in theory and practice.

To Menshevik objections that forced labour was always unproductive, Trotsky retorted that the shift 'from bourgeois anarchy to socialist economy without a revolutionary dictatorship and without coercive forms of economic organization' was unthinkable. He described the Menshevik programme as 'the Milky Way, without a grain monopoly, without eliminating the market, without a revolutionary dictatorship and without the militarization of labour'.[69]

Even allowing for the circumstances in which Trotsky read his report, it is plain that the Bolsheviks were not simply seeking a way out of the country's profound crisis, but were also laying the foundations of the totalitarian system. It was precisely during those years – the New Economic Policy was merely an attempt to introduce a correction – that the new society was initiated. Trotsky was not solely responsible for what was done, but with Lenin and the rest of the Bolshevik leadership he was an interpreter of Marxism in Russian conditions. As early as 27 December 1919, with Lenin's approval, the

Sovnarkom accepted Trotsky's proposal that a special commission under his, Trotsky's, chairmanship be established to draw up a plan for the introduction of labour conscription.[70] Within a few days Trotsky asked M.D. Bonch-Bruevich to estimate the number of people and the amount of transport and technical support the army would need to mobilize people for labour service, and requested Bonch-Bruevich to take charge of the preparatory work of the project.[71]

As for wages, Trotsky told the Trade Union Congress, 'for us they are above all not a way to secure the personal existence of the individual worker, but a way of valuing that which the individual worker gives the republic through his labour'. He spoke of the need to encourage those workers who 'collaborate in the general interest' more than others. But, he went on, 'in rewarding some, the workers' state cannot but punish others, that is, those who blatantly breach labour solidarity, undermine the general work, cause serious damage to the socialist rebirth of the country. Repression in the interests of achieving economic goals is a necessary weapon of the socialist dictatorship.' Repression was thus needed not merely for political purposes, but also for economic goals. None of this, he continued, had been written down in any book: 'We together with you are just beginning to write this book with the sweat and blood of the toilers.'[72]

But as Potresov wrote: 'The Bolshevik regime will disappear in time, just as every other despotism has disappeared, just as the Romanov dynasty disappeared when its utter decay was exposed.' But he warned that it was 'easier for capitalism to be reformed as socialism than to force an oligarchy to give up its privileges and to embark on the path of democratic statehood'.[73] Prophetic words, indeed.

Culture and Revolution

Trotsky's chief idol was the revolution, but there was another sphere of his activities that occupied an enormous place in his life, and that was literature and art. His dedication to a range of cultural values raised him above all his comrades-in-arms and the other revolutionaries, and he exerted his influence on the development of culture, while trying to employ it in the service of the revolution and to introduce the masses to the rudiments of European civilization.

The majority of Russia's scientists, poets, writers and painters were hostile to the October revolution, but many were not. Some vacillated and agonized, moving from outright rejection to wholehearted support, from ecstatic sympathy to disillusionment, from cautious circumspection to collaboration, from neutrality to enthusiastic collaboration in what they came to perceive as the good of the new society. Trotsky wanted to make culture an ally of the new order, but his approach was purely pragmatic and he envisaged only an auxiliary role for intellectuals and their institutions. In 1922 he began his book *Literature and the Revolution*, and when Lenin asked him in the middle of the year to take over as his deputy in the Sovnarkom, he declined, giving 'overload' of Party work as his reason. He took leave, settled down outside Moscow and forced himself to complete the book. While the Politburo was expressing its disapproval of his aloofness, he was surrounded by books and immersed in his writing.

Why did Trotsky decline to become Lenin's deputy, an event which for decades has remained without satisfactory explanation? On 14 January 1923 he wrote to the Politburo about a letter from Stalin on Gosplan and the Council of Labour and Defence, in which he mentioned 'personal appointments'. He wrote that 'a few weeks after I returned to work [from having been ill], Comrade Lenin asked me to be his deputy. I replied that if the Central Committee appoints me, then of course as always I would submit to its instructions, but that I would regard such a decision as profoundly irrational and in total conflict with all my views on organizational matters and the administration of the economy, my plans and intentions.' The 'very existence of [more than two] collegia of deputies', he went on, 'was harmful', but the reason he had refused was that the 'policy of the Central Committee Secretariat, Orgburo and Politburo was wrong on [the role of] the Soviets'.[74] Thus, the negative view he had of what was essentially Stalin's area of operations allowed him to rationalize the time he wanted to spend pursuing a more congenial occupation, writing.

It was only when he was later in exile that Trotsky realized that the order he had helped to introduce was unable to provide the spiritual space for genuine creativity. In his 1936 book *What is the USSR and Where is it Going?*, he would write:

> The Russian people have not known a great religious Reformation, like the Germans, nor a great bourgeois revolution, like the French. Leaving aside the Reformationist revolution of seventeenth-century Britain, it was from these two crucibles that bourgeois individuality emerged, playing a very important part in the development of human personality in general: the Russian revolutions of 1905 and 1917 signalled the first awakening of individuality in the masses ... that is to say, in truncated form and at an accelerated pace, these two revolutions carried out the educational work of the bourgeois reformations and revolutions of the West. Long before this work was even roughly finished, however, the Russian revolution was shunted onto socialist rails by the course of the class war ... Spiritual creativity requires liberty.

Lamenting conditions in the mid-1930s, he concluded that 'Great Russian culture, suffering as it is from the watchtower regime ... is living chiefly at the expense of the older generation that was formed before the revolution ... The youth are somehow being pressed down by a cast-iron slab.'[75]

When he wrote these words he did not know that the pre-revolutionary older generation was about to be virtually exterminated and that the cast-iron slab would crush the entire population. To the extent that he himself was involved in creating the dictatorship of the proletariat, and that it was responsible for wounding the soul of creativity from the outset, and of rejecting universal human values, he too shared the blame for this eventuality. Yet he did try to Europeanize the Russian way of life and to introduce the people to the rudiments of culture.

We have seen that Trotsky was in most senses a European in his outlook, and that he generally underrated the culture, history and the unique values of Russia. Before the revolution in *Kievskaya mysl* he wrote a scandalous article called 'On the Intelligentsia', which belittled many aspects of Russian achievement. To be sure, when he published this piece in his collected works in 1922, he tried to soften its effect on Soviet readers by adding in a note: 'The tone of this article was calculated to challenge the nationalist-circle messianism of the intellectual coffee-houses.'[76] Commenting on the fact that the invasions from the East and the pressure from a richer West had prompted the excessive growth of the Russian state, Trotsky claimed that this had not only impoverished the Russian labouring masses, but had also deprived the ruling classes of nourishment. As a result, the cultural veneer that had been laid over the virgin soil of social barbarism was barely perceptible.

How pathetic is the Russian nobility that history has given us! Where are its castles? Where were its tournaments, its crusades, its arms-bearers, minstrels and pages? Where is its chivalrous love? There is nothing, nothing whatever ... Where are the great strengths and the great names? ... Russia is a poor country, ours is a poor history ... The slavophiles wanted to perpetuate its social anonymity and slavish spirit – [of a people] that has never risen above the herd instinct – as 'meekness' and 'humility', the finest flower of the Slavic soul.[77]

After the revolution, Trotsky was more circumspect about Russia's past and her culture. Nevertheless, in rightly pointing out the back-wardness of the Russian way of life and her urban civilization, as well as the absence of other attributes of the coming machine-age, he put his finger on the unique and original quality of Russian history and culture which was indeed unlike anything to be found in Europe.

Trotsky's insulting views on Russia stemmed, it would seem, from the feeling of intellectual superiority that he felt towards his surround-ings and which he could not hide. It may be one of the reasons he lacked close friends: it was easy to admire him when listening to his speeches or reading his pamphlets, but it was not so easy to like him – he spoke, debated and wrote as if he were standing on a pedestal of his own making. Only towards the end of his life, when he was cornered by Stalin's hunters, did he change and express nostalgia for his homeland, frequently referring to its history or recalling great Russian writers and poets, thinkers and artists.

In order to write about culture, to share the literary interests of the intelligentsia and follow what was being published, Trotsky had to read a phenomenal amount, which he was able to do thanks to his ability to 'speed-read'. Apart from the library which he maintained on his armoured train, at the beginning of 1921 he ordered another one to be set up for him in Moscow. His aide, Butov, instructed Moscow District Military Commissar Dobroklonsky: 'A library on military, political and economic questions has been organized at

[Trotsky's] Secretariat. The number of books has reached 20,000 and is constantly growing . . . Referring to telephone conversations with you, I request you immediately appoint not less than three people who are suitable in all respects for work in this library . . .'[78] At Trotsky's request, A. Solts, the chief of libraries and literary supplies for the agitational department of the Central Committee, regularly sent him all the new books he could obtain at home or from abroad. In addition, Trotsky's office received a wide range of Soviet technical, political, economic, literary and artistic journals, as well as *Sotsialisticheskii vestnik*, which the Mensheviks were then publishing in Berlin.[79]

Trotsky was genuinely committed to exploiting the fruits of Russian culture for the good of the revolution – 'culture-mongering', he called it – and for this reason he wanted to carry out a revolution in the way of life, in rituals and speech. In his book *Questions of Lifestyle* (1923), he wrote: 'We must learn to work well: accurately, cleanly, efficiently. We need culture at work, culture in our lives, culture in our way of life. After long preparation we used the lever of armed uprising to throw off the supremacy of the exploiters. But there is no lever with which to raise culture overnight. For that a long process of self-education of the working class is needed, with the peasants alongside and in train.'[80] After dismissing the mockery of intellectual sceptics as empty chatter, he declared: 'Socialist construction is planned construction on the greatest scale. And through all the ebbs and flows, the mistakes and turns and all the contortions of NEP, the Party is following its great plan, it is educating the youth in the spirit of the plan, teaching everyone to connect his personal function to the general task which today commands him to sew on a Soviet button carefully, and tomorrow to die fearlessly under the banner of Communism.'[81] These views were an accurate reflection of ideas expressed by Lenin at the Third Congress of Soviet Youth.

Trotsky went beyond formulating the programme, however. He also proposed slogans and explained precisely how to carry them out, underlining as the chief links in the process of 'culture-mongering' the struggle against alcoholism, foul language, bad habits and loutish behaviour. In the early summer of 1923, while on holiday, he wrote to the Central Committee about a resolution that had been passed at a plenum in his absence:

It seems that once again the question was raised about allowing the unrestricted sale of [alcoholic] drinks for fiscal purposes, a question I have termed explosive. In view of the enormous importance of this matter and the exceptional responsibility those who have raised it have taken upon themselves, I think it essential I put my views in writing. It is entirely clear to me that our budget can be sustained only by success in agriculture, industry and export trade (export of grain, wood and so on). The attempt to shift the budget onto an alcohol basis is an attempt to deceive history, by freeing the state budget from dependence on our own successes in economic construction ... The working class generally feels in an uplifted mood. If alcohol gets into the picture, everything will go backwards and downwards.[82]

The letter had no effect. Trotsky, who was not a drinker, published an article in *Pravda* entitled 'Vodka, the Church and the Cinema', in which he wrote: 'The revolution inherited the abolition of the vodka monopoly as a fact and it adopted this fact, but for reasons of a deeply principled kind ... Abolition of [a system in which] the state turns the people into drunkards entered the iron safe of the revolution's conquests ... Our economic and cultural successes will be in inverse proportion to [alcoholic consumption]. There can be no concession on this.'[83]

Perceptively pointing out that 'culture-mongering' also focused attention on 'the oppressed position of housewives, mothers and wives', Trotsky remarked, in an article entitled 'To Build Socialism Means Liberating the Woman and Protecting the Mother': 'There is probably no hard labour that can compare to the life of drudgery and unrelieved misery of the peasant woman today, and not only those from poor families, but also from middle-peasant families. She has no rest, no holidays, no ray of hope!'[84] Without a general rise in cultural levels, he realized, there could be no socialism: 'Tuberculosis, nervous disorders, syphilis, alcoholism, all these diseases and many others are widespread in the population. We have to cure the nation. Without it, socialism is unthinkable. We have to get at the root and the source. And where is the source of the nation, if not in the mother? The struggle for homeless mothers must be first on the agenda.'[85]

When the workers at a shoe factory voted 'to abolish swearing', and 'to shame and educate' those who would not conform by fining them and publishing their names in the press, Trotsky at once responded with an article in *Pravda* entitled 'The Struggle for Cultured Speech'. Analysing Russian foul language as stemming from the class system – hunger, desperation, coarseness and hopeless slavery for the lower classes; superiority, lordliness, slave-owning and the security of their base for the upper classes – Trotsky noted that cursing had sickeningly coloured the whole of Russian life.[86] Going beyond the initiative of the shoe workers, he called for the language to be cleaned up, made clearer and more beautiful.

Trotsky was plainly over-optimistic about the 'civilizing' effects of the revolution on the denseness, ignorance, lack of culture and atavism of the people. Frequently he advocated 'new Soviet rituals': 'The revolutionary symbolism born of the workers' state is new, clear and powerful: the red banner, the hammer and sickle, the red star, worker and peasant, comrade, the Internationale.' He urged that everything that was created anew in everyday life be encouraged:

> There is a movement among the workers to celebrate their birthdays, rather than saints' days, and to name new-borns not with saints' names, but with new names that symbolize things, events or ideas that are close to us today. It was at a meeting of Moscow agitators that I heard for the first time that the new female name of Oktyabrina [derived from October] has already acquired a degree of civil right. There is the name Ninel (Lenin backwards). Rem has been used (from Revolution, Electrification and Mir [Peace, also sometimes Mechanization]). The link with the revolution is also expressed by giving babies the name Vladimir, as well as Ilyich, and even Lenin as a first name, Rosa, in honour of Rosa Luxemburg, and so on. Some births have been marked by a semi-serious ritual of 'inspecting' the baby in the presence of the factory committee and a special resolution registering the infant as a citizen of the RSFSR. Then the banquet would begin.

Not all new ideas would be successful, he conceded: 'Where's the harm? Natural selection will take its own course. The new life will establish the forms that suit it best...'[87]

Most of Trotsky's ideas in this area were doomed to failure: customs and rituals, no less than morals, take centuries to form and cannot be changed by a simple 'initiative'. On the other hand, it should be noted that the lack of culture against which he railed so passionately served as one of the fundamental props of Stalinist absolutism.

The struggle to raise the culture could not succeed without the support of the intelligentsia, and the intelligentsia was basically hostile to the new order. Many joined the Whites and in due course shared their fate, as hundreds of thousands drank the bitter cup of emigration. Those who remained were not trusted and were mockingly known as 'specialists' and relegated for the most part to carrying out the will of Party functionaries, who were often ignorant and militantly intolerant. While Lenin's entourage included many highly intelligent individuals, the lower levels of the bureaucracy were populated by workers elevated to administrative jobs, poorly educated revolutionaries 'from the people' whose political, moral and general culture was as a rule rather low. In the first decade of Soviet rule, at least, the very words '*intelligent*' and 'intelligentsia' – usually qualified by 'rotten' – were used disparagingly. The pre-revolutionary intelligentsia suffered hostility and distrust for many years, culminating in the monstrous purges of the late 1930s, but an ominous signal was sounded while Lenin was still alive: the deportation in 1922 of a large group of the most prominent figures in Russian culture, among them such philosophers and writers as Berdyaev and Bunin.

Despite its victory in the civil war, the Bolshevik state was not stable. There were internal disorders, riots and uprisings, and the Bolsheviks expected treachery to come from among the creative intelligentsia. Lenin gave the Justice Commissar, Krylenko, sinister advice when he recommended that legal form be given to the deportation abroad of intellectuals 'who have still not disarmed themselves' and who were suspected of anti-Soviet agitation. On the basis of a Politburo decision of 8 July 1922, reinforced by a VTsIK instruction of 10 August, 'hostile intellectual groupings' were to be exiled beyond the Soviet border. Although the complete lists have not been found, it is thought that some two hundred people were so despatched.

Among them was the eminent philosopher Nikolai Berdyaev, who, when later reflecting on his fate and the regime that had decided it, recalled that the GPU had granted him an exit visa on pain of execution should he ever appear on Soviet soil again: 'I was exiled from my country not on political grounds, but for ideological reasons. I became depressed when they told me I was to be deported.' The Russian revolution, he gloomily concluded, 'spelled the end of the Russian intelligentsia ... In Russian Communism the will for power is stronger than the will for liberty.'[88]

Trotsky explained the Soviet decision for these deportations in an interview with foreign correspondents: 'Given the new military difficulties . . . all these irreconcilable and incorrigible elements are a military-political agency of our enemies, and we prefer to deport them during a lull and in good time, and I express the hope that you will not refuse to acknowledge [this] prudent humanitarian [act].'[89] Bolshevik 'humanitarianism' was of a harsh kind. For Trotsky, 'to be outside the revolution means to be in emigration'.[90]

In the spring of 1918, Maxim Gorky, together with a number of other cultural figures, met the Commissar for Public Enlightenment [Education], Lunacharsky, and asked for permission to set up their own unions and societies and to run them 'without political inter-ference'. Lunacharsky responded by citing the Party line: 'We were against the political Constituent Assembly and are no less against a Constituent Assembly in the sphere of culture.'[91] There would be no cultural assemblies unless they were approved by the Party and were strictly monitored by the Central Committee's Agitprop Department. As for the deported intellectuals, they would, of course, become vigorously anti-Bolshevik in their pronouncements, and for years the most active of them would be kept under surveillance by Soviet intelligence and punitive agencies abroad. Their pronounce-ments and publications were regularly and promptly delivered to the Bolshevik leaders, including Trotsky, for their information and reflection.

As for the Russian Church, here action took the place of reflection. Like all the other leaders, Trotsky regarded religion as a rabid enemy of the Soviet state and the new culture. Speaking on 17 July 1924 at a meeting of workers' club organizers, he justified intensified anti-religious propaganda and added that the liquidation of religion by other means was also acceptable: 'In the anti-religious struggle, periods of open frontal attack alternate with periods of blockade, sapping, encirclement. In general terms we have now entered this phase, but it doesn't mean we won't go over once more to frontal attack. We just have to prepare for it.' Asserting that the Bolshevik attack on religion was a lawful one, he concluded: 'And has it produced results? Yes, it has.'[92]

The assault on religion had indeed been a mass frontal attack, its most appalling feature being the 'hunt' for priests. This began after

Lenin dictated a six-page letter to Molotov by telephone on 19 March 1922, prefaced with a warning that it was not to be copied, but was to be circulated to all members of the Politburo with instructions to write their comments on the original. A month earlier, an order of the VTsIK dated 23 February had unleashed a campaign of confiscation of Church valuables for famine relief. In the town of Shuya the inhabitants had resisted. Troops were called out and there were casualties. Lenin's response, as shown in the letter to Molotov, was harsh in the extreme:

> Concerning the events in Shuya, which is already under discussion at the Politburo, I think a firm decision should be taken at once in accordance with the general direction of the present plan. As I doubt if I'll be able to attend the Politburo meeting of 20 March, I shall outline my views in writing ... It is precisely now and only now, when the starving are eating people and corpses are lying in their hundreds, if not thousands, along the roads, that we can (and therefore we must) confiscate church valuables with the most furious and pitiless energy and not stop before any sort of resistance.
>
> Therefore I come to the inescapable conclusion that we must now launch the most decisive and merciless battle against the Black Hundreds clergy and crush their resistance with such ferocity that they will not forget it for several decades ... Only Comrade Kalinin [the official head of state] can officially announce some sort of measures – Comrade Trotsky must never under any circumstances write anything in the press or in print or say anything to the public in any form ... Confiscation of valuables, especially of the richest monasteries and churches, must be carried out with the most merciless determination, stopping at nothing and in the shortest possible time. The bigger the number of reactionary clergy and reactionary bourgeois we manage to shoot in the process, the better.[93]

Molotov's written comment on this letter was: 'Agreed. But I suggest the campaign not be extended to all provinces and towns, only to those where there really are major treasures, concentrating our forces and the attention of the Party accordingly.'[94] Next day, at a meeting of the Politburo attended by only four people – Kamenev, Stalin, Molotov and Trotsky – Trotsky submitted a draft instruction on confiscating Church valuables which was passed and circulated to all provincial Party secretaries. Trotsky attempted to give the campaign, already under way, an organized character. The seventeen points of his directive did not include any explicit instructions about executions, but he did call for the struggle against 'the princes of the Church' to be carried out with determination and in the shortest possible time.[95] Tribunals were set up. In Moscow eleven people – priests, deans and citizens – were sentenced to death and other forms of punishment. On Trotsky's intervention, six of the death sentences were commuted to prison terms.[96] Lenin had ordered that 'we must now teach these people so that for several decades they will not dare even to think about any kind of resistance.'[97] And now his orders were being carried out.

Trotsky headed the commission on the collection of valuables and was one of the most energetic executors of Lenin's desire to curb the Church's influence and drain it of its resources, although he was less aggressive than some other members of the Politburo. For instance, on 15 May 1922 he wrote to Lenin and the rest of the Politburo, as well as to *Pravda* and *Izvestiya*, suggesting broader and more active support for the clergy, led by Bishop Antonin (A.A. Granovsky), who were loyal to the Soviet regime under the slogan 'Changing Landmarks' (*Smena vekh*), and he noted that their appeal had appeared only as a small notice in *Pravda*. Meanwhile, he wrote, 'the utterly trivial Genoa [peace conference] nonsense occupies entire pages, whereas this the most profound of spiritual revolutions in the Russian people (or rather the preparation of this the most profound of revolutions), is relegated to the back pages'. On 15 May Lenin made a marginal note on this: 'Right! 1000 times right! Down with the nonsense!'[98] Despite their support for Bishop Antonin and others of his persuasion, the Bolsheviks based their relations with religion on force and coercion, and counted on speeding up the 'most profound of spiritual revolutions in the people'.

Trotsky was at the heart of the criminal campaign. Its ostensible aim of saving the starving was meant to be achieved by killing others. In addressing urgent social and economic problems, the Bolsheviks, as it were *en passant*, also settled the cultural issue of freeing the people's minds of religious dogma. This was a grave error, first, because religion was allied to morality, and secondly, because to struggle against ideas and convictions with weapons of violence was not merely criminal, it was ineffectual. For all his intelligence, Trotsky could not or would not see this. At the beginning of March 1922 he wrote to the Politburo and Central Committee Secretariat:

> The work of confiscating the valuables of the Moscow churches has become hopelessly confused because alongside the already existing commissions, the VTsIK has created its own commissions, using representatives of Famine Aid, provincial Party committees and provincial Party financial departments. Yesterday, my commission . . . came to the unanimous decision that a secret shock commission should be formed in Moscow, consisting of Comrades Sapronov, Unshlikht, Samoilova-Zemlyachka and Galkin. This commission will secretly handle the political and organizational side of the work. The real confiscation will start [this month] and be finished in the shortest possible time. I repeat, this commission must be entirely secret. Confiscation in Moscow will formally be the business of the central committee of Famine Aid, where Comrade Sapronov will have office hours.[99]

The 'shock commission' acted in the spirit of the times. Valuables were confiscated wherever they could be found: in churches, museums, from the middle classes, speculators and black marketeers. The treasures, some of them of immense cultural value, were converted into cash which was then distributed to various departments for various purposes, almost none of it for providing relief to the starving millions. Several major Party committees requested allocations of specific amounts of these so-called 'luxury items'. A Politburo minute of 12 January 1922, signed by Molotov, shows that a decision was taken to issue 'luxury items for the purpose of creating local funds in Moscow and Petrograd, and also an export fund. A commission, consisting of Comrades Zinoviev . . . Kamenev, Trotsky and Lezhava should be formed to determine the amounts and so on.'[100]

In striving to give a revolutionary twist to cultural activity, Trotsky was pursuing the belief that this would help to prepare the world revolution. In the talks he gave in various societies and clubs, he linked culture with international issues: 'From all the pulleys of trivial private matters drive-belts must be connected to the fly-wheel of the world revolution.'[101] Like Lenin, however, he did not want to recognize that there was such a thing as 'pure' proletarian culture. This was a complex issue. Vulgar educators, half-ignorant 'culture-mongers' of socialism were proclaiming a 'proletarian culture' based on class instincts and revolutionary values.

While attempting not to contradict the class approach, Trotsky wanted to convert 'proletarian culture' into 'culture of the transitional period'. This he identified as 'the remnants, still very active, of the culture of the gentry period – not all of it is useless: we will not throw out Pushkin and Tolstoy, we need them – and of the elements of bourgeois culture which we still need ... we are still living to a considerable extent on bourgeois specialists, we still haven't built our own factories and are working in those that we received from the hands of the bourgeoisie.'[102] To reinforce his argument he mentioned that Lenin had used the term 'proletarian culture' only in his polemics with a former rival, Alexander Bogdanov, before the First World War. Trotsky in effect was the first to argue against the wholesale nihilism of the Proletcult (the proletarian culture movement), and against deifying ignorance and praising class as a virtue in literature and art. At the same time, he firmly believed that exponents of the arts must be 'fighters for the Party'. In a letter to Kamenev and A.K. Voronsky, he wrote that an 'ideological union of writer-Communists was a good thing'.[103]

The ideas promulgated by Proletcult also penetrated the army. The victorious proletariat, it argued, must also create a purely proletarian military science which would sweep away the bourgeois military heritage. M.V. Frunze devoted an article to these notions entitled 'On a Unified Military Doctrine'. In a broad debate that took place in 1922 the views of Trotsky and Frunze clashed. Trotsky did not believe a special proletarian military science was possible, or that the proletariat would manage without the military experience of the past. Frunze later admitted that he had been wrong, and he recalled a conversation with Lenin, who had criticized the harmful ideas of Proletcult in military matters.

Although he was still War Commissar, Trotsky was also responsible to the Politburo for cultural affairs. In the second half of July 1924 he wrote to a group of literature specialists:

On the initiative of Nikolai Ivanovich Bukharin, I propose to convene a preliminary meeting of comrades who are involved in creative literature and literary criticism, for the purpose of establishing a more precise attitude of the Party towards literature. Some or other views and proposals (if they emerge after an exchange of opinion) may be submitted to the Politburo. The meeting is scheduled for Wednesday

26 July at 11 a.m. at the Revolutionary Military Council building (23, Znamenka).[104]

A list of Party representatives followed, including Bukharin, Kamenev and Trotsky himself from among the top leadership.

The effort to bring cultural figures under Party control succeeded after censorship was introduced. In June 1922 the Chief Directorate for Literature and Art (Glavlit) was created, quickly followed by the building of a network which would prevent the penetration of any free thought. When a year later the writer Yevgeni Trifonov tried to reply to Trotsky's slashing review of his work in the journal *Knigonosha*, his letter was rejected. The indignant Trifonov wrote to Trotsky: 'In your review in *Pravda* you subjected me to savage, annihilating criticism, both as a personality and as the author of an article that you did not like. I wanted to reply to you in the same newspaper ... but *Pravda* refused to print my reply ... A man of your stature has no need to resort to such methods to strike at an enemy whom someone else has obligingly grabbed by the hands and throat...'[105]

The delegation of social tasks to literature dates from this period. In September 1921 Trotsky wrote to the 'proletarian poet' Demyan Bedny ('Demyan the Poor'): 'Noulens is not only the representative of France on the International Commission, but, as the radio has announced, he is also chairman of the international commission for relief to Russia ... In my opinion, we should strike at him pitilessly and every day. Your couplets on Giraud seem to me to be a good beginning of the campaign, but only a beginning.'[106] Thus began a campaign against the former French ambassador to the tsar as 'a sworn enemy of the Soviet regime', who was at the same time head of the international commission dedicated to bringing relief to the starving of Russia. Demyan Bedny duly performed as he was expected to and submitted some doggerel that was meant to expose the two-faced and subversive purpose of the foreign aid-workers under Noulens's sponsorship.[107] As the civil war was approaching its end, however, Demyan Bedny wrote to Trotsky: 'I am now ready to salute you and return to my usual work. If you don't think I'm being premature, please tell the Central Committee that a need for my drum is no longer felt.'[108]

On a number of occasions, Trotsky's sense of intellectual solidarity overcame his radicalism, and he interceded for writers, gave them some cautious support or managed to deflect impending punishment. When Boris Pilnyak's book *Smertel'noe manit* (Fatal Attraction) was withdrawn in August 1922 and the clouds gathered over him, Trotsky wrote to Kalinin, Rykov, Kamenev, Molotov and Stalin:

> I'd like to raise the question of Pilnyak's book again. It was confiscated because of the story 'Ivan-Moskva'. Certainly Pilnyak does not give a very attractive picture of everyday life ... In his later works, 'The Blizzard' and 'The Third Capital' for the journal *Krasnaya nov'* [Red Virgin Soil], Pilnyak expresses a positive attitude to the revolution in his own way, admittedly with as much confusion and ambiguity as you like, and it is hard to know where he will end up. But in these circumstance it is a manifest error to confiscate his book ... I ask all members of the Politburo to give close attention to this question, to read the story, as far as possible, and to rescind the GPU's incorrect decision.[109]

Already the GPU could on its own authority withdraw a book if in its opinion it contained too many lice, black marketeers or foul language, all of which were an obvious 'insult to the revolution', and to ban an author's future output. Trotsky's efforts at limiting the worst effects of this censorship would later be used as evidence of his support for the class enemy.

In late September 1920, the well-known writer Fedor Sologub wrote to Trotsky in terms which graphically depict the circumstances to which the revolution had reduced the intelligentsia, although it should be noted that the entire country was in a dire condition at the time:

> I have come to Moscow for a few days and I earnestly request your help in obtaining permission to travel to Revel [Tallin], even for one month. I absolutely must organize my literary affairs, sell my new novel and acquire some of the things and clothes that I and [my wife] need badly – we are in rags and tatters, and to have to beg for every piece of bread, every log of firewood, a pair of galoshes or stockings is, you must agree, too humiliating and is not proper either for my age or my literary position. With all due respect, I ask you to show us justice and check the sincerity of our intentions, which exclude any kind of politics ...[110]

In a postscript, Sologub asked for a reply 'by Friday'. Two days later, on 30 September (the Saturday), Trotsky replied:

I will not enter into discussion of your observations about the 'humiliation' of having to bother about finding galoshes and stockings in this
exhausted and ruined country, and that this 'humiliation' is only made
worse by your 'literary position'. As for your business trip to Revel,
following my enquiries I have been informed that no obstacles to it
have been found. Taking the words from your letter, I have reported
that you have no intention of pursuing aims of a political character. I
need hardly add that any collaboration by you during the journey with
world exploiters against the toilers' republic will make it extremely
difficult for many other citizens to leave the country.[111]

A decade later, Trotsky might have felt that it had been a mistake
to put revolution invariably before culture. In his book *What is the
USSR and Where is it Going?*, he wrote prophetically: 'The dictatorship
reflects the barbarism of the past, not the culture of the future. Of
necessity it imposes strict limitations on all forms of activity, spiritual
creativity included. From the outset the programme of the revolution
envisaged such limitations as a temporary evil and was obligated, as
the new regime became more secure, to abolish all restrictions on
liberty, one after the other.' What he had in mind, however, was not
the dictatorship of the proletariat, but that of Stalin. He went on:
'With his rather "conservative" personal artistic tastes, Lenin was
always extremely politically cautious about art and readily admitted
his incompetence. He was occasionally upset by ... Lunacharsky's
support for any form of modernism, but he contented himself with
ironic remarks in private conversation and remained extremely far
from the idea of turning his personal taste into law. In 1924, Trotsky
had formulated the relations of the state to various artistic groupings
and tendencies as follows: 'While imposing on them the categorical
criterion, for the revolution or against the revolution, in the sphere
of artistic self-determination they should be given full freedom.'[112]

Of course, in practice there was to be no self-determination for
artists, and Trotsky shares the blame for that. Those practitioners
who served the revolution selflessly, though, could count on his support. His relations with the poet Alexander Bezymensky are instructive
in this respect. In a letter to Lunacharsky, Trotsky voiced high praise
of Bezymensky's work: 'Bezymensky is a poet and one of us, a real
October man to the marrow of his bones. He doesn't have to "accept"
the revolution, for the revolution accepted him on the day of his

spiritual birth.'[113] A poet who had dedicated himself to the revolution, in Trotsky's view, was worth supporting, but as an intelligent man, he was aware that in opening the sluice-gates of culture, the revolution had also impoverished it by alienating and destroying so many of its exponents.

Personality and Revolution

In the years since Stalin finally got rid of Trotsky, it has become increasingly clear that one of the greatest delusions of the twentieth century was the notion that it is possible to improve people's lives by bloody revolution. Among the biggest fanatics were the makers of the Russian revolution who believed it possible not merely to change economic relations, but also people's spiritual values, national self-awareness and even human nature itself. It was perhaps above all the Marxist idea that the dictatorship of the proletariat was an inevitability that pushed the revolution towards violence and led in turn to the emergence of a powerful authoritarian tendency in Bolshevism. For Lenin, the 'concept of a dictatorship means nothing other than unrestrained power based on the absence of any limits, laws and absolutely no rules'.[114] But this abstract formulation was quickly converted into practice by Lenin. In August 1918 he wrote to the Soviet in Nizhni Novgorod: 'A White Guards uprising is being organized in Nizhni. All forces must be harnessed, a troika of dictators must be appointed ... mass terror must be introduced at once, shoot and deport hundreds of prostitutes, drunken soldiers, former officers ... Not a minute's delay ... You must act with full force: mass searches, execution for concealing a weapon, mass deportation of Mensheviks and unreliables . . .'[115]

What had happened to pre-revolutionary assurances about sticking to democracy, humanism, justice? A sinister link was formed between the idea of the dictatorship of the proletariat, the use of force and totalitarianism which graphically illustrates the role of personality in revolution. Giving the working class the right to determine the lives of the people in general led inevitably to the consolidation of totalitarianism with its harsh division between the 'leader' and the 'masses'.

Naturally, it was only among the leaders that there could be 'personalities' and a hierarchy. The supreme 'leader', surrounded by 'outstanding leaders', was supported by a pyramid of other 'leaders' in descending order. This was the system which, by rejecting genuine democratic power, was established after the revolution in Russia.

Totalitarianism also established a division within the people, between the 'conscious' and the 'unconscious'. After the revolution the latter included the middle classes, the intelligentsia, tsarist administrators and almost the entire peasantry. The population was now reorganized and sub-divided in 'strata' and groups whose social 'purity' was determined by their class origins. But since it had been the war that had made the revolution possible, the Bolsheviks naturally adopted many methods that had been generated by the war, notably the instant resort to violence. Lenin's instruction to the Bolsheviks in Saratov in August 1918 to shoot not merely 'conspirators' but also 'the hesitant', and 'without wasting time on idiotic red tape', was a classic example of the trend.

As an orthodox Marxist, Trotsky was quick to understand Bolshevik authoritarianism, but he refrained from protesting because he also saw that there was a part for him to play as a leader in the emerging system. We have seen that he was congenitally well suited to the radicalism and maximalism of Bolshevik policies in 1917, and it was without a shadow of doubt that he could assert for years to come that the revolution of October was possible only because the masses were led by Lenin and himself. At the end of March 1935, he wrote in his diary:

> Had I not been present in 1917 in Petersburg, the October Revolution would still have taken place – on the condition that Lenin was present and in command. If neither Lenin nor I had been present in Petersburg, there would have been no October Revolution ... The same could by and large be said of the Civil War, although in its first period, especially at the time of the fall of Simbirsk and Kazan, Lenin wavered and was beset by doubts. But this was undoubtedly a passing mood which he probably never admitted to anyone but me. (I must tell about this in greater detail.)[116]

While this assertion is not an exaggeration of Trotsky's part in the events, its frankness, bordering on vanity, illuminates an important facet of his personality.

As Bolshevik-Communist custom quickly superseded social democratic tradition in the Party, it was enough for a 'leader' on any level
to declare that a measure was 'in the interests of the proletariat', or
that 'the working class demands' or 'the masses insist', for an action
to appear legitimate. The monopoly of power and thought meant that
only the 'leaders' could express the masses' interests, and the creation
by the Party 'old guard' of a new layer of Soviet leaders, all of them
outside any form of democratic control, soon led to the bureaucratization of the whole edifice of power. Party membership became the
irreplaceable and virtually the sole path to a successful career. Leaders,
intellectuals and Party workers, all of a new type, emerged, their
suitability being their absolute dedication, not only to Communist
ideology, but to the new leadership, and their outright hostility to all
things bourgeois. Henceforth, and especially from the end of the
1920s, meetings, conferences and congresses were dominated by loud
voices competing to support the 'general line of the Party', to praise
the 'wisdom of the leader' (now the sole leader), or the 'genius' of his
plans. Uniformity of ideas, indeed uniformity in everything, generated
the sinister atmosphere in which the poisonous tendrils of one-man
rule, bureaucracy and dogmatism could flourish. Party unity was
achieved at the cost of intellectual and moral liberty. The transformation of the Party into a state organization facilitated the emergence
of a new form of careerism.

These propositions are well illustrated by a letter from Adolf Ioffe,
dated 1 May 1920, requesting Trotsky's help in obtaining either the
post of Commissar of the Workers' and Peasants' Inspection (Rabkrin)
or an influential position in the Foreign Commissariat. Whether
intentionally or not, Ioffe's letter reveals the origins of the bureaucratization of the Party and state, and in particular the emergence of
Soviet careerism. Ioffe wrote that the new conditions in the country
meant that 'belonging to the Party, instead of having shackles on your
legs or a rope round your neck, brings with it access to the use of all
the real material goods', and that this was 'altering Party mentality
and Party morale'. There was, he went on, 'an unwritten law in our
Constitution' according to which 'the Party organization stands above
Soviet power, and this makes it possible for a demagogue to rise to
the top, a mercenary and politically amoral demagogue whose only
merit is a well-endowed tongue.' He continued: 'Given the lack of

material goods in Soviet Russia, the Party and Soviet bureaucracy enjoy what there is at the expense not only of the bourgeoisie, but also the proletariat, which is wrong. Why should commissars and commissarchiks [minor commissars] be able to move around freely, and we can't? Why is there always a seat for them on the train, but not for us? Why can they always get a place in a sanatorium, but we can't? And so on. I have heard this said at every non-Party conference I have spoken at.' There was, he said, a new psychological climate in which 'the leaders can do anything'.

He continued:

The inequality in Moscow is really enormous and one's material security virtually depends on one's job, a situation, you must agree, which is becoming extremely dangerous. I heard, for instance, that before the last purge of the VTsIK, its old members were anxious and concerned mainly because they were afraid they would lose the right to live in the Hotel National and would lose the privileges that went with it. From top to bottom and bottom to top, it's the same thing. At the lowest level it means a pair of boots and a tunic; higher up, an automobile, a railcar, access to the Sovnarkom dining room, an apartment in the Kremlin or the National, and at the very top, where they have all these things anyway, it means prestige, a prominent position and a well-known name. There is no room here for the old Party dedication and self-sacrifice, revolutionary endeavour and self-denial ... The young people are being brought up in these new traditions. How can one not be horrified for our Party and the revolution?[117]

Ioffe was citing facts that characterized the danger looming for the system and the Party, but he did not identify the deep well-springs from which it originated. After the Tenth Party Congress in March 1921, at which factions within the Party were banned, the bureaucratic ossification gathered pace. Once all 'platforms', 'deviations' and 'oppositions' were eliminated, the Party became an ideological order. Henceforth it would be necessary to demonstrate and prove one's purity and orthodoxy, and to expose anyone who stood out from the crowd in any way. The personalities of the revolutionaries were profiled and arranged in order of their Party importance. Having destroyed the middle classes, the Party had no one to consume but its own members who might depart in any way from the standards it set. A new type of leader emerged, one who served only the centre, who was suspicious of everyone, lacking in initiative, incompetent, uneducated but self-assured, a harsh executor of the Party line. He was, as Berdyaev wrote, psychologically 'congenial to Lenin's plan, he became the material of the Communist Party organization ... A new psychological type ... emerged from the milieu of the workers and peasants and was trained in military and Party discipline. These new people ... were alien to the traditions of Russian culture.'[118]

As one of the leaders of the Revolution, Trotsky made a substantial contribution to the canonization of Lenin's image, chiefly as a tribute to 'the greatest Russian revolutionary', but also no doubt because it would raise his own prestige still higher in society and in Comintern. By praising Lenin, Trotsky praised himself. When V. Sorin set about formulating the tasks of the Lenin Institute in 1925, Trotsky made many proposals for developing the project. It was decided to gather all of Lenin's manuscripts and to publish them as a collection, as well as to prepare a full biography and organize the systematic, widespread promulgation of his teachings.

The articles Trotsky wrote about Lenin, before and after Lenin's death, often approached the hagiographic tone of a later, more obedient generation. In his article 'Lenin on the Dais', which on 15 April 1924 his assistant Poznansky sent to three newspapers – *Pravda*, *Gudok* and *Krasnaya zvezda* – he wrote:

> Grabbing at his notes, Lenin would rush from the platform to try to evade the inevitable ... The roar of applause would grow, wave upon wave. 'Long live ... Lenin ... Leader ... Ilyich.' There in the glow of the electric lights glimmered that inimitable human head, lashed from all sides by the unbridled waves. And then when it seemed the whirlwind of ecstasy had reached the height of its frenzy, suddenly above all the roaring and yelling and clapping the sound of a young, intense, happy and passionate voice would cut through the storm, like a siren's: 'Long live Ilyich!' And from somewhere within the deepest palpitating depths of solidarity, love and enthusiasm, the reply would come like a threatening cyclone, in unison, making the rafters ring, the cry: 'Long live Lenin!'[119]

Trotsky would repeatedly employ his journalistic skill to inspire the masses with the thought of Lenin's divine nature. After Lenin's death such eulogies became even more essential to the leadership than when he was alive. Trotsky would do everything to underline how close he had been to the late leader and how much Lenin had trusted and liked him. Deep down, he wanted public and official recognition that he had been the second man of the revolution after Lenin. But, as he was to write in Norway after his deportation from Soviet Russia:

Up to now, every revolution has produced a reaction, even a counter-revolution ... The first victims of the reactionary wave were as a rule the pioneers, the initiators, the originators who had stood at the head of the masses during the offensive phase of the revolution; and the first place was taken by people of the second rank in alliance with yesterday's enemies of the revolution.[120]

The revolution dissolved personality, which was delivered up as a sacrifice to ephemeral ideals. The revolution could now be represented only by the personalities of the leaders who after Lenin's death began to dwindle sharply in number, as the post-revolutionary monster devoured them, one after the other.

5

The Outcast Revolutionary

Life is a paradox. Success alternates with failure. Grandiose plans and titanic efforts can end in historic defeat. The victor can become the outcast, and in this respect Trotsky's life was especially graphic. Having reached the crest of the wave in the October revolution, when the civil war came to an end he slithered steeply downwards. Not that he became less popular or less possessed by his idea, nor did he lose his touch as a brilliant pamphleteer and original thinker. His speeches were no less stirring, and he still believed that the lull in the revolution was only temporary, even if he now thought the new wave would come from the East. He did not change, but the times changed. The revolution by which he lived and found meaning in life receded.

The move to peace in the ruined country proved difficult. It was time to redeem the promises made to the population, and the debate on how this should be done exposed differences among the Boshevik leaders. The main stumbling block to new ideas was the cumbersome bureaucracy of a system created by a now hopelessly sick leader. Trotsky outlined his own ideas on how to rule the country in a memorandum to the Politburo, dated January 1923:

> The centrepiece of my written proposals to the Central Committee is the need to secure the correctly planned, day-to-day running of the state economy, with the reconstruction of state industry as the first priority. I have stated that we do not have a body that is directly responsible for the planned management of the state economy, endowed with its own rules, obligations and personnel, and that can carry out such management. I have stated that this is the precise cause of the growing tendency to pile up more and more new administrative and combined organs which in the end only get in the way of each

other. Apart from the Sovnarkom and Presidium of the VTsIK, we now have: the collegium of deputies [Deputy People's Commissars], the Council of Labour and Defence, the Finance Committee, the Little Sovnarkom, Gosplan [the State Planning Agency]. Moreover, absolutely all questions are also dealt with by the Central Committee (Secretariat, Orgburo, Politburo). In my view, this multiplicity of governing institutions, which have no defined relationship to each other and scattered responsibilities, is causing chaos at the top.[1]

At the Politburo, especially in Lenin's frequent absences, Trotsky repeatedly raised the question of the bureaucratic ossification of the system, the lack of proper monitoring of the administrative organization and the inefficiency of state government. His harsh and independent judgements were taken by many Party leaders to represent an unequivocal claim to the role of new leader, once Lenin's imminent demise became a fact.

The Stalinist Ring

A.P. Balashov, an old Bolshevik who had worked in Stalin's secretariat, told me that on one occasion at the Politburo when a row flared up between Zinoviev and Trotsky, 'everyone was supporting Zinoviev who burst out at Trotsky, "Can't you see you're in a 'ring'? Your tricks don't work any more, you're in the minority, a minority of one." Trotsky was enraged, and Bukharin tried to smooth things over. Often, before a meeting of the Politburo or some other gathering, Kamenev and Zinoviev would meet Stalin separately, no doubt in order to agree a position. In the secretariat these meetings of the triumvirate, with other members of the Politburo if needed, were known as "the ring", and they called them that themselves, like Zinoviev.'

Trotsky soon realized that there was a plot against him. At first he kept his peace, but then took every opportunity in his speeches to expose Stalin's 'technique'. In June 1927, at a meeting of the Central Party Control Commission, he declared:

You all of course know perfectly well that since 1924 a faction of seven has existed, consisting of all the members of the Politburo, except me.

My place has been taken by your former chairman, Kuybyshev, whose job is supposed to be chief custodian of the Party rules and Party morals, but who in fact has been the first to break the rules and pervert them. This 'group of seven' is an illegal and anti-Party body that has been deciding the Party's life behind its back . . . Its meetings have been used to devise ways of attacking me. In particular, it set a rule that Politburo members should not polemicize amongst themselves, but that they should all polemicize against Trotsky. The Party did not know about this, and nor did I. It has been going on for a long time.[2]

Under the guise of fighting for the interests of the people, the Party and socialism, a banal and utterly unprincipled struggle for leadership was going on at the summit of power, where the ruling group had ganged up against one of its own members because they feared he could lead the Party on his own. The warning that the Party could split, which Lenin had put in his so-called 'Testament', or 'Letter to the Congress', seemed about to be fulfilled. The 'ring', consisting of Stalin, Zinoviev and Kamenev, set about isolating and discrediting Trotsky and pushing him out of the main control centres. Events had to be accelerated in case Lenin's health should recover and he should bring Trotsky even more closely into his confidence. There can be little doubt that Lenin's suggestion, dated 4 January 1923,[3] that Stalin be removed as General Secretary if he, Lenin recovered, would have been quickly carried out.

The reason why Trotsky declined Lenin's proposal to enter into an alliance with him against Stalin over the Georgian affair* seems likely to remain a mystery. The triumvirate, however, must have been alarmed at the possibility of a union between the leader and Trotsky on such important issues as the national question, the monopoly on foreign trade, the struggle against bureaucratization and so on, and could not permit Trotsky to be so significantly reinforced.

Lenin's 'Testament', which was dictated in a series of sessions on 23, 24, 25, 26 and 29 December 1922, dealt at length with relations between Stalin and Trotsky, but it also examined the qualities of other Party leaders. It is therefore plausible to suppose that, once

---

* In 1922 Stalin, Dzerzhinsky and Ordzhonikidze had offended Lenin by using violent bullying tactics to bring the Georgian Bolshevik government into line.

the contents of the 'Testament' became known to the Politburo, the struggle for power was intensified. Lenin's secret document only added fuel to the flames. Had Lenin returned to active work, it would have been difficult for Stalin to count on retaining his 'unbounded power'. He needed to get rid of Trotsky, who was still seen by most of the Party as second only to Lenin, especially as in his 'Testament' Lenin spoke of Trotsky in immeasurably higher terms of praise than he did of any of the other leaders. Despite mentioning Trotsky's non-Bolshevik past, which 'can hardly be blamed on him personally', Lenin stressed that he was 'probably the most able man in the present Central Committee', with 'outstanding capabilities'.[4]

Trotsky had an interest in making Lenin's secret letter known; the other leaders did not. This much is clear from a top secret document which reveals how the Politburo and Presidium of the Central Control Commission felt about publishing the 'Testament'. The notes read:

TROTSKY: I believe the article should be published, unless there are formal reasons against it. [e.g. If] there were any differences in the way this article and others (about cooperatives, about Sukhanov) were transmitted.

KAMENEV: It should not be published: it is a speech that was not given at the Politburo. It is nothing more. The personal opinions are the basis and content of an article.

ZINOVIEV: N.K. [Krupskaya, Lenin's wife] was also of the opinion that it should only be given to the Central Committee. I didn't ask about publication as I thought (and still think) it is excluded. The question could be put. There were no differences in the conditions of transmission. Only the note (about Gosplan) was conveyed to me later, a few days ago.

STALIN: I suggest there is no reason to publish, especially as Ilyich gave no instructions to do so.

TOMSKY: I am in favour of Comrade Zinoviev's proposal that only members of the Central Committee should be shown it. It should not be published, as the general public will understand nothing in it.

SOLTS: V.I.'s note is not intended for the general public, which is why so much of it is given over to personal remarks. There is nothing of this in the article on cooperatives. It should not be published.

SLAVATINSKAYA: Comrades Bukharin, Rudzutak, Molotov and Kuybyshev are in favour of Comrade Zinoviev's proposal.[5]

The Stalinist triumvirate plainly wanted to suppress the 'Testament' because its publication would enhance Trotsky's chances and spoil their own. They were ambitious, especially Stalin and Zinoviev, and they actively sought support among the other members of the Politburo. They were reluctant, however, to come out openly against the victor of the revolution and civil war: the name of Trotsky still ranked alongside that of Lenin. On 14 October 1922, Radek wrote in *Pravda*: '[If] Lenin can be called the mind of the revolution, ruling by transmitting his will, then Trotsky can be seen as steel willpower restrained by reason. Like the voice of a bell summoning to work, Trotsky's speech rang out . . .' The triumvirate was well aware that, in order to unseat Trotsky, he first had to be distanced from Lenin, and then compromised in the eyes of the Party by greatly exaggerating his weaknesses and shortcomings.

Analysing this period later, when he was on Prinkipo, Trotsky noted that although the workers would have listened to Zinoviev and Kamenev, the pair's moral authority was weakened by the widespread knowledge of their flawed behaviour in 1917. Stalin, Trotsky declared, had been almost unknown beyond the narrow circle of old Bolsheviks. Against his own supporters' assurances that he was protected by his close association with Lenin in the public mind, Trotsky had argued that a hero during the rising tide of revolution can quickly be turned into an enemy by the slander of his opponents when the revolution is on the ebb.[6]

At Politburo meetings Trotsky felt ambushed, but the flames of the factional struggle were still prevented from spreading to the outside. In the autumn of 1923, when Lenin was already beyond being able to intervene, an important Party debate was planned with Trotsky as the target. It was to be described as a 'literary' debate. Trotsky, however, would be prevented from taking a direct part in it by illness: he had caught a chill when duck-shooting in the marsh country of Tver province earlier in the month, and he spent the entire winter confined on doctor's orders.[7]

In the absence of the chief antagonist and his potential ally, Stalin could now act with a free hand and measures were taken steadily to reduce Trotsky's authority and influence, beginning in a small way, and escalating into a major onslaught. Where at previous Party meetings an honorary presidium of Lenin and Trotsky had become customary, now the entire Politburo was so elected. Where in reports on Party gatherings Trotsky's name would normally have been listed after Lenin's, now all names – except Lenin's – were in alphabetical order. *Pravda*, *Izvestiya* and *Krasnaya zvezda* began omitting the epithet 'Trotsky, leader of the Red Army', while they mentioned Stalin more and more often. Stalin's secretariat, that is the Central Committee organization, began replacing Trotsky's supporters with new men who were loyal to the 'ring'. The political biographies of the leaders and their contribution to the victory of the revolution gradually started to come under review, and the steady, if barely noticed, reduction of Trotsky was under way, as Stalin proved himself to be a master of behind-the-scenes intrigue.

Trotsky recalled that a only few years later, when they were themselves struggling against Stalin, Zinoviev and Kamenev revealed the secrets of the plot to him. An inner Politburo of seven had been created, comprising all the other members except Trotsky, plus Kuybyshev who was head of the Supreme Economic Council. This centre settled all questions in advance and its members were bound by vows of secrecy. There were similar centres in the provinces which were subordinated to the Moscow centre's strict discipline and which communicated with it in code.[8] And, as he also learnt later, Party organizers were being selected on the single criterion that they must be 'against Trotsky'. The death of Lenin in January 1924 freed the conspirators to bring their campaign out into the open.[9]

Trotsky's personal authority was nevertheless still high enough for the Politburo to meet at his apartment, at Kamenev's suggestion and with Trotsky's agreement, if he were unable to attend the usual venue. These meetings were conducted with such heat and passion that, as Trotsky's wife recalled, he would run a high temperature after them: 'he came out of his study soaked through, and undressed and went to bed. His linen and clothes had to be dried as if he had been drenched in a rainstorm.'[10]

The chief cause of the heat generated at these meetings was Trotsky's letter to the Politburo of 8 October 1923. Addressed to all members of the Central Committee and Central Commission, the fifteen-page letter – it had taken a week for him to complete – contained eighteen theses on a wide range of topics. The 'ring' seized on it to show that Trotsky was engaging in factionalism and attacking the Party leadership. This letter, like a later one signed by forty-six of Trotsky's supporters, was in fact a response to the economic crisis of the summer and autumn of 1923, known as the 'scissors crisis'. In Trotsky's view the situation had been caused by serious errors of economic and political management on the part of the leadership and by the process of bureaucratization that had overwhelmed the Party. The 'extreme worsening of internal Party conditions' was due, he claimed, to the unhealthy internal Party system itself and also to the discontent of the workers and peasants caused by the harsh economic conditions imposed on them by the wrong policy.[11]

The letter, dictated while he was ill and in a state of nervous agitation, was not typical of Trotsky's usual style, but was awkwardly written and repetitious. It was nevertheless a prophetic warning about the future of a number of fundamental issues. He expressed concern about the work of the country's chief political organ: 'More than was the case before the Twelfth Congress, highly important economic issues are being settled by the Politburo in haste, without due consideration and outside their proper context.' The implication was that while Lenin was still on the job – even though he had been absent from the Twelfth Congress of April 1923 – the work had been done on a more solid basis and more democratically. He went on: 'The leaders of the country's economy describe Politburo policy as a policy of haphazard, unsystematic decisions ... There is no direction of the economy, the chaos comes from above.'[12]

The accusation of incompetence and lack of planning was justified, but he went further, accusing the Politburo of abuses in personnel policy:

> The appointment [instead of election] of provincial Party committee secretaries is now the rule. This means the secretary is virtually independent of the local organization ... The secretary in turn is the source of further appointments and replacements within the province. The secretarial organization created thus from above becomes more and more self-sufficient and draws all the threads to itself. Participation by the Party rank and file in the real formation of the Party organization is becoming more and more illusory.[13]

With uncanny perception, just as if he were able to see decades ahead, he went on:

In the last year and a half or so, a specific secretarial mentality has been created and its chief feature is that the secretary is capable of solving all and every question, without any knowledge of the essence of the issue at hand. All around us we see comrades, who showed no organizational, administrative or any other skills when they were running Soviet bodies, now imperiously settling economic, military and other issues as soon as they become secretaries. The practice is all the more dangerous because it dissipates and kills off any sense of responsibility.[14]

The system of selecting secretaries, Trotsky noted, and the 'secretarial hierarchy', made the frank exchange of opinion impossible, and a picture of 'automatic uniformity' in the organizations was the result.[15]

In his letter Trotsky also objected, albeit mutedly, to the pressure that was constantly being applied on him by the 'ring'. Once again he protested against the creation by a Party plenum in September 1923 of a new executive body alongside himself as Chairman of the Revolutionary Military Council, a measure he saw as another attempt to reduce his power. His suspicions had been further aroused when the plenum had proposed making Stalin and Voroshilov, and some others with whom Trotsky was not on good terms, members of the Revolutionary Military Council.[16] He had vehemently protested at the plenum, and when his words fell on deaf ears he had left the meeting, an act condemned as 'a challenge to the Party summit'. In his letter he described the decision of the plenum as the 'announcement of a new Revolutionary Military Council' and 'a shift to a new, i.e. aggressive, policy'.[17]

He ended his letter with the unequivocal conclusion that the internal Party 'regime cannot continue for long. It must be changed.' The Central Committee, he wrote, was pursuing a 'false policy'. The efforts he had been making 'for the last eighteen months' – i.e. since Stalin had been made General Secretary – had 'produced no result'.[18] Despite his complete isolation in the Politburo, Trotsky had had the courage to warn the Central Committee and the Politburo itself of the dangers of 'secretarial bureaucratism', but even though he had supporters in the Central Committee no one took serious notice of what he was saying.

While he was writing his letter Trotsky conferred with Ioffe, Sapronov, Muralov and other like-minded senior Bolsheviks, and having sent it he then composed a similar document to which he obtained the signatures of forty-six supporters. Dubbed by the Thirteenth Party Conference 'the Trotskyist Manifesto', the 'Statement of the 46' went further than Trotsky's letter. It stated categorically that 'the secretarial hierarchy, [i.e.] the Party hierarchy, increasingly selects the membership of conferences and congresses which in turn are more and more becoming executive meetings of this hierarchy ... The factional regime must be stopped and this must be done above all by those who installed it, it must be replaced by a regime of comradely unity and internal Party democracy.'[19]

This proved too much. On 16 October, when the letter was read at the Politburo, the triumvirate ordered an immediate emergency meeting of the Presidium of the Party Control Commission. This body found that 'the differences enumerated by Comrade Trotsky' were 'largely artificial and fabricated', and warned that such utterances could be fatal. The Control Commission effectively dismissed Trotsky's warnings and was only concerned that his letter not be circulated among the Party organizations.[20] For the triumvirate, however, this was not enough, and therefore, at Stalin's insistence, a joint plenary meeting of the Central Committee and Central Control Commission was held on 23–25 October 1923 to which were invited specially selected workers from ten of the biggest Party organizations.

A majority of this gathering condemned Trotsky's letter and the 'Statement of the 46' as a crude political mistake and as attacks on the Central Committee and Politburo. The Orgburo and Central Committee Secretariat – both of them in Stalin's pocket – proposed that the plenum condemn the declaration by Trotsky and his supporters as plainly 'factional'. It was then agreed that neither Trotsky's letter nor the 'Statement of the 46' be made known to the wider public. The Politburo did not want these documents to serve as the basis of the debate which it saw was inevitable, and it therefore authorized a critical article by Zinoviev to appear in *Pravda* as a signal for the debate to begin.

The barely perceptible split in the Politburo, which in early 1923 Lenin had so feared, was now obvious and out in the open. The old accusations of 'Menshevism' were again levelled at Trotsky. The Moscow Party bureau lamented that 'the disarray in the ranks of the Russian Communist Party will be the greatest possible blow to the German Communist Party and German proletariat that is preparing to seize power.'[21] The leadership did not want to hear sober voices urging caution. At the Thirteenth Party Conference held a few days before Lenin's death in mid-January 1924, using the resolution on Party unity passed by the Tenth Congress in 1921, the *de facto* leaders condemned Trotsky and his supporters' position as 'a Menshevik revision of Bolshevism'.

The issue flared up again at the combined plenum of the Central Committee and Central Control Commission, which took place two weeks after the Politburo had received Trotsky's letter. Trotsky wrote another long letter, defending the views he had expressed in early October[22] and adding that, in order to place him in opposition to Lenin, he was being accused of underestimating the peasantry, and noting in particular the personal attacks being made on him: 'The utterly incomprehensible accusation is being made that I have not paid enough attention to the army in recent years,' and hints were being made that he spent too much time on literary matters. Rejecting these charges, he reiterated the need 'to remove artificial walls within the Party'.[23]

On the last day of the plenum Stalin and Trotsky, for the first time in an open forum, exchanged mutual accusations, albeit in restrained form. Stalin was decidedly the more aggressive and demanded 'condemnation of Trotsky'. Regrettably, before Lenin's death, speeches at such meetings were not recorded verbatim and the hasty notes made by Stalin's assistant, B. Bazhanov, do not include all the arguments deployed by his rivals.[24] The plenum 'proposed to Comrade Trotsky that in future he participate more closely and directly in practical work'.[25] In other words, he was being told that if he had been doing his job, he would not have had time to engage in opposition.

The atmosphere at the plenum was extremely unpleasant for Trotsky, thanks to the campaign waged by the triumvirate. While we do not have a complete record of the speeches, there is a letter from Krupskaya to Zinoviev, which surfaced only recently, in which she objects to the attempts by the triumvirate to blame Trotsky for the split in the Party and to make him responsible for Lenin's illness. 'I ought to have shouted that this was a lie,' she wrote. 'It wasn't Trotsky who worried Vladimir Ilyich most, it was the national question and the morals that had taken over at the summit.' She expressed her

concern and indignation that in their campaign Stalin and his supporters had crudely trampled on the principles and norms of Party
life.[26]

Trotsky realized that his voice was going unheard. The 'ring' was
closing more tightly around him, and although after the Thirteenth
Conference he went for a rest to the Georgian Black Sea coast, the
grip of the apparatus was almost tangible. A creator of the Bolshevik
system himself, he did not understand that any attempt to improve it
would be fruitless, for the fundamental tenets of Leninism, based on
the monopoly of a single party, made reform impossible.

By the icy days of January, when Lenin was already dead, Trotsky
was profoundly isolated. Pacing alone along the shore of the Black
Sea, he agonized about what to do. The characteristic response of the
Russian intellectual when faced with such a challenge was to fight,
and Trotsky could not have acted otherwise.

'The New Course'

Reflecting on his life later in exile, Trotsky recognized that 1923–24
had been the turning point. Even while Lenin was still alive, he wrote,
the top echelon of the Party was developing the features of a caste,
with unwritten rules and regulations governing behaviour within
'one's own circle'. During the civil war, he mused, everyone had lived
according to the 'Party's tuning fork'. Once the tension of war had
subsided, 'and the nomads of the revolution went over to a settled
way of life, the philistine characteristics, sympathies and tastes of
self-satisfied functionaries were aroused, awakened and developed'. It
became the custom among the ruling élite, he recalled, to visit each
other's homes, to attend the ballet assiduously, to hold drinking parties
at which absentees would be pulled apart.[27] By remaining aloof from
this semi-bourgeois way of life, Trotsky only accelerated the already
rapid process of his exclusion from the caste of leaders.

The Bolshevik system itself was also at a turning point. The country
faced the need for major decisions. Besides a New Economic Policy,
a New Political Policy was also needed. Democracy in economic life
ought to have been accompanied by democracy in politics and a

change of course by the Party. But the single-party system already dictated its own laws on ideology, culture, the state and society as a whole. Despite recognizing the danger of bureaucratization, Trotsky did not link it with the one-party system. His, the subtlest of minds, was in the grip of the most erroneous Marxist dogmas about the defining role of the Party. In an article entitled 'Groupings and the Formation of Factions' he wrote: 'We are the only party in the country, and in the era of dictatorship there can be no other way.'[28] He believed, moreover, that the oppositionist views of various Communist groups were dangerous. He was in favour of like-mindedness, but it must be 'correct' like-mindedness, foreshadowing the way the regime would operate on this matter for the next seventy years. In his first letter to the Central Committee in early October 1923, he had gone further and asserted, while discussing informants, that 'informing on a Party organization that it is being used by elements that are hostile to the Party, is an elementary duty of every party member.'[29] He was somehow convinced that genuine people's power could develop within an environment where one party had a monopoly of power. The rest of the Party, and indeed most of the country for many long decades, felt much the same.

Even after having been publicly labelled a factionalist who wanted to revise Bolshevism in a Menshevik direction, Trotsky still wanted to change the 'distressing internal Party regime',[30] and plainly intended to do so by intellectual and political means. He believed that by his speeches at the Politburo and other Party bodies, and with the support of his relatively few followers, he could bring about a radical correction of the course, while the changes under NEP were still in train. His main forum, however, would be the press. On 11 December 1923 *Pravda* published his 'Letter to Party Meetings', which he entitled 'The New Course', at the end of the year he published 'Groupings and the Formation of Factions', 'The Question of Party Generations', 'The Social Composition of the Party' and 'Tradition and Revolutionary Politics', and on 29 December *Pravda* published two further pieces. All these articles came out as a collection, called 'The New Course',[31] during the Thirteenth Party Conference of 16–18 January 1924.

These publications did not represent a 'special' new course, distinct from that of Lenin's, as Soviet historiography always depicted them. The fact is, on 5 December 1923 the Politburo and the Party Control Commission jointly adopted a ruling on Party structure – which recognized the presence of bureaucratism – in which a number of measures were proposed to give the grassroots organizations greater democracy in internal Party life. Trotsky dared to hope that this might mean he had won the argument. Many Party members sincerely believed that a change towards democracy, freedom of opinion, openness on personnel matters, and an end to 'secretarial' bureaucratism were now all possible. Trotsky naturally did what he could through his writing to push the process forward. He would tell his assistant Sermuks that all was not lost, that the Party could be cured and that perhaps it was his medicine that would do the trick.

He was convinced that the resolution on 'the new course' would shift the centre of gravity towards 'a critically independent, self-governing Party, as the organized vanguard of the proletariat ... The Party must subordinate the organization to its authority, while remaining at all times a centralized body.'[32] None of this suggested that Trotsky was questioning the basic principle of the Party's governance by 'democratic centralism': the problem, as he saw it, was the excessive authority that had been invested in the *apparat*, or Party organization, especially since Stalin had taken over as its General Secretary. The omnipotence of the organization, he remarked, had induced a feeling of 'indisposition' in Party members. 'By killing independent initiative, bureaucratism inhibits a rise in the general level of the Party.'

By this time the Party was managed by orders and directives. Trotsky had himself been partly responsible for the formation of a strong and coherent organization, and now saw the importance of reversing the roles, so that it was the Party that controlled the organization, and not vice versa. At the same time, his articles create the impression that he did not know how to eliminate the problem. He saw Stalin and his group as the chief danger, but had no precise idea how to liberate the Party from the way secretaries were selected, especially the General Secretary.[33] He tried to address the entire Party, but he was neither heard nor understood. Most of the rank and file membership were of relatively low intellectual calibre, and in any case did not read his articles.

As a comrade-in-arms of Lenin, Trotsky could not openly come out against the ban on factions, adopted at the Tenth Congress, and indeed he frequently declared factions an evil to be avoided. Yet his arguments amounted to a disavowal of Lenin's resolution on Party unity. 'The ban,' he wrote, 'did not in itself represent an absolute or even partial guarantee of protecting the Party from new ideological and organizational groupings. The only guarantee is proper leadership, timely attention to all the needs of development ... flexibility in Party organization that did not paralyse but organized Party initiative, that was not afraid of critical voices and did not intimidate [members] with the charge of factionalism.' Cautiously approaching his main point, he concluded: 'The resolution of the Tenth Congress, banning factions, can only have an auxiliary character, and in itself it does not provide the key to all and every internal difficulty.'³⁴

In 'The New Course', Trotsky developed another idea which he hoped would not only breathe new life into the leadership, but also help him gain the new supporters he needed. He raised the question of generations in the Party. The underlying cause of present frictions, he wrote, 'is not that some secretaries have gone too far and must be slightly curbed, but that the Party itself is about to shift into a higher class'.³⁵ He related this shift to the active inclusion of the young – 'the surest Party barometer' that was also reacting sharply against bureaucratism – in the revolutionary process. 'Only the constant interaction of the older generation with the younger, within the framework of Party democracy, can preserve the old guard as a revolutionary factor.'³⁶ He hoped that by referring to the domination of the old generation, he would gain the sympathy of the young. It had got to the point, he wrote, 'that the Party inhabits two storeys, on the upper one they decide everything, and on the lower one they only hear about what has been decided'. The old guard must not decide everything for the whole Party without involving the young; the Party could not live only on the capital of the past. 'The old generation must not see the new course as a manoeuvre, a diplomatic ploy or temporary concession, but as a new stage in the Party's political development.' Trotsky's desperate plea fell, alas, on deaf ears.

Knowing how much depended on his efforts to find support, he wrote one more article, entitled 'Tradition and Revolutionary Politics', in which he urged the Party to base itself on Lenin, whom he called a genius. 'Leninism,' he wrote, 'means being free of the conservative glance backwards, free of precedents, formal references and quotations . . . Lenin should not be cut up by scissors into suitable quotations for every occasion, formula never took precedence over reality for him, but was always a means to master reality.' Having as it were thus recruited Lenin to his own side, he concluded with a remark that was an obvious challenge to Stalin: 'No one should identify bureaucratism with Bolshevism.'[37]

But in the struggle for a monopoly on Lenin, it was Stalin who in due course would win hands down. He would don his robe as the defender of Leninism and its chief interpreter. Trotsky was not able, or was too late, to adopt this device, which made Stalin invulnerable. Trotsky's attempt to recruit Lenin failed. Everyone who zealously attacked Trotsky made sure to refer to Lenin's resolution on unity, and this spelled Trotsky's defeat.

When the Thirteenth Party Conference was being prepared, Trotsky still thought there was a chance that his line on realizing the Politburo's resolution on a democratic renewal might succeed. He drafted a resolution and expounded a number of striking ideas. The text, written on 14 January 1924, contained the following:

> [It] would be dangerous in the highest degree to underestimate the conservative resistance of the bureaucratic elements who originated the Politburo's resolution on the need for a new course . . . Our Party's entire past shows that internal Party intrigue, including criticism of Central Committee policy, is entirely compatible with real unanimity and firm discipline . . . The Party must give warning of the danger of bureaucratism and it must guarantee a regime of independence for the Party rank and file.[38]

Following Stalin's speech, however, the conference passed a resolution branding the position taken by Trotsky and his supporters as 'a blatantly expressed petty bourgeois deviation' and a 'clear departure from Bolshevism'. It should be noted, however, that there was no 'new course' on internal Party democracy, and the struggle against bureaucratism was not implemented, despite there being a strong desire for it among the people. Trotsky had taken the Politburo resolution of 5 December 1923 as the signal for a new course, whereas the leadership had no such intention. The Party had been created by Lenin as enclosed, hierarchical, harsh and bureaucratic. Talk of 'democratization' was no more than a ploy to defeat Trotsky.

For a while, Trotsky sagged. He stayed indoors for days on end, saying he was ill. He took a trip for a cure, and went on several hunting expeditions with his friend N. Muralov, the head of the Moscow Military District. He wrote letters, put his huge archives in order and sorted his abundant correspondence. With the help of Sermuks and Poznansky, he collected his speeches, articles and notes for the next volume of his collected works. Among his papers were materials he had intended using in his campaign to aid invalids and civil war veterans. His wife had assisted in the attempt to set up an organization, called *Sobes*, or Social Security, to care for maimed soldiers, but the country's poverty and the rapidly burgeoning bureaucracy soon stifled that endeavour. At the end of 1922 he had drafted a memorandum to the Orgburo, saying that 'with the break-up of Sobes, the question of . . . civil war invalids has decidedly been left up in the air . . . There is no one who will concentrate all the responsible work in his own hands. As a result of Comrade Burdukov's transfer to Ukraine, and with the President of the All-Russian Aid Committee, N.I. Trotskaya, being on sick leave, Sobes has broken up. This threatens to paralyse the whole affair.'[39]

The leadership had first become aware of the problem of civil war invalids during a parade in honour of the Red Army, when a group of war wounded established themselves near the parade stands and began extorting money from the public. Trotsky was dismayed and angered by what he saw as a slur on his achievement as army chief, and wrote to Muralov: 'All invalids should be told personally that if they don't make their applications in the proper way, and choose instead to do so by disrupting parades, popular assemblies and so on, then the guilty will be deported from Moscow to a town in the provinces.'[40] He later involved the All-Russian Aid Committee, the Red Army Political Section and other bodies in organizing care for invalids, suggesting that the issue be dealt with on the level 'of material help and social education', in other words, to give work to war wounded within their capabilities.[41]

It seemed as if Trotsky had accepted his loss of influence and was not seeking to worsen his relations with the rest of the leadership. He carried out his duties as a member of the Politburo and Commissar for Military and Naval Affairs rather passively, using his main energies to prepare his collected works for publication. This project had been approved by Lenin and the Central Committee during the civil war, and much of what emerged is of great interest to the historian. While taking the waters at Kislovodsk in 1924, Trotsky wrote a great deal. He noted with irritation that the Party newspapers had taken to referring to his Menshevik past with growing frequency, and he was prompted to write the preface of his volume on the October revolution as a separate article, in a way that would both reply to his numerous critics and explain things as they had been. He wrote very fast and within three days the piece, nearly sixty pages long, was finished. Its main message was to inform the Party's mostly new and inflated membership of his achievements during the October revolution.

The article, entitled 'The Lessons of October', attracted the attention of the entire Party. In it, Trotsky gave high praise to Lenin, dismissed Zinoviev and Kamenev and referred directly to Stalin's insignificance. He quoted from Kamenev's letter to the press on the eve of the coup, which had declared: 'Not only I and Comrade Zinoviev, but also several organizer-comrades, feel that to take upon ourselves the initiative of an armed uprising at the moment, given the present relationship of forces, independently and only a few days before the Congress of Soviets, would be an impermissible, disastrous step for the proletariat and the revolution.' Trotsky asserted that people should learn what had happened in October. 'It would be wrong,' he wrote, 'to expunge a chapter of the Party's history, just because not all members had been in step with the proletariat. The Party can and should know everything about its past in order to have a proper evaluation and put everything in its rightful place.'[42]

But he, too, omitted to point out the significant fact that it had been easy to seize power because no one was prepared to defend it. The picture he painted, of wise leaders, perspicacious plans and a revolutionary population, was more romantic than the reality. The day after the uprising most of the inhabitants of Petrograd had no idea that the government had fallen and that the Bolsheviks had taken power. Trotsky's article was nevertheless illuminating for many people, but one of his chief purposes was to protect his own name.

The counter-attack came immediately, with all the 'heavy guns' being deployed. Kamenev published a long and dismissive article called 'Leninism or Trotskyism?', to which Stalin appended 'the facts about the October uprising'. An editorial in the journal *Bolshevik* described Trotsky as 'skimming over the surface, albeit like a maestro, beautifully, even brilliantly, like an ice-skating champion. The trouble is it is all nothing but patterns, remote from practical existence.'[43]

While Trotsky was awaiting a reply, the Politburo was devising a comprehensive programme to discredit him. The Central Committee Secretariat ordered all Party organizations to go over 'The Lessons of October' with a critical eye. Almost every member of the top echelon was expected to condemn Trotsky publicly. Dozens of articles appeared in the press within a short space of time. The criticism escalated from cool analysis to insinuation and outright abuse. Public speeches made by all the leaders – Stalin, Zinoviev, Kamenev, Bukharin, Rykov, Sokolnikov, Krupskaya, Molotov, Bubnov and others – were collected in a large anthology, called *For Leninism*. Many of the authors wrote diametrically opposite to what they had been saying before 1924.

At first, Trotsky read the daily dose of attacks, but when he started having chest pains and bad headaches and felt generally miserable, he stopped this form of self-punishment. He had not expected such a fierce offensive. His wife tried to reassure and distract him, making him go for walks and reading him letters from their sons. She later recalled that this attack of illness 'coincided with a monstrous campaign of persecution against him, which we felt as keenly as if we had been suffering from the most malignant disease. The pages of *Pravda* seemed endless, and every line of the paper, even every word, a lie. L.D. kept silent. Friends called to see him during the day and often at night . . . He looked pale and thin. In the family we avoided talking about the persecution, and yet we could talk of nothing else.'[44]

The press campaign hammered home the message that once a politician had been stained by Menshevism, the mark could never be washed away. Sermuks started selecting what to show Trotsky and which 'retorts to the renegade' should be filed in Trotsky's voluminous archives. Factory, regional and university cells throughout the country were unanimously passing resolutions condemning 'Trotsky's anti-Bolshevik assault on the foundations of Leninism', and calling on him to resign from the Party if he was not willing to carry out the policy laid down by the Thirteenth Party Conference.[45] The ripples of criticism widened steadily and the image of Trotsky created in revolution and civil war was gradually eroded.

Letters and telegrams of a different character were reaching Trotsky in Kislovodsk, however. Ioffe, Muralov and Rakovsky urged him not to remain silent, but to appeal to the Central Committee to put a stop to the scandalous clamour. Trotsky remained silent. Stalin's aim had been accurate. Trotsky's reputation had been based on the October revolution and the civil war, and Stalin succeeded in persuading the Party that it had been grossly inflated. All of Lenin's pre-revolutionary attacks on Trotsky were now published or republished and the hero quickly became a pariah. 1923 and 1924 were a unique watershed in Trotsky's life. He was still in the top echelon of the regime and his portrait still hung alongside that of Lenin. Quite a few towns and villages, streets, clubs and factories bore his name, yet his image as a revolutionary was growing dim and the aura had gone. His hopes for a 'new course' were unrealized. His attempts to retrieve his reputation were met either by indifference or outright hostility. And it was during this time that Stalin advanced his own 'theory' of 'socialism in one country'.

Many people who, as members of earlier oppositions, groupings and factions, had suffered defeat on other issues, were drawn to Trotsky and were expressing sympathy, since he was openly identified as an enemy of the present leadership. The Stalinist triumvirate of course seized on this and accused Trotsky of supporting anti-Party forces. For his part, Trotsky made little effort to draw on the help of his own supporters, and when he eventually came round to doing so, it would be too late. Meanwhile, expressions of support for Trotsky, though few, continued to arrive at the Central Committee. In one case, the railway-wagon workshop in Moscow voted by a small majority against the anti-Trotsky campaign as 'harmful and unworthy of the [Party] and damaging to the prestige of Comintern', and this despite a personal appearance by Molotov.[46]

Stalin, meanwhile, was also working behind the scenes to remove Trotsky's supporters from important posts in the Commissariat for Military and Naval Affairs. Within an eighteen-month period many district, army and section commanders lost their jobs. The appointments machine, which was in the hands of the Secretariat and Orgburo, i.e. Stalin's, advanced new men whose allegiance was simply to the triumvirate. Once, while he was taking the cure at Sukhumi after Lenin's death, Trotsky was visited by a number of members of the Central Committee – Tomsky, Pyatakov, Frunze and Gusev – who came to bring him up to date on the important changes of personnel taking place in the military administration. He was warned of the arrival of I.S. Unshlikht, whom he had never liked. The transfer of the Deputy Chairman of the GPU was a bad sign, but Trotsky was sick and unable to put up strong resistance. He particularly lamented the removal of Sklyansky, who had proved himself to be an excellent organizer and effective link between the War Commissariat and supply organizations during the civil war. A vacuum was being formed around Trotsky.

Stalin's campaign was greatly assisted by Trotsky himself. By virtually retiring from everyday life and the tasks facing the country and the Party in order to concentrate on his writing, by taking frequent sick leaves and by remaining silent during debates on important questions of current policy, he played into his enemies' hands. Also, by repeatedly affirming the correctness of Central Committee decisions, upholding the ban on factions and agreeing with the leadership's line, he created an inescapable impression of weakness, guilt and loss of self-assurance. In those two decisive years, he plainly overrated his power over people's minds, as well as his popularity. He had still believed he would ultimately triumph even after Lenin's death, and he was not prepared for the personal defeat that was moving inexorably upon him.

Against the powerful intellect and brilliant personal characteristics of this creative individual, stood the dull but mighty machine of the Party organization. The bureaucratic monster had come into being with amazing rapidity and was now capable of carrying out, unquestioningly and efficiently, orders issued by the centre, where Stalin was steadily strengthening his own position. The coming decisive battle would be an unequal one. Trotsky's defeat was certain.

The Duel of 'Outstanding Leaders'

From 1917 until the end of Trotsky's life, a thread of fierce rivalry and irreconcilable struggle connected the two revolutionaries whom Lenin in December 1922 called two 'outstanding leaders'. The thread was not severed until August 1940, when Trotsky was assassinated on Stalin's personal order. As we have seen, before 1917 the two barely knew each other, despite coming face to face several times. In 1905, at the Fifth Party Congress in London, Trotsky simply did not notice Stalin, who gazed at the motley crowd of revolutionaries with mixed feelings of curiosity and surprise. In the winter of 1913 another meeting took place, this time in Vienna, which Trotsky described in a note intended for his unfinished book on Stalin. He recalled sitting at the samovar in a cheap Viennese hotel with the Menshevik Skobelev:

> The son of a rich Baku miller, Skobelev was at the time a student and my political pupil; a few years later he would be my political opponent and a minister in the Provisional Government. We drank fragrant Russian tea and of course discussed the overthrow of tsarism. Suddenly, the door was opened without a prior knock and there stood a man I had not seen before. He was short of stature, thin, his face a swarthy-greyish hue and bearing the marks of smallpox. He was holding an empty glass in his hand. He was evidently not expecting to see me and there was no sign of friendship in his eyes. Muttering a guttural sound, which could be taken as a greeting, he approached the samovar, silently filled his glass and just as silently left the room. I glanced at Skobelev enquiringly. 'He's the Caucasian, Dzhugashvili, a fellow-countryman. The Bolsheviks have just made him a member of their Central Committee and he's already beginning to play a part, it seems.'[47]

No doubt, his later experience did much to colour Trotsky's recollection of that encounter.

During the summer of 1917, after his return to Russia in May, Trotsky, seeing Stalin at numerous meetings and conferences, committees and editorial boards, and also in Lenin's company, realized that the silent Georgian had become an integral part of the Bolshevik establishment, yet he did not arouse Trotsky's interest as a personality. Listening in silence to speakers as he smoked his pipe, Stalin would watch as people entered and left the room. Trotsky tried to recall if he had ever heard Stalin speak at one of these meetings, but could remember nothing. When they had met face to face or when he had felt those cold eyes on him, Trotsky would nod a cursory greeting and pass by. He saw Stalin less as a personality than a supernumerary, a member of the Party *corps de ballet*, such as will always be found in large numbers at all major historical events, and who will later embellish their reminiscences to enhance their true role.

Stalin was in fact not such a person. Almost imperceptibly, he was steadily and surely making his way up into the ranks of the leadership. Oddly, it was when they were not seeing each other that Trotsky got to know Stalin better, during the civil war when Trotsky was the dominant figure and Stalin was in charge of food supply and later a member of the Revolutionary Military Council on various fronts. There would even be occasions when Trotsky would give Stalin credit, as in May 1920 when he sent a telegram from his train to the Sovnarkom: 'As Comrade Stalin has devoted his main attention over the last year to military affairs, and as he is well acquainted with the South-western front, where the work is of the utmost importance, it would be highly desirable to make him a member of the Revolutionary Military Council of the Republic and thus use his abilities for central military work better than hitherto, in particular and especially for servicing the centre of the South-western front.'[48] Stalin had been a member of the Revolutionary Military Council of the Republic from 8 October 1918 to 8 July 1919 when it was reduced to a membership of six; he became a member again on 8 May 1920 until 1 April 1922.

Trotsky was right to point out that Stalin could be put to better use. In 1918, when Stalin was 'entrenched' at Tsaritsyn, a number of sharply worded cables had flown between him and the People's Commissar. They had both appealed to Lenin for support, and Lenin had tried to reconcile them, but their differences had proved too deep. For instance, Trotsky believed that former tsarist officers would help make a regular and battle-ready army, while Stalin supported commanders like Voroshilov, who put Party membership above military training and experience. In a telegram from Tsaritsyn to Trotsky, with a copy to Lenin, Stalin had reported that the headquarters staff of the Northern Caucasus front was 'totally unfit for the conditions of struggle against counter-revolution. It is not only that our "specialists" are psychologically incapable of decisive warfare against counter-revolution, but also that, as "headquarters" personnel who are only capable of "drawing charts" and producing redeployment plans, they are utterly indifferent to operational actions, questions of supply, the monitoring of different commanders, and in general they feel like outsiders or guests.'[49] Stalin had interfered in the work of head-quarters, removing staff who did not meet with his approval and applying repressive measures. He often used his staff of food-supply organizers, as well as staff from the Nationalities Commissariat, to carry out supervisory and inspection jobs that were outside their remit. The Centre and Trotsky started receiving complaints, to which at first he responded calmly. On one occasion he cabled the Balashov Revolutionary Military Committee that he was 'in complete agreement with Comrade Raskolnikov's protest against the interference of some comrades from the Nationalities Commissariat in arrangements at the front. I have made an appropriate statement to the Commissar for Nationalities. Comrade Bobinsky is leaving for the front today with full authority from me to act exclusively under the direction of the Revolutionary Military Committee.'[50]

Stalin and his people seemed to take no notice. He continued to issue orders and send demanding messages to Trotsky. On 27 September 1918 he requested an enormous quantity of all kinds of weapons, plus no less than 100,000 full sets of uniform, even though at that moment there were less than that number of troops on the southern front. He had personally penned the ending of his message in purple ink: 'We declare that if these demands (which are the minimum considering the number of troops on the Southern front) are not met with the utmost urgency, we shall be forced to cease military action and withdraw to the left bank of the Volga.'[51] Such ultimatums drove Trotsky to exasperation. The warehouses were empty and it was only with the greatest difficulty that a few munitions factories were able to function. Trotsky had cause to complain to Lenin that 'Stalin's actions are disrupting all my plans.'[52] His orders were being systematically ignored by Stalin, but it seems that it was not until the summer of 1918 that he sensed that the 'unremarkable Caucasian' was a man with a mind and a will of his own. After a number of such clashes, Trotsky tried to persuade Moscow to withdraw Stalin from the front, but Lenin and Sverdlov, who supported Trotsky in everything concerning the purely military aspects of his work, were in no hurry to take sides. Despite summoning Stalin to Moscow from time to time at moments convenient to Trotsky, and transferring Voroshilov and some other unsympathetic commanders to other sectors, Lenin declined to define such moves as the victory of one People's Commissar over the other. Hoping to effect a compromise, he urged them to sort out their differences themselves by making mutual concessions.

There were some short-lived moments of comparative improvement in relations between Trotsky and Stalin, and these were due to the latter's efforts. In his memoirs Trotsky remarked on these episodes:

> Because of his enormous envy and ambition, Stalin could not help feeling at every step his intellectual and moral inferiority. It seems that he tried to get closer to me. Not until much later did I realize the meaning of attempts to establish something approaching familiarity between us. But I was repelled by those very qualities that were his strength on the wave of decline – the narrowness of his interests, his empiricism, the coarseness of his psychological make-up, his peculiar cynicism of a provincial whom Marxism has freed from many prejudices without, however, replacing them with a philosophical outlook thoroughly thought out and mentally assimilated.[53]

Stalin took a number of small steps towards reconciliation. On the eve of the first anniversary of the October revolution, he published an article in which he effectively placed Trotsky side by side with Lenin by calling him the second chief organizer of the uprising – an original way of congratulating Trotsky on the occasion of his birthday, which also fell on 7 November (25 October Old Style). Later versions of this article omitted any celebratory remarks in this vein.[54]

Stalin's early telegrams to Trotsky, in 1918, were distinctly respectful in tone and signed 'Yours, Stalin'[55] – unimaginable a year hence. In fact, this phase lasted only while Stalin was preparing for the next stage of his military activities. By July, he was demanding that Moscow endow him with military authority and threatening that if he did not receive it he would without ceremony 'get rid of the officials and commanders who are destroying the cause' and that 'the absence of a bit of paper from Trotsky will not stop me.'[56] He was duly granted military authority and henceforth ignored orders whether issued by Trotsky or the Centre. The conflict was, as we have seen, momentarily resolved, on the one hand, by Lenin's softening Trotsky's blows against Stalin, and by Stalin's tactical decision not to contradict Trotsky.

Trotsky made no attempt to reciprocate Stalin's minimal efforts at reconciliation. He underestimated his rival as a politician and on the purely personal level found him uninteresting and unpleasant. It was therefore a surprise to him when suddenly, and with the onset of Lenin's illness, Stalin emerged among the top-ranking leaders, and this despite Trotsky's having recognized Stalin's tenacity and his ability to act decisively in a crisis. Indeed, he had even acknowledged this in a request for tough measures by Stalin and the Orgburo in 1919, when the Party's rules on mobilization were being regularly flouted: 'It would be helpful if Comrade Stalin would write an article in *Pravda* in this vein.'[57]

Until Lenin's death, Trotsky was convinced in his heart that the Politburo would call on him to replace the leader, and it was precisely in this sense that he later interpreted Lenin's 'Letter to the Congress': 'Unquestionably, his object in making the will was to facilitate the work of direction for me. He naturally wanted to do it with the least possible amount of friction. He talks about everyone most guardedly, softening the most devastating judgments. At the same time he qualifies with reservations the too definite indication of the one whom he thinks entitled to first place.'[58] He was convinced that Lenin intended him as his successor, and that the references to his character were a smokescreen to moderate the decisiveness of his choice.

The ongoing struggle between Stalin and Trotsky was greatly exacerbated by this ambiguity, which only provoked their mutual rivalry and made cooperation impossible. Trotsky, however, lost the fight from the outset. The fight itself was of course about something more than a matter of ambition, personal incompatibility or the clash of character. It was a contest between centrist and leftist tendencies in the Party. Stalin always embodied the centre, while Trotsky personified the leftists. In all times, whenever the centre collapses and either the left or right wing triumphs, society and the state will suffer. Here, however, something unexpected happened: having defeated the 'left' opposition, Stalin in effect armed himself with its programme and embarked on 'revolutions from above'. Hence, willingly or unwillingly, much of Trotsky's own methodology was appropriated by Stalin and put into practice.

An important distinction is called for here. It has often been said that Stalin carried out Trotsky's programme, and that if there were serious theoretical differences between them, they were about the future of socialism in the USSR. In fact, Stalin and Trotsky – and their respective supporters – represented two different social types. One, the pragmatists, were those who, in Trotsky's phrase, 'went over to a settled way of life' and wanted to build socialism in one country. The others, 'the nomads of the revolution', were romantics, full of faith in the triumph of their ideals. Both types were advocates of War Communism. If Trotsky and his supporters wanted to return to 'Lenin's' War Communism, with its Bolshevik zeal, revolutionary heroics, internal Party democracy (as they understood it) and working-class activity, then Stalin and his supporters wanted a bureaucratic society in which millions of functionaries and Party organizers would secure their own well-being by means of a dictatorship that would leave no room for democracy and in which the masses would be reduced to 'cogs'. Trotsky hoped to combine the revolutionary changes that were taking place in the cities and villages with the affirmation of a democratic regime in both the Party and the country – an impossible aim, given the one-party dictatorship.

An almost unending conflict began between the two rivals. While Lenin was alive it bore a more personal character and was less connected with 'platforms' and positions, apart from Trotsky's 'revolt' of October 1923. Mutual recrimination and argument went on at meetings of the Politburo and Central Committee, with minor injuries. For instance, a decision of the VTsIK in 1921 called for a review of the staff of People's Commissariats, and People's Commissars were asked for their views. Trotsky's office reported that in recent months Stalin had taken virtually no part in their work.[59] Trotsky plainly did not want inactive members on his team, but the bare statement of the facts suggested more significantly that he did not accept Stalin as a leader of the top rank.

Both rivals learnt of Lenin's 'Letter to the Congress' before Lenin died, and it did nothing to reconcile them, rather the opposite. In it, Lenin described Trotsky as 'probably the most capable man in the current Central Committee', while of Stalin he had written that he doubted if he would use the immense power he had in his hands with sufficient caution. The famous postscript of 4 January 1923, in which

Lenin suggested the Congress consider ways of removing Stalin as General Secretary, would appear to have settled the struggle in Trotsky's favour. In practice, however, things turned out very differently. Trotsky, who had already shown himself to be accident-prone politically, lost his bearings completely and dropped his guard, while Stalin carried on strengthening his position behind the scenes. It was probably Stalin who initiated the notion that Lenin had become incapable of further work.

As Trotsky later admitted, it was a big mistake on his part not to have attended Lenin's funeral. He claimed he had been misled by the telegram Stalin sent to the local Cheka in Tiflis (Tbilisi) on 22 January: 'Convey this at once and report when it was handed over. Mogilevsky or Pankratov to decode personally. Tell Comrade Trotsky. On 21 January at 6.50 p.m. Comrade Lenin died suddenly. Death followed the failure of the respiratory centre. Burial on Saturday 26 January.'[60]

Characteristically, Stalin did not send the telegram to the local Soviet authorities or even the Party committee, but to the Caucasian Cheka. It was also a Chekist, one Gerson, who had encrypted the telegram. Trotsky wanted to attend the funeral and cabled Moscow to this effect. Stalin replied with another telegram: 'The funeral is on Saturday, you won't be in time. The Politburo thinks that in your state of health you should go to Sukhumi.' The funeral, in fact, took place on the Sunday, 27 January, and Trotsky had thus been purposely prevented from taking part in an event of enormous political importance. At the All-Union Congress of Soviets on 26 January, Stalin stated his claim as a true Leninist to be the defender of Lenin's heritage. Cut off in Tiflis, Trotsky could do little more than cable a brief article, that was none the less full of feeling and that included the following words: 'How will we go forward, will we find the way, will we not go astray? Our hearts are now stricken with boundless grief, all of us who by the great grace of history were born contemporaries of Lenin, who worked alongside him, who learnt from him . . . How shall we go ahead? With the lantern of Leninism in our hands . . .'[61]

Trotsky's absence during the time of the funeral created a very unfavourable impression among the population, especially Party members, many of whom took it as a sign of disrespect for Lenin's memory. This was perhaps the decisive event leading to Trotsky's defeat. Trotsky was deeply moved by a letter he received from

Krupskaya in Sukhumi a few days after the funeral, and possibly it gave him some relief from the guilt and frustration he felt at having been absent. Krupskaya wrote that 'about a month before his death, as he was looking through your book, Vladimir Ilyich stopped at the place where you sum up Marx and Lenin, and asked me to read it over again to him: he listened very attentively, and then looked it over again himself. And here is another thing I want to tell you: the attitude of V.I. towards you at the time when you came to us in London from Siberia has not changed until his death. I wish you, Lev Davydovich, strength and health, and I embrace you warmly.'[62]

After the revolution, Lenin had indeed shown not only great confidence in Trotsky, but also concern for his well-being. On 20 March 1921 he had hand-written a draft order for the Politburo which stated that: '. . . on the basis of the physician Professor Rakhman's opinion that improper nutrition is one of the causes of Comrade Trotsky's illness and of the difficulty in curing it, the Orgburo is to organize adequate nutrition for Comrade Trotsky according to the doctor's orders, acting on the direct instruction of the Central Committee and via the Soviet agencies (VTsIK and the People's Commissariat for Food).'[63]

Trotsky often returned in his memories to the days of Lenin's funeral; they were not only a time of grief, but were the time when he lost hope of playing what he called 'the leading role' in the Party and the country. In Coyoacan, during the last year of his life, he wrote to his supporter Malamut on 17 November 1939:

On the way back to Moscow from Sukhumi with a few close comrades, when the conversation turned to the funeral – it was only touched upon, as three months had already passed – they told me that he (Stalin) or they (the triumvirate) had had no intention whatever of holding it on the Saturday, and were only concerned to ensure my absence. Who told me this? Perhaps V. Smirnov or N. Muralov, it was hardly E. Sklyansky, who was so reserved and cautious . . . I see now that the plot was more complex.

Trotsky then asserted that Stalin had regarded the Saturday as a fictitious date from the start. In a special personal coded telegram, he had summoned major Party leaders to Moscow from all over the country, men who were loyal to him: 'In view of the critical importance of the moment, Stalin mobilized his functionaries throughout the country. In the end, everyone turned up, except me, as I had been purposely misinformed by Stalin himself.'

Not long before his own death, on more than one occasion, Trotsky suggested and eventually came to believe – and tried to convince others – that Stalin had poisoned Lenin. In his article 'The Super-Borgia in the Kremlin' he described how G. Yagoda, a close confidant of Stalin's, 'had a special cupboard full of poisons from which he would take a flask when it was needed and give it to his agents with appropriate instructions. Stalin could not wait passively for Lenin to get better, for the fate of this Borgia depended on it. He knew that whether he was to become the boss of the organization and thus also of the country depended on it.' This was one occasion when Trotsky was wrong, or perhaps deliberately misleading, about Stalin's motives and behaviour. It is now possible to assert on the basis of documentary evidence that in fact Lenin himself, through Krupskaya, asked Stalin to obtain potassium cyanide for him to use when his suffering became unbearable. Stalin reported to his colleagues that Krupskaya told him she had even tried to poison Lenin herself, but her nerve had failed her. (A detailed account of this episode is to be found in my study of Lenin.[64])

After Lenin's death, the conflict between Stalin and Trotsky took on a more one-sided character: the former attacked, the latter defended. To be sure, Trotsky could still stir the public with his speeches and articles, but perceptive observers could see that he had lost the fight, and lost it badly. In January 1925 he was relieved of the posts of People's Commissar for Military Affairs and Chairman of the Revolutionary Military Council of the Republic. At the January 1925 Central Committee plenum where Trotsky's position was discussed in his absence, as he was ill at the time, Zinoviev and Kamenev unexpectedly proposed that his place as Military Commissar be taken by Stalin. The General Secretary at once objected, gazing askance at the other members. The proposal collapsed and Stalin remained at the helm of the fast-growing bureaucracy.

As long as Trotsky had been in charge of the armed forces, Stalin had feared him. He could not have forgotten that V.A. Antonov-Ovseenko had written to the Politburo in defence of Trotsky: 'Communists in the military are already saying that we must all as one support Comrade Trotsky.'[65] After consultation, the triumvirate found Trotsky three jobs that would shift him to the political sidelines and load him down with bureaucratic affairs. He was made head of the Chief Concessions Committee, the Electro-technical Board and chairman of the Scientific and Technical Industrial Board. He was no longer dangerous.

For a while Trotsky threw himself into his new work, grappling with technical problems and absorbed by the possibility of putting science to work for the new society. He toured laboratories, meeting scientists and holding conferences with engineering workers. He attended the Politburo rarely, citing his new work as an excuse. It seemed he was satisfied with his modest role as a 'technocrat' and the extra time it gave him for his literary work. Meanwhile, the anti-Trotsky campaign continued in the press, dragging up his old sins, and before long he felt constrained to drop his new jobs, retaining only the chairmanship of the Concessions Committee, in order to return to full-time politics.

By now, a split had developed within the triumvirate. Zinoviev and Kamenev eventually realized that by supporting Stalin they had reinforced the bureaucratic regime and prepared the ground for a dictator. The 'Bolshevik twins' turned to Trotsky. 'At our very first meeting,' Trotsky recalled, 'Kamenev declared: "It is enough for you and Zinoviev to appear on the same platform, and the Party will find its true Central Committee."'[66] But they had failed to take account of the work Stalin had been doing to surround himself with a loyal following by appointing dedicated functionaries to various key posts in the organization.

For his part, Trotsky was not particularly sanguine about his new allies. He simply did not trust them. In notes he entitled 'The Bloc with Zinoviev (for the diary)', made in December 1925, he remarked perceptively that the Leningrad (i.e. Zinoviev) opposition was a 'bureaucratic-demagogic adaptation by the organizational leadership to the alarm being expressed by leading elements of the working class about the general progress of our development'.[67] The alarm was being expressed in debates about the methods and pace of constructing socialism. Linking the progress of revolution in Russia to that of the world revolution, as was his wont, Trotsky still maintained radical, leftist views. In a 1926 draft he underlined several typical phrases:

'Why in fact rob the peasantry if socialism is impossible?'; '... we are regarded as "pessimists" and "faint-hearted" because we think the snail's pace is inadequate.'[68] He seemed to be contradicting himself, declaring on the one hand that without a world revolutionary conflagration it would be impossible to build socialism in the Soviet Union, while on the other hand calling for a decisive transformation of the country, and at a fast pace. Stalin was aware of this apparent weakness in Trotsky's thinking and waited for the chance to pounce.

At the Fourteenth Party Congress of December 1925, Zinoviev, as joint spokesman for the opposition, warned the Party of the danger of bureaucratic degeneration, but his arguments were weak. Kamenev gave a much tougher speech, declaring: '... we are against creating a "leader's" theory, we are against making a "leader" ... I personally do not think our General Secretary is the person who can unite the old Bolshevik headquarters around himself...'[69] But he only succeeded in arousing the delegates' indignation, and the ground under the 'left' opposition dwindled. Stalin tightened his grip. In June 1926 he wrote to Molotov that it was time 'to smash the mugs of Trotsky and Grisha [Zinoviev] and Kamenev' and turn them into renegades. By September he was more precise: 'It is quite possible that he'll fly out of the [Politburo] right now.'[70] In October 1926, Trotsky and Zinoviev were removed from the Politburo and a year later from the Central Committee. In November 1927 Trotsky was expelled from the Party.

The oppositionists issued a statement which declared: 'It is untrue that the opposition path would lead to an uprising against the Party and the Soviet regime. But it is indisputably true that the Stalinist faction coldly intends to unleash physical destruction on the way to achieving its goals. The opposition has given not the slightest hint of a threat of insurrection. But the Stalinist faction represents a real threat of further usurpation of the Party's supreme rights ... The opposition cannot be crushed by repression; what we think right we will defend to the last.'[71]

Having lost practically everything, Trotsky belatedly hastened to rally an anti-Stalinist organization within the Party. Illegal meetings were held, political struggle groups formed, attempts made to publish oppositional material, clandestine channels were opened. Throughout, however, Trotsky stressed that the opposition must limit itself to strictly ideological and political methods. He issued memoranda and instructions to his followers, defining their tasks. These appear in the reminiscences of one of his rank and file supporters, N.N. Gavrilov, who recalled some of the tasks he was called upon to perform: '1) to come out actively in support of my own views at Party meetings; 2) to spread the word of the opposition among the masses; 3) to collect money for paper and to help comrades who were being persecuted; 4) to make contact with other supporters; 5) to maintain contact with the leadership of the Leningrad opposition group.'[72]

Trotsky's position was further weakened when Zinoviev decided to repent before Stalin, hoping in this way to return to his former favour. Trotsky was not especially surprised by this turn of events, and recalled his son Seryozha's gloomy prediction that Stalin would deceive, and Zinoviev would run away.[73] The press campaign meanwhile did not slacken. Trotsky's efforts to justify himself were blocked by Stalin's orders to editors not to print his replies, but he would not surrender. The archives contain much material plainly intended for distribution in unofficial organs. For example, the following extract was printed on cigarette-paper:

Dear Comrades,
    After a long interval, Comrade Zinoviev and his close friends have resurrected the legend against Trotskyism ... in order to cover their own retreat. The legend of Trotskyism is a conspiracy by the [Party] organization against Trotsky. Bukharin has distinguished himself as the most productive practitioner of this underhand work. It would be a mortal punishment for this man if his collected works were published ... One should not trifle with ideas. They have a way of becoming attached to class realities and continuing to live their own lives independently.[74]

The duel of 'outstanding leaders' was only one of appearances. The face-to-face confrontation did not happen. Personally unattractive and uninteresting, but empowered by his command of the Party organization, Stalin was able to carry the majority of the Party with him. Sparkling and talented (even if somewhat faded after the civil war), Trotsky was virtually alone. What exiguous groups of support he managed to assemble entered the fray far too late, and their calls for a struggle against bureaucracy, Communist arrogance and organizational heavy-handedness were barely comprehensible to rank and file Party members, for most of whom Trotsky now appeared as nothing more than an oppositionist, a factionalist and a man who was at last revealing his former Menshevik leanings. The duel was indeed only one of appearances. In political contest, Stalin preferred murder to duelling.

The Thinning Ranks of Supporters

We have already seen that Trotsky was a man of paradoxes. While a convinced advocate of radical methods for solving social, economic and spiritual problems, he also simultaneously fought for the democratization of the regime in the Party. Perhaps his most puzzling feature was his vain attempt to combine the uncombinable: totalitarianism and democratism, militarism and culture. The hero of the revolution was a graphic expression of the contradictions of the Russian revolution itself. The revolution lit the torch of liberty, yet in carrying it forward, it also spread coercion. Proclaiming people's power, a handful of individuals decided the fate of millions; while trying to create the new, the revolution mercilessly destroyed the historically valuable, as well as that which had permanent importance for the future. Trotsky's paradoxical character was that of any revolution, especially the Russian revolution.

One such paradox was the disproportionate ratio of Trotsky's popularity to the number of his supporters. During the revolution and civil war, his name was known throughout the country and well beyond its borders. He was seen as the idol and symbol of the revolution, and many admired his energy, and his versatility as a military leader, state official, politician, public speaker, journalist and tireless advocate of world revolution. It seemed as if this veritable generator of revolution was capable of uniting millions by his indefatigable efforts. But the circle of people personally dedicated to him was narrow. He had set himself the task of becoming a leader, and leaders as a rule have few friends.

Like anyone else who wielded great power, Trotsky would respond to personal requests. With the help of his large secretariat he was willing to give help in various ways. For example, he forwarded a letter to the Orgburo from an old female revolutionary called Rozanova, with an accompanying note: 'I lived with her and her husband in Saratov, really as an illegal. I used her help in the sense of the apartment, addresses and so on. It was in 1902. I recall that Rozanova and her husband were Populists and, I think, later on in exile joined [the SR] Chernov . . . We ought to help the old woman.'[75] For Klara Zetkin, the German Communist and member of ECCI, he asked for 'more bearable conditions, as she's living in a cold room in the Lux Hotel. Perhaps we could give her an electric stove or find her another apartment.'[76] He did not turn away from people, he gave advice and did some good deeds.

But the revolutionary wave had subsided, and it suddenly appeared that the second man in the Party and the country had very few supporters. This provoked a discussion in the Party which was enlivened by Trotsky's letter to the Central Committee in October 1923, and again by the 'Statement of the 46', inspired by him, sent to the Politburo a week later.[77]

For Trotsky, the saddest thing was to realize that all his efforts to move the Party from its 'secretarial hierarchical' course had been doomed from the start. He had wanted what the revolution had proclaimed, what Marxism had declared and what met the interests of the Party members. The failure was due to a number of causes. First, most Party members were too ill-educated politically to understand what was at stake. The Party came into its own and grew in conditions of war, which explained the predominance of its military methods and use of military terminology, such as 'fronts', 'attacks', 'storming', 'treachery' and 'concentration'. Whoever stood at the Party's administrative helm could more or less determine the course of a debate, ensure the formation of the appropriate public opinion, create images of enemies and allies. Attempting to influence the Party line, Trotsky addressed the Party machine, the very 'secretarial hierarchy' – the 'ring' – which was set on stifling him. Since he was trying to reduce the influence of the organization, it was unlikely he would find supporters among it. And the power of the organization was spreading from top to bottom.

Furthermore, Trotsky was extraordinarily inept at choosing the moment to engage in political struggle. He was no tactician. He knew

very well the poor impression it would make on the Party, his supporters and the army if he, the second man of the revolution, were
absent from Lenin's funeral, even if it was through no fault of his
own. But he recognized the full magnitude of the omission only later.
Often at the most critical moments of the struggle he left the arena,
either through illness, or by taking a vacation in the Caucasus, or
going to Berlin for treatment. Once, when the Politburo was reviewing
his factional activity, he was on a hunting expedition with Muralov.
The fact is, the functionaries and Party members preferred to give
their allegiance to successful leaders, and Trotsky came across in the
political battle as a loser, which did nothing to swell the ranks of his
supporters.

Finally, his political opposition itself appeared as a naked struggle
for power, jobs and influence. Stalin had understood the importance
of appearing as the defender of Lenin and his heritage. All of his
speeches against Trotsky and the opposition were laced with quotations from Lenin and references to the dead leader. Trotsky, meanwhile, was having constantly to defend and justify himself, and to
demonstrate his loyalty to the Central Committee and Politburo. His
defensive posture created the impression that he was in the wrong,
that his views were dubious and harmful. This was morally depressing
for his supporters, who were dwindling steadily. From the late 1920s
many deserted him and recanted their views, and not only from fear
of sanction.

As a result of Stalin's efforts, and Trotsky's, too, the latter appeared
before the Communist masses as a malicious splitter of the Party.
And, after all, Lenin himself had stressed that a split would be more
dangerous for the Party than the White generals: the Party had to be
monolithic. Hence the hostility towards Trotsky and the support for
Stalin who, shoulder to shoulder with the Central Committee,
appeared as the upholder of unity. As for the ideological differences,
the majority of the Party, despite their belief in world revolution,
were impressed by Stalin's goal of building socialism in one country
first. The apparent lack of confidence shown by Trotsky and his supporters in the possibility of a socialist victory in the USSR, moreover,
was presented by Stalin as nothing less than a desire to bring back
capitalism.

Stalin spotted all of Trotsky's weaknesses and exploited them to the full. As the Party's chief administrator, he was in a position to ensure that only those who were against Trotsky were given important posts (in due course, any post). The policy was practised imperceptibly, but the effect was that Stalin's position was strengthened and Trotsky's weakened. Even those who saw the positive side of Trotsky's platform were doubtful that he could succeed. He soon became a general without an army. Who was supporting him?

In 1926, when Zinoviev and Kamenev went over to him, the list looked impressive, in quality if not in length. The 'Statement of the 46' had included the noteworthy remark: 'A wavering few are leaving the opposition, while tens and hundreds of convinced . . . Party rank and file are joining us.'[78] Only the first part of this statement was true. At the height of its popularity, the opposition could not muster more than seven or eight thousand members. To be sure, the number of those who did not accept Trotsky and his views may not have been many more, but the rest of the Party were objects of Stalin's manipulations, and it was precisely the amorphous nature of the rank and file membership that permitted Stalin to retain supremacy, for at decisive moments tens of thousands of members obediently followed the line laid down by the Central Committee, which was Stalin's to control.

In the spring of 1926 Zinoviev and Kamenev finally realized that they had underrated Stalin's strength and overrated Trotsky's. When in April 1926, after a three-year interval, the three politicians met at Kamenev's apartment, they were all aware of just how cleverly Stalin had beaten them. Unable to look Trotsky in the eye, Zinoviev and Kamenev talked at length, blaming him, too, for the mistake they had made in supporting Stalin. Why, they asked, had he insisted on raking up their conduct in October 1917? Why hadn't he come to Lenin's funeral? Did he not realize just how hopeless it was to come out against Stalin virtually alone?

Trotsky's new allies described the years they had spent with Stalin as a nightmare. They declared that they had each written letters, which they had hidden in safe places, stating that in the event of their sudden and unexplained death the world should know it was at Stalin's hands, and they told Trotsky to do likewise. Stalin, they said, had not yet liquidated Trotsky only because he feared that some young, convinced Trotskyist might take revenge on him. They went on, Trotsky's biographer Isaac Deutscher writes, that if the three of them were to unite and confront the people and the Party, it was possible to turn the Party back onto 'the true path'. With Trotsky's brilliant intellect and popularity, nothing would be easier than to remove Stalin from power.[79] They believed that they had not yet missed the train.

But in fact it was too late. Had this alliance emerged soon after Lenin's death, such an outcome might have been possible. But Trotsky also realized, with regret, that his new allies had only come over to him temporarily. He knew they were not capable of decisive struggle; they would not even seek a compromise, but would beg for Stalin's forgiveness. The less reliable of the two, Trotsky also knew, was Zinoviev, who had begun his adult life as a shop assistant in his native Kherson province. Trotsky had first met him at the turn of the century in Geneva and London. He had seen the potential in Zinoviev, then a chemistry student, later a law student at Berne University, and later had good cause to recognize the abilities of the young revolutionary with a keen intelligence and European culture. But even before the revolution, Zinoviev was known for his rapid changes of view, his weak resistance to political pressure and his lack of a philosophy.

It was due to Lenin that Zinoviev entered the upper ranks of the Party: as early as 1905, at the Fifth Party Congress in London, Lenin had put him forward for Bolshevik Central Committee membership, a position he was to hold for twenty years. In the spring of 1917 he would cross Germany with Lenin in the famous 'sealed train', as they travelled via Scandinavia to Petrograd. And it was with Zinoviev that Lenin would go into hiding from the Provisional Government in the summer of 1917. Zinoviev almost constantly followed Lenin. 'Almost', because he was against the April Theses at first, but chiefly because on 10 October, with Kamenev at a secret meeting of the Central Committee, he courageously spoke up against the policy of staging an armed coup. Courage, however, was not one of his main features. Despite his revolutionary pedigree, and the fact that he was the first President of Comintern, Zinoviev's inconsistency made him an object of political and in due course physical beatings.

Trotsky was not to know that Zinoviev would experience a host of further humiliations. When the GPU came for him on a December night in 1934, Zinoviev realized that it was the end. With a trembling hand, he wrote a hurried note to Stalin while his apartment was being searched: '. . . in no way, no way, am I guilty before the Party, before the Central Committee or before you, personally. I swear to you all by everything that is holy to a Bolshevik, I swear to you by Lenin's memory. I cannot even imagine what could have raised suspicion against me. I beg you to believe this, my word of honour. I am shaken to the depths of my soul.' Stalin merely speeded up the trial, and a month later, on 16 January 1935, his old Party comrade, a former member of his 'ring', would be sentenced to ten years' imprisonment, having first confessed all of his non-existent crimes and in addition undertaken to name 'all those I can and will remember as former participants in the anti-Party struggle'.[80]

Trotsky was right to call Stalin a sadist. He was the type who was not fully satisfied by the death of his victim: what he needed was complete moral surrender, and Zinoviev submitted completely on 14 April 1935. Looking back on the behaviour of Zinoviev and Kamenev in October 1917, it is impossible to deny that they had demonstrated considerable political courage in calling their leader's policy disastrous. And, indeed, on a number of occasions Zinoviev expressed what others believed in silence. In his book *Leninism*, for instance, which came out in 1925, he wrote: 'What is the direct source of power in the USSR? Who embodies the power of the working class? The Communist Party! It is in that sense that we have a dictatorship of the Party. Hence, the dictatorship of the Party is a function of the dictatorship of the proletariat.'[81]

Trotsky recognized that the alliance with Zinoviev had been provoked by the latter's loss of his post in the Politburo, his hostility towards Stalin and his unquenched political ambition. As anticipated, after their expulsion from the Party for factionalism, both Zinoviev and Kamenev sent a letter of repentance on 19 December 1927 to the presidium of the Fifteenth Party Congress, asking to be reinstated. The Party relented, but thereafter Trotsky's ephemeral allies were forced constantly to rehearse the unmasking of Trotskyism.

Trotsky had had better hopes of Kamenev, even though his disagreements with him were no less than with Zinoviev. However, Kamenev was not only Trotsky's brother-in-law, but was also endowed with more character than Zinoviev. At the April 1917 Party Conference, Lenin had described Kamenev and the work he had done for the Party for ten years as valuable,[82] and had nominated him as one of his deputies in the Sovnarkom and Council of Labour and

Defence. In the latter capacity, Kamenev had been effective in getting supplies into Moscow and Petrograd, particularly tens of thousands of tons of grain. He was also noted for having conducted personal negotiations with the Ukrainian anarchist guerrilla leader Makhno, which had led to an agreement. Trotsky was also aware, however, that Kamenev had frequently called for 'a struggle against the undermining of Leninism by Trotskyism'. In January 1925 Sermuks showed Trotsky an extract from an article by Kamenev condemning Trotsky: 'We were right not to allow Leninism to be undermined by some other teaching. Now that we are the ruling party, we have to manoeuvre skilfully within internal petty bourgeois and external capitalistic encirclement – we must be especially watchful, especially attentive to any form of deviation.'[83] When Kamenev came to Trotsky in April 1926 it was no doubt a courageous step for him to take. At the Fourteenth Congress four months earlier, as we have seen, he had declared prophetically: 'I have become convinced that Comrade Stalin cannot fulfil the role of unifier of Bolshevik headquarters . . .'[84] It was probably the only speech made at the congress giving the Party warning of a future dictator and virtually proposing that Stalin be removed.

Trotsky later combed the minutes of this congress, noting in particular this and other similar sentiments in Kamenev's speeches, and using the material in his books and articles in exile. He would never bring himself to admit that the many oppositions, factions and groups that he had personally inspired had been no more than ripples on the smooth surface of the vast Russian sea, and that its depths had remained undisturbed. His temporary allies did not strengthen his position. He had not grasped the fact that the sources of Caesarism and totalitarianism lay deeper than the office of the General Secretary. Stalin was not the cause. The burgeoning bureaucracy would have found its Stalin, regardless.

One of the last attempts by the opposition to give an account of itself, of its disagreement with the dictatorship of the Party and the emerging one-man rule, was undertaken in November 1927 on the tenth anniversary of the October coup. But any hopes that new supporters would emerge were dashed. Acting on Stalin's orders, the GPU did not stand on ceremony. The ranks of Trotsky's supporters were thinned. Some published personal statements, declaring that they were terminating their factional activity, others were exiled beyond the Urals, to Siberia and Central Asia, while yet others were given a more honourable exile as ambassadors or trade representatives. Some took a different path. Adolf Ioffe, for instance, an old Bolshevik and a long-standing friend of Trotsky, after a prolonged fit of depression shot himself. In his suicide letter he wrote that Trotsky had always been politically right, but that he did not have enough of Lenin's inflexibility and obstinacy.[85] Trotsky's speech at Ioffe's funeral was his last public address to his supporters in Russia.

Among Trotsky's longest-lasting supporters was Karl Berngardovich Radek, who was exiled to western Siberia after the opposition was smashed. Well-known as a brilliant journalist, Radek also had the reputation of being impulsive in both his personal and political life. Born in Poland – his pseudonym, K. Radek, was based on the Polish word for thief, *kradek*, as he had had to leave the Polish Social Democratic Party because of rumours of dishonesty – Radek never lost the political and cultural traditions of his native land. A witty polyglot and the reputed source of many jokes, he was a *bon vivant* with friends in many countries and in many walks of life. One of his chief characteristics was an ability to change political direction rapidly. A supporter of Trotsky during the Brest-Litovsk peace talks, he had managed simultaneously to side with Bukharin's group of Left Communists. On Lenin's orders he took part in helping to create the German Communist Party, and he was among the first to espouse the idea of the Popular Front.

Trotsky always viewed Radek with interest, but also with a measure of caution, as he was aware of his tendency to sudden changes of mind. When he was for a while the Rector of the Sun Yat-sen University in Moscow, Radek visited Trotsky frequently to discuss international issues, bringing news and lapping up Trotsky's prognostications. Most people seemed to find Radek likeable, even Stalin. At the same time, no one took him quite seriously. His wit and original turn of mind were recognized, as was his irrepressible optimism, but his apparent lack of systematic thought and the impression he gave of personal disorder concealed the powerful intellect of a penetrating analyst, who lacked, to be sure, sufficient willpower.

The first letter Trotsky received in exile in Alma Ata was from Radek, who was exiled in Tomsk together with Ivan Smilga, a Latvian Bolshevik who had risen to prominence during the civil war and who had later become a supporter of Trotsky. Radek wrote about the daily life of an exile, reflected on possible future developments, and urged Trotsky to take courage. Trotsky's replies, which have been gathering dust in the Party archives, include the following excerpts from various letters. On 27 February 1928 he wrote:

> Knowing how much you detest manuscripts, I am writing this on a typewriter. I recall the prophetic words of [my son] Seryozha: 'Don't make a bloc either with Iosif [Stalin], or with Grigory [Zinoviev]. Iosif will deceive and Grigory will run away.' I'm translating Marx's book *Mr Fogt* for the Marx-Engels Institute. I haven't been hunting again, yet. Sermuks is no longer with me; they arrested him and took him off ... I strongly urge you to organize a proper way of life in order to preserve yourself. Whatever it takes. We are still of much, much use ...[86]

Two days later, he wrote again: 'I'm reading a lot about China, world politics ... How are your kidneys? I shake you by your lazy hand with sympathy and reproach.'[87] On 7 March 1928, he wrote:

> Have you seen Bukharin's stupidity in *Pravda*? It's about my trip. Why do little people have to prostitute themselves when they've lost their principles? The GPU are creating obstacles ... I haven't been hunting once. I read a lot about the Chinese revolution ... I've had no news from Serebryakov. My correspondence with others is gradually being established. I got a letter of indignation over Pyatakov's letter. I have long regarded him as someone who can stand on his own two feet. He is an able man with a mathematically administrative turn of mind, but he is politically not very clever. Lenin turned out to be right about this, too, when he warned that one should not rely on Pyatakov in big political matters ... His letter to the press was his own epitaph.[88]

Trotsky had long regarded Bukharin as one of Stalin's chief main-stays – hence the abuse – but he also realized that Stalin was only exploiting Bukharin for as long as it suited him. On a number of occasions, Trotsky had approached Bukharin with proposals of various kinds in an effort to improve their relations. For instance, when a Jewish Communist wrote to Trotsky about antisemitism in his Party cell, where they were saying 'the Yids are making trouble in the Polit-buro', on 4 March 1926 Trotsky wrote to Bukharin:

You'll say it's an exaggeration! And I'd like to think so, myself. So I suggest we go to the cell together and see for ourselves. I think the two of us together, as two members of the Politburo, can combine sufficiently to make an effort calmly and with goodwill to check and see whether it is true, whether it is possible that in our Party, in Moscow, within a workers' cell, foul, slanderous antisemitic propaganda can go on without being punished.[89]

Whether Bukharin took up Trotsky's offer is not recorded.

Radek had still enough energy and courage to protest about the way Trotsky was being treated. On 25 September 1928 he wrote to the Central Committee:

Having heard that Comrade L.D. Trotsky is ill, I request the Central Committee move him to conditions offering the possibility of his recovery. You expelled us from the Party and exiled us as counter-revolutionaries without any regard for the fact that the elder among us have fought for Communism for a quarter of a century ... To keep in exile those who have fought with the kulaks is either lunacy or it is consciously giving aid to the kulaks. A revolutionary Bolshevik, whose past is not inferior to yours, is expected to restore his strength on thirty roubles a month. The story of Comrade Trotsky's illness is the last straw. You must raise the question of ending the exile of Bolshevik-Leninists, above all of Comrade Trotsky. Do this quickly, so that we who have seen Comrade Trotsky on all the fronts of the civil war shall not have the shame of having to raise our voices to save him. We have been deprived of our Party cards, but we do have a card stamped by the GPU with charges under Article 58.[90]

Although Radek was writing on Trotsky's behalf, it is equally clear that he was speaking for himself. His later letters to the Central Committee show a gradual surrender, an evolution typical not only of Radek and Smilga, but of the entire opposition. In a declaration to the Central Committee, dated Tomsk, 29 March 1929, Radek and Smilga wrote:

A number of articles by Comrade Trotsky have appeared in the bourgeois world press about his deportation and the situation in the USSR and the Party. Yaroslavsky is generating real slander on the basis of these articles, of which our own press has distorted the content and in places blatantly falsified the text. Yaroslavsky is trying to depict Trotsky as one who is selling his political conscience to the world bourgeoisie.

Not one worker, not a single Party member, who knows of the service
Trotsky has given to the cause of the revolution for more than thirty
years will believe this slander ... It was a political error for Trotsky
to publish these articles of an internal Party character. But we do not
repudiate the possibility of publishing in the bourgeois press articles
against the Bolshevik Party to which we want to return. Trotsky has
presented the struggle of recent years as a plot by Stalin against Trotsky,
but he has been silent about the danger from the right ...[91]

These are the words of people who have half-capitulated. The
number of those who were capable of staying their chosen course,
like Trotsky, was extremely small. It is one of the mysteries of the
Soviet period that after the death of Lenin there were so few revolutionaries with the courage to resist Stalin. There were many, as we
now know, who in the 1920s and 1930s did not share Stalin's concept
of 'building socialism in one country' by means of sacrifice. But the
majority adapted and made themselves believe that he was right. Much
of this was due to ordinary human weakness, the willingness to go
along with naked force, coercion and demagoguery. There is, however, another element that explains the compliancy of the revolutionaries of the time. They did not recognize the value of liberty. They
thought the liberty that had been thrown to them by the fortuity of
the First World War and Kerensky's mistakes was the prize for their
loyalty to Marxism. Their reverential attitude to the dogmatization
of Marxism, and then Leninism, meant that even the most obviously
wrong-headed policies of the leadership, embellished by the customary dozen or so quotations from holy writ, could be presented as if
inspired by a higher order.

When the opposition was criticized and abused and arrested to the
accompaniment of high-flown references to the usual dogmas, many
wavered, had doubts or lost their heads. Very few were capable of
overstepping the postulates that pushed the recently acquired liberty
into the shade. The opposition was a subconscious effort to find the
way back to that liberty. Dogmatic thinking, however, had already
closed the path to heterodoxy. The Trotskyite-Zinovievite opposition,
as it was called – although in effect it comprised the active elements
of the Party's left wing – faced the choice of either gradual extinction
or humiliating surrender. The overwhelming majority chose the latter.
Soon after their feeble protest to the Central Committee over the

treatment of Trotsky, Radek and Smilga wrote to the Central Control Commission to announce their 'agreement with the general line of the Party and our break with the opposition ... We have nothing in common with Trotsky's theory of permanent revolution ... We remove our signatures from the factional documents and request our reinstatement in the Party.'[92]

Radek's behaviour was typical of the majority of Trotsky's supporters. Whether it was Muralov or Preobrazhensky, Pyatakov or Serebryakov, each in his own way left the ranks of the opposition or was simply made to remain silent. Preobrazhensky, a leading Marxist scholar with whom Trotsky had been extremely frank in their discussions, accepted many of his propositions about the wrongheadedness of Stalin's policies, yet deep down he could not share Trotsky's radicalism, and by the end of 1928 the rift between them was complete. Pyatakov, whom Lenin described as a man 'with an administrative way of thinking', lacked the sophistication to detect political nuances and was among the first to abandon Trotsky. Antonov-Ovseenko, whose commitment to socialist ideals was boundless, saw the future not in Trotsky but in the further development of the revolution. Muralov, who had been close to Trotsky in the civil war and felt a close personal tie, frequently agreed that 'things are not right in the Party'. Trotsky thought very highly of Serebryakov, regarding him as an able and interesting man, and he trusted him. In April 1926 he wrote to him:

> The conversation you and I had with a few other comrades on Stalin's proposal and about agreement with him, has quite suddenly taken a fantastic turn. Two days after your departure rumours began circulating in the Party organization to the effect that, before [your] departure for Manchuria, [you] organized a faction with [me], Pyatakov and Radek, with Pyatakov serving as the link.[93]

This 'top secret' letter was an attempt to explain Stalin's motives and aims in unleashing such insinuations.

Such letters illustrate the fact that there were not only wide differences of thinking, but that there was a real political struggle going on, in which the issues were often overlooked in favour of personalities, ambition, and the egotistical claims of individual leaders. Stalin was not one to observe the 'rules' of Party comradeship or elementary ethics in this struggle. Nor for that matter was Trotsky. But Stalin had the huge apparatus, the GPU and the Party cadres at his disposal. Trotsky could not win. Despite the fact that he had many Party intellectuals on his side, it was Stalin who had the ability to raise the Party masses against the bogey of Trotskyism, invented by him and aided by Trotsky's own mistakes and omissions.

Before his deportation Trotsky had tried to rally his few supporters. According to N. Gavrilov, Trotsky went to Leningrad and held semi-legal meetings at the apartment of his first wife, Alexandra Sokolov-skaya, and once or twice at the home of the Raskins, who were also sympathizers. Trotsky stressed the importance of consolidating his support, otherwise 'the Party will degenerate. Democracy in the Party is in danger. A Thermidore is possible.' Despite a new suit, the clipped beard and short greying hair, he looked tired. Zinoviev was simultaneously organizing opposition meetings at the apartment of his old supporter Alexeev, most of them attended by forty or fifty people. Mass expulsions from the Party were, however, already well under way. The ranks of the opposition were thinning rapidly. Gavrilov himself had been expelled at the end of 1926.[94]

Each member of the opposition had something different to say. Contrary to what was said of them, none of them wanted to restore capitalism. Above all, they possessed the capacity for independent thought, the courage to take responsible political decisions, a readiness to doubt what seemed indubitable. To be sure, they inevitably included uncommitted people, but the weakness of the opposition lay mainly in the absence of clear and appealing alternatives which it could present to the Party. Rightly remarking that 'the Party is probably entering the most responsible period of its history with a heavy burden of mistakes committed by its leading organs,' Trotsky and his supporters also had only the vaguest of ideas of what must be done. They knew what must not be done. They knew it was necessary to combat 'secretarial psychology', 'bureaucratic placemanship' and 'false politics', but their criticism did not amount to a concrete alternative programme. In any case, it was not understood by most Communists.

Yet one cannot say that Trotsky had no programme. He did, but it was conveyed to the Party rank and file in an exaggerated and incomplete form. His enemies depicted him as an opponent of socialism in the USSR, as someone wanting to restore capitalism, regardless of the fact that he wanted the restructuring of society in the interests of world revolution. Like society, the Party had many layers. Trotsky usually addressed himself only to the top layer, but even the small cohort of Bolsheviks who did follow him quickly melted away under the pressure of the repressive Stalinist apparatus.

The Defeat of 1927

1927 was the year in which a line was drawn under Trotsky's political ambitions, and also when the rapid process of the totalitarianization of the Party and the society came sharply into focus. In that year Trotsky became the leader of the 'united left' opposition, whose programme had already been discussed at a Central Committee plenum in July 1926. The programme consisted of two documents, the 'Declaration of 13', and the 'Platform of 83', both of which in effect repeated the ideas contained in Trotsky's letter to the Central Committee and Central Control Commission of 8 October 1923, and in the 'Statement of the 46' of 15 October 1923. It is easy enough now to see that Trotsky's protest against coercion by the state and Party bureaucracy was far-sighted, but at the time his warning voice was easily stifled. According to the left opposition, the source of the country's problems lay in the Party's policy of building socialism in one country. As devotees of world revolution, Trotsky and his supporters viewed the localization of the tasks of revolution as heading towards isolationism, and hence the limitation of democracy and reinforcement of the totalitarian tendencies which were inevitable in the solitary 'socialist fortress', surrounded as it was on all sides. The main idea voiced in the opposition's discussions was that to make one country or one group of countries into a military camp would render democracy, or people's power, redundant. A 'fortress', 'citadel', and finally a 'camp', needs a leader, a Caesar, a dictator. Trotsky understood this fact better than anyone, and he believed that to set out to build socialism in one country, without linking it to the world revolutionary process, was profoundly wrong. It would also lead to huge problems in the country, he claimed.

In opposing the bureaucracy, however, Trotsky resorted to leftist formulas, and this immediately devalued his revolt against Stalin. The 'Platform of 83' emphasized that 'the incorrect policy is accelerating the growth of the kulak, the Nepman [traders and businessmen who were profiting from the New economic Policy] and the bureaucrat, all of them hostile to the dictatorship of the proletariat.'[95] These arguments, while in many respects justified, were a one-sided interpretation of the Party's policy, and they conflicted with the apparent desire of millions of people to continue along the present path. Impatience and a belief in the possibility of entering the promised land with one gigantic leap had already become an integral part of public awareness. The 'united left' opposition, with its global radical ideas and slogans, could find no way to attack the growing dictatorship of one man.

After his removal from the Politburo in October 1926 – formally on a proposal by the Leningrad Party organization – Trotsky concentrated his efforts on the written and oral defence of the opposition's ideas. According to Natalya Sedova, Trotsky's expulsion from the Politburo was best explained by Victor Serge. Shortly before it occurred, Serge reported, Trotsky had clashed with Stalin at a Politburo session when the latter declared that the opposition must recant at the forthcoming Fifteenth Party Conference. Trotsky angrily objected, arguing that such rulings were impermissible within the Party. The quarrel climaxed when Trotsky flung at Stalin: 'The First Secretary is applying for the job of gravedigger of the Party!' Stalin flared, then turned white, his eyes darkening. Choking on his words, he swept the rest of the members with an ominous look, turned away and hurried from the room, slamming the door behind him. Muralov, Pyatakov and Smirnov were waiting at Trotsky's apartment, and when he returned they clamoured to know why he had uttered those words. Stalin would now be his mortal enemy and would never forgive nor forget the insult. Trotsky, although pale, remained calm. He waved his hand as if to say, what's done is done. They all knew the rift was now final.[96] Stalin would now do everything in his power to remove Trotsky from the Politburo.

Until 1985 membership of the Politburo could be compared to belonging to an imperial family, although in terms of real power it was something incomparably higher. Outwardly, however, Trotsky appeared to have accepted the change in his status calmly. He threw himself into writing, meeting his supporters and trying to get his views known through the press. The newspapers and journals, however, blithely rejected everything he submitted. He protested to the Politburo on 16 May:

> On 12 May the Politburo ordered that my articles not be published. It seems two articles were at issue, one, 'The Chinese Revolution and Comrade Stalin's Theses', which I sent to *Bolshevik*, and 'The True Path', which I sent to *Pravda*. After this, somewhat unexpectedly, Comrade Stalin's theses appeared, representing the hardening and exacerbation of the most erroneous aspects at the heart of an erroneous policy ... Everything can be stifled temporarily: criticism, doubt, questions and indignant protest. But these are the methods Lenin called rude and disloyal ...[97]

Sensing that his chances of influencing the Party leadership were sharply reduced, Trotsky continued to display considerable courage. He wrote bitterly, in a personal letter to Krupskaya on 17 May 1927:

> Stalin and Bukharin are betraying Bolshevism at its very core, its proletarian revolutionary internationalism ... The defeat of the German revolution in 1923, the defeats in Bulgaria and Estonia, the defeat of the general strike in England, and the Chinese revolution in April, have all seriously weakened international Communism ... The decline in the international revolutionary mood of our proletariat is a fact that is strengthened by the Party regime and the false political education, such as socialism in one country, and so on. No wonder the left, revolutionary, Leninist wing of the Party has to swim against the tide in such circumstances. Stalin has now decided to turn the 'war of attrition' against the opposition of the last half-year into a 'war of destruction' ... We shall swim against the tide ...[98]

And several thousand, seeing the courage of their leader, swam with him.

Trotsky faced constant accusation and public attack, but invariably he fought back. For instance, in June 1927 at an extended sitting of the Central Control Commission chaired by Ordzhonikidze, he spoke for an hour and a half despite constant interruption by the chairman. Bitterly, Trotsky flung at Ordzhonikidze:

> I say that you are set on a course for the bureaucrat, for the functionary, but not for the masses. You've got too much faith in the organization. The organization operates as a vast internal mutual support structure,

mutual protection. That's why it's even impossible to reduce salaries. Independence from the masses is creating a system of mutual conceal- ment. And all this is considered the chief basis of the regime. Our Party now stakes everything on the secretary, not the rank and file member. That's what the Party regime amounts to . . .'[99]

One of the issues on which Trotsky chose to attack Stalin was the Chinese revolution, over which the General Secretary frequently wavered, while Trotsky stuck to a hard left position. He had retained a strong impression of the three-hour meeting he had had on 27 November 1923 with Chiang Kai-shek, the leader of the Nationalist movement, the Kuomintang, during which many important issues were made clear to him. He wrote a large number of articles on China, many of them in 1927, and also produced a book called *Problems of the Chinese Revolution*. But the pieces he published on China beginning in 1926 were all targeted on 'Stalin's mistakes', and were thus rather unbalanced in their analysis. In a long article of April 1927, entitled 'The Chinese Revolution and Comrade Stalin's Theses' and aimed at exposing the Party's mistaken policy in the East, Trotsky remarked that in China 'the revolutionary tempo has been lost' and the peasantry not politicized. In true left-wing manner, he asserted that 'whoever follows a peaceful policy in an agrarian revolution will perish. Who- ever procrastinates, hesitates, waits and misses the moment will perish.'[100] The manuscript of this article is covered with notes and underlinings, indicating how strongly Trotsky wanted to expose Stalin's political weakness, but his arguments were plainly debatable.

An article, 114 pages in length, entitled 'A New Phase in the Chinese Revolution' and intended for the Executive Committee of Comintern (ECCI), set out to prove the 'chain of errors' Stalin had made in international issues. 'The opportunistic Stalin-Bukharin line,' Trotsky wrote, 'after helplessly meandering this way and that, describes a sharp zigzag; the struggle with imperialism is vanishing and its place is being taken by the struggle with feudalism.'[101]

In focusing on events in China, Trotsky was not only exposing the flaws in Stalin's foreign policy, but repeating his earlier assertion that the East was still one of the most important revolutionary factors. He hoped that in addressing the Chinese question he would reinforce the opposition and weaken Stalin's faction. But the dénouement was approaching. Stalin and his new entourage were banking on the constant discrediting of Trotsky and his supporters, their gradual isolation from the mass of the Party and the creation of a 'capitulationist' and 'faint-hearted' image. By emphasizing world revolution as his chief goal, Trotsky appeared to be denying the possibility of building the socialist society in the USSR. Stalin succeeded in creating this image in the public mind partly with Trotsky's help. The statements, protests and enquiries that the latter addressed to the Central Committee and Politburo contained wholesale criticism of all spheres of Soviet life, as well as of Party and state policies.

Some of these documents were written by Trotsky's supporters, yet they still bore his imprint. A 100-page report on 'The Present Stage of the Revolution and Our Tasks', although signed by a group of oppositionists, was edited by Trotsky, and the origin of its central idea was unambiguous: 'The new theory of the victory of socialism in one country will lead to the betrayal of the international revolution for the sake of the security of the USSR . . . That means repudiating the Leninist formula of the entry of the capitalist countries into the era of wars and revolutions, and is a liquidationist [i.e. anti-Bolshevik] position in relation to the world revolution.'[102]

The oppositionists faced a grilling at Party plenums, meetings and assemblies of all kinds. Their leftist positions on the need to 'squeeze' the kulaks, to force industrialization, to initiate world revolution, on the impossibility of building socialism in one country – only made their situation worse. Most Party members did not accept the warning about the bureaucratization of society. For the ordinary worker or peasant, a bureaucrat was simply a procrastinator, a bribe-taker and sluggard. Party members did not realize that state bureaucracy meant the end of democracy. The level of discussion and political struggle was extremely low, even in the highest echelons of the Party. At the August 1927 Central Committee plenum, for instance, during a speech by Kamenev, who was trying to show that diversity of thought was natural, he was interrupted by Goloshchekin with: 'Who wrote that for you to read?' 'You're simply an idiot,' Kamenev retorted. 'Must you use such expressions?' Shkiryatov interjected. 'According to you everyone else is a fool, and only you are clever.' 'You'll only hear such things from a stupid man who has acquired the language of the fascists,' Goloshchekin added. 'It was you, Comrades, who sent me to Mussolini,' Kamenev replied.[103] He had just been appointed Soviet ambassador to Italy, diplomatic relations having been established in 1924.

The two sides were irreconcilable. The opposition was doomed, and its leader was saved from prison only by his fame. Yet Trotsky did not surrender. Stalin with the assistance of the Party organization continued to blacken Trotsky's image as a hero of the revolution and civil war. During a joint plenum of the Central Committee and Central Control Commission in October 1927, Stalin spoke disparagingly of Trotsky's role at the fronts, even hinting at cowardice. Trotsky at once wrote an indignant letter to L. Serebryakov: 'Stalin claimed that during the time he was working with you on the Southern front, I showed up only once, stealthily in my car with my wife for half an hour. He also said something to the effect that it was winter, and snowing, that Trotsky turned up and left at once because he was prohibited from going to the Southern front.' Trotsky went on to say that he had never been forbidden by anyone from going to the southern front, he'd never been at the front with his wife, and that as the train diary would show, he had spent weeks and months at the southern front. He requested confirmation that Stalin's utterances were rubbish.[104]

The story had first been concocted by Stalin in 1924, claiming falsely that the Central Committee had passed a resolution prohibiting Trotsky from visiting the southern front, and it had been repeated by Voroshilov in an article called 'Stalin and the Red Army'. But it was impossible publicly to repudiate the assertions of the General Secretary, whose utterances were circulated on a massive scale by *Pravda*, *Bolshevik* and many other organs, while only a narrow circle heard what Trotsky had to say. Stalin fought the battle on a broad front, leaving no room for the opposition either to defend itself or even to save face.

Since Trotsky had chosen to criticize the leadership with special vigour over its policy on the Chinese revolution, it was decided that the first surprise attack against him should be made at a joint session of the Presidium of the Executive Committee of Comintern and the International Control Commission. Stalin met the members of ECCI before the meeting to coordinate tactics. It was agreed that Trotsky should be thrown out of ECCI. It was also agreed that the conduct of the Yugoslav delegate Voislav Vujovic', who supported Trotsky on the executive Committee, be discussed. Since ECCI was funded entirely by the Kremlin, it had become the international arm of the Soviet leadership, and therefore no one objected to expelling Trotsky.

The meeting took place on 27 September 1927, and a few excerpts from its proceedings will suffice to give an impression of the character of this international 'court'. In the chair was Otto Kuusinen, the leader of the failed Communist revolution in Finland in 1918. He opened the meeting by declaring that the issue before them was the factional activity carried on by Trotsky and Vujovic'. He pointed out that on 30 May 1927 ECCI had categorically forbidden these two members from engaging in factional activity, yet within ten days the opposition, led by Trotsky, had organized an 'anti-Party demonstration at Yaroslavsky Station to mark the departure of Comrade Smilga . . . Illegal groups are being set up, with underground presses, and they are conducting a remorseless factional struggle. They call themselves "Bolshevik Leninists", but what does their behaviour have in common with Bolshevism and Leninism?'

TROTSKY (interrupting): The hero of the Finnish revolution is teaching me Bolshevism and Leninism . . .

KUUSINEN: When you have the floor, you can tell your tales. Personal insinuations have always been your way. You use them even against the best Russian revolutionary leaders, so I regard it as an honour to be slandered by you . . . The leadership of Comintern must intervene and expel the Trotskyists from their midst.

When he was given the floor, Trotsky listed twenty-five points, ranging from the Chinese revolution and the struggle against war to discipline and Party rules. Among his remarks he made the following observations:

TROTSKY: You accuse me of transgressing Party discipline. I'm quite sure you have your sentence prepared . . . Stalin, who is rude and disloyal, had the audacity to speak of a united front from Chamberlain to Trotsky . . . The Party is under orders to keep silent because Stalin's policy is a policy of bankruptcy. In your view, it is entirely in order to deny a crust of bread to Leninists who don't want to become Stalinists. For transcribing and distributing the opposition platform, [a group of] excellent Party members were expelled yesterday . . . Stalin is telling you what you must do: expel Trotsky and Vujovic' from ECCI. I think you'll do this. Stalin's regime is stupefying the Party with its one-sided discussions, expulsions and arrests ... Stalin's personal misfortune, which is fast becoming the Party's misfortune, is the colossal disparity between his intellectual resources and the power that the state and Party machine has concentrated in his hands ... The bureaucratic regime will lead irreversibly to one-man rule.

It was of course this 'colossal disparity' in favour of Stalin's machine that explains the further course of the meeting.

MURPHY [of the British Communist party]: We have just witnessed an extremely sad spectacle. Comrade Trotsky has come here this evening as the emissary of another party, not as a member of ECCI.

THOREZ [the French representative]: It's time to put a stop to the factional struggle of the opposition. When I was in the Donbass, the miners told me they were not inclined to go over to the Trotskyist opposition ...

PEPPER [USA]: Trotsky has always combined leftist phraseology and rightist actions with the methods of indecent personal slander. In the name of the American party I demand Trotsky's expulsion.

KATAYAMA [Japan]: We have heard you and we condemn you.

VUJOVIĆ [Yugoslavia]: I agree with what Trotsky has said. You are striking a blow against the Russian revolution.

BUKHARIN: If we examine Trotsky's speech, we see it is a platform of wild lies and slander against our Party and Comintern. We must ask Trotsky why he does not stand to attention before the Party, like a soldier?

TROTSKY: You have the Party by the throat ...

Kuusinen then summed up and formally proposed the expulsion of Trotsky as a member, and Vujovic' as a candidate member. Trotsky took the floor again. He declared that only recently Kuusinen would not have dared to make the false assertion that the last ten years had been a decade of Trotsky's struggle against Leninism. He cited Lenin at a meeting of the Petrograd Bolshevik Committee of 14 November 1917 when he had called Trotsky 'the best Bolshevik'. It was monstrous now to have to repudiate the slander of such people as Kuusinen and Pepper and their ilk.

KUUSINEN: Lenin called Trotsky a non-Bolshevik ...

TROTSKY: Everyone knows that Lenin would never have tolerated a non-Bolshevik in the Politburo ...

BUKHARIN: If you don't come to your senses soon, you will inevitably meet your political death ...

KREIBICH [Czechoslovakia]: Trotsky and Vujovic' have expelled themselves from ECCI ...

STALIN: The speakers here today have spoken so well, especially Comrade Bukharin, that there's little for me to add. What is it the Trotskyists are struggling against? Against the Leninist regime in the Party.

TROTSKY: You're lying ...

STALIN: Keep your strong words for yourself. You are discrediting yourself with this abuse. You're a Menshevik!

ROI [India]: I'm for Trotsky's expulsion from ECCI.

KABAKCHIEV [Bulgaria]: I'm also for his expulsion.

ANGARETI [Italy]: There's no place for them on ECCI.

SZAMUELY [Hungary]: It's time to put an end to the opposition.

A single proposal was put to the vote, and Trotsky and Vujovic' were unanimously expelled.[105] It was Trotsky's first official defeat of 1927. In 1925 he had lost his posts as Chairman of the Revolutionary Military Council and War Commissar, in 1926 he had been removed from the Politburo, and now he was thrown out of Comintern. More defeats were to come.

The Stalin–Trotsky conflict was closely observed abroad, and with particular acuity by the Mensheviks abroad. On 27 August 1927, in *Sotsialisticheskii vestnik*, the newspaper they still described as an organ of the RSDLP, they wrote that the conflict promised Russia new adventures and new misfortunes.

But it is all going on within the narrow circle of the Communist Party, causing concern outside it only among social democratic workers and those intellectuals who have not lost the habit of thinking politically. Beyond those boundaries, the masses, even in the cities, are curious but not passionately involved. Trotsky's fight against Stalin says little to the heart of the ordinary worker ... the opposition is afraid of the working masses and is hesitant about taking the quarrel to them. This is why the opposition in its present form is doomed. Their quarrel with the Stalinists will be settled unilaterally by their adversary.[106]

The Menshevik view was conveyed to the Politburo in July 1927 in a report by Menzhinsky's Foreign Section of the OGPU, which stated:

In the opinion of the Mensheviks, the authority of the Communist
Party is leading to the Party's downfall, thanks to Stalin's methods.
The atmosphere is becoming increasingly charged with electricity and
any spark could cause an explosion. In the Mensheviks' opinion, the
only man who can save the situation is Trotsky, as he enjoys the greatest
authority. He is already looked upon as a leader, and keeping him a
prisoner does not diminish his authority.[107]

As we see, the special services' reports were quite unlike the analytical material published in *Sotsialisticheskii vestnik*.

Trotsky was unusually active in the autumn of 1927. Almost every
day he met the leaders of his support groups either at home or in
Leningrad, made speeches at various institutes, while also writing
numerous declarations to the Central Committee, meeting foreign
correspondents, and cursing newspaper and magazine editors who
refused to accept his work. He felt the chances of remaining on the
political scene dwindling. He knew that if he did not succeed in keeping his foothold, the affair would not end in political rout alone. He
had frequent opportunity to lament the fact that back in 1923 and
1924 he had conceded so much ground without a fight by being absent
so often on holiday or on trips to Berlin for treatment. True, his
doctor, F.A. Guetier, whether independently or on someone else's
orders, had dissuaded Trotsky and his wife from travelling to Paris
in the summer of 1927 for treatment. He wrote to Natalya Sedova
on 4 May:

> To tell you the truth, I am not happy about your plans to go to the
> Paris environment for a malaria cure. I'm not happy, first because I
> don't know how healthy the place you intend to stay is, secondly,
> because I don't know in whose medical hands you will be. I saw Lev
> Davydovich yesterday (3 May). He looked quite well, much fresher and
> more robust than before the [recent] trip.
>   Yours ever, F. Guetier.[108]

In October a session of the Leningrad Soviet took place, and a
large demonstration was staged in its honour. Standing on the central
podium, Trotsky and Zinoviev drew special attention to themselves
and many of the marchers cheered them as they passed. Ordinary
citizens saw Trotsky not as the leader of the opposition, but as the
hero of the civil war and creator of the Red Army. Such occasions,

however, gave him no joy. He recognized that the cheers and applause were for his past. In the present, the opposition was losing ground fast.

At the end of October Trotsky was invited to yet another, and for him the last, joint plenum of the Central Committee and Central Control Commission. He would never again attend the Bolshevik headquarters. He harboured no illusions about the outcome of the forthcoming discussion of his oppositional activity. The meeting took place in an exceptionally stormy atmosphere. As soon as Trotsky was given the floor, shouts and insults were flung at him. His speech was passionate, but muddled. Adjusting his pince-nez and with one arm half outstretched, he read his text hurriedly, barely looking at his audience. The outstretched arm served a useful purpose, for apart from the insults, books, inkwells, tumblers and other objects were thrown at him. It was a degrading scene: the top echelon of the Party were crucifying one of their own leaders who had dared to swim against the tide. His voice – hurried and with an unfamiliar note – carried above the din: 'First, a word or two about so-called "Trot-skyism",' he began. 'Every opportunist is trying to use this word to cover his own nakedness. The falsification factory is working at full steam and around the clock to construct "Trotskyism" ... In our July declaration last year we predicted with complete accuracy all the stages of the destruction of the Leninist leadership of the Party and its temporary replacement by the Stalinist leadership. I say "temporary replacement" because the more "victories" the leading group sustains, the weaker it becomes.'

After pausing for the shouts and insults to subside, he glanced at the hostile assembly and continued:

> You want to expel us from the Central Committee. We agree that this measure emerges fully from the present course at the given stage of the Central Committee's development, or rather its ruin ... The rude-ness and disloyalty of which Lenin wrote are no longer simply personal qualities; they have become the hallmark of the leading faction, they have become its policy and its regime ... Lenin was worried about Stalin as General Secretary from the very beginning: 'This cook can only make peppery dishes.' Lenin said this to a small group at the time of the Eleventh Congress ...

As Trotsky spoke, Stalin sat calmly, gazing around the hall, correcting the text of the long speech he was about to make and to which he now added the title 'The Trotskyist Opposition Before and Now'. Casting occasional glances at the speaker, he busied himself by sketching a pack of wolves in the margin of his text, then took a red pencil and filled in a crimson background. Trotsky, meanwhile, was hurrying through his speech and counting the minutes as the end of his membership of the Party's élite approached.

> It's easy for Bukharin today to say 'Enrich yourselves' and tomorrow 'Get rid of the kulaks'. A few scratches of the pen is enough . . . You'll get nothing out of him. Behind the extreme organization-men there is a resurgent internal bourgeoisie . . . [And] behind that is the world bourgeoisie. Stalin's immediate task is to split the Party, isolate the opposition and teach the Party the methods of physical destruction. Fascist whistles, fisticuffs, throwing books or stones, prison gates – that's as far as Stalin's policy has gone, for the moment and until it moves further . . . Why should the Yaroslavskys and Shverniks, the Goloshchekins and the rest bother to argue about statistics, if they can throw a heavy book of statistics at an oppositionist's head? . . . Voices can already be heard saying 'We'll expel a thousand, shoot a hundred, and things will quieten down in the Party.' That is indeed the voice of the Thermidore.

Trotsky's closing remarks indicate how wrong he was to think that his position had a broad following: a few thousand intellectuals and some workers supported his ideas (though no peasants): 'The slander, expulsions and arrests are making our platform the most popular, most intimate and precious document of the international labour movement. You can expel us, but you won't prevent the victory of the opposition, that is, the victory of the revolutionary unity of our Party and Comintern!'[109]

Following a chorus of condemnation and violent demands for Trotsky's expulsion from the Central Committee and the Party, the man who had scripted, stage-managed and directed the entire spectacle took the stand. Stalin spoke softly for an hour and a half, looking at his text occasionally, vigorously gesticulating with his good right arm from time to time, as if cutting off the heads of the accused. 'The main attacks have been aimed against Stalin,' he explained, 'because Stalin knows all the tricks of the opposition, better perhaps than some of our comrades; it won't be easy to bamboozle him, [they say], so that's why they aim their blows above all at Stalin. Well, let them curse to their heart's content. Stalin is just Stalin, a little man. Try taking on Lenin.' Here he began to enumerate a long and precise list of Trotsky's sins, his 'hooligan slander of Lenin'. Once again he cited Trotsky's letter of 1913 to the Menshevik Chkheidze, in which he called Lenin a 'professional exploiter of any backwardness in the Russian revolutionary movement'. He then glared at the audience that was hungrily hanging on his every word: 'Quite a turn of phrase, you'll agree, Comrades, quite a turn of phrase. Trotsky wrote that. And he was writing about Lenin. Can you wonder that Trotsky, who could so unceremoniously dismiss Lenin, whose boot he is not worth, can now abuse one of Lenin's many pupils, Comrade Stalin, for no rhyme or reason?'[110]

Stalin had used the device of presenting himself as a pupil of Lenin's before, with the result that taking him on was like taking on the master himself. He then accused Trotsky of an inconsistent attitude to Lenin's 'Testament'. As early as 1925, he said, Trotsky had declared that even the conversations about Lenin's last wishes had been 'a malicious invention'. So 'on what basis can Trotsky, Zinoviev and Kamenev now run off at the mouth and claim that the Party and its Central Committee "are concealing" Lenin's "Testament"?' Stalin's carefully organized text took the opposition apart in eight points:

In 1921 Lenin proposed expelling Shlyapnikov from the Central Committee and the Party not because he had set up an anti-Party press, nor for his union with bourgeois intellectuals, but just because Shlyapnikov dared to make a speech inside a Party cell criticizing decisions of the Supreme National Economic Council (Vesenkha). Now compare what Lenin did with what the Party is doing in relation to the opposition and you'll see how far we've gone in allowing disorganizers and dissenters . . . They mention the arrest of disorganizers who have been expelled for their anti-Soviet activities. Yes, we are making arrests and will continue to do so, if they don't stop undermining the Party and the Soviet regime.

At the last plenum of the Central Committee and Central Control Commission in August this year, I was attacked by some members for my gentle approach to Trotsky and Zinoviev, for having dissuaded the plenum from immediately expelling [them] from the Central

Committee ... Perhaps I was too kind and made a mistake. It's time now for us to stand in the front rank with those comrades who are demanding their expulsion.

The meeting burst into tumultuous applause at these words. Within an order such as the Party had now become, the effect of psychological affinity with the leader is to suppress rational thinking and enhance feelings of fanatical solidarity, the herd-instinct, mindlessness.

Stalin then recalled Trotsky's 1904 pamphlet 'Our Political Tasks', and declared: 'This pamphlet is interesting, by the way, because Trotsky dedicated it to the Menshevik P. Axelrod. It says there: "To my dear teacher, Pavel Borisovich Axelrod". Well, good riddance to this "dear teacher Pavel Borisovich Axelrod"! Good riddance! But you'd better get a move on, esteemed Trotsky, because the decrepit "Pavel Borisovich" may suddenly die and you might be too late to see your "teacher".'[111]

The applause was long and, let it be said, genuine. Not all the delegates had paid particular attention to Stalin's words 'Good riddance', but I believe their utterance was not accidental. In 1927 Stalin was already wondering how he would get rid of Trotsky. He was not yet ready to deal with him physically, and exile to the east would only partially isolate this dangerous individual. He had more than once thought of deporting Trotsky abroad, as the Politburo five years earlier, under Lenin, had done with a large group of intellectuals. But at the October 1927 plenum Stalin was not yet ready to express any further thoughts on the matter.

Khristian Rakovsky had wanted to speak up in Trotsky's defence, but was not given the floor. He then tried in vain to publish his speech as a discussion paper for distribution in the Party. One excerpt from it will suffice to show the flimsiness of Stalin's argument:

Stalin's reasons for expulsion, for instance Comrade Trotsky's 1904 pamphlet which he dedicated to his 'dear teacher P.B. Axelrod', are not good enough. I don't know if Comrade Stalin has forgotten or if he ever knew that a little earlier than Trotsky, Lenin had also called Axelrod his 'dear teacher'. Nor should we consider as arguments all the rubbish, all the anti-biographical and biographical facts that have been cited in abundance here, but which are more than outweighed by the reasoned criticism that we hear from the opposition.[112]

But even if the plenum had listened to Rakovsky, they would not have heard him. The conflict had made both sides politically deaf to each other.

Trotsky had been expelled from the Central Committee, his second major defeat in the fateful year of 1927. He collected up his papers and stuffed them into his old briefcase, glanced expressionlessly at the platform and left the hall to the catcalls, hisses and insults of his former colleagues on the Central Committee. They had cast him out forever. Stalin and Trotsky saw each other for the last time that day, 23 October 1927.

Grey-faced, Trotsky got into the car that had not yet been taken away from him and went home to the Kremlin where, in the residence of the new rulers of the new empire, he had already begun to feel like an alien. His wife and his secretary, Grinberg, did their best to calm him. He had not expected a different outcome from the meeting, but the character and form of the proceedings had been oppressive. Now at last he felt himself to be a rejected revolutionary. 'But,' he protested to his family, 'they cannot tear me away from history!'

Next morning, having read the official transcript of the meeting, he dictated a letter to the Central Committee Secretariat:

> The minutes do not show ... that the platform systematically prevented me from speaking. They do not show that ... a glass was thrown at me from the platform (I understand by Comrade Kubyak). They do not show that one of the participants tried to drag me off the podium by my arm, and so and so on ... While I was speaking, Comrade Yaroslavsky threw a book of statistics at me ... employing methods that cannot be called anything but those of Fascist hooligans. While Comrade Bukharin was speaking, in reply to a riposte from me, Comrade Shvernik, a former Central Committee secretary and now head of the Urals Party organization, also threw a book at me. I hope his exploit will be recorded in the proceedings.[113]

Despite the plain fact that Stalin had won, Trotsky would not yield. He continued attending meetings of the opposition, he wrote statements and protests, and sent instructions to his support groups. He had little choice but to try to set up some kind of organized resistance, but it was too late. Mass arrests and expulsions from the Party were going on, and people were losing their jobs. The opposition was melting away. But he was determined to fight to the finish.

As the tenth anniversary of the October revolution approached, he consulted with Kamenev, Zinoviev, Smilga and Muralov, and suggested that their supporters take part in the demonstrations, but marching separately. Circulars were sent to Leningrad and elsewhere declaring that the opposition would proclaim its viability by taking part in the demonstrations under its own banners.

Trotsky's columns, when they turned out in Moscow and Leningrad, were not numerous. They carried portraits of Lenin, Trotsky and Zinoviev, and banners bearing ambiguous slogans, understandable only to the initiated: 'Down with the Kulak, the Nepman and the Bureaucrat!', 'Down with Opportunism!', 'Carry out Lenin's Testament!', 'Preserve Bolshevik Unity!'. Stalin had already issued the inevitable orders, however, and the columns were cordoned off by the militia and students of OGPU and the military academies. Trotsky in Moscow, and Zinoviev in Leningrad, toured the streets in their cars, trying to salute their supporters and the crowds that had come to celebrate. Many people called out greetings to the leaders of the opposition, voicing their solidarity and waving their arms. From the balcony of the former Hotel Paris, Smilga, Preobrazhensky and Alsky tried to address short speeches to the approaching columns, but the OGPU took rapid action. Smilga and Preobrazhensky were unceremoniously hustled from the balcony, the columns of sympathizers were scattered, and Trotsky's car was bombarded with stones, breaking its windows. The OGPU threatened to use weapons and fired some warning shots into the air.

It was all over. The attempt to address the people and the Party had come too late. In the eyes of rank and file Party members, Trotsky was already an enemy, a dissident, a disorganizer and a counter-revolutionary. He and his supporters tried to lodge a protest. Muralov, Smilga and Kamenev on the same day, 7 November, sent a note to the Politburo and the presidium of the Central Control Commission, which said, among other things:

> In sight of Budenny, Tsikhon and others, militiamen and soldiers fired on us as we left (evidently in the air). We stopped our car. A group of Fascists, five in number, rushed at the car, using foul language, and broke the horn and smashed a headlight. The militiamen did not even approach the car. After the journey, we arrived at the apartment of Central Committee member Comrade Smilga. Since the morning, a

banner saying 'Carry out Lenin's Testament' had been hanging above the windows of the apartment as well as a red banner with portraits of Lenin, Trotsky and Zinoviev ... The affair ended with 15–20 commanders of the Central Committee school and students from a military academy breaking down Comrade Smilga's door, smashing it to bits, and forcing their way into the rooms ... The 'criminal' banner mentioning Lenin's Testament was also torn up. The soldiers who broke in took away the banner with the torn portrait of Lenin as a trophy. Desks, splinters, broken glass, a broken telephone and so on were left all over the floor, as testimony to these heroic acts in honour of the October revolution.

The note ended: 'The fate of the Party is at stake, the fate of the revolution, the fate of the workers' state. The Party will judge. The working class will judge. We have no doubt about the judgment.'[114]

Smilga later noted that the destruction of his apartment had been led by the head of the Political Section of the Red Army, one Bulin, and that he had been accompanied by the secretary of the Krasnaya Presnya District Party Committee, the Soviet chairman of the same district, one of Kalinin's assistants, and other officials. Preobrazhensky, Mdivani, Ginzburg, Maltsev and other supporters of Trotsky were beaten up in the attack. Smilga remarked that it had been a real pogrom.

Trotsky also wrote to the Politburo to protest against the scattering of the opposition's columns and 'the accompanying beatings'. The attacks, he wrote, had been accompanied by 'unbridled shouts of a Black Hundreds and partly antisemitic kind'.[115] He demanded an investigation, publication of the results and punishment for the guilty. None of these demands, of course, was met. Instead, on 14 November, at Stalin's behest, the Central Control Commission expelled Trotsky and several other oppositionists from the Party. This was the third arranged defeat for the leader of the opposition in 1927. He called it 'the downward slide of the revolution' which carried him down with it. The last, thin thread connecting him with official circles had been broken. The day after his expulsion from the Party, Trotsky wrote to the Secretary of the Central Executive Committee of the USSR, that is, the head of government:

I hereby give notice that in connection with the decision taken yesterday, 14 November, concerning myself, I have been put out of the apartment in the Kremlin that I have been inhabiting. Until I find permanent accommodation, I shall be living temporarily at the apartment of Comrade Beloborodov (3, Granovsky Street, Apt. 62). As my son is ill, my wife and son will remain in the Kremlin for the next few days. I hope to free the apartment finally not later than 20 November.[116]

Arrests took place and opposition meetings were banned, often resulting in clashes. The press put out the view that the Trotskyists intended forming a counter-revolutionary party to oppose the Communist Party. In these circumstances, Trotsky wrote a 'Statement of the Opposition and the Position in the Party', which was not, of course, published, but was duplicated and passed from hand to hand. The tone of the statement was calm and conciliatory. It said, for instance: 'The idea of the Stalinist faction is that, by expelling many hundreds of the best Party members, culminating in the expulsion of Comrades Zinoviev and Trotsky, the opposition will be forced to take the position of a second party ... The opposition will not let itself be torn from the Communist Party and it will not undertake to organize a second party.'[117] Alas, little enough time would elapse before Trotsky was indeed torn away not merely from the Communist Party, but also from Moscow, his homeland and everything for which he had ceaselessly exerted himself all those years.

Exile and Deportation

In order to avoid the humiliation of forced eviction from the Kremlin, the day after the plenum friends helped Trotsky's family to move (temporarily, they believed) to the home of one his supporters, A.G. Beloborodov. This was the self-same Beloborodov who in July 1918 had transmitted the Centre's order, known to and approved by Lenin, to execute the tsar and his wife and children.

Trotsky spent his time writing articles, composing instructions for supporters, sending telegrams and meeting friends who were being sent into exile. His wife gently urged him to leave Moscow for a month or so and live in a nearby village. He had so much writing to do, and sooner or later the leadership was bound to see that he was right and call him back ... She knew this was not so, but she feared for his health. He had lost a lot of weight, and had become hollow-cheeked and sallow. Ioffe's suicide that month affected him badly. The shot in the Kremlin, where Ioffe was still living – exile had already been decided for him – had rung out like a protest at the violence against the opposition, against the great idea and revolutionary ideals. Trotsky attended his friend's funeral on 17 November 1927, and despite the fact that it took place during a working day, a large crowd turned up at the Novodevichy Cemetery. After friends and comrades had given their eulogies, Trotsky made a short speech, which ended: 'The struggle continues. Everyone is still at his post. No one will abandon it.' The crowd accompanied him to his car, greetings were called out, but there were also many hostile looks. Squinting myopically, Trotsky waved his hand to the assembled crowd. It was his last public appearance in Russia.

That evening a registered official letter was delivered to him. Signed by Rykov, Chairman of the Sovnarkom, it was an order relieving Trotsky of his post as Chairman of the Chief Concessions Committee, to be replaced by V.N. Kosandrov.[118] This had been Trotsky's last official post, and although he was technically still a member of the Central Executive Committee, that too was terminated a few days later.

With this final and complete severance of his links to the system, he had to start thinking seriously about making a living. Writing would hardly achieve this, since all the publishers were slamming their doors in his face. The state publishing house informed him that they were terminating the publication of his collected works. Undeterred, he wrote to his old friend David Ryazanov, director of the Marx-Engels Institute, and offered to translate the works of the founders of scientific socialism. Permission was granted and an agreement made, and Trotsky began spending his evenings reading Marx's *Mr Fogt* in the original. He would put aside the book and pace his small room in rapid strides, five paces to one corner, five back. Wearing an old sweater, felt boots, his hands folded behind him, he looked like a prisoner in a cell. In effect, that is precisely what he was, since OGPU sentries stood guard at the door of the apartment and the entrance to the building. Stalin was keeping an eye on his defeated rival.

What Trotsky thought about during those long winter evenings of 1927 is not known. Perhaps he still hoped for some good to emerge from the forthcoming Fifteenth Party Congress; perhaps he thought about all the mistakes he had made over Stalin. During the civil war, he had on several occasions tried to have him removed from the operational side of decision-making, but had never succeeded in getting Lenin to bring matters to a head. He had once called Stalin 'a most dangerous plague, worse than any treachery or betrayal by the military specialists', but on that occasion he stopped short of demanding his removal.[119] One of his most serious errors of omission was to have agreed to Stalin's appointment as General Secretary, even though he had a better notion than most of the harm Stalin could do. He could have done more to halt Stalin's rise when he still had the time and the power.

As he was to recognize later, he had waited too long to make an alliance with Zinoviev and Kamenev, and he had always been hostile to Bukharin, whom he had seen as the personification of rightist elements in the Party. And he had considered the rightists as potentially more dangerous than Stalin, who generally showed centrist tendencies. As Radek would write to him in Alma Ata, 'centrism is the ideological poverty of our Party', and Stalin was its carrier. Trotsky took the same view, and had even been prepared to form a bloc with Stalin against Bukharin, who, he believed, wanted to 'restore capitalism'. Trotsky and his supporters had attributed to Bukharin, Rykov and Tomsky the chief roles in the formation of policy, and his memoirs suggest he never changed his assessment of the rightists. He had accepted as logical that either the left or the right could make an alliance with the centre, but a bloc of the left – the genuine revolutionaries – and the right – the restorers of capitalism – would be going too far.

Trotsky could not understand Bukharin's moderate line. For him, the left represented the natural expression of revolutionary purity. At the beginning of 1927, his commitment to forced industrialization at the cost of the peasant was undiminished, as he called for the resolute socialist reconstruction of the village on the basis of harsh pressure on the kulak, and argued to replace annual planning with five-year plans. 'A loss of tempo,' he noted, 'would mean the transfer of a certain quantity of resources from the socialist channel to the capitalist channel.'[120] If only Trotsky had had more foresight, he would have realized that Stalin was about to commandeer the entire programme of the left and use it to smash the right. What Trotsky regarded as impossible would come to pass: Stalin would move from the centre to the left, liquidating both wings in the process.

Pacing his room and rehearsing his mistakes, Trotsky must also have realized that the defeat of the opposition had caused his allies to waver. Zinoviev and Kamenev had told him that it was time to have the courage to surrender. Trotsky had replied that 'if it takes courage to surrender, and that's all we have to do, then by now the revolution ought to have triumphed throughout the world.'[121] One evening, they brought the drafts of two declarations for the Fifteenth Party Congress. Both contained expressions of readiness to capitulate. Trotsky agreed to sign one of the variants only after the insertion of a phrase on the right of every oppositionist to defend his views. And he added: '. . . it is self-evident that the freeing of comrades arrested in connection with their oppositional activities is absolutely essential.'[122]

Stalin's response to the declaration came in his four-hour speech to the Fifteenth Congress on 3 December 1927. Noting that the opposition had undertaken to abide by all the Party's decisions, he pronounced to stormy applause: 'Comrades, I think nothing will come of this trick.' After a pause, he added: 'They say they're also raising the question of reinstating expellees in the Party. Comrades, I don't think this will happen, either.' When the second wave of applause died down, he summed up his view on the opposition: 'They must renounce their anti-Bolshevik views openly and honestly, before the whole world. They must openly and honestly, before the whole world, brand the mistakes they committed, mistakes which became crimes against the Party. Either that, or they can leave the Party. And if they don't leave, we'll kick them out!'[123]

Returning to the question of the opposition in his concluding speech on 7 December, Stalin said: 'I have nothing of substance to say about the speeches of Yevdokimov and Muralov, as there was nothing of substance in them. The only thing to say about them is, Allah forgive them, for they know not what they are talking about . . . Everyone knows that Rakovsky made a fool of himself at the Moscow conference on the question of war. He came here and spoke, no doubt to correct his foolishness. But he ended up looking more foolish than ever.' The delegates laughed and applauded the leader's wit. 'I now come to Kamenev's speech. This was the most mendacious, most hypocritical, most crooked and fraudulent of all the oppositionist speeches given from this podium.'[124] The speech Kamenev had made at the previous congress, when he had declared that Stalin was not fit to serve as a unifier of the Bolshevik headquarters, was no doubt in Stalin's mind. Reading Stalin's speeches in *Pravda*, Trotsky must by now have fully realized that Stalin would forgive nothing and forget nothing.

After the congress the ranks of the opposition thinned even more. Some, like Zinoviev and Kamenev, degradingly begged for forgiveness, others simply gave up political activity, while still others were arrested and sent into exile. Either Sermuks or Poznansky would visit Trotsky every day to bring him up to date: Rakovsky had been exiled to Astrakhan, Smirnov to Armenia, Radek was still in Tobolsk, Serebryakov, Smilga and Preobrazhensky were about to be exiled to Semipalatinsk, Narym and Uralsk, respectively. Trotsky's assistants read more and more new names, but the places of exile were all too familiar from another age: Irkutsk, Abakan, Kansk, Achinsk, Minusinsk, Barnaul, Tomsk. He felt he would be sent into exile himself any day now, although at the same time he harboured a faint hope that Stalin would not bring himself to treat Lenin's closest comrade-in-arms that way.

At the end of December Poznansky was called in by the OGPU and ordered to take Trotsky an offer to move to Astrakhan. Trotsky wrote to the Politburo the same day to say that he was prepared to work anywhere in the country, as long as it did not affect his health adversely. He would not agree to move to Astrakhan, as its humidity was not good for his malaria. A week later a minor OGPU official summoned him and announced that his request had been granted and that he could go to a dry place instead. The official then read the order in a flat, impersonal voice: 'In accordance with the law punishing anyone for counter-revolutionary activity, Citizen Lev Davydovich Trotsky is to be exiled to the town of Alma-Ata. The period of residence there is not specified. Date of departure for exile, 16 January 1928.' Trotsky gazed absently around the shabby little room and left. He felt no twinge of hesitation or repentance. He had long made up his mind. He would stick to his chosen path.

Natalya tried not to show her feelings at the miserable news he brought home. Their host, Beloborodov, had also received notice that he was to be deported to some unpronounceable place in the Komi republic. The packing-up process began. Constantly visited by oppositionist leaders who were still at large, Trotsky excitedly issued instructions, dictated telegrams, wrote out protests, enquiries and statements, in an effort to show his supporters that all was not yet lost. The Party must wake up. The cause of the revolution must not be ruined.

As Natalya Sedova later recalled, the packing was completed by 16 January. Trotsky had been particularly concerned that all his papers, books and archives be packed. Sermuks, Poznansky and his elder son, Lev, put them into more than twenty boxes. In the morning, his two wives, the sons, Ioffe's widow and two or three other relatives waited for the OGPU to come for Trotsky. He tried to make a joke, but the atmosphere in the small apartment was tense and unusually quiet. Then Rakovsky arrived and announced that a vast crowd had gathered at Kazan Station to see Trotsky off. The militia couldn't disperse them. There were portraits of Trotsky and some of the young people were lying on the line in front of the train.

Finally, the OGPU called to say the departure was delayed for two days, giving no reason. Next day, however, a large group of OGPU officers turned up. At first Trotsky refused to open the door, accusing 'the present leadership' of a breach of faith, and when he had to let them in he refused to submit to their order to quit the apartment, calling it illegal. Several OGPU men then picked him up bodily and carried him downstairs to a waiting car. His elder son ran ahead, knocking on all the doors and shouting, 'Look, Comrades! They're taking Trotsky away by force!' A few doors opened a crack to reveal a frightened or puzzled face, which quickly disappeared. Finally they were on their way, driving through the frozen streets of Moscow, empty-handed and unprepared for the journey, and were delivered not to Kazan Station but Yaroslav Station, where there was no one to see them off. The agents picked Trotsky up again and deposited him in a railcar. Escorts stood at the windows and doors of the compartment, and the neighbouring compartment was also occupied by OGPU agents. 'Where were we going?' Sedova later wrote. 'We didn't know. Our baggage had not been brought in when the locomotive started off with our solitary car. It was two o'clock in the afternoon. We found that we were going by a circuitous route to a small station where our car was to be attached to the mail-train that had

left Moscow from Kazan Station for Tashkent. At five o'clock, we
said goodbye to Seryozha and [Beloborodov's wife], who had to return
to Moscow. We continued on our way. I had a fever. L.D. was brisk
and almost gay. The situation had taken definite shape.'[125]

Two days before Trotsky's deportation, Stalin had left for Siberia to
deal with problems of grain deliveries, having first made the necessary
dispositions regarding Trotsky. Central Committee Secretary S.V.
Kosior sent him a coded cable to report that his orders had been
carried out: 'It proved necessary to use force and carry him out, as
he refused to go, and he locked himself in his room and they had to
break down the door. We're arresting Muralov and the others this
evening.' Stalin replied: 'I received your cable about the antics of
Trotsky and the Trotskyists.'[126]

In my book on Stalin I outlined this episode somewhat differently,
but now that additional information has become available, the picture
can be more fully described. The Politburo discussed the question of
Trotsky's exile several times. Bukharin and Rykov were against it.
Stalin was for it, with Voroshilov's zealous support. The rest were
hesitant. The discussions were not minuted, but clearly Stalin got his
way: his constant rival would be sent to the Chinese border, although
evidently the idea of putting him outside the borders of Soviet
territory was still a possibility.[127]

Beyond the detailed account of the journey to Alma-Ata given in
Trotsky's autobiography, it is worth adding that the OGPU had set
up a large special section, with branches in the localities, to deal with
the mass deportation of oppositionists to the eastern regions. Any
former Party member who had ever uttered a sympathetic word about
Trotsky was now arrested, and the number of suspects being watched
grew apace. The first category to be arrested were those who had
worked under Trotsky in the Revolutionary Military Council, the
War Commissariat and his secretariat.

Sermuks and Poznansky were arrested in Alma-Ata. Theirs was a
sad fate, as I learned from Nadezhda Alexandrovna Marennikova,
who had worked in Trotsky's secretariat in the 1920s. Sermuks and
Poznansky, she recalled, were highly intelligent, thoroughly dedicated
to their work and utterly convinced that Trotsky was right. Butov
served more or less as chief of the secretariat. 'We typists got 40
roubles a month, a small sum even then. Butov once mentioned this

to Trotsky who arranged to pay us an extra 23 roubles a month out of his earnings from publishing.' Marennikova's memory was patchy, as she was the first to admit: 'I can remember which row in the theatre I sat in with Sermuks, but I cannot remember Butov's first name.' Her memories of Sermuks were especially warm. 'He was arrested in 1928. He wrote to me from camp. His letters were stamped Medzhvezhegorsk, Cherepovets. He was moved somewhere else in 1929. He must have destroyed my letters, otherwise I'd have been arrested too. Everyone I knew in Trotsky's secretariat was arrested. They got long prison sentences and concentration camp, and in 1937–38 they were shot. Someone was very anxious that no one should remember Trotsky. They hunted down everyone who had worked with him in the People's Commissariat, or who had known him. And an awful lot of people had known him, so an awful lot had to be exterminated.'[128]

At the end of January 1928, Trotsky, his wife and son Lev were taken to Alma-Ata, then a minor provincial town in the borderlands. They would stay there a year. At first they were put up in the Hotel Dzhetysa, then soon found a small house. Sermuks and Poznansky were with them for a while, but, much to Trotsky's chagrin, were soon arrested.[129] The family organized a simple life for themselves, and Trotsky threw himself into his work. Whatever the circumstances, his sharp pen was never idle, and letters and telegrams were soon flying from Alma-Ata to Moscow and elsewhere. He was trying to establish as soon as possible where the other opposition leaders had been exiled, so that together they could work out their future strategy. Soon Trotsky's modest dwelling was inundated with correspondence.

His son was appointed 'office manager' and kept track of the incoming and outgoing mail. Between April and October 1928, 800 political letters and 550 telegrams were sent, while more than 1000 letters and 700 telegrams, most of them signed collectively, were received. As Lev recalled in his father's autobiography:

> All this refers chiefly to the correspondence with the region of exile, but letters from exile filtered out into the country as well. Of the correspondence sent us, we received, in the best months, not more than half. In addition, we received about eight or nine secret mails from Moscow, that is, secret material and letters forwarded by special courier. About the same number were sent by us in similar fashion to Moscow. The secret mail kept us informed of everything that was going

on there and enabled us, though only after much delay, to respond with our comments on the most important events.[130]

And the events that were taking place were important indeed. A grain crisis was mounting, as the peasants were refusing to give up their produce at low prices. Even though the Trotskyists had been hounded out of the Party, the Politburo was split. Stalin espoused the leftist course that Trotsky had been advocating, while Bukharin and his supporters warned of the danger of trying to force the issue. When Trotsky read Bukharin's 'Notes of an Economist' in *Pravda* in September, he exclaimed: 'The capitulationists could win! The revolution is in danger!' Bukharin was claiming that it was possible for industry and agriculture to develop without creating a crisis. Grain prices should be raised and the one-sided and excessive transfer of goods from the countryside to the cities for the needs of industry should be stopped. Everything should be done to widen the peasant market and not to force the transformation of the village. 'The maximum number of economic factors that work for socialism must be set in motion and made flexible,' he wrote. 'This means a complex combination of personal, group, mass, social and state initiative. We have over-centralized too much.'

Trotsky sensed that Stalin was inclined to repudiate Bukharin and take the route the opposition had proposed: restrict the kulaks, accelerate industrialization at the cost of the countryside, and take extreme measures to get out of the crisis. Like other opposition leaders, he was amazed that Stalin was coming over to their side. Many believed, as they wrote in their letters, that this change of course and the clash between Stalin and Bukharin would end with their being brought back from exile. Something similar is detectable in some of Trotsky's letters to his supporters.[131] In conversation with the few emissaries who managed, semi-legally, to reach him from Moscow and Leningrad, Trotsky expressed the view that Stalin's 'leftward' shift of policy meant that the opposition's strategy had been correct. And he declared that Bukharin's policies and ideas were more dangerous than Stalin's peasant policy.[132] It seemed to him that Stalin's attack, against his own will, on the kulaks would bring the General Secretary and his faction onto the left wing of the Party. The Party still needs us, he declared, optimistically.

Trotsky's hopes seemed to have been justified when one evening he was visited by a young man, calling himself an engineer, who shared his views. He enquired about the life of the exiles in Alma Ata, and then asked outright: 'Don't you think it is possible to take some steps towards reconciliation?' Trotsky replied: 'Reconciliation is impossible, not because I don't want it, but because Stalin cannot make peace.'[133] The visitor left and did not return, but Trotsky realized he had been sent to sound him out. He also understood that Stalin could hardly be expected to make peace with the 'left' opposition, as it would be seen by the rest of the Party as an admission of error on his part. Gradually, however, he came to the conclusion that Stalin had accumulated his enormous power in order to get rid of first the left and then the right. While formally remaining a centrist, Stalin was able nonetheless to appropriate much of Trotsky's platform.

Stalin would never again think of collaborating with Trotsky, as there was too much mutual hatred between them. But Stalin's pragmatic acquisition of some of the opposition's ideas led to their reshuffling. The old Bolsheviks, for whom membership of the Party virtually bore a mystical character, were prepared to ask for forgiveness from Stalin's organization. Among them, Radek and Preobrazhensky were especially vocal, while Rakovsky was absolutely opposed. Trotsky had already noticed a shift in Radek's position. Only a minority of Trotskyists, predominantly younger people, did not trust Stalin, believing that having taken over the ideas of the opposition, he was realizing them by shady methods. The opposition continued to melt away. In the six months following the Fifteenth Congress, more than three thousand of his supporters officially broke with Trotsky.[134] There remained only a few small groups, mostly in the large towns, which continued their illegal activities, and the colonies of exiles who went on belatedly arguing about the fate of their platforms and themselves.

The defamation of Trotsky, meanwhile, went on undiminished. When Moscow Party Secretary Uglanov announced that Trotsky was continuing his oppositionist activity under the cover of 'an imagined illness', Natalya lost patience and wrote a sharp letter, protesting that 'the imagined illness' continued the lies which had been used to raise a curtain around Trotsky. Signing herself Sedova-Trotskaya, she demanded an end to the harassment.[135]

By the autumn of 1928, the flow of letters addressed to Trotsky had been sharply reduced. Many vanished without trace, one of them in particular of special value to him. He had learned during the spring, in a letter from his elder daughter Zina, that Nina, the younger girl, was seriously ill. They were both living in very harsh conditions, finding corners to squeeze into and suffering constant persecution. Both were fanatical supporters of their father, and both felt acutely the knocks he had taken. Nina's husband had been arrested and she had lost her job for her 'Trotskyist convictions'. She became seriously ill, but there was no one to help, except her sister. For any doctor to attend the daughter of Trotsky would be tantamount to signing his own sentence. Nina died on 9 June 1928, aged twenty-six. It was seventy-three days later that Trotsky was informed. His elder daughter was also ill, but he could not make contact with her. The mail from Alma-Ata took an age: each letter was read, analysed and copied by the authorities. A special OGPU group summarized the correspondence and reported to Stalin through Menzhinsky. As he read the monthly secret police reports, Stalin became increasingly convinced that he must put an end to any kind of political activity by the Trotskyists on Soviet territory.

Trotsky, meanwhile, continued to send telegrams of protest, knowing that nothing would be done. On 3 December 1928 he addressed one to Menzhinsky, with copies to the Central Committee and Kalinin, the nominal head of state: 'A total postal blockade has been going on for more than a month. Even letters and telegrams about my daughter's health and the medicines she needs and so on are being seized.'[136] His courier, a driver with a local organization, suddenly disappeared. They had been meeting at the public baths, where they had furtively exchanged packets of papers. The driver had obviously been followed and arrested, and Trotsky's supplies of information were now being strictly rationed.

During breaks from the work he was doing on translations, Trotsky planned a large autobiography. He tried out several titles: 'Half A Century (1879–1929): An Experiment in Autobiography'; 'Flood Tides and Ebb Tides: The Autobiography of a Revolutionary'; 'In the Service of the Revolution: An Experiment in Autobiography'; 'A Life of Struggle: The Autobiography of a Revolutionary'; 'To Live is to Struggle: The Autobiography of a Revolutionary'.[137] Eventually he settled on *My Life*.

When he was not writing, Trotsky engaged in his favourite pastime, duck-shooting on the tributaries of the Ili River, some seventy kilometres away. Eventually the local OGPU was instructed to restrict his radius of travel to twenty-five kilometres. He sent a protest to Menzhinsky: 'A month ago the GPU banned me from hunting. Two weeks ago they said permission had been granted. Now they've limited me to 25 [kilometres], where there's nothing to hunt. I think there has been a misunderstanding and I am letting you know that I am going hunting on the Ili, beyond seventy [kilometres]. I request instructions to avoid unnecessary collisions.'[138] Nothing came back from the centre and Trotsky ignored the ban. Hunting almost alone in the great unspoiled territory of Central Asia, he would for a while at least gain some perspective on the events he had lived through: the excitement of 1917 and the triumphs of the civil war, but also the pettiness and squalor of the fights with Stalin and his camarilla.

After a spell of hunting, he would return to working on several books. He kept going back to the book he had begun on Lenin, and he wrote a long article called 'The Permanent Revolution and Lenin's Line', an attempt to reinterpret Lenin's writings. But he was too late, as Stalin had already seized the monopoly on Lenin. Without fresh information from the capital, furthermore, he found it increasingly difficult to continue this work. The postal blockade had been intensified.

Bukharin, feeling Stalin's iron grip closing around his throat, had decided he should make common cause with Zinoviev and Kamenev and, perhaps, also with Trotsky. Throwing caution to the wind, on the evening of 11 July 1928 he called on Kamenev at his apartment with the intention of establishing illegal relations with the half-destroyed opposition. Bitterly he told Kamenev how much he now regretted helping Stalin to destroy the opposition. As Trotskyists later reported in a leaflet dated February 1929, Bukharin had appeared crushed, and was constantly repeating, 'Stalin is Ghengis Khan, an intriguer of the very worst stripe,' and 'the revolution has been ruined.' But he had no clear plan of campaign. He visited Kamenev on several further occasions, but no practical steps were taken.

The OGPU, however, had intercepted these contacts and informed Stalin. At the same time, Menzhinsky reported that the 'Bukharinites' had established contact with Trotsky, and Stalin now brought forward a decision he had taken long before. According to Ivan Vrachev – a veteran political commissar of the 1920s and former Trotskyist who was finally expelled from the Party and exiled in 1936, and who was almost certainly informed by Bukharin – in the middle of January 1929, Stalin spoke for the first time at the Politburo of the need to isolate Trotsky. Bukharin objected, and Rykov and Tomsky expressed their doubt over the wisdom of such a move. Others supported Stalin, but with reservations. Stalin then took from his desk-drawer a note from Menzhinsky giving the quantity of oppositional correspondence being sent to Alma-Ata, and details of the couriers who came monthly to Trotsky, and he read several extracts from Trotsky's letters, commenting angrily: 'The degenerate was kicked out of the Central Committee and the Party, but he hasn't learnt his lesson. What, are we going to sit and wait for him to start organizing terror or a rebellion?' The rest fell silent. Stalin announced his decision: 'I propose we deport him abroad.' Then, after a pause: 'If he changes his mind, the way back will not be closed.'[139]

The other members of the Politburo were thinking more of themselves than of Trotsky. They were all aware that their positions depended increasingly on Stalin's favour, and were contradicting him less and less. He always had a cast-iron argument: 'Would Lenin have been sentimental?', 'Doesn't the Party govern through the dictatorship of the proletariat?', 'What are personal relations compared to the interests of the revolution?' Bukharin was no longer arguing with him. Soon, in April 1929, he would hear Stalin accuse him – 'this scholastic theorist' – of becoming 'a pupil of Trotsky . . . [Yesterday] he was still trying to form a bloc with the Trotskyists against the Leninists by the back door!'[140]

Stalin had acquired vast power, but he was not yet a dictator. He stood on the threshold of the most appalling 'revolution' to be unleashed from above. Under the guise of bringing socialism to the countryside he would bring back serfdom or, more accurately, Stalinist bondage, which would enslave tens of millions of people. He wanted no one to get under his feet during this huge and ominous operation, but he could not yet bring himself either to kill Trotsky or throw him into prison. Instead, Trotsky must be banished. Efforts were made on Stalin's orders to find somewhere to send him, but without success. Germany, Norway, France and England were among the countries that would not admit the legendary rebel. Finally, Turkey agreed.

Trotsky was still awaiting a reply to his protest about the postal blockade when on the evening of 16 December 1928 a special messenger arrived from Moscow. Accompanied by two OGPU agents, V. Volynsky entered Trotsky's apartment and delivered his message from the Centre: 'The work of your political sympathizers throughout the country has lately assumed a definitely counter-revolutionary character; the conditions in which you are placed in Alma-Ata give you full opportunity to direct this work; in view of this, the collegium of the OGPU has decided to demand from you a categorical promise to discontinue your activity; failing this, the collegium will be obliged to alter the conditions of your existence to the extent of completely isolating you from political life. In this connection, the question of changing your place of residence will arise.'[141]

To Trotsky it seemed obvious that he was about to be sent somewhere more remote, probably Siberia above the Arctic Circle, but the notion that he might be deported beyond the Soviet border did not enter his head. He at once wrote a long and detailed letter to the Central Committee and ECCI, explaining why he could not accept the ultimatum, citing in particular his lifelong commitment to the world revolution. A month later, on 20 January 1929, Volynsky reappeared with a large detachment of armed OGPU agents and handed 'Citizen Trotsky' the order for his deportation outside Soviet territory. Having read the order, Trotsky acknowledged its receipt by writing: 'The decision of the GPU, criminal in substance and illegal in form, has been announced to me, January 20, 1929. Trotsky.'[142] When he asked Volynsky where he was being deported, the messenger could only tell him that further orders were awaited.

Again the packing had to be done, this time only with the assistance of his elder son, but together they ensured that all of his papers and books were packed. They were both surprised the OGPU had not confiscated them. Within a year or two, when Trotsky's written output was unceasing and prolific, Stalin would rant and rage against those who had let him take his precious collection with him. Several people were arrested, notably the Chekists Volynsky, Bulanov and Fokin. It was as if Stalin himself had not realized that in his totalitarian system a directive from above had to be carried out to the letter, and the order for Trotsky's deportation had said nothing about his books and archives. Since the authorities had not expressly banned their removal from the USSR, any functionary would assume it must mean they were permitting it.

Almost one year after arriving in Alma-Ata, the Trotsky family left their nondescript, one-storey brick house and boarded the railcar that had been set aside for them and departed for the unknown, with their guards. Every day of the journey Trotsky asked to be given some explanation, and demanded to see his children in Moscow, Sergei and Zina. He also demanded a guarantee of safety, being only too aware that there were countless White Guard men in the countries to which he felt he might be exiled – Finland, the Baltic republics, Poland, Germany, France and Bulgaria – men whom the Red Army that he had created and led had thrown out of their native land, made homeless and miserable and vengeful. They would not let him forget their misfortunes. Every morning began with Trotsky's demanding to know where he was being taken. Finally, he declared a hunger-strike. The train pulled into an out-of-the-way halt on a single track, the car was detached and shunted into a siding. Trotsky was of course not allowed to go to Moscow, but Sergei and his wife were brought to say goodbye. A day or two later, on 7 February, Trotsky was informed that he was being deported to Constantinople in Turkey.

Again he wrote a protest to the Central Committee, the government and ECCI:

1. The GPU representative reported that the German Social Democratic government has refused me a visa. This means Mueller and Stalin agree on their political evaluation of the opposition.
2. The GPU representative reported that I will be handed over to Kemal* against my will. This means that Stalin has arranged for Kemal (a killer of Communists) to deal with the opposition as their common enemy.
3. [Trotsky deleted the following point when the statement was issued to the press in Constantinople.] The GPU representative refused to discuss minimal guarantees against White Guardists – Russian, Turkish or any other – for my forced deportation. Behind this lies Stalin's obvious expectation of cooperation from White Guards, which is essentially the same as the already secured cooperation of Kemal. The state-

---

* The Turkish president Mustapha Kemal, or Kemal Ataturk as he became known.

Above left: Polish caricature of Trotsky during the Civil War.

Above right: White caricature of Trotsky during the Civil War.

Left: Trotsky slaying the counter-revolutionary dragon: poster by Deni.

Lenin's funeral, Red Square, 27 January 1924.

On Lenin's tomb, 7 November 1924. Left to right: Voroshilov, Trotsky, Kalinin, Frunze, Budenny and Clara Zetkin.

Trotsky and Stalin carrying Dzerzhinsky's coffin, July 1926. From left to right: Rykov, Tukhachevsky(?), Kalinin, Trotsky, Kamenev, Stalin, unidentified, Bukharin.

Trotsky with group of Oppositionists expelled from the Party in 1928. Front row left to right: Serebryakov, Radek, Trotsky, Boguslavsky, Preobrazhensky; back row: Rakovsky, Drobnis, Beloborodov, Sosnovsky.

Trotsky's last holiday in the Soviet Union, at Sukhumi on the Black Sea, probably 1927.

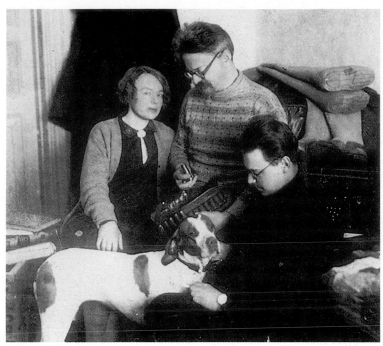

Trotsky with his wife Natalya and his son Lev Sedov in Alma-Ata, 1928.

Trotsky on Prinkipo, Turkey, 1929.

Trotsky depicted on a propaganda float in Leningrad, 1930, running at the heels of world imperialism.

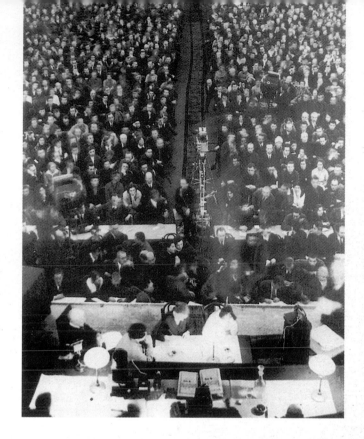

Above: One of the Moscow trials in progress.

Right: Anti-Trotskyist Soviet propaganda by Deni (following the Party line), 1930.

State Prosecutor Andrei Vyshinsky (centre) at the Moscow trials.

Workers demonstrating their support for the Moscow trials.

ment by the GPU representative to the effect that a 'security warrant' has been issued by Kemal for my possessions in exchange for my weapons, i.e. my revolvers, means I shall be unarmed while taking my first steps in front of the White Guards . . .

I report the above so that responsibility may be reinforced in good time and as the basis for the steps I regard it as necessary to take against this purely Thermidorean breach of faith.[143]

Moscow was unmoved: it must be Turkey. The train moved inexorably southwards, uncoupled and recoupled along the way. The family was not allowed to leave the train at any point. They reached Odessa on 10 February, where they took their farewell of Sergei and his wife. They would never see each other again. As he embraced his son, Trotsky said: 'Don't be sad, my son. Everything changes in life. Much will change even in Moscow. We'll be back . . . We'll definitely be back!' Chekist agent Fedor Pavlovich Fokin hurried them: 'Citizen Trotsky, it's time.'

Fokin, head of the passport section of the Chief Board of Militia, had the job of accompanying Trotsky from Alma-Ata to Constantinople. He regarded his charge with mixed feelings. Only recently, Trotsky's name had been spoken in awe, yet in the last two or three years the term 'Trotskyist' had become one of abuse at Party meetings. Fokin received the OGPU agents' report that Trotsky's luggage had been loaded, the trunks put in his cabin and the documentation completed. Trotsky donned an old topcoat over his worn-out sweater, picked up an attaché case with his most precious things, embraced Sergei and his wife once more, and set off towards the exit ahead of Natalya and Lev. Through the gloom of the unusually frosty night, they could discern the lights of Odessa, a city which had figured so large in his life. Holding his wife's hand, he went aboard the ship, just managing to make out the name painted on its hull, *Ilyich*.

As Trotsky took in the scene, he saw only a dense circle of soldiers. Sergei and his wife could not be seen; they had been whisked away at once. The steamer shuddered and moved slowly away from the quay. After nearly a day at sea, Trotsky sent Lev to invite Fokin to his cabin. Trotsky handed him an unsealed letter, suggesting he read it before passing it on to his superiors, and then added, 'I will not detain you.' Fokin went back to his cabin and looked at the letter. It was addressed to him, 'GPU Plenipotentiary Comrade Fokin', and read:

> According to GPU representative Bulatov, you are under strict orders, despite my protests, to put me ashore by force in Constantinople, that is, to hand me over to Kemal and his agents. You are able to carry out this order because the GPU (i.e. Stalin) has an agreement with Kemal for the forced settlement of a proletarian revolutionary in Turkey by the combined efforts of the GPU and the Turkish National-Fascist police. If at this moment I am compelled to submit to this violence, at the basis of which lies an unprecedented breach of faith by former pupils of Lenin (Stalin and Co.), I nevertheless think it necessary to warn you that the inevitable and, I hope, not too distant, rebirth of the October revolution, the Bolshevik Party and Comintern on genuinely Bolshevik foundations, will enable me sooner or later to bring to account both the organizers of this Thermidorean crime, and its executors.[144]

The letter was signed '12 February 1929, aboard the steamship *Ilyich* on the approach to Constantinople.'

On returning to Moscow, Fokin handed over Trotsky's statement to his superiors, but for some reason made a copy for himself, a fact he revealed to one of his colleagues at work. During the nightmare years of denunciation and counter-denunciation, this colleague informed on the 'Trotskyist document' that Fokin was harbouring, and in 1938 Fokin was arrested on Yezhov's personal order. He was chief of the Rostov militia at the time and was interrogated by Abakumov, then chief of the Rostov NKVD. The price Fokin paid for having kept Trotsky's warning was many years in the labour camps.

As the ship approached Constantinople, Trotsky drew up a chronology of the past year, beginning with the notice of his exile, supposedly to Astrakhan, and ending with his arrival in Constantinople.[145] It was a sad catalogue of his last year in his homeland, and the beginning of the last, eleven-year, chapter of his life. The man who with Lenin had laid the foundations of a mighty and sinister state system had been definitively rejected by it. Not because he was unsuitable, but because there was room only for one at the summit of the system. He was the first not to accept Stalin and his dictatorship. He was also the first to create and defend that dictatorship. Turkey would be the next place from which he would continue the struggle against the man who had betrayed the revolution and introduced the Russian Thermidore.

6

The Wanderer Without a Visa

As the *Ilyich* manoeuvred slowly alongside the quay, Trotsky had good reason to fear a trap. They could throw him into prison or send him on to a yet more distant country, but he was above all afraid that he would be a target for the White Guards who had settled in Constantinople after their evacuation by the Allies from the Crimea at the end of the civil war. Stalin may even have sent him to Turkey with that in mind. After all, since 1921 the Bolsheviks had been sending money to Constantinople for the purpose of spreading propaganda among these soldiers, and the mood among them was rabidly anti-Soviet and rife with the desire for revenge.[1]

Turkish authorities boarded the ship as soon as she docked on 12 February 1929. They found only the crew, Trotsky, his wife and son and four OGPU agents. Trotsky handed the senior Turkish officer a statement addressed to President Kemal:

Sir,
At the gates of Constantinople, I have the honour to inform you that I have arrived at the Turkish border not by choice and that I shall cross this border only under duress. Please accept my appropriate sentiments, Mr President.[2]

The officer folded the document and put it into his briefcase. On the quayside, Trotsky found an automobile and two surprisingly friendly representatives from the Soviet Consulate awaiting him. They installed his family in two rooms, brought in their luggage and generally displayed the marks of respect reserved for a high state official.

The future seemed uncertain. Trotsky at once started sending letters and telegrams to his many acquaintances in Paris, Berlin, Sofia,

Warsaw, Prague and London. He needed to know how he stood in the Consulate, how long he would be kept there, and what his family would live on. Just before the disembarkation, Fokin had handed him an envelope which turned out to contain fifteen hundred US dollars. Trotsky had been reluctant to accept it, but his pockets were empty and there was the family to think of.

They remained in the Consulate for about two weeks, at the beginning very much the honoured guests of its staff. But the atmosphere changed sharply for the worse once Trotsky's friends in Paris, Marguerite and Alfred Rosmer and Magdeleine and Maurice Paz, put the world's press onto him and his articles started appearing with an account of his deportation from the USSR. Soviet envoys in Paris, New York and Berlin now had to send a daily report to Moscow on what writings of Trotsky were being published, and what public and government opinion was saying about him.

Prinkipo Island and the Planet

As soon as Moscow heard about Trotsky's articles in the Western press, the Consul in Constantinople was instructed to suggest Trotsky find other accommodation, adding that he could remain for a few more days. Natalya and Lev starting looking for rooms, while Trotsky went on writing, meeting journalists and seeking channels of contact with his supporters in other countries. Messages of support and offers of help came from Rosmer and Paz in Paris, the critic Edmund Wilson in the USA, Sidney and Beatrice Webb, H.G. Wells and Herbert Samuel in England, among others. He felt much encouraged.

A few days later, however, the Consul asked him to leave and even threatened the use of physical force. On 5 March 1929 Trotsky issued a written statement to the effect that Constantinople was alive with White Guards and that he was being made an easy target for them. Sermuks and Poznansky had not been allowed to join him, and he accused the Central Committee of 'liquidating security for my family in the expectation that White Russians will take revenge on them.'[3] The Consul declined to accept this statement, as he was himself confused by the threatening telegrams coming from Moscow: he could not understand why there was so much anger and why Stalin was in such a hurry to deport a man who was better known to the world than the new master in the Kremlin.

Stalin was particularly irked by two articles which appeared in Paris at the end of February 1929. In one, entitled 'The Course of Events is Thus', Trotsky wrote: '. . . our attitude to the October revolution, to the Soviet regime, to Marxist doctrine and Bolshevism remains unchanged. We do not measure the historical process by the short yardstick of an individual life . . . I do not regard my expulsion from the Soviet Union as the last word in history. The issue is of course not about a personal fate. The paths of historical revenge are winding . . .' He then reproduced a long list of oppositionists who had been exiled and added: '. . . what is more important, however, is the politically indisputable fact that the services rendered by these exiles to the Soviet Republic are immeasurably higher than the services rendered by those who have exiled them.'4

The second article roused Stalin to even greater anger. Entitled 'How Could This Happen?', it represented the most savage criticism of Stalin yet published. Opening with the question 'What is Stalin?', Trotsky replied: 'This is the most outstanding mediocrity in our Party . . . His political horizon is extremely narrow. His theoretical level is equally primitive. His little book of compilations, *The Foundations of Leninism*, in which he tries to pay tribute to the Party's theoretical traditions, teems with schoolboy errors . . . He has the mentality of a dogged empiricist, devoid of creative imagination . . . His attitude to facts and to people is distinguished by an exceptional disregard. It is never hard for him to call white what yesterday he was calling black . . . Stalinism is above all the automatic work of an organization.'5 Stalin summoned Yaroslavsky, a member of the presidium of the Central Control Commission of the Party, and thrust Trotsky's article at him with, 'Read that and think of a way of replying to the swine.'

Trotsky meanwhile was looking for somewhere to live. One of the Consulate staff, who had served under him in the civil war, found an opportunity to let him know that the safest place to be was on one of the islands in the Sea of Marmora. The idea appealed to Trotsky, and by the evening of the following day the island of Prinkipo – Prince's Island – had been found, one and a half hours by sea from the capital. It contained a tiny fishing village at which once a day a small steamer called to deposit two or three passengers and collect fish. With the help of two supporters from Germany, Trotsky found a suitable old house in which the family could live and he could work, although he had no intention of remaining there long, and had already sent applications for permission to reside either in Paris or Berlin. In fact, the sojourn on Prinkipo would last four years.

Trotsky spent his time writing, apart from occasional fishing trips for which he developed a great liking. In a letter to Yelena Krylenko-Eastman he wrote: 'I have a big favour to ask you in the fishing area. Could you possibly buy me some line for underwater rods used for catching big fish? 200 metres would be good.' Six weeks later he wrote to thank her for the line.[6] But he needed money, as 'Stalin's gift' had lasted only a short time. Several donations came from the Rosmers and others, but they were not enough. He needed an income to support himself, his family and the two or three secretaries without whom he could not function, especially as he had now decided to publish a small journal of the 'left' opposition. He needed money, and only his writing could provide it.

Trotsky was well enough known for a host of publishers to want his work. He received $10,000 for his first articles for the *Daily Express*, *New York Herald Tribune*, *New York Times* and other newspapers. Soon he would receive an advance of $7000 from an American publisher for his autobiography, and for a series of articles entitled 'The History of the Russian Revolution' the *Saturday Evening Post* paid him $45,000.[7] While these were substantial sums for the time, they were all advances against books still to be written, and the writing of books is hard labour indeed. Fortunately, Trotsky enjoyed this particular form of punishment.

This was his third stint of exile. He still believed that either he would be called back to Moscow or that things there would change and he would be able to return, if not in triumph, at least with honour. Until 1934 he harboured the admittedly fading belief that the Party would not tolerate Stalin for much longer. The dictator must surely hang himself on the rope of collectivization and his struggle with the right. Meanwhile, Trotsky intended to do all in his power to debunk Stalin, to expose his limitations and the damage caused by his policies.

To increase the volume of information at his disposal, he sent his son with a fisherman he knew to Constantinople to buy a radio receiver so he could listen in to the crackly broadcasts from the USSR. In early March 1930 he heard Radio Moscow broadcasting a speech of Stalin's, published in *Pravda* as 'Dizzy With Success', in which the General Secretary stated: 'Up to 20 February this year already 50 per cent of peasant households in the USSR were collectivized. That means we have overfulfilled the five-year plan to 20 February 1930 more than twice over.' Instead of commenting on this success, however, the presenter started talking about 'bungled work', 'racing ahead', attempts to collectivize all and everything, and saying that 'such a policy can only be useful and good for our sworn enemies'.[8] Trotsky interpreted the article as a serious failure for Stalin and described the situation in a letter to his American friends: 'Stalin's new retreat, predicted so accurately by the opposition, will have major political consequences ... This retreat represents a savage blow to the revolution in general. The Stalinist faction will be severely shaken and there will be a new influx to the left opposition.'[9] Trotsky's conclusion was contradictory: on the one hand, he was claiming that a retreat from a left-wing policy would be unpopular in the Party, but more significantly, he seemed to forget that the power of the Stalinist organization, which had been the chief cause of his conflict with the leadership, could and would override ideological differences and rule by force. In other words, what he failed to consider was that, whether Stalin adopted a right-wing or a left-wing approach, he would carry the Party with him by means of organizational control.

After two or three months on Prinkipo, Trotsky and his wife could see how lonely their son was with nothing to do, and how much he missed the rest of the family. Letters from Moscow were few and far between, because they were being intercepted and retained by the OGPU. Lev was his father's pride. There was complete harmony in their political views, he had his father's combative character and the ability to grasp the intricacies of Party and international politics. After a long discussion, it was agreed that Lev should go to Moscow to see how things stood, and whether the rest of the family should remain in Moscow or try to join their parents. It was also necessary to clarify Sergei's position: he had become interested in science and was unlikely to agree to become a political nomad, like his elder brother.

Lev went to the Soviet Consul and requested permission to return to Moscow. He was promised an early reply, but weeks went by without news. With his father's help, Lev wrote to the OGPU, with a copy to the TsIK:

> On 13 July this year I made an enquiry at the Consulate General of the USSR in Constantinople as to whether or not, as a Soviet citizen, I require a visa to return to the USSR. The Consulate asked for my passport (which I surrendered) and promised to reply within a few days. A month has now passed. I applied to the Consulate a second time (on 8 August this year), also with no result. I earnestly request that you expedite this matter, as there can be no formal or substantive reason for a refusal. I have come here only temporarily, the family in Moscow is expecting me, and so on.[10]

The Consulate could, of course, decide nothing for itself. The bureaucratic machine turned slowly before Yenukidze finally informed Stalin of the request that had been made by Trotsky's son. Stalin merely smirked and said: 'For him it's all over. And the same for his family. Reject it.' The same day, 24 August 1929, Yenukidze told the OGPU to reject Sedov's application.[11] Now that he knew the way back home was closed to him, Lev committed himself wholeheartedly to serving his father, taking over the publishing operations, the contacts with the host of support groups throughout Europe and, finally, his father's personal security. Sermuks and Poznansky would, of course, have been of immense help, had they been allowed to join Trotsky. Instead they were moved from camp to camp and finally left to rot. Glazman was driven to suicide, Butov died in prison.

Two months or so after his first articles had appeared in Turkey, Trotsky read the Kremlin's reaction in the Moscow newspapers. *Pravda* published a statement signed by thirty-eight of his former supporters who now denounced him.[12] The heavy guns, however, were reserved for *Bolshevik*, the main theoretical journal of the Party, in which Yaroslavsky came out with two devastating articles. Trotsky had never liked Yaroslavsky. Even as early as the 1905 revolution he had thought him lacking in principles and prepared to serve whoever held power. Later, as the editor of *Derevenskaya Pravda* (Village *Pravda*), a member of the Party centre directing the uprising in Moscow, and First Commissar of the Kremlin, Yaroslavsky had displayed efficiency and imagination. When he began handling the history of the Party, however, he quickly revealed himself to be an obedient and nimble interpreter of Stalin's views. But he also supported Stalin's actions. Speaking in January 1938 at a Central Committee plenum, for instance, he 'reassured' his comrades that 'as well as our unmasked enemies, we are in a position to withdraw tens and hundreds of thousands of worthy people.'[13] For Yaroslavsky – Chairman of the Society of Old Political Prisoners, and of the Union of Militant Atheists, and of the Old Bolsheviks – the Stalinist terror was a natural extension of the revolutionary process. In 1936 a letter from Natalya Sedova, concerning Sergei and distributed to the leadership, ended up in Yaroslavsky's hands. He knew both of Trotsky's sons well, but he would do nothing for Sergei. His own death in 1943 would spare him the news of his son's suicide on 9 January 1947.[14] In 1929, he had no time for family sentiment.

With some disgust, Trotsky read Yaroslavsky's first article, 'Mr Trotsky at the Service of the Bourgeoisie, or L. Trotsky's First Steps Abroad', and then the second one, 'How Trotsky "Replies", and How the Workers Reply to Trotsky'. The terminology in both articles was typical Soviet usage of the period: 'Trotsky's calls for counter-revolution', 'a record of stupidity', 'the return to the Mensheviks', 'spitting in the face of the Soviet Union', 'the mischievous, renegade Trotskyist truth', 'Trotsky's utter intellectual bankruptcy and degeneracy'. It had become the norm to substitute abuse for argument. Claiming that Trotsky had exposed himself fully by accepting 'a large sum of dollars', Yaroslavsky added, 'the living political dead, the living renegade is negotiating the price of his slander', and concluded that, according to some sources, Trotsky had received $10,000 for his articles, while others put the figure at $25,000.[15] The second article condemned Trotsky simply for publishing his pieces in the bourgeois press at all. Yaroslavsky's sensibilities as a good Stalinist ideologist would not permit even the possibility of 'approaching the proletariat's class enemies and of using their services to publish such insinuations'.[16]

More important for Trotsky than replying to such hack criticism was the task of securing the regular publication of his *Bulletin of the Opposition* and its distribution in as many countries as possible, including the Soviet Union. He also wanted to establish a centre to focus the efforts of Marxists opposed to bureaucratic socialism, and to try to make contact with his supporters in the USSR. Rising from his desk after a long day of writing, and gazing over the calm sea burnished by the setting sun, he steadily lost hope that he would be recalled to Moscow and gradually adapted to the idea of himself as a man, as he put it, 'without a passport or visa'. For him, after falling from power, it was not enough to retire peacefully and write his memoirs, however. He had an aim, and it was to fight against his adversary in the Kremlin. He wrote to the Politburo that the opposition would not lay down its political weapons, but would fight Stalin to the end: 'Stalin's fate, as the perverter of the Party, the gravedigger of the Chinese revolution, the destroyer of Comintern and candidate for gravedigger of the German revolution, is sealed. His political bankruptcy will be among the most awful in history.'[17] Trotsky had chosen his weapons: political and ideological criticism, exposure of the Stalinist regime, establishing alternative structures to Comintern and struggling for influence among the workers of different countries.

Comintern, now virtually an arm of the Communist government in Moscow, was mobilized to use all its resources to discredit Trotsky as a politician, to compromise the numerous groups that were supporting him, and to conduct ideological war against Trotskyism on a broad front. Stalin also resorted to using White émigré dupes. Trotsky had always been known for his outright hostility towards the Whites. In September 1923, when he was at the peak of his power, he replied to a proposal by the Commander-in-Chief of Naval Forces, Ye. A. Berens, that Guchkov's group in Paris might be sounded out with a view to reconciliation: 'The talks must cease. Tell the negotiators that you regard continuing talks that will commit no one to anything as impossible.'[18] He wanted no truck with the Whites, and never changed his attitude. In November 1938, for instance, he advised his supporters: 'Assassins are being recruited from among the Whites . . . so you should under no circumstances enter into any kind of agreement with them . . .'[19]

The West responded to Trotsky's deportation cautiously, suspecting a trick. Russian émigrés saw it as a sign of a split in the Soviet leadership, a deep crisis and consequently, they hoped, the possibility of better times ahead. Two months after Trotsky's arrival in Turkey, Yagoda, Deribas and Artuzov, the high priests of the Soviet Inquisition, could report to Stalin, on the basis of reports from the Foreign Department of the OGPU: 'On 8 April P.N. Milyukov [former leader of the Russian liberals] gave a confidential speech in Prague in which he claimed that the Bolsheviks would fall this September and that it was now most timely to establish a Russian republican democratic party abroad . . . Kuskova, however, believes that there are no grounds for expecting a "big" revolution, but that the deportation of Trotsky may usher in a new and broader NEP which will give the country freedom of trade, labour and so on . . .'[20] Russia's former politicians had not taken long to become totally detached from the realities of Soviet political life.

Through its network of disinformation in the mass media, the OGPU let it be known that Trotsky had been deported from the USSR not as punishment for his opposition to the leadership, but in order to infiltrate him into the revolutionary movement in the West to revive it. This rumour was intended above all to inflame White officers against him still further.

As soon as Trotsky had settled on Prinkipo, he was put under Soviet surveillance, and strangers, who were neither journalists nor supporters, started appearing in the little village a few hundred metres from his house. On one occasion a certain Valentin Olberg urged Trotsky to take him on as his secretary, but was turned away after warnings came from friends in Paris. Olberg later gave evidence in the Moscow trials against Trotsky, Zinoviev and Kamenev.[21] Others offered their services as bodyguards, but Trotsky politely turned them all away. One night in March 1931, the house burned down. Trotsky wrote to Max Eastman's wife, Yelena, in Paris: 'Along with the house, everything we had with us and on us also burned. The fire happened in the dead of night . . . Everything, from our hats to our boots went up in smoke, including my entire library, although by chance my archive was saved, or at least the most important part of it.'[22] Later on, when he was in Mexico, he concluded that the fire had been started deliberately.

On the recommendation of Rosmer and Maring Sneevliet, a Dutch socialist, Trotsky hired two more secretaries, making five in all, and several bodyguards from among his most reliable supporters. One of them, a Dutchman called Jean van Heijenoort, remained with him until the last minute of his life and subsequently wrote a book entitled *With Trotsky in Exile: From Prinkipo to Coyoacan*. The Turkish government deputed half a dozen policemen to provide round-the-clock security, but it did not prevent the OGPU from maintaining its own constant surveillance on Trotsky's villa.

Thus, when Yakov Blyumkin – the assassin in 1918 of the German envoy to Moscow, Count Mirbach – visited Trotsky on Prinkipo en route back to the USSR from India, the OGPU knew about it at once. Blyumkin, a former Socialist Revolutionary and now a senior official in the OGPU, had reason to respect Trotsky, who had saved him from the death penalty over Mirbach's murder. The two men spent a day together, and when Blyumkin left in the evening, he took with him several letters from Trotsky, which he handed over to Radek on reaching Moscow. Radek advised Blyumkin to tell the OGPU about his meeting with Trotsky. Blyumkin left in a state of alarm and confusion, and Radek himself at once telephoned Yagoda and told him about Blyumkin's visit to Prinkipo, and also handed over Trotsky's packet, still sealed, to the security organs. Yagoda of course already knew about Blyumkin's movements.

Blyumkin was arrested immediately and shot a few days later, even though he was guilty of nothing more than having visited Trotsky, a fact he did not deny. When Trotsky heard what had happened, he wrote several angry articles, in one of which he declared: 'Blyumkin told Radek about L.D.'s thoughts and plans in the sense of the need for further struggle for his views. In reply, Radek demanded, according to his own words, that Blyumkin go at once to the GPU and tell them everything. Some comrades are saying that Radek threatened Blyumkin that if he did not do this, he would inform on him at once. This is very likely, given the present mood of this ruined hysteric. We have no doubt that this is what happened.'[23] Trotsky now realized that even contact with him was tantamount to a death sentence. He knew he was being followed and that he would be dealt with at the appropriate time. For the time being, he was saved by his convenient location and the security measures he had taken.

Soon, however, he read in a number of Western newspapers that a group of White officers, led by tsarist General Anton Turkul, had announced their intention of 'taking revenge on the Christ-seller and destroyer of Russia, Trotsky', and that they would put the blame on Moscow. There is no evidence that General Turkul had such a plan, but that was the rumour. Trotsky was convinced Moscow was establishing an alibi for itself and promptly, on 4 January 1932, sent the

Politburo a 'top secret' letter (by ordinary post), in which he declared that he knew 'about the work Stalin and General Turkul are sharing' against him.

> The question of a terroristic reprisal against the author of this letter was raised by Stalin long before Turkul: in 1924–25 at a small meeting Stalin weighed up the pros and cons. The main argument against was that there were too many young and dedicated Trotskyists who might react with their own counter-terror. I got this information at a certain time from Zinoviev and Kamenev ... Now Stalin has published the information which the GPU has collected about a terrorist act being prepared by General Turkul. Of course, I am not privy to the details of the scheme: whether Turkul will blame Stalin or Stalin will hide behind Turkul, I don't know, but someone around Yagoda does know. This document will be kept in a limited but adequate number of copies and in reliable hands in several countries. So, you have been warned![24]

Whether the Turkul 'affair' was a bluff or Stalin felt unable to 'reach out' to Prinkipo, Trotsky's days passed peacefully enough. He learned that Kamenev and Zinoviev heard about his letter to the Politburo and that they had reacted, as expected, by struggling for survival. They wrote to the Central Committee:

> Comrades Yaroslavsky and Shkiryatov have brought to our attention a letter from Trotsky of 4 January 1932 which appears to be a vile invention to the effect that in 1924–25 we and Comrade Stalin discussed the best time to carry out a terrorist act against Trotsky ... This is nothing but a disgusting slander aimed at compromising our Party. Only the sick imagination of Trotsky, that is totally poisoned by the thirst for creating a sensation in front of the bourgeois audience and that is always ready to blacken our Party's history with malicious words and hatred, is capable of dreaming up such a vile slander.[25]

Trotsky's letter was a blow to Zinoviev and Kamenev. Their position was shaky enough already, and now Stalin's chief enemy, in trying to strengthen his own security, was adding fuel to the fire. It was hardly ethical of Trotsky to refer to their past conversations, especially as his erstwhile temporary allies were bound to try to earn Stalin's indulgence by renewing their condemnation of Trotskyism. In any event, when they were accused three years later of involvement in Kirov's murder, Trotsky's letter would figure as incriminating evidence.

While he was adapting to the life of an exile, Trotsky did not cease his efforts to acquire the right of residence in a Western country, but nowhere could he find a government willing to accommodate the demon of October. Finally, in the autumn of 1932, Denmark allowed him and Natalya to come to Copenhagen for a week at the invitation of a student organization to give several lectures on the occasion of the fifteenth anniversary of the Russian revolution. He hoped he would be allowed to stay in Denmark for a long time, but the trip was not a happy one. He and Natalya were not permitted to leave their ship when it docked at Athens. In Italy they were allowed to disembark, but only under police escort. They travelled through France on a transit visa and were permitted to spend only one hour at the station in Paris. Obstacles were also placed in their path in Denmark, where Trotsky was under constant police surveillance, and where local Communists staged a demonstration against his visit. The monarchists also protested that he had been involved in the murder of the Romanovs, and the bourgeois press rehearsed his 'revolutionary sins'. The Soviet Consul demanded his immediate expulsion. Trotsky still managed to hold meetings with supporters from Germany, Denmark, France and Norway, and to give a number of interviews, but his hopes of remaining in Copenhagen were dashed. The Danish authorities told their 'guests' that they would have to leave when their seven-day visa expired, and so they did, retracing the journey to become outcasts again on Prinkipo.

Max Eastman's wife undertook to try to obtain a visa for Trotsky to visit the USA to lecture on the Russian revolution and the situation in the Soviet Union, but even before the formal refusal came, Trotsky knew it would not be issued. 'It was a mistake even to raise the question, given my present position,' he wrote to Yelena Eastman.[26] An attempt to go to Prague met a similar response. Forced to remain where he was, he set about putting his papers in order, the papers Stalin had allowed to slip through his fingers. Starting on Prinkipo and continuing in France, Norway and finally Mexico, he slowly worked through his speeches, orders, directives, letters and a broad array of documents, filing and annotating them in preparation for the literary work he saw ahead of him.

Already in March 1924 his assistant Butov had written a note to Glazman and Poznansky, asking them to begin sorting Lenin's letters and telegrams to Trotsky, which their boss needed for a book he planned to write on the late leader: 'I think the most difficult thing will be to find documents written by Lenin but located in secretarial files, i.e. non-confidential files, as there are so many of them. Lev Davydovich wants us to start collecting them without haste, carefully, but right away.'[27] Trotsky now leafed through all this material, feeling himself travelling back in time. One copy of almost all of the communications with Lenin was kept in the official archives in Moscow, and another in his personal archives. Among them was a note from Lenin in a file dated 1922: 'We're hiding my present location from everyone (including even [Dr] Guetier). I'm saying I'm in Gorki. Have you or Natalya Ivanovna said the opposite to Dr Guetier? If so, write to him so as not to offend him. If not, say nothing. If he comes to you, drop me a line.'[28]

Among the many notes from Lenin to Trotsky were also those dictated to his secretary Lydia Fotieva, or written by her. For instance: 'Vladimir Ilyich has told me to write to say he welcomes your idea of taking a gift from him to the children at the sanatorium at Podsolnechnoe. He asks you also to tell the kids that he thanks them very much for their cordial letter and the flowers, and is sorry he cannot accept their invitation; he has no doubt he would certainly get better being among them . . .'[29] Looking through his papers, Trotsky would also have come across a summary from a military tribunal reporting that 4337 men had been executed in the Red Army in 1921.[30] Or a note from Unshlikht offering him a place to recuperate: 'It is a two-storey house with ten rooms, Dutch heating system, good if variable furniture of Karelian birch, hand-made as well as simple. There are beds for seventeen bodyguards downstairs and seven upstairs, and five rooms for the Trotsky family. What is extremely inconvenient is that 1) the guards being downstairs will make a noise and disturb L.D., 2) the kitchen is about seventy yards away, 3) the telephone is downstairs in the room occupied by the manager, Shibanov, 4) there are no bells. If one needs something, one has to shout.'[31]

A note from Butov, dated 2 February 1922, reported that the Politburo administrative secretary, Comrade Buranova, was asking if he'd be coming to meetings and whether they should send him the questions the Politburo would be voting on outside its sessions. The note included a list of materials attached: a letter from Lenin, another from

Chicherin, material from Suvarin about the Communist movement in France, material from Profintern, his exercise book containing quotations from Shakespeare; it ended with a short list of papers that would be sent if Trotsky so chose, including a protest against the deportation of the Menshevik Sukhanov and an explanation of the arrest of one Comrade Borodulin.[32]

Butov had even sent him a copy of his own cardiogram, with the physician's notes: 'A heart attack occurred between 4 and 5 a.m. on 24 January [no year indicated], causing two brief blackouts. Arriving soon after the attack, I established that the heart was working quite normally. The same thing occurred the next day. L.D. felt some weakness for the next three to four days, but still went out, as usual, with his rifle. The weakness disappeared in due course and L.D. was back to his usual robust self.'[33]

Also among the papers was a note to GPU assistant chief Rudolf Gerson, requesting the chemical analysis of a packet of cooking salt, 'because the person who used it has had stomach pain for the last few days'. Gerson was able to report that the cooking salt contained 'a mixture of 3.71 per cent plaster of Paris and 17.25 per cent Glauber's salts [a popular laxative], and is harmful to the health and not to be used in cooking'.[34] A special commission was set up to investigate, but nothing came of it.

There was a letter in almost schoolboy handwriting from Raskolnikov, then the Soviet envoy to Kabul in Afghanistan:

> I have translated my latest conversation with Rabindranath Tagore and have started writing my reminiscences of the recent stormy years which you and I came out of alive by a miracle. Do you remember our night assault on the destroyer at Kazan when the boat died and we tied up to some barge or other in the light of the treacherous moon? The only reason we weren't shot at was that every last one of the White artillery officers was enjoying himself at the theatre. I'm now writing 'On the Eve of the October Revolution' and 'How the Black Sea Fleet was Sunk' . . . The Foreign Commissar doesn't seem able to fix a firm line . . . Either he empowers me to offer Afghanistan mountains of gold, or he orders me to give them the finger . . . I've established good relations with the Emir. He's a powerful politician and a decisive man, both in politics and in crime.[35]

As a member of the Politburo, Trotsky had received papers on every imaginable subject. He had kept his copy of the 'Manifesto of the Rightful Heir to the Russian Throne Cyril', signed in Paris on 31 August 1924. In it, Cyril listed the members of the royal family who had been murdered in Yekaterinburg in July 1918. In a phone call to Trotsky, Sverdlov had mentioned in passing that the Politburo had supported a proposal from the local Bolsheviks in Yekaterinburg to liquidate the Romanovs. Lenin had not objected, and neither had Trotsky, especially as the fate of the royal family had been a topic of discussion in the leadership on several occasions. They had wanted to take a decision, but it had never seemed the proper time. Neither then nor later did Trotsky ever express doubt that the decision had been the right one. What he thought of the murder of the empress and her children he never disclosed.

He could hardly believe it had all happened only ten years ago – the clatter of the wheels of his famous armoured train across the endless Russian plain, the Comintern congresses on which he had pinned such hopes, the death of Lenin who in his last months had seemed to want to tell him something very important. It was all gone. The only sounds he heard now were the lapping of a strange sea outside a strange window.

Deprived on 20 February 1932 of his Soviet citizenship, he was genuinely stranded on his lonely island and could do nothing but think about how to fight back. He and his wife still saw their present residence, the villa for which they paid around $4000 a year, as a temporary halt which they would leave any day now. All approaches seemed closed, until Maurice Parizhanin approached the former French premier, Edouard Herriot.[36] Permission for Trotsky and his wife to enter France was finally granted after many delays and disappointments.

Meanwhile, Trotsky's son Lev had moved from Berlin to Paris, where he had soon become an object of interest to the Soviet secret service. Through one Alexander Sevastyanovich Adler, an émigré from Leningrad, they had recruited an agent, 'B–187', whose name was Mark Zborowski.[37] Zborowski completed a number of questionnaires for the agency, outlining his autobiography and revealing that he had relatives in the USSR: two brothers, a sister and her husband, and giving their addresses. When his new bosses in Moscow, G. Molchanov and M. Rutkovsky, were informed that he had been recruited, they launched an in-depth check on his parents and his background in general.[38] Steps were now taken, in the summer of 1934, to infiltrate Zborowski into the company of Trotsky's closest and most trusted aide: his son Lev. Henceforth, many of the decisions, intentions, actions and documents emanating from Trotsky would become known to Moscow and to Stalin himself. Alexander Orlov (real name Leib Feldbin, aliases Lev Nikolsky and Igor Berg), a senior security official who had defected while serving in Spain, tried anonymously to warn Trotsky of the danger he was now in, but Trotsky never knew the truth about his son's new 'helper', who was in a position to feed Trotsky's mail and his writings straight to Stalin's desk in the Kremlin.

Who was this Mark Zborowski, thanks to whom Stalin was informed of practically every step Trotsky took from 1933 to 1939, even to the point of receiving books and articles before they had been published? Three days before he was assassinated in August 1940, Trotsky completed a long article, entitled 'The Comintern and the GPU', which was published posthumously. In it he correctly asserted that these two bodies were dissimilar yet indistinguishable: 'They are mutually coordinative, although the Comintern does not give orders to the GPU, rather the opposite, the GPU totally dominates the Comintern. Many Communists from different countries, being financially and politically dependent, carry out the shameful and criminal orders of the GPU.'[39] Mark Zborowski had carried out numerous missions already, as a member of the Polish Communist Party, both at home and abroad. He had been born in February 1908 in Uman in the province of Kiev and had emigrated to Poland with his parents in 1921, leaving behind in the Soviet Union a sister and two brothers. He had been imprisoned in Poland for organizing strikes, and with his wife, Regina Levi, had moved to Berlin and then Paris. Short of money, Zborowski was an easy plum for the OGPU agent to pick.[40] He was given the codenames 'Max', 'Mack', 'Tulip' and 'Kant'.

The Paris controller was soon able to cable Moscow:

> As reported, the source 'Max' has begun working in the Trotskyists'
> 'International secretariat', where the wife of Trotsky's son also works.
> [Lev's wife, Jeanne Martin, had left her previous husband, Raymond
> Molinier, for Lev.] In the course of his work, the source has befriended
> the son's wife and as a result has been transferred to the Russian section
> as a sort of personal assistant to the son. At the moment, the source is

meeting the son almost every day. We think this alone is evidence that your orders to infiltrate the source into Trotsky's entourage has been carried out.[41]

Moscow was delighted with this rapid success and signalled their agent 'Peter' in Paris: 'It is essential that the source "Max" strengthen his position in the organization. Give the source clear instructions on how to behave. Warn him not to undertake anything in the organiz- ation without your approval. We urge that he not go too far and thus ruin all our plans in this project.'[42]

'Max' soon earned Lev's trust so fully that he was granted almost complete access to Trotsky's papers. He was reporting regularly to Moscow about everything Trotsky and his wife were doing, as well as their intentions. Some of his reports were regarded as of special value. For example, after Trotsky's move to Norway, in the summer of 1935, the security services could not discover his address. The problem was solved when 'Max' sent Moscow an original letter from Trotsky to Lev which included Trotsky's address, as he was asking his son to send him the journal *Bolshevik* and other literature.[43] 'Max' eventually became entirely trusted by Trotsky and his son, as a letter from Lev to his father, dated 6 August 1937 – and of course copied at once to Moscow – shows: 'In my absence my place will be taken by Étienne [the name by which 'Max' was known to Lev], who is on the closest terms with me here, so the address stays the same and your missions can be carried out as if I were in Paris myself. Étienne can be trusted absolutely in every respect.'[44] Had Trotsky been aware of the web Stalin was weaving around him, he might have had a better notion of the police system he himself had been so zealous to create.

The One-Author Journal

Trotsky had hardly arrived on Prinkipo when he started to think of ways to bring out a small but regular journal. He was assisted in this venture by supporters, notably the Rosmers in Paris, but primarily by his son Lev. Trotsky established contact with the Spanish Communist Andrés Nin, the chairman of the Socialist Party of Holland, Maring

Sneevliet, the Belgian Van Overstratten, his French supporters Pierre Monatte and Boris Souvarine, the American socialist Michael Gold, and others who felt close to the Russian left opposition. Gradually, a number of tiny groups of Zinovievites in Germany joined him and sympathizers appeared in dozens of different countries. There was even a group in China, led by graduates of the Sun-yat Sen University in Moscow who had heard Trotsky speak while they were there.

Within a couple of months on Prinkipo, he was receiving visitors. They included those calling themselves Trotskyists, journalists, and some who, it later transpired, had been sent to infiltrate his household. He was often irritated by so many visitors and wrote to his son, then in Berlin, that he should prevent ordinary pilgrims, as 'these meetings exhaust me and take me away from my work'.[45]

Trotsky had arrived in Turkey in February 1929, and by July of that year the first issue of his journal appeared, called *Bulletin of the Opposition*, as unequivocal a name as it was possible to invent. He announced that the journal would be devoted to theoretical, political and factual articles about the Russian Communist Party, and to assisting the party of Lenin back onto the correct path. He promised his readers that he would examine problems of revolutionary internationalism and publish archival documents of the left opposition since its inception in 1923. A significant feature of the journal, which existed from July 1929 to August 1940, was that its chief, and often its only, contributor was Trotsky himself. It would be no exaggeration to say that he wrote something like 70 to 80 per cent of the entire contents of the sixty-five issues. (Some were double issues, which explains why the serial number reach 87.)

The journal was funded from Trotsky's royalties and from donations by supporters. Since he had no printing facilities of his own, it could only be produced where political circumstances permitted and financial arrangements could be made with printers where the journal's chief administrator, Lev, happened to be living. As the political situation in Europe was constantly changing, the *Bulletin* was printed in five different places. From July 1929 to March 1931 it was published in Paris. Lev then moved to Berlin, where not only were the terms better, but Trotsky's books were already being published, and there were contacts of sorts with the Soviet Union. When Hitler came to power in early 1933, however, Lev had to beat a hasty retreat back to Paris, where the next issue came out in March of that year. As the danger from Stalin's secret agents was mounting, the *Bulletin* remained there only until February 1934. Lev then moved to Zurich, but returned again to Paris in April 1935, where the last 'European' issue of the journal was published in the middle of 1939.

By that time, it was no longer Lev who was preparing the journal for the printer. He had died on 16 February 1938 in mysterious circumstances which, however, left little doubt that his death had been the work of Yezhov's agents. After the outbreak of the Second World War, the *Bulletin* came out in New York, which was chosen as being moderately close to its chief author, who was then living in Mexico. There was sufficient momentum in the operation for four issues to come out after Trotsky's death, and it then ceased publication.

Lev, as the chief administrator of the journal, was assisted at first by his father's strong supporter in Paris, Raymond Molinier, especially in financial and technical matters. Molinier engaged in commercial ventures of an unspecified kind and had wide contacts in the business world, a fact which for a time did much to alleviate Trotsky's material position. At first Trotsky addressed Molinier as 'my dear friend' and signed his letters 'With respect always'.[46] Then, suddenly, it all changed. Raymond's wife Jeanne left her husband for Lev. A scandal ensued and Molinier left the circle. Lev's new affair of the heart, however, brought him little joy. He was still receiving letters from the wife who had remained behind in Moscow with their small daughter, and who was now in despair. Furthermore, Jeanne turned out to be rather egocentric, which only heightened Lev's emotional distress. His only safety-valve was the work he did for his father, and here the hardest task was to find a channel by which to send a few dozen copies of the *Bulletin* into the Soviet Union.

The changes taking place in Europe and the USSR shaped the content of the *Bulletin*, which can be roughly divided into three broad periods. First, from its foundation until 1933–34, with the rise to power of Hitler and the consolidation of Stalin's position following the Seventeenth Party Congress in 1934. Many of Trotsky's articles on the German question formed the basis of his book on the German revolution. In 1932 he predicted: 'Fascism has not conquered in Germany. Gigantic forces still stand in its way. But if they are not brought into action, the irreversible could occur.'[47] During this period, the journal also persistently declared the need to return to the Leninist sources of Party life inside the country and in Comintern.

The second period of the journal, from 1933–34 to 1939 and the outbreak of the Second World War, was marked by Trotsky's stubborn efforts to create an alternative international union of Communists, the Fourth International. At the same time as the Stalinist bloodbath of terror was being perpetrated inside the USSR, Trotsky openly called for a 'political revolution' in the country and the immediate removal of Stalin.

The third and final period – one might say the unfinished period – is associated with the activities of the Trotskyist and other Communist organizations in the context of the war. The *Bulletin* formulated its unequivocal attitude both to Stalin and to Hitler, and defined the place of the 'Bolshevik-Leninists', as Trotsky dubbed his supporters, in defence of the first 'proletarian state' in the world.

The character of the *Bulletin*, of which we have given only the sketchiest outline, was conditioned not only by changes in international affairs, but also by the fact that after 1931 it became practically impossible to distribute copies inside the Soviet Union. By 1932–33, and of course later, showing the slightest interest in the journal was judged as tantamount to belonging to the 'Trotskyist bloc' and subject to punishment under Article 58 of the Criminal Code. Stalin himself was, naturally, immune from such sanctions. Indeed, B. Tal, the Central Committee functionary responsible for the press and publishing, ensured that the General Secretary regularly received a wide range of anti-Soviet publications, including Trotsky's *Bulletin*.[48] It was obtained from arrested Trotskyists and also by Soviet agencies abroad. The 'Sneevliet archive', held in the Party Archives,[49] shows that Stalin's secret agents kept Stalin fully informed of the contents of the *Bulletin*, well before Zborowski entered the scene. What he read there only inflamed his already seething hatred for the man whose deportation had been, in Stalin's own words, 'a big mistake'.

There were occasions when, thanks to Zborowski, Stalin knew the contents of an issue of the *Bulletin* even before it had been published. For instance, on 25 February 1938 Yezhov sent him extracts of two articles by Trotsky, dated 13 and 15 January 1938 and entitled 'Is the Soviet Government Still Following the Principles Established Twenty Years Ago?' and 'The Fuss About Kronstadt'. 'These articles,' Yezhov noted, 'are scheduled for publication in the March issue of the *Bulletin*.'[50] Trotsky had no conception that Stalin's tentacles could reach so deep. For his part, Stalin wanted to know the scale of the Trotskyist movement, its organizational scope and what it was publishing. In March 1937, the security organs submitted a list of Trotskyist publications abroad, showing that they amounted to fifty-four newspapers, journals and bulletins, printed in different countries. Stalin was surprised by the scale of these operations, but was reassured when told that most of these organs were published irregularly and only in a few hundred copies.[51]

Besides Trotskyist publications, there were also a host of other anti-Soviet organs published by leading émigré writers, Socialist Revolutionaries, Mensheviks and liberal politicians. Stalin issued his orders and the foreign section of the OGPU diligently collected and studied such publications, gleaning a mass of information about every shade of Russian political opinion abroad through its agents, who were as far as possible recruited from across this spectrum.

In his *Bulletin* Trotsky tried from the outset to report 'the revolutionary news from the USSR'. In the June–July 1930 issue, for instance, under the heading 'Letters from the USSR', he reported the beating of Trotskyists in a camp in the Urals, a protest from the 'Kamensk exile colony of Bolshevik-Leninists' and included an article entitled 'Stalin and the Red Army, or How History is Written'. On another occasion he argued, rather unconvincingly, that Soviet society was becoming 'bourgeoisified' because the number of workers in the leadership, already minimal, was shrinking, and they were being replaced increasingly by 'petty bourgeois elements'. As evidence, he cited the names of former White officers, all of them with unsavoury records, who had now been recruited into significant positions in the new hierarchy.[52]

Sometimes he commented on isolated facts. Having read in *Pravda*, for instance, of the disgrace of the poet Demyan Bedny in 1932, he wrote venomously: 'For a long time Demyan Bedny was dignified by the title of proletarian poet. Someone [the critic L.P. Averbakh] even suggested the "demyanization" of Soviet literature. That was supposed to mean giving it a truly proletarian character: he was a "poet-Bolshevik", a "dialectician", a "Leninist in poetry" ... In fact, Demyan Bedny personified everything in the October revolution except its proletarian current. Only the pathetic sketchiness, simple ideas and parroting of the [Stalinist] period can explain the astonishing fact that Demyan Bedny was called a proletarian poet.' Demyan Bedny, Trotsky concluded, had taken to the violence of the revolution 'like a fish to water'.[53]

The central theme of the *Bulletin* was, of course, Stalin, who was shown invariably in an extremely negative light, accompanied by devastating comment and ill-concealed hatred. Most of what Trotsky said of Stalin has now become common coin. For instance, replying to American friends about the part played by Stalin's minions in the murder of Sergei Kirov in 1934, even though he had no concrete evidence to go on, he wrote: 'There can be not the slightest doubt that the accusation made by Stalin against Zinoviev's group is false from beginning to end: in regard to the aim – the restoration of capitalism, and in regard to the means – terrorism ... Stalin is responding to Nikolaev's [the assassin's] act with intensified terror against the Party ... By following the tracks of the Zinoviev group, Stalin expects to reach "Trotskyism".'[54]

As he observed from afar, Trotsky came to the conclusion that Stalin was leading the revolution and socialism up a blind alley. True, his accusations included 'the return to the market', 'a shift towards a neo-NEP', 'the workers are paying for the mistakes in the country-side', and so on. In other words, he never doubted that the main danger for socialism would come from the right. But he was correct about one thing: '... after the assault on the left, sooner or later will come the assault on the right ... The chief danger for the USSR is Stalinism,' or what Trotsky perceptively called 'bureaucratic absolutism',[55] a term that probably better expresses the nature of the Soviet regime than 'the command-administrative system' which became current in the late 1980s and early 1990s.

As Trotsky rightly claimed, the use of force and coercion was integral to 'bureaucratic absolutism'. In every issue of the *Bulletin* he published the facts of Stalin's repression. More rarely he was able to include material provided by someone who had miraculously escaped, such as Anton Ciliga, a former member of the Yugoslav Politburo who had spent several years in the Gulag, and who recounted what he knew of the fate of many leading Bolsheviks and others: 'The OGPU-NKVD can repeat endlessly, automatically and without trial, sentences of imprisonment and exile for anyone who has ever been sentenced.'[56] Such testimony made a marked impression on Trotsky's meagre readership. The journal was generally passed from hand to hand and some of its material was reprinted in left-wing papers. The longer the *Bulletin* continued to exist, the more hatred it generated in the dictator, who on a number of occasions irritably asked his intelligence chiefs 'when they would end this slander of socialism?'[57]

As war approached, Stalin felt Trotsky's jabs with growing sensitivity. In the spring of 1939 Trotsky published two articles in a single issue which drove Stalin into a frenzy. They were entitled 'Hitler and Stalin' and 'Stalin Surrenders'. From Mexico, where he was now settled, Trotsky could observe the diplomatic game in which Stalin was engaged with Germany and the Western democracies. Each party wanted to guarantee its own security at the cost of the other. It was not yet clear how the game would end, but Trotsky declared that 'a rapprochement between Stalin and Hitler is most likely': they were two dictators who understood each other. Such an understanding, he believed, would be dangerous for everyone. 'Over the last three years,' he wrote, 'Stalin has labelled every one of Lenin's comrades-in-arms agents of Hitler. He has destroyed the flower of the command staff, shot, replaced or exiled around 30,000 officers [the real number was more than 43,000] – all on the same charge, namely that they were agents or allies of Hitler. Having destroyed the Party and decapitated the army, Stalin is now openly advancing his candidature as Hitler's chief agent.'[58]

Analysing the international situation from within his reinforced stockade in Coyoacan, Trotsky often indulged in wishful thinking, or saw what he wanted to see, including a place for himself in the great game. In January 1940 he published a routine article on 'The Dual Star: Hitler–Stalin'. Correctly defining the international situation, he noted that in the event of a war between Germany and the USSR, it was quite possible that both dictators would be swept away by a revolutionary war launched by their respective peoples. He quoted what the French ambassador in Moscow, R. Coulondre, had apparently said to Hitler on 25 August 1939: in case of war the real victor would be Trotsky. And he claimed, on the basis of a newspaper report, that 'Under the cover of darkness, revolutionary elements in Berlin are putting up posters in the working-class districts saying "Down with Hitler and Stalin!" and "Long Live Trotsky!"' He added, 'It's lucky Stalin doesn't have to black Moscow out at night, otherwise the streets of the Soviet capital would also be covered with equally meaningful posters.'[59]

At times, isolated as he was in his Mexican stronghold, Trotsky lost contact with reality. Still conditioned by the old dogmas, he believed that the world war might end in world revolution, and then the sixty-year-old revolutionary might get his last historical chance. Although he devoted most of his attention to his struggle with Stalin, Trotsky also persisted in his attempt to create an international Communist organization that could become an alternative to the one centred in Moscow. Thanks to his efforts, on the eve of the war Trotskyist groups were to be found in more than forty countries. They were, however, small in scale and quite unable to attract workers, not that this dampened Trotsky's zeal in any way.

The October 1933 issue of the *Bulletin* was devoted to the need to create a Fourth International, and all the articles were by Trotsky himself. Shortly before this time, Lev Sedov, representing the left Soviet opposition, and delegates from the German Socialist Workers Party and the Independent Socialist Party of Holland, signed a declaration outlining the principles of the emerging Fourth International, the basic one being that the Third International was incapable of carrying out its historic role. Commenting on this document in 'The Class Character of the Soviet State', Trotsky drew a number of conclusions. He stressed that the Twelfth Party Congress had been 'the last congress of the Bolshevik Party. The subsequent congresses have all been bureaucratic parades ... No normal "constitutional" paths for the removal of the governing clique now remain. The only way to compel the bureaucracy to hand over power to the proletarian vanguard is by force.' Stalin would henceforth use this assertion on every possible occasion to justify his mass terror, by accusing Trotsky of trying to change the existing system in the USSR by forceful means.

Trotsky, however, remained true to himself. In demonstrating the timeliness of the Fourth International, he was simultaneously asserting that 'only in the circumstances of the victorious development of world revolution is the root-and-branch reform of the Soviet state possible.'[60] Now a new ingredient was added to the older idea of the inevitability of world revolution: that it was permissible to use force to get rid of 'bureaucratic absolutism' in the USSR, to create a new party in a state that would itself have been reformed fundamentally. It was the task of the Fourth International to accomplish all these aims.

Writing in 1933, Trotsky realized that the parties and groups that shared his views were not all ready to join the new International. He was seriously committed to the idea, but he could not undertake the work of organization openly, as he was being hunted by Stalin's intelligence agents, as well as those of Comintern. Since there were many foreign Communist and labour parties which were prepared to help Stalin neutralize Trotsky, he had to observe extreme caution and secrecy. The founding congress of the Fourth International did not take place until September 1938, calling itself at Trotsky's suggestion the World Party of Social Revolution. While Trotsky's prognoses about Stalin and Stalinism were on the whole accurate, as far as the Fourth International was concerned, he obviously misjudged the position.

In October 1938 in Coyoacan, Trotsky recorded a speech on a gramophone record for a meeting of Trotskyists in New York, which he concluded by declaiming: '[In] the course of the next ten years the programme of the Fourth International will become the programme of millions, and these revolutionary millions will be able to take heaven and earth by storm!' So firm were his convictions that his supporters began to believe his ideas had a future.

In his *Bulletin* Trotsky was merciless in exposing the torchbearers of the coming war, but he looked upon the danger from his revolutionary ivory tower. 'It would be immeasurably better,' he wrote, 'if the proletarian revolution had prevented the war. But that did not happen and the chance of it happening is, frankly speaking, not great. The war is coming faster than new cadres of the proletarian revolution are being formed.' He concluded: 'Never has historical determinism taken on such fatal form as now: all the forces of old society, whether Fascism or democracy or social-patriotism or Stalinism, are equally afraid of the war and are equally heading for war.' These were not the sober views of an intellectual innovator, but the feelings of a fanatical revolutionary. 'Nothing will help them,' he wrote. 'They have provoked the war and they will be swept away by it. They have fully deserved it.'[61] Thus, Trotsky. When analysing general questions of civilization and society, he was a prophet and dialectician; when the issue was world revolution, a metaphysician and utter fanatic.

Although his financial position was chronically straitened, Trotsky bore all the costs of publishing the *Bulletin*, as well as providing for his family and two or three secretaries who doubled as his guards, out of his royalties. These were just sufficient for printing not more than a thousand copies per issue, and the journal produced no income whatever. The correspondence with his son and with his publishers shows how carefully he had to watch the marks, dollars and francs. Lev wrote to him from Berlin: '650 copies of the History have been sent out, and 2400 of the Autobiography. This is a record. No other Russian book has had such a print-run abroad. On 10 August they'll pay 500 marks for the History and the remaining 1,500 on publication ... I've received another 30 marks, but that crook Fuchtman hasn't sent any more ... Petropolis [the publishers] will print the index but don't want to pay ... I think they ought to pay at least 150–200 marks and I'm going to press them to do so ...'[62]

After the death of Lev in 1938, things became even harder for the journal. On the anniversary of his death Trotsky wrote: 'In constant danger from the GPU agents who followed on his heels, he knew he would die and his main concern was to ensure the future of the *Bulletin*. Its future and who would replace him troubled Sedov more than anything.'[63]

It had proved extremely difficult to distribute the *Bulletin* in the USSR. Only a few odd issues found their way there after 1933, brought in under diplomatic cover or smuggled in through merchant navy channels. It was therefore unknown to the Communist Party with the exception of a few NKVD officials and Stalin's entourage. The NKVD did its best to hamper publication of the journal and even to influence its contents. Since Trotsky's articles were sent to Lev in Paris, and thus came into Zborowski's hands, it was decided in Moscow that an attempt should be made to alter and distort the sense of some of his writings, and even to include in the journal material written by the NKVD. The following is a coded telegram from Moscow to Paris, from 'Oleg' to 'Peter':

Further to our telegram No. 969 about slipping into the next issue of the *Bulletin* a few articles or paragraphs, it is essential that the following be borne in mind. There are two possibilities: first, to insert our articles under L.D.'s name, and second, to dilute all the articles with our paragraphs. Which choice shall we make? We think the second, but it is the more difficult one, as our insertions have to be done so well that the article should not lose its meaning, while clearly unmasking the face of Trotskyism . . . The first choice is easier, but it gives the publisher the trump card of being able to find us out during the typesetting. The articles cannot pass us by, they will come to us via 'Mack', but all this has to be done without blowing his cover, so it is essential that we recruit the printer.[64]

In fact, the Soviet secret service was unable to put the plan into effect, thanks to the vigilance of L. Estrin, who read the proofs for the *Bulletin*. Estrin, a female assistant of Lev's who was identified in OGPU correspondence as 'Neighbour', was a relation of the Menshevik leader Fedor Dan, and had been working in the Mensheviks' organization abroad for some time. Then she became closely acquainted with Lev, and began working for the Trotskyists. She met Dan on several occasions, and he tried in vain to alter her political views. Like Dan and the rest of the Menshevik leaders abroad, Estrin knew perfectly well that she was under surveillance by the OGPU-NKVD. The blanket watch kept on this group of Russian Social Democrats is noted in a special report to Moscow by the secret service in Paris.[65] In another report from Paris of July 1939, agent 'Ajax' gave details of Dan's relatives in the USSR: his brother M. Gurvich, his nephew L. Gurvich, his wife's relatives the Tsederbaums (she was Martov's sister) and Kranikhfelds. It was also noted that Dan received news of his family from Yekaterina Peshkova* when she travelled abroad.[66]

After Lev's death the *Bulletin* started appearing on the American continent, as NKVD 5th Section security agent Gusakov reported, adding that its publisher in New York was Sara Weber, who had visited Trotsky on Prinkipo.[67] The deputy chief of the 5th Section, P.A. Sudoplatov, reported that the journal of the Fourth International, currently being printed in Paris by the French section of the Popular Revolutionary Party (a Trotskyist grouping), would be coming out in

---

* Peshkova was a leading figure in the Political Red Cross, which tried, mostly in vain, to intercede for writers and intellectuals who were in trouble with the authorities.

Brussels from July, edited by individuals identified as S. Lesual and Don.[68] The Soviet secret service knew practically everything about the Trotskyists, their organizations and their publications. In March 1937 the chief of the 7th Section of the NKVD security service sent Yezhov a highly detailed list of all the Trotskyist publications in all countries and continents, and outlined their main contents.[69]

After Lev's death Trotsky maintained contact with his circle, especially Estrin and Zborowski. 'Dear Comrades,' he wrote, 'I enclose material for the *Bulletin*. If there's too much, you don't have to print all these articles and commentaries, just a part. You can delete the signatures under the articles, but the dates must definitely be left in. We are not replying yet to your letter about Lev; we still have to find the strength. N[atalya] Iv[anovna Sedova] is very weak and cannot write at all. What are the material possibilities and outlook for the *Bulletin*?'[70] One way or the other, the journal had to survive the death of its manager and chief administrator.

Family Tragedy

It was dangerous to be a relative of Trotsky's. This became clear as early as the civil war. In February 1920 a coded message was sent by the Odessa revolutionary committee to his armoured train: 'In December 1919 on Denikin's orders Comrade Trotsky's family was arrested, including his uncle and aunt Gersh and Rakhiel Bronstein, who were arrested in Bobrinets, and his cousin Lev, a Communist. They have been transported to Novorossiisk as hostages. According to some reports, they are being exchanged for Kolchak's nephew. Relatives of those arrested are asking for urgent measures to be taken to effect their release by means of exchanging hostages.'[71] Trotsky did not see the telegram as he was at the front, but Butov took the necessary measures.

Trotsky's closest relatives watched his meteoric rise with joy. Until the emergence of the left opposition in 1923, the slightest connection with the Bronshtein-Trotsky clan or acquaintanceship with his relatives gave the revolutionary young a reverential thrill and a feeling of being close to something great. The number of his relatives grew, most of them completely new to him. On 2 August 1921, for example, he received a letter: 'I am M.L. Ginzburg of Yekaterinoslav (husband of your cousin Olga Lvovna, née Zhivotovskaya), and I need to see you on a matter of great urgency to me, so I beg you not to refuse to give me a few minutes of your time.'[72] It transpired that the Ginzburgs were being persecuted and living in poverty.

Trotsky's daughters, Nina and Zina, did their best to defend their father when the press starting attacking him. They rarely asked him for material help, although they always lacked money. His two families – the two daughters from his first wife, Alexandra Sokolovskaya, and two sons from his second wife, Natalya Sedova – were Trotsky's personal drama. The two wives felt a strong mutual hostility, and he had to exercise considerable tact to avoid arousing an outburst of female emotion. He occasionally remembered to send a birthday card to his daughters, but took virtually no part in their upbringing. They nevertheless grew up with a strong sense of pride in their famous father, even though they also harboured resentment against both of their parents for their ambiguous position and the feeling of inferiority it engendered.

The younger daughter, Nina, died in June 1928, when Trotsky was in exile in Alma Ata. She was twenty-six. Her husband, Nevelson, had already been arrested and would eventually be shot. Apart from her sister, Nina received help from no one. The stigma of having a rebellious father worsened her situation and hastened her death, although her tuberculosis no doubt saved her from prison and the Gulag. Her daughter Volina, born in 1925, may have been with her grandmother, Sokolovskaya, but when she in turn was arrested and exiled the child disappeared without trace and her fate is unknown. She may still be alive, having survived the orphanages without knowing either her real name or origin. As we have seen, Trotsky learnt of Nina's death only several weeks after the event, and it hurt him to know that its main cause was his defeat in the political struggle. His elder daughter Zina had sent him a telegram: 'Nina is calling for you all the time, hoping that if she sees you she will get better.' It arrived seventy-three days after it was sent, when Trotsky was under guard. Nina's death heralded the start of a long series of deaths in Trotsky's family.

Zinaida, in whose arms Nina had died, was broken by the dramatic change in the family's circumstances, her father's exile, the arrest of her husband Platon Volkov, the death of her sister, her son's illness and the dire need and rejection which had become her lot. As if all this were not enough, she too suffered from tuberculosis. She began to make efforts to go to Trotsky in Turkey and, after a long ordeal and humiliation, she finally succeeded in obtaining permission and in early 1931 arrived with her son on Prinkipo. By this time, however, she was plainly showing signs of psychological instability, having, like her sister, lived for the last few years in a state of mortal terror. In addition to her tuberculosis, she became deeply depressed and suffered anxiety attacks. She missed the daughter she had left behind in Moscow and she did not know what was happening to her husband. She felt her presence was a burden to her father. She stayed with him on Prinkipo for ten months, but during that time no deep feeling developed between them. She was eager to help him in his political work, but he, aware that she must one day return to her daughter in Russia, kept her, for her own sake, at a distance in that sphere. Furthermore, despite his best efforts, the ill-concealed hostility between his second wife and his daughter remained as a barrier.

Although Trotsky was troubled by his lack of fatherly affection for his elder daughter, it seemed he could do nothing about it. She, feeling unwanted and unloved, competed for his affection with her stepmother, and the atmosphere in the home became unbearably strained. Finally, Zinaida took her father's advice to seek treatment in Berlin, and, after considerable efforts on his part, she left her six-year-old son Seva temporarily with him and went to the German capital, with return to the USSR ultimately in view. Requesting a re-entry visa for her from the Turkish foreign minister, Trotsky wrote: 'In order to avoid any misunderstanding, I think I ought to point out that the journey my seriously sick daughter is making is not connected directly or indirectly with any political purpose and is purely in her therapeutic interests.'[73]

Soon after Zinaida began her treatment in Berlin Trotsky received a letter from his friend Alexandra Ramm, who had undertaken to look after his daughter. She wrote that 'Zina's condition is complicated not only by the lung disease, but above all by her psychological state . . . It undoubtedly started in Constantinople. She went there full of the greatest expectations of her famous father and so on, but soon suffered deep disappointment. This expressed itself as, they don't love me. Who's to blame? Apart from that, she feels she is alone and sick. Her sister died. Constant illness . . .'[74] Alexandra Ramm was right. The chief cause of Zinaida's illness was that she was alone. Her father was cold to her, her husband had been arrested, her daughter was in Moscow. Ramm went on: 'Dear Lev Davydovich, I don't want to hide my personal thoughts from you. In a sense she has been disappointed here, too. She thought she would enter Lev and Jeanne's life here. That hasn't happened, nor could it. She said to me once, don't you know a man or woman with nothing to do who could visit me, it's so hard for me to be alone.'[75]

In about a dozen letters, Lev wrote in a similar vein to his father:

> Zina remembers a lot and talks about Nina's death . . . She was count-ing very much on your writing to her yourself . . . She is more depressed than she has ever been. She doesn't attack Mama [Natalya], but she says you cannot write to her and that you won't and she understands that. Zina is terribly oppressed, depressed, she looks utterly destroyed, I pity her, Daddy, very, very much. It's painful to look at her. I talked to Dr Mai in detail. He thinks she could return to the [Soviet] Union in eight to ten weeks. He says she needs more tenderness. In other words he gave me to understand that he thinks it very important for you to write to her and to exert a direct influence. Maybe her last postcard to you will give you the opportunity? The line I am taking with her (one has to take her condition into account) is that she herself, by her own behaviour, with facts, the nature of her letters and so on, must create the preconditions for establishing normal relations with you. She responds with utter pessimism: 'No, you know what I've done to Papa, he'll never write to me.'[76]

In none of the archives where Trotsky's papers are held has it proved possible to trace a single letter from him to his tormented elder daughter. Perhaps, had he written to her, her life might not have ended as tragically as it did, but his hardness towards her proved too much. Father and daughter were separated by a barrier of incom-patibility which he, as the father, ought to have sought to overcome. Perhaps his heart had been hardened by the revolution, or, having left his daughters with their mother so early in their lives, he could not find in himself any fatherly feelings towards them. Be that as it may, soon after Zinaida arrived in Berlin she suffered another blow, and a blow that could not be remedied: on 20 February 1932 the

Soviet government deprived not only Trotsky of his Soviet citizenship, but also his wife and all the members of his family who were abroad on that day. On 26 February Trotsky wrote to Yelena Eastman-Krylenko, suggesting that perhaps her brother, Nikolai Krylenko, might take an interest in the case.[77] Krylenko was People's Commissar for Justice of the RSFSR, i.e. of the Russian Republic rather than the Soviet Union, though he would have only two more years in the job, as he was shot in 1938.

Zina had been bursting to go home to the Soviet Union, to her daughter Alexandra, and to be reunited with her husband who was then in exile. Despite the fact that Trotsky had managed to organize the return of her son Seva (his full name was Vsevolod) to her in Berlin – he too had been deprived of his Soviet passport – she became still more depressed. She could not take the last blow: at the insistence of the Soviet embassy, only one week after Seva arrived, the German police ordered Zina and her son to leave Berlin. She had no passport and no money. Where was she to go? On 5 January 1933, she left Seva with some neighbours and turned on the gas in her apartment. She was just over thirty. Seva was adopted by Lev and now calls himself Esteban.

A week later Lev wrote to his parents with the details:

> The morning before, Zina phoned me to say she wanted to see me, she asked me to come straight away (our slight estrangement disappeared once Seva arrived). There was simply no way I could go that morning. I urged her to come over that evening or during the day or any other morning: I insisted and she replied with some reluctance but promised to come. I never saw her again. Platon [her husband] must be written to, he loved Zina very much. If it's too much for Papa to do, I'll write, but at least give me some advice . . . [The] world's press has already reported the death of Trotsky's second daughter.[78]

Trotsky was shaken by what had happened in Berlin. He had lost both his daughters in less than eight years. Their health and their mental states had been too unstable to withstand their father's defeat, and he knew it. His immediate reaction to the news was to write in anger to the Communist Party leadership in the USSR:

> The persecution . . . of my daughter was completely senseless politically. Depriving her of her citizenship, taking away her last remaining

hope; allowing her to live normally and recuperate and then to expel her from Berlin (obviously the German police were doing Stalin a favour) were politically pointless acts of naked revenge and nothing more. My daughter knew what was happening to her. She knew that, in the hands of European police who were tormenting her to gratify Stalin, she had no hope . . . I will restrict myself to this communication without further comment. The time for comment will come.[79]

Lev succeeded against the odds in getting through to his younger brother Seryozha in Moscow by telephone, and Seryozha duly reported the tragic news to Zina's mother in Leningrad. Alexandra Sokolovskaya was not yet sixty, but when she heard about Zina's death she turned into an old woman overnight. She now took on the care of her grandchildren. In one of Zina's last letters, Alexandra Sokolov-skaya had been bitterly reproached for not having been able to keep the family together and for making them all miserable. Trotsky had heard the same thing from his elder daughter. The wife of Trotsky's younger son, Olga Eduardovna Grebner, was right when she told me: 'Regardless of what he would have wanted, Trotsky brought grief to all his family and relatives.' His grandchildren were not spared. Nina's daughter Volina, as we have suggested, disappeared into the Soviet orphanage system, while Zina's daughter Alexandra was sent into the Gulag when she reached maturity. She died in 1989. Seva-Esteban now lives in Mexico, where he is the curator of the museum devoted to his grandfather.

Trotsky knew that Stalin would not stop. Although he became accustomed to life on Prinkipo, it was difficult to keep in touch with his supporters, hard to publish the *Bulletin* and, in case of emergency, difficult to hide or escape. He felt Yagoda's agents closing in on the villa and he longed to move to Western Europe. He had tried as early as 1929 to gain entry to a European country, but first Germany and then England, after some hesitation, declined his application. He had written for help to a number of luminaries of the British left, such as the Webbs, George Bernard Shaw, Harold Laski, and Labour Cabinet Ministers, including the Chancellor of the Exchequer, Philip Snowden, reminding him that he had received him in the Soviet Union,[80] but nothing worked. He then turned to the French who replied, after a lengthy silence, that the order expelling him from France to Spain in 1916 was still in effect. Enquiries were made in

Prague which at first met with an encouraging response and then, suddenly, an outright refusal. Similar results came from Holland, Luxembourg, Austria and Norway.

Many people abroad believed that his deportation was a move in a game being played by Stalin and Trotsky: he had been sent abroad to export revolution. He realized he must sit tight and wait, as his wife urged him to do: 'You must be patient. Everything in its own time. Your hour has not come yet.' As usual, he thought, she was right. During the years of revolution and civil war, Natalya had worked in the Cultural Department of the Commissariat of Enlightenment [Education],[81] and there is plenty of archival testimony to her responsibility and competence. For instance, on 6 July 1920 she wrote to Foreign Commissar Chicherin: 'The department for the protection of art and antiquities has no objection to the return to Finland of artistic and archaeological objects that have no special value for Russia.'[82] At a time when much of the country's cultural heritage was being pilfered and destroyed, she succeeded in saving a great deal by protecting it under revolutionary law.

The couple would often recall those days, as they sat on the veranda of their Turkish villa and watched the lights of the fishing boats. They might have reminisced about the time Trotsky had had to apply to the chief of supply just to get Natalya some new stockings.[83] Perhaps he owed some of the firmness of his convictions to his stalwart wife. His letters to her show not only their tenderness towards each other, but also how much he valued her attitude to him and his cause.[84] Stoically she bore all the hardships and misfortunes of their exile and remained a strong support for her husband. She had to endure the bitterest of suffering, that both her sons would die before her and that she would not be able to bury either of them, and then to survive her husband by more than fifteen years. During her long life, she did much to organize and safeguard Trotsky's rich archive and to transfer it to Harvard University.

Trotsky had two sisters and a brother. One of his sisters, Yelizaveta Melman, died of natural causes in the Kremlin in 1924. The other, Olga Kameneva, the wife of Lev Kamenev, would suffer all the hardships that could be inflicted on a relative of Stalin's chief enemy. First she was exiled, then in 1935 arrested and sentenced to prison and concentration camp, and finally shot in the autumn of 1941. In that

year, following the German invasion, Stalin set about clearing the
prisons of those judged by the NKVD to be a 'dangerous political
burden', and many thousands were summarily executed.

Trotsky's elder brother Alexander worked during the 1920s and
1930s as an agronomist in the Novokislyaevsk sugar mill in the province of Voronezh. As I was told by an inhabitant of the district, A.K.
Mironov, Alexander was a learned expert who enjoyed the respect of
the villagers. He apparently rode in a beautiful phaeton drawn by two
fine horses. When Trotsky came under attack, Alexander was expelled
from the Party, exiled, and made publicly to repudiate his brother.
He underwent a marked change, shrinking into himself as if from the
pangs of conscience. The recantation did not help him, however, and
in the summer of 1936 he was suddenly arrested at night and the
following year shot in Kursk prison as 'an active, un-disarmed Trotskyist'. Stalin's long arm had reached them all, except the main target
himself, his wife and his two sons.

After the deaths of Nina and Zina there was real fear for the safety
of Trotsky's sons, especially Sergei. He had not wanted to leave the
country with his father, preferring to devote himself to his scientific
interests. Uninterested in politics, Sergei had first wanted to be a
circus performer, but then became interested in technology, completed polytechnic and became a teacher there. He was a professor
before he reached the age of thirty. He married twice and his daughter
from his second marriage, Julia, is still alive in the USA. His first wife,
Olga Grebner, a lively and intelligent elderly woman when I spoke
to her in 1989, naturally endured Stalinist camp and exile. She recalled
Sergei only fragmentarily: he had been a mischievous boy, and an
amusing and talented man. Plainly, in the family it was the elder boy,
Lev, who was the favourite. Olga and Sergei had married when he
was twenty and she was nineteen.

'When the family was kicked out of the Kremlin to Granovsky
Street,' she recalled, 'we had nowhere to live. We took shelter in any
corner we could find. Lev Davydovich was always welcoming. I was
especially impressed by his lively, clever blue eyes. Outwardly, Natalya
Ivanovna was not an interesting woman. She was short, fat and
unattractive. But it was obvious how much they meant to each other.
As I said, Sergei was talented, whatever he turned his hand to, he
succeeded. When Trotsky was deported, Natalya Ivanovna said to

me: "Look after Seryozha." He was arrested on 4 March 1935. It seemed like a tragic play. Five of them arrived. The search took several hours. They took Sergei's books and a portrait of his father. My husband was taken to the Lubyanka. He was there two or three months. They told him the charges: espionage, aiding and abetting his father, wrecking. Anyway, they sent him to Siberia. He was doomed.'

In January 1937, *Pravda* published an article under the heading 'Trotsky's Son, Sergei Sedov, Tries to Poison Workers With Exhaust Gas'. At a meeting at the Krasnoyarsk Engineering Works, a foreman called Lebedev declared: 'We have working here as an engineer the son of Trotsky, Sergei Sedov. This worthy offspring of a father who has sold himself to Fascism attempted to poison a large number of workers at this factory with gas.' The meeting also discussed Zinoviev's nephew Zaks and the factory manager Subbotin, who was alleged to be protecting him and Sergei. All three were doomed. 'Sergei was soon sentenced,' Olga Grebner recalled. 'Some time that summer I received a postcard which he had somehow managed to send. It said: "They're taking me to the North. For a long time. Goodbye. I embrace you."' There were rumours that he was shot in 1941 somewhere in Kolyma, but Olga Grebner was not sure. In fact, he had been executed on 29 October 1937.

For a long time Sergei's parents remained unaware of what had happened to him. In his last letter to his mother, on 9 December 1934, he had written that the 'general situation is proving extremely difficult, much more difficult than you can imagine'.[85] On 1 June 1935 Trotsky wrote in his diary: 'Seryozha has been arrested; he is in prison; now it is no longer guesswork, something almost certain but not quite; we have a direct communication from Moscow . . . He was arrested, evidently, about the time our correspondence stopped, i.e. at the end of December or beginning of January . . . Poor boy . . . And my poor Natasha . . .'[86]

Natalya, with Trotsky's help, addressed an appeal to public opinion and leading cultural figures in which she called for 'an international commission of authoritative men of goodwill, naturally friends of the USSR. This commission should check all the repressions connected with the murder of Kirov; in the process, it should also throw light on the case of our son Sergei.' She added: 'Surely Romain Rolland, André Gide and Bernard Shaw and other friends of the Soviet Union could undertake this initiative?' She wrote that 'Seryozha remained as far from politics in recent years as he always had ... And the regime, from Stalin down, knows this very well; Seryozha, after all, grew up in the Kremlin, Stalin's son was a frequent visitor to our boys' room; the GPU and the university authorities have kept a double watch on him, first as a student and then as a young professor.'[87] But it was all in vain. Sergei had vanished from sight. Right up until his death, Trotsky tried to convince himself that Seryozha was still alive in some remote concentration camp 'without the right of correspondence'. He would say to Natalya, 'Maybe my death will save his life?'[88]

In November 1935, without waiting for a response to his wife's appeal, Trotsky, now in Norway, wrote to a friend enclosing three copies of Natalya's letter about Sergei. 'Apart from the usual agencies and newspapers, it should be sent to Romain Rolland, André Gide, Malraux and other famous "friends of the USSR" by registered post, reply paid.'[89] Natalya again appealed to public opinion through the *Bulletin* and the press: 'For the last three months I have been sending a very modest amount of money by bank transfer to my son's wife in order to assist her, as far as possible, in helping Sergei ... But the reply I got was that the addressee could not be found ... Thus my son's wife has also been arrested ... One cannot dismiss the thought that in these new circumstances the rumour, started by the Soviet authorities to the effect that my son "is not in prison", has acquired a particularly ominous and irremediable meaning. If Seryozha is not in prison, where is he? And where is his wife?'[90] Her appeal was met by the terrible silence of the Gulag.

Stalin was impenetrable. He, like his organization, replied tersely to such appeals for mercy. When the wife of his closest aide since 1928, A.N. Poskrebyshev, was arrested, to the pleas of his faithful arms-bearer he replied: 'Don't panic. The NKVD will sort it out.' Just how this was done was already clear to many, and Stalin, moreover, assisted the NKVD in their efforts. In August 1938 Yezhov sent a series of notes to Stalin, the first saying 'Here is a list of those arrested subject to trial in the first degree by the military collegium.' The return order, signed by Stalin and Molotov, was laconic in the extreme: 'All 138 to be shot.' The second note enclosed four lists of accused, numbering 313, 208, fifteen 'female enemies of the people and 200 army employees. I request your approval to shoot them all.'

Stalin and Molotov responded with the single syllable 'For.'[91] It was into this bloody maw that Sergei was flung, the innocent object of Stalin's insatiable revenge.

With Sergei's arrest, Trotsky and his wife had to think even more seriously about the life of their elder son Lev, his father's genuine emissary. Apart from publishing the *Bulletin*, Lev was also involved in two international bodies created by Trotskyists: the International Secretariat and the International Bureau. These two centres of 'Bolshevik-Leninists' were intended to rally the scattered groups of Trotsky's supporters into the monolithic World Party of Social Revolution. Trotsky gave Lev as a party alias the name of one of his friends from the far-off revolution, the sailor Markin, who had arrested senior officials of the foreign ministry in November 1917.

Lev was the family favourite. He entered the Party early, idolized his father and was a fanatical believer in his ideas. When Trotsky came under attack in the mid-1920s, Lev dropped out of the technical school where he was studying and became in effect his father's closest assistant. Although formally he was not himself exiled, he joined his parents in exile without hesitation and accompanied them when they were deported to Turkey as a sign of solidarity. He was, however, no mere executive: he had a flexible and strong political mind of his own and he wrote well. Among his brilliantly written pamphlets and articles is one, entitled 'The Red Book on the Moscow Trials', which is noteworthy for its solid argument and penetrating analysis.[92]

While his parents were on Prinkipo and Lev was travelling around Europe on his father's business, he reported that he realized on several occasions that he was being followed. He knew Yagoda's agents had him in their sights. The Moscow trials began in 1936 and thousands of people whom Stalin had decided might be dangerous to him were sent to their deaths. Progressive opinion in Europe was aghast. Even some Soviet intelligence agents were embarrassed and were ready to break with the criminal policy. The first to do so was the prominent agent Ignaz Reiss, to whom we shall return.

Stalin's report to the Central Committee plenum of February–March 1937 constituted in effect an exposition of the methodology of terror, repression, the hardening of the 'class approach' in relation to internal and external enemies. Secret circulars went abroad after the plenum hammering home Stalin's argument: 'We shall smash enemies in the future as we are smashing them at present and as we smashed them in the past.'[93]

When Trotsky was installed in Mexico, he repeatedly warned Lev of the danger he was in. Some of Lev's friends urged him to leave Europe, even temporarily, and rejoin his father. After prolonged hesitation, Lev expressed his misgivings to Trotsky and again said he was being followed. He suspected there was an 'outsider' in his circle, and asked his father for advice. Lev was living in somewhat straitened circumstances, and Trotsky could do little to help, burdened with debt as he was, living on advances for unwritten books and still publishing the *Bulletin* with its meagre circulation and no revenue. Lev's relationship with Jeanne became difficult. Every day seemed to bring new cares. The Trotskyist organizations were more often at odds with each other than in harmony. Lev experienced some sort of mental crisis, especially after receiving Trotsky's letter from Coyoacan dated 18 November 1937, in which his father advised against leaving Paris as it would 'slow things down'. Zborowski reported this to Moscow. In a report from Paris, the agent 'Peter' wrote:

> On the occasion of his son's birth, 'Mack' invited 'Sonny' [the OGPU's codename for Lev] to dinner. 'Sonny' spent the entire day over the bottle at 'Mack's' and drank a lot ... Having drunk a great deal, but without passing out, 'Sonny' felt terribly upset. He apologized to 'Mack' and almost in tears begged his forgiveness for having suspected him of being an agent of the GPU when they first met. At the end of all these 'revelations', 'Sonny' said that right from the start in the [Soviet] Union the opposition struggle had been hopeless and that no one had believed it could succeed, that as early as 1927 he had lost all faith in revolution and now believed in nothing at all, that he was a pessimist. The work and the struggle that was going on now was nothing but a continuation of the past. Women and wine were more important to him ...[94]

Lev was unable to hide his pessimism when he wrote to his parents. On 14 November 1937 'Mack' reported via the local agent to the Foreign Section of the NKVD that 'Sonny' was depressed and 'has left a will in which he says where his archives are kept and so on'.[95] It later transpired that the archives were being held in a bank safety-deposit to which Jeanne had the key. Trotsky tried to reassure his son, but also criticized him for the 'unsatisfactory content of the

Bulletin'. As for a trip to Mexico, even a temporary one, Trotsky was not enthusiastic, replying that his son would gain nothing by leaving France: the United States was not likely to admit him and Mexico would offer even less security than France. As Deutscher comments, Trotsky did not wish his son to shut himself up in the Coyoacan 'semi-prison'.[96] How he would punish himself for those words two months later. Why did he not see the mortal danger hanging over his son? Alas, even prophets who can discern the shape of things to come through the present gloom are sometimes unable to see what is standing right before them.

On 8 February 1938 Lev had a severe attack of appendicitis. While Zborowski telephoned around the private clinics, Lev wrote his last letter which he asked his wife to open only if something happened to him. Absurdly, as Deutscher rightly says, he avoided French hospitals because of the fear that the OGPU would find him, and opted for the most dangerous alternative, a small private clinic run by Russian émigré doctors, where he registered as Monsieur Martin and was supposed to speak French only. They operated on him the same evening and it seemed he was recovering well. He was already walking and getting ready to discharge himself when, four days later, he suffered a severe relapse with signs of poisoning. After a series of blood transfusions and an agony of pain, on 16 February 1938 Lev died, aged thirty-two.

Zborowski reported Lev's illness to his Paris controller and Moscow was informed the same day. There is no direct evidence in the NKVD archives to indicate that the secret police had a hand in his death. Perhaps, as their chief source of information on the Trotskyist movement, Lev was more useful to them alive than dead. On the other hand, in 1938 the NKVD had been ordered by Stalin yet again to intensify their efforts to get rid of Trotsky, and since Lev was by then in a state of depression, it may well be that his value as a source had greatly diminished.

When Trotsky and Natalya heard that Lev had died they were profoundly shaken. They locked themselves in their room and received no visitors for several days. Once he came to himself, Trotsky began demanding an immediate investigation of the circumstances of his son's death. Almost nobody doubted that he had been poisoned, but if this was so, the murder had been carried out so professionally that it left no clues. (The NKVD had a special section for developing poisons.[97])

On 20 February, a week after Lev's death, Trotsky wrote what Deutscher has eloquently described as 'a threnody unique in world literature', his obituary for his son:

> The old generation with whom ... we once embarked upon the road of revolution ... has been swept off the stage. What Tsarist deportations, prisons, and *katorga* [hard labour], what the privations of life in exile, what civil war, and what illness had not done, Stalin, the worst scourge of the revolution, has accomplished in these last few years ... The better part of the middle generation, those ... whom the year 1917 awakened and who received their training in twenty-four armies on the revolutionary front, have also been exterminated. The best part of the young generation, Lyova's contemporaries ... has also been trampled down and crushed ...

He spoke of the great help his son had given him in his writing, help that was possible 'only because our intellectual solidarity had entered our blood and our nerves'. Blaming the OGPU and their master in Moscow for Lev's death, Trotsky ended: 'Farewell, dear and incomparable friend! Your mother and I never thought, never expected, that fate would lay this task on us ... that we should have to write your obituary ... But we have not been able to save you.'[98]

As Zborowski reported to Moscow, the Politburo of the French Trotskyists proposed he take over all the work of the Russian section, even before 'Starik' (i.e. 'the Old Man', as the NKVD codenamed Trotsky) sent his own instructions.

> 1) The French will recognize only 'Mack' as the representative of the Russian group. 2) With 'Neighbour' [L. Estrin] on 18 February [1938] 'Mack' will send a letter to 'Starik' in which they will give the details of 'Sonny's' death. 3) 'Neighbour' has told 'Mack' that there are three archives: a) an old archive, which is in a bank safety deposit for which Jeanne has the key; b) an old archive which 'Mack' is looking after (and which is known to us); c) one (the Ajax archive) hidden by 'Neighbour'. 'Sonny' did not know its location. 4) 'Mack' and 'Neighbour' have a good relationship. She regards herself as equivalent to 'Sonny's' successor. It has been suggested to 'Mack' that he shouldn't snub her, but rather to get everything she knows out of her. This is very important

... 5) 'Mack' has been instructed by us to take over future links with the 'International Secretariat' himself.[99]

Having in all probability murdered Lev, the NKVD was determined not to lose the valuable links it had set up to the Soviet regime's most wanted man.

Trotsky did not know what had happened to his granddaughters in the USSR after the arrest of his first wife, and the one remaining offspring of that generation abroad was Zina's son Seva, who was barely ten years old when Lev, his adopted father, died. Trotsky felt a sense of deep guilt for the deaths of his children and wanted to take on the task of raising his remaining grandson himself. He knew that his political struggle had made both his families deeply unhappy and had been ultimately responsible for all their fates. He judged himself harshly, within the concrete stockade in Mexico, for having done so little to help his sick daughters, for failing to make real human contact with Zina, for not having persuaded Sergei to come with him to Turkey, and for not responding to Lev's wish to take a break from France. But he had always put the cause before his children, and for that he would bear the guilt until the end of his life.

The matter of his grandson was not simple, however. A struggle with Jeanne over his archives did much to spoil the atmosphere when he tried to persuade her to come and live with the boy in Coyoacan. Their relations deteriorated so badly that he finally resorted to the courts to obtain custody. The case dragged on for a year, but Jeanne would not yield. Trotsky then wrote to the French Minister of Justice to explain that the boy had no parents and no blood relatives, except himself: 'Your authoritative intervention, Monsieur Ministre, would be sufficient to cut through the knot in twenty-four hours.'[100] But it was not until October 1939, after Marguerite Rosmer had torn Seva from Jeanne's clutches, that the child finally joined his grandfather in Mexico.

For more than a third of his life Trotsky had lived abroad. He had been rejected by his homeland and condemned to wander. It was only after the deaths of his sons that he felt deep in his heart that he would never see his country again. Several years earlier, shortly before leaving Prinkipo, he had given Moscow a signal that in the interests of the revolution he was prepared to compromise. He had agonized for a long time then, in March 1933, before writing the letter. He did not want it to look as if he was surrendering. That he would never do, but he did harbour a faint hope of at least reducing the hostility to the point where he might once again see his homeland.

He had not been able to bring himself to write to Stalin, although he knew that of course only the General Secretary would decide the outcome. Instead he wrote to the Politburo, putting 'Secret' at the head of the paper:

> I regard it as my duty to make one more attempt to appeal to the sense of responsibility in those who are presently ruling the Soviet state. You are better able than I to judge the situation in the country and the Party. If internal development continues along its present path, a catastrophe is unavoidable. It is utterly hopeless and fatal to think that the present situation can be overcome by repression alone. What must be done? First, the party must be reborn. It is a painful process, but it must be done. I have not the slightest doubt that the 'left' opposition is willing to give the Central Committee its full cooperation to put the Party back on the rails of a normal life without shocks or with as few as possible ... The fate of the workers' state and the international revolution for many years to come are at stake.

Sensing what today would be called historic failure, Trotsky nonetheless saw the means to avoid it in one-sided, metaphysical terms. He attacked the bureaucracy and totalitarianism, but still believed in the revolutionary methods of the single party. It did not occur to him to doubt the axioms of Bolshevism. He believed that agreement between the 'left' opposition and the leadership was possible: 'However strained the atmosphere, it could be relaxed in a few successive stages, given goodwill on both sides ... The purpose of this letter is to declare the existence of goodwill in the "left" opposition.' The Politburo, he concluded, could choose the ways and means, if it 'thought it necessary to enter into preliminary negotiations without any publicity'.[101]

Naturally, there was no reply, nor could there be. Stalin was waiting for news of a quite different kind. Having read the letter, he cursed ominously and snapped that Menzhinsky 'can't catch mice any more' and that it was time he had Trotsky silenced. Menzhinsky was ill, and had he not died soon after there can be little doubt that he would not have survived much longer in this world, let alone at his post. This episode demonstrates that, even when he and his family had been placed in the position of permanent nomads, Trotsky had made one last naive effort at reconciliation, one last attempt to restore the Party to the democratic ideals of the revolution. The gesture was rejected and the persecution intensified.

In May 1938 a warning was published in the *Bulletin*, in which the editor claimed to know the NKVD's intentions towards Trotsky: 'As long as L.D. Trotsky is alive, Stalin's role as destroyer of the Bolshevik old guard is unfinished. It is not enough to pass the death sentence on Comrade Trotsky, along with Zinoviev, Kamenev, Bukharin and the other victims of the terror. The sentence has to be carried out.' The journal published a list of suspicious individuals who had followed Trotsky from country to country.[102] Among the warnings of the growing danger was a letter which carried great weight. It spoke with apparent inside knowledge of the NKVD's plans to murder Trotsky. In due course it was revealed that the letter was sent by Alexander Orlov, a senior intelligence officer who had defected while abroad. He would later write a sensational book, *The Secret History of Stalin's Crimes*. Orlov warned that Trotsky was in danger from someone known as 'Mark' – he couldn't recall 'Mark's' surname – and he advised against trusting anyone who turned up with an introduction from 'Mark'. He suggested that 'the Old Man' put a notice in a local paper to say he had received the letter.[103] Trotsky duly posted the announcemement 'Your letter received and noted. Please come for personal conversations.'[104] Orlov, however, did not show up, and Trotsky assumed the letter to have been an NKVD provocation. His confidence in 'Mack' remained undiminished.

The Moscow Trials

The four years on Prinkipo had been extremely productive in terms of Trotsky's writing. Apart from his *History of the Russian Revolution* and *My Life*, he had given dozens of interviews in which he never tired of repeating that Leninism was not dead, that the idea of world revolution was not utopian, and that Stalinism was no more than a tragic hiccup in Russian history. In the years that followed he would write little, apart from a small book called *The Revolution Betrayed*, of which even Victor Serge, who edited it for publication, declared: 'It is cumbersome, hastily written and of small literary value.'[105] He had sacrificed even his literary talent, along with everything else, to the political issues of the day. The French, Norwegian and Mexican stages of his wanderings would pass as time committed to his new brainchild, the creation of the Fourth International. He would quickly discover how ill-assorted and unpromising that body would turn out to be, even if many other people have continued for decades to believe in its viability.

In July 1933, with Natalya and two secretaries, Trotsky boarded an old Italian steamer, the *Bulgaria*, and left Constantinople for Marseilles, hoping that his appearance in the West would activate his supporters. Natalya later recalled that Trotsky had felt unwell on the trip. 'It was very hot. The ship was draughty and it ended with him getting lumbago. We called the ship's doctor. The pain was excruciating. The patient couldn't get out of bed. On 24 July the ship stopped off Marseilles. A motor-launch came alongside with our son, Lev Sedov, and R. Molinier.'[106] After travelling around the south of France and living in a host of small towns on the way, in July 1933 they settled in Grenoble for eleven months. In mid-December 1933, Trotsky managed to spend just one day in Paris.

As soon as Mark Zborowski joined Trotsky's organization, it became clear to the family that Trotsky was being followed. He said as much to his secretaries, Rudolf Klement and Sara Weber, as well as to Raymond Molinier, and security measures were stepped up. Zborowski would extract as much information as possible from Lev Sedov about Trotsky's movements in France, although Lev was at first suspicious and even wondered if Zborowski was not an agent of the NKVD. Trotsky soon realized that France was bristling with Soviet agents. Despite all the measures he took to remain anonymous, he was several times recognized by reporters, as well as officials of various political parties and Russian émigrés. The Communist newspaper *L'Humanité* several times published protests against lifting the ban on Trotsky's entry into France. Despite this, Trotsky received his supporters from many countries in Europe, the USA and even China, although he took careful precautions. He told them all that a new wave of revolution was coming, that they must prepare for it and intensify their work among the masses; he took soundings on the possibility of unifying the multitude of Trotskyist groups into a single major international organization. To his distress, however, many of his supporters were not convinced that a new revolutionary wave was approaching.

At a meeting in Paris in August 1933 at which fourteen parties and groups were represented, only three of them could agree on the proposal to create the Fourth International at once. Trotsky, who had not taken part in the meeting as a matter of security, was disappointed. He had devoted considerable effort to preparing the documents and resolutions for this conference, and had expected a better result. But at least it revealed to him just how little support he had. The world situation was different from what it had been on the eve of the October revolution.

Trotsky, too, felt that there would be no more meteoric rises, either revolutionary or for him personally. His letters of September 1933 from St Palais near Royan on the French Atlantic coast to Natalya in Paris, where she was undergoing medical treatment, were sad and disconsolate: 'Dearest, dearest mine, it was quieter on Prinkipo. Already the recent past seems better than it was. Yet we looked forward with so much hope to our stay in France. Is this definitely old age already? Or is it only a temporary, though all too sharp decline, from which I shall still rally? We shall see.'[107]

The pressure on him was building up. In the spring of 1934 he was asked to leave Barbizon, an hour's journey from Paris, because the police could no longer guarantee his safety. Following a hasty withdrawal from Barbizon, he spent just over another year in France, but without finding peace and security anywhere. At times his escapes were conducted in humiliating conditions, as for example when he had to shave off his beard and disguise himself. Once he had to hide for several days in the attic of one of his son's friends. He was threatened by local Nazis and Communists alike, and the OGPU was hunting for him. He was supported throughout all this, and indeed until the end of his life, by his Dutch assistant van Heijenoort, whose dedication reminded Trotsky of Sermuks and Poznansky. Often Trotsky changed his abode without Natalya, usually accompanied by Molinier and van Heijenoort with one or two French bodyguards. At times he was changing hotel rooms five or six times a month, but always he was followed by silent, mysterious-looking policemen.

He became anxious, and seriously regretted leaving Prinkipo. Only in a small village near Grenoble was he able to settle quietly for a few months, and there he tried to complete the book on Lenin for which he had already signed contracts with a number of publishers. But his inspiration had been driven out by the anxiety. Instead, he waited every day for his secretary to bring him the newspapers: after the murder of Kirov, the situation in the USSR was becoming ominous. The Western press – he saw few Moscow newspapers – were daily reporting new arrests, the search for plotters everywhere, even within the Politburo, and incomprehensible events throughout the country. In the evenings he tuned in to Radio Moscow and occasionally managed to catch its distant chimes, reminding him of his days in the Kremlin. Radio Moscow was constantly talking about the criminal activity of Zinoviev and Kamenev, as responsible for the murder of Kirov, and stating that all these 'unfinished enemies' were inspired and guided by 'the Fascist hireling Trotsky'.

Trotsky was appalled by the degeneration of the Soviet system. Shortly before he and his wife left France, he would write an article in which he would recall that in March 1929 he had warned everyone that Stalin was bound to link the 'opposition with assassination attempts and staging armed uprisings and so on'. Knowing full well that Stalin was the organizer of the Moscow trials that were just beginning, he declared openly that Stalin had given Zinoviev and Kamenev an ultimatum: they themselves must devise the formula for him that would justify his repression of them. It was all being done so as to be able to accuse Trotsky. Venomously, he mocked Stalin's attempts to find more and more fabricated excuses to unleash mass arrests in the country.[108]

Within two months he learned that soon after Kirov's murder Alexandra Sokolovskaya had been arrested and exiled to the north, forced to send his granddaughters to an aunt in Ukraine. For decades the woman who had introduced the young Bronshtein to Marxism bore the heavy cross of the lonely and abandoned woman, on whom ever more savage blows were rained. In numerous interrogations she was asked how she carried out her husband's orders to assist the activities of Trotskyist groups, what instructions he had sent her from abroad and who brought them to her. Both Trotsky's sons-in-law, Volkov and Nevelson, as they awaited the end of their sentences in exile, were rearrested and sent to camp, where they both soon disappeared without trace.

As for Trotsky, his prolonged petitioning at last bore fruit: the Norwegian government issued a permit for him to enter the country, and on 15 June 1935 he and Natalya arrived in Oslo. His friends found them a small hotel a two-hour journey from the capital. Life was hard there, as Trotsky and Natalya had left France with practically no money. Two years in France, not working but worrying about security, had eaten up Trotsky's small savings. He now wanted to work: to write letters to the supporters who shared his dream of a new type of international organization, capable of raising the international banner that had been trampled in the mud; to earn a living, to publish the *Bulletin*, to support his elder son and his grandson, Seva. But he had to work in a country where he was regarded as a leper. The authorities had insisted he sign an undertaking not to engage in political activity. The opposition in parliament raised the question of his 'temporary' stay in the country. No one was willing to let him a house or apartment, and hotels were costly. The press was full of hostile articles. Soon agents of Yagoda appeared within his orbit: Zborowski, who monitored Trotsky's correspondence with his son, was able to give Trotsky's Norwegian address to his OGPU controller.[109]

In such difficult moments, Trotsky recalled, he had always been able to find moral strength and certainty in his wife. He wrote in his diary: 'Natalya and I have been together for thirty-three years (a third of a century!), and always in tragic moments I am amazed by her reserves of character. I can say one thing: Natalya has never "reproached" me, not in the most difficult times; she doesn't reproach me now, either, in the worst days of our life, when everyone has ganged up against us . . .'[110]

Eventually they found a suitable place to live just north of Oslo in the family of the Norwegian Social Democrat Konrad Knudsen. They were now without bodyguards and assistants. Since the Norwegian Minister of Justice, Trygve Lie – the future Secretary General of the United Nations – had forbidden Trotsky to engage in politics while he was in the country, he determined to concentrate on his writing, while keeping a keen eye on events in Europe and the Soviet Union.

But his literary work was greatly hampered by the huge volume of correspondence he was compelled to maintain with his supporters. As before, he had to try by letter to reconcile hostile factions and groupings, especially in France, and to receive representatives of these groups. It seemed the 'revolutionary army' was good for nothing but endless petty squabbling, trivial intrigue and loud rhetoric. For a man who had stood on the very crest of the Russian revolution, none of this could increase his enthusiasm.

In the middle of August 1936 Trotsky was on holiday with Knudsen when they heard on the radio that a major trial had opened in Moscow and that the chief defendants were Zinoviev, Kamenev and their 'accomplices', who were all being charged with organizing terrorism in the USSR. The main charge was that the murder of Kirov and a planned attempt on Stalin, Voroshilov and other leaders had been conducted 'under the direction of Trotsky'. Hearing these revelations, the 'organizer of Fascist terror' hurried home and for the next few days was glued to his radio. He was shaken by what he heard. The whole thing was incomprehensible. Kamenev, Zinoviev, Mrachkovsky and Bakaev were saying monstrous things, there wasn't a grain of truth in it, not a grain! Dispassionately, Zinoviev said he was the political inspirer of Kirov's murder, in effect the organizer. Trotsky was named as the leader of an entire 'terrorist' bloc. 'Trotskyism,' Zinoviev averred, 'is a variation of Fascism.' Kamenev testified that 'he himself served Fascism and with Trotsky and Zinoviev had prepared a counter-revolution in the USSR'. Trotsky could not believe what he heard. What had been done to make these people say such things? He was being called the chief plotter and organizer, a terrorist and murderer.

What he did not know was that just before the opening of the trial, Zinoviev and Kamenev had been brought from prison to Stalin's study, where he had made them an offer: if they 'confessed' to everything at the trial and demonstrated that Trotsky was the chief organizer of hostile, terroristic activity against the Party and the country, he would do his best to save their lives. He would do his best. While there is no document to support this account of the meeting, indirect evidence suggests that the two old Bolsheviks were made to understand that they had no choice, and that death was the only alternative. Although they knew that Stalin had no equal in cunning and deceit, they could not but agree. Nor would they have the courage to deny everything in public.

The Moscow trials, more graphically than anything, confirmed Trotsky in his belief that Stalin had undermined everything the revolution had stood for. On 4 August 1936 he had finished his book *The Revolution Betrayed*. It had taken him a year to write and it was full of prediction, harsh judgement and categorical but often contradictory conclusions. The book's chief target was the new bureaucratic caste in the USSR:

> Why did Stalin win? It would be naive to suppose that he had emerged from behind the scenes, unknown to the masses, with a great strategic plan. No. Before he found his way, the bureaucracy found him . . . The bureaucracy conquered not only the 'left' opposition. It also conquered the Bolshevik Party . . . It conquered all those enemies . . . not with ideas and argument, but by its own sheer weight. The leaden backside of the bureaucracy weighed more than the brains of the revolution . . . That is the secret of the Soviet Thermidore.[111]

Then, however, he suddenly came to the conclusion that the bureaucracy, as a new class, might bring about the restoration of capitalism in the USSR.

This kind of thinking was not untypical of Trotsky. Having conducted a deep and accurate analysis and made startling predictions, he was capable at times of drawing false conclusions – an effect, no doubt, of his being constantly primed for revolution. Since the bureaucracy had 'consumed' the revolution, he argued, it could end in bourgeois reaction. In fact, Trotsky's position was closer to Stalin's than that of more sober Marxists: 'Giving the land to the collective farms for their eternal use is not a socialist measure and will only preserve the desire for private property.' He believed that kulak psychology had not been eliminated, that personal private plots (a concession of 1932 designed to alleviate the worst effects of collectivization) were a seedbed of the old private-ownership outlook. In agrarian matters, he was completely bound by the old Marxist dogmatic and utopian notions according to which it would be possible to bring about 'truly socialist transformation' only as a result of the total nationalization of the land and other property. He still believed that 'the task of the European proletariat lies not in perpetuating frontiers, but on the contrary getting rid of them by revolutionary means. Not the status quo, but the United States of Europe!'

The chief argument of *The Revolution Betrayed* was that 'the Soviet bureaucracy will not surrender its positions without a fight.' Therefore, the working class, having carried out the first socialist revolution in history, now confronted the need for a new 'supplementary' revolution, not a social one, but a 'political revolution against bureaucratic absolutism ... There is no peaceful way out of the crisis. A clash between the people and the bureaucratic oligarchy ... is inevitable. The political revolution will overthrow the Stalinist system of government, but will not alter the existing property relations.'[112]

The call for revolution was tantamount to calling for a coup d'état, an utterly utopian and futile desire with no chance of realization. On the other hand, leaving aside the form, the timing and the character of his desperate appeal, Trotsky was perhaps the first person to place on the open agenda the need to liquidate Stalinism as a system, as an ideology, as a mode of operations and as a way of thinking. For Trotsky, Stalinism was the worst form of totalitarianism, comparable only with Fascism. Genuine democratic development could only occur if the Stalinist system was first dismantled. Only then could socialism have a future.

The publication of *The Revolution Betrayed* had a fatal consequence outside its author's control. Having completed the manuscript and in August 1936 sent it to his Paris publishers, Trotsky also sent a copy to his son Lev, with instructions to publish extracts in the *Bulletin of the Opposition*, or some bourgeois newspapers. This was duly done, but, thanks to Zborowski, the manuscript, or at least parts of it, turned up on Stalin's desk even before it was published in Paris in the summer of 1937. Indeed, Trotsky had scarcely sent the manuscript to France when the head of the 7th Section of the Main State Security Board of the NKVD, Slutsky, had reported to Yezhov, who reported to Stalin: 'Sedov is negotiating with various publishers over this book. It is intended to publish it in several languages. It will be translated in French by V[ictor] Serge (publisher Grassi). The German translation will be done by [Alexandra Ramm] the wife of the German Trotskyist, Pfemfert. B. Burian will do the Czechoslovak edition. An offer has also been received from the Polish publishing house Wydawnicwo Polske.'[113]

Indirect information about Trotsky's publications also occurs in the 'Sneevliet collection' which the Central Party Archives of the Institute of Marxism-Leninism received from the Party History Institute of the Polish Workers Party. The collection came into the hands of the Polish Communists because it was purportedly discarded by the Germans in Poland in 1944–45, and it contains several hundred documents, reports, letters, circulars and minutes dating from between 1922 and 1940. It no doubt includes material that had earlier reached Moscow by way of the NKVD.[114]

It is known that, when trying to save his archives, Trotsky transferred part of them to the Paris Institute of Historical Research at 7, rue Michelet. Lev Sedov, in the company of Zborowski, had handed over the documents to the curator of the Institute, the Menshevik Boris Nikolaevsky. A few days later, on the night of 6 November 1936, there was a break-in and some of the material was stolen. Apart from Trotsky and Lev, the only people who had known the new location of the archives were Nikolaevsky and Zborowski. Like Lev, Nikolaevsky was being watched by Soviet intelligence. A report to Moscow by OGPU agent 'Gamma' noted that 'in view of the agreement between Norway and the [Soviet] Union, Trotsky's correspondence is being opened.'[115] Plainly, Moscow could learn practically everything that could be known about Trotsky from a variety of sources.

Thus it was that extracts of his manuscript of *The Revolution Betrayed* turned up in Moscow. Zborowski had given Stalin long notice of its impending publication, and it is not difficult to imagine the effect Trotsky's call for a 'political revolution' had on him. It is not impossible that this played a part in Stalin's decision to carry out a major purge in the country. The manuscript might have been a factor in his decision to launch mass repression, although he was ready enough as it was to begin the process. *The Revolution Betrayed* finally convinced Stalin that Trotsky was a real danger, and that by his pen he could still inflict telling ideological blows. Stalin, moreover, had determined to liquidate the potential soil for Trotskyism in the country. The main attack in the forthcoming trials in Moscow would be aimed at Trotsky.

Meanwhile, as the Moscow press was reporting, the trial of Zinoviev and Kamenev and their 'accomplices' was depicting Trotsky as the mastermind of terrorist 'bands'. The chief prosecutor, Andrei

Vyshinsky – who had incidentally moved into Trotsky's apartment on Granovsky Street the minute its disgraced tenant moved out and was exiled to Alma-Ata – claimed that Trotsky was directing terrorist operations from Norway. The reporters descended on Trotsky, who told them with his customary eloquence that everything being said about him in Moscow was 'the lie of the century', fully in keeping with 'the chief creator of this lie, who is hiding himself behind the walls of the Kremlin'.

On 29 August 1936 the Soviet ambassador in Norway carried out the instructions he had received from Moscow and demanded Trotsky's expulsion by the Norwegian authorities.[116] The Norwegians, however, had already taken their own measures and placed Trotsky under house arrest. He had fallen ill from the shock of what was being said about him at the Moscow trials. After reading a letter from Natalya to Lev Sedov in Paris, Zborowski duly informed Moscow that '"the Old Man" is very sick, has stopped going out altogether, he is sweating profusely which weakens him drastically. He should be in a sanatorium, but the Norwegian authorities are making his position more difficult.'[117] To Moscow's undoubted disappointment, however, Trotsky had a tough constitution and soon recovered.

Trotsky's semi-arrest had been prompted by his efforts to use the Western press to counter Stalin's accusations. He was in a kind of quarantine, in which journalists were denied access to him, his mail was opened and he was not allowed to leave the house. He remained in these circumstances until mid-December 1936, when he finally heard that Mexico was prepared to admit him. The Norwegian government chartered the oil-tanker *Ruth* and on 19 December Trotsky and Natalya left the inhospitable shores of Norway. The Atlantic at that time of year was not a more hospitable place, and Trotsky, who feared the ship might sink, sent his will to Lev in Paris before embarking.

The trip turned out be uneventful, and in early January the passengers were safely put ashore in Mexico. Three days after Trotsky's departure from Norway, 'Mack' reported to Moscow that Lev had received a telegram on 23 December saying that his father and mother had left for Mexico: '"Sonny" is very upset by this, as he had expected "the Old Man" to pass through France and meet him and his friends. The French transit visa had already been received ... "Sonny" at once decided to send van [Heijenoort] and Jan Fraenkel to Mexico as completely trustworthy people.' He further reported that in future all the mail would be addressed to van Heijenoort *poste restante* in Mexico. 'Important letters will be sent to the address of Diego Rivera and less important ones to that of one of the more serious American Trotskyists or other.'[118]

The year 1937 has gone down in Russian history as synonymous with Stalin's unbridled terror against his own people. For Trotsky it was a year of monstrous slander and ostracism. Stalin's campaign against him had, of course, begun much earlier. In February 1934, for instance, G.A. Molchanov, head of the OGPU's Secret Political Section, had signed an indictment of the so-called 'Case of the All-Union Trotskyist Centre', leading to the arrest and sentencing of dozens of people, almost all of whom were to be executed in 1937–38. The apotheosis of collective madness to which Stalin brought the Party, the society and the state, occurred at the Plenum of the Central Committee which took place in February–March 1937. This meeting effectively approved and reinforced the most savage methods for dealing with 'enemies of the people'.

According to the information Trotsky was receiving from Moscow, Stalin had told the plenum that the 'counter-revolutionary Fourth International was made up of two-thirds spies and saboteurs', and that the Norwegian Schöffle's 'group of scoundrels was harbouring the super-spy Trotsky and helping him to blacken the Soviet Union'.[119] The plenum, which lasted two weeks, was essentially dedicated to one issue, 'the lessons of the sabotage, the diversionary actions and espionage by Japanese-German and Trotskyist agents'. It is plain from the proceedings that absolutely no attempt was made at a rational analysis or to make sense of the charges, simply because the object under judgement was a mirage.[120] Nevertheless, every speaker unanimously condemned Trotskyism.

The chief arguments were of course made by Stalin himself in his report 'On the Deficiencies of Party Work and Measures to Liquidate Trotskyist and other Double-Dealers'. Speaking in a soft voice, making the delegates strain to hear his words, Stalin put the question: 'What does present-day Trotskyism consist of?' After a brief pause he explained: 'It is a frenzied band of saboteurs. Seven or eight years ago it was a false anti-Leninist political tendency. Kamenev and

Zinoviev denied they had any political programme. They were lying. Pyatakov, Radek and Sokolnikov did not deny there was such a platform at their trial in 1937: it was to restore capitalism, dismantle the Soviet Union territorially (Ukraine to the Germans, the Maritime Provinces to the Japanese), and in the event of an attack by enemies, to use wrecking tactics and terror. That is precisely the platform of Trotskyism.'[121] The 'Trotskyist wreckers and spies', he told the plenum, aimed to carry out terroristic acts against the Soviet leaders, and it was therefore necessary to 'smash and root out the Japano-German agents of Trotskyism'.[122] The unanimous applause that greeted the speech was needed by Stalin to legitimize, or give the appearance of legitimizing, the huge scale of the terror then being perpetrated throughout the country.

Stressing the importance of the Party organization as the foundation of the regime, Stalin outlined its scale very much as a general would define his army: 'Our Party has 3–4000 senior leaders. I would call this the top brass. Then, 30–40,000 middle-ranking leaders make up the Party's officer corps; 100–150,000 lower ranks are the Party's NCOs.'[123] In this militarized order, which was the way he wanted to see the Party, and which, incidentally echoed Lenin's vision of the Party at the turn of the century, the entire personnel must go through stringent checks for 'utter reliability'.

Many delegates to the plenum, on hearing the call 'mercilessly to unmask the Trotskyists', fell to the task at once. Kosior, for instance, reported that 'in the Central Committee of the Ukrainian Communist Party there have been quite a few Trotskyists. We have removed many already and we shall continue to do so.'[124] He then proceeded to read a long list of names. Other delegates were quick to follow suit. Kaganovich, the People's Commissar for Transport who loved to make precise, concrete statements, peppered his report with statistics on how the great work of 'uprooting the Trotskyists' and other enemies had begun: 'In the political organization of the Transport Commissariat we unmasked 220 people. Transport has dismissed 485 former [tsarist] police, 220 SRs and Mensheviks, 572 Trotskyists, 1415 White officers, 285 wreckers and 443 spies. All of them had ties with the Right-Trotskyist Bloc.'[125] It is doubtful if anyone at the plenum accepted at face value that all these spies and wreckers had been merely 'dismissed', as if they were now free to find other jobs.

People's Commissar for Military and Naval Affairs Voroshilov then reported on how Trotskyists were being dealt with in the armed services: 'In 1923-24 the Trotskyists had practically the entire Moscow garrison. Almost all the military academies, the government school, the artillery school, the Moscow Military District Headquarters, where Muralov was in charge, and other units were all for Trotsky.'[126] Voroshilov was wrong: while it was the case that the army followed Trotsky, he never used it in the political struggle, although that was the accusation against him.

Reports were followed by sinister resolutions calling for the intensification of the struggle with Trotskyism at home and abroad. Yezhov complained that 'the struggle with Trotskyism and the Trotskyists has been started at least four years too late, as a result of which the traitors to the motherland – the Trotskyists and other double-dealers, working with the German and Japanese intelligence services – have been able to carry out their wrecking diversionary spying and terroristic activities with relative impunity.' He went on: 'The People's Commissariat of Internal Affairs has been pursuing an incorrect, lenient punishment policy towards the Trotskyists ... and the Secret Political Section of the NKVD's Security Department had the possibility as early as 1932-33 of exposing the monstrous Trotskyist plot (there was the link between Soviet officials and Trotsky's son and so on). Molchanov, the head of the section, was linked to the Trotskyist Fourier.' The plenum passed a resolution 'instructing the People's Commissariat for Internal Affairs to deal with the unmasking and smashing of Trotskyist and other agents to the very end, in order to crush the least sign of their anti-Soviet activity. The staff of the Security Department and the Secret Political Section must be strengthened with reliable people. Reliable agencies at home and abroad must be organized. Intelligence officials must be strengthened.'[127]

The Secret Political Section of the Main Administration of State Security of the NKVD has already been mentioned as an agency which, alongside the Foreign Section of the OGPU was responsible both for intelligence gathering and, 'when necessary', the elimination of political and ideological opponents abroad. Many hundreds of people died at the hands of the elaborate network of operatives at their command. Personnel from these bodies had been hunting Trotsky and his entourage for a long time. The Secret Political Section was directly subordinate to the People's Commissar of Internal Affairs, while especially important tasks, such as those connected with eliminating Trotsky, were assigned by Stalin himself.

On 23 January 1937, before the Central Committee Plenum, the so-called 'Trial of the Seventeen' took place in Moscow. Pyatakov was the chief defendant, and the object of the trial was to show that Trotsky, with the aid of the defendants, had organized wrecking actions in preparation for the restoration of capitalism in the USSR. Pyatakov told the court everything he had been ordered to under torture. He described in graphic detail his meeting with Lev Sedov in Oslo, where he had never been in his life, and recounted that Trotsky's orders included two variants 'for our coming to power'. In the first, the Trotskyists would have to deliver a major terroristic blow before the war, simultaneously wiping out Stalin and other Party and state leaders. The second variant would operate during the war as a result of military defeat. Trotsky allegedly thought this latter course the more realistic.[128] Zborowski had reported from Paris that he had managed to establish, in a cautious conversation with Lev Sedov, that Trotsky had never spoken to Pyatakov.[129] The Chief Prosecutor and Yezhov, however, were not guided by the need to establish the truth. Their justice was dictated by the supreme leader.

The transcript of the trial is peppered throughout with the words 'Trotsky', 'Trotskyism', 'Trotskyist murderers', 'Trotskyist sabotage', and nothing could have been plainer but that the chief defendant was indeed the absent Trotsky. However, the most painful impression on world opinion was perhaps created in March 1938 by the trial of Bukharin, Rykov, Krestinsky, Rakovsky and the rest of the twenty-one defendants, the so-called Right-Trotskyist Bloc. Stalin used this grandiose show trial in an effort to deliver a mortal blow to Trotsky and his supporters, accusing Trotsky of being a terrorist, spy, murderer and 'international scum'. After such 'unmaskings', he calculated, no government in the world would give Trotsky shelter, and eventually he would be handed over to the Soviet authorities. He also calculated that public opinion abroad would not overreact to the liquidation of Trotsky. The fact that he had long before deprived Trotsky of his Soviet citizenship and thus put him beyond the reach of Soviet claims was of no consequence to Stalin. In this trial, as in the other Moscow trials, the chief target was Trotsky. In the indictment of Pyatakov,

Radek, Sokolnikov et al Trotsky's name is mentioned no less than fifty times. The same was true of the indictments of Bukharin and his co-defendants.

From distant Mexico Trotsky issued protests and mocked the monstrous spectacle whose director remained firmly behind the scenes. He had already anticipated the outcome of the trials and their purpose. Countless failures in Soviet industry, agriculture and construction, and the slow rise in the standard of living, meant that 'wreckers' would have to be found: such was the logic of Stalin's method. Abnormal, forced rates of construction, for instance, led to poor workmanship, a vast number of accidents and breakdowns. There could only be one explanation: 'sabotage'. And one man was responsible for all this . . . But Trotsky was far away, across the ocean, and therefore Vyshinsky could only spray the wretched defendants in Moscow with the epithets of Stalinist justice: 'stinking carrion', 'pitiful scum', 'damned vermin', 'chained curs of imperialism'. *Pravda* described Soviet justice as 'the most democratic people's court in the world'.[130]

At all the show trials, one of the most alarming accusations was that of 'terrorism', 'plots to assassinate the leaders of the Party and government', the intent 'to kill Stalin'. Not a single concrete fact was, however, ever brought as evidence for such intentions. Today, it is relevant to ask whether in fact there was at least an intention to get rid of Stalin. Is there any documentary evidence to support such a possibility, and how reliable is it? In order to address this question, it is necessary to digress slightly.

In June 1938 the name of Genrikh Samoilovich Lyushkov would not have been heard on Soviet radio nor seen in the Soviet press, yet early on the morning of 13 June 1938 this former NKVD Chief of the Far Eastern Region, taking with him his code-books, a number of lists and some operational documents, crossed the Soviet–Manchurian border and asked the Japanese for political asylum. Lyushkov was well known to Yezhov, and even enjoyed the confidence of Stalin himself, having been appointed a deputy to the Supreme Soviet of the USSR with Stalin's knowledge. Having worked in the Cheka-OGPU-NKVD since 1920, Lyushkov was familiar with the rules and conventions of Soviet intelligence. He had taken an active part in the purge of state, Party and military senior ranks, so when two of Stalin's special trusties, Mekhlis and Frinovsky, arrived in the

Far East on Stalin's orders, Lyushkov knew that his own hour had come. He was told laconically that his job was 'to sort out Blyukher'.[131] Lyushkov realized that by not sending a timely signal to Moscow about Marshal Blyukher's 'wrecking activities', he had condemned himself. Such omissions were not forgiven. Before crossing the frontier he managed to arrange for his family to get out of Russia to Finland. Once in Manchuria, he actively cooperated with Japanese intelligence in the hope of being given passage to a third country, but he was to be disappointed. According to a book by the Japanese historian E. Hiyama, *Plans to Assassinate Stalin*, Japanese intelligence was planning to use Lyushkov to kill the Soviet leader. It has not proved possible to confirm or refute this claim.

Light can be thrown on the question of plots to kill Stalin from another angle. In the first half of February 1937, Fedor Dan read a report to a group of fellow-Mensheviks in Paris which essentially recapitulated the contents of two of his articles in *Sotsialisticheskii vestnik*, entitled 'The Death Sentence on the Bolsheviks' and 'The Political Crisis in the Soviet Union'. Dan noted that 'among the Mensheviks were some who recognized the positive side of terrorism'. Solomon Schwartz argued that he was 'against terror in general, but under certain circumstances it can play a positive role. The murder of Stalin would arouse the widest masses which would be beyond the control of Voroshilov or Kaganovich or anyone else who took Stalin's place.' The content of this meeting was reported to Moscow by the NKVD agent present.[132] However incapable this small group of Mensheviks might be of influencing events in the USSR, it is easy to see how such 'theoretical' views could be used by the suspicious Stalin to support his arguments at the February–March plenum.

There is, however, another source of evidence concerning the idea of getting rid of Stalin, this time connected directly with Trotsky. Among the numerous reports sent from Paris by Zborowski are two curious documents. The first, in Zborowski's hand, was dated 8 February 1937:

> On 22 January at [Zborowski's] apartment, speaking of the second Moscow trial and the role of the various defendants (Radek, Pyatakov and others), L. Sedov declared: 'There's no point in hesitating any longer. Stalin has to be killed.' I was so surprised by this, that I had no time to react. L. Sedov at once changed the subject. On 23 January

in my presence and that of L. Estrine, L. Sedov uttered something of the same sort as on the twenty-second. Estrine snapped 'Bite your tongue.' They did not return to this topic.[133]

Possibly the report was a fabrication designed to add fuel to the prosecution's arguments at the forthcoming trial. Yet it was not used by Vyshinsky or Ulrikh: no doubt they did not want to expose their secret agent in Paris. In any event, the document remained in Zborowski's dossier. Perhaps Sedov uttered the phrase in an outburst of hatred for Stalin, perhaps he was revealing a genuine intention. It should, however, be noted that several months before this event, the Chief of the Foreign Section of NKVD Main Directorate of State Security, Commissar Second Class Slutsky, reported to Yezhov:

On 21 June [1936] Trotsky's son, Lev Sedov, proposed to our source ('Mack') that he should go to the USSR to do illegal work. L. Sedov said to the source literally the following: 'We will give you missions, money and a passport. You will go for two or three months and go to several places at the addresses which we'll give you. It won't be easy. There is unfortunately no centre you can go to. The people are isolated and you'll have to look for them ...' Sedov gave no indication when this trip might take place.[134]

A month later a note was written in blue pencil on the report: 'Nothing happened.' Whether Zborowski declined the proposal or, more likely, Trotsky and his son changed their minds, is unknown.

The second document from the Zborowski collection, dated February 1938, is more lengthy and included the following:

Since 1936 'Sonny' has not talked to me any more about terror. He used to start conversations about it indirectly: 'Terrorism does not contradict Marxism. There are situations when terrorism is necessary.' While reading the newspapers, he said: 'The whole regime in the USSR depends on Stalin and if he were killed the whole lot would collapse.' He repeatedly returned [to this theme] and stressed that the murder of Comrade Stalin was necessary. During this conversation 'Sonny' asked me if I was afraid of death in general and was I capable of carrying out a terroristic act? In reply to my answer that it would depend on the need and the practicality, 'Sonny' said the whole thing depended on someone being ready to die. Like the members of the People's Will [a terrorist organization in nineteenth-century Russia]. He then said I was too soft for such a job. The conversation was abruptly terminated by the appearance of 'Neighbour' [Estrine] and the theme was not raised again.[135]

There are several possible explanations of this document. It may have been fabricated by the NKVD to be used should it be decided to recall Zborowski to Moscow for trial and liquidation. Nor can the possibility be ruled out that Zborowski was simply fantasizing. Or perhaps Lev, who was of a nervous and unstable disposition, had become obsessed by the idea of murdering Stalin. It is not inconceivable, either, that Trotsky himself was testing the ground to see if someone was capable of performing this act of terror in his name in order to rid the USSR of the Stalinist pollution. Trotsky's own attitude to terror and violence had been amply demonstrated by his strong-arm tactics during the civil war. Whatever the explanation, there is not a single shred of evidence that the Trotskyists carried out or prepared for any high-profile act of terrorism.

Speaking at the February–March plenum of the scale of the 'Trotskyist wrecking', Molotov quoted Stalin's words: 'How is it possible for the wrecking to have assumed such proportions? Who is to blame for it? We are to blame.'[136] He then regurgitated the argument that the NKVD had delayed liquidating the Trotskyists for four years. That delay would now be made up for with interest. Anyone who had ever had the slightest contact with Trotsky was placed under surveillance, arrested, exiled or executed. And, perhaps uniquely in history, the archives became a dangerous place. NKVD officials descended on the archives of the Red Army, the Central Committee and October Revolution, and systematically checked Trotsky's orders, directives and correspondence, collecting all the names found there for further 'processing'.[137] Practically all of the people discovered in this way would be executed in due course, whether they had served in the Revolutionary Military Council, the People's Commissariat, the armoured train, or were no more than acquaintances in Trotsky's Party or literary work. Hundreds of thousands of people were sucked into the vortex of the political trials, all of them, in Stalin's twisted logic, 'directed' by Trotsky. It should have been asked how such a vast army of conspirators could have come into being, considering that at the end of 1920s the 'left' opposition had numbered no more than three to five thousand people. As Trotsky himself wrote mockingly in an article entitled 'The Results of the Trial':

Judging by the results of the last series of trials, Vyshinsky must conclude that the Soviet state emerges as a centralized organization of state treason. The head of government and most of the People's Commissars . . .; the most important Soviet diplomats . . .; all the leaders of the Comintern . . .; all the economic chiefs . . .; the best leaders of the Red Army . . .; the most prominent worker-revolutionaries produced by Bolshevism over the last thirty-five years . . .; the head and members of the government of the Russian Republic . . .; the heads of all three dozen Soviet republics without exception . . .; the GPU chiefs of the last ten years . . . and finally and most important, members of the all-mighty Politburo, the supreme power in the country – all these people were involved in a conspiracy against the Soviet regime, even when it was in their hands. All of them, as agents of foreign powers, strove to tear the Soviet Federation that they had built into shreds and to enslave in Fascism the peoples they had struggled for decades to liberate.

In their criminal activity, premiers, ministers, marshals and ambassadors were invariably subordinate to one man. Not an official leader, but an outcast. Trotsky had only to lift his finger and veterans of the revolution became agents of Hitler and the Mikado. On 'Trotsky's instructions' leaders of industry, transport and agriculture destroyed the country's productive forces and its culture. On an instruction sent from Norway or Mexico by an 'enemy of the people' the railway workers of the Far East organized the derailment of military trains and venerable Kremlin physicians poisoned their patients . . . There is a problem, however. If all the key points of the system were occupied by Trotskyists under my orders, how is it that Stalin is in the Kremlin and I am in exile?[138]

The Moscow trials were not only a general purge, they were staged so as to destroy Trotsky morally, politically and psychologically; the order to annihilate him physically had been given long before. The people, fed on disinformation and deception, blindly supported the regime's actions. Meetings were held with such slogans as, 'Death to the Fascist hirelings!', 'Crush the Trotskyist vermin!', 'Trotskyism is another form of Fascism!'. On 6 March 1937 *Pravda* asserted that 'the Trotskyists are a find for international Fascism . . . The insignificant number of this gang should not reassure us, we have to increase our vigilance tenfold.' On 15 March 1938 *Vechernyaya Moskva* (Moscow Evening News) wrote: 'History knows no evil deeds equal to the crimes of the gang from the anti-Soviet Right-Trotskyist Bloc. The espionage, sabotage and wrecking done by the *ober*-bandit Trotsky and his accomplices Bukharin, Rykov and the others, arouses feelings of anger, hatred and contempt not only in the Soviet people, but all progressive mankind.'

Tens of millions of people were seized by one of the greatest confidence tricks in history. The vast, unhappy country condemned its fake enemies. The security and intelligence services also underwent a fearful purge. In 1937–38 23,000 NKVD officials were arrested. Most of those interrogated informed on others in order to survive. Suspicion turned people into scoundrels. The Chief of the First Section of the Main Intelligence Directorate of the Red Army A.I. Starunin sent a report 'upwards', and as a result of its 'hostile leadership', the Red Army was left virtually without any intelligence organization. On the eve of the Second World War, the army had no 'eyes and ears'. Between 1938 and 1940 three heads of Red Army intelligence were liquidated: Ya.K. Berzin, S.P. Uritsky and I.I. Proskurin, along with almost all deputy heads of directorate and most department chiefs. Before his own arrest, Proskurin reported, as if it were a great achievement: 'More than half of the intelligence personnel have been arrested.'[139]

As Alexander Orlov, a senior intelligence official who, as we have seen, defected from the USSR in the 1930s, wrote: 'Although Trotsky was thousands of kilometres from the courtroom, everyone knew that it was precisely he who was the chief defendant, here as in the previous trials. It was precisely because of him that the gigantic machine of Stalinist falsifications was set in motion again, and each of the defendants could clearly feel Stalin's hatred pulsating here, and Stalin's thirst for revenge, aimed at the distant Trotsky.'[140] It is plain now that the trials, which were fabricated from start to finish, occasionally touched on facts which did have a degree of relevance to Trotsky.

Trotsky responded to Stalin with equally burning hatred, though rather more justification: nearly all his family and loved ones had been destroyed directly or indirectly by Stalin's actions. He did not, however, want to be thought of as vengeful or full of hatred. He had never expected the struggle of the 'left' opposition to end in a personal battle. Things were far more complex. Therefore, when he continued with his biography of Stalin, he wrote in the preface:

Certain circles speak and write of my hatred for Stalin which inspires me with gloomy judgements and predictions. I can only shrug my shoulders at this. Our paths have diverged so far and so long ago, and he is for me a tool of such inimical and hostile historical forces, that my personal feelings towards him hardly differ from my feelings for Hitler or the Japanese Mikado. Whatever personal feeling there was has long been burnt out. The observation point that I have occupied has not permitted me to identify the real human person with the gigantic shadow he throws on the screen of the bureaucracy. I therefore think I have the right to say that I have never raised Stalin in my mind to a feeling of hatred for him.[141]

Did Trotsky not remember, however, that as the 'second man' in the country he had himself laid the foundations of lawlessness? In November 1922 the Bolshevik leaders in Baku reported to the Politburo on a trial of Socialist Revolutionaries, indicating that of the thirty-eight defendants, eight had been sentenced to death and the Baku people wanted the Politburo's approval of the sentences, which they themselves regarded as essential. Lenin, Trotsky, Stalin and Molotov voted in favour without hesitation.[142] Stalin had been well trained by Lenin and Trotsky.

Even after Trotsky had been murdered, Stalin feared his shadow. As late as December 1947 he ordered the Ministry of the Interior to build top security prisons and camps for especially dangerous state criminals, above all 'for Trotskyists, terrorists, Mensheviks, SRs, nationalists'. Stalin's personal archive contains Interior Minister S.N. Kruglov's reply in early February 1948: 'In accordance with your instructions I herewith present a draft decision of the Central Committee for organizing strict regime camps and prisons to contain especially dangerous state criminals. I request your decision.'[143] Stalin gave his decision, which the Council of Ministers rubber-stamped on 21 February 1948 and the Ministry of the Interior carried out one week later.

The documents show that these prisons and camps for 'Trotskyists and other enemies' were to be built in Kolyma and Norilsk in the Komi Autonomous Soviet Republic, at Yelaburg, Karaganda and other sites which formed the 'Gulag Archipelago'. The judicial foundation was provided by the appropriate section of the infamous and much amended Article 58, according to which even the family of the 'criminal' were subject to inhuman punishment.[144] The Minister of the Interior, following Stalin's orders, issued instructions that 'Chekist work must be done in order to expose any Trotskyists and other enemies of the state still at large,' and that there should no 'reduction of the term of punishment for such people nor the granting of any other privileges', instead, when their terms of imprisonment and exile came to an end, 'freed prisoners must be held for further registration'.[145]

Until his dying day, Stalin regarded Trotskyists as dangerous enemies, the embodiment of a universal evil. His henchmen therefore continued to hunt for them as long as Stalin was alive. Kruglov was soon requesting Stalin's personal permission 'to increase the size of the special camps' from the present 180,000 'by another 70,000 to bring them up to 250,000 prisoners'.[146] Stalin of course agreed, and no doubt would have liked to turn the whole country into a camp. Indeed, in many respects it already resembled one. The peasants were denied internal passports and were therefore unable to move around the country, fixed like serfs in their settlements. In every work-group and army company, in every university department and workshop there were secret informers, but no one was prepared to say that the Soviet Union was moving towards a state of slavery. Anyone who might have done so was liquidated, while the rest thought things were as they were supposed to be. The system had turned the people into a tool for achieving utopia. The revolution to which Trotsky had dedicated himself had turned into the pathology of social development.

The Loneliness of Coyoacan

Trotsky had never led the life of a hermit. He was used to being surrounded by large numbers of people, and this remained true to the end of his life. Yet in Mexico he and his wife felt a deep inner loneliness. The gradual loss of the ideals to which he had dedicated his entire life, the deaths of all his children and so many friends, and the passing of the days inexorably gnawed at the core of his being. More than once he thought of suicide, but did not want to leave such a stain on his record as a fighter and revolutionary.

Against their expectations, the couple were welcomed in Mexico with something approaching genuine friendliness. When the empty tanker *Ruth* docked at Tampico on 9 January 1937, Trotsky refused to disembark before he could see they were being met by friends. He was not disappointed. More significantly, perhaps, he was warmly greeted by official representatives of President Lazaro Cardenas, who put his personal railcar at Trotsky's disposal. In fact, Trotsky was the guest of the president and the painter Diego Rivera. A small group of American Trotskyists were also there to meet him. It had been arranged that Trotsky and Natalya would stay with Rivera in his house, Casa Azul, on London Street in Coyoacan, a suburb of Mexico City, designed and built by the artist himself as a refuge for art, inspiration and creativity.

Trotsky and Natalya were ecstatic over their new abode. In his first letter to his son Lev he wrote: 'The Mexican authorities have treated us with utterly exceptional courtesy . . . The President is carrying out a radical and bold policy. He is helping [Republican] Spain openly and has promised to do everything to make our stay here comfortable.'[147] According to a report from NKVD agent 'Oscar' to Moscow, Diego Rivera was making speeches in which he called on 'true Marxists to break with the police-reactionary spirit represented by Iosif Stalin'. As for Rivera's own agenda, 'Oscar' reported, he dreamed of creating a worldwide 'congress which would officially consecrate the founding of an international federation of arts workers. We want: independent art for the revolution; revolution for the ultimate liberation of art.'[148] Trotsky was cheered by Rivera's message, he admired his work as an artist, and all in all was much buoyed by his first impressions of Mexico.

After briefly recounting the pleasure of arriving in the new country, Trotsky in his letter to Lev soon passed on to business matters. While on board ship he had completed his book on the Moscow trials, which would eventually appear under the title *Stalin's Crimes*, and he needed publishers. The main item of news he passed to Lev was that he had decided with his friends George Novak and Max Shachtman to organize a counter-trial at which the lies, slander and insinuations of the Moscow trials would be exposed. It was hoped the trial would be held

either in New York or Paris, or as a last resort in Switzerland. He
then gave Lev a string of orders, to find certain documents, contact
his supporters, analyse the European press reaction to the Moscow
trials, indicate what should go into the next issue of the *Bulletin*, and
so on. He seemed to expect Lev to perform as if he had a large
secretariat at his disposal, but he spared himself no more than he did
his son. His subsequent letters were similar in content, except that he
also reported that Natalya had contracted malaria, and described
his own state of mind and the wonderful fruits and vegetables of
Mexico.

During this first year, while enjoying excellent relations with the
hospitable Rivera, Trotsky set about preparing the counter-trial. He
hoped that with Rivera's help he would be able to arouse world public
opinion against Stalin's tyranny. To each accusation levelled at him
in Moscow, he scrupulously prepared factual, documentary or logical
refutations. The work also occupied both his secretaries and an assistant he had been lucky to find. She was the daughter of a Russian,
she had not lost her native language and she could type very well.
She was also connected with the NKVD, and her job was naturally
to pass on information about what was happening within Trotsky's
entourage. It has been suggested that she was also working for the
FBI.[149] The small team of assistants worked from dawn till dusk, and
Trotsky was looking forward to staging a major event that would
condemn Stalin.

Quite soon after arriving in Mexico, Trotsky became in effect the
object of two diametrically opposed forces, both of them eminent
artists. On the one hand, Diego Rivera, who had been one of the
founders of the Mexican Communist Party but was no longer a
member, was at first a cordial, attentive and concerned host. The
other artist was David Alfaro Siqueiros, who wanted Trotsky expelled
from the country. Trotsky had become used to being the centre of
conflicting attention, and was therefore not particularly concerned by
calls that were also coming from the head of Mexican trade unions,
Vincente Lombardo Toledano, to 'despatch the enemy of the socialist
revolution from all four corners of the country'. Trotsky recognized
the cautious and discreet concern the Mexican president showed by
way of police protection, and expressed his gratitude on a number of
occasions. But he did not meet Cardenas once in his three and a half

years in the country, though he could understand that his presence had placed the head of state in an awkward position.

Trotsky had barely set foot on Mexican soil before secret agents from Moscow arrived there, among them a man whose testimony is of exceptional importance. Pavel Anatolievich Sudoplatov was a Soviet intelligence agent with enormous experience. His life was in a sense doubly wasted, for he was imprisoned for fifteen years when Beria was arrested in 1953, and he had pursued his grisly career in the sincere belief that he was carrying out the higher will of the proletariat. Sudoplatov described for me not only the details of the hunt for Trotsky on Stalin's personal orders, but also the climate inside the NKVD at the time. The Secret Political Section of the NKVD Main State Security Administration, which from early 1937 had been strengthened by new cadres for its overseas work,[150] like the Foreign Section, responded actively to Trotsky's crossing the Atlantic.[151] According to Sudoplatov, experienced undercover agents were despatched to Mexico to keep a watch on Trotsky and to carry out his extermination.

The preparation of the counter-trial was greatly helped by the vast amount of material sent from Paris by Lev Sedov.[152] Some of the evidence took great efforts to prepare. Simply to prove that Trotsky had visited Copenhagen in 1932 for the sole purpose of giving lectures, his helpers were required to interview forty people and send their depositions to Mexico. The Social History Institute in Amsterdam contains eloquent evidence of the efforts made by Lev to assist his father's campaign to repudiate the charges made against him in the Moscow trials.[153]

The American Committee for the Defence of Leon Trotsky was a broad-based group comprising hundreds of members, many of them distinguished writers, trade union leaders, lawyers and journalists, naturally from the left of the US political spectrum. Its president was the eminent educationist and philosopher John Dewey, and it was assisted by a companion body in France, the French Commission of Inquiry into the Moscow Trials, set up by Trotsky's close friends the Rosmers and their circle, and comprising writers, lawyers and public figures from the front rank of the large and influential left wing of French politics. The Soviet embassy in Washington and the Communist Parties of America and Mexico were invited to send representatives to the counter-trial, thus giving them an opportunity to question Trotsky directly, but the Soviet ambassador ignored the invitation, and the Mexican trade union and Communist Party leaders, Lombardo Toledano and Hernan Laborde, sent abusive replies.[154]

Since a US visa for Trotsky was ruled out and his presence in Paris was already prohibited, the inquiry, which was launched by a preliminary commission under Dewey, was held in Mexico. Dewey opened the proceedings in Rivera's Casa Azul on 10 April 1937 by declaring that 'no man should be condemned without a chance to defend himself' and that the Commission's purpose was 'to ascertain the truth as far as is humanly possible . . . If Leon Trotsky is guilty of the acts with which he is charged, condemnation cannot be too severe.'[155] The hearing ranged over the entire list of charges against Trotsky, but under cross-examination he was able to refute every one of them with documentary and factual evidence. He proved false Goltsman's claim that they had met in Copenhagen in 1932, Romm's that they had met in the Bois de Boulogne in 1933, showed that Pyatakov could not have flown to Norway in December 1935, and so on. The officially notarized receipts and train tickets that he was able to produce for the Commission totally undermined the false testimony given in Moscow. As 'Mack' had reported to Moscow, Lev Sedov 'had seen Pyatakov at the Unter den Linden in Berlin on 1 May 1931. Pyatakov had recognized him but turned away and did not want to speak to him. Pyatakov then went off with someone else, apparently Shestov.'[156]

Trotsky made a deep impression on the hearing when he declared: 'If the Commission finds that I am in the slightest degree guilty of the crimes ascribed to me by Stalin, then I undertake beforehand to hand myself over voluntarily to the GPU executioners.' He requested that his statement be published in the press. It was a brave move, since the Commission was not composed entirely of his supporters. If, however, the Commission did not corroborate Stalin's accusations, 'it would stand as an eternal curse of the Kremlin leaders'. The hearing lasted a week and Trotsky's hour-long concluding speech was so passionate, and the Commission so profoundly moved by his rhetoric, that Dewey, when he finally found his voice, closed the hearing with: 'Anything I can say will be an anti-climax.'

The Dewey Commission did not reach a formal verdict until 13

December 1937. It covered 247 points and the 627-page manuscript was eventually published by Harper Brothers of New York in a volume 600 pages long. Its conclusion was that Trotsky and his son were innocent of all the charges.[157] Trotsky had expected that publishers would fall over themselves to publish the rich collection of material he had gathered for the hearings, and he had been convinced that both the counter-trial and his speech would find a ready outlet in the press. But the US coverage was less than universal, and the European press was preoccupied with the rising tension in international relations. The monumental labour carried out by the Dewey Commission, lasting almost 300 days, in effect gave Trotsky little more than personal satisfaction. The counter-trial was not going to influence either Moscow or the world, as he had hoped.

The effort involved and the results obtained from the counter-trial left Trotsky feeling devastated and isolated. Apart from a small group of his supporters and some cultural figures and intellectuals, the world had shown indifference. Stalin, of course, had not been indifferent, and this only added to Trotsky's sense of failure. All his efforts had not succeeded in pushing back the evil by so much as an inch. He had to accept that for some truths to be acknowledged, much time was needed. Moreover, most of the world had come to see that nothing good would come of a new revolution. For his part, Trotsky remained forever locked within the 'magic circle' of revolution, and for that reason the world had been uninterested in the counter-trial. Interest in him as an individual and revolutionary remained high, but not in his revolutionary illusions.

The Kremlin observed Trotsky's activities in Mexico closely. The embassies in Washington and Mexico and the intelligence bodies sent regular reports on every aspect of his behaviour, not only to the 'summit' of Stalin, Molotov and Yezhov, but also to the Soviet ideological centres which were expected to mould propaganda accordingly. For instance, an article entitled 'Trotsky in Coyoacan' by the American journalist Joseph Freeman, which had been published in several US and Mexican newspapers in April 1937, was circulated to the following Central Committee departments: Stetsky, Head of Culture and Propaganda; Angarov, Head of Arts; Koltsov, chief editor of *Pravda*; Stavsky of the Writers' Union; Yudin, Head of the Press Department. Freeman had written: 'On his arrival in Coyoacan,

Trotsky received a group of bourgeois journalists; they asked him about his differences with Stalin and his relations with the Gestapo. Trotsky let loose a torrent of frenzied abuse against the Soviet Union and Stalin, but said nothing about Hitler and Mussolini.' The article went into detail about 'the day and night police sentries' guarding Trotsky: 'No one has ever attempted to do him any harm, although Trotsky never stops referring to the danger threatening his person ... Trotsky's statements bore the character of rabid attacks on his own country and the cause with which he has never been associated.'[158] It is worth noting that soon Freeman would be writing reports from Moscow on the Bukharin trial which his New York newspaper, the *Daily Worker*, would find too frank to publish. He was soon expelled from the American Communist Party.

The leaders in the Kremlin, while monitoring Trotsky's reactions to the trials, were also keeping a close watch on the American reaction. Soviet diplomats and intelligence agents across the ocean were reading dozens of newspapers and magazines and sending in their reports and prognoses. An entire volume of such reports was sent to Voroshilov in the first three months of 1937 alone. It contains cuttings from a wide range of the US press on Trotsky's arrival in Mexico. However much they tried, these Soviet researchers could find nothing positive to say, and they were therefore compelled to send critical accounts to Moscow. 'With Trotsky's move to Mexico,' they reported, 'the Trotskyists in the USA stepped up their publishing activities. There have been recent announcements of the publication and writing of several Trotskyist books. Thus, Shechtman's *Behind the Scenes of the Moscow Trials* is out; soon Trotsky's *The Revolution Betrayed* is to be published, as well as *Stalin's Crimes*.'[159]

Such reports only succeeded in stoking up the fires of Stalin's hatred for Trotsky, who even in his present position was able to land painful blows on the General Secretary's feelings, and cast a shadow over his policies, but most of all show him in the most unpleasant light. Stalin became increasingly convinced that both the Foreign Section of the NKVD and its Secret Political Department were doing their jobs. Yezhov obviously lacked proper control of the international part of his 'mission'. The sources of information, to please their masters, were also twisting the facts and fabricating forgeries about Trotsky. In January 1938, for instance, the Washington embassy reported that

Trotsky had said in one of his speeches that 'Stalin has placed himself above any Party criticism and above the state. The only way to replace him is by murdering him.'[160] Trotsky had said nothing of the kind, but such 'evidence' would figure in the 1938 trial of the 'Right-Trotskyist Bloc' as particularly telling.

On Stalin's orders, the ambassador in Washington, Troyanovsky, and his counsellor, Umansky, published articles and gave interviews to American journalists with the aim of altering the negative US view of what was happening in Moscow. An extract from one such piece by Troyanovsky gives an idea of their general character:

> After the tolerance that was shown to these people [the accused], after the Soviet leadership, and especially Stalin, showed themselves willing to help these people and to save them from falling into the abyss of counter-revolution, no informed person can believe that these people were accused without preliminary and careful investigation. I myself have personally witnessed the gentleness Stalin showed towards Pyatakov, Soklonikov, Radek and others. Any suggestion of personal vengeance and settling of scores from base feelings is not worthy of reply ... Nearly all the accused enjoyed a cordial attitude and trust on Stalin's part, even after Stalin knew they had once been ardent Trotskyists.[161]

In an interview with the *New York Herald Tribune* on 13 February 1938, Umansky declared that Trotsky's demand for a dispassionate review of the charges that had been levelled at him 'is so ludicrous that it's not worth discussing ... The Trotskyists are trying to force a war in order to seize power and carry out their plans for the restoration [of capitalism] ... Two facts speak for themselves: the complete support the Soviet people is giving to the new Constitution, and the support Trotsky is giving Fascism and the support Fascism is giving Trotsky.'[162]

Soviet diplomats had become victims of 'bureaucratic absolutism', as had the population itself. The wild words to be found, for example, in *Bolshevik* reflect the blindness of a people deprived of conscience, memory and the capacity to think:

> The sentence of the court is the sentence of the people. With unanimous approval the Soviet people greeted the sentence of the military collegium of the Supreme Court on the participants in the anti-Soviet

Trotskyist centre. In factories and mills, on collective farms, at town meetings of workers a stormy wave of the people's wrath rose up against the base traitors and betrayers of our motherland, against the murderers of workers and Red Army men, against the German and Japanese spies, the warmongers who were working under the direct orders of the ferocious enemy of the people, Trotsky . . . Enemy of the people Trotsky gave an undertaking to German Fascism that if he could seize power he would liquidate the state farms, disperse the collective farms, terminate the policy of industrialization and restore capitalist relations to Soviet territory . . . The Trotskyist bands were eager to repay their Fascist bosses in the bloody coin given them by the most sworn enemy of the people, L. Trotsky.[163]

Sad to say, people sincerely and for many years believed this delirium, as they believed Vyshinsky when he said at one of those monstrous trials: 'I do not make these accusations alone! Alongside me, Comrade Judges, I feel as if the victims of these crimes and these criminals are standing here, on crutches, crippled, half-alive, perhaps with no legs at all, like the signal-woman of Chusovskaya Station, Comrade Nagovitsyna, who wrote to me today in the pages of *Pravda* and who at the age of twenty lost both legs; she warned of the destruction being planned by these people here.'[164]

The barefaced rabble-rousing did its work, and the population came to believe that Trotsky was indeed a 'terrorist, spy and murderer'. Reading such material, Trotsky was shaken by the depths to which the Party and people could sink in barely a decade. Amazingly, he managed to retain his self-control and the will to fight.

Trotsky made mistakes of his own in this uneven contest. He was critical of the part played by the Popular Front in the Spanish civil war, and by dismissing out of hand the activities of the Communist Parties that did not accept his approach, only added to the difficulties already facing the defenders of the Republic. In the numerous interviews he gave to the press, he was not always discreet in his choice of words, condemning not only Stalin and his henchmen, but also the people and the state as a whole, forgetting the part he himself had played in bringing that state into existence. None of this went unnoticed.

In 1938, at the height of the Moscow trials, many of Trotsky's intellectual friends began asking themselves at what point and from what source the Stalinist terror and the violent, anti-democratic character of the Soviet regime had originated. For Max Eastman, Victor Serge and Boris Souvarine the rot had begun with the crushing of the Kronstadt revolt in March 1921.* They now publicly raised the question of Trotsky's personal responsibility. Serge declared unequivocally that this use of force against those who thought differently from the Bolsheviks had signalled a shift to repressive policies in the Soviet republic while Lenin and Trotsky were still in power. Had Trotsky not led the punitive expedition himself? In what way was he superior to Stalin? Trotsky had never described the Kronstadt revolt: no doubt like others involved in crushing it he found it unpleasant to recall. But the criticism from his recent supporters was serious and required answering.

In an article entitled 'Once More on the Suppression of Kronstadt', Trotsky replied to his critics in characteristic style:

> In his book on Stalin, that faded Marxist-turned-sycophant Souvarine claims that in my autobiography I purposely said nothing about the Kronstadt revolt: there are, he says ironically, feats one is not proud of ... The fact is I took not the slightest part in the suppression of the Kronstadt revolt itself, nor in the repressions that ensued ... As far as I recall, it was Dzerzhinsky who dealt with the repressions, and he (rightly) never permitted any interference in his work ... However, I am willing to admit that a civil war is not a school of humanitarianism ... Let those who wish to reject the revolution as a whole on these grounds (in their little articles) do so. I do not reject it. In this sense, I fully and entirely bear responsibility for the suppression of the Kronstadt revolt.[165]

Trotsky was not entirely honest in dealing with this issue. With Lenin's knowledge, he had indeed been one of the organizers of the bloody suppression of the revolt. The criticism coming from his

---

* The soldiers and sailors of the island garrison had risen up against the Bolshevik government they had helped bring to power. The economic crisis of early 1921, combined with a sense of political betrayal, led to a rebellion which the Red Army, under Trotsky's leadership, crushed with extreme violence. Trotsky had responded to the rebels' attempts to negotiate with a demand for unconditional surrender, otherwise they would be 'shot like partridges'. Fifty thousand Red Army troops made the final assault, killing hundreds in combat and later as prisoners.

former friends had found a raw nerve and he felt constrained to respond in a further long polemical article, entitled 'The Fuss About Kronstadt', written at the end of 1937 and beginning of 1938. It quickly found its way via Zborowski to Stalin's desk.[166] This was one occasion when the General Secretary could not have found fault with his former rival, for the line Trotsky took on Kronstadt coincided precisely with the official Soviet line at the time. Indeed, Stalin could have put his own signature to it. Among other things, Trotsky wrote: 'The Kronstadt revolt was nothing more than the armed reaction of the petty bourgeoisie against the difficulties of the socialist revolution and the dictatorship of the proletariat . . . The [rebels] wanted a revolution that would not lead to a dictatorship, and a dictatorship that did not use coercion.'[167] This was pure Stalinist, or rather Bolshevik, cant. Trotsky and Stalin may have been diametrically opposed in personal terms, but they both remained typical Bolsheviks, obsessed with violence, dictatorship and coercion.

Simultaneously, Trotsky was having to repudiate the Stalinist slander, the criticism of his former supporters and the attacks of the Mexican Communist and labour organizations that were demanding his deportation from the country. Feelings of loneliness and isolation grew in him and at times led to depression. He did not give in, however, and tried to keep up the front of the committed revolutionary, reminding the world community that he was alive and had not yet spoken his last word. Only his wife knew how low he really felt.

The two years they lived in Diego Rivera's house seemed idyllic, in terms of their physical well-being. Then, suddenly, a rift occurred. The bone of contention was President Cardenas, whom Trotsky regarded with the greatest respect for having provided a refuge. Then, unexpectedly, Rivera published a blistering attack on the president as 'an accomplice of the regime in Moscow'. Trotsky and Rivera attempted to solve their differences, but they only grew deeper, until Trotsky announced he no longer found it possible to accept the painter's hospitality.

At almost the same time other events were taking place in the Trotsky family which complicated matters further. When Trotsky first arrived in Mexico he had met Rivera's wife, the painter and actress Frida Kahlo. She was a woman of great beauty and delicacy, and living in the same house, she and Trotsky saw each other constantly. Suddenly, at the age of fifty-seven, Trotsky felt an overwhelming attraction to this intelligent and enchanting woman. By nature a puritan, he had strict views on family relations and still loved his wife sincerely, yet he almost lost his head, even becoming oblivious to the social good conduct he normally observed by openly displaying obvious signs of attention to Frida. In July 1937, at Rivera's suggestion, he went on his own to stay for three weeks at the village of Gomez Landero, where he relaxed, rode, did some fishing and wrote. A few days after his arrival there, Frida joined him. The true nature of the relationship between the worn-out revolutionary of a certain age and the twenty-eight-year-old beauty is not known. But it is plain he was infatuated with her. This much is revealed by the few notes he sent her that have recently been discovered among the papers of Frida's friend Teresa Proentso, by the Mexican journalist Xavier Guzman Urbiola.[168]

The notes show the depth of feeling Trotsky was experiencing. His relations with Frida became known to Natalya and Diego, and difficult moments ensued. Trotsky had the good sense not to take things so far as to break with Natalya. He managed to shake himself free of Frida's charms and to tell Natalya everything. His secretary, van Heijenoort, wrote in his book *With Trotsky in Exile: From Prinkipo to Coyoacan* that after a brief moment of 'torment', Trotsky's common sense had triumphed over his feelings.

Relations with Diego, however, could not be so easily repaired. In his last note to Frida, Trotsky wrote: 'I still hope it will be possible to restore my friendship with him, both political and personal, and I sincerely hope you will share this opinion. Natalya and I wish you the best of health and real artistic success and I embrace you as our good and sincere friend. As ever, Yours, L. Trotsky.'[169]

With the help of American friends, in the spring of 1939 Trotsky acquired a large but uncomfortable house on Vienna Street in Coyoacan, and at once assumed a financial burden beyond his means. He published whatever he could, received advances for his unfinished book on Stalin and tried to reissue his old books. He still needed to pay two or three secretaries, a bodyguard, a housekeeper and a typist. Under these circumstances, he felt compelled to sell his archives to the Houghton Library at Harvard University for the astonishingly small sum of $15,000. As before, he was helped in the crisis by friends, notably Albert Goldman, and was thus able more or less to maintain his way of life.

The first task to which his friends and his guards turned their attention was to see to the security of the house. They raised a high fence and strengthened the doors and gates to the property. A high tower with a searchlight was erected and an alarm system installed inside the house, which now took on the appearance of a small fortress. The doors to Trotsky's study and his bedroom were lined with sheet-iron. The outside of the house was patrolled day and night by the police and the inside by his secretaries and bodyguard. Monitoring arrangements were organized for visitors. People Trotsky did not know were admitted into his presence only if they were carrying nothing and were accompanied by the bodyguard. Journalists continued to call and supporters still came from different countries, as well as publishers and Trotskyist activists. From one of the secretaries, Zborowski learnt that Trotsky 'has a weakness for visitors from the [Soviet] Union and Spain', and passed this intelligence on to his masters in Moscow.[170] It was valuable information.

Trotsky planned his days in strict order. Rising early, he would work at his desk for two hours before lunch, after which he carried on with his literary labours until dinner. Life in the little fortress was tense and nervous. Its inhabitants noticed that the number of unfamiliar faces around the place seemed to be growing. For a time, an observation point was established in a neighbouring property. It appeared at first as if there was some digging going on, but then it became clear that each shift of three or four men was spending more time observing Trotsky's house than working in the trench. NKVD officials who had had to flee Spain in the aftermath of the civil war seemed to have found an alternative base next door to Trotsky. He redoubled the security of his walls and doors. Taking exercise, usually in the evenings, he would pace thirty steps in the yard in one direction, then thirty back. He was immersed in his book on Stalin, and he confided to Natalya that now his mind was ranging over the gamut of his experience, from the turn of the century to October 1917, to the mistake he and Lenin had made in not having seen through the 'wonderful Georgian', as Lenin had described Stalin so many years ago.

In a letter to the editor of the *Bulletin* in March 1938, Trotsky wrote:

> I am committed to write a book on Stalin and to finish my book on Lenin in the next eighteen months. All of my time, at least over the next few months, will be devoted to this work ... I will need your help with the book on Stalin. Tomorrow I'll send you the list of books I have on Stalin. I can tell you now that I don't have Barbusse's book. I don't know if there are any special files on Stalin in Lev's archive.[171]

It is not hard to imagine the effect of this letter on Stalin when it landed on his desk. In eighteen months a book on him, written by his best-informed enemy, would be published. It must not happen. It was precisely at this time, late 1938 and early 1939, that Stalin's verbal instructions to liquidate Trotsky became frantic. Trotsky meanwhile was writing to his friends for more material on Stalin. In May 1938 he asked Kogan 'to look through the journal *Krasnaya Nov*' from the point of view of Stalin's political evolution, or rather his zigzags, and the methods he used to fight the opposition. I will be much obliged to you for any information of this sort, as I have very few books here, and I have to finish the book on Stalin within five months.'[172]

Occasionally, early in the morning, accompanied by two or three men, Trotsky would disguise himself and, tucking into a corner of the car, escape from the fortress for a brief outing. They would drive twenty or thirty kilometres into the mountains and fields, wander around looking for original kinds of cactus, find a village and have lunch and return home quickly under cover of darkness. Every such 'expedition', as he called these trips, was fraught with risk. On several occasions when an open attack was expected, Trotsky would go to a remote village for two or three weeks and stay in a secretly hired peasant hut, in disguise and under an assumed name. Quite a few letters from him to Natalya during these periods have survived, and they reveal his intimate and tender feelings for her. Almost never did he discuss political or ideological topics in them, and they testify to his growing sense of isolation and his awareness that she was the last remaining person in the world who was close to him.

In one of his letters, he wrote: '... as I read your letter I wept ... Everything you said to me about our past is right, and I have said the same thing to myself hundreds and hundreds of times. Isn't it monstrous now to torment oneself over the way things were more than twenty years ago? Over details? But still some trivial question sticks in my mind, as if our entire life depended on answering it . . . So I run for a piece of paper and write the question down.'[173] The death of his last son had filled his heart with desolation, pain and sadness. He recognized that his present efforts were ephemeral, but he still maintained one last goal, to preserve his reputation as a revolutionary, so that history would allocate a niche for him that would last forever.

The loneliness of the unhappy couple was relieved when their last true friends, the Rosmers, came to Coyoacan in October 1939, bringing with them Trotsky's grandson Seva. They stayed in the gloomy house for eight months. Trotsky and Natalya were overjoyed by the boy's arrival, although Seva, who had been transported from one country to another and constantly surrounded by new faces, did not understand much of what was happening. He had attended schools in German and French, and since his Uncle Lev's death, no one had spoken to him in Russian, so that he spoke his native language like a foreigner. The tragedy of the family was as it were etched on the boy's mind as a kaleidoscope of names, places, and rivalries between people who claimed a right to him. Now, at least, the boy could bring his grandfather joy in his last few months.

The Illusion of the International

While still on Prinkipo, and as the thought of being able to return to Moscow began to fade, Trotsky realized that what was needed was an organization inside the Communist movement to resist Stalin and Stalinism. He recognized that such an organization could succeed only if it had a clear programme, aims and means. As a political and ideological trend, from the outset Trotskyism was at a serious disadvantage: it set out to do battle not only with capitalism, the bourgeois political parties and governments, but also with everyone who in Trotsky's opinion had betrayed Marxism and Leninism. Among these he included all the Communist and workers' parties which had joined the Third International and recognized its programme.

By the early 1930s, in several European countries and North and

South America, parties and groups had emerged which shared the ideas of the 'Bolshevik-Leninists' – who were in step, that is, with the views of the crushed Left opposition of the Soviet Communist Party. Trotsky conducted a wide-ranging correspondence with these people and their representatives visited him for advice and inspiration, but he soon came to feel that there were far too few of them, numbering only a few hundred. In an interview in March 1937, he confessed: 'It is hard to be sure of the exact number, especially as there are constant shifts within the working class: there are semi-supporters and demi-semi-supporters, and so on. I think today one could speak of several tens of thousands of them.'[174] Plainly this was a considerable exaggeration.

It was a disappointment and a surprise to Trotsky that these parties and groups were constantly riven by discord, splits and mutual hostility. Many of them were sectarian, leftist formations whose members had been expelled from Communist and workers' parties. Among them also were many provocateurs and OGPU agents whose purpose in joining was anything but revolutionary. Indeed, the NKVD was extremely well informed about most of the activities and conferences of the Trotskyists. Copies and the originals of many of their documents are to be found in the NKVD archives. For example, in March 1937 Yezhov sent Stalin 'the continuation of Sedov's letter to Trotsky of 3 March. The information from the USSR that he cites in this letter allegedly came via Menshevik circles from a French newspaper representative or the agent Havas who left Moscow recently. Measures have been taken to find out more about this individual. The letter contains some omissions and lack of clarity, which is explained by the fact that it was taken down while being dictated.'[175]

To be named in Trotsky's correspondence as a supporter inside the USSR led, of course, to immediate arrest. In a note from Moscow to agent 'Skif' in June 1939, orders were given to ensure that Zborowski 'should be directed above all to finding out about espionage, terrorist centres, counter-revolutionary contacts with the USSR, preparation of any transfers to the USSR and so on'.[176] This largely explains the high number of arrests and murders, not only of Trotsky's supporters, but of anyone who was even indirectly connected with them inside the USSR. Outside the country, especially in Spain during the civil war and under the guise of dealing with the Soviet Union's enemies, NKVD operatives carried on the work of their comrades at home and arranged the assassinations of many Trotskyist sympathizers. Any Soviet citizen sent abroad on official business was liable to arrest as a Trotskyist spy immediately upon return to the Soviet Union.

As the documents in the 'Sneevliet' collection and in the archive obtained with Zborowski's help make clear, 'Tulip', as Zborowski was also codenamed, was deputed to work on the members of the Fourth International Secretariat, and to provide information on French Trotskyists and Lev Sedov. 'With his assistance,' reads one report, 'the archives of the International Secretariat and part of Trotsky's archive were lifted.'[177] Through the work of agents like Zborowski, Moscow aimed at blocking the 'subversive actions' of the Trotskyists.

In a letter of July 1935, Trotsky told leading 'Bolshevik-Leninists' in Poland that they must form opposition groups inside the Polish Social Democratic Party, 'penetrating [it] surreptitiously, and also working illegally inside the Communist Party. You must also slip into the [Jewish] Bund. You must cease pointless discussion and become more actively linked with the left elements of Polish Social Democracy.'[178] While Trotsky said nothing about terror of any kind, he certainly advocated illegal and other ways of strengthening his influence in socialist and Communist parties, and such 'instructions' found their way not only into the offices of the NKVD, but also the Party Central Committee.[179]

Although plans for the formation of the Fourth International were ready as early as 1933, Trotsky held back from putting them into effect, and when he finally committed himself, the moment had passed. In relative terms, the early 1930s were the most propitious time the Trotskyists may have had. By 1938, when the founding congress took place in Paris, the Trotskyist wave, itself barely noticeable, had virtually merged into the smooth surface of the post-revolutionary scene. In the USSR the last of Trotsky's supporters were being mercilessly wiped out or dying in the camps. In Germany, Hitler was dealing with the Marxists in the same way. In Austria, Czechoslovakia and Italy the Nazis and Fascists were trampling everyone underfoot. The time of the popular fronts had passed. Trotskyism had never enjoyed a high profile, but with the defeat of the Republican cause in Spain, it became nothing more than a symbol of its leader. Without him, it is unlikely many people would have heard of this particular branch of Marxism.

Trotsky did everything possible to make the founding congress a success. He had already proposed that the new international be called the 'World Party of Social Revolution'.[180] The new body, he declared, should 'gather together everyone who is for the [new union], even if they have serious differences among themselves'.[181] In practice, the founding congress comprised merely twenty-one delegates from eleven countries. It took place on 3 September 1938 in Alfred Rosmer's villa outside Paris. Fearing that French right-wingers or the OGPU might stage a provocation, the delegates hastily approved the documents that had been prepared, with barely any discussion. There were, among others, resolutions on the war in the Far East, on victims of class warfare, on international solidarity, and on the current position in the USSR, where 'all the conquests of the October revolution are threatened with destruction' and 'the basic task of the Russian section of the Fourth International is to call for a new social revolution'.[182] The manifesto proclaimed the new International 'proudly the successor and continuation of the cause of Marx's First International, the Russian revolution and Lenin's Communist International'.[183] The congress lasted no longer than one day.

To conceal the whereabouts of the delegates, the press release announced that the congress had taken place in Lausanne, but of course such measures were futile since the sole member of the Soviet 'delegation' was none other than Mark Zborowski, who since Lev's death had been representing Trotsky's interests in Paris. Zborowski reported to the NKVD: '"The Old Man" has arranged for me to join the secretariat and to be invited to all sessions of the International Secretariat.'[184] On 20 June 1938, even before the Paris meeting took place, Zborowski had informed Moscow that a special commission had been formed 'to combat the police and the GPU'. In the same report he gave Moscow details of the forthcoming founding congress.[185] Following the congress, he rapidly transmitted details of the participants, along with the resolutions passed, including, of course, the call to step up the task of infiltrating Trotskyists into various mass organizations, especially among the youth and the student population. Trotsky, indeed, had already indicated that 'the Fourth International will be a Youth International'.[186] Zborowski, in his zeal, also compiled

a complete list of the documents he had managed to photograph in
the International Secretariat and in Trotsky's personal archive and
sent it to Moscow.[187]

The NKVD's resources for penetrating Trotsky's manifold circles
were of course numerous and varied. For example, according to
recently published documents from the archives of the KGB, Sylvia
Franklin and Ruby Weil, two secret American Communists, were
introduced to the NKVD in 1937 and 1938 by the American Communist Louis Budenz. In due course Sylvia Franklin became secretary to
James Cannon, the American Trotskyist leader, and was thus made
privy to a large part of Trotsky's own plans, since Trotsky relied very
much on Cannon. Meanwhile, under instruction by the NKVD, Ruby
Weil, who posed as a Trotskyist, cultivated Sylvia Agelof, a social
worker from Brooklyn who devoted her vacations to working for
the Trotskyists. Agelof was known to Zborowski through their work
together in the secretariat, and she acted as interpreter at the meeting
in Paris. The NKVD arranged for Weil to introduce Agelof to a
young Spaniard calling himself Jacques Mornard.[188] The couple soon
became lovers. Mornard was also an agent of the NKVD's Foreign
Section.

Awaiting news of the congress in Coyoacan, Trotsky imagined that
the new body would announce the formation of the World Party of
Social Revolution, a political force to be reckoned with. Not for the
first time, however, he had miscalculated politically. The International
was destined forever to remain a sect which, especially once its founder
had departed the scene, would fade rapidly and within a decade be
barely noticeable. The European press greeted the founding congress
with deafening silence. The radio was reporting the agony of the
Spanish Republic. There was economic news and music. The telephone failed to ring, until finally on 5 September Trotsky received a
telegram announcing that 'the new-born promises to be a hero'. He,
his wife and his secretaries rejoiced, thinking that at last their efforts
had borne fruit.

Two weeks later 200 pages of the documents approved by the
congress arrived in Coyoacan. Trotsky was especially moved by a
letter which had been adopted in the last few minutes of the meeting
and which expressed the delegates' feelings towards their absent
leader:

The Fourth International sends you warm greetings. The barbaric repressions directed against our movement, and against you especially, prevented you from being among us and contributing your important viewpoint as an organizer of the October uprising, as the theorist of permanent revolution and direct heir of Lenin's teaching. As enemies of Stalinism, Fascism and imperialism, great trials have befallen us . . . You are yourself the object of constant murder attempts . . . However harsh it may be, this persecution can only strengthen further our conviction in the correctness of the Marxist programme, whose chief interpreter since Lenin's death you have become for us. That is why our greetings contain something more than recognition of a great contemporary theorist of revolutionary Marxism . . . We express the hope that for a long time to come you will share the spoils of victory, just as for so long you have shared the vicissitudes of the struggle . . .[189]

Two weeks after the congress Trotsky met its chairman Max Shachtman, and quickly realized that the 'World Party' was a great illusion. At the most, the congress had united some eight to ten thousand members of disparate small groupings which too often were calling themselves 'parties'. As honorary president of the new International and a member of its executive committee, Trotsky felt that, against a background of the rise of the totalitarian regimes in Germany, Italy and the USSR, the growing threat of war and the decline of the labour movement, success was unlikely. The founding of the Fourth International went virtually unnoticed by the main political forces in the unfolding drama. Trotsky had hoped to use the slogans of the First World War: 'For Marxists the struggle against war means the struggle against imperialism. The means to accomplish this is not "disarmament", but the arming of the proletariat for the revolutionary overthrow of the bourgeoisie and the creation of a workers' state. Not a League of Nations, but the United States of Europe and of the entire world . . . Whoever wishes to struggle against the war must rally to the banner of the Fourth International.'[190]

This notion was also illusory, yet as long as Trotsky was the head of the new International, it might have something to say. His major miscalculation was to imagine that the Fourth International would replace Comintern, which was in decline and which had become, as everyone knew, an auxiliary arm of Soviet policy and totally subservient to the ruler in the Kremlin. Trotsky nevertheless set out to compromise Comintern by publishing a number of articles, one of which, 'Comintern and the GPU', was published posthumously. In it, he showed that Comintern, and the leaders and officials of many Communist Parties, were financially dependent on the Central Committee of the Soviet Communist Party. Comintern's entire budget came from the Central Committee's, and often also from that of the GPU.[191] He completed the article three days before his death. He knew that Stalin was capable of using Comintern as a cover for terror against disobedient and difficult or suspicious individuals, as is evidenced by documents in the archives dating from as early as May 1931.[192]

In fact, Comintern had been in the hands of the Soviet Party from the moment of its inception. Lenin's unpublished papers contain a great deal of evidence that the leadership funded foreign parties in order to stimulate the revolutionary process, and Trotsky himself had been closely associated with this practice. In 1921 he had written to Raskolnikov, the Soviet envoy to Afghanistan, asking for his views on further action to be taken in Persia: 'Would I be right in thinking our hands are free to penetrate deep into Persia, if a revolt occurs in Persia and a new government calls on our help?'[193] In other words, by engineering a revolt, the Soviets would have an open door through which the Red Army could pass in order to ensure the creation of a Soviet-friendly regime. Similarly, in August 1919 the chairman of the Kalmyk Bolshevik Central Executive Committee, A. Chapaev, wrote to Lenin: '1) We must equip an armed detachment and send it through Mongolia and Tibet to India; 2) The detachment should take arms and ammunition for distribution among the population; 3) We have to introduce the Buddhist peoples of the East to the world revolution . . .' Lenin marked the letter to be 'forwarded to Chicherin for action'.[194] Thus, Comintern activity, through the introduction of arms, propaganda and agitation, was seen as an integral part of the policy being implemented by the People's Commissar for Foreign Affairs. Such requests for Soviet financial and other aid for revolutionary causes, routed through the Soviet Foreign Commissariat, were commonplace.

The Fourth International was to be, Trotsky had hoped, a proletarian force free of Stalinism, but he also knew that unless the situation in the USSR changed, any plans and programmes drafted in Coyoacan would remain nothing but pieces of paper. It was impossible to channel any influence from the Fourth International to the workers in the Soviet Union. It is even unlikely that anyone there, apart from the leadership and NKVD officials, knew that such a body had come into existence. Churchill's 'iron curtain' had come down well before the start, let alone the end, of the Second World War. Trotsky's influence on Soviet political and social life was minimal, if not totally non-existent. Occasionally and indirectly, for example by producing a reaction in a foreign Communist Party, might the muffled echoes of Trotsky's attacks on 'bureaucratic absolutism' find their way to the USSR. Apart from the financial and logistical restraints, there was no state in the world that would permit Trotsky to broadcast to the USSR from its territory.

After much thought, he decided in April 1940 to write an open letter to the Soviet workers, hoping, not very enthusiastically, that it would get through and be copied and passed from hand to hand. After crafting several variants, he finally settled on what sounded like a combined personal manifesto and an appeal from the Fourth International. In three dense pages, he managed to compress history, politics, ethics, philosophy and psychology. The letter included assessments of the situation in Russia, the causes of degeneration of the Soviet system, and a pointer to the way the country could get out of the deep crisis into which Stalin had taken it. Headed 'You are being deceived!', the letter opened with:

> Greetings to the workers, kolkhozniks, Red Army men and Red sailors of the USSR from distant Mexico, where I ended up after being expelled to Turkey by Stalin's clique and chased by the bourgeoisie from country to country ... Whoever raises his voice against the hated bureaucracy is called a 'Trotskyist', an agent of a foreign power, a spy – yesterday a spy for Germany, today a spy for England and France – and subject to execution by shooting. Tens of thousands of revolutionary fighters have perished.

This was a serious underestimate. From my own study of reports in the Stalin archive, the NKVD's own statistics and the archives of the former Central Committee, by the time Trotsky wrote his letter, between 1937 and 1939 from five to five and a half million people had been arrested. Not less than a third of them had been shot, and many of the rest died in the camps.

Trotsky went on:

Stalin has destroyed the entire Bolshevik old guard, all of Lenin's collaborators and assistants, all the fighters of the October revolution, all
the heroes of the civil war. He will go down in history under the
despised name of Cain.

He then came to the main point of the letter:

Honest leading revolutionaries have organized the Fourth International
abroad and already it has its sections in most countries of the world
. . . In taking part in this work, I remain under the same banner I stood
under with you or your fathers and older brothers in 1917 and the
years of the civil war; the same banner as that under which together
with Lenin we built the Soviet state and the Red Army. The aim of
the Fourth International is to spread the October revolution throughout the world and at the same time to give rebirth to the USSR by
cleansing it of the parasitic bureaucracy. This can only be done by way
of an uprising of the workers, peasants, Red Army men and Red sailors
against the new caste of oppressors and parasites. A new party is needed
to prepare this uprising . . . Learn how to create closely tied and reliable
revolutionary circles in the Stalinist underground . . . The present war
. . . will bring the whole world to new revolutionary explosions.[195]

Dated 25 April 1940 and published on 11 May, the letter ends with
an appeal to strengthen the USSR as a 'fortress of toilers', and to
prepare for the 'world socialist revolution' by getting rid of 'Cain-
Stalin and his camarilla'.

The call for creating an illegal underground organization and staging an uprising suggests that Trotsky was prepared to go to the limit,
but it also shows the degree of his desperation. It was also totally
unrealistic. Every vestige of opposition inside the Soviet Union had
been destroyed, and any attempt to move against the regime would
have been crushed, not merely because of the monstrously efficient
security and penal system, but also because the population was too
stupefied by propaganda even to recognize the status of slave it had
come to occupy.

The creation of the Fourth International was the last expression of
Trotsky's vast egoism, of his inability to accept that the time of his
meteoric rise had passed and that his brainchild was stillborn. It was
the most unrealistic venture of this Gulliver among a mass of Lilli-

putians, the squabbling Trotskyists. Whatever trace the Fourth International might have left is due only to the name of its founder. In attempting to infuse new blood into the anaemic new body, Trotsky reverted to the Marxist dogmas that had already been shown in Stalinist practice to be limited and historically vulnerable. This was true above all of the theory of class war and the dictatorship of the proletariat, the monopoly of the single party and the exclusion of the social democrats. Trotsky envisaged fighting on two fronts: against the imperialistic bourgeoisie and Stalin's 'bureaucratic absolutism'. And to do so without the help of allies, for he had dismissed the social democrats as servants of the bourgeoisie. But neither Trotsky and the 'World Party of Social Revolution', nor any other political force of the time, was capable of shouldering this task. Trotsky's new venture only exposed still more sharply the hopelessness of his position, this Don Quixote of the twentieth century.

Still he continued to present the desirable as the real, never failing, for instance, to remind the world that the most powerful section of the Fourth International was that of the Soviet 'Bolshevik-Leninists', despite the fact that there was not a single delegate from the Soviet Union, unless one counts the NKVD agent Zborowski. Even before the new organization was proclaimed to exist, in 1936, for instance, Trotsky was claiming that the ideas of the Left opposition were penetrating the USSR 'notably through our *Bulletin*'. After 1933 the *Bulletin* came into the hands of the OGPU-NKVD only, yet Trotsky declared in his 1936 article 'The Soviet Section of the Fourth International': 'Already today the Fourth International has in the USSR the strongest, most numerous and most battle-hardened of its sections.'[196] He dearly wished to believe his own myth.

It is important, however, to note that in striving to create his new party, Trotsky was also exposing the political forces that were preparing for war. In 1937 he predicted that a second world war would break out in two or three years, and before many politicians had realized it he had seen that the rise to power of Nazism in Germany would lead to war sooner or later. Such articles as 'Germany, the Key to the International Situation' (1931), 'The Only Way' (1932) and 'What is National Socialism?' (1933) were prophetic indicators of what Nazism would do.[197] In 1933 he wrote that 'Hitler stood out only because of his big temperament, a voice much louder than others, and an intellectual mediocrity much more self-assured ... But his harangues resounded, now like commands and now like prayers ... Sentimental formlessness, absence of discipline.'[198] And in the summer of 1937 he predicted that Stalin would make an alliance with Hitler.[199]

While he may have seen clearly that a new world war was coming, Trotsky was woefully off target in seeking to avert it by starting a new revolution: 'If [the revolution] does not come about before the war, then the war itself will bring about the revolution, as a result of which both the Stalinist regime and the Fascist regime will collapse.'[200] Even when the Second World War was already raging, in February 1940, he wrote to an American sympathizer called Welch: 'In this terrible time of rampant world chauvinism ... the only way for humanity to survive is by way of socialist revolution.'[201] The old revolutionary hymns were, however, drowned by the clanging of tanktracks and the thunder of guns. And Trotsky, unheard, continued to live in his dream world of a bygone age.

7

Outcast of the Era

In the last eighteen months or so of his life, Trotsky and Natalya
would go out into the back garden of their small fortress and sit on
a wooden bench, silent for the most part, occasionally exchanging a
word or two, and watch the Mexican night descend. However doomed
a man may be, he still has the great luxury of freedom of thought that
can carry him soaring over the past and the future, the single attribute
that can never be taken away by tyrant or circumstance. Thinking
as always of the world revolution, Trotsky may have remembered
receiving an inventory from Bazilevich, a special appointee of the
Sovnarkom, in 1918:

> This is to report that on 8 March in the [Kremlin] Armoury, upon
> opening chests containing the property of the former empress, State
> Repository representative Chinarev found contents to the value of 300
> million gold roubles. The jewellers, Kotlyar and Frants, base their
> valuation on the following: if a buyer were found who was able to buy
> these treasures as objects, then the value would be 458.7 million gold
> roubles . . . And the coronation treasures, which are contained in two
> separate chests, are valued at over 7 million roubles.[1]

Trotsky had forwarded the note to Lenin in the usual way, and
Lenin for his part would have given routine instructions for the disposal of these riches for the good of the world revolution. A year
later, A. Alsky, head of the State Repository, was reporting the distribution of an additional 2.2 million gold roubles to Comintern, mostly
in the form of jewellery for sale.[2]

In his masterly biography of Trotsky, Isaac Deutscher calls him a
prophet. He undoubtedly was a prophet, but some of his prophecies

sound more like Utopian dreams. In argument with Herter, the Dutch representative, at a session of the ECCI on 24 November 1920, Trotsky had called himself 'one of Eastern Europe's outcasts'.[3] He was yet to discover that he was in fact an outcast of the era.

The Prophet and his Prophecies

The Bible says, 'If a prophet speaks in the name of the Lord, and the word comes not to pass and is not fulfilled, then it is not the Lord who spoke the word, but the prophet in his audacity.' Trotsky spoke in the name of the revolution, and for his 'audacity' he could only count on Marxist indulgence. If in the 1905 revolution he had thought and acted within the Russian national framework, then in the months following the October victory of 1917 he called on the proletariat of Europe 'to close ranks ... under the banner of peace and social revolution!'[4] After the creation of Comintern in 1919, he never tired of telling himself - or the next congress or the whole world - that this was 'the beginning of the triumph of the proletariat'. In an article of 1919 entitled 'Thoughts on the Course of the Proletarian Revolution (en route)', he wrote:

> History has always taken the path of least resistance. The revolutionary epoch burst in through the door that was the least barricaded ... If today the centre of the Third International is Moscow, then, we are profoundly convinced, tomorrow the centre could move west to Berlin, Paris or London ... An international congress in Berlin or Paris would signify the complete triumph of the proletarian revolution in Europe and, therefore, in the whole world.[5]

Trotsky was deeply convinced that what he said and wrote was right. His speeches were so passionate that they were believed not only by workers and students, but also by the revolutionaries who came to hear him. They believed because they passionately wanted Trotsky's prophecies to come true. He seemed to be able to see further and predict more surely than others. He spoke of the world revolution as inevitable, irreversible, already decided. And he did so even when it seemed obvious that the wave of revolution had subsided in Europe.

In June 1923 an institute named after Karl Liebknecht, the German revolutionary murdered in 1919, was opened in Moscow, and Trotsky was invited to give the inaugural address. As always he was greeted with an ovation. Also as always, his theme was optimistically revolutionary:

> The German working class moves on asphalt, but its hands and feet are bound in class slavery. We stride over ruts, ditches, potholes and puddles, but our feet are free. That, Comrades, is what distinguishes us from the European proletariat ... The world that surrounds us is more powerful than we are, and the bourgeoisie will not surrender its positions without fierce fighting. The battles will be the more terrible as the Communist Party becomes stronger, and it is getting stronger ... The approach of the world Communist revolution means we will have to go through more big battles.[6]

The revolution had ebbed, yet Trotsky could speak of the approaching world revolution, and warn that class war would become more intense as the Communist Party became stronger, an idea in many respects foreshadowing an argument advanced by Stalin in the 1930s. Trotsky's prediction was unambiguous: world revolution was inevitable and it was imminent. What grounds had he for such certainty? First, like all orthodox Russian revolutionaries, he believed in Marxism. While everything else could be subjected to doubt and analysis, the writings of the great German thinkers Marx and Engels were sacrosanct. It was profoundly paradoxical that a man with so powerful an intellect as Trotsky could believe so fanatically in the Utopian idea. Lenin had been equally convinced. In 1919, closing the First Congress of Comintern, he had proclaimed: 'The victory of the proletarian revolution throughout the world is guaranteed. The founding of the International Soviet Republic is approaching.'[7] This confidence, like that of Trotsky, was founded on the experience of October 1917, when power had been seized with extraordinary ease. If it could happen in Russia, why not everywhere else in the world? This view was reinforced by the apparent rise of the revolutionary movement on different continents. Communist Parties were coming into being. There was revolution in Hungary, Germany and China. The optimism of the Leninist International captivated millions, and nourished Trotsky's faith in the possibility of the impossible. He thought that,

alongside Comintern's active ideological work, concrete organizational steps should be taken to give a revolutionary push to the world
community. He proposed that a cavalry corps be sent to India to
start a revolution, that the White Poles be smashed and that the
revolutionary gates to Europe be opened. These ideas seemed to him
realistic.

The Bolsheviks had wanted to act in the west, the south and the
east. At the end of the First Congress of Comintern, Lenin wrote to
the Bolshevik Yelava in Turkestan of the urgent need for an independent revolutionary base to be established there: 'Money is no object,
we'll send sufficient gold and foreign currency ... The affair must
be carried out in total secrecy (as we used to work under the tsar).
Greetings, Lenin.'[8] And the deed was done. Karakhan, of the Foreign
Commissariat, even calculated the exact cost of financing each agitator
in northern China and Korea at 10,000 gold roubles.[9] There were
not enough weapons to defend Soviet Russia and also give help to
the world proletariat, and in October 1921 Trotsky proposed an
additional allocation of 10 million gold roubles to purchase weapons
in America. Lenin approved the proposal.[10]

It is amazing that Trotsky managed to keep alive his prophecy of
world-wide Communist revolution for so many years. In May 1938,
shortly before the founding congress of the Fourth International, he
drafted an extensive programme of activities which he submitted for
discussion by the International secretariat and the national sections.
Eloquently entitled 'The Agony of Capitalism and the Tasks of the
Fourth International', the programme asserted that 'the Fourth International's strategic task is not to reform capitalism, but to overthrow
it.'[11] As always, he accused the social democrats of aiding and abetting
the capitalists, denied the trade unions a revolutionary role and called
for the formation of parties of the Fourth International and the arming
of the proletariat. All these measures were, he believed, the prerequisites of world revolution: 'Any talk about the historical conditions not
having "ripened" for socialism is the result of ignorance and conscious
deception. The objective prerequisites of proletarian revolution have
not only "ripened", they have already begun to rot. Without socialist
revolution, and at the earliest historical period at that, the whole of
human culture is threatened by a catastrophe.'[12] If the vanguard were
willing, he claimed, the masses were ready for revolution.

Above: Trotsky's elder son,
Lev Sedov.

Right: Trotsky's younger son,
Sergei Sedov.

Below: Olga Kameneva, Trotsky's
sister and Kamenev's wife.

Right: Trotsky in Mexico, 1938, with (from left)
Diego Rivera, Frida Kahlo, Natalya, Reba Hansen,
André Breton, a Mexican Trotskyist, Jesús Casas (head of
the police garrison guarding Trotsky's house), one of Rivera's
drivers and Jean van Heijenoort.

Below: Trotsky dictating to one of his secretaries in the 1930s.

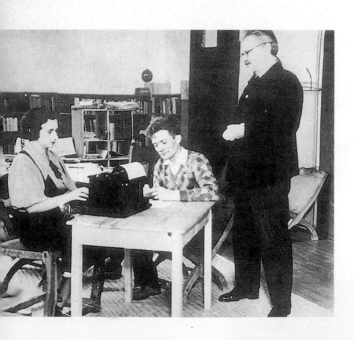

At the Dewey Commission's hearings in Mexico City, April 1937. From the left: Jean van Heijenoort, Albert Goldman (Trotsky's US lawyer), Trotsky, Natalya, and the Czech Trotskyist Jan Frankel.

Trotsky with two of his security guards in Mexico.

Trotsky with Natalya on a cactus-collecting expedition, Mexico 1940.

Trotsky feeding his rabbits, 1940.

Above: Trotsky's study after Ramon Mercader's attack, 20 August 1940.

Left: Mercader after his arrest.

Mercader re-enacting his attack during the investigation.

Trotsky on his death-bed.

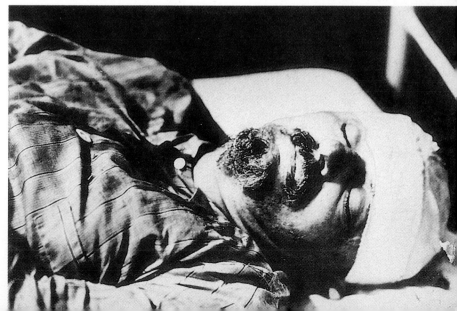

Trotsky's funeral procession, Mexico City, 22 August 1940.

Trotsky's grandson, Esteban (Vsevolod-Seva) Volkov, at his grandfather's grave in Mexico City in 1989.

Soon after the founding of the Fourth International, on 18 October 1938, Trotsky sent greetings to the American Trotskyist party, predicting that the urge for world revolution represented by the new organization would become the programme for millions over the next ten years, and that they 'will be able to take heaven and earth by storm'.[13] Like Lenin, he often set a deadline for the arrival of the radiant future. And, also like Lenin, he was often seriously wrong. Speaking at an All-Union Librarians' Congress in 1924, he declared that, 'Before you know it, in ten, fifteen or twenty years the French and English proletariat will have overtaken us in socialist construction, because of their greater cultural development. Of course, we shall not be offended. Go ahead, overtake us, we have been waiting long enough.'[14] His words were greeted by laughter and applause. But fifteen years later he was still talking of the same time-frame.

The Second World war had begun, mankind was being rocked by the roar of guns and the voice of reason was drowned by the grinding of tank-tracks. Trotsky could see the only way out in revolution. On 27 February 1940 he wrote his will, in which he declared: 'My faith in the Communist future of mankind is no less ardent, indeed it is firmer today, than it was in the days of my youth.'[15] The country where Lenin, Trotsky and the other Bolsheviks had made their revolution, leaving a trail of victims in their wake, was moving towards the spectral goal of Communism, a seventy-year experiment that failed by almost any reckoning. If, as Marx said, the 'basic principle' of communism was 'the full and free development of every individual',[16] then the country where this social experiment took place has provided a picture of spiritual and physical outrage against the individual as monstrous as history has seen or, one would hope, is ever likely to see.

Although the great Soviet prophet and his prophecies have been repudiated in theory, logic and reality, it does not follow that Communism cannot exist as a variant of Utopian theory. The search for a system in which the people exercise real power and where humanism and justice prevail does not have to end because it failed universally in its twentieth-century Communist guise. The Communist Utopia, in which Trotsky – and millions of other Soviet citizens – believed, could not be accomplished, partly because the methods applied by the Bolsheviks were simply criminal, but also because the concept of liberty, as a primary social, economic and spiritual value, was absent from the core of the teaching. The prognoses of the 'audacious prophet' were doomed when the Bolsheviks adopted the dictatorship of the proletariat as a fundamental principle - a principle in which Trotsky believed to his dying day.

On the other hand, Trotsky's prognostications about the future of the Soviet Union were rather accurate, while those he made about Stalin were extraordinarily so. His boldest predictions occur in his book *What is the USSR and Where is it Going?*, reworked as *The Revolution Betrayed*. In it he wrote: 'The trampling of Soviet democracy by the omnipotent bureaucracy, and the crushing of bourgeois democracy by Fascism, derive from the same cause: the world proletariat's delay in dealing with the historic task set before it. Stalinism and Fascism, despite the profound difference of their social bases, are symmetrical phenomena. In many ways they are murderously similar.'[17] The present regime in the USSR, he repeatedly claimed, had no future: 'Will the bureaucrats consume the workers' state, or will the working class overcome the bureaucrats? The fate of the USSR depends on the outcome of this question.'[18] He argued that a political, as distinct from a social, revolution was inevitable and that it would alter the form of government by getting rid of the Party and the state bureaucracy. 'The right of criticism and genuinely free elections must be restored,' he wrote. There must be 'freedom for Soviet parties', and 'the expensive toys', by which he meant lavish palaces for Party purposes, must be curtailed 'in favour of workers' housing', while 'ranks should immediately be abolished and trinket medals be thrown into the crucible. Young people should have the chance to breathe freely, to criticize, to make mistakes and become adults. Science and art will be unshackled. Finally, foreign policy must return to the traditions of revolutionary internationalism.'[19]

After several more decades, to be sure, 'bureaucratic absolutism' was eliminated in the Soviet Union, the population was given the right to vote freely, and freedom of criticism was embodied in the *glasnost* of *perestroika*. Trotsky had seen that the society constructed by Stalin and his henchmen would end in a blind alley. 'The chief danger for the USSR,' he wrote in 1935, 'lies in Stalinism.'[20] Two years later, in an article entitled 'It is Time to go Over to the Attack Against Stalinism', he declared: 'We confidently challenge the Stalinist

gang before all of mankind ... Some of us might yet fall in this
struggle. But its outcome is ordained. Stalinism will be crushed,
smashed and buried in dishonour forever.'²¹

Trotsky's predictions about Stalin and Stalinism alone have earned
him a place in history, even if he chose never to recall his own role
in laying the foundations of totalitarianism, a role second only to that
of Lenin. Despite this, when it appeared that the monolithic empire
was unshakeable and the position of its leader impregnable, Trotsky
continued to alert world opinion to the dangers of Stalin's dictatorship
and to predict his inevitable fall. Undoubtedly, personal hostility, even
hatred, played a part, but the main motivation was intellectual and
ideological: the analysis of Soviet conditions, the USSR's international
position and the profound problems associated with the degeneration
of the Party and state. At times by rational means, at times through
intuition, Trotsky formulated the notion of 'bureaucratic absolutism'
as a temporary coercive means of strengthening the system, and he
concluded that the system could not long survive the grip of a regime
that was girded for war and held in place by punitive organs. Yet any
loosening of that grip would inevitably lead society, the population
and the Party to the realization that freedom, democracy and respect
for pluralism of thought – all long lost in the USSR – were eternal
values. As early as 1926, Trotsky was speaking of Stalinism as
doomed.

On the eve of the war, Trotsky closely observed the political
manoeuvres of the powers. He had predicted the Second World War
in the early 1930s, and in an article from the late summer of 1939,
entitled 'Stalin – Hitler's Quartermaster', he wrote:

... the author of these lines has the right to refer to the continuous
series of his statements in the world's press, beginning in 1933, to the
effect that the basic task of Stalin's foreign policy was to reach agreement with Hitler ... The general causes of the war lie in the irreconcilable differences within world imperialism. The immediate trigger for
the opening of military action, however, was the signing of the Soviet-
German Pact ... Stalin is afraid of Hitler. And not for nothing. The
[Red] Army has been decapitated. This is no idle phrase, it is a tragic
fact. Voroshilov is a fiction. His authority was artificially created by
totalitarian agitation. At his dizzy height, he has remained what he
always was, a limited provincial with no vision, military capability, nor
even the capabilities of an administrator.

The Soviet-German Non-Aggression Pact, he wrote further, 'secures for Hitler the opportunity to exploit Soviet raw materials'. Thus, he declared, 'Hitler conducts his military operations, and Stalin acts as his quartermaster.' He further asserted that 'Germany is bound to open an offensive against the Soviet Union in the autumn of 1941.' It was extremely likely, he wrote, that two years after the occupation of Poland 'Germany will attack the Soviet Union. In exchange for Poland, Hitler has given Moscow freedom of action in the Baltic [states]. However great these "advantages" may be, they are merely temporary, and their sole guarantee is Ribbentrop's signature on a scrap of paper.'[22]

Trotsky may have been a Utopian dreamer where world revolution was concerned, but his analysis of the world situation, and especially of the forthcoming war, was almost faultless. In a series of articles written on the eve of the war, notably in 'The Dual Star: Hitler-Stalin' of December 1939 but published posthumously, he correctly analyzed the manoeuvres along the perimeter of the great triangle of the USSR, Germany and the Western democracies. Each side was trying to guarantee its own security at the expense of the others. Cynical deals, embellished by declarations, deceit, the carving up of 'spheres of interest', secrecy and the concealing of ultimate goals, all this and more characterize the diplomatic practice of those years. Trotsky's analysis has much in common with that of present-day historians and political scientists, but he preceded them by decades.

Trotsky's life following the revolution had been closely associated with the army, and it was therefore not surprising that he would frequently revert to the military theme in his articles. In *What is the USSR and Where is it Going?* he included a chapter on the Red Army and its doctrine, singling out Tukhachevsky for special mention several times. He remembered that in 1921 Tukhachevsky had suggested that Comintern create an 'International General Staff' under its Executive Committee (ECCI). Tukhachevsky had subsequently published his letter to Comintern in a collection of articles called *The War of the Classes*. Trotsky described Tukhachevsky as 'talented, but inclined to be impetuous, like most military leaders'.[23] When he wrote this article, Trotsky was not aware that virtually at that moment the youngest Marshal of the Soviet Union, aged forty-three, was under surveillance and suspected of harbouring secret intentions, although what they might be the security organs had not yet decided. Certain 'signals' had been received. When in early 1936 Tukhachevsky had visited London and Paris on official business, the chief of the 1st Section of Red Army Intelligence, Corps Commissar Steinbruk, had reported regularly to Voroshilov on what was being written in the bourgeois press about Tukhachevsky.

On the whole, the Paris newspapers were well disposed towards the handsome young Marshal, who impressed everyone with his flexible and original mind and courtly manner. Significantly, Voroshilov's red pencil marked what Tukhachevsky had said about the French officers he had met when he was in German captivity during the First World War: 'I will never forget our friendship. We have met again after twenty years, just like [the Three Musketeers] . . .' He then added: 'You are coming to Moscow . . . Now we are not parting for twenty years: now we're going to see each other much more often.'[24] With a thick red line Voroshilov marked a passage in another report: 'Marshal Tukhachevsky, a former ensign in the Imperial Guards, is of course the most brilliant military man in the USSR . . . At the age of twenty-six he was commander-in-chief of the Red Army that marched on Warsaw.'[25] Voroshilov did not enjoy reading such glowing praise of his deputy, and then at the end of 1936 he became aware of Trotsky's flattering remarks about the Red Army's most brilliant officer.

Trotsky would never know the details of the hurried trial of the senior officers Tukhachevsky, Yakir, Uborevich, Kork, Eideman, Feldman, Primakov and Putna that took place on 11 June 1937, but he was right to assert that the Red Army had been decapitated and rendered unprepared for war with Hitler. It is worth quoting Marshal Budenny's report of the trial to Voroshilov. Budenny served as one of the judges and described his 'impressions of the recent trial of the counter-revolutionary Fascist organization'. Among other things, he wrote that 'the conspirators were oriented towards Trotsky and his bloc', that 'Putna, a patent spy, was a convinced Trotskyist of the modern type, acting under the banner of Fascism'. Putna had confessed, Budenny reported, that after the civil war he 'had become a firm supporter of Trotsky', and 'believed that Trotsky spoke the truth.' Primakov 'was given a more serious task by Trotsky, namely to raise an armed uprising in Leningrad . . . In connection with this special task from Trotsky, Primakov won over the 25th Cavalry Division commanded by ... Zybin. In his words, Zybin was supposed to meet Trotsky on the frontier once the insurgents had captured Leningrad. They had prepared one rifle division and an armoured corps for the purpose ... From the start of the trial, when the charges were being read out and during the questioning of all the other defendants, Tukhachevsky shook his head, as if to say all this is false, none of it corresponds to reality.'[26] The twenty-page report is virtually all in this vein, and is full of coarse abuse of Budenny's former comrades, especially Tukhachevsky.

Trotsky was right about the military condition of the USSR, even if he did not know everything that was happening in the country: the decapitated Red Army would find it extremely hard to resist the Wehrmacht. He knew Budenny and Voroshilov all too well from the civil war, and they duly demonstrated their utter lack of ability during the Second World War. But he could not have known, for example, that security chief Yezhov wrote to Voroshilov in 1937: 'Corps Commander Comrade Kapulovsky has sent me a letter from Kiev and asks you to accept it. I summoned him to Moscow where he told me a number of facts that I suggested he write down. I enclose two copies of his statements.'[27] Ivan Kapulovsky, an ensign in the tsarist army and a brave officer, was being harassed by suspicion and imminent arrest. What he wrote in his letter to Yezhov was simply a fantastic jumble of statements about more than twenty senior officers, including some of those who would be tried with Tukhachevsky. It did not save him. He was arrested the same year and shot.

It is doubtful if any military system could have remained steadfast if, for instance, it took no more than a single telegram from the chief of NKVD security in the Far East, Mironov, to effect the arrest of twelve senior officers. Mironov's telegram closed ominously: 'The arrest of the others is being prepared.'[28]

Even though he was not informed in detail as to what was happening in the USSR, Trotsky could imagine it with a high degree of accuracy. Pacing the small yard of his home in Coyoacan, he could not but wonder if his predictions would come true.

The Portraitist's Brush

Some of the most successful and striking of Trotsky's literary output was in the form of political biographies. In Paris before the First World War, and again after the revolution, he published a wide range of sketches – of Russian and European politicians, revolutionaries, writers and artists – which constitute most of the eighth volume of his collected works. With the onset of the purges and the terror, his portraits tended increasingly to be obituaries. Among his best biographical writing his own autobiography, *My Life*, must hold pride of place as a work of remarkable self-analysis, as well as imaginative history. Although he wrote it at the relatively early age of forty-eight, soon after his deportation, his life up to then had been eventful enough to merit recording.

For many years, however, the lives of two other revolutionaries, Lenin and Stalin, stood awaiting his portraitist's brush, and both studies remained unfinished. Trotsky had planned to write a biography of Lenin while his subject was still alive, and he had asked his assistants, Sermuks and Butov, to file everything they could find on his relations with the leader. He did not start work on the book until Lenin died, intending at first merely to publish a book of reminiscences. The Trotsky archives contain a typescript of more than two hundred pages, including published and unpublished articles, some of it published in 1924 as a book entitled *On Lenin: Materials for a Biographer*. The most striking pieces in this rather fragmentary publication were entitled 'On his Fiftieth Birthday', 'Wounded', 'Ill' and 'Deceased'. Trotsky noted in the preface that he had intentionally omitted 'several circumstances as too closely related to the evils of the present day'.[29] The publication of the book was evidently decided in haste, as the manuscript bears a note dated 16 October 1924: 'With the agreement of the State Publishing House, the net proceeds of this publication will be used to provide relief for the men and women worker-victims of the floods of Leningrad . . .'[30]

Among Trotsky's papers there are many indications of his intention 'to write a book on Lenin', 'to speed up the work on the manuscript', and 'finally to complete this book'. From Prinkipo he wrote to the Rosmers in Paris that by the autumn he wanted to write a book called

'Lenin and his Imitators', and also a collection of 'personal sketches (of friends and enemies)' in which Lenin would occupy pride of place.[31] Four years later, on 20 February 1934, he would write to his Paris publisher: 'My work on Lenin has not yet emerged nor will it quickly emerge from the preparatory stage ... The first chapters will hardly be ready for translation before July ...'[32]

Only a month before leaving Prinkipo, he had written to his supporter Sara Weber in New York: 'Our move to France coincides with financial difficulties ... In the coming months, nine tenths of my time will be devoted to the work on Lenin.'[33] But the time Trotsky and his wife spent in France was not conducive to creative writing, and both in Norway and later in Mexico he was too distracted by persecution, deportation, the Moscow trials and the counter-trial, the founding of the Fourth International, and finally his book on Stalin to be able to concentrate on and complete his study of Lenin. He did not want to rush the writing of this work, which was important to him. After Prinkipo he began to sense that he would end his life in exile, and that his hopes of positive changes in the Soviet Union were increasingly less likely to be realized. The book on Lenin was intended to be a sort of settling of the score with history, and a witness to the rightness of his own case. Lenin, both in the USSR and to the world at large, was still a figure of epoch-making scale, and Trotsky believed, with good reason, that his biography would show that as the second man of the revolution he, Trotsky, had done everything possible to maintain its achievements, its ideals and its hopes. A book of such import could not be written in two or three months, like *The Revolution Betrayed*. Above all, it must show that it was Trotsky together with Lenin who had tried to save the revolution; the book was to be about the 'two leaders' of the Russian revolution.

Trotsky had of course already written of this at length in his autobiography, but he was well aware of Berdyaev's comment, that 'this book was written to glorify Trotsky as a great revolutionary and still more to diminish his mortal enemy, Stalin, as a non-entity and pathetic imitator. Undoubtedly, Trotsky stands head and shoulders above the other Bolsheviks in many respects, if one does not count Lenin. Lenin was of course more powerful and a more significant figure, the head of the revolution, no less, but Trotsky was more talented and more brilliant.'[34]

The former Bolshevik-turned-Menshevik Nikolai Valentinov wrote of the leaders of the October coup in a different tone: 'Lenin's originality lay in the fact that his view of himself lacked what is there in most other people's self-assessment, namely trivial vanity and self-admiration. There was an inordinate amount of just this, for instance, in Trotsky, who was the most prominent figure of the revolution after Lenin. He was not yet forty-eight when he began to write his autobiography and to describe his life and the revolutionary feats he had accomplished in terms of self-glorification.'[35] It could as well be argued that Trotsky's autobiography shows him to be as much a talented writer as a great revolutionary. Being perhaps aware of this, he intended his book on Lenin to reveal his own qualities in greater depth and detail. Regrettably, it remained uncompleted.

As he lived through the vicissitudes of the last phase of his life, Trotsky was obsessed by the idea that he could not make his final exit before he had answered Stalin. To be sure, he had written dozens of devastating articles about the tyrant in the Kremlin. Indeed, he could barely write any political article that did not include some scathingly worded disclosure about Stalin. But nothing would satisfy the craving to utter the last word better than to write a major analytical biography. He had been thinking along these lines for some time. As early as August 1930 he had written a long article entitled 'Towards a Political Biography of Stalin',[36] which was in effect a short outline of the future book. His objective was not merely to show Stalin as Cain, but also to illuminate the genetic origins of Stalinism as the embodiment of 'bureaucratic absolutism'.

In many respects Trotsky's incomplete biography of Stalin was one of his least successful books, and in places Trotsky's talent as a political journalist, historian and thinker seems to have deserted him, subverted by the bile and hatred that motivated him. Despite this, he did succeed in defining many sources of Stalinism, in the growth of the state and Party organizations, the rapid strengthening of the all-powerful bureaucracy, and the elimination of political, spiritual and intellectual alternatives in society. Trotsky, however, was also utterly un-self-critical, unable to write of his own shortcomings and seemingly unaware that the chief flaws in the system which he began to attack after October 1923 had emanated from himself and Lenin, the Jacobins-in-chief of the revolution. Many of Trotsky's totalitarian ideas materialized in the new state. He was one of the chief architects of 'bureaucratic absolutism', though he showed no awareness of it in any of his writings.

He regarded his deportation as illegal, even if, as his son Lev pointed out on Prinkipo, it had undoubtedly saved his life – for the time being. Yet the practice of deporting political undesirables had first been used when he was in power, and far from denouncing it, he had been in strong support of it as normal revolutionary practice. In an article entitled 'Our Differences', written in 1924 but not published at once, Trotsky wrote: 'Revolutions have often failed because the working masses were spineless, indecisive and too good-natured ... A revolution can survive only if it changes its very character into a more severe form and arms itself with the sword of Red terror ... The Red terror was an essential weapon of the revolution.'[37] Once in exile, Trotsky rightly condemned Stalin's terror, while managing to omit his own previous views on the role of violence in the revolutionary restructuring of society. He rationalized this by stressing the difference between the civil war years, when he had used terror against the state's enemies, and the peaceful conditions of the 1930s, when it was being used against the state's own people. As late as 1938 he could still justify the 1918 decree on hostage-taking by calling it 'a necessary measure against the oppressors'.[38]

Trotsky found writing the book on Stalin extremely hard. He felt himself unable to apply his usual standards of analysis, comparison and objective scrutiny of the factors that would give colour, shape and form to the sinister portrait he was creating, and complained to Natalya: 'It's hard going. It's incredibly hard to write calmly about the swine. It's easier to pour a bottle of black ink on the paper. I can only write about this Cain that way.' He showed her a fragment of what he had written. It read: 'Stalinist methods take to the limit, to the highest tension and to the point of absurdity, all the lying, cruel, base devices that constitute the mechanism for ruling any class society. Stalinism is a clot of all the deformities of the historic state, its malign caricature, a revolting grimace.'[39] All this was undoubtedly justified, but when a text is dominated by the endless incantation of such phrases as 'the political gangrene of Stalinism', 'Stalinism is the hangover of the revolution', or 'Stalinism is counter-revolutionary banditry', the effect is bound to pall eventually. Hatred is not the artist's best friend.

Recalling the last days of his membership of the Central Committee, Trotsky wrote that by 1927 Central Committee sessions had become disgusting spectacles. Questions were not discussed on their merits, but everything was decided behind the scenes in private session with Stalin. The line of attack against the opposition was prearranged, with roles and speeches previously assigned:

When the comedy was staged, each time it more closely resembled an obscene and rowdy bar-room burlesque. The tone of that baiting became more unbridled. The more impudent members, the climbers most recently admitted to the Central Committee, exclusively in recognition of their capacity for impudence towards the Opposition, continuously interrupted ... veteran revolutionists with senseless repetitions of baseless accusations, with shouts of unheard-of vulgarity and abusiveness. The stage director of all this was Stalin. He walked up and down at the back of the praesidium, looking now and then towards those to whom certain speeches were assigned, and made no attempt to hide his approval when the swearing addressed to some Oppositionist assumed an utterly shameless character.[40]

To the extent that he concentrated on depicting his subject's image in the most damaging light, Trotsky began to lose sight of the essential, but then he seems to have become aware of this and again focused on the social and political analysis of the phenomenon of Stalinism, rather than its progenitor.

On the question of Stalin as the natural heir of Lenin, Trotsky was especially scathing:

The current official comparisons of Stalin to Lenin are simply indecent. If the basis of comparison is sweep of personality, it is impossible to place Stalin even alongside Mussolini and Hitler. However meagre the 'ideas' of Fascism, both of the victorious leaders of reaction, the Italian and the German, from the very beginning of their respective movements displayed initiative, roused the masses to action, pioneered new paths through the political jungle. Nothing of the kind can be said about Stalin. The Bolshevik Party was created by Lenin. Stalin grew out of its political machine and remained inseparable from it.[41]

The creation of Stalin's portrait by Trotsky may be the only occasion in history when the sitter killed the painter before the work was done. At least, it was fitting that Trotsky was working on it when he was assassinated.

Chronicler of the Revolution

Trotsky's historical writing bears the clear imprint of personal experience. Perhaps it is for this reason that we find in it not only the 'stages', 'periods' and 'epochs' of human evolution that are the stock-in-trade of most historical literature, but also feel the surge of emotions, the will and the mind of the *dramatis personae* who populate its pages. For Trotsky, history was an endless gallery of individuals, fighting, confused, possessed, acting in accordance with the objective (and Marxist) laws of development. Compared with many other writers of the revolutionary period, Trotsky did not confine himself merely to chronicling events, but strove for the philosophical heights of history-writing. The past for him was a drama of ideas and of people.

No other Marxist ever attempted, as Trotsky did, to write the history of the three Russian revolutions, and throughout it is the Bolshevik version that he gives. Of 1905 he wrote: 'The revolution came and completed the period of our political childhood. It consigned to the archives our traditional liberalism and its sole attribute: its faith in the successful replacement of government figures.'[42] As a radical revolutionary, he blamed the indecisiveness of the liberals for the failure to bring about a nationwide uprising. The revolution that was to be organized by the Marxists, therefore, would come as the result of a 'merciless struggle with liberalism for the minds of the masses'.[43] The numerous articles he wrote on the 1905 revolution were less true history than impulsive responses to events, but he was nevertheless sufficiently attached to what he had written to submit significant amendments to the Institute for Party History in 1921, when it was researching the period.[44] At this point, when he was as it were measuring himself for the historian's mantle, there was only a very rare mention of himself in his writings, none of the historical egocentrism of which later historians would accuse him.

Trotsky made his first serious attempt to recount the October revolution only a matter of months after the event. At the Brest-Litovsk peace talks he spent his evenings writing a brief account which went into many editions, in Russia and abroad, as a short book. But it was not until he reached the age of fifty that he became a real historian. It was then that he wrote his *History of the Russian Revolution*, a work agreed by most to be his best, alongside his autobiography. Had he never written another word, his reputation as a talented historical writer would have been assured by these two works.

The *History*, a work of nearly fifty chapters and appendices, unfolds a vast canvas in two acts, February and October 1917. The sole existing draft of the book is now located in the Hoover Institution at Stanford, California. It found its way there because Boris Nicolaevsky, who had fled Europe for the USA on the eve of the Second World War, transferred his archives – and himself – to Stanford in 1963. How Trotsky's manuscript came to be in Nicolaevsky's hands is not entirely clear. Before leaving Norway for Mexico, Trotsky had transferred part of his archives to the Institute of Historical Research in Paris, where Nicolaevsky was then working. On the night of 6 November 1936, as we know, a burglary took place and the material, weighing some eighty kilograms, was taken. Most of the papers, including manuscripts, articles and correspondence, were spirited away bit by bit to Moscow, many of them being shown personally to Stalin. Notes from Yezhov were passed regularly to Stalin by his assistant, Poskrebyshev, for example: 'Top secret. To Central Committee Secretary, Comrade Stalin. I enclose 103 letters taken from Trotsky's archives in Paris. The letters contain Trotsky's correspondence with the American Trotskyist Eastman and his wife Yelena Vasilievna Krylenko for 1929-1933.'[45]

A Menshevik, Boris Nikolaevsky had spent many years as the unofficial archivist of the Russian Social Democratic Workers Party, and had amassed a large and important collection in the process. He arrived in the USA in the year of Trotsky's death, and in New York he continued the work of sorting, classifying and editing the vast quantity of correspondence and research that was in his hands. Assisted for many years by Anna Mikhailovna Burgina, the long-time companion of another Menshevik, Irakli Tsereteli, and who became Nikolaevsky's wife late in life, Nikolaevsky realized in time that a proper institutional home was needed for his important property. As the Russian exile community dwindled and resources, such as they were, disappeared, he approached several universities for a solution. Only the Hoover Institution realized that the custodian was inseparable from the collection, and in 1963 it offered both Nikolaevsky and Burgina tenured posts as official curators of the Nikolaevsky

Collection at Stanford. The Trotsky part of the collection includes manuscripts of books and correspondence dating from the first half of his last exile, when he was on Prinkipo. One of the great rarities of the collection is the manuscript of his *History of the Russian Revolution*.

There is no evidence that Trotsky gave his papers, numbering more than four hundred items, to Nikolaevsky. A letter from Zborowski to Moscow, dated 7 November 1936, sheds some light, however, and as we have seen the part played by Mark Zborowski was crucial:

> [Lev Sedov] summoned me at noon. 'Neighbour' [L. Estrin] also came to the café. 'Sonny' announced that during the night the GPU had stolen the 'Old Man's' archives from the Institute. 'Sonny' said there and then that only four people knew of its location: himself, 'Neighbour', Nikolaevsky and myself. The first three are beyond suspicion. That leaves 'Mack' [i.e. Zborowski]. We have only known him [Sedov said] for two years. But, after a pause, 'Sonny' said he personally trusted 'Mack' one hundred per cent. We have to make sure [Sedov said] that the second archive, which is in a secret location, is still secure. [At this point, in the margin of his letter, Zborowski noted: 'We have already photographed this archive.'] They are worried about a police investigation which, although it will not find the archive, may uncover other things. I discovered that in my absence Nikolaevsky, 'Sonny' and 'Neighbour' had discussed the possibility that 'Mack' had stolen the archive. But they finally abandoned their suspicions and told the police, 'This is the work of the GPU.' [The French police in fact suspected Boris Souvarine, whom they held to be a 'dangerous Communist'.[46]] When 'Mack' was suggested as the culprit, 'Neighbour' declared: 'No way. You'd have to be a genius to play a game like that for two years. I remember very well the way he reacted to the executions in Moscow.'[47]

As a sort of mediator between Lev Sedov and the Paris Institute, Nikolaevsky clearly came into possession of part of the archive, and after Trotsky's death felt free to deal with it as he saw fit. Thus it was that Trotsky's *History* found its way to the Hoover Institution.

Trotsky's interpretation of the events of 1917 is severely constrained within the canonical framework of Marxist theory, and is thus fundamentally limited and narrow, rejecting the possibility that any other view may be valid. 'The main thing,' he wrote, 'was that the February revolution was only an outer shell within which the nucleus of the October revolution lay concealed. The history of the February revolution is the history of the way the October nucleus freed itself of its conciliatory defects. Had the vulgar democrats dared to state the course of events objectively, they too would hardly have been able to invite anyone to return to February, just as you cannot ask an ear of corn to return to the seed that gave it birth.'[48]

The predetermined, pre-ordained nature of the values and arguments used by Trotsky, the rigid class point of view and absolute certainty in the historical correctness of the approach, undoubtedly constitute the weakest feature of his otherwise outstanding *History*. Adhering to the well-established landmarks of 1917, he doggedly repeats the extremely dubious contention that the February revolution was doomed from the start, and that by the end of June it was politically exhausted.[49] He could not or would not see that February had only opened the door to democracy. Nor did he understand that it was not the Bolsheviks who had made the October revolution, but above all the First World War, the weak regime, and the profound social crisis, the indignation of the 'lower orders'. The Bolsheviks turned out to be the most receptive and radically oriented force capable of exploiting these conditions. Trotsky was unable to recognize that 'skipping over' the democratic stage, represented by the February revolution, implied a willingness to resort to the use of force.

Trotsky saw the use of force as the trigger of revolution. Once the proletariat activated that trigger, it would carry out its just cause. The end – revolution – thus justified the means. In his *History* Trotsky explained the inner mechanism of the revolution in a few simple strokes:

> What gave the coup the character of a sharp blow, with the minimum number of casualties, was the combination of a revolutionary conspiracy, a proletarian uprising and the struggle of the peasant garrison ... The Party directed the coup; the main moving force was the proletariat; armed workers' detachments were the fist of the uprising; but the outcome was decided by the struggle of the heavyweight peasant garrison.[50]

Unlike later mendacious Soviet accounts, Trotsky stated that the coup had taken no more than twenty-four hours and that 'perhaps no more than 25-30,000 people' had taken part in it.[51]

Trotsky was prepared to admit that the democracy brought about by the February revolution had been a great achievement, but he claimed it had done nothing to advance 'class war'. In other words, first the fabric of society must be destroyed, and then it must be reconstructed on new lines. The assumption that social change can succeed only when old structures have been destroyed lay at the heart of the failure of the Bolshevik experiment. Having first reduced everything to ashes, the Bolsheviks then proceeded to build their barracks-style socialism. He dismissed as pointless the question of whether the revolution justified the number of victims it caused. And he added: 'If gentry culture gave the world such words as tsar, pogrom and knout, then October has internationalized such terms as Bolshevik, Soviet and Five-year Plan. This alone justifies the proletarian revolution, if it needs justification.'[52] Writing these words in 1932, Trotsky might perhaps be forgiven for not advancing as even more characteristic terms of Soviet reality such words as Gulag, totalitarian bureaucracy and primitive dogmatism. Even when he was perfectly aware of the extent of Stalin's terror, Trotsky did not abandon his optimistic view of the future, nor his activism. Writing from Mexico on 3 February 1937 to his supporter Angelica Balabanova, he asked: 'What is pessimism? It's a passive and pathetic complaint against history. But how can one complain against history? You have to take it as it is, and when it commits extraordinary swinishness, you have to pummel it with your fists. It's the only way to survive on this earth.'[53] Pummelling history, and hoping everything would find its proper place, was all that was left for him to do.

Trotsky's methods as a historian deserve mention. Having read a vast array of the most varied literature, he would collect the quotations, speeches and documents most suitable for his purpose, and stick them in a logical sequence on sheets of paper in accordance with his plan for the current work, whether it was an article, a chapter or a book. Between the mounted quotations on these long 'scrolls' he would then insert the appropriate commentary, argument or reflection. That would provide the first draft. Usually a second draft would then be written, with additional material and further refinement. And finally a third draft would be regarded as the finished version. Some parts of the *History* were only inserted after much more rewriting. The manuscript in the Hoover Archives includes chapters that were never published.

As a synthesis of history and memoirs, Trotsky's *History* was a literary achievement the like of which he would never attain thereafter. Although, as we have seen in his letter to Balabanova, he was putting on a brave face, the Moscow trials knocked the wind out of him. *The Revolution Betrayed* presented its editor, Victor Serge, with a tough job, as he wrote to Lev Sedov in June 1937: 'The book has not been well written or constructed, but has been hurriedly sewn together out of various material . . . a mass of almost literal repetitions and longueurs . . . He shouldn't have killed the book by overloading it . . .'[54] Trotsky was writing the book, however, in Norway, with the combined threat of the NKVD and deportation hanging over him. Prinkipo by comparison had been a writer's paradise.

Despite the authorial egocentrism, which is only to be expected in view of the author's intense involvement in the events, Trotsky's *History* is a masterly account of the vast Russian drama of 1917, written for the most part in a reserved and detached style. It contains philosophical and psychological insight, combined with the vigorous argumentation needed to refute the lies being peddled in Moscow and elsewhere. As he wrote in 1933: 'Just as shopkeepers when they grow rich invent new and more appropriate genealogies for themselves, so the bureaucratic class that has emerged from the revolution has created its own history. Hundreds of duplicating machines are at its service. But the quantity will do nothing to raise its scholarly quality.'[55] He wrote in virtually the same terms in the preface to his book *The Stalinist School of Falsification*, which was published at nearly the same time as the *History* and which consists of a number of original documents, three unpublished speeches and his letter to Istpart.

The basis of this letter of more than one hundred pages, listing seventy points, was the response he had made to a Party history questionnaire of 1927 (see p. 80). Citing a host of documents, he exposed the way the rewriting of history had evolved in Moscow, and apart from Stalin he also blamed Zinoviev, Bukharin, Yaroslavsky, Olminsky and Lunacharsky, the latter three of whom, he claimed, carried out whatever order the secretariat chose to issue.[56] Rejecting the accusation that he was a Menshevik, and pointing out that he had broken with Menshevism in 1904, he wrote: 'I never called myself nor regarded myself as a Menshevik . . . As I have stated several times, in my differences with the Bolsheviks on a number of questions of principles, I was in the wrong.'[57]

Writing in 1931, Trotsky knew that Stalin was exerting himself to discredit his, Trotsky's, position during the Brest-Litovsk treaty negotiations. He wrote that the policy of delaying 'the moment of capitulation to the Hohenzollerns' had been approved by the majority of the Bolshevik leadership: 'During the Brest negotiations the question was entirely about whether or not the revolutionary situation in Germany in early 1918 had developed so far that by not continuing the war (we had no army!) we would nevertheless not have to sign the peace. Experience was to show that this was not the situation.'[58] Stalin was now trying to create the impression that Lenin had decided his policy only after consulting him.

The 'tradition' of twisting the truth about the past to suit present policy would last for many decades. As we have seen, Sorin and Stasova wrote to Stalin in May 1938 with suggestions for 'amendments' to Lenin's notes concerning him at the beginning of 1918.[59] Trotsky now bitterly regretted not having taken with him from Moscow many documents relating to the pre-Revolutionary period and the first years of Soviet rule, especially the minutes of the Revolutionary Military Council, as well as his orders and instructions as People's Commissar for Foreign Affairs, Military and Naval Affairs and Transport, and his voluminous correspondence. He particularly felt the absence of the archives of the Society of Former Political Prisoners and Exiles. He had been admitted to the Society in 1924, when his star was already on the wane. In his membership application he had dutifully entered that his address was the Kremlin, his profession 'writer-revolutionary', his education high-school level, that he was the son of a 'colonist-landowner', and that he had served prison terms in Nikolaev, Odessa, Irkutsk, Alexandrovsk and Moscow.[60] From its inception, the Society gradually accumulated a rich fund of memoirs, documents and notices, and published a magazine, *Katorga i ssylka* (Hard Labour and Exile). Trotsky had intended to dip into this fount of information for his *History*.

When he completed his *magnum opus*, he was not aware that the Society had only a matter of months left to live. Following 'checks and inspection', Ya. Peters and P. Pospelov reported to the boss of the Party Control Commission, Yezhov, and his deputy M.

Shkiryatov, that 'on 1 April, 1935 there were 1307 Party members in the Society and 1494 non-Party members. Former members of other parties represent 57 per cent of the membership.' They further reported that former SRs and Mensheviks were 'closely united by old ties'. Following the assassination of the Leningrad Party boss Kirov in December 1934, 'forty to fifty members of the Society were arrested'. Peters and Pospelov clearly felt that their masters would want to know that 'the SR Andreev, the Mensheviks Driker, Tipulkov and Feldman and others call the NKVD "the Okhranka" [the nickname of the old tsarist secret police]', and that 'in their publications they refer to Bakunin, Lavrov, Tkachev, Radishchev, Ogarev, Lunin et al'. Half of the writers in the journal were Populists, SRs and Mensheviks, there were articles on Nietzsche and Kerensky, and 'one of the articles stated that "there would have been no October had there been no February".' The Society idealized the Cossacks and indirectly cast doubt 'on some of the classic positions taken by Comrade Stalin'. Things had gone so far, indeed, that the former convicts shared the belief that 'the Society must defend its members should they be arrested by the Soviet regime as well.' The report concluded by effectively raising the question of liquidating the Society.[61] Stalin of course approved this proposal, and the Society was disbanded soon after. Gorky obtained Stalin's permission to remove most of its library for the Union of Writers, while Voroshilov took over the Society's rest home at Sochi for his own commissariat.[62]

Trotsky shared the view of many members of the Society that the revolution had occurred not only because the old world had reached a crisis point, but because unsustainable impatience had erupted to cause the explosion. Catastrophes and upheavals of any kind can often facilitate the eruption of revolution, and in the case of the Russian revolution, Trotsky wrote, the necessary catastrophe was the First World War. Superficially, his *History* may seem to be an account of the activities of the Central Committee, the Soviets and so on, but in fact he unobtrusively wove into his narrative the idea of the underlying links between the mood of the masses, the classes and different nations with the situation as it was. As an orthodox Marxist, however, he could not doubt for an instant the 'historic right' of the Communists to remake the world by force.

An original feature of the *History* is Trotsky's constant awareness of the French revolution as a point of reference. All the leaders of the Russian revolution were Jacobins, and they often measured their own efforts by the benchmarks established by Robespierre, Marat, Danton and Saint-Just. During critical moments in 1918–19 Trotsky mentally placed himself in the Convention and the Committee of Public Safety. His most powerful analytical weapons he reserved for the 'Thermidore', or Stalinist reaction. He interpreted Stalin's emergence as occurring naturally, at the stage when genuinely revolutionary forces lose their vigilance and a new privileged caste takes root in the fertile soil of change. When the festival of the revolution ends, he wrote, it is followed by grey, cold and hungry workdays. Not everyone, he said, was able to grasp that 'the deprivation is not a result of the revolution, but merely a step towards a better future'. The grey workdays, however, always chilled the spirit of the revolution, and this was a source of the reaction. Comparing the French and Soviet periods of reaction, Trotsky sought the inner logic of the process itself: 'The French Thermidore, begun by left-wing Jacobins, eventually turned into reaction against the Jacobins in general. Terrorist, Montaignard and Jacobin became terms of abuse. In the provinces they cut down the trees of liberty and trampled tricolour cockades underfoot.' Things were different in Russia: 'The totalitarian party included in itself all the elements required for reaction and it mobilized them under the official banner of revolution. The Party suffered no competition even in the struggle with its enemies. The struggle against the Trotskyists did not become a struggle against the Bolsheviks, because the Party swallowed this struggle whole, setting certain limits for it, as if in the name of Bolshevism.'[63]

Returning repeatedly to the theme of the relationship between 'the leaders, the Party, the class and the masses', Trotsky asserted that these elements were rarely in balance. His depiction of the enemies of October was generally graphic and on the whole correct, but whether writing about Nicholas II, Kerensky or Prokopovich, he was universally dismissive. He was of course no less scathing at times about personalities in his own camp, but in this he conformed perfectly to the norms set by Marx and brought to perfection by Lenin, Stalin and most of the other Bolsheviks when they were involved in theoretical debate with friend or foe.

Naturally, Trotsky wrote a great deal about Lenin, eloquently and with great psychological insight, yet, after reading his *History* one is left with the sense that the cult of Lenin, against which both he and Lenin had protested, may well have had its origins in Trotsky's own writings. The notion that Trotsky could find only positive qualities in Lenin is hard to swallow. Before the revolution Trotsky had uttered many unflattering things about the Party's leader, but after it he adopted a note of pure praise. He certainly failed to take account of the fact that Lenin was not averse to flattery, even if he knew how to hide it. Angelica Balabanova, who had known Lenin well, noted that he 'needed accomplices rather than collaborators. Trustworthiness to him meant absolute certainty that an individual would carry out all orders, including those contrary to his conscience.'[64]

There were other flaws in the founder of Bolshevism to which Trotsky was blind, among them his defence of the dictatorship of the proletariat, his making an absolute value of the class struggle, his conviction that social democracy was fundamentally wrong, and much else that Trotsky accepted as the postulates of divine teaching. Since he was firmly convinced that the October revolution could not have happened without Lenin, Trotsky depicted Lenin not merely as a messiah, but as the person bearing responsibility for the act of revolution itself. But, of course, in raising Lenin to the very summit of historical justification, Trotsky was surreptitiously also placing himself on the pedestal of history, since he had so often been named as the second man of the revolution. And he used his defence of Lenin as a weapon in the fight against the new leader. He was therefore particularly outraged when the Soviet press began putting Stalin alongside Lenin. On 5 August 1935 *Pravda* published an article by David Zaslavsky, celebrating the fortieth anniversary of the death of Engels and proclaiming that 'the wonderful friendship of Marx-Engels, which is worthy of study, was repeated not by accident in the wonderful collaboration, the great friendship of Lenin-Stalin'. Trotsky responded with an article entitled 'How They Write History and Biography', in which he wrote: 'After this, the son of a bitch squats and awaits encouragement.'[65]

Apart from writing historical studies of the revolution, Trotsky was to a certain extent also a military historian. It was on his initiative that his orders, directives and speeches as Chairman of the Revolutionary Military Council were published in a five-volume collection

in 1923–24 under the title *Kak vooruzhalas revolyutsiya* (How the Revolution was Armed). As early as February 1920 he had written to the
Chief of the Field Staff, the Political Direction of the Red Army and
the Military History Commission: 'It seems that it will be absolutely
necessary in the coming months to compile at least a brief history of
the Red Army. Such a history will be needed above all in Western
Europe and America ... It must become the source-book for many
other countries which have either already entered or are about to
enter the revolutionary epoch.'[66] He indicated that the history of the
Red Army should reflect its different stages, that of partisan warfare,
voluntary and regular service, the role of the commissars and aspects
of strategy in the civil war.

The civil war occupies a special place in Trotsky's writing, and the
seventeenth volume of his collected works is devoted to its history,
and an analysis and description of the widest possible range of events.
At the Sixth Congress of Soviets in November 1918 he had proclaimed
that 'the first army of Communism in the history of the world' had
been created and was operating victoriously.[67] Most of his writing on
military themes took the form of narrative, or chronicles of events,
but he also believed that by peopling scenes of battle and front-line
activity with sharply etched personalities, he could strike sparks of
revolutionary enthusiasm and raise the exhausted and tormented
population once more to continue the fratricidal conflict. While his
multi-volume history of the civil war lacked formal structure, it
succeeded in recreating the atmosphere of the time.

Much of the material in the collection testifies to Trotsky's enormous contribution to the thinking and decision-making that went into
building the new army. Speaking in November 1920 at a commission
charged with making use of the experience of the civil war, and long
before the military reforms of 1925, he put forward the idea of a
regular army based on the foundation of a militia.[68] When the civil
war was over, Trotsky repeatedly raised the question of spreading
knowledge about its history in the interests of the world revolution.
The idea, promoted in speeches by a number of other leaders besides
Trotsky, was to familiarize the masses with the military history of the
Russian revolution, on the assumption that awareness of it was essential as a manual of instruction and source of revolutionary strategy for
the coming civil wars in other countries. The Soviet military leaders

believed that their advice would soon be needed elsewhere. 'We must compile a strategic and tactical calendar of October,' Trotsky said. 'We must show how events rose in wave after wave, and the way they were reflected in the Party, in the Soviets, the Central Committee and military organization.' It would all be of use to 'our class brethren'.

In his 1920 report Trotsky also spoke of the need to be able to combine a defensive war, forced on the Red Army, with the civil war conditions in the enemy camp.[69] Practical experience thus became a definite weapon. When in 1924 D. Petrovsky, the editor of the journal *Voennyi vestnik* (Military Messenger), sent B. Shaposhnikov's article 'The History of One Campaign. Summer 1920' to Trotsky for comment, Trotsky crossed out the author's words, 'Because of our military loss, the link was broken between the October revolution and that of Western Europe.'[70] Shaposhnikov's article had been devoted to an analysis of Tukhachevsky's lecture 'The Vistula Campaign', and Trotsky was not prepared in 1924 to share this defeatist view in public.

He had in fact been the initiator of a large number of significant studies by military thinkers, including Anishev, Kakurin, Bubnov, Kamenev, Tukhachevsky and Eideman, but by the end of the 1920s his own name no longer figured in them. Many other important features of the Soviet Union's military history with which he had been associated were also suppressed. For instance, on Trotsky's orders the former commander of the 3rd Cavalry Corps, G. Gai, sent him a full report on the fate of Red Army units in Poland in 1920. After suffering severe losses in heavy fighting, the 3rd Corps had become separated from the main front and was forced to enter Germany, where its troops were interned.[71] Trotsky had also been informed that the retreating 1st Cavalry Army under Budenny had brought with it a wave of pogroms, although no mention of this is to be found in the Soviet military literature. As Commissar Zilist reported to Lenin: '1st Cavalry Army and 6th division destroyed the Jewish population as they went, looting and killing on the way . . . 44th Division was also not idle . . .'[72] Lenin marked the report 'for the archives', but Trotsky did not have the right to use such material in his writings.

At the end of the 1920s the process began whereby the roles of individuals were altered in the writing of Soviet history to suit Stalin's purposes better, and military history was not neglected in this regard. When Trotsky read a panegyric by Voroshilov in *Pravda* on the occasion of the leader's fiftieth birthday in 1929, he became enraged. Voroshilov asserted that the saviour of the Soviet regime in the civil war was none other than Stalin, whose 'iron will and strategic talent' were demonstrated in his able and skilful leadership. On the other hand, according to Voroshilov, 'the defeat of our troops at Warsaw, which was the result of the treacherous orders of Trotsky and his supporters in Red Army Headquarters, disrupted the Cavalry Army which was preparing to attack Lvov.'[73] During the civil war Trotsky had tried and failed to persuade Lenin to remove Voroshilov, and now the worm had turned and was having his revenge by piling one myth on the other.

Trotsky chose to reply to Voroshilov in an article entitled 'Stalin and the Red Army, or How History is Written', using almost exactly the same sub-headings as Voroshilov – 'Tsaritsyn', 'Perm', 'Petrograd' and 'The Southern Front' – but providing on the basis of the documents, step by step and paragraph by paragraph, an entirely different picture in each case. In his introduction he wrote that Voroshilov's article contained 'not a single line of truth, not one'.[74] He realized, of course, that while millions would read Voroshilov's travesty, virtually no one in the Soviet Union would have the chance to judge it by comparison with his own factual version, apart from some NKVD officials, a few diplomats and Stalin himself.

Trotsky did not know that in December 1928, when he was en route from Alma-Ata to Odessa, Voroshilov was enlisting Stalin's assistance in having certain cuts made to a book by Yegorov on the Warsaw campaign. In particular he wanted to delete references to Stalin's telegram which prevented the Cavalry Army from going to Tukhachevsky's assistance. Voroshilov wrote to Stalin in their customary familiar way:

Dear Koba,
    I have read your letter to Yegorov about keeping the telegram of 13 August 1920 in his book Lvov-Warsaw. I am in full agreement with the essence of your letter ... But unfortunately Comrade Yegorov gives his own interpretation of the telegram. I urge you to cast your eye over the few pages (127–130) of Lvov-Warsaw which show why I am concerned. If you still think the explanation of Berzin's correspondence with Trotsky and Yegorov's commentary are adequate, tell Comrade Tovstukha to call me, or give me a call on the phone yourself.

My own view is against including the telegram with such a peculiar commentary as that given by Yegorov.[75]

Yegorov wrote to the publishing house, protesting: 'This book is my monograph and to make changes without my knowledge means to deprive it of its author and, as the author, I cannot accept public responsibility for the alteration carried out in the book by other hands.'[76] It was of course the view of Stalin and Voroshilov that prevailed, not the author's. It had become a rule that all sins, past and present, all defeats and failures, must be blamed on the chief opponent, the distant exile Trotsky.

Voroshilov would soon become even more explicit. In his Order No. 072 of 7 June 1937, the successor of Trotsky and Frunze as Defence Commissar stressed that

> the Soviet court has already more than once justly punished the gangs of terrorists, saboteurs, spies and murderers exposed amid the Trotskyites and Zinovievites who have been doing their treacherous deeds with money from the German, Japanese and other foreign intelligence agencies under the command of the brutal Fascist, traitor and betrayer of the workers and peasants, Trotsky . . . As an agent of Japano-German Fascism, Trotsky will now have to recognize yet again that his faithful accomplices, the Gamarniks and Tukhachevskys, the Yakirs, Uboreviches and all the other scum who served capitalism as lackeys, are to be wiped off the face of the earth and that their memory will be forever cursed and forgotten.[77]

All this had only an indirect relation to the writing – and rewriting – of history. From the early 1930s, indeed, Trotsky was no longer able to devote himself wholeheartedly to such luxuries as historical research. He was consumed by the problem of self-preservation. History, however, is not only to be found in the pages of researchers. The drama of the historian himself may become elevated to the level of the highest tragedy.

Forty-Three Months in Mexico

Despite the fact that his name figured in every condemnatory remark made at the Moscow trials, officially Trotsky could not be sentenced

by the Soviet court, even *in absentia*, since in 1932 he and his entire
family had been deprived of their Soviet citizenship. As Vyshinsky's
concluding three-hour speech revealed, however, it was the regime's
intention that Trotsky should be morally and politically annihilated:
'Together with our entire people, I accuse these most heinous of
criminals, who deserve only one kind of punishment, shooting, death!'
His words were greeted by the customary stormy applause. At
7.15 p.m. on 30 January 1937, the court adjourned, ostensibly to
consider its verdict, although this had been decided long in advance
of the trial. While Vyshinsky and Ulrikh were reporting to Stalin,
and tea was taken behind the scenes, the court waited. The accused
had to wait eight long hours while their fate was decided. Finally it
emerged that four of them were to be spared – for the time being.
Concluding his reading of the sentence, Ulrikh declared that on the
evidence given at the trial the court had shown that Trotsky and his
son Lev had been directing the treasonous activities of the 'Trotskyist
anti-Soviet Centre', and that should they ever be found on Soviet
territory, they would be arrested and tried by the Military Collegium
of the Soviet Supreme Court.[78] What Ulrikh did not know was
that the order to liquidate Trotsky physically had been given long
before.

As we have seen, for the first two or three years of his exile Trotsky
still entertained some fragile hope of being able to return to the USSR.
He knew that this could only happen if Stalin were removed from the
leadership, or in the event of a dramatic change of course by the
regime. In any case, he sent signals from Prinkipo on two occasions
indicating his readiness for reconciliation without preconditions. He
saw the international revolutionary movement as the basis for such
reconciliation, maintaining the hope that the movement would rise
and would convince the leadership in Moscow that he had been right
all along.

From early 1931 Trotsky had been urging that the fate of the
revolution in Spain depended crucially on the Spanish Communist
Party's readiness to fight and to lead with authority, and he wrote a
letter to the Politburo warning that defeat of the Spanish Republic
would automatically lead to the installation of a Fascist regime, as real
as that of Mussolini. 'There is no need,' he concluded, 'to speak of
the consequences this would have for the whole of Europe and the

USSR.' In the letter, however, he also pointed to the opportunities for a world revolution contained in the situation in Spain, and urged the Soviet leadership to make 'an honest attempt' to heal its rift with the international labour movement, and 'to form a united front in the arena of the Spanish revolution'. The word 'honest' cannot have come easily from Trotsky's pen, knowing Stalin as he did. Noting the fact that 'nine-tenths of these differences' had nothing to do with Spain, he had decided not to complicate matters further by making his case in the press, and therefore restricted himself to this confidential address to the Soviet leadership.

Trotsky could not, however, bring himself to send the letter. He feared it would be read as a sign of surrender, and let it lie on his desk until 27 April 1931, when he added a short concluding sentence to the effect that his proposals required urgent action, and sent it by ordinary post to Moscow.[79] Without waiting for a reply, he then lost patience and published the letter in the May–June issue of the *Bulletin of the Opposition*.[80] The Politburo had in fact seen his letter in May, and Stalin had then made it clear that action must be taken to eliminate Trotsky politically. His note, scrawled in red ink across Trotsky's typed letter, reads: 'To Molotov, Kaganovich, Postyshev, Sergo, Andreev, Kuibyshev, Kalinin, Voroshilov, Rudzutak. I think that Trotsky, this criminal gang-boss and Menshevik charlatan, has to be bumped on the head through ECCI. He has to know his place.'[81]

Most of the Politburo added short approving comments, Molotov's remark being more lengthy: 'I suggest no reply be made. If Trotsky publishes this, a reply should be made along the lines proposed by Comrade Stalin.' Exactly what this meant is unclear, since Stalin spoke only of 'bumping Trotsky on the head'. It is noteworthy that Stalin did not name all the members of the Politburo for circulation: Kirov is missing, as are Mikoyan, Petrovsky and Chubar, who were candidate members, while Andreev was no longer a candidate member and was chairman of the Party Control Commission. It is not always possible to follow the serpentine path of Stalin's thinking, but here at least it is clear that he wanted Trotsky silenced. He often issued orders in oblique or elliptical language, for instance 'first category sentence', which meant the death penalty. In Trotsky's case, Stalin's will would be carried out literally – after a nine-year delay.

Why did Stalin indicate Comintern as the means for getting at

Trotsky? Did he intend the action to be carried out as the result of a propaganda resolution of ECCI, or similar action by the Spanish Communist Party? Evidently not. The issue was more complex. As early as the end of the 1920s, a special group had been formed by the OGPU under Menzhinsky, with the task of carrying out operations abroad against Russian counter-revolutionaries, including the liquidation of opponents of the Stalinist order. The work of this group was regarded by the leadership as especially patriotic, representing the highest form of class vengeance against the enemies of socialism. The perpetrators of these terroristic actions were well rewarded and given rapid promotion in the service. In due course the Foreign and Secret Political Sections of the Security Directorate of the NKVD were formed and staffed by senior intelligence officials, of whom the most notable were Zubov, Serebryansky, Sudoplatov, Kolesnikov, Eitingon, Shpigelglas and Fitin.

One of the most valuable sources of information on these activities is Pavel Sudoplatov, with whom I conducted lengthy interviews, and who has since published an authoritative account of the KGB and his life as a secret operative.[82] Sudoplatov was not only an intelligence agent. Like others in his group, he also engaged in the assassination of the USSR's enemies among the White émigrés and oppositionists. Some of these operatives themselves served prison terms or died, like Serebryansky, in Soviet custody, their work having exposed them to too many suspicious contacts for their masters' liking. For most, however, their work on behalf of the system was valued as heroic and gladiatorial. Menzhinsky, Yagoda, Yezhov and Beria successively reported personally to Stalin on the work of their special 'legionaries'.[83]

Before the Second World War the Foreign Section of NKVD Security carried out the orders of the highest authority. As Sudoplatov wrote to the Procurator General of the USSR in 1989: 'For the thirty or more years that I worked in intelligence, all the operations I took part in emanated not from Beria, but from the Party Central Committee. Intelligence and diversionary operations abroad and behind the Fascist German lines were under the direct orders of the Party Central Committee [to which Sudoplatov and his colleagues reported back[84]]. All the reports on my special operations are to be found in the General Department of the Central Committee, and one of them is a one-page report in my own hand.'[85] This handwritten report was on the assassination of Trotsky in Mexico.

Arrested in 1953 – like many other senior officials of the secret service whose recent careers had been closely associated with Beria, who was himself arrested when Stalin died – Sudoplatov spent the next fifteen years in prison. In 1982 he applied for rehabilitation, but it was not granted until 1992.[86] In a second application for rehabilitation in 1987, Sudoplatov mentioned other operatives of the Foreign Section, among them a number of foreign refugees and exiles, better known as Comintern personalities, who had been recruited into the Special Group, including Dimitrov, Manuilsky and Dolores Ibarruri, nicknamed 'La Pasionaria'.[87] The use of foreign Communists in NKVD intelligence operations was also confirmed in letters and reminiscences of Kolesnikov and Eitingon, and has been documented in a collection of KGB archives.[88] A number of other other senior Comintern figures, as well as diplomats, were also used by the Special Group for intelligence-gathering rather than active operations. These included the Bulgarian ambassador to Moscow, Ivan Stamenov, who, according to Sudoplatov, suggested a radio receiver and embroidered Russian felt boots be presented as a gift to the Bulgarian king, Boris.

Following Stalin's decision 'to bump Trotsky on the head', Menzhinsky and Yagoda attempted to carry out their master's wish on Prinkipo, covering their tracks by launching rumours in the Communist-friendly press about an impending attempt on Trotsky's life by White émigrés. Efforts were indeed made to provoke Whites into carrying out the murder, but Trotsky left Prinkipo for France at the crucial moment. Thus ended the first, rather slack, attempt to fulfil Stalin's wishes.

France, with its much larger Russian community and far larger contingent of OGPU agents than there had been in Turkey, presented a greater threat to Trotsky. His location was soon discovered and he was forced to move often, living like a wanted criminal in hiding. It was impossible for him to disappear from view, however, because among his son's assistants was the OGPU agent Zborowski.

Early in 1935, Soviet intelligence agent Mikhail Shpigelglas received verbal instructions from Yagoda, who had received them in turn from Stalin, to 'speed up the liquidation of Trotsky'. An experienced operator, Shpigelglas mobilized the entire agency in France, including Ignaz Reiss, a Polish Communist who worked for the OGPU from 1925 to 1937 in Germany, France, Austria and Switzerland, successively.

Trotsky was very careful. He had received warning via Reiss that he was a marked man.[89] Reiss himself defected in 1937 over the bloodletting of the Moscow trials, proclaiming himself a Trotskyist and supporter of the Fourth International. He wrote to the Central Committee: 'I have come thus far with you, but I will not go one step further ... Whoever remains silent now becomes an accomplice of Stalin and a traitor to the cause of the working class and socialism.' He enclosed with his letter the Order of the Red Banner that he had received as 'a heroic fighter for Communism', adding: 'To wear it while the executioners of the best representatives of the working class are also wearing it is beneath my dignity.'[90] Six weeks after writing this letter, on 4 September 1937, Reiss was murdered in Zurich. He had probably warned Trotsky to get out of France as early as the spring or summer of 1935, which Trotsky duly did. It was at this period that Trotsky virtually went under cover. Shpigelglas and his men located him several times, only to find that their prey had slipped the noose at the crucial moment.

Deep frustration was felt in Moscow, and when Trotsky escaped to Norway in June 1935, Shpigelglas was summoned home, only to find a witch-hunt in progress, with himself under suspicion. Eighteen months later, at the February–March 1937 Central Committee Plenum, Stalin declared: 'The one thing we lack is the willingness to liquidate our own carelessness, our own placidity, our own shortsightedness.'[91] He accused the special services of spinelessness and indecisiveness. Not surprisngly, the resolution on Yezhov's report – Yezhov having replaced Yagoda – confirmed that the NKVD Security Directorate had had the chance in 1932–33 to expose 'the Trotskyist conspiracy' and liquidate it. This was an implicit and sinister reproach that the chief enemy had been allowed to remain alive. The resolution spoke of the surviving links between Soviet officials and Sedov in Berlin, of the 'criminal' relations betwen the chief of the NKVD's Secret Political Section, Molchanov, with the Trotskyist Fourier, and so on. This confirmed that senior Soviet officials abroad were under surveillance themselves, as reports from the Paris agency also showed.[92]

The plenum resolution also called for the process of 'exposing and smashing the Trotskyists' to be carried out to the end, a formula which, issuing from Stalin, could only mean physical annihilation. The NKVD special services were to be reinforced. Having failed to carry out Stalin's order, Yagoda was soon arrested as a member of the 'Right Trotskyist Bloc', and in 1938 was shot, although the charges specified at his trial did not, of course, include that of failing to organize the murder of Trotsky.[93] Yagoda stated at the trial: 'I already know my sentence, I've been expecting it for a whole year.'[94] In his prosecution speech, Vyshinsky declared significantly that 'Yagoda and his vile treacherous activity' had not been exposed by the 'treacherous security organ that he organized and that he directed against the interests of the Soviet state and our revolution, but by the real, the genuine Bolshevik intelligence service that is headed by one of the most remarkable Stalinist comrades-in-arms, Nikolai Ivanovich Yezhov'.[95] The fact is that, when Trotsky sailed away from Turkey in July 1933, both Menzhinsky and his deputy, Yagoda, had known that Stalin would never forget it. Menzhinsky died a natural death in his bed, but Yagoda was fair game as a defendant in the 'right-Trotskyist' trial. The resolution unambiguously decreed that steps be taken 'to strengthen a reliable agency in the country and abroad'.[96]

The implication was that not only had Yagoda and his subordinates 'penetrated the NKVD agencies as Trotsky's accomplices',[97] but that such agents and Shpigelglas and his group had done so too. He had been sent abroad, knowing that his operation had been sanctioned by the highest authority, and he had failed. Although he was allowed to continue analyzing the reports that Zborowski was sending back to Moscow from Paris, he was no longer trusted,[98] and was soon arrested, condemned and eventually shot. Sudoplatov's comment on Shpigelglas was laconic: 'He didn't carry out the job of killing Trotsky. So he couldn't be forgiven.'

After the Eighteenth Party Congress of March 1939, the Foreign Section became the NKVD First Directorate, headed by Fitin with Sudoplatov as his deputy. A Special Group, under the former SR Serebryansky, continued to function within the First Directorate, and after June 1941 it was detached to form a strong, independent unit, reporting directly to the People's Commissar for the Interior.[99]

As operations behind enemy lines during the war expanded, the unit became the Second Independent Section of the NKVD, and then in 1942 the Fourth Section.[100] Sudoplatov was made its chief with the rank of Lieutenant-General, and his deputy, Naum Eitingon, was made a Major-General. Both of them were decorated with the Order of Suvorov. The NKVD's Special Group and similar units produced no less than twenty-two Heroes of the Soviet Union. As Sudoplatov wrote to the Politburo, his agency – Section C – had run a special bureau to gather information on the research being conducted on atomic weapons abroad, material that was put to use by Soviet physicists and arms manufacturers.[101] Yet when Beria was arrested in the summer of 1953, Sudoplatov, Eitingon, Serebryansky and others of their kind were also arrested for having been particularly trusted by their fallen leader. In practice, their work had been devised and supervised by a special section of the Central Committee, but as a unit under the formal authority of the Interior Commissariat, they became especially vulnerable when its sinister chief fell from grace.

Stalin's determination to get rid of Trotsky stiffened when he learned late in 1936 that Trotsky was writing *The Revolution Betrayed* and continuing his biography of Stalin himself, books that would expose the worst of the regime and the criminal nature of its leader. After the death of Lev Sedov, the Special Section had to decide the future role of Lev Zborowski. Agent 'West' reported that 'Tulip's' (Zborowski's) position had become difficult. The greatest threat was posed by Estrin, who did not hide her distrust of him, although Zborowski dismissed this as unimportant. Noting that Zborowski was 'very lazy by nature', 'West' requested Moscow's permission to tell him to concentrate on gathering information on the Trotskyists, continuing his work on the *Bulletin* and assisting the 'Russian Section of the Fourth International'. But the chief task the Special Section proposed giving to its underemployed undercover agent was to 'get to "the Old Man"'. First, he must join Trotsky's security staff. But van Heijenoort had not replied to a letter from Zborowski suggesting that he (Zborowski) come to Mexico to join Trotsky's staff.[102] Another would be sent by the next ship to Mexico. 'West' then referred to the 'Sofia method' (an attempt made by the NKVD to blow up an apartment in Sofia), adding that if Zborowski failed to penetrate Trotsky's personal security, 'two or three German Trotskyists should be despatched via the International Secretariat. These people could be very valuable to us in the future, also in other ways.'[103]

'West's' proposals were accepted by Moscow, and new agents were despatched from Spain and the Soviet Union. Soon it was decided that Zborowski should be sent to Mexico: 'Send a draft letter from "Tulip" to "the Old Man", but only after you have received our sanction should the letter be sent.'[104] Moscow was thus considering various paths by which to penetrate Trotsky's defences. Early in 1939, Stalin convened a small meeting to discuss the sole question of how to liquidate Trotsky. The 1938 issues of the *Bulletin* had contained the most vitriolic and devastating condemnation yet of the purge of the Red Army. Under the title 'Totalitarian Defeatists', Trotsky had accused Stalin of rendering the country defenceless in the face of war: 'Defeatism, sabotage and treason are lodged in Stalin's *oprichnina* [special guards]. The *ober*-defeatist is the "father of the people" – he is also their executioner ... The slogan of Soviet patriotism should be "Down with the totalitarian defeatists, out with Stalin and his *oprichnina!*"'[105]

In an article entitled 'Behind the Kremlin Walls', dated January 1939, Trotsky revealed that Abel Yenukidze had been shot for trying 'to stay the hand that was raised above the heads of the old Bolsheviks'.[106] The same issue of the *Bulletin* was meant to have included an article commemorating the first anniversary of Lev's death, but Trotsky could not find the strengh to write it. Instead, he asked Zborowski to do it for him: 'You are doing a great service in publishing the *Bulletin* so punctually and with such care. This is to your credit.'[107]

Stalin wanted to read or hear no more of Trotsky's poisonous barbs. He was tired of waiting while a succession of henchmen failed to deal effectively with the issue, and decided to settle the matter by giving the orders himself. In March 1939 he summoned Sudoplatov and told him that 'this Fascist hireling must be liquidated without further ado. Spare no expense. Bring in whoever you want.' At a later meeting it was decided that Eitingon, with his greater experience and knowledge of Spanish, should head the expedition. Finally, Stalin reminded Sudoplatov that the order to liquidate Trotsky had come from the Central Committee: 'I don't have to tell you what that means,' he added significantly. Eitingon (who spent twelve years in prison along with other secret service officials who were tainted by association with

Beria, who was arrested after Stalin's death in 1953), wrote to Khrush-
chev in September 1963 in the hope of rehabilitation, and stated
plainly that from 1925 he had worked abroad on Central Committee
missions, adding that his team had never carried out any personal
commissions of the People's Commissariat of the Interior.[108]

If Trotsky knew that the NKVD had been given orders to liquidate
him, he also knew that such practices had been in use when he was
still a leading political figure in the USSR. For instance, in May 1924
the head of the Foreign Section of OGPU, M. Trilisser, wrote to
one of his agents in Germany: 'Arthur Koch, Winkler, Kuhsfeld,
Benimann, Spange, Elsa Stuerz, Maderkrebs and Senger have been
adequately instructed in the use of hypodermic syringes and should
have mastered them fully. San, Kaiser, Stuetter and Neumann must
be eliminated in any event. Contact must be made with anyone
arrested and instruction given as to how they should behave. Any
reference to us is absolutely impermissible.'[109]

The practice of assassinating undesirables was even acknowledged
by Vyshinsky at the trial of Yagoda, when he declared on 11 March
1938: 'Yagoda stood at the peak of the technology of killing people
in the most devious ways. He represented the last word in the "science" of bestiality.'[110] Amid the welter of mendacity that characterized
the show trials, this is one piece of testimony, at least, that can be
accepted as true and accurate.

Of his part in the operation against Trotsky, Sudoplatov wrote to
the Politburo: 'At the end of 1938, thanks to the efforts of Dekanozov,
the new chief of the Foreign Section, as well as of Beria, I was accused
of having "criminal links with Shpigelglas". I was threatened with
arrest. And so was Eitingon. I remained in this state of limbo until
March–April 1939. Then, just in time, Eitingon and I were given
our new assignment by the Central Committee; everything around us
calmed down and we began active preparations for the operation in
Mexico. And we carried it out in August 1940.'[111]

Sudoplatov remained in Moscow 'to supervise and cooordinate' the
operation, while Eitingon and a large group of agents, most of them
from Spain, set off for Mexico. Among them were the Spanish military
graduates Martinez, Alvarez, Ximenez, and the Chekists Rabinovich,
Grigolevich and others who were well acquainted with Latin America.
They were to have been joined by Zborowski, but by the time he

arrived Trotsky was already dead, and his involvement was no longer required.[112] He later made an effort to get out of the game and even managed to collaborate with the American anthropologist Margaret Mead on a study of the Jews of Eastern Europe, *Life is for People* (1952). He was suspected of espionage and arrested in the USA in 1956, but was soon released. Rearrested in 1962, he was given a four-year prison sentence. He managed to write another anthropological study, *People in Suffering*, but in none of his writings did he ever refer to his work as an agent of the NKVD.[113] And there was much he could have said, especially as his indirect role in the operation against Trotsky in Coyoacan was significant, as we shall see.

The group settled in Mexico City as refugees from Spain. First, however, a noisy Comintern-inspired campaign was organized, calling for Trotsky's expulson from the country. The Mexican Communist Party published an array of materials, sent by Moscow, purporting to expose Trotsky's 'treachery to the working class', his links with German and English intelligence services, and his participation in terroristic attempts on the lives of Soviet leaders. Notices were posted in the streets to the effect that Trotsky was organizing a revolution in Mexico with the aim of establishing a Fascist dictatorship. In effect, these fabrications simply regurgitated the charges of the Moscow trials.

In Moscow, efforts were being made to find supplementary 'evidence' of Trotsky's crimes. At the end of 1938, Yezhov and Beria sent a top-secret memorandum to the Politburo – apparently the last thing Yezhov wrote – in which it was claimed that additional evidence had been found that showed Trotsky as having collaborated with German intelligence even before the October revolution.[114] The blatant falsity of this material was too much even for the Politburo, and no more was made of it.

Meanwhile, Trotsky and Natalya felt the noose tightening around their last refuge. Their guards watched as strangers and vehicles circled the house slowly. A careful scrutiny was made of all visitors, and Trotsky asked the city authorities for police reinforcements. He had been warned of the looming danger by Alexander Orlov, who had worked with Eitingon in Spain. When a relative of Orlov's in Kiev – one Katsenelson – had been arrested, Orlov saw the writing on the wall, seized $60,000 of the Agency's funds, and absconded to

America with his wife and daughter. Trotsky, however, had not taken Orlov's warning seriously, especially in regard to Zborowski, who had taken over the *Bulletin* after Lev's death.

Many of Trotsky's supporters were similarly under siege, thanks to Zborowski. In August 1937 he had reported that Lev had left Paris, handing over the organization's affairs to him, Zborowski, to manage, including all the current correspondence along with the despatch of documents to Trotsky. Lev had given him a small notebook containing all the addresses: 'As you know,' Zborowski wrote to his masters in Moscow, 'we have dreamed about getting hold of it for a whole year, but we never managed it before, because "Sonny" would never let it out of his hands. I enclose herewith a photo of these addresses. We shall research them in detail shortly and send you [the results]. There are quite a few interesting addresses here . . .'[115] They included those of Trotsky's entourage in Mexico.

The NKVD knew too much about Trotsky for him to survive. Trotsky arranged for an article to appear in the press under the headline 'L.D. Trotsky's Life in Danger', in which it was made plain that the threat came from Stalin: 'As long as L.D. Trotsky is still alive, Stalin's role as the destroyer of the Bolshevik old guard has not been accomplished. It is not enough to condemn him to death with Zinoviev, Kamenev, Bukharin and the other victims of the terror. The sentence has to be carried out.' The article mentioned that an attempt had already been made on his life in Coyoacan: 'In the guise of an exile bringing a gift, a suspicious-looking man had attempted to get into the house. The attempt had failed because the man's behaviour had aroused suspicion. He managed to get away, but left behind a package containing explosives.'[116] The article also named Stalin's agents who had come from Spain to Mexico, but the list does not include Eitingon, Mercader or Grigulevich, nor indeed any of the chief members of the group that had arrived to carry out the act. They were, of course, all operating under assumed names.

Trotsky wrote two letters to the *Bulletin* editors. In the first he informed them that they should not expect any major new articles for the next two or three months: 'I am under an obligation to write my book on Stalin and to complete my book on Lenin over the next eighteen months.' In his second letter, written two days later, he noted that articles by Alexander Barmin, the former Soviet envoy to Athens who had defected, had arrived 'just when we were in a state of alarm (from an attempt of the sort made in Bulgaria . . .) I had to leave the apartment for a while without my manuscripts and documents . . .'[117]

Copies of Trotsky's letters to the *Bulletin* were already on their way to Moscow when he went into hiding. Agent 'West' reported to the Foreign Section that the *Bulletin* would be coming out on 15 April: 'You have already received by the latest post, or will be receiving, nearly all the "Old Man's" articles.'[118]

It was known in Moscow that Trotsky was aware of the operation mounted against him. At the end of the 1930s Yakov Serebryansky, a major Soviet intelligence agent, had managed to steal part of the Trotskyists' archives in Paris, with the help of Zborowski. In it were documents showing that an attempt on Trotsky's life was known to be a possibility. For instance, in a document dated 19 November 1935, a meeting is mentioned at which a letter from Freda Zeller, who had visited Trotsky in Norway on returning from the Soviet Union, was discussed. The letter, which contained a proposal 'to kill Stalin', was seen by the Trotsykists as a blatant provocation.[119] The myth of an attempt by the Trotskyists on Stalin's life provided a satisfactory justification not only for the mass terror in Russia, but also for the activities of the Foreign Section of the NKVD abroad. The Sneevleit archive, which also ended up in NKVD hands, contains numerous examples of documents which testify to the general fear and awareness among Trotsky's entourage. For example, a certain Kruks wrote to a fellow-Trotskyist, Keller: 'A mortal danger from the GPU is hanging over Comrade "Ts" [Trotsky]; we have to take measures to save him.'[120]

Meanwhile Eitingon continued his preparations, using two alternative strategies, as agreed in Moscow: one by means of the Mexican Communist Party and the other through individual agents. David Siqueiros, the well-known Mexican painter, has described in some detail the motives and intentions of his accomplices, who had determined that 'Trotsky's headquarters in Mexico must be destroyed, even if it means resorting to force.'[121] Siqueiros, however, did not know the whole truth, or could not utter it. He says nothing of the role of the Communist Party of Mexico, nor of the non-Mexicans who planned the operation, and attempts to depict the operation as merely the expression of discontent by Mexican internationalists at the activities of the Trotskyists in Spain. His discussion of this topic is strained

and historically unsound, to put it mildly, and it is impossible to
believe that it was the intention of this large group to do no more
than 'to seize as many documents as possible, but to avoid bloodshed
at all costs'.[122] One wonders why they required a machine-gun for the
purpose. It seems that all this was said for the Mexican court, for
public opinion and to camouflage the savage action guided by Moscow. Siqueiros describes the attack on Trotsky's life as virtually a
spontaneous outburst of internationalists who had fought in Spain
and who were intent on taking their revenge on him for the split in
Republican ranks brought about by the POUM, a Marxist party under
Trotsky's influence. In his book *The Spanish Communists*, Jesus Fernandes Tomas writes that the crime of the POUM leaders, Andrés
Nin and Joaquin Maurin, had consisted in not wishing blindly to copy
the Soviet experience. As early as 1932, Maurin had written: 'The
Soviets are a Russian creation which cannot be adapted to just any
other country ... To submit oneself prematurely to any concrete
structures means condemning oneself to defeat.' Andrés Nin shared
these views, a fact, Fernandes wrote, that condemned the leaders of
POUM to destruction. The liquidation of Nin was carried out by
Alexander Orlov. The legend still exists of a Trotskyist plot and uprising in Spain.[123] If Siqueiros is to be believed, the operation against
Trotsky would amount to no more than revolutionary revenge. He
had commanded the 82nd Brigade in Spain and had been especially
successful at Teruel. He formed a combat group for the terrorist
operation in Mexico.

Eitingon's group, in which Eitingon himself never appeared openly,
continued intensive operations. Everything was foreseen: ways of neu-
tralizing the police on the perimeter of Trotsky's house, of disarming
the interior guards, breaking telephone contact, the order in which
groups designated to seize, burn and destroy archives should function,
and so on. The two main objectives were to exterminate the master
of the house and to destroy his papers. Everything seemed ready, but
chance intervened.

On 1 May 1940 thousands of Mexican workers paraded through
the squares and streets, bearing Communist placards and slogans calling on the President to throw Trotsky out of the country. Although
he was used to them by now, the slander and insults were hard for
Trotsky to bear. He spent the whole of May feverishly writing the

next chapter of his book on Stalin as well as two articles, 'The Role of the Kremlin in the European Catastrophe' and 'Bonapartism, Fascism, the War', and answering letters. On the eve of the attempt on his life he wrote to Sara Weber, who was responsible for publishing the *Bulletin* in the USA, reassuring her that she should not become depressed over the lack of money: 'We'll publish the issue when there is money to do so.'[124] He wrote a polemical letter to his opponent Weissbord, whom he accused of devaluing the work of the left opposition: 'Of course you won't find anything in Lenin about democratic centralism, because Stalin's faction was formed after Lenin's death.'[125]

By mid-May Trotsky was risking an hour or two beyond the gates of his fortress with a couple of bodyguards. As one of them, identified only by his initials, KM, recalled: 'Usually each excursion was a small military expedition. We had to work out a plan in advance and arrange a precise timetable. "You treat me like an inanimate object," he sometimes said, hiding his impatience with a smile.'[126]

In the early hours of 24 May Trotsky was still working. The rest of the family had long retired. At about 2.30 a.m., unable to sleep and agitated, he took a sedative and fell into a deep sleep. The most detailed account of what then transpired is given by Natalya in her book, written with Victor Serge, *The Life and Death of Leon Trotsky*. At about 4 a.m. the household was awoken suddenly by the sound of wild gunfire outside. The police guards had been disarmed by a large group of armed men led by a portly 'major'. Fragments of concrete were already flying off the walls before the inhabitants realized what was happening. The room filled with gunsmoke, and a constant stream of bullets flew in through the open window. Natalya pushed Trotsky into a corner behind the bed, shielding him with her own body. The gunfire lasted twenty minutes. From the next room came the piercing shriek of Trotsky's terrified grandson: 'Grandfather!' Trotsky later recalled that the child's cry had been the worst moment of the night. In the ensuing silence, they thought the boy had been kidnapped. With intense relief the grandparents found Seva safe, with no more than a graze from a ricochet on his face. In a state of shock the guards told Trotsky what had happened. Among those in the house were a terrified Marguerite and Alfred Rosmer. They had been staying for several weeks, having brought with them a large number of books and letters, and part of Trotsky's archives. During one of their first conversations, Rosmer had described meetings with the wife of Ignaz Reiss, Estrin and Zborowski, in which they had discussed how they had all betrayed Trotsky. As for Zborowski, Rosmer said he 'vouched for his reliability with his life', and gave the best account of his character.[127]

The picture they all reconstructed of the attack was that more than two dozen men. in police and army uniforms, armed even with a machine-gun, had suddenly driven up and instantly disarmed the guard. Robert Sheldon Harte, who had been on the gate, had opened it when told to do so by the 'major', and the raiding party had driven through, disarmed another guard and opened fire on the windows and doors of Trotsky's study and bedroom. It seemed that no one could have survived the onslaught. Trotsky and Natalya had been saved by a small space in the corner beneath the window – a chance in a thousand. The countless bullets had ricocheted onto the bed, which protected them. Fate had once again been kind to the exile.

The early morning found the shaken residents of the house behind their concrete stockade gesticulating and talking in amazement of the narrow escape. Even the fact that Trotsky's Ford and Dodge cars had been stolen seemed trivial by comparison. A small fire that had been started by the shooting had been quickly extinguished and Trotsky's papers saved. A bomb, thrown into the house after the firing, had mercifully not exploded. The same morning a coded telephone message was sent from Mexico to New York. It was decoded and transmitted to Moscow later that day, and delivered to Stalin: 'Operation carried out. Results known later.'

When Mexican secret police arrived to investigate, they found that more than two hundred bullets had been fired into the bedroom alone. Their enquiries dragged on for weeks without result. The Mexican Communist Party blamed reactionaries and American imperialism, and the Mexican Confederation of Labour, which was a Communist front, declared that the attack had been a provocation aimed at Mexico, and that Trotsky should be expelled. So intense was Communist propaganda about a 'put-up job' that three of Trotsky's young companions, Charlie Cornell, Otto Schüssler and Jean Bazin, were arrested and interrogated about the 'alleged attack that Trotsky himself had set up'.[128] The public was being fed the story that Trotsky had organized an attempt on his own life in order to compromise

Stalin, a notion reinforced when journalists learned what Trotsky had said to the police chief the morning after: 'The attack was carried out by Josef Stalin with the help of the GPU. It was Stalin!'

Trotsky wrote to the President of Mexico, stating that 'the house had been attacked by GPU gangs, but the investigation has taken a false path. I am not afraid to make this statement as every new day will refute the shameful theory of a fabricated event . . .'[129] His letter had an effect, especially when Robert Sheldon Harte, who had been kidnapped, was found dead not far from the house. This gave Trotsky grounds for asserting that any attempt to represent the affair as a provocation was baseless. On the other hand, the fact that Harte had opened the gate on Eitingon's order, and without resistance, and had left with the attackers, leaves open the question of whether he had been an undercover GPU agent who was murdered to make sure he did not 'squeal' under interrogation. Trotsky, however, insisted that Harte had been loyal and was an innocent victim, and ordered a metal plaque to be fixed to the wall of the house to commemorate him.

In his book Sudoplatov explains that the NKVD had an agent inside the house. She was Maria de la Sierra, who had provided Siqueiros with a detailed plan of Trotsky's house and character analyses of his secretariat before being recalled to Moscow shortly before the attack.[130] But it seems there may be another secret to be revealed. Sudoplatov said little of it, recalling only that in Trotsky's house 'we had our woman' who was keeping Soviet intelligence informed. Her help was crucial. She had taken part in other operations, and died unnamed by Sudoplatov in Moscow in the 1980s.

In addition, according to present-day American Trotskyists, the FBI and US secret service were also involved in the operation. In a two-volume book published in the USA in 1985 and entitled *The Gelfand Case*, which contains a large collection of Mexican court papers, letters, notes of interrogation and the depositions of witnesses, it is asserted that the NKVD was in some indirect way linked with the FBI, or at least that some of the Soviet operatives were double agents. Analysis of the documents gave rise to this suggestion, and in May 1975 the International Secretariat of the Fourth International began to explore it. In particular, the author, Alan Gelfand, accuses Joseph Hansen, Trotsky's former personal secretary, of protecting Sylvia Franklin, a closet American Communist and NKVD agent, who was also working for the FBI. It is difficult now to determine unequivocally the truth of this allegation. The fact that the chief operatives were Stalin's own is plain enough, but there remains the possibility that the American special services were following, and perhaps in some sense influencing, events in Coyoacan.

After the turbulence had settled, it was felt acutely that Trotsky was doomed. Stalin would not stop until he had been exterminated. Trotsky's entourage and his comrades-in-arms did what they could to protect their leader. They suggested he go to another country and go underground, mentioning France and the capitals of several Latin American countries. He listened but at once rejected the idea. He felt old, and was tired of running. Above all he had no intention of keeping silent, and if he continued as before to expose Stalin, his whereabouts would soon be discovered. James Cannon, one of the American Trotskyist leaders, later wrote that people from various organizations who now visited Trotsky felt they were seeing him for the last time: 'After meeting Lev Davidovich, it was decided to launch a new campaign to strengthen his security. We collected . . . several thousand dollars to reinforce the house; all party members and sympathizers responded generously and unselfishly to the call.'[131]

As Sudoplatov confirms, news of the failure of the assassination attempt sent Stalin into a rage. Beria had to endure his angry words, while those associated with the operation could expect a fate similar to that of Shpigelglas, who was under arrest. Everything would now be staked on the action of an individual operator who had long been installed in Mexico, and who was preparing to carry out his mission.

August 1940

Every morning, after feeding his rabbits and chickens, and before breakfast, Trotsky would sit at his desk. The book on Stalin was going badly. Over the last decade he had written so much about this man that he was left feeling creatively ruined. He knew this was his worst book. The hatred froze his mind the minute he sat down to write. Yet he had to finish it, if only because the publishers were nagging him and threatening to demand repayment of their advances.

Stalin was pressing Beria to get on with the 'operation'. After the failure of Siqueiros's efforts it would have been unwise to turn again to the Mexican Communists. Siqueiros himself had to go into hiding for a long time, then serve a prison term and finally go into exile. Yet he had the courage in later years to admit that taking part in the attack on Trotsky had been a crime.[132] This was not something that those who were working for the NKVD would ever confess. Right up to the collapse of Bolshevism, they and their successors in the KGB pretended they knew nothing of the affair, asserting that there were no relevant documents in their custody. (Indeed, it was so difficult for me to obtain material that in certain circumstances I have been able to give no references to sources, since I obtained them unofficially. This book was already at the presses for its Russian edition when the events of August 1991 in Moscow occurred, bringing the downfall of the totalitarian system.)

In the eyes of the Soviet Party's leadership Siqueiros was not only a famous artist, but above all an orthodox Communist, capable of 'revolutionary action'. Indeed, in 1966 he was awarded the International Lenin Prize for 'the strengthening of peace between the peoples'. Perhaps it was his dedication in May 1940 that was being recognized. Be that as it may, after the failure of the attempt, Eitingon could no longer accept the help of Siqueiros's people.

While Eitingon was working out a new plan, life in the little fortress gradually returned to something like normal. When the police finally ceased to suspect that the attempt had been engineered by Trotsky's supporters, Trotsky and his friends set about strengthening the walls, building brick balustrades on the veranda, installing additional alarms and lighting the approaches. Despite the hubbub of all this activity, Trotsky and Natalya felt a new wave of depression and isolation. The Rosmers, who were so dear to them, had left for Paris, never to see them again.

Trotsky displayed an air of indifference to the warnings of his friends about the need to increase his vigilance and to avoid any contact with unknown people. After all, the claim given by his 'well-wisher' Orlov, that a murderer was hiding among his entourage, had proved groundless. The attack had been the work of an entirely outside force, and had not come from within, he was sure. He remembered how both he and Lenin had received warnings of imminent danger to themselves soon after the revolution. On one occasion in 1919, as he arrived at a Central Committee meeting in Moscow, Lenin had passed him a telegram from a Red Army man at Saratov: 'Comrade Lenin, Allow me the opportunity at once to tell you about secret military actions against the Soviet regime. Your enemies, all of whom I know, want to kill you and Trotsky.'[133] Trotsky had merely smiled and pushed the paper back to Lenin. He had received such naive warnings repeatedly, and would continue to do so. In April 1921, for instance, he received a letter from a Party member called Stepan Zvanov: 'With Communist greetings, Lev Davydovich Trotsky! Respecting you as I do as the leader of the world proletarian revolution, I urge you to be careful in [Petrograd]. I have learnt through rumours that the chief of army communications, Comrade Dmitriev, harbours some sort of ill will towards you. I am known to you. We worked together in America.'[134]

Now such warnings were no longer necessary. Everyone realized perfectly well that Stalin's sword hung over the hideously reinforced villa. But how would the blow be delivered? Explosives? Machine-guns? Poison? Not even Stalin knew the answer, nor was he interested in such details. Only the end result mattered. As Sudoplatov remembered from his meeting with Stalin in the spring of 1939, the leader pronounced unequivocally: 'War is coming. Trotskyism has become an accomplice of Fascism. We must strike a blow at the Fourth International. How? Decapitate it.' A blow had been attempted in May, but a miracle had saved the leader of the World Party of Social Revolution. Eitingon knew there could be no more such errors. At stake were not only the life of the man who had barricaded himself in his Mexican villa, but Eitingon's own and those of his family. He had to find a way to infiltrate his man into Trotsky's house, but as since the May attempt Trotsky had virtually given up his expeditions into the hills for cactuses. An attempt had already been made by Zborowski to install someone from Paris among Trotsky's security personnel. He had written first to Trotsky and then his secretary, van Heijenoort, but Trotsky had been cautious and unwilling to extend the circle of people around him.[135]

Eitingon was therefore compelled to resort to his second plan, which was centred on a Spanish Communist called Ramon Mercader who had been in America since the beginning of 1939, first in the

USA and then in Mexico. He had first moved from Spain to France under the name of Jacques Mornard. There, with Zborowski's help, he had been introduced by US Communists to Sylvia Agelof, an active Trotskyist and a member of one of the American organizations of 'Bolshevik-Leninists'. Sylvia's mother was Russian and Sylvia, apart from English, French and Spanish, also spoke Russian. In September 1938, while attending the founding congress of the Fourth International, she met Jacques Mornard and a stormy romance ensued. He took the twenty-eight-year-old Sylvia – who was not especially attractive – to restaurants and theatres, and proposed marriage. They spent three happy and carefree months together; Jacques was good-looking and attentive, and not short of cash. Three or four months after Sylvia returned home to the USA in February 1939, Mornard turned up, giving business as the reason for his visit. He was now presenting himself as a Canadian called Frank Jacson, a metamorphosis, he explained to Sylvia, necessitated by the evasion of military service. In effect, Sylvia played the role of a reverse Mata Hari: she did not seduce the people she needed, they seduced her. She was head over heels in love, and with her help Mercader-Mornard-Jacson finally penetrated Trotsky's household.

Ramon Mercader, captivated by revolutionary zeal since his youth in Spain, was also in the grip of the Soviet special services, and would remain so until the end of his life. His full name was Jaime Ramon Mercader del Rio Hernandez. One of the most interesting books on him is by Isaac Don Levine, entitled *The Man Who Killed Trotsky*,[136] and I have also learnt much about him from David Semenovich Zlatopolsky, who with his wife, Conchita Brufau, was close to Mercader during his Moscow period. The testimony of Ramon's brother Luis, who became a professor at Madrid University, is also revealing.[137] The most complete information, however, on this victim of Stalinism comes from Sudoplatov and the secret files of the OGPU's Foreign Section.

Sudoplatov described Mercader as highly intelligent and strong-willed, fanatically convinced of the historic justification of the cause to which he had devoted his life. Either his grandfather or great-grandfather had been Spanish ambassador to St Petersburg, while his mother's father had been the Governor of Cuba. Ramon's mother, Eustacia Maria Caridad del Rio, was an impulsive, energetic, determined woman. During the Spanish civil war, as the young mother of five sons – Jorge, Pablo, Ramon, Monserrat and Luis – she had left her devout husband, joined the Communist Party and become an agent of the NKVD. The Soviet Resident at the time was Alexander Orlov and his deputy was Naum Eitingon. From this moment Eitingon became closely associated with Caridad and her son Ramon, recognizing the reliability and determination of the young officer of the Republican army. It was from this time also that Mercader became a secret agent of the NKVD. The alias Frank Jacson was acquired when the NKVD special laboratory in Moscow gave him a fabricated passport concocted from the documents of a Canadian volunteer who had died in Spain.

Ramon's younger brother Luis associates Ramon's fate with the character of their mother, a beautiful and adventurous woman who exerted a powerful influence over her son. It was these chief players that Eitingon prepared to act out the last scene of Trotsky's life. No money was spared. To return to Moscow with empty hands would have meant for Eitingon the same fate as that of Shpigelglas. It was not open to him to disappear into thin air, as Orlov had done: his sense of duty was too strong. He told Ramon: 'You must carry out the sentence.' According to Luis, who spent nearly forty years in the USSR and personally knew Kalinin, Beria, Kobulov, Sudoplatov and Eitingon, the whole operation cost not less than $5 million.

Mercader, having settled in Mexico, invited Sylvia to join him, and at the beginning of 1940 she soon fixed herself up as a secretary to Trotsky, her sister Ruth Agelof having held the same position earlier. Trotsky liked the modest, plain young woman, who was extremely helpful to him. When Eitingon found out that Sylvia was going to work for Trotsky, he was delighted: the penetration had begun.

Sylvia and Ramon lived together at the Hotel Montejo, and Ramon would take her to work in his elegant Buick. As a smartly dressed businessman, he would get out of the car, open the door for her, help her out, kiss her cheek and wave an affectionate goodbye. Often he would also pick her up after work. The guards at Trotsky's villa soon grew accustomed to Sylvia's tall, handsome lover, and gradually they accepted him as one of their own. On one occasion he gave the Rosmers a lift into town, and they afterwards told Trotsky that Sylvia had 'a very sympathetic fiancé'. It was with Marguerite Rosmer's help that Ramon finally managed to enter the fortress. The guests from France had returned from a shopping expedition and asked him to help them carry their packages into the house. Once there, he was able to confirm what he had learnt from the female Soviet agent who was already in place about the disposition of the rooms, the doors, the outside alarms, the locks, etc.

At first the young Spaniard did not expect that he would have to bloody his own hands with the murder of Trotsky, but on 26 or 27 May 1940, a few days after the unsuccessful attempt on Trotsky's life, Eitingon closeted himself with Mercader and made clear how things stood. It was impressed on him that he would be merely 'carrying out a just sentence' issued in Moscow, and that this enormous honour would make him a hero forever. Mercader could not disobey. He had already seen in Spain how disobedience could end. When one of his Republican acquaintances was suspected in Catalonia of connections with the POUM, he disappeared without trace. Mercader had learned that this was the law of the revolution: the weak and unreliable are liquidated.

Like Sudoplatov and Eitingon, all the other participants in the operation expected a successful outcome. Eitingon conducted the uninterrupted psychological preparation of his agent. He managed to convince Ramon not only that the action was possible, but also reminded him that 'Mexico is the ideal country for an act of vengeance. They don't even have the death penalty. But you should know that if you don't manage to escape we will save you. Absolutely!' Mention of the death penalty must have sent a chill down Ramon's spine, but the psychological massage did its work. After a brief depression in June, he took heart and began energetically preparing himself for the 'action'.

Eitingon, a member of his team called Rabinovich, and Mercader met on several occasions to make plans and discuss details. Naum Isaakovich Eitingon had enormous experience. It is not generally known that he had worked in Shanghai with the Comintern agent Richard Sorge, or that he had controlled the activities of the British spy Kim Philby, as well as other Soviet agents. It was Eitingon who carried the greatest risk: one more failure and he would be summoned to Moscow and his inevitable doom. But it was Ramon who was the most tormented. He had seen Trotsky, spoken with him, met the

Rosmers and Natalya, and they had all treated him in a friendly and sympathetic way. And this was how he would repay them?

Some time before Trotsky met his killer, he had had intimations of his impending death. Before the attack on 24 May he decided to write his last will. Above all he wanted to leave his supporters and friends posthumous guidance, and to let later generations know that he had remained true to the Idea. Half of the testament is devoted to his wife and the other half to the political struggle. Not his homeland, not the Fourth International, not even Seva, his grandson, figure: only two names occur, Natalya and Stalin.

First published in 1958 in *Trotsky's Diary in Exile*, the testament was written in three parts, two on 27 February 1940, and a personal addendum on 3 March. Characteristically, Trotsky reaffirmed his dedication to revolutionary ideas: 'For forty-three years of my conscious life I have remained a revolutionist; for forty-two of them I have fought under the banner of Marxism. If I had to begin all over again I would of course try to avoid this or that mistake, but the main course of my life would remain unchanged. I shall die a proletarian revolutionist, a Marxist, a dialectical materialist, and, consequently, an irreconcilable atheist. My faith in the communist future of mankind is not less ardent, indeed it is firmer today, than it was in the days of my youth.' On 3 March he added: 'But whatever may be the circumstances of my death I shall die with unshaken faith in the communist future. This faith in man and in his future gives me even now such power of resistance as cannot be given by any religion.'[138]

We have already seen how much Trotsky loved his second wife. Nearly fifty letters from him to her in the Houghton Library offer poignant testimony to this. The episode with Frida Kahlo was entirely out of character and rather confirmed the steadfastness of his love for one woman. What he writes about Natalya in his testament is tender and full of meaning. Having thanked his friends for remaining loyal at the most difficult moments of his life, he did not wish to name or single out any individual: 'My high (and still rising) blood pressure is deceiving those near me about my actual condition. I am active and able to work but the outcome is evidently near.' He believed he would die of a brain haemorrhage, and even hoped for such an end: 'If the sclerosis should assume a protracted character ... then I reserve the right to determine for myself the time of my death. The "suicide", if such a term is appropriate in this connection, will not in any respect be an expression of an outburst of despair or hopelessness. Natasha and I said more than once that one may arrive at such a physical condition that it would be better to cut short one's own life, or, more correctly, the too-slow process of dying.'[139]

Even after the attack in May Trotsky continued to scrutinize and analyse the world situation. In his last months he wrote a great deal about the war, predicting that Hitler, who had built his state on racial principles, and Stalin, who had built his on class principles, must inevitably clash. Trotsky must have asked himself on more than one occasion how Hitler, with his advocacy of the master-race, differed from Stalin, who continued to assert the old Marxist postulate of class leadership. Yet in placing the two leaders on the same level, Trotsky could not bring himself to attack the 'leading role' of the proletariat. Indeed, in the Manifesto of the Fourth International, which he wrote and which was approved at a special conference two days after the 24 May attack, it was plainly stated: 'The essence of our programme can be expressed in two words: proletarian dictatorship.'[140] Without this formula the entire programme of world revolution would have collapsed. Trotsky linked the two dictators by their shared criminal mentality, but it never occurred to him that for millions of Soviet citizens Stalinism was not an anomaly, but something that had grown organically out of Marxism and Leninism, adapted to fit the needs of the day.

Throughout this period, despite his illness and the atmosphere of tension around the house, Trotsky continued to engage in businesslike correspondence with the organization. His letters continued to examine methods of bringing his anti-Stalinist ideas to the Soviet people. The question arises of whether Trotsky wished for a Soviet defeat in the war. Perhaps for him the removal of Stalin superseded the national interest? It was not so simple. In the programme of the Fourth International he wrote: 'For us the defence of the Soviet Union coincides in principle with preparing the international proletarian revolution. We utterly reject the theory of socialism in one country as the ignorant and reactionary brainchild of Stalinism. Only the international revolution can save the USSR for socialism. But the international revolution will bring inescapable death to the Kremlin oligarchy.' The line of Trotsky's thinking is clear: the Soviet Union must be defended in order to save the world revolution, which itself would remove Stalin and his regime. He wanted to imbue Soviet public opinion with these ideas, but meanwhile, as he himself wrote, part of the published Trotskyist literature 'should be kept on the shelf'. Trotsky never realized that the idea of carrying out a revolution against Stalin on the wave of a Nazi invasion was Utopian.

Trotsky was disquieted by the internal problems that afflicted the American Socialist Workers Party, which was a major element in the Fourth International, and in which a split had occurred. The majority, led by James Cannon, continued to support Trotsky, while the minority, led by Trotsky's old personal friends Shachtman and Burnham, had for practical purposes split both with Trotskyism and traditional Marxism altogether. Shachtman's defection was especially hurtful, as Trotsky had considered him his loyal pupil. It is worth noting that splits, factional squabbles, mutual recrimination and intellectual dissension had characterized the Trotskyist movement from the outset, much as it had the Russian revolutionary movement of an earlier generation. This mutual irreconcilability is explained by the profound internal inconsistency of the movement in general. Trotsky had declared intellectual war on virtually everyone: on the bourgeoisie, on social democracy, and on Stalinism. He did not change the point of view he had expressed in 1931, when he said: 'The struggle with social democracy is the struggle with the democratic wing of imperialism.'[141] Many of Trotsky's supporters believed the main thrust of his strategy was the struggle with Stalinism, and that the rest of his targets were mere appendages.

After the death of Lev, the links with Paris were somewhat weakened. Letters from Estrin and Zborowski continued to arrive, along with the books and magazines Trotsky requested, but when Lev died something inside Trotsky himself snapped. When Estrin came out to Mexico Trotsky and Natalya sat for a whole evening and listened as their friend talked about Lev, reliving the tragedy of his death.[142]

Zborowski meanwhile continued to seek permission to come to Mexico,[143] but Trotsky felt no need for new people. He was tired of visitors, tired of the danger and tired of the struggle. Almost every day he would assemble a pile of documents and in agony try to write something new about Stalin, but he had written so much about him already, one article much like the other, that he felt he could produce little that was original. The book on Stalin was going slowly, partly also because very little information was coming out of the USSR. Apart from what he could glean from the fabrications of *Pravda* – a month after they had appeared – and the radio broadcasts from Moscow, which were barely audible, there was almost no information. In the forty-three months that Trotsky had lived in Mexico he did not know that Stalin had become a real earthly god, and that blind adoration of him had virtually become the chief feature of Soviet public life. The situation had gone so far that shortly before his own removal, Yezhov, referring to 'countless requests from workers', could propose the unthinkable: his department prepared a draft decree of the Supreme Soviet renaming Moscow as Stalinodar. The draft was sent to the Politburo and the Praesidium of the Supreme Soviet. Stalin, however, was cautious and no fool, and did not agree to the proposal.[144] Instead he concentrated on perfecting punitive measures against his enemies on all sides. Almost every day he confirmed hundreds of lists of names of those considered 'Trotskyists' and condemned as 'first category', i.e. to death. On 12 December 1938 alone, Stalin and Molotov sanctioned the shooting of 3167 people.[145] Trotsky was cut off from much that was happening in his homeland, and he knew that angry abuse would not by itself save his last book. Anxiously he delved into the newspapers and urged his supporters to find factual material about the regime.

While he was trying to consolidate his movement and lead it in the right direction, the Moscow group of Chekists in Mexico was not idle. From all of the available evidence – Sudoplatov, the trial proceedings of Mercader, Natalya's memoirs, the evidence of the Mexican chief of police, of Trotsky's secretary Joe Hansen, and more – it is possible to trace step by step Eitingon's chief task, the penetration of Mercader into Trotsky's circle.

Mercader-Jacson first entered the house some time at the end of April 1940, when he helped Marguerite and Alfred Rosmer take their bags to their room, returning at once to his car. On 28 May, shortly before the departure of the Rosmers, Mercader was invited to dinner as 'Sylvia's friend' who would drive them to their ship. At the Rosmers' request Mercader was brought into the dining room, accompanied on Trotsky's orders by Harold Robins, who was in charge of security.

On 12 June 1940, before leaving for New York 'at the command of his firm's boss', Mercader entered the house to ask Trotsky if he might leave his Buick in the yard during his absence.

On 29 July, Natalya invited Sylvia and Ramon for a chat about their future over a cup of tea. Natalya was sure they would get married, and she talked with tact and humour about family life and its diversions.

On 1 August, Ramon drove Sylvia and Natalya on a shopping expedition to the city centre. On their return, he carefully carried the packages and bundles into the house and deposited them where Natalya indicated. He left at once, mentioning urgent business.

On 8 August, giving no obvious reason for the visit, Mercader appeared with a bouquet of flowers and a box of sweets. In conversation with Trotsky, he said he would gladly take him on an excursion into the mountains. Trotsky thanked him, but made no commitment.

On 11 August, coming to collect Sylvia after dinner, Mercader did not wait for her at the car, but came into the house. The guards regarded this as normal, as he had become such a familiar face. The couple soon left the house and drove away.

On 17 August, the new 'friend of the house' arrived uninvited and asked Trotsky for a few minutes of his time. He wanted him to look over an article he had written in which he criticized those, like Burnham, who were attacking Trotskyism. The conversation was brief and Mercader left. For some reason he had been wearing a dark suit and carrying a raincoat, although it had been hot.

It appears that Mercader was in the house about ten times, apparently with no definite plan of action. He may have wanted to confirm the interior lay-out for himself, but we now know it had already been revealed to him by the female agent.

There would be one more fateful visit. It took place at 5 p.m. on Tuesday 20 August 1940. The description of the last day of Trotsky's life is best left to his widow. The morning post had brought news that at last Trotsky's manuscripts had been received safely at Harvard. Their despatch had had the character of an undercover operation, as Trotsky was so concerned for their safety, and he was also pleased with the $15,000 the university had paid him for the privilege of keeping his papers.

Trotsky usually fed his rabbits and chickens at around eight in the morning. Natalya would watch him through the window; she always watched him, even when he was at his desk. 'From time to time,' she wrote, 'I would open the door a little so as not to disturb him, and saw him in his usual position bent over papers and magazines, pen in hand.' Trotsky himself acknowledged that he worked better when he knew that she was nearby. Even in his testament he found it possible to speak of her in the most unconventional way: 'Natasha has just come up to the window from the courtyard and opened it wider so that the air may enter more freely into my room. I can see the bright green strip of grass beneath the wall, and the clear blue sky above the wall, and sunlight everywhere. Life is beautiful. Let the future generations cleanse it of all evil, oppression and violence, and enjoy it to the full.'[146]

Having fed the animals, Trotsky would sit down to write. That day, he intended to reply to the Mexican newspaper *El Popular* and to continue working on the biography of Stalin. Natalya recalled:

At about five o'clock we had tea. Twenty minutes later, I saw Leon Davidovich at the bottom of the garden near the rabbit hutches. He had a visitor with him, but I did not recognize him until he came up to me and took off his hat. It was Jacson-Mornard . . . 'I am terribly thirsty,' he said. 'Could I have a glass of water?' 'Wouldn't you like a cup of tea?' 'No, I had a late lunch . . .' His face looked green and he seemed singularly nervous. 'Why are you wearing your hat and raincoat,' I asked, 'in such fine weather?' 'Because it might rain,' he replied absurdly . . . He drank a glass of water and told me that he had brought an article, typed this time, for Leon Davidovich to see.[147]

After the rehearsal of 17 August, when Ramon had visited with his raincoat on his arm, he had now come to do the terrible deed itself. Eitingon had worked long and hard to prepare him for the final act, but Mercader was not a robot. Fifty years after the event, his brother Luis declared: 'My brother was not simply a murderer, he was a man who believed in the Communist cause.' For this agent of the NKVD Trotsky was an agent of world imperialism and a mortal enemy of Communism.

There were, I believe, other motives which prompted Mercader. He was acting under compulsion. His mother was in Mexico – indeed, she was waiting for him in the car with Eitingon not a hundred metres from the house. One can well imagine the tension they were feeling.

If Ramon's nerve failed, none of them would survive. They were his hostages. As was his young brother Luis, who at Eitingon's insistence had been sent from Paris to Moscow. The greenish colour of Mercader's visage showed his mental struggle as he faced the thin line between life and death, the line beyond which he must now despatch another human being.

The account continues with the evidence Mercader gave at his trial:

> I laid my raincoat on the table in such a way as to be able to remove the ice-pick which was in the pocket. I decided not to miss the wonderful opportunity that presented itself. The moment Trotsky began reading the article gave me the chance, I took out the ice-pick from the raincoat, gripped it in my hand and, with my eyes closed, dealt him a terrible blow on the head. Trotsky gave a cry that I shall never forget. It was a long 'aaaa', endlessly long, and I think it still echoes in my brain. Trotsky jumped up jerkily, rushed at me and bit my hand. Look, you can still see the marks of his teeth. I pushed him away and he fell to the floor. Then he rose and stumbled out of the room.[148]

Natalya describes what happened next: 'Three or four minutes went by. I was in the room next door. There was a terrible piercing cry ... Leon Davidovich appeared, leaning against the door-frame. His face was covered with blood, his blue eyes glittered with his spectacles, and his arms hung limply by his side.'[149] Sudoplatov commented: 'In any affair there are unavoidable accidents. And one occurred here. How could Trotsky find the strength both to struggle and to utter that inhuman cry after Mercader, who was very strong physically, had delivered such a crushing blow with the ice-pick? If Trotsky had died instantly Mercader might have escaped.'

A great din was raised in the house. Mercader was seized and beaten by the guards. Natalya recalled that he cried out, 'They made me do it ... They've got my mother ... They have put my mother in prison ...' 'What shall we do with him?' Natalya asked. 'They'll kill him.' Trotsky replied slowly, 'No, he must not be killed, he must talk,' dragging out each word. Charlie Cornell, Joe Hansen and Harold Robins had fallen on the assassin, who yelled, 'Kill me now or stop beating me!'[150] It was his one display of weakness, and in the long months of the investigation and the trial he would not repeat those words. He would stick to the line that it was he who had planned and carried out the whole operation. He knew of no GPU, nor had he any accomplices. It was his decision and his alone.

According to Sudoplatov, during the first six months of his twenty-year sentence, Mercader was often beaten in prison in an effort to find out just who he was. For a full five years he was kept in solitary confinement, with no window, but Eitingon's special agent kept control of himself and would not recant his first testimony, even though at the trial documentary proof had been produced to show that he was not who he claimed to be. As Luis stated: 'After the first shock he came to himself and always believed he had done a necessary deed.' Twenty years later, after his release, when he was in the USSR, Ramon, commenting on events in Colombia, declared: 'Terrorism is necessary in the struggle for Communism.'[151] In fact, he was quoting Trotsky's own words from Terrorism and Communism, where his victim had written: 'Terror can be very effective against a reactionary class that does not want to leave the scene.'[152] In these utterances we find an unexpected resonance between the victim and the murderer. The ideas of Bolshevik Jacobinism, so firmly implanted by Trotsky in the Russian revolution, had come back to strike at him with the force of a boomerang.

A letter found in Jacson's pocket stated that he had become disillusioned with Trotskyism and Trotsky. It gave as a trigger for his action Trotsky's having told him of his intention to go to the USSR to liquidate Stalin. The letter had plainly been written by others. The court quickly established that Trotsky had been alone with Jacson only twice, on 17 August, for five to seven minutes, and on the day of the murder, for an even shorter time. It is inconceivable that in those brief moments Trotsky would have revealed such an intention to a virtually complete stranger, yet Jacson claimed that he had done precisely this. The court did not of course recognize the well-practised hand of the NKVD. Similar letters were found in 1938 on the bodies of Rudolf Klement, Trotsky's murdered secretary, and several other defectors who were killed after allegedly accusing Trotsky of espionage and terrorism. Possibly the letter found on Mercader had been inspired by a report from Zborowski to Moscow in February 1938 – if it was not a fabrication of the NKVD – in which he stated that Sedov had raised the question of finding a terrorist because, he had said, 'It is enough to murder Stalin for everything else to collapse.'[153]

In this case, however, the falsity of the letter concocted by Eitingon's group is not open to doubt. It seems that the organizers of the murder made no great effort to establish an alibi. The world still knew little about the event, yet the Party newspaper, *Pravda*, could state on 24 August 1940 that 'Trotsky has died in hospital from a fractured skull, received in an attempt on his life by one of his closest circle.'[154] The letter in Jacson's pocket and the information for *Pravda* came from a single source. In fact the world's press never doubted the identity of the murderer.

All those who planned the operation managed to escape, except Mercader. The car, its engine already running, took off the moment there was a stir at the gates and the alarms went off. Eitingon, Mercader's mother and some others escaped from the capital by various means. Eitingon and Caridad waited in California for instructions to come from Moscow. Within a day they learnt from the radio and press that the operation had been a success. Stalin's order to 'decapitate the Fourth International' had been carried out. Eitingon was afraid that the excitable Caridad, having lost her son, might fall apart and commit some indiscretion. Within a month Moscow reported, by special channels, that it was grateful the task had been accomplished, and ordered Eitingon to find out from his agency in Mexico the condition of the 'patient', i.e. Mercader, and to see what could be done to help him. After having done this, Eitingon would be permitted to return to Moscow. In May 1941, a month before the entry of the Soviet Union into the war, Eitingon and Caridad returned to Moscow via China, a journey taking more than a month. Sylvia's movements during the incident, and indeed after it was all over, have not been accounted for. Presumably, as an innocent tool in the conspiracy, she returned to her normal life in Brooklyn.

Trotsky survived the attack for twenty-six hours. Everything was done to save him, but it was clear that all the vital centres of his brain had been damaged. Two hours after the attack, Natalya recalled, Trotsky fell into a coma. Shortly before this, 'pointing to his heart, he said to Joe Hansen in English, "I feel . . . here . . . that this is the end . . . This time . . . they've . . . succeeded."' Before operating, the nurses began cutting his clothes off. Natalya recalled that he said to her, distinctly and very gravely: 'I don't want them to undress me . . . I want you to do it . . ."' These were his last words to me. I undressed him and pressed my lips to his. He returned the kiss, once, twice and again. Then he lost consciousness.' Concluding her sad reminiscence, Natalya wrote that in the evening of the following day, after trepanation, the doctors 'lifted him up and his head slumped onto his shoulder, but his features retained their pride. I had seen him ride out crises . . . I still believed he could do it again. He would suddenly regain his strength, open his eyes, and take charge of his life again . . . Two doctors in white stood before me . . . Leon Davidovich had died peacefully a moment before, at 7.25 p.m. on 21 August 1940. He was sixty years old.'

Obelisk in a Foreign Country

A huge anti-Stalinist demonstration was occasioned by his funeral, on the day after his death, following Mexican custom. Trotsky was buried at the house on the quiet little street in Coyoacan. Natalya insisted on it. All she had left was her grandson Seva, and Trotsky's grave, which provided a link to the memory of everything that mattered to her. She was above all his wife and the mother of his sons, and she had never played an active political part in his struggle.

Soon after the funeral a meeting of the leaders of the American Section of the Fourth International decided to erect an obelisk on the grave, and to look into the possibility of building a museum in Trotsky's name. The obelisk was soon raised, but it would be fifty years from his death before the museum was opened. The memorial itself was rather primitive. A hammer and sickle was engraved on a concrete slab nine feet tall and inscribed simply 'Leon Trotsky'. Later, behind the simple column, a flagpole was erected with a red flag at half-mast. For as long as she was alive Natalya ensured that the grave was surrounded by fresh flowers. The strange monument is still there, guarded by Trotsky's grandson Seva, now known as Esteban Volkov. It seems that the obelisk is the chief monument both to Trotsky and to the ephemeral idea of world revolution.

Indeed, it may be Trotsky's only surviving monument. Of the three chief leaders of the revolution, Trotsky was worst served as far as 'monumental propaganda' is concerned. Stalin had his monuments by the thousands, and they only began to disappear gradually after his death. The greatest number of such sculptural symbols, however, was dedicated to Lenin. Had Trotsky died, say, during the civil war, his monuments would still be standing. Paradoxically, perhaps, his tragic death has preserved his memory better than that of some of his other comrades-in-arms.

The leaders of the revolution, having demolished the tsarist symbols, within a few years began populating the centres of Soviet citities with their own statues, and Trotsky was no exception. In September 1920 Leonid Krasin, an old Bolshevik and a senior figure in Soviet diplomacy, wrote to Lenin that an English sculptress was 'travelling around with Kamenev and it is absolutely necessary that you should allow at least once in your life a halfway decent bust of yourself, which she is entirely capable of making and very quickly'.[155] At the time when this note was written, the country was convulsed by civil war, starvation and ruin, but the bust of the leader could be regarded as 'absolutely necessary'. Soon, very soon, banal representations of the leader would be scattered throughout the land. In the same month Trotsky received a letter from a school friend, the artist Nikolai Skoretsky, in which he reported: 'The talented sculptor Grinshpun is dying to see you, as he wants to properly complete the bust he has begun of you in the spirit of Rodin's Rochefort.'[156] Whether this was ever done has not been established. On the other hand, the author has met a ninety-year-old retired colonel called Filip Mikhailovich Nazarov, a St George's cavalryman who in his own words 'was five times wounded and took the oath five times', who evidently made a large sculpture of Trotsky in 1921, on the orders of the Red Army Political Section. 'The sculpture turned out quite big,' he recalled, 'some ten feet tall. I made it out of plaster, then coated it with a protective glaze in khaki. I moulded the head separately. Trotsky was shown with his coat unbuttoned and his arms folded behind him.' Asked whether Trotsky knew of this monument, the amateur sculptor replied: 'The monument was erected in the village of Klementievo in the Mozhaisk district of Moscow Province in a large artillery camp. Soon after it was set up, an order from Trotsky was read out before the assembled ranks encouraging me in my work.' As for the fate of the statue, 'some time in 1927 or 1928 it was taken down. In the 1930s I was dead scared they might suddenly remember it was I who had made it. In good time, of course, I destroyed all the photographs and sketches of it and the notice of Trotsky's thanks.'

In November 1923 Trotsky's assistant Sermuks laid before him a note from Max Eastman: 'The sculptor Joe Davidson, of whom I'm sure you've heard, is in Moscow. He has made busts of nearly all the famous people in the West and was the official sculptor of the Allied heroes of the World War, but he himself is a radical and a good friend of mine. He has already done busts of Kalinin, Radek, Chicherin, Rakovsky, Litvinov, Ioffe, Krasin and others. You don't have to pose for him, as he can complete a model of you in one session of three or four hours while you are working.'[157]

The artist V. Deni wrote in July 1921: 'Would you find it possible, before the arrival of the Petrograd artists Brodsky and Voshchilov, to give an hour to the popular sculptor Andreev to sketch you in pastels?'[158] Of course, since the rest of the Bolshevik leaders were immortalizing themselves so rapidly, Trotsky could hardly refuse. Where the Davidson and Andreev busts disappeared to after his ostracism is not hard to imagine.

These trivial facts serve to show yet again how all triumphant revolutionaries fall into the trap of personalizing their victory. Monuments created during their subjects' lifetime cannot serve human memory, only vanity. These mass monuments were the shameful landmarks of idolatry.

Trotsky avoided the epidemic of the 'monument harvest', not because he was more self-effacing than the others, but simply because there was not time to plant his plaster, bronze and marble image throughout the country. He was lucky in this sense. His concrete obelisk in Mexico is a genuine memorial, more perhaps to his personality than to his political life. What has in fact remained in our memory? Why has the name of Trotsky for so many decades attracted the attention of historians, philosophers, writers and film-makers? What does the obelisk in a foreign country signify? The chasm of history is uniformly deep for everyone, and only major historical figures, such as Trotsky, do not disappear from view. Stalinism imbued the Soviet mind with a strictly negative image of Trotsky, as having brought the people nothing but suffering and terror. Certainly, Trotsky had believed that by perfecting the dictatorship of the proletariat the regime could solve all social questions. In June 1927, while still a member of the Central Committee, he remarked in his unpublished notes on the national question that 'coexistence and collaboration between different national groups, and the equalization of economic and cultural development, are restrained by force from the centre . . . precisely over the national question our fundamental differences might acquire the sharpest expression.' He proposed that the solution to these questions could be found 'only by preserving and strengthening the proletarian dictatorship of the centralized workers' state and the planned economy.'[159] As always, the dictatorship.

The obelisk in Mexico reminds us that it was Trotsky who first understood Stalin and Stalinism from within, who first saw the outline of the reaction and signs of Bolshevik degeneration. The bitterness and tragedy of his fate make his life memorable. After all, the grey, everyday and ordinary have little chance of surviving in the human memory. The grave in Mexico bears witness that the image of the revolutionary, which becomes sharper with time, plays a great role in historical memory.

Stalin's silhouette, however camouflaged, has always been bloody. His name is a synonym for political cruelty. Lenin was wrapped up in sugary phrases and swathed in official propaganda, his biographers, and indeed the inertia of Russian thinking, wanting only a 'good tsar'. But Lenin was not a god, he was a mortal man. As N. Valentinov wrote, Lenin, 'having drawn a circle around himself, trampled underfoot and cut down with the axe everything outside that circle'. Valentinov, who had spent many hours in conversation with Lenin, had been amazed to discover in him 'blind intolerance and rage'. Lenin rewarded him 'with a stream of abuse, as soon as he realized I did not share his views'.[160] Soviet citizens for decades were permitted to know only the shining genius of Lenin. The unbounded hagiographic literature distorted the image of a man who had been wrong in many ways, theoretically and politically, and whose actions were to have such dire consequences for Russian history.

Trotsky was not an ideological idol, but a personality with the widest possible spectrum of strong intellectual and moral qualities mixed with uncompromising Leninist intolerance and vanity. The obelisk in Mexico reminds us neither of a fearful tyrant nor an 'unsurpassed genius', but of the advocate of revolution who became its victim and at the same time the bearer of the violence which corrupted that same revolution. Berdyaev remarked that Trotsky, 'the organizer of the Red Army, the advocate of world revolution, in no way arouses the feeling of terror which is aroused by the genuine Communist in whom personal self-awareness, personal thought, personal conscience have been utterly extinguished, and who has become one with the collective'. This man, Berdyaev wrote, 'is like Lenin but is less vicious in polemics'.[161]

The obelisk also reminds us of the international organization that Trotsky created. For a long time he protested and became indignant when his opponents manipulated the term 'Trotskyism'. When he was expelled from ECCI, cornered and showered with abusive criticism from his former comrades, he denied the existence of 'Trotskyism', and would recognize only a 'left' opposition movement.[162] He stuck to this position in the early 1930s. At the end of December 1932, while still on Prinkipo, he wrote to his translator Alexandra Ramm that he was sending her the manuscript of a long article entitled 'Lenin's Testament'.[163] The article was typical in its anti-Stalinist tone, but it also contained a section called 'The Legend of "Trotskyism"'. This legend, he wrote, had been created by Zinoviev and Kamenev. With Stalin's agreement it was they who had dubbed the 'left' opposition 'Trotskyism'. To be precise, however, the term had been put into official circulation by Stalin, when he had declared in his article 'Trotskyism or Leninism' that it was necessary to see 'Trotskyism as a peculiar ideology that is incompatible with Leninism'.[164]

After that time, those Communists who shared Trotsky's political views began to be called 'Trotskyists'. From the beginning of the 1930s to have this label attached to one in the USSR was tantamount to a death sentence. Trotsky protested that these people were genuine 'Bolshevik Leninists', and he was right in principle: all Bolshevik Leninists were the same, believing as they did in the dictatorship of the proletariat, and they were all convinced that the world could be remade according to the Communist blueprint. Zinoviev might assert that 'Trotskyism was (and to a certain extent still is) only a "left" nuance of "European" (i.e. opportunist) pseudo-Marxism, which is fundamentally hostile to Bolshevism,'[165] but by 1926 he would declare that his struggle against Trotskyism had been the biggest mistake of his life, 'more dangerous than the mistake of 1917', when he had opposed the armed uprising of October. A year later, however, in begging Stalin's forgiveness, Zinoviev would again speak of the 'danger of Trotskyism' as a manifestion of 'pseudo-Marxism'.[166]

None of this is to deny the existence of Trotskyism, which we have already described as one of the three basic trends in Russian Marxism, the other two being Leninism and Stalinism. Lenin regarded Marxism primarily as a means to advance his ideas for the revolutionary movement. Apart from his theoretical reflections on the revolutionary party and organizational issues, he brought little that was new to Marxism. Stalinism emerged as a grotesque form of Leninism. In its turn, Trotskyism on the theoretical level can be seen as the most radical form of Marxism, and applicable not only to Russia but to the entire 'world Communist revolution'. It is possible therefore to say that Trotskyism is the most sharply expressed attempt to apply European Marxism in Russia as its extreme radical variant. This view has been taken as the point of departure by the Israeli scholar Baruch Knei-Paz in his authoritative study of Trotsky's ideas, namely, 'that Trotsky's theory of a Russian revolution constituted the only sustained attempt to explain the manner in which both Marxism and a socialist revolution were immediately relevant to the Russia of the early twentieth century ... And following the events of [1917] Trotsky did not hesitate to claim that it had been confirmed by these events.'[167]

Trotskyism was an extreme form of Marxism, many elements of which Stalin borrowed in practice, naturally without acknowledgement. Trotskyism can only be understood by taking into account its unshakeable belief in class postulates, the highest justification of revolutionary violence and its faith in the inevitability of a world Communist future. At the Third Comintern Congress on 23 July 1921, Trotsky declared: 'Only crisis can be the father of revolution, while a period of prosperity is its gravedigger.'[168]

Trotskyism is an expression of Lenin's belief that it was possible by means of unbridled violence 'to give history a shove' and to achieve fundamental social change in the shortest possible time. As one of the Menshevik leaders, R. Abramovich, recalled, with the introduction of 'War Communism' Lenin at first believed that the strategic goal of revolution was close. At the beginning of 1918, wrote Abramovich, 'at virtually every session of Sovnarkom Lenin insisted that it was possible to realize socialism in Russia in six months. Trotsky remarks that when he first heard the timetable he was surprised – six months, not six decades, or at least six years? But no, Lenin was insisting on six months.'[169] Trotsky may have been surprised, but he did not object. As we have seen, after 1917 his own timetable for the world revolution also fluctuated between five and eight years, although later he avoided fixing any deadline for the universal conflagration, or postponed it for decades.[170] The Russian social democrats, by contrast, advocated a more peaceful path of social change, fearful as they were that a new 'time of troubles' would erupt in the country, but they, of course, were excluded from politics after October. This did not save some of their leaders, however, from the attentions of the NKVD who, even when they were abroad in exile, maintained surveillance and reported on their doings to Moscow.[171]

Trotskyism expressed the Marxist postulates in their most refined form. As a counterweight to Stalin it formally rejected totalitarianism, although it is not clear how the dictatorship of the proletariat could be applied in such circumstances. Thus, Trotskyism was a Utopian attempt to combine dictatorship and democracy, the monopoly of one party with political pluralism. In fact, Trotskyism represented the Utopia of radical Marxism in Russia.

It would appear that the obelisk in Mexico was the final act in the drama of the movement founded by Trotsky. And yet it was not. Trotskyism lives on. Why? What is it that nourishes the hopes of his followers? Surely the historic failure of socialism in Eastern Europe and the USSR has disappointed their hopes and dreams? Present-day Trotskyists still believe that the revolutionary renewal of the world is not only necessary but possible. One need only glance at the *Journal of International Marxism*, which is still published by the International Committee of the Fourth International. In 1988, on the fiftieth anniversary of the founding of that body, the Committee passed a resolution stating that the world was on the threshold of new revolutionary convulsions, and that Trotsky's theory of permanent revolution 'is confirmed by all of life'. In the *Journal*'s words, at a time when 'Gorbachev is grovelling before Wall Street, the rapid restoration of capitalism in the USSR is taking place ... The defence of the conquests of October demands as a historic necessity the overthrow of the bureaucracy by means of political revolution.' It was as if time for the Trotskyists had stood still: what in 1936 in *The Revolution Betrayed*

Trotsky had demanded in relation to Stalin and Stalinism, was being repeated fifty years later by his followers in regard to Gorbachev. Such regurgitation of the outmoded idea of permanent revolution nevertheless displays the viability of left radicalism, above all the idea that the world can be reshaped by audacious proletarian action.

Reading the *Journal* gives one the illusion of plunging decades back into history. The following appeared in the 1989 issue:

> The great historical goal of uniting the various national units of the international proletariat into a single army can be achieved at once. The battle cry of revolutionary Marxism − 'Proletarians of all lands, unite!' − will become the basis of class struggle in every country. The old Stalinist and social democratic parties, and the rotten remains of the long-dead Second and Third Internationals, cling with growing desperation to an outmoded national state system and the capitalist lords. Thus the epoch of the Fourth International has come. The tasks of the International Committee are to assemble the cadres that are ready to act decisively according to these plans, to rally the working class under the banner of the Fourth International, and to prepare for the victory of the forthcoming world socialist revolution.[172]

This resolution was passed in August 1988.

Over the last fifty years many organizations, parties and even entire states have disappeared, yet the international party of Trotskyists remains alive. One reason for this remarkable fact must be the robust historical authority of its founder. The obelisk in Mexico bears witness therefore not to the death of Trotsky, but to the fact that revolutionism in its classic form still has life. Revolutionism for Trotsky was like the Bible for a believer. Even when everything indicated the 'ebb', in his words, of world revolution, he would speak of its imminent 'flow'. On 21 June 1924, addressing the Fifth All-Union Congress of Health Workers, he drew loud applause as he concluded:

> The Communists say to the European worker: if you come to power, if you create a Soviet United States, you will at once unite two mighty continents, you will acquire wonderful technology, limitless space and natural wealth, and the huge enthusiasm of the revolutionary class that is already in power. If you have to fight the armed world counter-revolution − and you will − you will build your own Red Army, but you won't have to start from scratch, as you will get a good start from

the Red Army of the Soviet Union which is already singed by war and winged with victory.[173]

The question arises of whether Trotsky tried by any practical means to broadcast the ideas of the left opposition inside the USSR, or other Communist parties. The Trotsky archives at Harvard, as well as the Sneevliet archive and other materials held by the NKVD, show clearly that concrete efforts were indeed made to revive and activate the struggle against the Stalinist regime. In the autumn of 1932, for instance, Lev Sedov in Berlin sent his father notes of a conversation he had had with Goltsman, a supporter who helped to despatch Trotskyist literature into the USSR and to receive political information for the exile. Sedov wrote, among other things, that the hopes they had had for creating a bloc with Zinoviev, Kamenev and Lominadze had collapsed. They were 'broken'. He reported, however, that his 'packages' to Moscow and Leningrad so far were arriving and falling into the proper hands.[174]

It is clear that in 1932 Trotsky still had links with the thinning ranks of his supporters in the USSR. Sedov's correspondents were reporting that thousands of people in the Ukraine were swollen with hunger and fleeing the villages. Kolkhoz chairmen who had failed to fulfil delivery quotas were being stripped naked on the ice on the orders of the chief prosecutor of the Ukraine. It was alleged that an anti-Stalinist document, written by Bukharin, was being passed from hand to hand. Lominadze's group was more or less functional, but was being very cautious. Robbery was rife. Special retail outlets for Party workers were being established. Factories were being built and left unfinished when yet others were begun. Right-wing Communists had not accepted defeat.[175]

From these fragmentary reports it was clear that the opposition, although much weakened, still survived, and Trotsky therefore felt justified in attempting cautiously to re-ignite the embers of dissatisfaction with Stalin's policies in the early 1930s. While he was still in Europe he sent letters to his supporters calling on them to reactivate the struggle against Comintern and Stalin.[176] He did not, however, restrict himself to giving instructions of a purely ideological kind, but also advised his supporters 'to work completely illegally'.[177] In an NKVD file marked simply 'Publications' there are many hundreds of printed papers and leaflets of an anti-Stalinist content published by Trotskyist organizations. While the distribution of such literature inside the Soviet Union may have been severely limited, the fact is that some of it nonetheless got through.[178]

All this material confirms that Trotsky did make an effort to wage not only ideological but also political struggle against the Stalinist Communist Parties and the Russian Communist Party itself. Despite all these efforts, however, it was clear to him that the revolutionary tide had subsided. The left movement never became widespread. He did not give up, but continued to strike the bell of revolution in the form of his *Bulletin*. The notes sounded, however, dim and indistinct.

Even these slight efforts were, however, noted by the NKVD. Deliveries of literature that were intercepted, and the arrest of a number of people found with the *Bulletin* in their possession, led to an increase in repressive measures. Any contact between Soviet citizens and individuals suspected of Trotskyism was registered at once. For instance, a certain Baldoni, an 'assumed Trotskyist' who was under surveillance in Moscow, met Budu Mdivani, among others, and Preobrazhensky's and Donat's families. As soon as this was known, Agent 'West' informed the NKVD, and all these people were arrested.[179]

According to data supplied by Yezhov, at the end of 1936 and the beginning of 1937, in the central institutions of Moscow alone, thousands of 'Trotskyist wreckers' were arrested. Between October 1936 and February 1937 the following numbers of employees in the People's Commissariats were arrested and sentenced: Transport – 141, Food Industry – 100, Local Industry – 60, Internal Trade – 82, Agriculture – 102, Finance – 35, Education – 228; and the list continues.[180]

It was not necessary to have known Trotsky or served under him in the civil war to qualify as a state criminal: the mere mention of his name, or the possession of a book of his, or any indirect suggestion of association, would bring prison or worse. Widespread searches were conducted as Trotskyists were rooted out. An unspoken competition arose, so that, for instance, the Party Committee of the Finance Commissariat, which exposed the least number of Trotskyists, was itself purged. Figures were sent to superiors, as if reporting on conditions at the front: the numbers unmasked and the numbers arrested.

At a general meeting of the History Faculty of the Institute of

Red Professors, for example, Professor A.V. Shestakov gave a lecture entitled 'The Methods and Devices of Wrecking Work on the Historical Front'. Among other things, he declared: 'In his letter to the editors of *Proletarskaya revolyutsiya*, Comrade Stalin indicated that the Trotskyists are carrying out their subversive activity by distorting historical reality. For example, in discussing the tyranny of the [sixth-century] Greek colony at Pantikapea, Drozdov discredits the idea of democracy when compared with Fascist tyranny.'[181]

In this lecture and elsewhere mention was made of the 'Trotskyist definition of [the nineteenth-century Caucasian fighter] Shamil's dictatorship', also that 'despite the indications of Comrades Stalin, Kirov and Zhdanov, it is asserted that Alexander I's foreign policy was ambiguous', and that 'Professor Piontkovsky masked his wrecker's snout while attempting to restore capitalism in the USSR.'[182] All these ludicrous and ominous statements were uttered by people who held scientific degrees and academic titles. The mental tyranny crippled these people, teaching them to see enemies everywhere, and to display the harshest intolerance towards anything that might seem suspicious. Of course, such activities were far from restricted to the shameful public trials of the period.

A report from the acting director of the Institute of Red Professors of 27 December 1937 indicates that of the 408 teachers recruited between 1931 and 1937, 296 were fired, having been 'unmasked and arrested as enemies of the people'.[183] It is noteworthy that directors were being replaced so rapidly that such reports were commonly submitted by 'acting directors'.

While Trotsky was writing his addresses, printing his *Bulletin* and seeking means to infiltrate his writings into the USSR, Stalin was following his own agenda. There were perhaps no more than three or four hundred genuine Trotskyists in the whole country, but in order to liquidate them Stalin destroyed hundreds of thousands of people. It therefore seems appropriate to suggest that the obelisk should stand not only as a memorial to the leader of the 'left' opposition, but also to those who remained loyal to him in those dreadful years.

People read Trotsky's books about the Bolshevik revolution not merely because they are interesting in themselves, but because he was so closely associated with the events they describe. As early as 1921

G.A. Ziv in his book on Trotsky could write: 'The name of Lenin will rightly enter the history of Bolshevism as its father and prophet; but for the broad contemporary masses, triumphant Bolshevism (and for as long as it triumphs) is naturally associated with the name of Trotsky. Lenin personifies the theory, the idea of Bolshevism (even Bolshevism has its idea), while Trotsky embodies its practice.'[184] This assessment is too simple. Trotsky personified both the theory and the practice of Bolshevism. In the sphere of theory Trotsky's name will always be associated with permanent revolution, while in that of practice his name evokes the idea of world revolution.

A large number of papers in the Houghton Library consist of material on the first four congresses of Comintern, with Trotsky's letters to many foreign leaders of that organization. Trotsky recognized that even the highest functionaries of Comintern were gradually losing their independence, while also being turned into undercover agents for the NKVD. But even he could hardly have imagined that such figures as Dimitrov, Togliatti, Bela Kun and Kolarov would have to beg ignominiously for Yezhov's permission to open a club for political émigrés in Moscow.[185] Or that the Society of Political Exiles, among whose leaders were all the most prominent revolutionaries, including Stalin, was reporting on their 'work' on a regular basis to Yezhov.[186] Even Maxim Gorky, who discussed a personal request from the veteran revolutionary Vera Figner with Stalin, reported on this to Yezhov.[187] No doubt Gorky was taking no chances.

Realizing that Mexico was his last refuge, and lacking solid information about the situation in the USSR, Trotsky seems to have resorted increasingly to old arguments and recollections. The more he gazed into the dim future, the more he seemed to see shades of the distant past: conversations with Lenin, ecstatic crowds, the Red Cavalrymen, and his armoured train. Yet surprisingly in his writings we find nothing nostalgic or sentimental about his motherland, or his children and the other relatives who died there. Perhaps Ziv was right to declare that 'Trotsky is morally blind'.[188] On the other hand, Trotsky had spent more than twenty years in two phases of emigration and exile. He was by nature a cosmopolitan and lived entirely in the sphere of the political and intellectual. If he had any longings they were for revolution. He loved the first years of the Bolshevik regime, from 1917 to 1924, and detested the 1930s. In the early years he had enjoyed affection and respect, but in exile he was vilified and hated by millions of brutalized citizens whom the Stalinist functionaries knew how to manipulate.

In order to gain an impression of how far public opinion had deteriorated, it is enough to read extracts of the Soviet press or some of the books of the period. For instance, in the memoirs of the labour hero Alexei Stakhanov – ghosted in fact on Moscow's order by I. Gershberg – the author 'recalled':

> When the trials were going on in Moscow first of Zinoviev and Kamenev and then of Pyatakov and his gang, we immediately demanded they be shot . . . In our village even women who had never been interested in politics clenched their fists when they heard what was in the newspapers. Both old and young demanded the bandits be destroyed. When the court gave its sentence and said in our name that the Trotskyist spies should be shot, I wanted to see the newspaper that would announce they had been executed. When I heard on the radio that the sentences had been carried out, my spirits rose . . . If these vermin had fallen into our hands, any one of us would have torn them apart. But the old swine Trotsky is still alive. I think that his time will come, too, and we will deal with him in the proper way.[189]

More than fifty years have elapsed since Trotsky's death, yet his ideas, although they never seized the minds of millions, still live. They express fanatical rebelliousness, commitment to the revolutionary tradition and the hope for a global, social cataclysm, as the result of which a new world will arise. The obelisk on his grave marks not only the tragic fate of a human being, but also the simplicity of the idea that moved him. At the end Trotsky left no verse about his distant childhood in Yanovka, or the cobblestones of the Kremlin, or the vast Russian plain. It is not known whether he read the poems of Zinaida Gippius, who wrote in 1929, the year of Trotsky's deportation, the lines:

> Lord, let me see!
> I pray in the small hours.
> Let me once more see my native Russia.[190]

Trotsky suffered, but memories of his native land were swallowed in the global scale of his suffering. The thirst for revolution had long ago taken the place of sentimental yearnings, but there was nothing with which to slake his thirst. Where there should have been a longing to see his country once again, there was only a desire for revolution.

EPILOGUE

The Prisoner of an Idea

All his life Trotsky had thought in terms of epochs, continents and revolutions. When he addressed crowds of thousands of workers, peasants and soldiers he created the impression that he was bringing the future closer with his words. He did not dissemble, his faith in what he said was genuine. Speaking on 24 October 1918 in the city park of Kamyshin, he said as he stood gesticulating on the former tsar's Packard: 'We shall create our kingdom of labour, and the capitalists and landowners can go where they like, to another planet or the next life . . . A new world revolutionary front is emerging, on one side of which stand the oppressors of all lands, and on the other the working class . . . This moment will sound the death-knell of world imperialism and then we shall achieve the kingdom of freedom and justice.'[1] His audience felt that a reign of prosperity was at hand, and they applauded him zealously.

Trotsky was convinced that history would justify all the sacrifices that would have to be made to achieve the kingdom of freedom. Sometimes in his fanaticism, however, his proposals were apocalyptic. A few weeks before the speech at Kamyshin, he told Party workers and Soviet employees at a meeting in the theatre in Kazan: 'We value science, culture and art, and we want to make art and science and all the schools and universities accessible to the people. But if our class enemies were once again to show that all this exists only for them, then we shall say, death to theatre, science and to art.' After loud approving noises from his audience, he continued: 'We, Comrades, love the sun which illuminates us, but if the rich and the oppressors wanted to monopolize the sun, we would say, let the sun go out and let darkness reign, eternal gloom!'[2]

It seemed that the speaker in his shiny leather outfit was a free man, who was capable of achieving the impossible. The intoxicating power of the Idea captivated not only Trotsky but millions of others. Some became accustomed to believing part of it. Others saw in the revolutionary idol a chance to change the world for the better, while yet others were simply caught up in the momentum of the revolutionary upheaval.

Trotsky wrote a large number of books and articles, yet it is impossible to find in them any explanation of his fanatical faith in Marxism and the revolution. Berdyaev asks: 'Why did Trotsky become a revolutionary, why did socialism become his faith, why did he devote all his life to social revolution?'[3] These questions are nowhere answered satisfactorily in Trotsky's writings, but it may be said that the faith he held, and which went beyond rational explanation, was close to fanaticism. All his strivings were aimed towards revolution, and while such dedication implied great mental strength, it also denoted a great weakness: strength because such people are capable of influencing human life, and weakness because they are prisoners of the Idea. They do not have the capacity to change or adapt to new circumstances. For such people this kind of Marxism is a revolutionary religion. Their values, however, are not the universal human values of the world's great religions, but are embodied in the dictatorship of the proletariat, the class struggle and the unlimited predominance of a single party.

Trotsky was the prisoner of the Communist idea. When he wrote on 27 February 1940 in his testament, 'My faith in the Communist future of mankind is no less ardent, indeed it is firmer today, than it was in the days of my youth,' he was not mouthing a ritual formula. What were the consequences of this 'imprisonment'? Why should blind, fanatical devotion to the Idea lead to defeat, and how was this expressed in Trotsky?

First of all, he recognized only social revolution, and despised reformism. He never questioned the Leninist thesis that the transfer of power from one class to another was the fundamental sign of a revolution in every sense.[4] The historic fallacy of this notion consists in speaking of the dominance of a class, not of the people, while in fact it is impossible to achieve justice by placing one class above others. We ourselves have witnessed that infinitely more can be achieved by means of reform. The revolutions that have taken place in Europe at the end of the twentieth century are all based on non-violent reform and have given rise to such terms as 'the velvet revolution'. In the Bolshevik ideology such evolution was rejected at the outset, and Trotsky was one of the most consistent advocates of the 'traditional' violent solution of world problems. Shortly before his death he declared: 'The only worthy way for mankind to develop is by the path of socialist revolution.'[5] He was indeed a prisoner of the Idea, but he had chosen this path for himself.

In the draft of his speech to the Ninth Party Congress, entitled 'Routine Tasks of Economic Construction', Trotsky wrote that what was needed was 'regular, systematic, persistent and harsh struggle against labour desertion, in particular by publishing lists of penalties for desertion, by creating penal workers' teams out of deserters, and finally imprisoning them in concentration camps'.[6]

It is not too far fetched to suggest that such methods eventually became a normal means of 'socialist construction'. In March 1947 the Minister of the Interior, S. Kruglov, reported on the camps to Beria: 'In the second quarter there will be a need to build for a further 400,000 people. We shall have to allocate 50,000 to Dalstroy [the Far East], 60,000 to BAM [the Baikal–Amur Railway], 50,000 to Special Construction, 50,000 to logging camps, 40,000 to Vorkuta-Ukhta-Norilsk, and 100,000 to make up for losses [i.e. those who had died]. I request that the additional obligation to supply this labour force not be placed on the Ministry of the Interior at the present time.'[7] Despite the astonishing scale of the repressions, there were still not enough slaves. Such was the logic of violence: from the militarization of labour to penal labour teams and thence the Gulag industry.

Trotsky did not differ from the other leaders about the role of the Party in the socialist revolution. He firmly believed, with Lenin, in the dictatorship of one party, and in its monopoly on power, ideas and all decision-making, the very factors leading to the emergence of totalitarianism. Speaking on 7 December 1919 at the Seventh Congress of Soviets, he declared: 'I must say that in the form of our commissars and leading Communists we have a new order of Samurai, who without caste privileges will know how to die and will teach others to die for the cause of the working class.'[8] Within four years he would change his position somewhat, and would speak against the 'bureaucratization of the Party organization', and the 'false internal

Party line of the Central Committee' and 'secretarial omnipotence',[9] but he would never question the right of that single party to determine the fate of the vast population. He merely wanted to 'democratize the organization of the working class', without realizing that the monopoly would inevitably turn that organization into a weapon of totalitarianism. Trotsky strove to move ahead, but the totalitarian goals of the Party monopoly forced him to face the past.

Twenty years before the Twentieth Party Congress of 1956, Trotsky predicted the inevitable collapse of the Stalinist tower of lies. He himself did much to bring this about, although he was not without fault. Whether intentionally or not, Trotsky brought people to see that the chief idea to which he devoted his life was Utopian. The more he preached the inevitability of world revolution, the more ephemeral it seemed. In his own lifetime fewer and fewer people came to believe in the cleansing mystery of a world cataclysm. His nemesis in the USSR – Stalin – was showing what Bolshevik radicalism could lead to in one country, and it was not hard to imagine what would happen if the entire planet were consumed by the revolutionary fire.

Trotsky was loved as a leader of the revolution, yet by the end of the 1920s his name had become a term of abuse. It took Stalin no more than five years to turn a hero into a pariah. Trotsky himself was partly responsible for this. His tragedy lay in the fact that in his tireless and passionate struggle with Stalin, he facilitated Stalin's seizure of power in the Party. It was Trotsky's own doing that allowed Stalin to surround him with a circle of schismatics, heretics and other 'internal enemies'. Paradoxically, it was Trotsky's furious fight against Stalin that helped Stalin to become a bloody dictator. The new Party leader labelled Trotsky's statements as just another 'deviation', but Stalin himself took many of the left opposition's ideas for his own use. In his draft notes 'On the Building of Socialism in One Country', Trotsky defined the possibility of broad social reform as 'a social democratic deviation'. He pushed Stalin towards 'revolutionary tempos'. 'They regard us as pessimists and sceptics,' he wrote, 'because we regard the snail's pace as inadequate.'[10]

It may be argued that Trotsky inadvertently urged Stalin to adopt radical policies in the draft 'Platform of the Bolshevik Leninists' which he presented to the Fifteenth Party Congress of 1927. He declared that: 'Stalin's group has proved powerless to avert the growth of those forces which want to turn our country onto the capitalist path and which want to weaken the positions of the working class and poorest peasants against the growing strength of the kulak, the Nepman and the bureaucrat ... The growing strength of the farmer class in the countryside must be opposed by a faster growth of the collectives ... Rental relations are coming increasingly under the influence of the kulaks.'[11]

In view of these and similar statements, we may assume that, had Trotsky come to power, he would have carried out this programme with energy. In practice, however, it was Stalin who conducted the savage struggle against 'the growing strength of the Nepman and kulak'. While responsibility for the tremendous sufferings imposed on the Soviet people belongs squarely with the Communist Party under Stalin and his circle, the ideological origins of the policy of coercion and the forcing of social change should be laid at the door of the left opposition.

After the murder of Trotsky, the NKVD at home and abroad soon lost its interest in Trotskyism. Without its leader, the Fourth International was no threat to anybody. This fact highlights the paradox that lay in the contrast between his massive personality and the puny ideological movement to which Trotsky gave birth. Sooner perhaps than by other agencies, this was recognized by the NKVD. On 1 July 1941, a week after Hitler's armies had begun ploughing up Trotsky's native land with their tank-tracks, state security officials Agoyants and Klykov drafted a memorandum 'closing the agency's case on Trotsky and Trotskyist publications abroad'. The final document stated that 'all this material is no longer of any operational interest'.[12]

Beria's functionaries may have lost all interest in Trotsky once they had destroyed him, but he remains a major figure in the history of twentieth-century politics. He cannot be described in grey colours, for he combined the rebellious spirit of the Russian revolutionaries, their radicalism and dedication, with extreme Jacobinism and a readiness to serve the Idea fanatically. As Berdyaev perceptively observed:

> Trotsky is a very typical revolutionary, a revolutionary with great style, but he is not a typical Communist. He does not understand the main point of what I call the mystique of the collective ... The collective and the general line of the Communist Party are analogous to a church congregation and anyone who wishes to remain orthodox must submit

to the conscience and consciousness of the collective ... Trotsky still attributes importance to the individual, he thinks individual opinion, individual criticism and individual initiative are still possible, he believes in the role of heroic revolutionary personalities and he despises mediocrity and lack of talent.[13]

Trotsky's individuality lay primarily in his obsession with the Idea. For him the Idea was the equivalent of a philosophical temple, in which everything created within it belonged to eternity. For him the greatest spiritual luxury consisted in the ability to think and reflect freely. We shall never know everything about this man, for the more unusual the personality, the more enigmatic it remains.

Notes

Introduction

1 Central State Archives of the Soviet Army (TsGASA), f.33 987, op. 2, d.32, ll.279–80.
2 Ibid., l.282.
3 Ziv, G.A., *Trotskii: Kharakteristika (Po lichnym vospominaniyam)*, New York, Narodopravstvo, 1921.
4 TsGASA, f.4, op. 14, d.55, l.8.
5 Marx-Lenin Central Party Archive (TsPA IML), f.17, op. 2, d.612, vyp.III, l.7.
6 Kropotkin, P.A., *Rechi buntovshchika*, St Petersburg, 1906, p. 85.
7 TsPA IML, f.325, op. 1, d.228, l.20.
8 *Byulleten' oppozitsii*, No.87, August 1941, p. 5.
9 Trotskii, L., *Moya zhizn'*, Berlin, vol.2, 1930, p. 336.
10 *Byulleten' oppozitsii*, No.87, August 1941, p. 8.
11 More than sixty years passed before the Soviet taboo was lifted. 1990–91 saw the publication in the Soviet Union of Trotsky's *History of the Russian Revolution, Political Silhouettes, Stalin, The Stalinist School of Falsification, My Life* and *Literature and the Revolution*.
12 TsPA IML, f.130, op. 1, d.3, l.24.
13 TsPA IML, f.2, op. 1, d.22 947, l.6.

Chapter 1

1 TsGASA, f.33 987, op. 3, d.60, l.21.
2 TsPA IML, f.325, op. 2, d.14, l.1.
3 Trotskii, *Moya zhizn'*, op. cit., vol.1, p. 17.
4 Ibid., p. 36.
5 TsPA IML, f.325, op. 1, d.14, l.1.
6 Ziv, *Trotskii*, op. cit., p. 12.
7 Trotskii, *Moya zhizn'*, op. cit., vol.1, pp. 99–100.
8 Ibid., p. 36
9 Trotskii, L., *Dnevniki i pis'ma*, New Jersey, 1986, p. 154.
10 Letter to V.I. Nevsky, 1921. TsPA IML, f.325, op. 1, d.17, l.1–2.
11 The incident was described by I.M. Vasilevsky after the revolution in his *Nikolai II*, pp. 4–46.
12 Ziv, *Trotskii*, op. cit., p. 18.
13 TsPa IML, f.325, op. 1, d.14, ll.4–8.
14 Trotskii, *Dnevniki i pis'ma*, op. cit., p. 43.
15 TsPA IML, f.325, op. 1, d.1, l.1.
16 Shura, Shurochka, Sasha and Sashenka are only some of the diminutives of the name Alexandra.

17 TsPA IML, f.325, op. 1, d.1, ll.2–3.

18 Trotsky, *My Life*, Scribner's, New York, 1930, p. 124.

19 Trotsky, L. (trans. Elena Zarudnaya), *Trotsky's Diary in Exile*, Faber & Faber, London, 1959, pp. 61–2, 71.

20 TsPA IML, f.325, op. 1, d.178, l.9.

21 Ibid., d.18, ll.19–20.

22 *Sochineniya Gleba Uspenskogo*, SPB., 1889, vol.II, pp. 139–40.

23 TsPA IML, f.325, op. 1, d.2, l.1.

24 Ibid., l.3.

25 Ibid., l.8.

26 Trotskii, *Sochineniya*, vol.8, Moscow, 1926, pp. 14–15.

27 Trotsky, *My Life*, op. cit., p. 19.

28 Berdyaev, N., *Samopoznanie: opyt filosovskoy avtobiografii*, YMCA, Paris, 1949, p. 275.

29 Lenin, *Polnoe sobranie sochinenii* (PSS), vol.46, p. 277.

30 Trotskii, N., *Nashi politicheskie zadachi*, Geneva, 1904. (The initial 'N' was commonly used at the time by those writing under aliases, e.g. N. Lenin.)

31 Trotskii, *Sochineniya*, vol.8, op. cit., pp. 66–8.

32 Deutscher, I., *The Prophet Armed: Trotsky, 1879–1921*, Oxford University Press, 1954, p. 62.

33 Trotskii, *Sochineniya*, op. cit., pp. 65–6.

34 Houghton Library, Trotsky coll., bMS.Russ.13.1 (8680–3).

35 Houghton Library, Trotsky coll., bMS.Russ.13.1 (10634–41).

36 TsGASA, f.33 987, op. 1, d.21, ll.35–41.

37 Houghton Library, Trotsky coll., bMS.Russ.13 (T.866.3S).

38 Houghton Library, Trotsky coll., bMS.Russ.13.1 (8680–3).

39 These comments are from Sedova's notes, which Trotsky used in *My Life*, op. cit., p. 148.

40 *KPSS v rezolyutsiyakh i resheniyakh s'ezdov, konferentsyii I plenumov TsK*, 8th edn, vol.1, Moscow, 1970, p. 71.

41 Trotsky, L., *My Life*, op. cit., p. 163.

42 Lenin, *Sochineniya*, vol.34, p. 137.

43 Trotsky, *My Life*, op. cit., p. 164.

44 Martov, Y.O., *Mirovoi bol'shevizm*, Berlin, 1923, pp. 25–35.

45 Trotskii, *Sochineniya*, vol.8, op. cit., p. 67.

46 Trotsky, *My Life*, op. cit., p. 171.

47 Trotskii, L., 'Vtoroi s'ezd RSDRP (Otchet Sibirskoi delegatsii)', cited in Deutscher, *The Prophet Armed*, op. cit., p. 83.

48 Stalin, I.V., *Sochineniya*, vol.10, Moscow, p. 205.

49 Trotskii, *Nashi politicheskie zadachi*, op. cit., p. 55.

50 Houghton Library, Trotsky coll., BMS.Russ.13.1 (10 872–10 873).

51 Lenin, PSS vol.49, p. 390.

52 TsPA IML, f.325, op. 1, d.6, l.1. See also Deutscher, *The Prophet Armed*, op. cit., pp. 232–3 for part of this letter in the Houghton Library. As Deutscher notes, the letter was also intercepted by the Russian secret police, and it can be found in the Hoover Institution under Okhrana, XVIIc, fol.2, as well as in the Nicolaevsky Collection, also at the Hoover.

53 *Trotsky's Diary in Exile*, op. cit., pp. 83–4.

54 Lenin, PSS vol.18, p. 363.

55 Valentinov, N., *Vstrechi s Leninym*, New York, Chekhov, 1953, p. 338.

56 *Iskra*, No.92, 10 March 1905.

57 Trotskii, *Sochineniya*, vol.2, pt.1, Moscow, 1926, p. 246.

58 Ibid., pp. 248–9.

59 Ibid., pp. 251–4.

60 *Polnyi sbornik Platform vsekh*

Russkikh politicheskikh partii, n.a., St Petersburg, 1906, pp. 1–2.

61 Trotsky, *Die Russische Revolution 1905*, Munich, 1907, pp. 93–7.

62 Trotskii, *Sochineniya*, vol.2, pt.1, op. cit., p. 128.

63 Ibid., pp. 307, 309, 311.

64 TsPA IML, f.325, op. 1, d.201, l.15.

65 Ibid., d.211, l.1.

66 *Luch*, No.67, Paris, 21 March 1913.

67 Zinoviev, G., *Istoriya Rossiiskoi Komunisticheskoi Partii (bol'shevikov)*, Moscow, 1924, p. 198.

68 TsPA IML, f.325, op. 1, d.95, l.12.

69 TsGASA, f.33 987, op. 3, d.1103, l.146–9.

70 Ibid., op. 1, d.178, l.287.

71 *Trotsky's Diary in Exile*, op. cit., pp. 139–40.

72 TsPA IML, f.325, op. 1, d.3, ll.1–2.

73 Trotskii, L., *Permanentnaya revolyutsiya*, Berlin, Granat, 1930, p. 167.

74 TsPA IML, f.325, op. 1, d.190, l.55.

75 Ibid., d.213, l.1.

76 *Ugolovnoe Ulozhenie Rossiiski Imperii*, St Petersburg, 1903.

77 TsPA IML, f, 325, op. 1, d.212, l.12.

78 Trotsky, *My Life*, op. cit., p. 191.

79 TsPA IML, f.325, op. 1, d.24, ll.2–3.

80 Trotskii, *Sochineniya*, vol.2, pt.1, p. 478.

81 Trotsky, *My Life*, op. cit., pp. 192–8.

82 TsPA IML, f.325, op. 1, d.24, l.1.

83 Trotsky, *My Life*, op. cit., p. 200.

84 Trotskii, *Nashi politicheskie zadachi*, op. cit., pp. 68, 73, 78.

85 *Byulleten' oppozitsii*, August 1930, No.14, p. 7.

86 Lenin, PSS vol.47, p. 137.

87 Trotsky, *My Life*, op. cit., pp. 213–14.

88 Trotskii, *Sochineniya*, vol.8, pp. 47–8.

89 TsGASA, f.4, op. 14, d.30, l.8.

90 *Bol'sheviki. Dokumenty po istorii bol'shevizma s 1903 po 1916 god byvsh. Moskovskogo Okhrannogo Otdeleniya*, Moscow, 1918, pp. 111–12.

91 Trotskii, *Sochineniya*, vol.8, p. 71.

92 Ibid., pp. 71–2.

93 *Bol'sheviki. Dokumenty po istorii bol'shevizma s 1903 po 1916 god byvsh. Moskovskogo Okhrannogo Otdeleniya*, op. cit., pp. 194–5.

94 Trotskii, *Sochineniya*, vol.6, Moscow, 1926, pp. 415–20.

95 Ibid., p. 10.

96 TsPA IML, f.325, op. 1, d.229, ll.42–3.

97 Trotskii, *Sochineniya*, vol.9, Moscow, 1927, p. 240.

98 TsPA IML, f.325, op. 1, d.229, l.1.

99 Ibid., d.243, l.9.

100 Ibid., d.229, l.11.

101 Trotsky, *My Life*, op. cit., p. 236.

102 TsGASA, f.33 987, op. 2, d.86, l.6.

103 Trotsky, *My Life*, op. cit., p. 232.

104 Houghton Library, Trotsky coll., bMS.Russ.13.1 (8675–9).

105 TsPA IML, f.325, op. 1, d.388, l.1.

106 TsGASA, f.33 987, op. 2, d.141, l.274.

107 Trotskii, *Sochineniya*, vol.9, p. 3.

108 Trotsky, *My Life*, op. cit., p. 236.

109 Trotskii, *Sochineniya*, vol.9, p. 6.

110 TsGASA, f.33 987, op. 1, d.178, l.286.

111 *Arkhiv russkoi revolyutsii*, vol.11, Berlin, 1923, p. 200.

112 Arkhiv INO OGPU, f.17 548, d.0292, t.1, l.262.

113 TsGASA, f.33 987, op. 1, d.32, ll.341–4.

114 TsPA IML, f.325, op. 1, d.10, l.1.5.

115 *Trotsky's Diary in Exile*, op. cit., pp. 83–4.

Chapter 2

1 Trotsky, *My Life*, op. cit., p. 268.
2 Trotskii, *Sochineniya*, vol.3, pt.1, pp. 45–6.
3 Lenin, PSS vol.31, p. 115.
4 *Leninskii sbornik*, vol.4, Moscow, 1925, p. 303.
5 Lenin, PSS vol.32, p. 442.
6 Trotskii, L., *Fevral'skaya revolyutsiya*, Berlin, Granat, 1931, p. 321.
7 TsPA IML, f.325, op. 1, d.360, ll.1–5.
8 TsGASA, f.33 987, op. 2, d.79, l.90.
9 Ludendorff, E., *Meine Kriegserinnerungen, 1914–1918*, Berlin, 1919, p. 47.
10 Arkhiv INO OGPU, d.501, t.III, ll.469–470.
11 Trotskii, *Sochineniya*, vol.3, pt.1, pp. 165–6.
12 Sukhanov, N., *Zapiski o revolyutsii*, vol.4, Berlin-St Petersburg-Moscow, 1922, p. 511.
13 Raskolnikov, F., [In Kerensky's Gaol], TsPA IML, f.325, op. 1, d.19, pp. 36–37.
14 Kerenskii, A., *Izdaleka*, Paris, 1922, p. 11.
15 *Arkhiv russkoi revolyutsii*, vol.2, p. 89.
16 Sukhanov, *Zapiski o revolyutsii*, op. cit., vol.4, pp. 306–7.
17 Ibid., p. 188.
18 Trotskii, L., *Stalinskaya shkola fal'sifikatsii: Popravki i dopolneniya k literature epigonov*, Berlin, Granat, 1932, pp. 5–7.
19 *Velikaya Oktyabr'skaya sotsialisticheskaya revolyutsiya*, Entsiklopediya, Moscow, 1987, p. 18.

20 Melgunov, S., *Kak bol'sheviki zakhvatili vlast'*, p. 15.
21 TsPA IML, f.325, op. 1, d.11, l.10.
22 Sukhanov, *Zapiski o revolyutsii*, op. cit., vol.7, p. 91.
23 Lenin, PSS vol.34, pp. 435, 436.
24 TsGASA, f.33 987, op. 3, d.76, l.24.
25 Trotsky, L., *The History of the Russian Revolution*, London, Gollancz, 1934, pp. 960–1.
26 See e.g. Lenin, N. (V. Ulyanov), *Sobranie sochinenii*, Moscow-Petrograd, vol.14, 1923, p. 482.
27 Stalin, *Sochineniya*, vol.6, pp. 328–9.
28 Trotskii, *Stalinskaya shkola fal'sifikatsii*, op. cit., p. 13.
29 *Proletarskaya revolyutsiya*, No.10 (22), 1923, pp. 150–2.
30 Trotskii, *Stalinskaya shkola fal'sifikatsii*, op. cit., pp. 18, 19, 20.
31 Ibid., p. 25.
32 Ibid.
33 Ibid., p. 26.
34 Ibid., p. 27.
35 Ibid., pp. 33–4.
36 Ibid., pp. 37–8.
37 Trotsky, *My Life*, op. cit., pp. 294–5.
38 Cited in Trotsky, *The History of the Russian Revolution*, op. cit., p. 926.
39 TsPA IML, f.325, op. 1, d.11, l.5.
40 Trotsky, *My Life*, op. cit., p. 295.
41 Arkhiv INO OGPU-NKVD, f.17 548, d.0292, t.II, l.159.
42 *Rabochii i soldat*, No.3, 19 October (1 November) 1917.
43 Trotskii, *Sochineniya*, vol.3, pt.2, p. 380.
44 *Rabochii put'*, No.39, 18 October 1917.
45 Trotskii, *Sochineniya*, vol.3, pt.2, pp. 52–3.
46 Sukhanov, *Zapiski o revolyutsii*, op. cit., vol.7, p. 91.
47 *Novaya zhizn'*, 31 October 1917,

TsPA IML, f.325, op. 1, d, 11, l.14.

48 Milyukov, P., *Vospominaniya (1859–1917)*, New York, Chekhov, 1955, p. 391.

49 Sukhanov, *Zapiski o revolyutsii*, op. cit., vol.7, p. 33.

50 Cited in Trotsky, *The History of the Russian Revolution*, op. cit., p. 1004.

51 TsPA IML, f.325, op. 1, d.11, l.19.

52 Ibid., l.1.

53 Ibid., l.16.

54 In *Rabochaya gazeta*, TsPA IML, f.325, op. 1, d.11, l.11.

55 TsGAOR, f.130, op. 1, d.1, l.20.

56 Ibid.

57 Trotskii, *Stalinskaya shkola fal'sifikatsii*, op. cit., p. 119.

58 Ibid., p. 97.

59 Trotskii, *Sochineniya*, vol.17, pt.1, p. 190

60 TsGASA, f.33 987, op. 2, d.47, l.21.

61 Savinkov, B., *Nakanune novoi revolyutsii*, Warsaw, 1921, pp. 19–20.

62 Lenin, PSS vol.34, pp. 344–5.

63 Cited in Melgunov, *Kak bol'sheviki zakhvatili vlast'*, op. cit., p. 268.

64 See *Izvestiya Vserossiiskoi po delam o vyborakh v Uchreditel'noe Sobranie komissii*, Nos.16–22, November 1917.

65 Cited in Anin, D., *Revolyutsiya 1917 goda glazami ee rukovoditelei*, Rome, 1971, p. 463.

66 Lenin, PSS vol.35, pp. 153–4.

67 Trotsky, *My Life*, op. cit., pp. 327–8.

68 TsPA IML, f.325, op. 1, d.11, l.9.

69 Trotsky, *The History of the Russian Revolution*, op. cit., 1934, p. 1197.

70 TsPA IML, f.325, d.365, ll.78–9.

71 Ibid., op. 2, d.11, l.21.

72 *Pravda*, 7 November 1919.

73 *Proletarskaya revolyutsiya*, No.10, 1922, pp. 52–64.

74 Trotskii, *Sochineniya*, vol.3, pt.2, p. 94.

75 Trotsky, *My Life*, op. cit., p. 468.

76 TsPA IML, f.17, op. 2, d.317, vyp. 1, ch.1, l.81.

77 Trotsky, *My Life*, op. cit., p. 394.

78 Trotskii, *Sochineniya*, vol.3, pt.2, p. 157.

79 Trotsky, *My Life*, op. cit., pp. 339–40.

80 TsGAOR, f. 130, op. 1, d.3, l.18.

81 Czernin, O., *Im Weltkriege*, Berlin, 1919, p. 232.

82 Trotskii, *Sochineniya*, vol.17, pt.1, p. 5.

83 Czernin, *Im Weltkriege*, op. cit., pp. 319, 335.

84 Lenin, PSS vol.35, p. 225.

85 *Vladimir Ilyich Lenin. Biograficheskaya khronika*, Moscow, 1974, p. 176.

86 Trotskii, *Sochineniya*, vol.17, pt.1, p. 18.

87 Ibid., p. 31.

88 These speeches are to be found in Lenin, *Sochineniya*, 2nd/3rd edition, vol.22, pp. 277, 248.

89 TsGASA, f.33 987, op. 3, d.1075, ll.36–42.

90 *VII s'ezd Rossiiskoi kommunisticheskoi partii (bol'shevikov). Stenograficheskii otchet*. Moscow-Petrograd, 1923, pp. 126–9.

91 Trotskii, *Sochineniya*, vol.17, pt.1, p. 65.

92 Wheeler-Bennett, J. W., *Brest-Litovsk: The Forgotten Peace*, London, 1963, p. 186; also cited in Deutscher, *The Prophet Armed*, op. cit., pp. 379–80.

93 In *Pravda*, 30 November 1924.

94 Trotskii, *Sochineniya*, vol.17, pt.1, pp. 103, 105, cited here from Wheeler-Bennett, *Brest-Litovsk: The Forgotten Peace*, op. cit., pp. 22–7.

95 Trotskii, *Sochineniya*, vol.17, pt.1,

p. 104, cited here from Wheeler-Bennett, *Brest-Litovsk: The Forgotten Peace*, op. cit., p. 227.

96 Trotskii, *Sochineniya*, vol.17, pt.1, p. 115.
97 Ibid., p. 116.
98 Ibid., p. 111.
99 Ibid., p. 659.
100 Ibid., pp. 134–44.
101 Ibid., pp. 141–2.
102 *Istoriya VKP(b): Kratkii kurs.* Moscow.
103 *VII s'ezd Rossiiskoi kommunisticheskoi partii (bol'shevikov). Stenograficheskii otchet*, op. cit., p. 86.
104 Merezhkovskii, D., *Polnoe sobranie sochinenii*, vol.15, pp. 22–3.
105 Plekhanov, G., *God na Rodine: Polnoe sobranie sochinenii i rechei, 1917–1918 gg.*, Paris, 1921, vol.2, p. 75.
106 Lenin, PSS vol.30, p. 133.
107 TsPA IML, f.325, op. 2, d.11, l.25.
108 Kerenskii, *Izdaleka*, op. cit.
109 TsGASA, f.1, op. 1, d.37, l.212.
110 Ibid., d.123, ll.100–1.
111 Trotskii, *Sochineniya*, vol.17, pt.1, p. 213.
112 Ibid., p. 157.
113 Ibid., p. 160.
114 Ibid., p. 201.
115 Ibid., p. 205.
116 Ibid., p. 214.
117 TsPA IML, f.325, op. 1, d.270, ll.1–4.
118 Trotskii, *Sochineniya*, vol.17, pt.1, pp. 164–5.
119 TsPA IML, f.325, op. 2, d.1, ll.5–6.
120 Trotskii, *Sochineniya*, vol.17, pt.1, pp. 183–4.
121 Ibid., p. 207.
122 *Russkaya mysl'*, Paris; cited in *Fevral'skaya revolyutsiya. Revolyutsiya i grazhdanskaya voina v opisaniyakh belogvardeitsev*, Moscow-Leningrad, 1925, p. 121.

123 Trotskii, *Sochineniya*, vol.17, pt.1, pp. 187–8.

Chapter 3

1 Arkhiv INO OGPU, f.17 548, d.0292, t.1, ll.106–7.
2 *Grazhdanskaya voina 1918–1921*, Moscow, 1928, vol.1, p. 15.
3 TsGASA, f.4, op. 14, d.7, l.79.
4 Trotsky, *My Life*, op. cit., pp. 349–50.
5 Ibid., pp. 351–2.
6 Trotskii, *Sochineniya*, vol.17, pt.1, pp. 686–7.
7 Ibid., pp. 267–8.
8 Ibid., p. 362.
9 Ibid., pp. 363, 369–70.
10 Ibid., p. 329.
11 TsGASA, f.33 987, op. 1, d.329, l.106.
12 Arkhiv INO OGPU, f.17 548, d.0292, t.2, ll.202–18.
13 *Arkhiv russkoi revolyutsii*, vol.12, pp. 89–93.
14 Lenin, PSS vol.36, p. 79.
15 Ibid., p. 95.
16 TsGASA, f.33 987, op. 2, d.361, l.170.
17 Ibid., d.85, l.29.
18 Ibid., op. 1, d.146, l.125.
19 TsPA IML, f.325, op. 1, d.40, l.9.
20 TsGASA, f.33 987, op. 1, d.41, l.2.
21 Ibid., op. 2, d.41, l.7.
22 TsPA IML, f.325, op. 1, d.40, l.19.
23 TsGASA, f.33 987, op. 2, d.40, l.29.
24 Trotsky, *My Life*, op. cit., p. 397.
25 Trotskii, *Sochineniya*, vol.17, pt.1, pp. 507–8.
26 Ibid., pp. 509–11.
27 Arkhiv INO OGPU, f.17 548, d.0292, t.2, l.212.
28 Trotskii, *Sochineniya*, vol.17, pt.1, pp. 451–76.
29 Ibid., p. 476.
30 Trotsky, *My Life*, op. cit., p. 396.

31 TsPA IML, f.325, op. 1, d.40, l.21.

32 Lenin, PSS vol.50, p. 133.

33 TsGASA, f.4, op. 1, d.16, l.239.

34 TsGASA, f.176, op. 3, d.171, l.2.

35 *Direktivy komandovaniya frontov Krasnoi Armii (1917–1922)*, Moscow, 1978, vol.4, p. 38.

36 Trotsky, *My Life*, op. cit., pp. 402–3.

37 TsPA IML, f.325, op. 1, d.403, l.84a.

38 Ibid., l.86.

39 Trotsky, *My Life*, op. cit., p. 408.

40 Trotskii, *Sochineniya*, vol.17, pt.1, p. 519.

41 *Arkhiv russkoi revolyutsii*, vol.7, p. 273.

42 Trotsky, *My Life*, op. cit., pp. 407–8.

43 TsPA IML, f.325, op. 1, d.40, l.29.

44 TsGASA, f.33 987, op. 3, d.46, l.301.

45 *Direktivy komandovaniya frontov Krasnoi Armii (1917–1922)*, op. cit., vol.2, p. 790.

46 Ibid., p. 410.

47 TsGASA, f.33 987, op. 2, d.40, l.29.

48 *Leninskii sbornik*, vol.37, Moscow, 1970, p. 106.

49 TsGASA, f.33 988, op. 2, d.289, ll.19–20.

50 Lenin, PSS vol.51, pp. 206–7.

51 Ibid., p. 208.

52 TsGASA, f.33897, op. 2, d.32, l.533.

53 Golovin, N.N., *Rossiiskaya kontrrevolyutsiya, 1917–1918 gg.*, vol.5, Paris, 1937, pp. 129, 131.

54 *Arkhiv russkoi revolyutsii*, vol.10, p. 183.

55 Denikin, A.I., *Ocherki russkoi smuty*, vol.5, Berlin, 1926, p. 136.

56 Arkhiv INO OGPU, f.17 548, d.0292, t.II, l.208.

57 Savinkov, B.V., *Nakanune novoi revolyutsii*, p. 27.

58 Trotskii, *Sochineniya*, vol.17, pt.2, p. 349.

59 Ibid., pp. 196–7.

60 Ibid., p. 189.

61 Lukomskii, A.S., *Vospominaniya*, Berlin, 1922, pp. 165–7.

62 Denikin, *Ocherki russkoi smuty*, vol.1, p. 1.

63 Ibid., pp. 357–8.

64 TsGASA, f.33 987, op. 1, d.475, ll.350–4.

65 Ibid., op. 2, d.682, ll.57–9.

66 Ibid., op. 3, d.864, ll.408–10.

67 Berdyaev, *Samopoznanie*, op. cit., p. 269.

68 Trotskii, *Sochineniya*, vol.17, pt.2, p. 182.

69 Ibid., p. 184.

70 TsPA IML, f.325, op. 1, d.12, ll.1–10.

71 TsGASA, f.33987, op. 1, d.475, l.178.

72 Ibid., d.195, l.73.

73 Ibid., op. 2, d.41, l.5.

74 TsPA IML, f.17, op. 65, d.34, ll.163–5.

75 TsGASA, f.100, o;.3, d.192, l.277.

76 TsGASA, f.33 987, op. 1, d.306, ll.111, 125.

77 Ibid., d.146, ll.111, 125.

78 Ibid., l.72.

79 Ibid., op. 2, d.89, l.375.

80 Ibid., l.373.

81 Ibid., d.3, l.52.

82 Ibid., op. 1, d.266, l.556.

83 Trotskii, *Sochineniya*, vol.17, pt.2, p. 149.

84 TsGASA, f.33 987, op. 2, d.3, l.66.

85 Ibid., op. 1, d.229, l.213.

86 Trotskii, *Sochineniya*, vol.17, pt.2, p. 212.

87 Ibid., pp. 256, 260.

88 TsGASA, f.33 987, op. 1, d.146, l.254.

89 Trotskii, *Sochineniya*, vol.17, pt.2, pp. 265–7.

90 TsGASA, f.33 987, op. 2, d.141, ll.790–3.

91   Trotsky, *My Life*, op. cit., p. 413.
92   TsGASA, f.33 987, op. 1, d.25, ll.16–44.
93   TsGASA, f.4, op. 7, d.125, ll.5.
94   Ibid., d.34, l.60.
95   TsGASA, f.33 987, op. 2, d.40, l.314.
96   Trotsky, *My Life*, op. cit., pp. 419–20.
97   TsGASA, f.33 987, op. 1, d.45, l.3.
98   Ibid., op. 2, d.47, l.66.
99   Ibid., op. 1, d.41, l.218.
100 Ibid., op. 2, d.42, l.460.
101 Ibid., op. 1, d.45, l.17.
102 Ibid., d.13, l.13.
103 Trotsky, *My Life*, op. cit., pp. 416.
104 TsGASA, f.33 987, op. 2, d.86, l.92.
105 Ibid., l.105.
106 Ibid., op. 1, d.260, l.17.
107 Ibid., d.262, l.115.
108 Ibid., d.229, l.31.
109 Ibid., l.83.
110 TsGASA, f.8, op. 1, d.310, l.24.
111 TsGASA, f.33 987, op. 1, d.260, l.124.
112 Trotsky, *My Life*, op. cit., pp. 418–19.
113 TsGASA, f.33 987, op. 1, d.229, l.84; f.1, op. 1, d.123, l.265.
114 Ibid., d.142, l.98.
115 Ibid., op. 2, d.41, l.223.
116 Ibid., l.225.
117 Ibid., d.126, l.28.
118 Ibid., op. 1, d.266, l.218.
119 Ibid., d.229, l.216.
120 Ibid., op. 2, d.41, l.183.
121 Ibid., l.170.
122 Ibid., l.183.
123 Trotsky, *My Life*, op. cit., p. 420.
124 Semenov, G., *Voennaya i boevaya rabota partii sotsialistov-revolyutsionerov za 1917–1918 gg.*, Berlin, 1922, pp. 18–33.
125 Lenin, PSS vol.44, p. 159.
126 TsGAOR, f.130, op. 1, d.19, ll.126–35.

127 Trotskii, *Sochineiya*, vol.17, pt.2, pp. 218–19.
128 TsGASA, f.33 987, op. 2, d.41, l.146.
129 Trotsky, *My Life*, op. cit., p. 411.
130 TsGASA, f.33 987, op. 1, d.216, l.174.
131 TsGASA, f.4, op. 14, d.7, l.14.
132 TsGASA, f.33 987, op. 2, d.41, l.5.
133 Ibid., l.86.
134 Lenin, PSS vol.37, p. 174.
135 TsPA IML, f.325, op. 1, d.403, l.87a.
136 Olikov, S., *Dezertirstvo v Krasnoi Armii i bor'ba s nim*, Moscow, 1926, pp. 27–8.
137 Ibid., pp. 124, 125, 126.
138 TsPA IML, f.325, op. 1, d.40, l.27.
139 Denikin, *Ocherki russkoi smuty*, vol.3, p. 145.
140 Ibid., vol.4, p. 91.
141 TsGASA, f.33 987, op. 2, d.41, l.62.
142 Ibid., l.63.
143 Ibid., d.86, l.96.
144 Ibid., d.3, l.76.
145 Ibid., op. 1, d.392, l.108.
146 TsPA IML, f.17, op. 2, d.5.
147 TsGASA, f.33 987, op. 1, d.420, l.350.
148 Ibid., d.87, l.459.
149 Ibid., d.146, l.72.
150 TsPA IML, f.325, op. 1, d.40, l.37.
151 TsGASA, f.33 987, op. 2, d.40, l.308.
152 Ibid., l.418.
153 *Arkhiv russkoi revolyutsii*, vol.7, Berlin, p. 246.
154 TsGASA, f.33 987, op. 2, d.141, l.179.
155 Ibid., d.195, l.132.
156 Ibid., d.32, l.253.
157 Ibid., op. 3, d.717, ll.202–7.
158 Ibid., op. 2, d.32, ll.346–53.
159 Ibid.
160 Ibid., l.166.
161 Ibid., l.307.
162 Lenin, PSS vol.38, p. 350.

163 Lenin, PSS vol.37, p. 535.
164 Gorkii, M., *Nesovremennye mysli*, Moscow, St Petersburg, 1990, p. 84.
165 TsGASA, f.33 987, op. 2, d.32, ll.74–740b.
166 Ibid., d.3, l.54.
167 Ibid., op. 1, d.2, l.131.
168 Lenin, PSS vol.38, p. 317.
169 Anishev, A., *Ocherki istorii grazhdanskoi voiny*, Leningrad, 1925, p. 229.
170 TsPA IML, f.17, op. 2, d.11, ll.1–2.
171 Ibid., 1.ob.
172 TsGASA, f.33 988, op. 2, d.88, l.96.
173 *Izvestiya*, VTsIK, 25 February 1919.
174 *Izvestiya*, TsK KPSS No.9, 1989, p. 181.
175 *VIII s'ezd RKP(b). Mart 1919. Protokoly*, Moscow, 1959, p. 147.
176 Partarkhiv Instituta istorii partii Leningrada (filial TsPA IML), f.1, op. 1, d.336, ll.1–36.
177 TsGASA, f.33 987, op. 2, d.86, l.155.
178 Ibid., d.96, l.10.
179 Ibid., d.40, l.29.
180 TsPA IML, f.41, op. 2, d.1, l.15.
181 Ibid., d.3, l.29.
182 TsGASA, f.33 987, op. 1, d.448, l.27.
183 *Leninskii sbornik*, vol.37, Moscow, 1970, pp. 138, 139.
184 *Izvestiya*, TsK KPSS. No.11, 1989, p. 174.
185 Tukhachevskii, M.N., *Izbrannye proizvedeniya*, Moscow, 1964, vol.2, p. 226.
186 *Iz istorii grazhdanskoi voiny v SSSR*, vol.2, p. 205.
187 Kamenev, S.S., *Zapiski o grazhdanskoi voine i voennom stroitel'stve*, Moscow, 1963, p. 63.
188 TsGASA, f.33 987, op. 2, d.32, l.18.
189 *Grazhdanzkaya voina 1918–1921*, Moscow-Leningrad, 1930, vol.3, p. 10.

Chapter 4

1 Trotskii, *Dnevniki i pis'ma*, op. cit., p. 162.
2 TsPA IML, f.325, op. 1, d.122, l.3.
3 Ibid., d.368, l.17.
4 Marx K. and Engels, F., *Sochineniya*, 2nd edn, vol.7, p. 261.
5 Trotskii, L., *Itogi i perspektivy*, Moscow, 1919, pp. 4–5.
6 Parvus's commercial and revolutionary interests are definitively described by Michael Futrell in *Northern Underground*, London, 1963, and the issue of financial aid to the Bolsheviks by the present author in *Lenin: Life and Legacy*, London and New York, 1994.
7 Ludendorff, E. (trans. Kriegserinnerungen,), *Moi vospominaniya o voine 1914–1918*, Moscow, 1924, p. 89.
8 Spiridovich, A.I., *Istoriya bol'shevizma v Rossii*, Paris, 1922, pp. 355–6.
9 Lenin, PSS vol.11, p. 222.
10 Trotskii, L., *1905*, Moscow, 1922, pp. 4–5.
11 Ibid., p. 285.
12 Trotskii, L., *Permanentnaya revolyutsiya*, Berlin, 1930, p. 12.
13 Ibid., p. 167.
14 Ibid.
15 TsPA IML, f.325, op. 1, d.139, l.1.
16 TsGASA, f.4, op. 14, d.51, l.147.
17 Struev, I., *Teoriya permanentnoi revolyutsii tov. Trotskogo*, Rostov on Don, 1925.
18 Ibid., p. 2.
19 Trotskii, *Sochineniya*, vol.18, p. 72.
20 Ibid., p. 92.
21 Ibid., pp. 83–7.

22   Lenin, PSS vol.44, p. 36.
23   Trotskii, L., *Istoriya russkoi revolyutsii*, vol.1, p. 22.
24   Ibid., p. 506.
25   Ibid., p. 32.
26   Trotskii, *Permanentnaya revolyutsiya*, op. cit., p. 125.
27   TsGASA, f.33 987, op. 1, d.145, l.245.
28   Ibid., d.498, ll.787–8.
29   TsPA IML, f.17, op. 2, d.78, l.2.
30   TsPA IML, f.325, op. 1, d.292, ll.1–5.
31   Trotskii, L., *Novyi kurs*, Moscow, 1924, pp. 40–6.
32   TsGASA, f.33 987, op. 2, d.147, ll.90–1.
33   Ibid., ll.51–2.
34   Ibid., l.52.
35   Ibid., l.188.
36   Ibid., d.89, l.22.
37   Ibid., op. 3, d.13, ll.23–39.
38   Ibid., d.101, ll.517–26.
39   Trotskii, *Sochineniya*, vol.12, p. 342.
40   Ibid., pp. 369–70.
41   Ibid., p. 371.
42   Ibid., pp. 371–2.
43   TsGASA, f.33 987, op. 1, d.266, l.71.
44   Ibid., d.409, l.724.
45   Ibid., op. 3, d.40, l.10.
46   Ibid., l.47.
47   Trotskii, *Sochineniya*, vol.12, p. 395.
48   Ibid., p. 402.
49   Ibid., p. 177.
50   TsGASA, f.33 987, op. 2, d.97, l.5.
51   Potresov, A.N., *V plenu u illyuzii*, Paris, 1927, pp. 12–17.
52   Trotskii, *Sochineniya*, vol.12, pp. 25–6.
53   TsGASA, f.1, op. 1, d.142, l.20.
54   Savinkov, B., *Nakanune novoi revolyutsii*, p. 48.
55   TsGASA, f.33 987, op. 3, d.80, l.78.
56   Ibid., op. 2, d.141, l.287.

57   Trotskii, *Sochineniya*, vol.12, pp. 38–9.
58   Potresov, *V plenu u illyuzii*, op. cit., p. 50.
59   Trotskii, *Sochineniya*, vol.12, p. 47.
60   Ibid., pp. 50, 55, 59–60.
61   Ibid., p. 105.
62   Ibid., p. 110.
63   Arkhiv INO OGPU, d.343, t.III, l.135.
64   Ibid., ll.14–24.
65   TsGASA, f.33 987, op. 14, d.7, l.59.
66   Trotskii, *Sochineniya*, vol.12, pp. 128, 129.
67   Ibid., p. 131.
68   Ibid.
69   Ibid., p. 136.
70   TsGASA, f.33 987, op. 1, d.229, l.647.
71   Ibid., op. 2, d.97, l.1.
72   Trotskii, *Sochineniya*, vol.12, pp. 142–3.
73   Potresov, *V plenu u illyuzii*, op. cit., p. 45.
74   Houghton Library, Trotsky coll., bMS Russ.13 (T.773).
75   Trotskii, L., *Chto takoe SSSR i kuda on idet?*, Paris, 1936, pp. 142–3, 145.
76   Trotskii, *Sochineniya*, vol.20, p. 327.
77   Ibid., pp. 330, 332.
78   TsGASA, f.33 987, op. 1, d.428, l.91.
79   Ibid., ll.19–25.
80   Trotskii, *Sochineniya*, vol.21, p. 4.
81   Ibid., pp. 4–5.
82   Houghton Library, Trotsky coll., bMS Russ.13 (T.801.1S).
83   *Pravda*, 12 July 1923.
84   Trotskii, *Sochineniya*, vol.21, p. 55.
85   Ibid., p. 57.
86   Ibid., p. 27.
87   *Pravda*, 14 July, 1923.
88   Berdyaev, *Samopoznanie*, op. cit., p. 263.
89   *Izvestiya*, VTsIK, 30 August 1922.

90 TsPA IML, f.325, op. 1, d.99, l.36.
91 *Novaya Zhizn'*, 26 April, 1918.
92 Trotskii, *Sochineniya*, vol.21, p. 153.
93 TsPA IML, f.2, op. 1, d.22 947, ll.1–6.
94 Ibid., l.1.
95 TsPA IML, f.17, op. 3, d.283, ll.6–7.
96 Ibid., d.293, l.12.
97 TsPA IML, f.2, op. 1, d.22 947, l.6.
98 Ibid., d.27 072.
99 Houghton Library, Trotsky coll., bMS Russ.13 (T.440.1S).
100 TsGASA, f.33 987, op. 2, d.141, l.10.
101 Trotskii, *Sochineniya*, vol.21, p. 162.
102 Ibid., p. 159.
103 TsGASA, f.33 987, op. 1, d.498, l.639.
104 Ibid., l.560.
105 TsGASA, f.4, op. 14, d.13, l.225.
106 TsGASA, f.33 987, op. 1, d.450, l.188.
107 Ibid., l.196.
108 Ibid., op. 3, d.60, ll.66–66a.
109 Ibid., op. 1, d.498, l.622.
110 TsGAOR, f.9430, op. 1, d.19, l.1.
111 Ibid., l.2.
112 Trotskii, *Chto takoe SSSR i kuda on idet?*, op. cit., p. 146.
113 TsGASA, f.4, op. 14, d.13, l.254.
114 Lenin, PSS vol.41, p. 383.
115 RTsKhIDNI, f.2, op. 1, d.6615, l.1.
116 *Trotsky's Diary in Exile*, op. cit., pp. 53–4.
117 TsGASA, f.33 987, op. 3, d.46, ll.142–3.
118 Berdyaev, N., *Istoki i smysl russkogo kommunizma*, Paris, 1955, p. 101.
119 TsGASA, f.f, op. 14, d.32, l.278.
120 Trotskii, *Chto takoe SSSR i kuda on idet?*, op. cit., p. 74.

Chapter 5

1 Houghton Library, Trotsky coll., bMS.Russ.13 (T.773.4S).
2 *Arkhiv Trotskogo: Kommunisticheskaya oppozitsiya v SSSR*, Moscow, 1990, vol.3, p. 87.
3 Lenin, PSS vol.45, p. 346.
4 Ibid., p. 345.
5 *Arkhiv Trotskogo*, vol.1, p. 56.
6 Trotsky, *My Life*, op. cit., p. 491.
7 Ibid., p. 498.
8 Ibid., p. 500.
9 Ibid.
10 Ibid.
11 TsPA IML, f.17, op. 2, d.685, ll.53–68.
12 Ibid., ll.58–62.
13 Ibid., l.61.
14 Ibid., l.62.
15 Ibid., l.63.
16 Ibid., d.103, ll.2–3.
17 Ibid., d.685, l.65.
18 Ibid., l.68.
19 Ibid., op. 3, d.388, l.3.
20 Ibid., op. 2, d.685, ll.96–7.
21 Ibid., ll.94–5.
22 TsPA IML, f.51, op. 1, d.21, ll.540b–570b.
23 Ibid., l.570b.
24 TsPA IML, f.17, op. 2, d.104, ll.31–8.
25 Ibid., ll.3–4.
26 *Izvestiya TsK KPSS*, No.2, 1990, p. 202.
27 Trotsky, *My Life*, op. cit., p. 504.
28 *Pravda*, 23 December 1923.
29 TsPA IML, f.17, op. 2, d.685, l.53.
30 Ibid., l.66.
31 Trotskii, *Novyi kurs*, op. cit.
32 *Pravda*, 11 December 1923.
33 TsPA IML, f.17, op. 2, l.685, ll.58–9.
34 *Pravda*, 28 December 1923.
35 *Pravda*, 29 December 1923.
36 *Pravda*, 11 December 1923.
37 Trotskii, *Novyi kurs*, op.cit., pp. 40–9.

38 TsPA IML, f.325, op. 1, d.115, ll.1–2.

39 TsGASA, f.33 987, op. 1, d.478, l.109.

40 Ibid., p. 68.

41 Ibid., p. 25.

42 Trotskii, L., *Uroki Oktyabrya*, Moscow, 1924, p. 54.

43 *Bol'shevik*, Nos.12–13, 1924, p. 108.

44 Trotsky, *My Life*, op. cit., p. 515.

45 TsPA IML, f.35, op. 1, d.318, ll. 2, 3, 6.

46 TsGASA, f.33 987, op. 2, d.167, l.188.

47 Houghton Library, Trotsky coll., bMS.Russ.13.1 (7710–40), folder 2/5.

48 TsGASA, f.33 987, op. 2, d.100, l.264.

49 Ibid., op. 1, d.572, l.27.

50 TsGASA, f.4, op. 1, d.243, l.95.

51 TsGASA, f.33 987, op. 2, d.19, ll.16–17.

52 Ibid., d.40, l.30.

53 Trotsky, *My Life*, op. cit., p. 477.

54 Stalin, *Sochineniya*, vol.4, p. 152.

55 TsGASA, f.33 987, op. 2, d.19, l.2.

56 Stalin, *Sochineniya*, vol.4, p. 120.

57 TsGASA, f.33 987, op. 1, d.498, l.8.

58 Trotsky, *My Life*, op. cit., pp. 479–81.

59 TsGASA, f.33 987, op. 1, d.306, l.188.

60 Ibid., op. 3, d.80, l.587.

61 TsPA IML, f.2, op. 1, d, 27 088, l.1.

62 Houghton Library, Trotsky coll., bMS.Russ.13.1 (8967–86) folder 1/2, pp. 1–2.

63 Ibid.

64 Volkogonov, *Lenin: Life and Legacy*, op. cit., pp. 425–7.

65 TsPA IML, f.51, op. 1, d.21, l.290.

66 Trotsky, *My Life*, op. cit., p. 521.

67 *Arkhiv Trotskogo*, vol.1, p. 154.

68 TsPA IML, f.325, op. 1, d.355, ll.14–15.

69 *XIV s'ezd Vsesoyuznoi kommunisticheskoi partii (bol'shevikov). Stenograficheskii otchet*, Moscow-Leningrad, 1926, pp. 274–5.

70 *Izvestiya TsK KPSS*, No.7, 1991, pp. 123, 135.

71 Houghton Library, Trotsky coll., bMS.Russ.13 (T.136), p. 3.

72 Gavrilov, N.N., *Moya rabota v oppozitsionnoi gruppe*. In *Pamyat'*, Paris, 1980, vyp. 3, pp. 385–7.

73 Trotsky, *My Life*, op. cit., p. 521.

74 TsPA IML, f.325, op. 1, d.361, ll.1–5.

75 TsGASA, f.33 987, op. 1, d.498, l.100.

76 Ibid., l.80.

77 TsPA IML, f.17, op. 2, d.685, ll.53–68; f.17, op. 3, d.388, ll.1–4.

78 Houghton Library, Trotsky coll., bMS.Russ.13 (T.736.1S).

79 Deutscher, I., *The Prophet Unarmed: Trotsky, 1921–29*, Oxford, 1959, p. 263.

80 *Izvestiya TsK KPSS*, No.7, 1989, p. 80.

81 Zinoviev, G., *Leninizm*, Moscow, 1925, p. 76.

82 *VII Vserossiiskaya konferentsiya RSDRP, Protokoly*, Moscow, 1958, p. 624.

83 Kamenev, L., *Lenin, Marks, Oktyabr', Perspektivy/Prozhektor*, No.3, 1925, p. 5.

84 *XIV s'ezd Vsesoyuznoi kommunisticheskoi partii (bol'shevikov), Stenograficheskii otchet*, Moscow-Leningrad, 1926, p. 274.

85 Deutscher, *The Prophet Unarmed*, op. cit., p. 382, citing Houghton Library, Trotsky coll.

86 TsPA IML, f.326, op. 1, d.113, l.72.

87 Ibid., l.75.

88 Ibid., ll.73–4.
89 Houghton Library, Trotsky coll., bMS.Russ.13 (T.868), p. 2.
90 TsPA IML, f.326, op. 1, d.23, l.1.
91 Ibid., d.29, l.1.
92 Ibid., d.33, l.2.
93 Arkhiv Trotskogo, vol.1, pp. 187–8.
94 In Pamyat', pp. 389–91.
95 TsPA IML, f.17, op. 2, d.308, l.2509.
96 Serge, V., La Vie et le Mort de Leon Trotsky, Paris, 1954, pp. 180–1.
97 Arkhiv Trotskogo, vol.3, pp. 43, 46.
98 Ibid., pp. 57, 58, 59.
99 Ibid., p. 126.
100 TsPA IML, f.325, op. 1, d.357, ll.37–41.
101 Ibid., d.359, ll.3–7.
102 Ibid., ll.196–7.
103 TsPA IML, f.17, op. 2, d.317, vyp. 1, ch. 1, ll.75–6.
104 Ibid., l.75.
105 TsPA IML, f.505, op. 1, d.65, ll.1–35.
106 Sotsialisticheskii vestnik, No.15 (157), Berlin, 1 August 1927, p. 14.
107 Arkhiv INO OGPU, d.672, t.1, l.196.
108 Arkhiv Trotskogo, vol.3, pp. 41–2.
109 Ibid., vol.4, pp. 219, 221–2, 223, 224.
110 Stalin, Sochineniya, vol 10, pp. 172–3.
111 Ibid., pp. 191, 204–5.
112 Arkhiv Trotskogo, vol.4, p. 243.
113 Ibid., pp. 230–1.
114 Ibid., pp. 250–2.
115 Ibid., p. 255.
116 Ibid., p. 264.
117 Ibid., p. 269.
118 TsGAOR, f.5446, op. 2, d.33, l.19.
119 Houghton Library, Trotsky coll., bMS.Russ.13 (T.119.1S).
120 Houghton Library, Trotsky coll., bMS.Russ.13 (T.946), pp. 2–6.
121 I. Deutscher, Interval, London, 1963, p. 618.
122 Arkhiv Trotskogo, vol.4, p. 275.
123 Stalin, Sochineniya, vol.10, p. 351.
124 Ibid., pp. 354–7.
125 Trotsky, My Life, op. cit., pp. 539–41.
126 Izvestiya TsK KPSS, No.5, 1991, p. 201.
127 APRF, f.45, op. 1, d.19, 20.
128 Personal interview with the author.
129 Arkhiv INO OGPU, f.17 548, d.0292, t.2, l.216.
130 Trotsky, My Life, op. cit., p. 556.
131 Houghton Library, Trotsky coll., bMS.Russ.13 (T.2918), pp. 1–4.
132 Deutscher, Interval, op. cit., p. 618.
133 Trotskii, Dnevniki i pis'ma, op. cit., p. 73.
134 Yaroslavsky, Y.M., Za poslednei chertoi. Trotskistkaya oppozitsiya posle XV s'ezda, Moscow-Leningrad, 1930, p. 64.
135 International Institute of Social History, Amsterdam, No.740, 2363.
136 Houghton Library, Trotsky coll., bMS.Russ.13 (T.2912.1S).
137 Arkhiv INO OGPU, f.17 548, d.0292, t.1, l.21.
138 International Institute of Social History, Amsterdam, No.740, 2363.
139 Interview with the author in 1988.
140 Stalin, Sochineniya, vol.12, p. 79.
141 Trotsky, My Life, op. cit., p. 558.
142 Houghton Library, Trotsky coll., bMS.Russ.13 (T.2948), p. 2; Trotsky, My Life, op. cit., p. 562.
143 Houghton Library, Trotsky coll., bMS.Russ.13 (T.2949.1S).
144 From the personal archives of Lieutenant-General of Justice B.A. Viktorov, who was involved in the

rehabilitations of 1956, including that of Fokin.

145 International Institute of Social History, Amsterdam, No.740, 2374.

Chapter 6

1 TsPA IML, f.2, op. 2, d.612, l.1; d.711, l.2.
2 Trotskii, L., *Chto i kak proizoshlo. Shest' statei dlya mirovoi burzhuaznoi pechati*, Paris, 1929, p. 9. See also Deutscher, I., *The Prophet Outcast: Trotsky, 1929–1940*, Oxford, 1963, p. 4, which cites this document from the Houghton Library, Trotsky coll.
3 International Institute of Social History, Amsterdam, No.740, 2374.
4 Trotskii, *Chto i kak proizoshlo*, op. cit., pp. 10–11.
5 Ibid., pp. 25–7.
6 Arkhiv INO OGPU, 17 548, d.0292, t.1, ll.194–5.
7 Carmichael, J., *Trotsky*, Jerusalem, 1980, p. 237.
8 Stalin, *Sochineniya*, vol.12, pp. 191, 197–8.
9 Arkhiv INO OGPU, 17 548, d.0292, t.1, l.1.
10 TsGAOR, f.3316, op. 2, d.83, l.1.
11 Ibid.
12 *Pravda*, 29 April 1929.
13 TsPA IML, f.17, op. 2, d.639, l.28.
14 TsGAOR, f.9401, op. 2, d.168, ll.31–2.
15 *Bol'shevik*, No.5, 1929, p. 67.
16 Ibid., No.9, 1929, p. 30.
17 Trotsky, *Dnevniki i pis'ma*, op. cit., pp. 42–3.
18 TsGASA, f.33 987, op. 3, d.1049, l.96.
19 Houghton Library, Trotsky coll., bMS.Russ.13.1 (7710–40), folder 2/4.

20 Arkhiv INO OGPU, f.17 548, d.1017, t.1, l.202.
21 See Deutscher, *The Prophet Outcast*, op. cit., pp. 26–7.
22 Arkhiv INO OGPU, f.17 548, d.0292, t.1, l.106.
23 *Byulleten' oppozitsii*, No.9, 1930, p. 10.
24 Houghton Library, Trotsky coll., bMS.Russ.13.1 (8703).
25 Ibid., folder 1.
26 Arkhiv INO OGPU, f.17 548, d.0292, t.1, l.217.
27 TsGASA, f.33 987, op. 2, d.192, l.318.
28 Ibid., d.1425, l.35.
29 Ibid., l.46.
30 Ibid., l.179.
31 Ibid., d.141, ll.39–42.
32 Ibid., l.165.
33 Ibid., d.192, l.317.
34 Ibid., d.141, l.263.
35 Ibid., ll.270–1.
36 Arkhiv INO OGPU, f.17 548, d.0292, t.1, ll.262–3.
37 Ibid., f.31 660, d.9067, t.1, ll.2–4.
38 Ibid., ll.9–15.
39 *Byulleten' oppozitsii*, No.86, 1941, pp. 8–10.
40 Arkhiv INO OGPU, f.17 548, d.0292, t.1, l.298.
41 Ibid., l.44.
42 Ibid., l.25.
43 Ibid., l.28.
44 Ibid., l.144.
45 Ibid., l.298.
46 Houghton Library, Trotsky coll., bMS.Russ.13.1 (9134–58), folder 1/2.
47 Trotskii, L., *Nemetskaya revolyutsiya i stalinskaya byurokratiya*, Berlin, 1932, p. 30.
48 TsGASA, f.33 987, op. 3, d.173, l.36.
49 TsPA IML, f.552, op. 1, d.173, l.36.
50 Arkhiv INO OGPU-NKVD, f.17 548, d.0292, t.2, l.160.

51 Ibid., ll.54–9.
52 *Byulleten' oppozitsii*, Nos.12–13, 1930, pp. 25–7.
53 Ibid., No.28, 1932, p. 18.
54 Ibid., No.41, 1935, pp. 3, 7.
55 Ibid., No.42, 1935, p. 4.
56 Ibid., No.47, 1936, p. 2.
57 TsPA IML, f.17, op. 2, d.612, vyp.III, l.10.
58 *Byulleten' oppozitsii*, Nos.75–6, 1939, p. 4.
59 Ibid., No.81, 1940, p. 5.
60 Ibid., Nos.36–7, 1933, p. 10.
61 Ibid., Nos.77–8, 1939.
62 Arkhiv INO OGPU, f.17 548, d.0292, t.1, ll.185–8.
63 *Byulleten' oppozitsii*, No.74, 1939, p. 2.
64 Arkhiv INO OGPU-NKVD, f.31 660, d.9067, t.1, ll.104–5.
65 Ibid., d.22 918, l.11.
66 Ibid., ll.76–8.
67 Ibid., d.31 660, d.9067, t.1, l.78.
68 Ibid.
69 Ibid., f.17 548, d.0292, l.17.
70 Ibid., l.97.
71 TsGASA, f.33 987, op. 2, d.113, l.39.
72 Ibid., op. 1, d.467, l.108.
73 Houghton Library, Trotsky coll., bMS.Russ.13.1 (10634–44), p. 1.
74 International Institute of Social History, Amsterdam, No.67, 2634/1.
75 Ibid.
76 Ibid., No.91, 330/23, 16/6.
77 Arkhiv INO OGPU-NKVD, f.17 548, d.0292, t.1, l.208.
78 International Institute of Social History, Amsterdam, No.111, 322/1, 2(2).
79 *Byulleten' oppozitsii*, No.33, 1933, p. 30.
80 Deutscher, *The Prophet Outcast*, op. cit., p. 17.
81 TsGASA, f.33 987, op. 1, d.382, l.164.
82 Ibid., l.415.
83 Ibid., l.375.
84 Houghton Library, Trotsky coll., bMS.Russ.13.1 (10598–631), folder 1/10.
85 *Trotsky's Diary in Exile*, op. cit., p. 100.
86 Ibid., p. 116.
87 *Byulleten' oppozitsii*, No.44, 1935, pp. 11–12.
88 Serge, V. and Sedova, N. (trans. Arnold J. Pomerans), *The Life and Death of Leon Trotsky*, London, 1975, p. 219. The translation is ambiguous, and I have rendered the Russian original differently, in order to emphasize that Trotsky thought his son was indeed still alive. The English edition of the book has: 'Perhaps my death would have saved Sergei.' [HS]
89 Houghton Library, Trotsky coll., bMS.Russ.13.1 (10031–248), folder 4/16.
90 *Byulleten' oppozitsii*, No.46, 1935, p. 6.
91 TsAMO, f.32, op. 701 323, d.38, ll.14–16.
92 Sedov, L., *Le Livre Rouge sur le Procès de Moscou*, Paris, 1936.
93 TsPA IML, f.17, op. 2, d.612, vyp.III, l.10.
94 Arkhiv INO OGPU-NKVD, f.31 660, d.9067, t.1, l.122.
95 Ibid., ll.144–5.
96 Deutscher, I., *The Prophet Outcast*, op. cit., p. 393.
97 Andrew, C. and Gordievsky, O., *KGB: The Inside Story of its Foreign Operations from Lenin to Gorbachev*, London, 1990, pp. 128–129.
98 Deutscher, *The Prophet Outcast*, op. cit., p. 401 and *Byulleten' oppozitsii*, No.64, 1938, pp. 2, 4, 8.
99 Arkhiv INO OGPU-NKVD, f.31 660, d.9067, t.1, l.141.
100 Trotskii, *Dnevniki i pis'ma*, op. cit., p. 156.
101 Ibid., pp. 44–5.

102 *Byulleten' oppozitsii*, Nos.66–7, 1938, p. 32.

103 See Deutscher, *The Prophet Unarmed*, op. cit., pp. 408–9, n.1.

104 Arkhiv INO OGPU-NKVD, f.31 660, d.9067, t.1, l.254.

105 Ibid., f.17 458, d.0192, t.2, l.127.

106 Trotskii, *Dnevniki i pis'ma*, op. cit., pp. 56, 58.

107 Houghton Library, Trotsky coll., bMS.Russ.13.1. (10598–631), folder 1/10, p. 2. Cited from Deutscher, *The Prophet Outcast*, op. cit., p. 265.

108 *Byulleten' oppozitsii*, No.42, 1935, pp. 7–8.

109 Arkhiv INO OGPU-NKVD, f.31 660, d.9067, t.1, ll.81–2.

110 Trotskii, *Dnevniki i pis'ma*, op. cit., pp. 98, 124.

111 Trotskii, L., *Predannaya revolyutsiya*, Paris, 1937, pp. 26–7.

112 Ibid., pp. 67–71, 79, 81.

113 Arkhiv INO OGPU-NKVD, f.17 548, d.0292, t.2, ll.130–2.

114 TsPA IML, f.552, op. 1–2.

115 Arkhiv INO OGPU-NKVD, f.31 660, d.9067, t.1, l.73.

116 *Izvestiya*, 30 August 1936.

117 Arkhiv INO OGPU-NKVD, f.31 660, d.9067, t.1, ll.81–2.

118 Ibid., ll.88–9.

119 TsPA IML, f.17, op. 2, d.612, vyp.III, l.21.

120 Ibid.

121 Ibid., ll.1–5.

122 Ibid., ll.18, 37.

123 Ibid., l.10.

124 Ibid., ll.15–19.

125 Ibid., l.34.

126 Ibid., ll.77–8.

127 Ibid., op. 2, d.577, ll.1–7.

128 *Sudebnyi otchet po delu antisovetskogo trotskistkogo tsentra*, Moscow, 1937, pp. 42–5.

129 Arkhiv INO OGPU-NKVD, f.31 660, d.9067, t.1, l.83.

130 *Pravda*, 9 December 1948.

131 TsGASA, f.33 986, op. 3, d.1084, l.38.

132 Arkhiv INO OGPU-NKVD, d.22 918, ll.26–8.

133 Ibid., f.31 660, d.9067, t.1, l.98.

134 Ibid., l.42.

135 Ibid., l.140a–c.

136 TsPA IML, f.17, op. 2, d.612, l.31.

137 TsGASA, f.33 987, op. 2, d.79, l.316.

138 *Byulleten' oppozitsii*, No.65, 1938, pp. 3–4.

139 TsGASA, f.33 987, op. 3, d.122, ll.125–6.

140 Orlov, A., *Tainaya istoriya stalinskikh prestuplenii*, New York, 1983, p. 279.

141 Trotskii, L., *Stalin*, New York, 1985, vol.1, p. 7.

142 TsPA IML, f.2, op. 2, d.1268, l.1.

143 TsGAOR, f.9401, op. 2, d.199, l.197.

144 *Ugolovni Kodeks RSFSR. S izmeneniyami na 1 iyulia 1938*. Moscow, 1938, pp. 26–33.

145 TsGAOR, f.9401, op. 2, d.199, ll.198–200.

146 Ibid., t.1, ll.169–70.

147 Houghton Library, Trotsky coll., bMS.Russ.13.1 (10091–248), folder 9/16.

148 Arkhiv INO OGPU-NKVD, f.17 548, d.0292, t.2, l.228.

149 *The Gelfand Case*, Labour Publications, London, 1985, vol.1, p. 11.

150 TsPA IML, f.17, op. 2, d.577, ll.35–41.

151 Arkhiv INO OGPU-NKVD, f.31 660, d.9067, t.1, l.16.

152 Ibid., f.17 548, d.0292, t.2, l.131.

153 International Institute of Social History, Amsterdam, No.137, 330/350.

154 Serge and Sedova, *The Life and Death of Leon Trotsky*, op. cit., pp. 219–21.

155 Ibid., p. 221.

156   Arkhiv INO OGPU-NKVD, f.31 660, d.9067, t.1, l.79.
157   Preliminary Commission of Inquiry, *The Case of Leon Trotsky*, New York and London, 1937.
158   TsGAOR, f.5413, op. 4, d.14, ll.15–27.
159   TsGASA, f.33 987, op. 3, d.987, l.170.
160   Ibid., d.989, l.260.
161   Ibid., d.987, op. 3, d.989, ll.253, 304.
162   TsGASA, f.33 987, op. 3, d.989, l.308.
163   *Bol'shevik*, No.3, 1937, pp. 1–2.
164   Ibid., p. 2.
165   *Byulleten' oppozitsii*, No.70, 1938, p. 10.
166   Arkhiv INO OGPU-NKVD, f.17 548, d.0292, t.2, l.190.
167   Ibid., ll.202–18.
168   *Situras*, 8 September 1990.
169   Ibid., p. 3.
170   Arkhiv INO OGPU-NKVD, f.31 660, d.9067, t.1, l.163.
171   Houghton Library, Trotsky coll., bMS.Russ.13.1 (7710–40), folder 1/2, p. 2.
172   Houghton Library, Trotsky coll., bMS.Russ.13.1 (8699–702), p. 1.
173   Houghton Library, Trotsky coll., bMS.Russ.13.1 (10598–631), folder 1/10, p. 2.
174   *Quatrième Internationale* No.3, 1937, p. 12.
175   Arkhiv INO OGPU-NKVD, f.17548, d.0292, t.1, l.61.
176   Ibid., f.31 660, d.9067, t.2, l.251.
177   Ibid., t.1, l.312.
178   TsPA IML, f.552, op. 2, d.1, ll.2–3.
179   Arkhiv INO OGPU-NKVD, f.31 660, d.9067, t.1, l.141.
180   TsPA IML, f.552, op. 2, d.1, l.1.
181   Ibid., op. 1–2, d.1, ll.199–200.
182   *Quatrième Internationale*, Nos.12–13, 1938, pp. 172–81.
183   *Byulleten' oppozitsii*, No.72, 1038, p. 4.
184   Arkhiv INO OGPU-NKVD, f.31 660, d.9067, t.1, l.262.
185   Ibid., ll.184, 186.
186   TsPA IML, f.552, op. 2, d.1, l.1; Arkhiv INO OGPU-NKVD, f.31 660, d.9067, t.1, ll.184, 186.
187   Arkhiv INO OGPU-NKVD, f.17 548, d.0292, t.2, ll.159–65.
188   Klehr, H., Haynes, J.E., Firsov, F.I., *The Secret World of American Communism*, New Haven and London, 1995, p. 142.
189   *Quatrième Internationale*, Nos.12–13, 1938, p. 218.
190   TsPA IML, f.552, op. 2, d.1, l.115.
191   *Byulleten' oppozitsii*, June 1941; see also Volkogonov, *Lenin: Life and Legacy*, op. cit., pp. 399ff, for a detailed account of Moscow's funding of foreign Communist Parties.
192   TsPA IML, f.558. op. 2, d.6118, l.35.
193   Trotsky, *Dnevniki i pis'ma*, op. cit., pp. 160–2.
194   TsPA IML, f.2, op. 2, d.293, l.3.
195   Ibid., d.1299, l.1.
196   *Byulleten' oppozitsii*, No.48, 1936, p. 4.
197   See Howe, I., *Leon Trotsky*, New York, 1978, pp. 124.
198   Arkhiv INO OGPU-NKVD, f.17 548, d.0292, t.2, l.258.
199   Serge and Sedova, *The Life and Death of Leon Trotsky*, op. cit., p. 248.
200   *Byulleten' oppozitsii*, Nos.58–9, 1937, p. 5.
201   Houghton Library, Trotsky coll., bMS.Russ.13.1 (10788), p. 2.

Chapter 7

1   TsPA IML, f.2, op. 2, d.1165, l.1.
2   Ibid., d.621, ll.1–3.
3   Trotskii, *Sochineniya*, vol.13, p. 101.

4 Ibid., vol.3, pt.2, p. 209.
5 Trotskii, *Sochineniya*, vol.13, pp. 27–8.
6 TsGASA, f.4, op. 14, d.32, ll.121–124.
7 Lenin, PSS vol.37, p. 490.
8 TsPA IML, f.2, op. 2, d.202, l.1.
9 Ibid., d.1318, ll.1-3.
10 Ibid., d.914, l.1.
11 *Byulleten' oppozitsii*, Nos.66–7, 1938, p. 3.
12 Ibid., p. 2.
13 Ibid., No.71, 1938, p. 16.
14 TsGASA, f.4, op. 14, d.32, l.34.
15 Deutscher, *The Prophet Outcast*, op. cit., p. 479; Trotskii, *Dnevniki i Pis'ma*, op. cit., p. 165.
16 Marx, K., *Kapital*, vol.1, p. 86.
17 Trotskii, *Chto takoe SSSR i kuda on idet?*, op. cit., p. 229.
18 Ibid., p. 235.
19 Ibid., p. 237.
20 *Byulleten' oppozitsii*, No.42, 1935, p. 4.
21 Ibid., Nos.60–1, 1937, p. 4.
22 Ibid., Nos.79–80, August–October 1939, pp. 14–16.
23 Trotskii, *Chto takoe SSSR i kuda on idet?*, op. cit., p. 173.
24 TsGASA, f.33 987, op. 3, d.864, l.241.
25 Ibid., l.248.
26 Ibid., d.828, ll.56–9.
27 TsGASA, f.3, op. 2, d.1006, l.3.
28 TsGASA, f.33 987, op. 3, d.1006, l.30.
29 Trotskii, L., *O Lenine. Materialy dlya biografa*, Moscow, 1924, p.vi.
30 TsPA IML, f.325, op. 1, d.347, l.2.
31 Arkhiv INO OGPU, f.17 548, d.0292, t.1, l.2.
32 Houghton Library, Trotsky coll., bMS.Russ.13.1 (9452–7), p. 1.
33 Houghton Library, Trotsky coll., bMS.Russ.13.1 (10793–805).
34 *Novyi grad*, No.1, Paris, 1931, p. 92.

35 Valentinov, N., *Maloizvestnyi Lenin*, Paris, 1972, p. 184.
36 *Byulleten' oppozitsii*, No.14, 1930, pp. 6–12.
37 *Arkhiv Trotskogo*, vol.1, pp. 135–6.
38 *Byulleten' oppozitsii*, Nos.68–9, 1938, p. 14.
39 TsPA IML, f.2, op. 2, d.478, l.13.
40 Trotsky, L., *Stalin*, Universal Library, New York, 1941, pp. 413–14.
41 Ibid., p. 336.
42 Trotskii, *Sochineniya*, vol.2, pt.1, p. 56.
43 Ibid., p. 57.
44 See Sverchkov, D., *Na zare revolyutsii*, Moscow, 1922, pp. 5–9.
45 Arkhiv INO OGPU-NKVD, f.17 548, d.0292, t.1, l.193.
46 Ibid., f.31 660, d.9067, t.1, l.83.
47 Ibid., ll.60–7.
48 Trotskii, *Istoriya russkoy revolyutsii*, op. cit., vol.1, p. 6.
49 Ibid., p. 501.
50 Ibid., vol.2, pt.2, p. 314.
51 Ibid., p. 319.
52 Ibid., pp. 376–377.
53 Houghton Library, Trotsky coll., bMS.Russ.13.1 (7314–18).
54 Arkhiv INO OGPU-NKVD, f.17 548, d.0292, t.2, ll.127–8.
55 *Byulleten' oppozitsii*, no.35, 1933, pp. 20-21.
56 Trotskii, *Stalinskaya shkola fal'sifikatsii*, op. cit., 1932, p. 38.
57 Ibid., pp. 96–7.
58 Ibid., p. 38.
59 TsGASA, f.33 987, op. 3, d.1075, l.42.
60 TsGASA, f.4, op. 14, d.49, ll.3–4.
61 TsGAOR, f.3316, op. 2, d.1613, ll.3–18.
62 TsGASA, f.33 987, op. 3, d.773, l.297.
63 Trotskii, *Stalin*, op. cit., vol.2, p. 218.

64 Balabanova, A., *Impressions of Lenin*, Ann Arbor, 1964, p. 82.

65 *Byulleten' oppozitsii*, No.45, 1935, p. 16.

66 TsGASA, f.33 987, op. 2, d.113, l.209.

67 Trotskii, *Sochineniya*, vol.12, pt.2, p. 31.

68 TsGASA, f.33 987, op. 2, d.113, l.209.

69 TsGASA, f.4, op. 14, d.32, l.187.

70 TsGASA, f.33 987, op. 3, d.80, l.319.

71 Ibid., op. 1, d.573, ll.238–65.

72 TsPA IML, f.2, op. 2, d.454.

73 Voroshilov, K., *Stalin i Krasnaya Armiya*, Moscow, 1929, p. 27.

74 In Trotskii, *Stalinskaya shkola fal'sifikatsii*, op. cit., p. 201.

75 TsAMO, f.112, op. 1260, d.7, l.8.

76 Ibid., l.9.

77 *Prikazy Narkoma oborony Soyuza SSR (1937-1941)*, Moscow, 1941, pp. 18–19.

78 *Sudebnyi otchet po delu antisovetskogo trotskistkogo tsentra*, Moscow, 1937, p. 258.

79 TsPA IML, f.558, op. 2, d.6118, ll.35–6.

80 *Byulleten' oppozitsii*, Nos.21–2, 1931, p. 17.

81 TsPA IML, f.558, op. 2, d.6118, l.35.

82 Sudoplatov, P., *Special Tasks: The Memoirs of an Unwanted Witness – a Soviet Spy-Master*, London, 1994.

83 Arkhiv INO OGPU-NKVD, f.17 548, d.0292, ll.190–3.

84 Ibid., f.31 660, d.9067, t.1, l.141.

85 DV personal archives. *Kopiya zayavelniya P.A. Sudoplatova ot 27 vi 1989 g. General'nomu Prokuroru SSSR Sukharevu, A.Ye.*

86 Sudoplatov, *Special Tasks*, op. cit., pp. 479–82.

87 DV personal archives. *Kopiya pis'ma P.A. Sudoplatova v Komissiyu Politburo TsK KPSS po rassmotreniyu zayavlenii o neobosnovannykh represssiaykh ot 17 fevralya 1987.*

88 Klehr et al, *The Secret World of American Communism*, op.cit.

89 Serge and Sedova, *The Life and Death of Leon Trotsky*, op. cit., p. 225.

90 *Byulleten' oppozitsii*, Nos.58–9, 1937, p. 23.

91 TsPA IML, f.17, op. 2, d.612, v. 111, l.10.

92 Arkhiv INO OGPU-NKVD, f.31 660, d.9067, t.1, ll.79, 83.

93 *Sudebnyi otchet po delu pravotrotskistskogo bloka*, Moscow, 1938, p. 343.

94 Ibid., pp. 343–75.

95 Ibid., p. 331–2.

96 TsPA IML, f.17, op. 2, d.577, l.39.

97 Ibid., l.37.

98 Arkhiv INO OGPU-NKVD, f.17 548, d.0292, t.3, l.218.

99 TsOA KGB, f.6, op. 1-7, d.161, l.88.

100 Ibid., l.105.

101 DV personal archives. *Kopiya pis'ma P.A. Sudoplatova v Komissiyu Politburo TsK KPSS po rassmotreniyu zayavlenii o neobosnovannykh represssiaykh ot 17 fevralya 1987.*

102 Arkhiv INO OGPU-NKVD, f.33 660, d.9067, t.1, l.163

103 Arkhiv INO OGPU-NKVD, f.31 660, d.9067, ll.158, 159, 163–4, 216.

104 Ibid., l.216.

105 *Byulleten' oppozitsii*, Nos.68–9, 1938, p. 4.

106 Ibid., No.73, 1939, p. 15.

107 Arkhiv INO OGPU-NKVD, f.31 660, d.9067, t.1, l.232.

108 DV personal archives. *Kopiya pis'ma N.I. Eitingona Pervomu Sekretaryu TsK KPSS N.S. Khrushchevu.*

109 Politisches Archiv, Geheime Akten, R-31514, Russland, Pol.2, adh.2.

110 *Sudebnyi otchet po delu antisovetskogo trotskistkogo tsentra*, Moscow, 1937, p. 332.

111 DV personal archives. *Kopiya pis'ma N.I. Eitingona Pervomu Sekretaryu TsK KPSS N.S. Khrushchevu.*

112 Arkhiv INO OGPU-NKVD, f.31 660, d.9067, t.1, l.312.

113 *New York Times*, 6 November 1958; 30 November 1962; 14 December 1962.

114 TsGASA, f.33 987, op. 3, d.1103, l.149.

115 Arkhiv INO OGPU-NKVD, f.31 660, d.9067, t.1, ll.128–9.

116 *Byulleten' oppozitsii*, Nos.66–7, 1938, p. 32.

117 Houghton Library, Trotsky coll., bMS.Russ.13.1 (7710–40), folder 1/4.

118 Arkhiv INO OGPU-NKVD, f.31 660, d.9067, t.1, l.166.

119 TsPA IML, f.552, op. 2, d.1, l.174.

120 Ibid., l.18.

121 Siqueiros, D., *Menya nazyvali likhim polkovnikom. Vospominaniya*, Moscow, 1986, p. 220.

122 Ibid., p. 223.

123 Fernandes Tomas, J., *Españoles del Comunismo*, Madrid, 1976, pp. 191–4.

124 Houghton Library, Trotsky coll., bMS.Russ.13.1 (10806–48), folder 3/4.

125 Houghton Library, Trotsky coll., bMS.Russ.13.1 (10806–49), folder 2/5.

126 *Byulleten' oppozitsii*, No.87, 1941, p. 11.

127 Arkhiv INO OGPU-NKVD, f.31 660, d.9067, t.1, l.270.

128 Serge and Sedova, *The Life and Death of Leon Trotsky*, op. cit., p. 259.

129 Trotskii, *Dnevniki i pis'ma*, op. cit., pp. 163–4.

130 Sudoplatov, *Special Tasks*, op. cit., p. 74

131 *Byulleten' oppozitsii*, No.84, 1940, p. 8.

132 Siqueiros, *Menya nazyvali likhim polkovnikom*, op. cit., p. 225.

133 TsGASA, f.33 987, op. 2, d.60, l.15.

134 Ibid., d.426, l.218.

135 Arkhiv INO OGPU-NKVD, f.31 660, d.9067, t.i, l.163.

136 Levine, Isaac Don, *L'Homme qui a tué Trotsky*, Paris, 1960.

137 See *El Mundo*, 31 July 1990.

138 *Trotsky's Diary in Exile*, op. cit., pp. 139-40, 141.

139 Ibid., pp. 139–41.

140 *Byulleten' oppozitsii*, No.84, 1940, p. 25.

141 Ibid., Nos.21–2, 1931, pp. 7–35.

142 Arkhiv INO OGPU-NKVD, f.31 660, d.9067, ll.143, 159, 215.

143 Ibid., l.216.

144 *Izvestiya TsK KPSS* No.12, 1990, pp. 126–7.

145 TsAMO, f.32, op. 701 233, d.38, ll.14-16.

146 *Trotsky's Diary in Exile*, op. cit., p. 140.

147 Serge and Sedova, *The Life and Death of Leon Trotsky*, op. cit., pp. 266–7.

148 Levine, *L'Homme qui a tué Trotsky*, op. cit., p. 10.

149 Serge and Sedova, *The Life and Death of Leon Trotsky*, op. cit., p. 267.

150 Ibid., pp. 267–8; *Byulleten' oppozitsii*, No.85, 1941, pp. 1–5.

151 *El Mundo*, 31 July 1990.

152 Trotskii, *Sochineniya*, vol.12, p. 59.

153 Arkhiv INO OGPU-NKVD, f.31 660, d.9067, t.1, l.140.

154 *Pravda*, 24 August 1940.

155 TsPA IML, f.2, op. 2, d.414, l.1.
156 TsGASA, f.33 987, op. 3, d.60, l.55.
157 TsGASA, f.4, op. 14, d.17, l.217.
158 TsGASA, f.33 987, op. 1, d.467, l.56.
159 Ibid., l.156.
160 Valentinov, *Vstrechi s Leninym*, op. cit., p. 313.
161 *Novyi grad*, No.1, pp. 93–4.
162 TsPA IML, f.505, op. 1, d.65, ll.1–32.
163 Houghton Library, Trotsky coll., bMS.Russ.13.1 (9508–678), folder 13/14.
164 Stalin, *Sochineniya*, vol.6, p. 324.
165 Zinoviev, G., *Leninizm. Vvedenie v izuchenie Leninizma*, Leningrad, 1925, p. 160.
166 Houghton Library, Trotsky coll., bMS.Russ.13.1 (9508–675), folder 13/14.
167 Knei-Paz, B., *The Social and Political Thought of Leon Trotsky*, Oxford, 1978, p. 5.
168 Trotskii, L., *Mirovoi khozyaistvennyi krizis i novye zadachi Kominterna*, Moscow, 1921, p. 26.
169 Aronson, G. (ed.), *Martov i ego blizkie*, New York, 1959, p. 77.
170 Trotskii, L., *Zapad i vostok*, Moscow, 1924, p. 120.
171 Arkhiv INO OGPU-NKVD, f.31 660, d.9067, t.1, l.60.
172 *Chetvertyi Internatsional. Zhurnal Internatsional'nogo Marksizma*, 1989, pp. 1–63.
173 Trotskii, L., *Pyat' let Kominterna*, Moscow-Leningrad, 1925, p. 604.
174 Houghton Library, Trotsky coll., bMS.Russ.13.1 (1882).
175 Houghton Library, Trotsky coll., bMS.Russ.13.1 (13–205).
176 TsPA IML, f.552, op. 2, d.1, l.1.
177 Ibid., l.113.
178 Arkhiv INO OGPU-NKVD, f.17 548, d.0292, t.1–2.
179 Ibid., f.31 660, d.9067, t.1. l.164.
180 TsPA IML, f.17, op. 2, d.577, l.25.
181 TsGAOR, f.5143, op. 1, d.614, l.21.
182 Ibid., d.615, ll.18-35.
183 Ibid., op. 4, d.2, ll.6, 26.
184 Ziv, *Trotskii*, op. cit., p. 95.
185 TsGAOR, f.3316, op. 2, d.1613, l.33.
186 Ibid., ll.102–8.
187 Ibid., ll.131–2.
188 Ziv, *Trotskii*, op. cit., p. 93.
189 Stakhanov, A., *Rasskaz o moei zhizni*, Moscow, 1937, pp. 125–6.
190 Gippius, Z., *Stikhotvoreniya*, Paris, 1931, p. 126.

Epilogue

1 TsGASA, f.33 987, op. 2, d.16, l.198.
2 Ibid., d.18, l.309.
3 *Novyi grad*, No.1, p. 92.
4 Lenin, PSS vol.31, p. 133.
5 Houghton Library, Trotsky coll., Russ.bMS.13.1 (10788).
6 TsGASA, f.33 987, op. 3, d.2, l.60.
7 TsGAOR, f.9401, op. 2, d.176, t.2, l.361.
8 Trotskii, *Sochineniya*, vol.17, pt.2, p. 326.
9 TsPA IML, f.17, op. 2, d.685, ll.54–68.
10 TsPA IML, f.325, op. 1, d.355, l.15.
11 Ibid., d.167, ll.7, 24–25.
12 Arkhiv INO OGPU-NKVD, f.17 548, d.0292, t.2, l.468.
13 *Novyi grad*, No.1, 1931, p. 93.

Index